WITNESS TESTIMONY IN SEXUAL

Evidential, Investigative and Scientific Perspectives

WITNESS TESTIMONY IN SEXUAL CASES

Evidential, Investigative
and Scientific Perspectives

Edited by

PAMELA RADCLIFFE
GISLI H. GUDJONSSON CBE
ANTHONY HEATON-ARMSTRONG
DAVID WOLCHOVER

OXFORD
UNIVERSITY PRESS

UNIVERSITY PRESS

Great Clarendon Street, Oxford, OX2 6DP,
United Kingdom

Oxford University Press is a department of the University of Oxford.
It furthers the University's objective of excellence in research, scholarship,
and education by publishing worldwide. Oxford is a registered trade mark of
Oxford University Press in the UK and in certain other countries

Published in the United States of America by Oxford University Press
198 Madison Avenue, New York, NY 10016, United States of America

British Library Cataloguing in Publication Data
Data available

Library of Congress Control Number: 2015957073

ISBN 978–0–19–967293–6

Printed and bound by
CPI Group (UK) Ltd, Croydon, CR0 4YY

To our families

FOREWORD

The investigation and trial of sexual offending has always been an inherently complex task. The misuse of the internet and other technology has added to that complexity. Deficiencies in the traditional approach were recognized. Parliament has made significant legislative change. The Criminal Procedure Rule Committee, through the Criminal Practice Direction read in conjunction with the Criminal Procedure Rules, has also addressed the need for change. It has provided clear rules and firm guidance for all court users, including judges, particularly when dealing with vulnerable witnesses. For example, the use of 'Grounds Rules Hearings', an essential tool in the effective and appropriate case management of proceedings involving a vulnerable defendant or witness, is now recognized as invaluable to judges. Their importance and relevance in day-to-day practice and appropriate management of the trial process is being emphasized in judgments of the Court of Appeal. In *R v Cokesix (Lubemba)* [2014] EWCA Crim 2064, Lady Justice Hallett highlighted the importance of both practitioners and judges being aware of the wealth of guidance available to them when dealing with complex evidential issues and vulnerable witnesses.

As a result, practices have been developed which provide proper support to complainants not only when they report the offence but throughout the investigation and trial, whilst at the same time safeguarding the defendant's right to a fair trial. It is good fortune that these developments have taken place before the very recent steep rise in reporting of all types of sexual offending and the significant time such cases now occupy in the Crown Court.

It is against this background of significant change and improvement and a steep rise in the reporting of this type of offending that the importance of this book must be judged. It has set about the ambitious task of assisting investigators, legal and other professional practitioners, and judges in understanding the importance of evidence in sexual cases and evaluating its probative value. It has done so by bringing together in a carefully structured series of chapters what investigators, practitioners, and judges need to enable the fairest assembling, presentation, and evaluation of evidence to take place. The chapters range from a comprehensive analysis of the disclosure regime to an analysis of forensic science in sexual crimes. They serve to highlight the depth and variety of topics which have been covered in a series of essays by a highly experienced team.

The result is not only a source of much practical assistance structured in an accessible and coherent manner but also a series of very valuable insights. I very much hope that all those engaged in this type of work heed the advice given as to proper approaches to the potential legal and procedural complexities in dealing with complex sex cases with the requisite sensitivity and robustness that is required.

The Right Hon. The Lord Thomas of Cwmgiedd
Lord Chief Justice of England and Wales

ACKNOWLEDGEMENTS

First we extend our gratitude to the Oxford University Press team for their assistance throughout. *Witness Testimony in Sexual Cases* was a particularly challenging enterprise for editors, authors, and publishers, primarily because of its sensitive subject matter and the delicate treatment this warranted. The preparation of the book has outlasted some staff whose input at the outset was critical. We especially appreciate the assistance rendered in the early stages by Roxanne Selby former Senior Commissioning Editor. Latterly, Vicky Pittman, Amy Jones, Fiona Sinclair, and Peter Daniell have ensured its completion. Finally, we thank Andy Redman, Editorial Director, whose steady presence in the background and wise guidance in times of crisis was invaluable.

Our gratitude is also extended to a number of serving and retired members of the judiciary, who have provided sage advice and encouragement, notably Sir Anthony Hooper, Dame Brenda Hale, Peter Rook QC, Nicholas Browne QC, Nicholas Philpot, and Sam Katkhuda. Our thanks also go to members of the Bar and legal professionals who assisted us along the way, particularly, Alison Levitt QC and John Riley, Alix Beldam at the Criminal Appeal Office, and Laura Hoyano of Oxford University.

We pay tribute to each of our authors to whom we extend our unreserved thanks for their loyalty and dedication and for completing their respective chapters.

Someone who requires special mention is the late Lord Bingham of Cornhill who was a supporter of and contributor to the book's two predecessors. He persistently avowed their worth to judges and practitioners. We trust that *Witness Testimony in Sexual Cases* would have been similarly commended by him. We have continued to derive a sense of spiritual inspiration from his endorsement of the central theme underpinning the Witness Testimony series.

Last but by no means least, a heartfelt tribute to our respective families whose unswerving forbearance, loyalty, and encouragement through thick and thin has enabled us to bring the undertaking to its conclusion.

Pamela Radcliffe
Gisli H. Gudjonsson CBE
Anthony Heaton-Armstrong
David Wolchover
1 June 2015

PREFACE

This is the third volume in the *Witness Testimony* series. The first and second books[1] paved the way for a far broader, deeper, and more fundamental appreciation of the frailties and foibles of narrative testimony in the trial process than had hitherto been prevalent among criminal justice professionals. In the Preface to the first book in the series, *Analysing Witness Testimony*, the then editors set out its primary objective:

> There has been considerable resistance amongst lawyers to the acceptance of wisdom from scientists as to mental processes. This may have been caused by and is undoubtedly reflected in the absence of reference to learning from other disciplines in professional training courses. Legal education has, understandably, been apt to focus on legal concepts but the drawback of such a narrow approach is that the importance of significant areas of knowledge which might assist lawyers in forensic practice, whether as practitioners or members of the judiciary tends to be minimized or even sneered at. ... We do not seek to revolutionize the law on the admissibility of expert evidence concerning the reliability of expert testimony and recognize that change, if [it is] to be valuable must come slowly on mature consideration.

These words are as apt now as they were in 1999. The first book was endorsed in its Foreword by Lord Bingham, then Lord Chief Justice, who commended the authors on 'making available learning not readily available to lawyers'. In his Foreword to the second book Lord Justice Judge, as he then was, noted that it was concerned, 'with the much deeper and more complex and subtle problem of the search for the truth in the forensic process'. The aim of the *Witness Testimony* series was, he said, 'to change the mindset of key decision makers concerning the reliability and accuracy of witness evidence'. Both books brought about an increasingly open-minded approach to witness testimony and promulgated the requirement for a more critical analysis of the topic.

The overriding objective in criminal courts is that cases be dealt with 'justly'.[2] The key theme of *Witness Testimony in Sexual Cases* is to apply that essential aim, encouraging a better understanding not only of those factors which tend to undermine the reliability of witness testimony, but focusing positively on factors which

---

[1] See: Heaton-Armstrong, A., Shepherd, E., and Wolchover, D. (1999) *Analysing Witness Testimony*, London: Blackstone Press; and Heaton-Armstrong, A., Shepherd E., Gudjonsson, G., and Wolchover, D. (2006) *Witness Testimony: Psychological, Investigative and Evidential Perspectives* Oxford: Oxford University Press.

[2] The Criminal Procedure Rules, 2015 Pt 1 1.1. (1) and (2).

may conduce to enhancing witness quality. In seeking to attain the overriding objective of doing justice, the book draws together learning not readily available and encourages an integral and rigorous approach to the analysis of witness testimony in the special context of sexual cases. It is not generally concerned with the analysis of legal processes or reiterating current law as it relates to sexual cases, but it will be noted that a minority of chapters do consider legal principles where they touch on the issue of witness testimony.

Although the first two books continue to provide a host of important lessons in the assessment of witness reliability the clock never stops. Empirical research and clinical experience are continuing apace. Our knowledge is expanding rapidly and while it may supplement or reinforce, refine or even redefine, the scope of our comprehension of already well-understood areas of human behaviour and cognition, research along other perhaps less well-trodden paths of inquiry will modify or even alter conceptual principles. Moreover, changes in substantive and adjectival law may expose new fields of interaction between testimony and the forum in which it is rendered. It is only to be expected therefore that some elements of the content of the first two books will no longer be found at the cutting edge of research and the development of ideas. Nonetheless, their chapters on such a diverse range of topics as the workings of the faculties of perception and memory, the influence of drugs on testimony, witness demeanour,[3] witness testimony in sleep and dream related contexts, hypnotically induced testimony and the interpretation and translation of foreign languages will contain much of continuing general value and interest in the arena of trials for sexual crime, if not also of specific application. As such they are to be commended as complementing this new treatment of the subject and at the very least may serve to provide reference points for locating more recently published material.

Witness Testimony in Sexual Cases is not intended to replace other authoritative texts but to supplement the knowledge in this area from practitioner, academic, and scientific perspectives. It concentrates exclusively on cases involving allegations of sexual crime. The challenges to the criminal justice system wrought by witness testimony in this crime category are many and complex. It is now recognized as a specialist area calling for an understanding that straddles law and science. Updated training initiatives for investigators, prosecuting lawyers, and advocates are occurring or about to be 'rolled-out'. It is hoped that this volume will provide a timely and welcome contribution.

---

[3] See Fife-Schaw, C., 'The influence of witness appearance and demeanour on witness credibility' in Heaton-Armstrong, et al., (1999) cited at n.1, chap. 16; Bingham, T 'Assessing Contentious Eyewitness Evidence: A Judicial View' n Heaton-Armstrong, et al., (2006) n.1, chap. 18. For more recent treatment of the subject, which also addresses some of the difficulties involved in 'historic' cases, see the text of a speech delivered by Mr Justice Mostyn in December 2014 accessible at *https://www.judiciary.gov.uk/wp-content/uploads/2014/12/bristol-speech.pdf.*

The collective experience of the editorial team renders a strong practical under-tow for the book. Radcliffe, Heaton-Armstrong, and Wolchover have exten-sive experience of defending in both contemporary and historic sexual cases and Heaton-Armstrong also prosecutes these. The editorial team is particularly indebted to the support and contribution of Professor Gudjonsson CBE. His work as a forensic clinician and researcher in the field of vulnerable witnesses, mem-ory distrust, and false confessions is of international renown. His guidance and patience, keeping the 'ship on course' has proved invaluable.

The book is aimed primarily at criminal justice professionals working in the field of sexual crime. This includes the judiciary, advocates, investigators, probation offic-ers, and social workers. In addition, it is hoped that the book will also prove useful to law and psychology students and the interested layman.

Finally, the four editors pay tribute to all author contributors without whom this book would not have been possible. Their unfailing trust and support for the pro-ject during its long gestation was humbling. We express our gratitude to them.

The editors
Pamela Radcliffe
Gisli H. Gudjonsson CBE
Anthony Heaton-Armstrong
David Wolchover

CONTENTS

TABLE OF CASES

EUROPEAN COURT OF HUMAN RIGHTS

JAMAICA

JERSEY

MAURITIUS

SCOTLAND

UNITED STATES

TABLE OF LEGISLATION

Canada

TABLE OF STATUTORY INSTRUMENTS

OTHER LEGISLATION

Australia

Iceland

New Zealand

EUROPEAN DIRECTIVES

LIST OF EDITORS AND CONTRIBUTORS

EDITORS

Pamela Radcliffe
barrister and
Visiting Research Fellow, Department of Psychology,
University of Portsmouth

Gisli H. Gudjonsson CBE
Professor Emeritus of Forensic Psychology,
Institute of Psychiatry, Psychology and Neuroscience, Kings College London
Professor of Psychology at Reykjavik University

Anthony Heaton-Armstrong
barrister in independent practice

David Wolchover
barrister in independent practice

CONTRIBUTORS

R. Christopher Barden
Scientist, psychologist, and attorney USA

Christine Bassindale
Consultant Forensic Physician

Diane Birch OBE
JC Smith Professor of Law,
The University of Nottingham

Ray Bull
Professor of Criminal Investigation,
University of Derby

Mark Castle OBE
Chief Executive Officer,
Victim Support

Andrew L.-T. Choo
Professor of Law, The City Law School,
City University London

Graham Davies
Professor Emeritus of Psychology,
University of Leicester

Charles C. Dike
Director of Whiting Forensic Division,
Assistant Professor of Psychiatry,
Law and Psychiatry Division,
Yale University School of Medicine, USA

Bruce Durno
Justice of the Superior Court of Justice
(Ontario), Canada

Seán Enright
Circuit Judge, England

Brendan Finucane QC
barrister in independent practice

Rebecca Foulkes
barrister in independent practice

Christopher C. French
*Professor of Psychology,
Head of the Anomalistic Psychology
Research Unit,
Goldsmiths, University of London*

Fiona Horlick
barrister in independent practice

Ian Hynes
Chief Executive Officer of Intersol Global

Robert Kane
*barrister in independent practice,
Adelaide, Australia*

Reena Kapoor
*Associate Professor of Psychiatry, Law
and Psychiatry Division,
Yale University School of Medicine, USA*

Paul Keleher QC
barrister in independent practice

Sam King
barrister in independent practice

James Leonard
barrister in independent practice

Nevada McEvoy-Cooke
Former legal researcher; student solicitor

Rebecca Milne
*Professor of Forensic Psychology,
Centre of Forensic Interviewing,
Institute of Criminal Justice Studies,
University of Portsmouth*

Jacqueline Yek-Quen Mok
*Former Lead Paediatrician for Child
Protection in Edinburgh*

Amanda Naylor
*Manager of Victim Support's Children
and Young People's Service*

Mary A. Newton
Independent forensic consultant

Nigel North
*Consultant Clinical Psychologist
and Neuropsychologist,
Salisbury District Hospital,
Visiting Professor at Bournemouth
University*

Amy J. Ohler
*barrister in independent practice,
Toronto, Canada*

David Ormerod QC
*Law Commissioner for England
and Wales,
Professor of Criminal Justice, Queen
Mary University
of London*

James Ost
*Reader in Applied Cognitive Psychology,
Department of Psychology,
University of Portsmouth*

Gavin E. Oxburgh
*Senior Lecturer in Psychology,
Newcastle University*

Jason Payne-James
*Consultant Forensic Physician
and Specialist in Forensic
& Legal Medicine*

Cleo Perry
barrister in independent practice

Bridget Pettitt
Former researcher at Victim Support

Martin Picton
Circuit Judge, England

Mary Pillai
*Consultant in Obstetrics
and Gynaecology*

Jean Price
*Formerly Consultant Paediatrician
for Southampton City Primary
Care Trust*

John Price QC
barrister in independent practice

Keith Rix
*Consultant Forensic Psychiatrist
and Visiting Professor,
University of Chester*

Andrew Roberts
*Senior Lecturer, Melbourne Law School,
University of Melbourne, Australia*

Paul Roberts
*Professor of Criminal Jurisprudence,
University of Nottingham*

Jon F. Sigurdsson
*Professor of Psychology and Clinical
Director at Reykjavik University
and Professor of Psychology,
University of Iceland*

Robert R. Spano
*Judge of the European Court
of Human Rights
Professor of Law, University of Iceland*

Simon B.N. Thompson
*Associate Professor of Clinical Pyschology
and Neuropsychology,
Bournemouth University, Visiting
Professor at Université Paris X
Ouest Nanterre La Défense,
Paris, France*

Alex Verdan QC
barrister in independent practice

Lina Wallace
*Senior Manager for Witness Services
Development,
Victim Support*

Tony Ward
Reader in Law, University of Hull

Gerard Winter C.R.H
District Court Judge, New Zealand

Harry N.W. Wood
*Consultant Clinical and Forensic
Psychologist*

Harry Zeitlin
*Emeritus Professor Child and
Adolescent Psychiatry,
University College London*

EDITORS' CURRICULA VITAE

Pamela Radcliffe was called to the Bar in 1979. Her practice has spanned both criminal (defending) and family jurisdictions, encompassing a broad range of complex and grave allegations, including serious sexual assault. Radcliffe's academic interest lies in the interface between psychology and the law, especially memory science and criminal justice issues associated with serious sexual allegations. She advocates an interdisciplinary approach towards professional legal education. Radcliffe is also interested in European justice models and comparative approaches towards the investigation and trial treatment of serious sexual crime. She is a Visiting Research Fellow with the International Centre for Research in Forensic Psychology at the University of Portsmouth. She has addressed criminal justice professionals, academics and charitable organizations on aspects of serious sexual crime and related criminal justice issues.

Gisli H. Gudjonsson CBE is a Fellow of the British Psychological Society. He is a registered practitioner (clinical and forensic) with the Health Care Professions Council (HCPC). He is an Emeritus Professor of Forensic Psychology at the Institute of Psychiatry, Psychology and Neuroscience, King's College London and a Professor of Psychology at Reykjavik University. Prior to his retirement from King's College London on 1 January 2012 he was the Head of Forensic Psychology Services for the Lambeth Forensic Services and Medium Secure Unit at the South London and Maudsley NHS Trust (SLaM). He has extensive experience as an expert witness in cases involving witness testimony and was a lay magistrate in Croydon between 1990 and 1999. Professor Gudjonsson has been awarded two lifetime achievement awards and was appointed CBE in 2011 for his contribution to clinical psychology. He is still active in conducting research and publishing academic papers relevant to psychology and law.

Anthony Heaton-Armstrong is a practising barrister and author of numerous published texts concerning criminal investigations and procedure and lead editor of the book's two predecessors, *Analysing Witness Testimony* and *Witness Testimony: Psychological, Investigative and Evidential Perspectives*. He has very extensive experience of acting as a defence and prosecution advocate in cases involving allegations of serious sexual assault and is on the Crown Prosecution Service panel of specialist rape prosecutors. He has served on a number of Government Committees tasked to consider improvements to the England and Wales criminal justice system and is legal editor of *Medicine Science and the Law*, the journal of the British Academy of Forensic Sciences. He is chairman of Witness Confident, a charity which encourages the engagement with the police by victims of and witnesses to crime and the General Council of the Bar's representative on the Forensic Science Regulator's Quality Standards Specialist Group.

David Wolchover has been a barrister in independent practice for well over forty years, specializing in criminal defence work at all levels of complexity and gravity. For over ten years he was Head of Chambers at 7 Bell Yard (now Church Court Chambers). He is the author or co-author of a number of textbooks and numerous articles and papers mainly on criminal evidence and procedure, is an acknowledged expert on, among other topics, PACE, bail, visual identification procedures and certain aspects of the trial of sexual offences, and has been instrumental in securing a number of legislative and procedural criminal justice reforms. His particular interest in the recording of witness statements and visual identification has led to his becoming an acknowledged expert on the Lockerbie Bombing, the destruction of Pan Am flight 103.

INTRODUCTION

The Editors

A. Setting the Scene

The ultimate objective of any democratic criminal justice system should be one **Int.01** that succeeds in combining a fair trial process with humane treatment for all participants. There is no inherent conflict between the rights of the accused and those of any other witness within this process. The witness who brings the criminal complaint may claim no special privilege over any other witness, including the defendant. All who enter the criminal justice arena do so with parity. However, there is a palpable tension within the legal system. It springs from the twin prosecution duties, to support and protect victims of crime whilst also treating the accused 'justly'. As Lord Macdonald of River Glaven QC, observed, Crown Prosecutors need to keep a 'cool head' and 'avoid going on a mission and losing perspective'.[1] The interests of justice are ill-served by over-zealous prosecutors or biased investigators.

Sexual crime now occupies about a third of crown court trial days. It is anticipated **Int.02** that there will be a 30 per cent rise in the number of rape cases going to trial in 2015.[2] Ensuring and enhancing the efficiency and integrity of the investigation and trial of sexual crime in England and Wales is of paramount importance.

---

[1] Hamilton, F., Gibb, F., Simpson, J., and Pitel, L., ('Prosecutors in dock as sex case MP is cleared' *The Times*, 11 April 2014. His remarks were particularly applicable to 'historic' cases.

[2] Bowcott, O., 'Rape trials rise by 30% as courts fight to clear caseload. Director of public prosecutions says increase is good as it suggests that more victims feel they will be believed' *The Guardian*, 8 January 2015 *http://www.theguardian.com/society/2015/jan/08/rape-trials-30-percent-rise.*

Int.03 Sexual crime concerns the most intimate human conduct. It involves inherently private behaviour, making it immeasurably more challenging for victims to report, and for professionals to investigate and evaluate.

Int.04 Making a formal complaint about sexual misconduct, talking to police, and being questioned in a public forum is an intimidating and for many, a frightening experience. Recent research continues to support the suggestion that only a fraction of victims make a formal complaint to the police.[3] The high attrition rate in sexual crime cases is also well known.[4]

Int.05 Difficulties for prosecution decision-making are compounded when witnesses may be confused about what has taken place, for instance, as with a young child who may not understand what has occurred, or an adult suffering from a mental impairment or learning disability. Further difficulties may arise for instance when a young victim of grooming behaviour may have convinced him or herself they were in a romantic relationship. Prosecutors are now better informed and approach these cases with increased understanding. However, as the 'gang-grooming' cases have demonstrated, many victims have been left marooned, without justice.[5] New genres of sexual crime are continually emerging.

Int.06 The National Crime Agency recently disclosed a surge in the incidence of trafficking gangs enslaving children and adults. Nearly seven out of ten potential victims were children.[6] Within this crime category the United Nations has warned that, 'hundreds of children have been abducted from their families in Africa' and trafficked to London. These children are being raped or sexually abused within 'voodoo' ceremonies. Greater awareness and increased action is required. Police are being urged to do more to tackle the problem.[7]

Int.07 The investigation and criminal justice treatment of historic sexual allegations, variously described as non-recent, delayed complaints, or historic child sexual abuse (HCSA), is a category of sexual crime that has featured prominently in recent years.[8] Since Operation Yewtree[9] commenced in October 2012, there has been

---

[3] Only 15% of victims of serious sexual offences said they reported the incident to police: Ministry of Justice, Home Office and The Office for National Statistics. (2013) *An overview of sexual offending in England and Wales: Statistic Bulletin. https://www.gov.uk/government/uploads/system/uploads/attachment_data/file/214970/sexual-offending-overview-jan-2013.pdf.*

[4] See Chapter 1.

[5] Jay, A. (2014) *Independent Inquiry into Child Sexual Exploitation in Rotherham 1997–2013.* Rotherham: Rotherham Metropolitan Borough Council, *http://www.rotherham.gov.uk/downloads/file/1407/independent_inquiry_cse_in_rotherham.*

[6] Barrett, D., 'Branded like cattle: the tattooed victims of human traffic gangs' *The Telegraph,* 30 September 2014.

[7] 'UN Warns Britain over child voodoo victims', *http://www.rt.com/uk/167376-child-voodoo-rituals-pedophile/* 20 June 2014.

[8] There is no official definition of what is meant by the term 'historic'.

[9] A Metropolitan Police Service investigation collating all sexual crime reports made against the late Jimmy Savile, a high profile English entertainer and charity worker.

an increase in historic sexual complaints. There are no recent statistics for trials featuring historic sexual complaints[10] but existing data suggests they comprise a significant proportion of reported sexual crime. For the year ending June 2013, 24 per cent of crimes reported were said to have occurred between one and twenty years previously and 11 per cent more than twenty years previously.[11]

Historic allegations present challenges to criminal justice professionals because of the complex procedural and investigative issues that frequently accompany them. However, witness testimony arising from a delayed complaint is not processed or treated any differently from contemporary complaints within the justice process. Readers seeking an analysis of the procedural and substantive law issues in these cases are referred to Rook and Ward's seminal work.[12] **Int.08**

This volume is concerned with witnesses and their testimony, not 'black letter' law or explaining legal procedure. Historic allegations will therefore be considered from a purely witness testimony perspective. The hallmark of the delayed complaint is the dependence on long-term memory recall to prove the Crown's case. Consequently, given that accurate memory recall underpins reliable witness testimony, references with relevance to delayed complaints can be found throughout the volume. Where other aspects pertaining to delayed complaints warrant special mention they are drawn to the reader's attention within individual chapters. **Int.09**

The spectrum of witnesses and crime type continue to expand. Obtaining, understanding, and evaluating witness testimony, is dynamic and challenging territory. Obtaining good quality witness testimony lies at the heart of a 'just' process. **Int.10**

B. The Objective of Witness Testimony in Sexual Cases

The overarching objective of this book is to assist investigators and all justice professionals to understand factors that enhance the quality and probative value of witness testimony by identifying factors that assist or undermine witness accuracy and witness communication. The second, linked, objective is to assist decision-makers evaluate the reliability of witness testimony. This volume encourages an inter-disciplinary approach and draws together essential information from the law, medicine, psychology, and forensic science. **Int.11**

---

[10] Bowcott (2015), cited at n.2.

[11] Office for National Statistics (2013) *Sexual Offences in England and Wales for the year ending June 2013,* http://www.ons.gov.uk/ons/rel/crime-stats/crime-statistics/period-ending-june-2013/info-sexual-offenses.html, 3.

[12] Rook, P. and Ward, R. (2014) *Rook and Ward on Sexual Offences, Law and Practice,* 1st sup to 4th edn, London: Sweet & Maxwell, Ch. 26, Historic Cases. See also, Lewis, P. (2006) *Delayed Prosecution for Childhood Sexual Abuse,* Oxford: Oxford University Press, for an extensive academic discourse on both legal and psychological issues.

Int.12   Sexual crime is now recognized as a specialist field in its own right and a radical overhaul of practice and procedure is currently underway.[13] No other crime category is so heavily dependent on oral witness testimony as that pertaining to sexual assault.

Int.13   The book's approach focuses on investigative and evidential archaeology in a complex and evolving field of law. The overall editorial compass endeavours to steer a neutral and inclusive course, taking into account both prosecution and defence perspectives. However, in some chapters, the subject matter dictates an approach favouring one particular perspective, as for instance in Chapter 2, dealing with the prosecution of sexual offences in England and Wales.

Int.14   Over the past fifteen years, the legal landscape in sexual crime cases has transformed beyond recognition. Legislative and procedural changes and witness support measures have reformed substantive law, the law of evidence and the adversarial trial. Reform is still ongoing at the time of writing.[14] These have been wrought by society's increased understanding of the impact of sexual violence upon children, vulnerable witnesses, and all complainants. Consistent research findings showed that too many complainants were being deterred from reporting sexual crime by investigative prejudice and the abusive trial process. The justice system reacted.

Int.15   The Sexual Offences Act 2003 (SOA) came into force on 1 May 2004. Rape[15] was redefined, conclusive[16] and evidential[17] presumptions were introduced and new offences identified. Evidential safeguards to prevent complainants from unfair questioning about previous sexual history have been bolstered.[18] Trial modifications, via 'special measures', now enable testimony to be given by video recorded interview for all witnesses in sexual crime.[19] Witness support has been enhanced[20] and most recently a code of practice drawn up for victims of crime.[21] There has been an 'avalanche' of new rules, protocols, and procedural guidance for investigators and all criminal justice professionals to learn in respect of sexual crime. Most, if not all, of these reforms and modifications impact in some way on witness testimony whether at the investigative, or trial stage.

Int.16   It has been a challenge to keep abreast of the abundance of legal developments in the field of sexual crime since the idea for the book was conceived. The book reflects those developments.

---

[13] See Chapters 1, 8, and 15.
[14] The implementation of s 28, Children and Young Persons Act, 1999—following pilot schemes.
[15] SOA, s 1(1), extended rape to vaginal and anal penetration and penetration of the mouth.
[16] Section 76(2)(a), SOA.
[17] Section 75(1), SOA.
[18] See Chapter 5.
[19] See Chapters 13 and 14.
[20] See Chapter 15 for a round-up of witness support measures.
[21] Ministry of Justice (2013) *Code of Practice for Victims of Crime*, London: The Stationery Office.

C. The Role of Memory Science within Witness Testimony

Eliciting accurate memory recall is essential in every police interview and central **Int.17** to reliable witness testimony. Understanding how memory works is critical for fact finders when assessing testimonial reliability; for instance, when considering whether memory flaws, revealed in an interview, may have arisen via a neurological disorder, ordinary memory decay or trauma, or whether memories are sincere albeit false or simulated.

It is for the above reason that references to memory science are a recurring feature **Int.18** throughout the book. Witnesses are not robots, able to churn out a memory on cue. 'Memory' is known to be a highly malleable, plastic concept. 'Historic' or delayed complaint cases, where memory recall may reach back decades, present an acute problem for investigators, prosecutors, and the defence. Where memory ends and imagination or innocent 'confabulation'[22] begins is extremely difficult to discern, for all criminal justice professionals and lay fact finders.

The four overriding factors that all ensure optimum memory recall and quality **Int.19** witness testimony are:

(a) competent interviewing from the outset;
(b) appropriate professional practice by investigators and lawyers with an open mindset;
(c) identification of vulnerabilities and appropriate witness support throughout the criminal justice process; and
(d) understanding the importance of context.

D. The Structure and Content of the Book

The editors appreciate that some readers may consider the order of chapters to be **Int.20** somewhat arbitrary. For instance, the book could have been alternatively structured by choosing topics sequentially from complaint through to trial. However, it is hoped that by separating out the law from the science, the book is more easily navigable. Topics are readily identifiable and a 'mix and match' reading method may be adopted. Alternatively, the book may be 'read' chapter by chapter. Whichever way the book is approached, it is intended as a useful supplemental text, and an inter-disciplinary resource for investigators, and all criminal justice professionals.

---

[22] Confabulation 'refers to problems with memory processing where people replace gaps in their memory with imaginary experiences that they believe to be true': see Gudjonsson G.H. (2003) *The Psychology of Interrogations and Confessions. A Handbook*, Chichester: John Wiley & Sons Ltd, 364.

Int.21 Readers will also notice that writing styles are not uniform. Some chapters are written in an informal narrative style, whilst others are more academic in appearance and tone. This inconsistency reflects the varying approaches of practitioners and academics. The strength of *Witness Testimony in Sexual Cases* lies in its practical approach to the application of legal principles.

Int.22 **Part I** discusses core legal topics. Case studies are used throughout to highlight points made. *Chapter 1, Witness Testimony: Vulnerabilities, Context, and Issues*, provides an introduction to key issues in witness testimony and emphasizes the central importance of 'context'. It also cross-references other significant topics within the book, in particular the challenges posed by historic or delayed complaints as they relate to witness testimony.

Int.23 *Chapter 2, Prosecuting Sexual Offences in England and Wales* examines prosecution responsibilities and the new 'merits based' approach. It also discusses recent developments in the prosecution of delayed complaints.

Int.24 *Chapters 3 to 10* explore aspects of law and practice applicable to witness testimony in sexual crime cases. The chapter headings are self-explanatory. They do not, in the main, set out the substantive law but discuss the application of the law or rules together with recent case studies.

Int.25 *Chapter 4, Abuse of Process and Delayed Prosecutions*, merits special comment. An application to stay the proceedings on the basis that their continuance constitutes an abuse of process, applies predominantly to historic complaint cases. Whilst recent case law has firmly reduced the scope for these applications, they are not rendered redundant. The chapter provides an essential overview of case law developments. The law is never static and judgments in this field are often fact-specific.

Int.26 *Chapter 10* briefly sets out the English Family Court practice and procedure when assessing child sexual allegations. Criminal practitioners unfamiliar with the family court process should find this chapter immensely useful.

Int.27 *Chapters 11 and 12* add an important international dimension. *Chapter 11* provides three international perspectives from Canada, New Zealand, and South Australia. *Chapter 12* provides guidance on the conduct of abuse enquiries drawing on the Icelandic experience.

Int.28 **Part II** explores investigative and scientific issues. *Chapters 13, 14, and 15* discuss measures and procedures that will equip and inform investigators from receipt of the complaint.

Int.29 *Chapter 16* focuses on psychiatric perspectives of child testimony. Investigators and practitioners will find this an invaluable chapter. Increasing numbers of ever-younger children are giving witness testimony.

Chapters 17 to 20 provide relevant information about forensic and genital examina- **Int.30** tions, mental health conditions, and forensic science.

Chapters 21, 22, and 23 relate to the application of memory science within the **Int.31** legal process. *Chapter 24, Pathological Lying* concerns a rare and little known topic, but such cases do occur. It comprises a valuable contribution; there is a dearth of literature on this topic.

E. Clarifying Terminology

Whilst some chapters refer to 'victims', others refer to 'complainants'. In the context **Int.32** of this book, both terms are interchangeable. They relate to people—whether male or female, child or adult—who make a sexual complaint. The Crown Prosecution Service protocols and guidance refer to 'victims' from the outset of complaint. This terminology is maintained whether or not a conviction follows. On the other hand, lawyers and statute, tend to use the neutral term, 'complainant'; no disrespect towards genuine victims is implied. The fulcrum of the criminal trial is based upon the presumption of innocence. Lawyers by virtue of their training adopt an objective and legalistic approach. Therefore, unless or until a guilty verdict is reached, there is, strictly, no crime 'victim'. In cases in which identification is the sole issue it would not be inconsistent with this approach for the defence to concede the term victim.

The term 'victim' usually denotes the complainant. However, it may also properly **Int.33** describe those 'failed' more broadly by the criminal justice process. This may arise where the criminal process provided insufficient support for a vulnerable witness from the outset, with resulting withdrawal from the process,[23] or because the investi- gator failed to ask the right questions and failed to secure the best witness testimony.

The term 'victim' may also embrace those 'falsely accused' of sexual crime. Just **Int.34** as rape victims suffer serious psychological trauma and even commit suicide,[24] so too do the 'falsely accused'.[25] There is little scientific research into the prevalence of false or unreliable complaints or mental health follow-up of these victims. An unpopular cause, false accusers and falsely accused transect all social boundaries.[26]

---

[23] See Chapter 15.

[24] See Chapter 15.

[25] Knight, K. and Brooke, C., 'One man killed himself, the other had his life destroyed. All because one girl falsely cried rape. So what does she have to say for herself?' *MailOnline*, 2 June 2010; Martin, E., 'Envoy had breakdown over bogus claim he touched woman's bottom' *Evening Standard* 5 June 2013, 28; 'Charity boss was "destroyed" by fake teenager who invented rape' *The Times*, 18 October 2013.

[26] Hoyle, A., 'BBC personality made 40 false rape allegations against her ex-boyfriend whose life remains blighted by her lies' *MailOnline* 25 January 2009; Grace, M. and Siemaszko, C., 'TV weatherwoman Heidi Jones pleads guilty to lying about being assaulted by "Hispanic" man'

Reported cases range from high-profile individuals to the unhappy and depressed. Criminal justice professionals should remain vigilant to detect and prevent injustice to all witnesses in the justice process, including the defendant.

F. Controversies Not Addressed

Int.35 This volume does not set out to be controversial, however, any publication dedicated to sexual crime is likely to touch upon sensitive issues where polarized viewpoints are apt to prevail. Consequently, this book does not venture an opinion on the *conviction rate versus the false allegation debate*. However, false and unreliable evidence is an unavoidable feature of witness testimony and the book does not flinch from this topic.

Int.36 Neither does the book debate the future of the English adversarial system. Concerns about the appropriateness of the English trial model for witnesses in sexual crime cases and what future reforms may be on the horizon are outside its scope.

G. The Inter-disciplinary Nature of the Law

Int.37 Kapardis observes that although psychology and the law 'are inextricably bound together by virtue of their common role in relation to the regulation of human behavior and their responsibility for maintaining the social fabric in a civilized society … a gap remains between the two disciplines'.[27]

Int.38 The law is inherently conservative and understandably slow to react to scientific ideas. It is hoped that this volume will go some way to bridge the information gap between science and the law and that lawyers and investigators will be encouraged to approach their task through a wider lens. Learning the law is simple; applying connected learning with insight and understanding is more challenging.

NYDailyNews.com/local 14 September2011; Tozer, J., 'Facing jail, woman whose sex attack lies led to anguish of four men' *Daily Mail*, 19 June 2010 (complainant ripped her own clothes, inflicted injury on herself, hacking off her hair, scratched her breasts).

[27] Kapardis, A. (2014) *Psychology and Law: A critical introduction*, 4th edn, Cambridge: Cambridge University Press, ch.1, 16, n.24, and 18.

PART I

EVIDENTIAL PERSPECTIVES

1

WITNESS TESTIMONY: VULNERABILITIES, CONTEXT, AND ISSUES

Pamela Radcliffe and Gisli H. Gudjonsson CBE

A. Introduction

'The principle of accurate fact-finding is the ultimate golden thread tying criminal **1.01** proceedings to the public interest. It must never be allowed to become too badly frayed or torn, for criminal process unconcerned with the truth is the instrument, not of justice, but of despotism.'[1]

The fact-seeker in criminal proceedings is the police investigator; the fact-giver, the **1.02** witness. The person who tests the facts is the advocate. The investigator's role is to obtain a detailed and reliable account of events whilst remaining sensitive to the needs and vulnerabilities of the witness.[2] The investigator must ensure that fairness and justice are served by enabling the witness to provide their 'best evidence'.[3] The basic

---

[1] Roberts, P. and Zuckerman, A. (2010) *Criminal Evidence*, 2nd edn, Oxford: Oxford University Press, ch 1, 19.

[2] Gudjonsson, G., (2003) *The Psychology of Interrogations and Confessions: A Handbook*, Chichester: John Wiley & Sons Ltd.

[3] Gudjonsson, G. 'Psychological vulnerabilities during police interviews. Why are they important?' (2010) 15 *Legal and Criminological Psychology*, 161–75.

premise of this chapter is that good quality witness testimony obtained from the outset furthers successful prosecutions, whilst poor quality evidence can result in a miscarriage of justice, including a wrongful acquittal.

1.03 An early pioneer in the scientific assessment of the reliability of witnesses' account of sexual offences emphasized the need to separate the two main components of credibility: 'eyewitness ability' and 'eyewitness motivation'.[4] The first relates the capacity of the witness to observe, consolidate, retrieve, and accurately report salient features of the offence. Motivation relates to the willingness of the witness to 'tell the truth'. These two components may be difficult to separate in real-life cases and sophisticated methods have been devised to address these issues.[5]

1.04 A 'witness' in criminal proceedings is any witness deposing to fact, expert opinion, or character. The witness may be the complainant, the accused, or a witness called at trial by either the prosecution or defence. This chapter will focus primarily, but not exclusively, on the testimony of the complainant.[6] The first part of the chapter will explore the central role of witness 'testimony' in the trial process. It will briefly discuss the problems associated with erroneous beliefs about autobiographical memory, delayed reporting, (including historic child sexual abuse (HCSA)), and the identification of vulnerable witnesses (including child witnesses), and highlight the importance of context.

1.05 The second part of the chapter will examine witness testimony in the context of trial outcomes in sexual crime. It will briefly touch upon the topical attrition and conviction rate debate and consider how the data might better serve the criminal justice process. It will be suggested that rather than focusing on maximizing the conviction rate, policy-makers and criminal justice professionals should concentrate on ways to enhance reporting rates and optimize the quality and evaluation of witness testimony.

B. Witness Testimony, Vulnerable Witnesses, and Context

(1) Complainant witness testimony and the investigation

1.06 'Testimony' is traditionally understood to be 'the oral statement of a witness made on oath in open court and offered as evidence of the truth of that which is asserted.'[7]

---

[4] Undeutsch, U. (1982) 'Statement reality analysis' in Trankell, A. (ed.), *Reconstructing the Past: The Role of Psychologists in Criminal Trials* Deventer, the Netherlands: Kluwer, 27–56.
[5] Vrij, A. (2008) *Detecting Lies and Deceit: Pitfalls and Opportunities* Chichester: John Wiley & Sons Ltd.
[6] Neutral terminology of 'accuser' and 'complainant' is used.
[7] Keane, A. and McKeown, P. (2014) *The Modern Law of Evidence*, 10th edn, Oxford: Oxford University Press, ch 1, 10.

However, since 1988, the content of video-recorded interviews with children has been admissible as their evidence-in-chief, subject to adherence to the Memorandum of Good Practice, as it then was.[8] Since 2011 the content of video-recorded interviews with adult sexual complainants has also been admissible as evidence-in chief, subject to the witness' choice.[9] (Alternatively, the adult witness may still choose to make a traditional written statement.) In addition, recently revised guidance to advocates reduces the nature and scope of cross-examination in cases of young and vulnerable witnesses.[10] The video interview conducted prior to trial is now capable of being treated as the witness testimony at trial for both children and adults and the content may in future go before the jury largely unchallenged. Recent research by Westera, Kebbell, and Milne shows that video interviews in cases of rape allegations provide a better opportunity for detailed and good quality evidence from a witness than live evidence-in-chief.[11]

In sexual cases, the oral account of the complainant is often the sole evidence of **1.07** the alleged crime, given that most sexual (mis)conduct occurs in private. Martin Hewitt, the Association of Chief Police Officers (ACPO) lead for adult sexual offences, recently commented: 'As an investigator I can think of very few other types of crime where so much emphasis is based on the victim and their testimony to carry the case through.'[12] In the case of contemporary complaints made proximate to the alleged incident, investigators may be able to locate useful crime scene evidence, for instance, forensic evidence or CCTV or eye-witness evidence but it still may not corroborate the actual incident. If there is a long delay between the incident complained of and the complaint to police, crucial supporting evidence may be lost and eye-witness evidence and witness memory recall rendered less reliable as memory deteriorates with time and the potential for contamination increases.[13]

The investigative interview is the evidential cornerstone for both the initial charg- **1.08** ing decision and the jury's verdict. It is the 'gateway' to further enquiries. The importance of obtaining accurate answers, gathering reliable testimony, and neutrally exploring all investigative pathways, is of fundamental importance to the investigative process.[14]

---

[8] Criminal Justice Act 1988, s 32A.

[9] Youth Justice and Criminal Evidence Act 1999, s 22A as inserted by the Coroners and Justice Act 2009, s 101. It came into force on 27 June 2011.

[10] The new guidance is found at *http://www.theadvocatesgateway.org/a-question-of-practice*.

[11] Westera, N.J., Kebbell, M.R., and Milne, B. (2013) 'Losing two thirds of the story: a comparison of the video-recorded police interview and live evidence of rape complainants' [2013] Crim LR, 290.

[12] Newman, M. and Wright, O., 'Juries need to be taught about the reality of rape, says DPP' *The Independent*, 6 May 2014.

[13] Schacter, D.L. (2007) *How the Mind Forgets and Remembers*, London: Souvenir Press.

[14] Williamson, T., 'Towards greater professionalism: minimizing miscarriages of justice' in (2006) Williamson, T. (ed.) *Investigative Interviewing: Rights, Research Regulation*, Cullompton, Devon: Willan, 147–66.

1.09 In delayed complaint cases the investigator must take particular care when exploring distant memory during the interview. (See Chapter 14.) Where historic complainants are accompanied by neurological or psychological disorders, additional complications may arise. Investigators and legal professionals are advised to identify any vulnerable features that may further impact on delayed recall and testimonial reliability as early as possible. (See Chapters 20 and 21.)

1.10 According to an unnamed judge consulted by Baroness Stern for her independent review:

> If there were always a proper investigation and evaluation by the police and the CPS of all the evidence uncovered in the initial stages of the investigation (not just the parts which support the prosecution case), I am confident the conviction rate would be improved in two ways. First, if the investigation reveals a serious flaw in the prosecution case the decision should be made that the prosecution should not proceed. Second, if the investigation reveals a sensible answer to or explanation for the apparently damaging evidence, the chances of obtaining a conviction will be greatly improved.[15]

(2) Understanding memory and factors undermining reliability

1.11 Eliciting accurate memory recall is essential in every police interview and central to reliable witness testimony. Understanding how memory works is critical for fact-finders when assessing testimonial reliability, for instance, whether memory flaws may have arisen via a neurological disorder, ordinary memory decay, trauma, or are genuinely held but false beliefs, or whether the interviewee is telling deliberate lies.

1.12 Whilst it is recognized that understanding general memory principles may be helpful to the Court,[16] individual differences, the nature of the event remembered, and the conditions under which memory is consolidated and elicited also need to be considered.[17]

1.13 In the USA, most wrongful convictions in sexual cases based on DNA exoneration involve flawed eye-witness identification and testimony.[18] However, as Roberts and Ward point out in Chapter 7 of this book, the identity of the alleged perpetrator is known to the victim in most indictable sexual offences committed against adults and the focus of expert testimony is therefore typically on witness credibility rather than identification.

---

[15] Stern, V. (2010) *The Stern Review: A report by Baroness Vivien Stern CBE of an independent review into how rape complaints are handled by public authorities in England and Wales*, Government Equalities Office and Home Office. London: HMSO, 88.

[16] For example, it is well established that memory is an error-prone reconstruction process, which can have serious consequences for the judicial process. See Schacter, *How the Mind Forgets and Remembers* cited at n.13.

[17] Roediger, H.L., 'Relativity of remembering. Why the laws of memory vanish' (2008) 59 *Annual Review of Psychology*, 225–54.

[18] Garrett, B.L. (2011) *Convicting the Innocent: Where Criminal Prosecutions Go Wrong*, London: Harvard University Press.

Evaluating the reliability of historic or delayed witness testimony is inherently **1.14** problematic for investigators and fact-finders because of the (usually exclusive) reliance placed upon the complainant's evidence and the vagueness or inconsistency that may accompany genuine historic recall. In such cases, problems sometimes arise due to one or more of the memory flaws described in the literature in relation to 'recovered' and 'false' memories, the two main ones being 'misattribution' and 'suggestibility'.[19]

Historic complaints may relate to alleged events from one to twenty or more years **1.15** prior to the official report to the police. The longer the time delay, the greater is the opportunity for memory decay and contamination.[20] It is uncontroversial memory science that memory is not reproductive but reconstructive; however misconceptions remain amongst the public and legal professionals. Chapters 21, 22, and 23 explain how memory works and consider issues that may arise.

Expecting witnesses in historic abuse cases to recall events accurately after many **1.16** years or even decades is problematic and early memories rarely contain the kind of specific details targeted by investigators.[21] Much has been written about recovered memories in the context of remembering trauma and historic[22] sexual abuse allegations.[23] Interestingly, over 90 per cent of historic cases from a large Canadian study involved alleged continuous[24] rather than recovered memories and 68 per cent of the complainants claimed repeated abuse rather than a single incident.[25] The authors of the Canadian study concluded that 'there is a paucity of empirical research on the retention of emotional or traumatic childhood events recalled after many years'. The study included only criminal prosecutions and it is possible that the sample was biased towards cases involving reported continuous memories where prosecution is more likely to be successful.[26]

---

[19] Schacter, cited at n.13.

[20] Here the term 'contaminate' refers to the way in which memory may be corrupted by post-event information. See Gudjonsson, *The Psychology of Interrogations and Confessions* cited at n.2.

[21] Wells, C., Morrison, C.M., and Conway, M.A., 'Adult recollections of childhood memories: What details can be recalled?' (2014) 67 *The Quarterly Journal of Experimental Psychology*, 1249–61.

[22] There is no official definition of 'historic'. A Canadian study incorporated cases where two or more years had elapsed from the abuse incident to trial: Connolly, D. and Read, J.D., 'Delayed prosecutions of historic child sexual abuse: Analyses of 2064 Canadian criminal complaints' (2006) 30 *Law and Human Behavior*, 409–34.

[23] See e.g. Davies, G.M. and Dalgleish, T. (eds) (2001) *Recovered Memories: Seeking the Middle Ground*, Chichester: John Wiley & Sons; McNally, R.J. (2003) *Remembering Trauma*, Harvard: Belknap Press of Harvard University Press; and Brainerd, C.J. and Reyna, V.F. (2005) *The Science of False Memory*, New York: Oxford University Press.

[24] The methodology involved reviewing judicial 'decisions' and identifying terminology indicative of 'repression' in addition to any declared belief in continuous memory by the witness. The study data may not be an accurate guide to the overall prevalence of discontinuous or 'repressed' memories as witness interview transcripts were not reviewed.

[25] Connolly and Read, 'Delayed prosecutions of historic child sexual abuse' cited at n.22, 426.

[26] Gudjonsson, G., 'Members of the British False Memory Society: the legal consequences of the accusations for the families' (1997) 8 *Journal of Forensic Psychiatry*, 348–56.

1.17   Gudjonsson and colleagues[27] have emphasized the role of 'memory distrust' in cases of false memories, which involves up to five sequential steps: (1) **a trigger** (i.e. false beliefs are usually provoked by something people see, hear, are told, or dream about); (2) **plausibility** (i.e. the event is perceived as if it could have happened); (3) **acceptance** (i.e. the person accepts that the event did happen even if they cannot recall it); (4) **reconstruction** (i.e. the person then tries to make sense of it by constructing in their own memory what could or may have happened and this is where post-event suggestions are important); and (5) **resolution** (i.e. the person realizes that he or she has had a false memory and given a false account of event). Resolution may not occur in cases of false memories due to the persistence of the false memory.[28] Gudjonsson and his colleagues argue that these five sequential steps are equally applicable to cases of HCSA as internalized false confessions.[29]

1.18   Where the complaint has surfaced in the context of ongoing therapeutic support, the belief systems, methodology, and qualifications of the counsellor/therapist should be examined. Registration with a professional body is not mandatory. Many unregulated 'therapies', with varying degrees of scientific efficacy exist; they may generate irreversible 'false memories'.

1.19   Whether or not a complaint is made proximate to the alleged event, or surfaces within a therapeutic context years later, witness demeanour can be an unreliable indicator of truth or accuracy. Fact-finders in sexual cases inevitably draw upon demeanour and non-verbal behaviour when reaching their verdicts. Research shows that confidence in detecting truth/lies, bears a poor relationship to accuracy. Reliance upon witness demeanour to evaluate witness truthfulness is inherently risky and may lead to unjust verdicts.[30]

(3) Identifying vulnerable witnesses and optimizing interview quality

1.20   A vulnerable adult for the purposes of special measures directions,[31] includes someone suffering from a mental disorder, significant impairment of intelligence

---

[27] Gudjonsson, G., Sigurdsson, J.F., Sigurdardottir, A.S., Steinthorsson, H., and Sigurdardottir, V.M., 'The role of the memory distrust in cases of internalised false confessions' (2014) 28 *Applied Cognitive Psychology*, 336–48. doi: 10.1002/acp.3002; Gudjonsson, G., Kopelman, M.D., and MacKeith, J.A.C., 'Unreliable admissions to homicide: A case of misdiagnosis of amnesia and misuse of abreaction technique' (1999) 174 *British Journal of Psychiatry*, 455–9.

[28] In cases of historic allegations of sexual abuse a retraction only occurs in about 5% of cases; see Gudjonsson, G.H., 'False memory syndrome and the retractors: Methodological and theoretical issues' (1997) 8 *Psychological Inquiry*, 296–9.

[29] See also: Ost, J., Costall, A., and Bull, R., 'False confessions and false memories? A model for understanding retractors' experiences' (2001) 12 *The Journal of Forensic Psychiatry*, 549–79.

[30] The average accurate detection rate after 30 years of research is 57%. Kapardis, A., (2014) *Psychology and the Law: A Critical Introduction*, 4th edn, Cambridge University Press, 4th edn, 262, citing Vrij, A. (2000) *Detecting Lies and Deceit: The Psychology of Lying and the Implications for Professional Practice*, Chichester: John Wiley & Sons Ltd.

[31] These are generally not applicable for the accused, although the use of registered intermediaries with defendants in court is growing. See also Chapter 8 in this volume para 8.14; and The Criminal Procedure (Amendment) Rules 2015 (S.I. 2015/13); Hoyano, L. (2015) 'Reforming

and social functioning, or physical disorder or disability that the court con-cludes is likely to diminish the quality of their evidence.[32] There is however, no internationally agreed definition of the word vulnerable.[33] Gudjonsson[34] has suggested a generic definition applicable to all witnesses, to identify potential 'risk factors' that may undermine reliability of witness testimony.

It is statistically more likely that vulnerable witnesses will have been victims of sex-ual crime.[35] Equally, miscarriages of justice have occurred when psychological vul-nerabilities were subsequently detected and revealed that incriminating interview answers were rendered potentially unreliable.[36] In addition, the early detection of vulnerabilities will be vital to the subsequent determination of legal capacity to testify. It is therefore imperative that STOs[37] are trained to identify those witnesses who require expert assessments prior to the interview so that appropriate adults or other support may be arranged and the interview questions planned accordingly. **1.21**

Detecting psychological and mental health problems is challenging and requires education, training, vigilance, and appropriate implementation. Recent studies reveal that despite the concerns raised by the Bradley Report[38] and subsequent reforms, police perform poorly at identifying vulnerable or intimidated suspects and witnesses and often fail to act when vulnerabilities are identified.[39] The larg-est unidentified groups are those with developmental disorders, particularly those **1.22**

---

the adversarial trial for vulnerable witnesses and defendants' [2005] Crim LR 107–29; Mahony, B.M. (2010) 'The Emerging Role of the Registered Intermediary with the Vulnerable Witness and Offender: Facilitating communication with the Police and Members of the Judiciary' *British Journal of Learning Disabilities*, 38, 232–7. See also Gudjonsson cited at n.2 , on the use of a clinical psychologist throughout the two trials of Barry George to ensure that he was able to cope with the trial process.

[32] Youth Justice and Criminal Evidence Act 1999, s 16.

[33] Bull, R., 'The investigative interviewing of children and other vulnerable witnesses: Psychological research and working professional practice' (2010) 15 *Legal and Criminological Psychology*, 5–23 cited in Gudjonsson, 'Psychological vulnerabilities during police interviews' cited at n.3, 161–75.

[34] Gudjonsson, 'Psychological vulnerabilities during police interviews' cited at n.3. 'Psycho-logical characteristics or mental state which render a witness prone, in certain circumstances to providing information which is inaccurate, unreliable or misleading', 66. See also Gudjonsson, G.H., 'The psychological vulnerabilities of witnesses and the risk of false accusations and false confessions' in Heaton-Armstrong, A., Shepherd, E., Gudjonsson, G., and Wolchover, D. (eds) (2006) *Witness Testimony. Psychological, Investigative and Evidential Perspectives*, Oxford: Oxford University Press, 61–75.

[35] Pettitt, B., Greenhead, S., Khalifeh, H., Drennan, V., Hart, T., Hogg, J., Borschmann, R., Mamo, E., and Moran, P. (2013) *At Risk, Yet Dismissed: The Criminal Victimization of People with Mental Health Problems*, London: Victim Support and Mind.

[36] Gudjonsson, 'Psychological vulnerabilities during police interviews' cited at n.3, 161–75.

[37] STOs are Specially Trained Officers, trained in sexual offence investigation techniques.

[38] Bradley, K. (2009) *The Bradley Report: Lord Bradley's Review of People with Mental Health Problems or Learning Disabilities in the Criminal Justice System*, London: Department of Health.

[39] Burton, M., Evans, R., and Saunders, A. (2006) *Are special measures for vulnerable and intimi-dated witnesses working? Evidence from the Criminal Justice Agencies On-line Report*, London: Home Office; cited in Gudjonsson, G. 'Psychological Vulnerabilities during Police Interviews. Why are they Important?' (2010) 15 *Legal and Criminological Psychology*, 161–75.

with attention deficit hyperactivity disorder and mild intellectual disabilities.[40] 'The findings suggest there still remains a huge unmet need among vulnerable witnesses with regard to identification and implementation of special measures.'[41] Whether police training and resources will be able to meet the increasing demands of more vulnerable witnesses entering the Criminal Justice System (CJS) remains to be seen.

1.23 A recent study[42] measured the suggestibility of 90 children suspected of having been sexually abused, aged between 7 and 16 years. Test results suggest that these children have heightened suggestibility under interrogative pressure. In addition, analysis of scores from children abused by a family member, indicate those children are even more vulnerable to giving in to interrogative pressure than children abused by acquaintances and strangers. The study has important implications for all professionals when questioning child witnesses or assessing credibility. Apparent unreliability may simply reflect heightened suggestibility from an honest child witness.

(4) Child witnesses and legal capacity to testify

1.24 Much has been written about the vulnerabilities of child witnesses and their capacity to give evidence.[43] The general thrust of the research is that child witnesses' accounts should be elicited by free recall, direct and leading questions should be avoided as far as possible, and a validated interview protocol should be used.[44] In their detailed analysis of 285 video recorded evidential interviews of children suspected of sexual abuse, Gudjonsson and colleagues[45] found that most of the younger children (3 ½ to 5 years) were able to act as witnesses to basic facts about a distinct and personally experienced event. For example, over 90 per cent of these young children were able to distinguish truth from a lie, understood the basic rules of the interview, had reasonable memory for basic personal information, and

---

[40] Young, S., Goodwin, E.J., Sedwick, O., and Gudjonsson, G., 'The effectiveness of police custody assessments in identifying suspects with intellectual disabilities and attention deficit hyperactivity disorder.' (2013) 11 *BMC Medicine 2013*, 248, doi:10.1186/1741-7015-11-248. This study does not include an assessment of high functioning autism, but similar problems with identification are likely to be present.

[41] Gudjonsson, G. 'Psychological vulnerabilities during police interviews. Why are they important?' (2010) 15 *Legal and Criminological Psychology*, 161–75.

[42] Vagni, M., Maiorano, T., Parjardi, D., and Gudjonsson, G., 'Immediate and delayed suggestibility among suspected child victims of sexual abuse' (2015) 79 *Personality and Individual Differences*, 129–33.

[43] Lamb, M.E., Hershknowitz, I., Orbach, Y., and Esplin, P.W. (2008) 'Tell me What Happened: Structured Investigative Interviews of Child Victims and Witnesses', Chichester: John Wiley & Sons Ltd; Ceci, S.J. and Bruck, M. (1995) *Jeopardy in the Courtroom. A scientific analysis of children's testimony*, Washington, DC: American Psychological Association.

[44] Gudjonsson, G., Sveinsdottir, T., Sigurdsson, J.F., and Jonsdottir, J.K., 'The ability of victims of childhood sexual abuse (CSA) to give credible evidence. Findings from a National Child Advocacy Centre' (2010) 21 *The Journal of Forensic Psychiatry and Psychology*, 569–86.

[45] Ibid.

were able to give satisfactory answers to general questions. In comparison with the older children, their limitations related to describing events immediately following the alleged abuse, giving details of conversation with the abuser, ability to answer open-ended questions, reporting the precise timing of the abuse, and describing their feelings whilst being abused. However, one also needs to consider the individual characteristics of the child, such as cognitive and emotional development, and context.[46]

Risks of contamination are associated with multiple interviews due to the possible impact of implicit social demands and explicit suggestions.[47] However, multiple interviews may be necessary, particularly where children have been abused on more than one occasion. On such occasions, 'young' victims of abuse would generally not be expected to provide the precise time and date for each incident, but their account will require information about the place, time, descriptions of participants, and relevant contextual details.[48]   **1.25**

(5) Context

There are a number of contextual factors that are relevant to the interview and court   **1.26**
process and potentially impact on reliability. These include: (a) the status of the witness (i.e. complainant, witness to fact, or suspect); (b) the nature and seriousness of the offence; (c) the relationship between the witness and the accused; (d) the length of time since the offence; (e) how the reporting of the offence emerged (e.g. did the person volunteer the information or was it elicited by another person, such as a parent or police officer?): (f) whether the 'memory' of the offence has always been recalled (i.e. continuous memory)[49] or 'recovered' (e.g. during therapy, extended self-rumination or reference to victim self-help literature); (g) how the witness is interviewed and the quality of that interview; (h) the number of interviews conducted; (i) whether there is only one reported offence or multiple offences; (j) the support provided to the witness prior to and during the police interview and court process; and (h) any external event proximate to the complaint, for instance, a child custody hearing, birth of a child, marriage, divorce, or death.

The greater the delay between the alleged incident and the complaint to the police,   **1.27**
the less likely any recovery of independent evidence that either supports or undermines the reliability of the complaint. Evaluating the credibility and reliability of a sexual complaint, that is, determining whether a crime occurred (beyond

---

[46] See section 5.
[47] See Poole, D.A. and Lamb, M.E. (1998) *Investigative interviews of children. A guide to helping professionals* Washington, DC: American Psychological Association.
[48] Brubacher, S.P., Malloy, L.C., Lamb, M.E., and Roberts, K.P., 'How do interviewers and children discuss individual occurrences of alleged repeated abuse in forensic interviews?' (2013) 27 *Applied Cognitive Psychology*, 443–50. These authors cite the case of *Podirsky v R* (1990) 3 WAR 128.
[49] Although it is important to note that a confident and genuinely held belief in continuous memory recall may not always be accurate. See Schacter, cited at n.13.

reasonable doubt), is not simply about the answers given to cross-examination at trial, but inexorably reaches back to the conduct of the video interview. Evaluating witness testimony, whether it is at the initial charging decision, or behind the door of the jury room, is a daunting and complex task for which there is little guidance.[50] It is uncommon for jurors to hear expert scientific psychological or psychiatric evidence specifically about contextual issues, although it may form an important part of the clinical evaluation. Expert evidence on memory science is not always positively received by the courts.[51]

1.28 As Williamson noted, there is a 'knowledge gap' between science and the law.[52] Investigators, legal professionals, and jurors are often unaware of the complex psychological processes involved when considering the reliability of witness testimony. The approach of the English Court of Appeal appears to be that jurors can be relied on to apply their commonsense in these often highly complex cases.

1.29 Much time and expense is applied to promoting public awareness of victim issues. However, ensuring the integrity of witness testimony by equipping investigators with the knowledge and skills to obtain reliable evidence underscores the entire justice process.

C. Attrition and Conviction Rates and False Allegations

(1) Attrition and conviction rates: How does the data assist?

1.30 The focus of policy-makers, particularly since Kelly's groundbreaking research in 2005,[53] has been to reduce the high attrition rate in rape cases and enhance conviction rates.[54] The working hypothesis is that the sexist attitudes, myths, and stereotypes towards victims of rape have been applied by police investigators, legal professionals, and the general public, causing non-reporting of sexual crime, wrongful discontinuance of complaints, biased/flawed investigations, and wrongful acquittals.

1.31 However, understanding the implications of different perspectives and drawing conclusions from the plethora of studies and official statistics is not easy. Victim

---

[50] Judicial Studies Board (2010) *The Crown Court Bench Book* (March 2010), ch. 17, setting out specimen judicial directions in trials for sexual offences.

[51] *R v Anderson (Stephen)* [2012] EWCA Crim 1785.

[52] Newburn, T., Williamson, T., and Wright, A. (2007) *Handbook of Criminal Investigation*, Cullompton: Willan, ch. 4 on Psychology and Criminal Investigation, 68.

[53] Kelly, L., Lovett, J., and Regan, L. (2005) 'A gap or a chasm? Attrition in reported rape cases' Home Office Research Study, 293.

[54] The 'attrition rate' is the percentage of sexual complaints that are 'lost' or discontinued between complaint to the police and final trial verdict. There are various 'attrition points' where complaints may be discontinued, for instance before the initial charging stage, between charge and trial, and finally during the trial itself when a 'half-time' submission of 'insufficient evidence' or 'no case to answer' may be successfully advanced.

advocates remonstrate that conviction rates are too low, that rape myths abound and false allegations are rare. Their arguments sound compelling, but are sometimes misconstrued[55] and are open to debate.[56] Reece opines that 'regressiveness' of public attitudes may have been 'overstated' and that there is scant evidence that 'myths' are widespread.[57]

Thomas' research on jury verdicts indicates that verdicts in sexual assault cases **1.32** are within the bounds of reasonableness when juxtaposed against other categories of crime.[58] Her study analyzed 551,669 trial outcomes in England and Wales between 2006 and 2008 and found that cases with the strongest direct evidence had the highest conviction rates. For instance, the conviction rates for making indecent images of a child, possession of drugs with intent to supply, and dangerous driving were respectively 89, 84, and 85 per cent. Cases requiring the jury to assess the state of mind of the defendant had lower conviction rates, for example, those for attempted murder and causing grievous bodily harm were respectively 47 and 48 per cent. In contrast, that for rape (usually dependent on determining state of mind) was 55 per cent.

In 2010, Baroness Stern cautioned prosecutors against being propelled into **1.33** prosecuting more cases when 'well trained and dedicated professionals' had identified the case as 'weak' and that this approach was 'not in accordance with the Code for Prosecutors, which requires a realistic prospect of conviction'.[59] She opined that 'scarce prosecution resources should be focused on prosecuting well the cases where the evidence base is strong'. Stern commented it was unhelpful to focus on the conviction rates, taking into account the complex issue of consent usually before the jury; she said, 'it is not easy to see how the conviction rate could reach a much higher level'.[60] Critically, she concluded that in her view the implementation of best practice would increase the number of successful outcomes and that it was time to take a 'broader approach' to measuring success in dealing with rape than using the conviction rate as the yardstick of success. On the matter of the prevalence or otherwise of false sexual allegations, Stern noted the absence of empirical data and recommended further research be conducted.

---

[55] Ibid. For instance, this research showed that only 8% of reported complaints of rape in the study resulted in a conviction. However, the 8% figure has been misunderstood to represent the conviction rate of those cases taken to trial, which is not accurate. See table at p 40 of the research paper.

[56] Reece, H., 'Rape Myths: Is Elite Opinion Right and Popular Opinion Wrong?' (2013) 33(3) *Oxford Journal of Legal Studies*, 445.

[57] Ibid.

[58] Thomas, C., 'Are juries fair?' Ministry of Justice Research Series 1/10, February 2010, confirming an earlier statistical comparison by Wolchover, D. and Heaton-Armstrong, A., 'Rape, myths and statistics' (2008) *Counsel*, May 2008, 29, and 'The truth about rape: forget the myths and look at the statistics' *The Times*, 15 October 2009.

[59] *The Stern Review*, cited at n.15, 94.

[60] Ibid., 94.

1.34 Wolchover and Heaton-Armstrong have commented that instead of focusing on conviction rates, government efforts should be redirected to educating vulnerable witnesses on risk-avoidance, providing further witness support, facilitating quality investigations and case preparation, and refining ways of detecting unreliable allegations.[61]

(2) The 2013 review on 'cases involving allegedly false rape'

1.35 Notwithstanding Stern's findings, there is an escalating public imperative that the conviction rates for sexual crime should be higher. The conviction rate for sexual offences in general and rape had been on a steady upward trend, until 2013.[62] However, in the light of continuing professional and public concerns about the prevalence of 'false' allegations, the DPP conducted a seventeen-month study reviewing all cases identified as suspected false allegations of rape or domestic violence.[63]

1.36 At the outset, the report identifies a 'misplaced belief' that false allegations of rape and domestic violence are 'rife' and seeks to convey a 'more accurate picture'. The review considered pre-filtered cases of potentially 'false' allegations.[64] This posed a potential methodological limitation to the study. For instance, the CPS case workers appear to have known that the charging decision for selected suspect cases would be reviewed by the DPP. This may have rendered decision-making more cautious, by de-selection of cases perceived as borderline.

1.37 The high watermark of the review was that out of 5,651 prosecutions for rape, only 121 (2.1 per cent) suspect cases of false rape complaints were identified. Of those suspect cases, only thirty-five were prosecuted for perverting the course of justice or wasting police time. The conclusion drawn in the report was that only a very small number of individuals were detected and prosecuted for false complaints and thus false allegations were not prevalent within the criminal justice system as a whole.

---

[61] Wolchover, D. and Heaton-Armstrong, A., 'The rape myths myth' (2008) *Counsel*, March 2008, 11–12.

[62] *The Stern Review*, cited at n.15, for a background review. See also Ministry of Justice, Home Office and Office for National Statistics 'An overview of Sexual Offending in England and Wales', January 2013, 1.

[63] Levitt, A. and CPS (2013) 'Charging perverting the course of justice and wasting police time in cases involving allegedly false rape and domestic violence allegations', A joint report to the DPP by Alison Levitt QC, Principal Legal Advisor and the Crown Prosecution Service Equality and Diversity Unit, March 2013.

[64] *Guidance for Charging Perverting the Course of Justice and Wasting Police Time in Cases involving Allegedly False Allegations of Rape and / or Domestic Abuse* http://www.cps.gov.uk/legal/p_to_r/perverting_the_course_of_justice_-_rape_and_dv_allegations/. 'A person who deliberately makes a false allegation in the knowledge that there is a risk that the police will conduct an investigation may be guilty of perverting the course of justice. But, in reaching a decision to prosecute, the prosecutor must be able to prove that the allegation was in fact false. If there is any question as to whether the original allegation might in fact have been true, then there is not a realistic prospect of conviction, and no charge of perverting the course of justice should be brought.'

Whilst the review is of interest, it does not ineluctably lead to the conclusion drawn, **1.38** namely, that 'false' sexual allegations are rare.[65] What the report does reveal is the complex decision-making process and high evidential threshold when considering charges of perverting the course of justice. The CPS guidance instructs that prosecutors must approach suspected false complaints with an abundance of caution, prosecutions of persons under 18 requiring 'very great care'.[66] In summary the guidance demonstrates a highly measured approach to these cases. The case studies showed that prosecutions were only made where incontrovertible direct evidence could be shown proving that the complaint was false. Therefore, the actual rate of false allegations may be higher than the 2.1 per cent identified.

Other relevant information revealed by the study, not so widely broadcast, was the **1.39** extent of third-party reporting and the relationship between these reports and the relative youth of the suspects. In 38 per cent of suspicious crime reports, the initial complaint of rape or domestic violence had been made by someone other than the suspect.[67] In 51 per cent of the cases, the suspect was 21 years or under.

Turvey and McGrath's findings from studying crime data in the United States sug- **1.40** gest that abduction and sexual crime comprise the majority of false crime reports and that false allegations are 'commonplace', constituting a 'significant drain' on resources.[68] However, they highlight the scarcity of sound scientific studies on false reports for sexual assaults. Such studies are required before firm conclusions can be reached about the prevalence of false allegations.

A precise definition of what constitutes a 'false allegation' remains elusive.[69] **1.41** Confining the definition to successful prosecutions for perverting the course of justice is unduly restrictive, inviting unrealistic conviction rate targets. Cases are discontinued and juries acquit defendants for a variety of reasons. A holistic understanding of the attrition and acquittal rates entails acceptance that evidence may sometimes be insufficient to found a conviction. As has been seen, it is difficult to forensically prove an allegation to be false.

---

[65] Commenting on the study, Keir Starmer, the DPP, noted: 'From the cases we have analysed, the indication is that it is therefore extremely rare that a suspect deliberately makes a false allegation of rape ... purely out of malice': Starmer, K., 'False Rape Allegations Rare, But "Damaging Myths" Harm Real Rape Victims', *Huffington Post*, 13 March 2013, *http://www.huffingtonpost. co.uk/2013/03/13/false-rape-allegations-ra_n_2865823.html*.

[66] Guidance Perverting the Course of Justice—Charging in cases involving rape or domestic violence, *http://www.cps.gov.uk/legal/p_to_r/perverting_the_course_of_justice_-_rape_and_dv_allegations/*. Cited at n. 67.

[67] Wolchover and Heaton-Armstrong, 'The rape myths myth' cited at n.64, para 19.

[68] Turvey, B.E. and McGrath, M. 'False allegations of crime' in Turvey, B.E. (2014) *Forensic Victimology: Examining Violent Crimes in Investigative and Legal Contexts*, 2nd edn, Oxford: Academic Press, ch. 9, 253–85 at 253 and 261.

[69] Saunders, C.L., 'The Truth, The Half- Truth and Nothing Like the Truth. Reconceptualising False Allegations of Rape' (2012) 52(6) *British Journal of Criminology* 1152–71. See also, Lisak, D., Gardinier, L., Nicksa, S.C., and Cote, A.M. 'False Allegations of Sexual Assault: An Analysis of Ten Years of Reported Cases' (2010) 16(12) *Violence Against Women*, 1318–34.

1.42   The escalation in historic complaints coupled with the absence of any forensic test confirming witness veracity or falsity, means investigators must be vigilant to ensure a neutral and fair investigation. In historic cases, investigating beyond the allegation to confirm a fact in issue that may corroborate or undermine the main complaint, is sometimes overlooked or not pursued until the last minute. Prosecutors should conduct disclosure enquiries expeditiously so that charging decisions are fully informed and discharge their disclosure duties promptly towards the defence. Defence advocates must scrutinize the Unused Material schedules with care and make relevant applications for outstanding material that may assist their case. (See Chapter 3.)

1.43   Investigators must be scrupulous to maintain an independent investigation and all professionals and fact-finders should tread with equal care to ensure a fair trial occurs. Miscarriages of justice are more likely when neutrality and critical scrutiny is abandoned.

D. Conclusion

1.44   There is tension within the criminal justice system between maximizing the progress of sexual complaints through the justice system via reliable witness testimony on the one hand, and ensuring unreliable complaints are swiftly detected and discarded on the other. False or mistaken complaints in sex cases do occur and may not always be easily identified or proven. Improved identification of these cases is urgently needed.

1.45   Much progress has been made in recent years in identifying vulnerable witnesses and ensuring that they are assisted in giving their best possible evidence. Whilst it may be important for the Court to understand the general principles about memory, individual differences, the nature of the event remembered, and the conditions under which memory is consolidated and elicited, also need to be considered. Context does matter.

1.46   Rather than focusing on maximizing the conviction rate, policy-makers and criminal justice professionals should concentrate on ways to enhance reporting rates and optimize the quality of the investigation and evaluation of witness testimony.

Further Reading

Schacter, D.L. (2007) *How the Mind Forgets and Remembers*, London: Souvenir Press.
Turvey, B.E. (2014) *Forensic Victimology. Examining Violent Crimes in Investigative and Legal Contexts*, 2nd edn Oxford: Academic Press.

2

PROSECUTING SEXUAL OFFENCES IN ENGLAND AND WALES

Diane Birch and John Price QC

A. The Decision to Prosecute and the Merits-Based Approach

There are two stages to the decision to prosecute.[1] First, is there sufficient evidence **2.01** to provide a realistic prospect of conviction? If there is not, then the matter may not proceed however desirable a prosecution may otherwise be. If there is, then is it also in the public interest to proceed? It does not necessarily follow that there ought to be a prosecution in every case where the evidence would justify it.

(1) The evidential stage

The so-called 'merits-based approach' to the assessment of evidence in cases of **2.02** sexual crime has been presented as a recent innovation, and of exclusive application to such crime, designed to encourage the prosecution of cases that previously might not have been prosecuted. It is neither. Rather it is an affirmation of the application

---

[1] *The Code for Crown Prosecutors*, January 2013.

of sound reasoning, basic fairness, and the avoidance of prejudice or unwarranted assumptions in the decision-making process.

2.03 The clearest expression of relevant principle is in *R (FB) v Director of Public Prosecutions:*[2]

> There are some types of case where it is notorious that convictions are hard to obtain, even though … the crown prosecutor may believe that the complainant is truthful and reliable … If the crown prosecutor were to apply a purely predictive approach based on past experience of similar cases (the bookmaker's approach), he might well feel unable to conclude that a jury was more likely than not to convict the defendant…. On the … 'merits based' approach, the question whether the evidential test was satisfied would not depend on statistical guesswork.[3]

2.04 The case concerned an application for judicial review of a decision by the Crown to abandon a prosecution, not in a case of sexual crime, but of causing serious injury. The claim was upheld. The complainant suffered from recurrent mental illness, the symptoms of which included occasional auditory and visual hallucinations. This illness did not mean, however, that he was unreliable; merely that what he said might on occasion be unreliable. In other words, to state the obvious, he was much the same as most others who give evidence in a criminal court! Scrutiny of his account, both internally and in conjunction with other evidence, including the account of the suspect, showed much of what he said to be accurate. The real issue in the case was the narrow one of identification. To have abandoned the prosecution solely because of his medical history was not only 'irrational'—it was a violation of his rights.[4] On either ground the decision had been unlawful.

2.05 It would equally be not only irrational but unlawful to base a decision not to prosecute on similar unwarranted and unthinking assumptions about how a juror might believe a victim of sexual crime should be expected to behave before, at the time of, and immediately after, the conduct complained of, or in court when giving evidence about it, or about what circumstances mark out a true or a false complaint, however widely held such beliefs might be. The prosecutor, when examining the merits of the actual evidence, should instead take account of the fact that a jury will be directed by the judge to beware of such assumptions. The prosecutor must assume that they will do so, not that they will not.

(2) The public interest

2.06 Contrary to an impression which may appear to be given in *R (FB) v Director of Public Prosecutions*[5] this exercise should not involve a prediction of the likely impact of the relevant considerations upon a jury. A jury is not the judge of issues of

---

[2] [2009] EWHC 106 (Admin); [2009] 1 Cr App R 38.
[3] Ibid, at para [50].
[4] The court found that there had been a breach of ECHR Article 3.
[5] Cited at n.3, para [51].

public interest which may arise for consideration in any given case any more than is the judge, be they matters of mitigation or anything else. Jury trials proceed upon the basis that jurors obey their oath (to decide upon *the evidence*) and apply the legal directions they are given by the judge.[6]

In cases of sexual crime the issue is most likely to arise where the suspect and/or **2.07** the presumed victim are very young. In *R (E) v Director of Public Prosecutions*,[7] the Divisional Court quashed as unlawful a decision to prosecute a very young child for sexual offences allegedly committed against her even younger siblings. The ratio of the decision is fact-specific,[8] but the judgment is conspicuous for observations made by the court on matters of principle on this topic arising from the *Code for Crown Prosecutors* and published *CPS Legal Guidance*,[9] which otherwise find little echo in the public statements of senior prosecutors:

(i) There is no legal obligation in this exercise *to seek* the views of a complainant, only to have regard to any such views which may have been expressed.

(ii) There is no primacy in the interests of the victim. The law and the guidance require a proper balancing of the interests of the defendant, of the victim and indeed of the public at large.

B. The Choice of Charge and the Merits-Based Approach

Assuming the case falls to be charged under the Sexual Offences Act 2003, the **2.08** wide range of available offences means that the same facts may give rise to the commission of more than one offence. Here the choice of charge is mainly an issue of policy.[10] Cases involving children again illustrate some of the more difficult issues which may frequently arise.

Whereas it is meaningless in both law and fact to think in terms of consent where **2.09** the complainant is a young child, the issue of actual consent will be relevant to the choice of charge in the case of an older child. Although consent is not a defence to sexual activity, proof of the absence of consent would be a factor of very significant aggravation and the choice of charge should reflect that, so that a jury may decide upon the matter. Accordingly, a complaint by an older child which in the case of an adult would be regarded as a complaint of rape, should be so charged.

At the same time, however, the guidance discourages, in such a case, the use of an **2.10** alternative charge, for example alleging a contravention of section 9[11] especially

---

[6] *R v Christou* [1997] AC 117.

[7] [2011] EWHC 1465 (Admin); [2012] 1 Cr App R 6.

[8] The reasons for the decision wholly failed to address reliable information as to the likely deleterious effect upon the family.

[9] *Rape and Sexual Offences*, ch. 11.

[10] Ibid., chs 2 and 10.

[11] Sexual activity with a child.

where the suspect admits to the sexual activity but asserts that it occurred with actual consent.[12] Essentially this approach is justified in order to avoid 'sending a signal to the jury that the prosecution is not confident of its case. It may also serve to give a jury an easy option'.[13] The reasoning behind this guidance is suspect and sits uneasily with a 'merits-based' approach to charging decisions.

2.11 The decision whether to include a lesser alternative charge in an indictment should not be based upon a hunch that it may be misinterpreted or misused by a jury. It is reasoning of this kind that led to the unlawful decision to abandon the prosecution in the case of *R (FB) v DPP*. If there is a proper evidential foundation for its inclusion and it does not trivialize the case and thereby act as a distraction from the real issue, it should be included. It should be assumed by the prosecutor that the jury will examine the evidence and reach its verdict on the genuine merits of the case. Ensuring that they do so is not achieved by a manipulation of the form of the indictment, but by clear advocacy on the part of the prosecutor and proper direction from the judge. Such a decision being based other than on the merits of a case may well give rise to injustice (to either party), in this instance by presenting a jury with a stark choice between what they might reasonably perceive to be two false alternatives; convicting an accused of the primary offence where satisfactory evidence of an important element may be lacking, or acquitting him entirely, when it is obvious or even has been admitted by him, that he is guilty of an alternative lesser, but still very serious, offence. In such circumstances a court may still have the power to intervene and will do so, but only where Section 6(3) Criminal Law Act 1967 applies.[14] It cannot insist on an amendment to the indictment.

C. Credibility, Complainants, and the Merits-Based Approach

(1) Credibility and the merits of the account

2.12 In the vast majority of prosecutions for sexual offences, the testimony of the complainant forms the central plank of the case. Applying the merits-based approach, the prosecutor must base decisions about credibility on the credibility of the *account*, rather than the *complainant*, avoiding value judgments about personal characteristics and lifestyle (particularly as victims may have been targeted because they are in some way marginalized by their circumstances, for example adolescents in a care home). Myths and stereotypes must not cloud judgement. A person groomed and abused in childhood may repeatedly go back to the suspect, genuinely believing

---

[12] It may be still considered a very serious offence if, for example, he is very much older than the child or occupies a position of trust.

[13] *Rape and Sexual Offences*, cited at n.9, ch. 10 (Alternative charges).

[14] *R v Foster* [2007] EWCA Crim 2869, [2008] 1 Cr App R 38.

that theirs is a loving relationship. So as not to be misled by such indications, prosecutors must adopt 'a sophisticated and informed' approach at the pre-trial stage[15] and challenge the making of false assumptions at trial. Common examples of false assumptions are set out in prosecutorial guidance and in the judicial Bench Book, with some experienced judges giving the jury a steer away from them at the outset of a trial, rather than waiting until the summing-up.

This represents a conscious attempt to turn the tide in terms of how credibility **2.13** has traditionally been viewed. Complainants in sexual cases used to attract mandatory corroboration warnings, on the basis that their allegations were easy to invent and difficult to refute. Child witnesses, even if competent, were regarded as inherently unreliable and potential fantasists. Both propositions were peddled on the basis that 'everyone knew' these truths.[16] The law having purged itself of these false assumptions, the concern is that society has not,[17] so that the trial must furnish a proper understanding of the context, including how victimization affects behaviour.

Shocking revelations about the crimes of the late Jimmy Savile, and others who **2.14** exploited the power that society's misperceptions helped to confer upon them, may force juries to accept the new orthodoxies of the dynamics of sexual offending. But the merits-based approach faces other challenges, particularly where, as is frequently the case, the prosecutor is entirely dependent on the complainant's evidence to prove what occurred, or that it was without consent.[18] While a jury can still convict on the basis of one person's word against another's, the danger of false assumptions is greatest where the credibility of the complaint and the complainant merge. Furthermore, the traditional indications of lack of credibility that continue to form part of the trial process, such as inconsistency, lies, and bad character, centre primarily on the complainant rather than the complaint, potentially militating against the merits-based approach.

(2) Inconsistency

Any real and significant inconsistency is bound to be exploited at trial: the rules **2.15** of evidence subscribe to the proposition that inconsistency is an indication of unreliability, and the statutory reworking of the hearsay rule builds on tradition by allowing the inconsistent statement to be evidence of the facts stated.[19] But the prosecutor should consider alternative explanations, particularly in the

---

[15] Levitt, A. and Emerson, T., 'After the "Watershed": The New CPS Guidelines on Prosecuting Cases of Child Sexual Abuse', *Blackstone's Criminal Practice Quarterly Update*, Spring 2014.

[16] *DPP v Hester* [1973] AC 296.

[17] See e.g. the *Joint CPS and Police Action Plan on Rape*, June 2014, where it is said that not only police and prosecutors, but also communities must 'reject the out of date myths'.

[18] *CPS Policy for Prosecuting Cases of Rape*, s 5.1.

[19] Criminal Justice Act 2003, s 119.

case of children, where the CPS Guidance explains that piecemeal or seemingly contradictory disclosure is so commonplace that it can potentially be regarded as symptomatic of abuse rather than as an indication of untruthfulness.[20] In such cases the standard judicial direction that it is 'unwise to assume that an inconsistent account is always untrue'[21] may fall well short of the mark in providing a balanced picture.

2.16 In the case of adult witnesses too, inconsistency may be explained on other grounds: for example a traumatized witness may suffer lapses of memory.[22] In *R v PR*[23] the complainant testified that she could only clearly remember one act of incest by her father when she was a child; if, as the prosecution claimed, there were more, she had no clear recollection of them. In cross-examination she was asked about a previous statement in which she suggested that there were other occasions: a strategy which backfired when it was held that the jury was entitled to convict on the strength of the 'inconsistent' statement.

(3) Lies

2.17 Many complaints termed 'false' by police and prosecutors merely contain a demonstrable lie rather than disclose no offence.[24] In all cases where the complainant has lied, careful thought must be given to the implications, but it by no means follows that the complaint itself is false. The reasons for lying may, as with inconsistency, be far from straightforward, but ultimately a jury may be convinced that, despite the falsehood, the complainant is telling the truth about core matters.[25] A common example is the case of an adolescent complaining truthfully of sexual abuse by an adult, but covering embarrassment by untruthfully asserting an absence of actual consent. A prosecutor should look behind the falsehood to see whether there is a convincing reason for it, and/or some independent evidence supporting the core elements of the complaint. Appeals are often mounted on the ground that the judge should have instructed the jury to look for independent confirmation of a witness who has lied (the *Makanjuola* warning [26]) but the emphasis on what is effectively corroboration has begun to look heavy-handed in light of current thinking about the likelihood of evasiveness and denial in the disclosure process, and appeals seldom succeed if the jury's attention has been properly directed to the lie in the summing-up.

---

[20] CPS, (2013) *Guidelines on Prosecuting Cases of Child Sexual Abuse*, para 40.
[21] *Crown Court Bench Book*, ch. 17 (Sexual Offences).
[22] Ibid.
[23] [2010] EWCA Crim 2741.
[24] Saunders, C., 'The Truth, The Half-Truth, And Nothing Like The Truth' (2012) 52 *Br J Criminol* 1152.
[25] See, for example, *P* [2013] EWCA Crim 1426, where there was supporting evidence but no obvious reason for the lies, and *Joshi* [2012] NICA 56 where there was neither.
[26] [1995] 2 Cr App R 469.

(4) Bad character and lifestyle

Statutory restrictions on the use of bad character evidence mean that a complain- **2.18**
ant's convictions, though disclosable, will not necessarily be admissible to attack
credibility at trial: even previous convictions for dishonesty have been found to
be of insufficient relevance where the issue is consent.[27] The same is true of other
evidence of misconduct such as a confession of murder.[28] If there was once an
'anything goes' approach to discrediting complainants, those days are past.[29] As
understanding of the link between victimization and criminal behaviour becomes
more widespread, patterns of offending particularly associated with abuse might
instead form part of the prosecution case.

At the same time, the greater freedom to make use of the accused's bad character **2.19**
means that evidence of a relevant discreditable propensity may enhance the credibility of a complaint, for example where a child alleges sexual assault against a
man who, unknown to him or her, uses pornography indicating a sexual interest
in children.[30]

The sexual behaviour of the complainant on other occasions is irrelevant both to **2.20**
consent and to credibility:[31] a hard-won statutory rule that there are no plans to
change. False complaints made on other occasions fall outside the statutory prohibition, but the courts are careful to ensure that there is evidence that a complaint
was indeed false, and that this is not an indirect way of introducing the sort of
prejudicial evidence that the prohibition was intended to catch.[32] But convictions
obtained since the merits-based approach was introduced suggest that juries may
be less susceptible to prejudice than is traditionally thought. In *Gjoni*[33] G was convicted of raping the complainant after she had been out drinking with G and his
male friends, invited them into her home, taken cocaine and had consensual sex
with one of them. Despite inconsistencies in her account the jury believed her. The
evidence that was (rightly) excluded—a claim that she had previously been intimate with one of the other men—was arguably less likely to prejudice a jury than
the colourful account of the night in question, but the result was still a conviction.

(5) Pre-trial witness interviews

Since 2008, prosecutors have been allowed to conduct pre-trial witness interviews **2.21**
(PTWIs) in order to make a better-informed decision about any aspect of the case

---

[27] Criminal Justice Act 2003 s 100; *Garnham* [2008] EWCA Crim 266.
[28] *B* (2104) (unreported, 19 March).
[29] *W* [2014] EWCA Crim 545.
[30] Criminal Justice Act 2003, s 101; *Latham* [2014] EWCA Crim 207, applying *D* [2012] 1 Cr
App R 8.
[31] Youth Justice and Criminal Evidence Act 1999, s 41.
[32] *M* [2009] EWCA Crim 618.
[33] [2014] EWCA Crim 691.

including the reliability of testimony.[34] A PTWI should always be considered as part of the decision-making in rape cases, and is regarded as an effective tool especially in borderline cases.[35] PTWIs break with the tradition that prosecutors should not contact their witnesses before trial; a tradition that sometimes left the prosecutor over-dependent on the thoroughness and judgement of the investigator. An early study showed that PTWIs are useful to obtain information omitted from a complainant's original statement, and to follow up on information coming to light subsequently, including the emergence of material that might fuel cross-examination.[36] However, much if not all of this information could be acquired by a follow-up interview conducted by the investigator rather than a prosecutor. While experienced lawyers may have the edge over investigators in assessing how a complainant will come across in court where it is 'one person's word against another's', there is a risk that this may be seen either as impermissible coaching[37] or as an exercise in focusing on the complainant rather than the complaint (which would be contrary to the merits-based approach). Provided these pitfalls are avoided, the PTWI may provide a useful step in building the case.

D. Holding Prosecutors to Account

2.22 Only in highly exceptional cases will the courts disturb the decision of an independent prosecutor. The rule reflects the separation of powers and the breadth of the discretion entrusted to the prosecutor, and recognizes that prosecutorial decision-making is 'polycentric', taking account of a range of policy and public interest considerations that a court is not competent to second-guess.[38] 'Polycentric' is particularly apt as a description of the decision-making in sexual cases.

(1) Challenging decision to discontinue proceedings

2.23 *The Victims' Right to Review Scheme* (VRR) provides a time frame and procedure within which victims can seek an internal review of a decision to terminate proceedings. VRR gives effect to Article 11 of the EU Directive on the Rights of Victims of Crime,[39] and reflects the decision of the Court of Appeal in *Killick*[40]

---

[34] CPS, *Pre-Trial Witness Interviews—Guidance for Prosecutors*, http://www.cps.gov.uk/legal/p_to_r/pre_-trial_witness_interviews/.

[35] *Rape and Sexual Offences*, cited at n.9, Guidance, ch.7.

[36] Roberts, P. and Saunders, C., 'Piloting PTWI: A Socio-Legal Window on Prosecutors' Assessments of Evidence and Witness Credibility' (2010) 30(1) *Oxford Journal of Legal Studies*, at 101. Rape and other sexual assaults accounted for about a third of cases in the study.

[37] McGowan, L., 'Prosecution Interviews of Witnesses: What More Will Be Sacrificed to "Narrow the Justice Gap"?' (2006) 70 *J.C.L.* 351.

[38] Lord Bingham in *R (On The Application of Corner House Research and others) v Director of The Serious Fraud Office* [2009] UKHL 60.

[39] 2012/29/EU 'victims, in accordance with their role in the relevant criminal justice system, have the right to a review of a decision not to prosecute'.

[40] [2011] EWCA Crim 1608.

that it would be disproportionate to expect an aggrieved victim to resort to judicial review in the first instance. The courts have welcomed VRR,[41] on the grounds that internal review is a better process for checking that all relevant considerations have been taken into account, and allows the victim to succeed if the decision is merely wrong rather than manifestly unreasonable.[42] Where a decision not to prosecute has followed a 'painstaking' review, it is likely to be only in 'very rare' cases that judicial review proceedings will show up a flaw in the outcome. For example in *R (F) v DPP*,[43] F claimed that she had agreed to intercourse with D on the condition that he would not ejaculate, which he then did. An internal review determined that there was not enough evidence to support a charge of rape, but judicial review was granted so that the reviewer could factor in a later authority about consent,[44] that underlined the importance of a complainant's choice in relation to crucial features such as the risk of pregnancy.

(2) Challenging decision to prosecute

Judicial review of a decision to prosecute will rarely be entertained, as an alternative remedy will be available at trial,[45] through either abuse of process, or a successful submission of no case to answer. In exceptional cases it appears that the court may intervene where there has been a manifest failure to follow policy, as in *R (E) v Director of Public Prosecutions*[46] where the decision to prosecute a girl for sexual offences committed against her younger siblings when she was aged 12 was quashed. However, the later decision in *A*[47] suggests that *E* was exceptional only because the court was also considering the adverse effect of prosecution on E's siblings: had E's case stood alone, judicial review would not have been appropriate. **2.24**

While the court may not be the right forum to enforce policy, courts certainly exercise considerable influence over its formulation. In *A*, the applicant had been convicted of perverting the course of justice for falsely retracting an allegation of rape by her violent and abusive husband. The Court of Appeal promptly quashed her custodial sentence, expressing the hope that the prosecution of vulnerable rape victims would be 'very exceptional'. In consequence, fresh guidance was issued to prosecutors under which A would not have been prosecuted.[48] This change to policy did not, however, afford a ground of appeal against conviction. **2.25**

---

[41] *L v DPP* [2013] EWHC 1752 (Admin).

[42] Starmer, K., 'Finality in Criminal Justice: When Should the CPS Reopen a Case?' [2012] Crim LR 526.

[43] [2013] EWHC 954 (Admin).

[44] *Assange v Swedish Prosecution Authority* [2011] EWHC 2849 (Admin).

[45] *R v DPP ex p Kebilene* [2000] 2 AC 326 (Lord Hobhouse).

[46] [2011] EWHC 1465 (Admin) [2012] 1 Cr App R 6, considered above at para 2.07.

[47] [2012] EWCA Crim 434.

[48] [2010] EWCA Crim 2913.

(3) Finality and promises not to prosecute

2.26 A person who has been officially notified that he or she will not be prosecuted for a crime has a legitimate interest in the finality of prosecutorial decision-making, but his or her interest has to be balanced against the need to review incorrect decisions, and the interests of victims in seeing justice done. Where an initial decision not to prosecute is overturned, it is unlikely that this alone will give rise to an abuse of process. Particular factors may, however, render it 'unfair to prosecute' and thus an abuse. The leading authority of *Abu Hamza*[49] suggests that this is 'unlikely' unless (i) there has been an unequivocal representation by the relevant authorities that the defendant will not be prosecuted; and (ii) the defendant has acted on that representation to his or her detriment. But Lord Phillips CJ was careful also to stress that these considerations might yield to the discovery of new facts that were not known when the representation was made: a qualification that might be of particular importance in relation to sexual offences where, for example, other complainants come forward. In *Gripton*[50] the court stressed that this was not an area of law best served by comprehensive binding rules: rather the courts are 'concerned with considerations of fairness and they must be free to respond to the circumstances of each case'. Thus a stay may be the right course of action whether or not the defendant has acted to his detriment: it all depends on the strength of the competing interests to be weighed.[51]

(4) Private prosecutions

2.27 In the event of a decision not to prosecute, a complainant could in theory bring a private prosecution. However, such proceedings may be taken over and discontinued by the CPS, using the same evidential threshold that applies to a public prosecution.[52] Additionally, the private prosecution may be judged to be an abuse of process, in that the complainant ought instead to have sought a review of the original decision.[53]

E. Non-recent Offences and the Effect of Previous Stays

2.28 Until recently, any prosecutor deciding whether to charge where an offence is said to have occurred many years ago would be mindful of the risk of a stay of proceedings being imposed on the ground of abuse of process occasioned by delay. With

---

[49] [2007] QB 659; and see *Killick* cited at n.40; *R v Croydon justices, ex p Dean* [1993] QB 769.
[50] [2010] EWCA Crim 2260; and see *Bloomfield* [1997] 1 Cr App R 27.
[51] In *R v John Downey* 24 February 2014, the key consideration was the public interest in holding officials of the state to undertakings linked to the peace process in Northern Ireland 'in full understanding' of the importance of keeping to their part of the bargain. Although there was some evidence of detrimental reliance by D, it seems highly unlikely that the outcome would have been different in the absence of detriment: *http://www.judiciary.gov.uk/wp-content/uploads/JCO/Documents/Judgments/r-v-downey-abuse-judgment.pdf*.
[52] *R v Gujra* [2012] UKSC 52.
[53] *Jones v Whalley* [2007] 1 AC 63.

the decision in *F(S)*[54] this risk has effectively vanished unless, exceptionally, a fair trial is no longer possible owing to prejudice to the defendant occasioned by the delay which cannot fairly be addressed in the normal trial process. In some cases there is instead a new and intriguing challenge to be addressed.

In today's more sympathetic climate increasing numbers of adult complainants may feel **2.29** emboldened finally to come forward about events in their childhood. New evidence of serious offending may emerge in respect of suspects previously prosecuted based upon the complaints of others, where proceedings were stayed in circumstances that would now lead to a rejection of such an application; where a fair trial was and remains possible. The new complaints and the old may be of a similar vintage, and allege very similar circumstances; for example, complaints by former boys at the same school against the same teacher. The situation may therefore arise where it is possible to try the later complaints but not those made earlier. This has already happened.[55] Such a situation is a recipe for legitimate and profound grievance; is there anything that can be done?

As we have seen, an incorrect decision by a prosecutor not to prosecute may be **2.30** reversed, even where notified to an accused.[56] In the tension between the right [as it is] to an adjudication upon the merits and the need for finality of notified decisions, the balance has moved firmly in the direction of the former. Even if the accused has acted to his detriment in reliance upon the notification, 'if facts come to light which were not known when the representation was made, these may justify proceeding with the prosecution despite the representation'. [57]

Is a court able therefore to reverse an incorrect decision not to try the case where **2.31** the same applies; in other words where, for example, since the stay was imposed, new evidence of a similar kind has emerged against the same suspect and it is plain to a court applying the law as now clearly stated in *F(S)*, that a fair trial of all of the complaints is possible and therefore desirable?

The problem is one of jurisdiction. A prosecutor may change a decision because it is **2.32** wrong. It is elementary, however, that one Crown Court judge exercises no appellate jurisdiction in respect of a decision by another. It is insufficient therefore, in seeking to lift a stay, simply to establish that the earlier ruling was wrong.

A 'stay of proceedings' is not a final disposal, because it is not an adjudication of **2.33** the merits:

> I am of the opinion that the effect of a stay is that it is not equivalent to a discontinuance, or to a judgment for the plaintiff or the defendants. It is a stay which can be and may be removed if proper grounds are shown …[58]

---

[54] [2011] EWCA Crim 1844, [2011] 2 Cr App R 28.
[55] *R v Roland Peter Wright* Aylesbury CC, December 2013.
[56] *R v Killick* [2012] 1. Cr App R 10; [2011] EWCA Crim 1608 cited at n.40.
[57] *R v Abu Hamza* [2007] 1 Cr App R 27; [2006] EWCA Crim 2918.
[58] *Cooper v Williams* 1963 2 QB 567 (Lord Denning MR) at 580.

2.34   It has been acknowledged that a Crown Court has the power to lift a stay it has imposed,[59] or even to 'sidestep' a stay imposed by examining justices.[60] The problem, however, is that where a stay has been imposed on the ground of delay, there is no doubt that it was *intended* by the judge and understood by the parties to be final; an effective and permanent end to the proceedings in question. After all, the passage of time is hardly likely to cure the perceived defect.

2.35   The question which therefore arises for authoritative decision is whether, as in *Killick*, in the case of a prosecutor's decision, a subsequent and significant change of circumstance is sufficient to confer the power for a stay to be lifted or whether, in addition, it is necessary to establish a defect in the process by which the stay was initially obtained, such as, for example, by demonstrating that the court was misled or mistakenly informed as to a critical fact. If it is the latter, then it is likely to prove very difficult to succeed in such an application.

2.36   Alternatively, and subject to it being admissible,[61] there would seem to be no good reason in such a case why the previous stay, wrongly imposed but otherwise inviolable, should of itself operate to prevent the admission of the evidence of the complainants from the earlier case. It has long since been established that even a previous acquittal is not a bar to the admission of the evidence that lay behind the charge.[62] In deciding questions of legal admissibility, nothing more than the conventional law of evidence is to be applied. Recent authority confirms that this basic principle of admissibility applies to evidence originally adduced in proceedings the subject of a stay, whatever the reason for its imposition and including a case where it was imposed on the grounds of delay.[63] A relevant previous history involving, for example, an acquittal or a stay may, of course, be relevant to the consideration of the exercise of the discretion to exclude.

2.37   The aggrieved complainants, however, will be likely to view this as poor, if any, consolation. This chapter has been primarily concerned with the public policy objective of ensuring that all serious cases of alleged sexual offending are prosecuted and tried on their true merits. The hangover of stays wrongly imposed to prevent the trial of complaints that are worthy of prosecution, may be a real impediment to it being fulfilled.

2.38   A very recent case, however, points to an alternative solution. In *R v Paul Gadd* [aka Gary Glitter][64] the accused had been the subject of a complaint of serious sexual assault made to the police by a woman in 1998 relating to an alleged event in about 1975, when she was still a very young child. At the committal proceedings

---

[59]   *R v Butterfield* (1999) unreported 30 July 1999; No 98/4198/W5, 98/4202/W5.
[60]   *R v C (Committal Proceedings)* (1995) 159 JP 205.
[61]   Under s 101(1)(d) Criminal Justice Act 2003 as evidence of bad character.
[62]   *R v Z* [2000] 2 AC 483.
[63]   *R v Smith (David)* [2006] 2 Cr App R 4; and *R v Wright* [2014] EWCA Crim 1790.
[64]   [2014] EWHC 3307 (QB).

the charge was stayed by the stipendiary magistrate as an abuse of the process of the court on the ground of delay. An application by the prosecution for leave to appeal by way of judicial review was refused by the Divisional Court.[65] In October 2012, in the wake of publicity surrounding the activities of Jimmy Savile, further complainants came forward to report serious sexual assaults by Mr Gadd in respect of which he was charged in 2014. In the light of these developments the prosecution applied to the High Court for leave to prefer a voluntary bill of indictment in respect of fresh charges arising from the 1998 complaint which had been stayed. The stay having been granted by a magistrates' court, authority existed in a similar case to indicate that the use of this procedure disposed of the issue of jurisdiction.[66] So much was conceded in the High Court which was therefore freed to consider the matter on its merits. Notwithstanding the difficulty caused by the adverse ruling of the Divisional Court in 1998, the application was granted. In February 2015 Mr Gadd was convicted of an offence of attempted rape in respect of a complaint that had been stayed seventeen years earlier on the grounds of delay. It remains to be seen whether this procedure may overcome the issue of jurisdiction in the case of a stay granted by a Crown Court but there would seem to be no reason in principle why not. If so, then here also the High Court would be free to consider the matter on its merits.

Author Biographies

Professor Diane Birch OBE is JC Smith Professor of Law at the University of Nottingham. She has written widely in relation to the presentation of the evidence of vulnerable witnesses and helped to produce the original 'Achieving Best Evidence' materials. She is also a contributing editor to the evidence sections of *Blackstone's Criminal Practice*.

John Price QC practices criminal law at 23 Essex Street, London. He was called to the bar in 1982, appointed a Recorder in 2007 and Queen's Counsel in 2009. He prosecutes and defends in all forms of major criminal cases and has extensive experience in the conduct of complex trials of serious sexual offences, including cases where the alleged offence occurred many years before the trial. He appeared for the Crown before the Court of Appeal Criminal Division in the leading cases of *R v F(S)* (abuse of process arising from delay) and *R v H and others* (guideline in sentencing 'historic' cases).

---

[65] CO/3970/98. CO/3742/98, 9 July 1998.
[66] *R v C (Committal Proceedings)* (1995) 159 JP 205.

3

DISCLOSURE ISSUES IN THE INVESTIGATION AND TRIAL OF ALLEGATIONS OF SEXUAL ASSAULT

Anthony Heaton-Armstrong, HHJ Seán Enright, David Wolchover, and Paul Keleher QC

A. Introduction

(1) The distinction between disclosure issues in sexual assault cases and others

3.01 In contrast with other cases, allegations of sexual assault very frequently involve events where the complainant and the accused were together in private and where there is little, if any, independent evidential support for the accounts of either. In contested trials the issues necessarily focus on whether the complainant is dishonest or—due to a wide variety of mental processes—honestly mistaken. It is thus inevitable that the disclosure process concentrates on factors peculiar to the complainant's background, such as the history of his or her mental health and relevant involvement with third parties such as social services departments and therapeutic counsellors, and any prior engagements with the police. The fact that so many sexual assault cases now involve events said to have occurred many years previously brings all these issues into sharper relief. In such 'historic' cases the disclosure process is critical. All of this concern reflects the experience of the courts that, in a small proportion of cases, the complaint proves to be unreliable or the complainant's account simply false. Occasionally, this emerges only at a late stage of a trial, or even afterwards.

3.02 In some cases the reasons for a false allegation may be obvious but in others, much less so. And here lies one of the paradoxes of the adversarial process: the duty of making disclosure does not rest with an independent body, it lies with the prosecution. It is a difficult and time-consuming process which involves making unpalatable decisions which may impact on the privacy of complainants. Although the disclosure process is carried out well in the majority of cases there are, however, others where the operation of the process is patently inadequate.

(2) Purpose of this chapter

3.03 The readers' knowledge of the detail and mechanics of disclosure law is assumed, since this is adequately covered in other texts.[1] It is sufficient to say that the statutory

---

[1] *Archbold: Criminal Pleading, Evidence and Practice*, London: Sweet & Maxwell, and *Blackstone's Criminal Practice*, Oxford: Oxford University Press, are published annually with supplements. For other works on disclosure in general, see e.g. Epp, J.A. (2001) *Building on the Decade of Disclosure*

regulation of disclosure law is set out in the Criminal Procedure and Investigations Act 1996 (CPIA) and its accompanying Code of Practice which provides guidance as to how the prosecution should approach their role, and imposes a duty on the investigator to 'pursue all reasonable lines of inquiry, whether these point towards or away from the suspect.'[2]

The Attorney General's *Guidelines on Disclosure* have been revised in a number **3.04** of editions, most recently published on 3 December 2013,[3] contemporaneously with the also revised version of the *Judicial Protocol on the Disclosure of Unused Material in Criminal Cases*.[4] The Crown Prosecution Service (CPS) is bound by its own Manual and guidance—on disclosure in all cases,[5] in rape and sexual cases,[6] on prosecuting cases of child sexual abuse[7] and, as endorsed in the 2013 *Judicial Protocol*, on 'Disclosure of information in cases of alleged child abuse and linked criminal and care directions hearings'.[8]

That is simply a summary because this chapter is not a discourse on disclosure law **3.05** or its defects but concentrates on the need for the correct mindset, how problems arise during the trial process, and the sources of potentially disclosable material. We will also suggest appropriate strategies for advocates to follow. Finally, we make some suggestions for systemic improvements.

B. Getting the Mindset Right

(1) Apparent confidence and fundamental error

The late Lord Bingham of Cornhill memorably observed that 'the common law **3.06** is nothing if not pragmatic. It lives and it learns. So it has learned ... less obvious lessons: that witnesses ... may be completely honest, entirely confident, very persuasive, but quite wrong.'[9] There is no shortage of reported cases which exemplify

---

in *Criminal Procedure*, London: Cavendish; Corker, D. and Parkinson, S. (2009) *Disclosure in Criminal Proceedings*, Oxford: Oxford University Press; Heaton-Armstrong, A., Corker, D., and Wolchover, D. (2006) 'Disclosure of unused material by prosecution authorities and third parties' in Heaton-Armstrong, A., Shepherd, E., Gudjonsson, G., and Wolchover, D. (eds), *Witness Testimony: Psychological, Investigative and Evidential Perspectives*, Oxford: Oxford University Press, ch 21. See also Rook, P. and Ward, R. (2010) *Sexual Offences, Law and Practice*, 4th edn, London: Sweet & Maxwell, ch 25 and 1st supp., March 2014.

[2] CPIA Code of Practice under Part II para 3.5.
[3] *https://www.gov.uk/government/publications/attorney-generals-guidelines-on-disclosure-2013*.
[4] *https://www.judiciary.gov.uk/publications-and-reports/protocols/criminal-protocols/protocol-unused-material-criminal-cases*.
[5] CPS Disclosure Manual, *http://www.cps.gov.uk/legal/d_to_g/disclosure_manual/*.
[6] *http://www.cps.gov.uk/legal/p_to_r/rape_and_sexual_offences/*.
[7] *http://www.cps.gov.uk/legal/a_to_c/child_sexual_abuse*.
[8] *http://www.cps.gov.uk/publications/docs/third_party_protocol_2013.pdf*.
[9] Bingham, T. Foreword in Heaton-Armstrong, A., Shepherd, E., and Wolchover, D. (eds), (1999) *Analysing Witness Testimony*, London: Blackstone Press.

this proposition, some of them involving convictions of those who were later exonerated.

(2) Prosecutor's crucial need for objective open-mindedness

3.07 Investigators and prosecution lawyers need to keep a clear head and a mind uncluttered by bias caused by a plausible complainant, remembering the nature of their roles—to be not the complainant's advocates but impartial and unprejudiced professionals.

(3) Irrelevance of the apparent strength of evidence

3.08 Regardless of any personal view of the probable outcome of court proceedings, investigators and prosecution lawyers need to be alert to the broad range of motives and explanations that give rise to false complaints—and to remember that in a very small number of cases complainants have been known to fabricate evidence (by concocting real evidence) in their efforts to strengthen the credibility of their accounts.[10] We should stress that there is no evidence that false complaints are more likely to emanate from any particular demographic grouping in society—the phenomenon is simply one of the problems faced during the investigative and trial processes.

C. How Problems Arise

(1) At the police station

3.09 The first opportunity for disclosure of any information concerning an allegation arises at the police station following the suspect's arrest. The process by which this is effected is not legally controlled, the consequence of which is that what a suspect or his or her legal representative is told by the police will depend on the discretion of the investigating officer. Experience shows that such disclosure is not always in writing and may not be accurate. It is important to bear in mind that inadequate disclosure often leads police station lawyers to advise their clients in favour of making no comment in interview, an option which may have a direct impact not only on the charging decision but later, during the trial, on invoking the licence to draw adverse inferences under section 34, and related sections, of the Criminal Justice and Public Order Act 1994. Comprehensive recording of disclosures made is therefore essential.[11]

---

[10] For a discussion of this and other issues raised in this chapter, see Wolchover, D. and Heaton-Armstrong, A., 'Rape Trials' (2010) 174(17) *Criminal Law and Justice Weekly* (24 April), 244–9; and Heaton-Armstrong, A. 'Rape—myth and reality and the need for balance' (2010) 50 *Medicine Science & the Law*, 111–15.

[11] For extensive consideration of these issues see Cape, E. (2011) *Defending Suspects at Police Stations*, 6th edn, London: Legal Action Group.

(2) Appointment of the disclosure officer

3.10 'Unused' material—that is, material which does not form part of the prosecution case and, thus, the subject of potential disclosure to the defence—is, at least in the early stages of the investigative and forensic processes, accessible only to the investigating police. There is a process for this material to be passed on to the prosecution legal team. But access to unused material by the defence is, thus, initially dependent on decisions made by the police. The experience of the appellate courts shows that many past decisions made by the police not to disclose have been clearly mistaken and that such errors continue to be made.

3.11 In recognition of the risk that the investigating officer might not perform the police disclosure obligation with sufficient independence of mind, the CPIA Code makes provision for two different officers to be tasked with these roles, but with the proviso that in certain circumstances one can perform both. This relaxation of the principle has, in all but the most complex cases, resulted in a single officer being both in charge of the investigation and responsible for disclosure. The tension this creates in the system has often been a source of non-disclosure.

(3) The distinction between the initial and continuing disclosure processes

3.12 The CPIA and its Code provide for two stages in the performance of the prosecution's disclosure obligations—initial and continuing. Initial disclosure is required to be performed before the defendant has served his defence statement. Initial disclosure comprises, first, the evidence which the prosecution intends to adduce at trial, and second, any 'unused' material which, essentially, has the capacity to undermine the strength of the prosecution allegations. In a sexual assault case the latter ought, typically, to include, for example, records of the complainant having made false complaints or having criminally offended. Such disclosure does not depend on the notification of any prospective defence provided by the defendant in police interview, although this can—and in appropriate circumstances should—be taken into account.[12]

3.13 Continuing disclosure should occur after a defence statement has been served. Material disclosed to the defence at the 'continuing' stage being, in effect, the prosecution's response to any additional factual issues raised in the defence statement.

3.14 In spite of these carefully delineated requirements, the experience of many practitioners has shown that material which ought to have been disclosed at the initial stage is disclosed only in response to defence requests for disclosure. The implication

---

[12] Paragraph 7.3 of the CPIA Code of Practice specifically requires the disclosure officer to provide the prosecutor with copies of any material that casts doubt upon the reliability of a confession or of a prosecution witness, regardless of whether any defence has been advanced.

of this tendency is that without a specific defence request the material might never have been disclosed at all.

3.15 Leaving aside the resource implications of initial disclosure failures, another consequence is that whether or not comprehensive disclosure takes place may depend, in part, on the competence and experience of the defence lawyer.

(4) Disclosure schedules—sensitive and non-sensitive schedules

3.16 It is the disclosure officer's responsibility to list every item of unused material on either a non-sensitive (referred to by police as the MG6C) or sensitive (MG6D) schedule. The MG6C, but not the MG6D, is served on the defence as part of initial disclosure. If the defence have not been copied an item listed on the MG6C they can make a section 8 CPIA application to the court for an order requiring disclosure of this but for obvious reasons the defence cannot make such an application in relation to an item listed on the MG6D.

3.17 In some prosecuting advocates' experience certain items which ought to have been listed on the non-sensitive schedule are wrongly listed on the sensitive schedule, thus precluding the defence from applying for an order for disclosure: it is something to guard against.

(5) Adequacy of disclosure schedules

3.18 It is obligatory that schedules of unused material are comprehensive and are described in such a way as will enable the prosecution case lawyer to make informed decisions as to whether they require sight of the item listed.[13] The defence have little means of challenging effectively either the comprehensiveness or the specificity of the non-sensitive disclosure schedule.

(6) Failures in communication

3.19 The disclosure process involves several complex steps by different participants in positions of responsibility on the prosecution team. Its success depends on an open-minded approach and meticulous attention to minutiae. One particularly egregious example of a failure of communication occurred in a recent rape case. The complainant said she had had no prior sexual experience and this was a relevant feature of the evidence. The original police disclosure officer, his substitute, and the prosecution reviewing lawyer had viewed the complainant's medical records and informed prosecution counsel that they contained no disclosable material. On the first day of trial the medical records were viewed by prosecuting counsel and found to contain references to the complainant having had a prior sexual relationship. In

---

[13] This is a specific requirement of the CPIA Code of Practice, para 6.11, emphasized in the Attorney-General's Guidelines, para 23.

that case a serious error in the disclosure process was revealed. It is no satisfactory answer to say that the material came to light just in time for the trial.

Success in the disclosure field hinges on the maintenance of effective and efficient **3.20** lines of communication between the three prosecution participants—the police disclosure officer, the reviewing lawyer, and the prosecuting advocate. Common problems that arise include material sent electronically to the prosecuting lawyer not reaching its target, the police failing to pass relevant material on to the prosecuting lawyer, and prosecuting lawyers not reading or adequately considering the implications of material sent to them by the police. These all occur all too frequently. How much is not revealed because it gets missed?[14] But at least understanding that this is part of the problem allows solutions to be formulated.

(7) Efficiency—or otherwise—and the eleventh-hour experience

It is often only after a trial has begun and occasionally when it is well advanced **3.21** that a vital piece of undisclosed unused material comes to light, owing to persistent defence requests or simply by chance, rather than to the methodical operation of the disclosure regime. It is a reminder of the need for vigilance and following proper procedures. A piecemeal, eleventh-hour and reactive approach to disclosure not only risks unjust convictions but also puts in peril truthful complainants—because the credibility of their evidence may be irreparably damaged by late disclosure implying an unfair prosecution. Prompt and methodically based disclosure, properly undertaken in accordance with the legal regime, militates in favour of just verdicts.

Funding and remuneration are also issues. CPS case lawyers are overworked and **3.22** under-resourced; self-employed prosecuting counsel are normally not paid for their role in the disclosure process and may attend to their obligations at a late stage. For various reasons defence advocates who are insufficiently experienced in sexual assault cases may be instructed. Such matters are unpalatable but real influences on the disclosure process.

(8) Defence failures

As the *Judicial Protocol* and other guidance make clear, disclosure failures are **3.23** not always attributable to prosecution inaction or bad decisions. Poorly drafted and insufficiently detailed defence statements result in the prosecution being ill-equipped to carry out their disclosure obligations. Disclosure requests, now commonly tacked on to defence statements, are apt to be too formulaic and make 'blanket' requests for the disclosure of unused material which are not tailored to disputed evidence.

---

[14] The revised 2013 Judicial Protocol and Attorney General's *Guidelines* recognize this and emphasize the responsibility of the prosecution to act in a 'thinking' and proactive manner, and the responsibility of the court to manage this.

(9) The absence of a dedicated and strategic forensic approach to the disclosure operation and suggested provision for this

3.24 This is an area where a more focused approach may pay dividends. The Criminal Procedure Rules make no provision for a dedicated disclosure management document such as that recommended for large and complex cases in the most recent edition of the Attorney General's *Guidelines on Disclosure*.[15] Such a document might include a chronological list of actions taken by the prosecution with additional detail including:

(a) the allocation of disclosure responsibilities between the disclosure officer, the case lawyer, the prosecution advocate and, if appointed, the disclosure advocate, and the identities and contact details of these;

(b) a brief summary of the prosecution case;

(c) a brief summary of the defence case, including information provided by the suspect during police interview;

(d) steps taken or proposed to be taken by the prosecution in accordance with their disclosure obligations, including:

  • reasonable lines of enquiry pursued by the police (e.g. those relating to CCTV evidence, the credibility of a complainant or other prosecution witness, the Individual Nominal Index, police collators' records, the Criminal Records Office, witnesses not yet interviewed, including those named by the defendant);

  • details of third parties (e.g. social services departments, holders of the complainant's medical and educational records, the Criminal Injuries Compensation Authority, previous employers of the complainant and defendant) approached by the police, whether information requested from them has been accessed and, if so, with what result;

(e) details of material served on the defence during the initial disclosure process including dates of service;

(f) date of receipt of the defence statement;

(g) response to the defence statement and date of service of this;

(h) details of correspondence with the defence concerning disclosure issues and dates of sending and receipt of this;

(i) the history of communications between the disclosure officer, the prosecution reviewing lawyer, and the prosecution advocate; and

(j) details of court hearings at which disclosure issues were raised and their outcomes.

3.25 It may be that a Disclosure Management Document of the type suggested by the Attorney General's *Guidelines* would be useful in all cases and would be quite straightforward to complete in simple cases. Paragraph 52 of the *Guidelines* states:

---

[15] Cited at para 3.04 and n.3, paras 51(a)–(d), and 52.

[T]he prosecution should follow the Disclosure Management Document. They are living documents and should be amended in the light of developments in the case; they should be kept up to date as the case progresses. Their use will assist the court in its own case management and will enable the defence to engage from an early stage with the prosecution's approach to disclosure.

The obvious implication is that the Document itself will be disclosable to the defence. **3.26**

D. Sources of Disclosable Material and their Potential Significance to the Prosecution and Defence

(1) Previous statements by the complainant: inconsistencies and their import to the parties

'Previous statements' in this context are those which do not form part of the prosecution case and evidence. Where these are inconsistent, they have the obvious potential to undermine the credibility of the complainant's account. Examples include statements to parents and other relatives, friends, associates, schoolteachers, doctors and other medical personnel, social workers, therapeutic counsellors, and police officers. **3.27**

In addition to the statements themselves, the context and circumstances in which they were made may be disclosable. These are likely to include not only what complainants themselves said but also things said to them by the person to whom the statements were made. Leading questions posed to a complainant by a parent may be particularly significant. **3.28**

(2) 'Complaint' statements made on a complainant's behalf by others

In some circumstances a complaint will be made to a civilian or to the police by a third party before the complainant does so. This may be because the complainant lacks the courage to come forward, would prefer to forget their ordeal, is reluctant to submit to the forensic process, or owing to other factors which are nonetheless consistent with the reliability of their complaint. Alternatively, it may be that the complainant knows that the allegation is ill-founded and regrets having originally complained. Whatever the reason, however, the detail of what the third-party complainant informed either another civilian or the police and the circumstances in which the third party's complaint was made are likely to be disclosable. **3.29**

(3) Police knowledge of a complainant's interest in advantages to be gained by making a complaint

The experience of investigators and courts has shown that concealed behind a complaint there may be hidden influences which have caused a complainant to report **3.30** a sexual assault to the police. The fact that they may exist does not establish that the complaint is false but might throw light on the reliability of the complainant.

3.31 Well documented examples include a desire for compensation; the avoidance of an embarrassing situation; self-seeking publicity; the settling of a score; a wish to move to alternative housing; gaining of an upper hand in a divorce, separation or custody dispute; or a pretext for remaining in the UK in a dispute with the immigration authorities.

(4) Previous complaints of crime by a complainant

3.32 Where a complainant has previously complained of crime and this has not resulted in a conviction sustained in any appeal it will usually be desirable, especially if the previous complaint is of a sexual assault, for the full circumstances of this to be disclosed to the defence to enable them to assess whether there are grounds for suggesting that the previous complaint was false.

(5) Records of complainants' and other witnesses' reprehensible conduct held by the police and others

3.33 Previous convictions and police cautions have an obvious potential to undermine credibility. This will particularly be the case if the prior offences involved dishonesty or interference with the course of justice or where, in the case of a conviction, this followed a contested trial in which the witness (as defendant) had given evidence on oath and been disbelieved. Dependant on the circumstances, an acquittal may also be significant, notably if this follows an aborted trial in which no evidence has been offered owing to the absence of a crucial prosecution witness.

3.34 In either event, disclosure of the files may be necessary to allow the defence to consider what steps need to be taken.

(6) Complainant's knowledge of complaints of sexual assault made by friends or associates

3.35 A complainant may have heard of similar complaints made by another person. It is conceivable that this might have influenced the complainant. In order to discover if any contact between the complainant and the other person may have provided the opportunity for collusion, the circumstances of such knowledge or contact must be made known. This may be particularly relevant where the complainant is a child who appears to have sexual knowledge beyond his or her years.

(7) Complainant's health records

3.36 The complainant's health records may contain entries which support or contradict claims made of genital injuries, or the lack of them, or of previous sexual history which contradicts a complainant's assertion that he or she was sexually inexperienced at the time of the alleged offence. The records may show previous mental ill-health, for example, brought on by alcohol or illicit drug abuse, psychosis or schizophrenia, which may indicate that the complainant has a tendency to become confused because of prescription drugs whose side effects include hallucinations. The records may also show a history of making false claims.[16]

(8) The possible origins of a confabulated account—a complainant's history of nightmares, bad dreams, 'daydreams', and hallucinations

The debate as to whether a person can become confused between complex real **3.37** events and what they have dreamt is fraught with controversy.[17] Research in this field is problematic, since it is patently impossible to prove, first, whether a dream occurred, second, what the ambit of the dream might have been, and third, whether, assuming a dream occurred, this was reflective of real events in the past. Some support for the suggestion that dreamers can come to believe that dreamt events are real is found in a series of cases where dental patients anaesthetized with the same drug reported sexual assault by the dentist on recovering from the drug's anaesthetic affects. Only after the common thread had been established was it realised that one of the side effects of the drug was to cause the patient to suffer dreams of apparently real events.[18] Narcolepsy, where the sufferer involuntarily falls asleep for short periods, has also been said to give rise to vivid dreaming episodes and it has been argued that these may form the origins of a false complaint.[19]

Those involved in the disclosure process may be very sceptical of this body of **3.38** research and its applicability to the case in hand. The point is that these issues have been raised in criminal trials and will be raised in future. Prosecutors need to be aware of this body of research and deal with the factual issues that arise in a way which is consistent with the proper application of the disclosure regime.[20]

---

[16] For a discussion of CPS compliance with its disclosure obligations concerning medical records and counselling notes see HMCPS Inspectorate (2013) *Disclosure of medical records and counselling notes, http://www.justiceinspectorates.gov.uk/crown-prosecution-service/wp-content/uploads/sites/3/2014/04/DOMRACN_thm_Jul13_rpt.pdf.*

[17] The evidence of a psychologist called by the defence at the second trial of the veteran TV broadcaster Stuart Hall to the effect that some of the several complaints of sexual abuse by him which it was claimed had not occurred might have been dreamt, was described as 'psychobabble' in prosecution counsel's closing speech to the jury, who, nonetheless, acquitted Hall of most of the counts he faced.

[18] See Dundee, J.W., 'Fantasies during sedation with intravenous midazolam or diazepam' (1990) 58 *Medico-Legal Journal*, 29–34, cited by Lader, M., 'The influence of drugs on testimony' in Heaton-Armstrong et al., cited in n.9.

[19] *http://www.sleepfoundation.org/sleep-topics/sleep-related-problems/narcolepsy-and-sleep.* See also Warnsley, N. et al. 'Delusional Confusion of Dreaming and Reality in Narcolepsy' (2014) 37(2) *Sleep*, 419–22.

[20] For further discussion of the potential influence of drugs on testimony, including alcohol and illicit drugs, see Curran, H.V. 'Effects of Drugs on Witness Testimony' in Heaton-Armstrong et al., cited at n.1. For a detailed discussion on the affects of dreams on testimony, see Fenwick, P., 'Witness testimony in sleep and dream-related contexts' in Heaton-Armstrong et al., cited at n.9. For a comprehensive multi-authored treatise on confabulation, see Hirstein, W. (ed) (2009) *Confabulation: Views from Neuroscience, Psychiatry, Psychology and Philosophy*, Oxford: Oxford

(9) Counselling records

3.39 A complainant may have taken part in therapeutic counselling sessions, either before or after complaining to the police, although the latter is officially circumscribed, albeit not forbidden, until after the conclusion of trial.[21] What was said during such sessions might have a bearing on the reliability of an evidential complaint, particularly where what is said by or to the counsellor concerns the subject matter of the allegation. The professionalism and qualifications of counsellors differ widely. Some carefully abide by official guidance as to what is appropriate; others do not. Records of things said and techniques used during counselling sessions are notoriously scanty. Some counsellors consider that books such as the infamous, now discredited, and in many respects extraordinary, volume by Bass and Davies provide useful pointers to 'diagnosis' of sexual abuse in a patient along the lines of 'if you think you might have been abused you probably have been'.[22] If a complainant has, on the recommendation of their counsellor, read such 'self-help' books there may, thus, be a risk that false or unreliable memories are strengthened or even generated. Litigators and advocates should therefore be astute to discover whether volumes such as these have been relied upon by a counsellor or consulted by a complainant and be aware of the possible consequences of this.

3.40 In addition to the counselling records themselves, disclosure needs to be sought of the counsellor's CV, professional qualifications, the extent of their experience, the techniques used during counselling sessions, and any reliance placed during these on published texts.[23]

(10) Educational and employment records

3.41 Educational and employment records (including the suspect's) may throw light on a number of relevant issues: a history of reprehensible or dishonest behaviour in the school or workplace or the making of false or exaggerated complaints against others. In cases of historic abuse, work records may provide support for an alibi.

(11) CCTV recordings

3.42 CCTV footage has the potential either to confirm or refute assertions by a complainant that, for example, they were forcibly taken to the location of the alleged

---

University Press. See also, McNally, R.J. and Clancy, S.A., 'Sleep paralysis, sexual abuse and space alien abduction' (2005) 42 *Transcultural Psychiatry*, 113–22; and Mazzoni, G., Lombardo, P., Malvagia, S., and Loftus, E., 'Dream Interpretation and False Beliefs' (1999) 30(1) *Professional Psychology: Research and Practice* 45–50.

[21] See CPS, *Guidance on the Provision of Therapy for Adult and Child Witnesses Prior to a Criminal Trial*, *https://www.cps.gov.uk/publications/prosecution/pretrialadult.html* and *https://www.cps.gov.uk/publications/prosecution/therapychild.html*.

[22] See 'Believing it Happened' unnumbered chapter in Bass, E. and Davies, L. (2002) *The Courage to Heal*, London: Vermilion, 86–91.

[23] See Chapter 1, para 1.18

attack, or that the suspect was pressing his or her attentions in an unwelcome way, or that the complainant was incapable of consenting to sexual activity owing to intoxication. Experience has shown that, in these instances, recovered CCTV recordings have established prior consensual intimacies between the complainant and suspect, obviously willing association en route to the scene of the alleged attack, or the complainant being in a physical state which suggests full awareness and an ability to make informed decisions.

Recovery of CCTV recordings often presents practical difficulties. Cameras may **3.43** have been 'pointing in the wrong direction'. Footage may be deleted within specified periods of the recording having been made. Police investigators and litigators acting on behalf of suspects must be alert to the need to identify the presence of CCTV cameras at relevant locations and to recover these before the footage has been 'wiped'.

(12) Police records created during the course of an investigation

Crime Reporting Information System (CRIS) reports, CAD messages (elec- **3.44** tronically recorded exchanges between police personnel and with the emergency services), '999' tapes and transcripts, Sexual Offences Investigative Technique (SOIT) logs (kept by police officers with responsibility for liaison with complainants in sexual assault cases), domestic violence report books, police collators' records and intelligence reports, and records maintained on the Individual Nominal Index, are all sources of potentially relevant material. They are apt to include records of conversations of varying degrees of formality with complainants and other witnesses, details of other crimes said to have been committed by prosecution or defence witnesses or complaints of these, the identities of potential witnesses not yet interviewed and a wide variety of other potentially disclosable material.

(13) Social services records

Where a complainant or other civilian witness or their family has been the subject **3.45** of intervention by a local authority social services department a file will have been created to reflect such contact. Social services files frequently contain disclosable material—records of relevant things said by complainants or by other witnesses or of other relevant events; social workers' reports containing potentially disclosable assertions; details of therapeutic or medical support offered to or received by a complainant; psychiatric and psychological reports; histories of contact between complainants and others.

(14) Family Court documents

Associated Family Court proceedings may have arisen independently of the mak- **3.46** ing of the instant complaint or as a consequence of this. They include factually based pleadings, affidavits of witnesses, judicial rulings, reports by social workers or court welfare officers, and psychiatric and psychological reports.

3.47 All such material is potentially disclosable. It may comprise statements by witnesses concerning the subject matter of the complaint in the criminal proceedings, which have a bearing on the credibility of the instant complaint and the complainant or other witnesses associated with the complainant. Where the Family Court proceedings involve matrimonial, partnership, or custody or access disputes between a complainant's parents or where the complainant is or has been in care, the likelihood of the Family Court documents becoming disclosable in the criminal proceeding is increased.

3.48 A real difficulty in this area is the prohibition on disclosure imposed by the Family Courts. Application to the Family Court may be required to secure disclosure, even to the police.

E. Proactive Defence Involvement in the Disclosure Process

3.49 As the Attorney General's *Guidelines* and the *Judicial Protocol* make clear, defence litigators and advocates ('the defence') should take a far more proactive stance in the disclosure process than is required in the statutory provisions of the CPIA.

(1) Timeliness

3.50 Timeliness and efficiency are essential, and this will increasingly be needed in cases involving pre-trial cross-examination of witnesses under section 28 of the Youth Justice and Criminal Evidence Act 1999.

(2) Challenging inadequate disclosure at the initial disclosure stage

3.51 As we have indicated, it may be that the police schedule of unused material is deficient either because it fails to list non-sensitive items known to exist or because they are not particularized with sufficient detail or clarity to enable the defence to decide whether, in certain circumstances, to make a section 8 CPIA application for disclosure of the item in question. In that event, the defence should challenge the prosecution to remedy the defects and bring to the court's attention any failure to do so. This might involve an application for the Plea and Case Management Hearing to be adjourned until initial disclosure has been effected comprehensively.[24]

---

[24] The 2013 Judicial Protocol explicitly addresses this issue in paras 28–29 and concludes 'The regime established under the Criminal Justice Act 2003 and the Criminal Procedure Rules gives judges the power—indeed, it imposes a duty on the judiciary—actively to manage disclosure in every case', para 56.

(3) The fundamental importance of the defence statement

The importance of the defence statement being sufficiently particularized to ena- **3.52**
ble the disputed factual issues to be identified and the potentially harmful consequences for the defendant if they are not is already the subject of significant
guidance in the texts we have listed[25] and we do not, therefore, provide further
discussion of the topic here.

It is now common practice for the defence statement to be followed by a list of **3.53**
disclosure requirements, requests, and suggestions, which is highly recommended
for the reasons we have already explained. These should be numbered, individually
tailored to the issues in the case, and provide reasoned and logical explanations
as to why any required or suggested material, such as that listed above, may be
relevant and disclosable. The defence statement might also make suggestions as to
further reasonable lines of enquiry to be pursued by the prosecution. Blanket or
formulaic requests for disclosure of material by general category, for example, 'Any
material which undermines the complainant's allegations', 'The CRIS Report',
'Social Services Records' are likely to waste time and act as an unhelpful diversion
from what is needed.

The list should conclude with two requests to the prosecution: (i) to confirm **3.54**
that the defence statement has been copied to the prosecution advocate, experience having shown that the defence statement may only reach the prosecution
advocate at an excessively late stage of the proceedings; and (ii) to provide their
section 7 CPIA response to the defence statement and its disclosure requests
by reference to its own paragraph numberings. This reduces the risk of misunderstanding as to which aspects of the defence statement the section 7 letter
provides responses.

To minimize the risk of disclosure correspondence being mislaid or, as not infre- **3.55**
quently happens, the CPS claiming not to have received it, both defence and prosecution advocates would be well advised to copy it to each other.

(4) Involving the court

The re-introduction of court case progression officers would be a useful case **3.56**
management tool. It is suggested that court's overall control of the disclosure
process would be assisted by the existence of an up-to-date and comprehensive Disclosure Management Document in all but the most straightforward
cases involving allegations of sexual impropriety. The *Judicial Protocol* makes
clear that it is the judge's responsibility to actively manage the disclosure
process.

---

[25] At n.1 and para 3.04.

F. The Future

(1) Training

3.57 All participants in the disclosure process—police investigators and disclosure officers, prosecution case lawyers and workers, litigators and advocates, require mandatory training for the performance of their roles. That this is necessary is clear from the fact that disclosure failures and inefficiencies continue to recur. Training programmes should be consistent throughout the jurisdiction to prevent the proliferation of variable practices amongst different CPS areas, police forces, and courts which, whilst they may be locally useful, cause difficulties elsewhere, especially when more complex cases cross administrative boundaries.

(2) Forensic strategies

3.58 We have already extolled the value of the proposed Disclosure Management Document, which has the potential to make a significant difference in sexual assault cases.

3.59 That there is no effective penal sanction for disclosure failures may require correction.[26] The courts might be given the power to impose a fine on any government body found responsible for reprehensible failure during the disclosure process. This would act as an effective deterrent to inefficiency.

(3) Consistency of practical approach

3.60 There is also a need for a co-ordination and conformity of practical approach, not least amongst social services authorities when disclosure of their files to the police is requested. Whereas the various legal resources to which we have referred mitigate in favour of the same procedure to be adopted by every social services department, they do not preclude these from developing different local protocols. The justification for this is hard to fathom, since there is nothing to distinguish between the legal obligations, or the way these ought to be obeyed, from one social services department to another. Inconsistent local protocols are not helpful and, in any event, conflict with the requirements of the 2013 model protocol, which is specified as being nationally applicable.[27]

---

[26] See Judiciary of England and Wales (2012) Further review of disclosure in criminal proceedings: sanctions for disclosure failure. November 2012, *https//www.judiciary.gov.uk/publications/further-review-disclosure-criminal-proceedings-november-2012/*.

[27] Cited at n.8.

G. Conclusion

It should be remembered that after conviction there is no continuing duty on the **3.61**
police or prosecutor either to disclose material or to respond to whatever enquiries
the defendant may make for access to the case materials to allow re-investigations.[28]
The ruling of the Supreme Court in which that principle was declared, reinforces
the need for disclosure to be managed comprehensively at first instance.

Disclosure problems will continue to arise in sexual assault cases. We live in an **3.62**
imperfect world subject to all kinds of constraints but the system we have must be
made to work and work effectively in a way which benefits the community.[29]

Author Biographies

Anthony Heaton-Armstrong was the Criminal Bar Association's representative on
the working group which formulated the 2001 edition of the Attorney General's
Guidelines on Disclosure and is the author of numerous published articles concerning disclosure issues. See also under Editors' details.

Seán Enright was called to the Bar in 1982. After twenty-six years of practice in
criminal cases he was appointed as a Circuit Judge in 2008.

David Wolchover In his many years experience as practitioner David Wolchover
has inevitably encountered a comprehensive range of disclosure issues, and has also
written on the subject jointly with Anthony Heaton-Armstrong.

Paul Keleher QC has been in criminal practice since 1980 and was appointed
Queen's Counsel in 2009. He is the author of an Archbold Criminal Research
Paper on Disclosure, which was copied to all CPS branches.

---

[28] See the judgment of the Supreme Court in *R (Nunn) v Chief Constable of Suffolk Constabulary*
[2014] UKSC 37, 18 June.
[29] Whether the Criminal Procedure Rules of 5 October 2015 (https//www.justice,gov.uk/courts/
procedure-rules/criminal/rulesmenu) the Better Case Management scheme (see, for its essence:
https//www.justice.gov.uk/courts/procedure-rules/criminal/formspage) and the onset of digital
working will have the effect of causing the operation of the disclosure process to become more efficient
and reliable remains to be seen.

4

ABUSE OF PROCESS
AND DELAYED PROSECUTIONS

*Andrew L.-T. Choo**

A. Introduction

Delayed prosecutions of sexual offences continue to generate publicity and **4.01** controversy,[1] and to raise difficult and conflicting issues. On the one hand, as a result of the passage of time, a defendant on trial for 'historical sexual offences' might well encounter significant forensic disadvantage in defending himself. Such disadvantage might stem, for example, from 'the fact that any potential witnesses

---

* This chapter was completed on the basis of materials available in May 2014, although it has been possible to incorporate references to subsequent developments in places.

[1] See e.g. Topping, A., 'Historic Sex Case Prosecutions Will Continue, Vows Chief Prosecutor', *The Guardian*, 20 February 2014, online; Gibb, F., 'Prosecutors Pledge Fresh Pursuit of Historical Abuse Cases', *The Times*, 27 February 2014, online; Pidd, H., 'DPP Defends Failed Prosecutions of Celebrities over Historic Sex Claims', *The Guardian*, 27 February 2014, online; Hamilton, F., Gibb, F., Simpson, J., and Pitel, L., 'Prosecutors in Dock as Sex Case MP Is Cleared', *The Times*, 11 April 2014, online; Mason, R. and Bowcott, O., 'Attorney General Demands Answers from CPS over Failed Sex Offence Cases', *The Guardian*, 11 April 2014, online; Mason, R., Halliday, J., and Pidd, H., 'CPS Defends Decision to Bring Assault and Rape Charges against Nigel Evans', *The Guardian*, 11 April 2014, online; Rustin, S., 'Alison Saunders, Director of Public Prosecutions: "I Think Women Have Had, as Witnesses and Victims, a Raw Deal"', *The Guardian*, 2 May 2014, online.

have died or are not able to be located'[2] or from 'the fact that any potential evidence has been lost or is otherwise unavailable'.[3] 'Obviously', the Court of Appeal has noted, 'as a matter of commonsense, if someone is facing allegations relating to events that have occurred a long time ago there will be difficulties in recollection, not only for those who make the allegations but for those who have to defend themselves against them'.[4] On the other hand, delays in making complaints of offences of this nature might be perfectly understandable: 'Some victims of sexual abuse may not feel confident or strong enough to report until many years after the abuse has taken place, and often not until they are adults. This delay in reporting can be for a wide range of reasons …'.[5] The task of ensuring that relevant legal principles accommodate these conflicting considerations is a complex one. This chapter examines one such principle: the abuse of process doctrine.[6]

B. Why the Abuse of Process Doctrine is the Chief Mechanism for Protecting Defendants Charged with Sexual Offences

4.02 It is worth clarifying two points which explain why the abuse of process doctrine is the chief mechanism potentially protecting defendants charged with sexual offences after undue delay from facing trial.

(1) No time limit

4.03 While section 127 of the Magistrates' Courts Act 1980 prevents a magistrates' court from trying an information unless it was laid within six months of the commission of the offence, no time limit of this nature applies to the commencement of trials on indictment (which are the forum in which prosecutions of sexual offences will be tried).

(2) Limited applicability of right to be tried within a reasonable time

4.04 The second point is that the right to be tried 'within a reasonable time', guaranteed by Article 6(1) of the European Convention on Human Rights, and made directly

---

[2] Evidence Act 1995 (New South Wales), s 165B(7)(a); Evidence (National Uniform Legislation) Act 2011 (Northern Territory), s 165B(7)(a).

[3] Evidence Act 1995 (New South Wales), s 165B(7)(b); Evidence (National Uniform Legislation) Act 2011 (Northern Territory), s 165B(7)(b).

[4] *R v M (Brian)* [2007] EWCA Crim 1182 [17].

[5] Crown Prosecution Service (2013) *Guidelines on Prosecuting Cases of Child Sexual Abuse Issued by the Director of Public Prosecutions*, para 96. See also *R v Wright* (Amersham Crown Court, 6 February 2014) (sentencing remarks); *R v Cullen* (Derby Crown Court, 24 March 2014) (sentencing remarks); *R v Clifford* (Southwark Crown Court, 2 May 2014) (sentencing remarks); *Attorney General's Reference (No 14 of 2015)* [2015] EWCA Crim 949 [15].

[6] I have drawn here on some of my earlier analyses in Choo, A.L.-T. (2008) *Abuse of Process and Judicial Stays of Criminal Proceedings*, 2nd edn, Oxford: Oxford University Press, ch. 3.

enforceable in domestic law by the Human Rights Act 1998, has limited applicability in the present context. This right has generated a very large volume of jurisprudence from Strasbourg; indeed, it was commented in 2007 that: 'Length of judicial proceedings is … the issue that has most occupied the European Court of Human Rights in quantitative terms—so much so that since 1968 it has accounted for almost 30% of the judgments handed down by the Court.'[7] In terms of the implications of the right, the Strasbourg Court has explained that

> in criminal matters, the 'reasonable time' referred to in Article 6, §1, begins to run as soon as a person is 'charged'; this may occur on a date prior to the case coming before the trial court … , such as the date of arrest, the date when the person concerned was officially notified that he would be prosecuted, or the date when preliminary investigations were opened … 'Charge', for the purposes of Article 6, §1, may be defined as 'the official notification given to an individual by the competent authority of an allegation that he has committed a criminal offence', a definition that also corresponds to the test whether 'the situation of the [suspect] has been substantially affected'.[8]

In essence, therefore, it is only delay *after* the defendant has been officially notified in some way of the relevant allegation against him or her that falls within the scope of the right to be tried within a reasonable time.[9] Delayed prosecutions of sexual offences, however, are typically caused by delay occurring well before that stage. For this reason, the right is of limited significance in the present context.

C. The Abuse of Process Doctrine: General Principles

The judicial power to stay criminal proceedings which constitute an abuse of the process of the court[10] is well established, having being refined in modern times by the House of Lords in *Connelly v DPP*[11] and in subsequent cases such as *R v Horseferry Road Magistrates' Court, ex p Bennett*,[12] *R v Latif*,[13] and *R v Looseley*,[14] **4.05**

---

   [7] Edel, F. (2007) *The Length of Civil and Criminal Proceedings in the Case-Law of the European Court of Human Rights*, 2nd edn, Strasbourg: Council of Europe Publishing, 6.
   [8] *Korshunov v Russia*, App no 38971/06 (ECtHR, 25 October 2007) [68], quoting from *Deweer v Belgium* (1980) 2 EHRR 439 [46].
   [9] Contemporary authorities in which such a right is discussed include *Boolell v State of Mauritius* [2006] UKPC 46, [2012] 1 WLR 3718; *Tapper v DPP of Jamaica* [2012] UKPC 26, [2012] 1 WLR 2712; *Celine v State of Mauritius* [2012] UKPC 32, [2012] 1 WLR 3707; *Rummun v State of Mauritius* [2013] UKPC 6, [2013] 1 WLR 598.
   [10] See generally Choo (2008), cited at n.6; Wells, C. (2011) *Abuse of Process*, 2nd edn, Bristol: Jordan Publishing; Young, D., Summers, M., and Corker, D. (2014) *Abuse of Process in Criminal Proceedings*, 4th edn, Haywards Heath: Bloomsbury Professional.
   [11] [1964] AC 1254.
   [12] [1994] 1 AC 42.
   [13] [1996] 1 WLR 104.
   [14] [2001] UKHL 53, [2001] 1 WLR 2060.

and, most recently, by the Supreme Court in *R v Maxwell*.[15] The abuse of process doctrine is considered to have two limbs. In the words of Lord Dyson JSC:

> It is well established that the court has the power to stay proceedings in two categories of case, namely (i) where it will be impossible to give the accused a fair trial, and (ii) where it offends the court's sense of justice and propriety to be asked to try the accused in the particular circumstances of the case. In the first category of case, if the court concludes that an accused cannot receive a fair trial, it will stay the proceedings without more. No question of the balancing of competing interests arises. In the second category of case, the court is concerned to protect the integrity of the criminal justice system. Here a stay will be granted where the court concludes that in all the circumstances a trial will offend the court's sense of justice and propriety ... or will undermine public confidence in the criminal justice system and bring it into disrepute ...[16]

4.06   It is clear that the concern of the first limb is with epistemic considerations. A 'fair trial', therefore, may be seen as one which facilitates accurate fact-finding or truth discovery; its concern is with what Bentham called 'rectitude of decision'.[17] To put it simply, pursuant to the first limb, criminal proceedings may be stayed to prevent the wrongful conviction of an innocent person. This reflects a recognition that '[p]eople have', as Dworkin has explained, 'a profound right not to be convicted of crimes of which they are innocent'.[18] In the words of another commentator, '[t]he extreme unfairness of depriving a person of freedom for an offense she did not commit is beyond dispute'.[19] The second limb of the abuse of process doctrine, on the other hand, has at its root deontological concerns with values that are unrelated to the promotion or achievement of accurate fact-finding. This limb therefore 'represents a political-moral judgment that certain values are more important than accuracy in fact-finding. As such, it limits the truth that is allowed to appear at trial in favour of social goals which transcend the importance of factual truth.'[20] A trial may be stayed on the basis of the second (and, arguably, more controversial[21]) limb of the abuse of process doctrine not because of any danger that to allow the prosecution to continue may result in an inaccurate verdict, but because to do so may undermine particular values that are deemed worthy of protection.

---

[15] [2010] UKSC 48, [2011] 1 WLR 1837. See also the decision of the Privy Council in *Warren v Attorney General for Jersey* [2011] UKPC 10, [2012] 1 AC 22.

[16] *R v Maxwell* [2010] UKSC 48, [2011] 1 WLR 1837 [13].

[17] Bentham, J. (1827) *Rationale of Judicial Evidence, Specially Applied to English Practice* (5 vols), London: Hunt and Clarke, vol i (reprinted New York: Garland Publishing, 1978) 1.

[18] Dworkin, R. (1986) *A Matter of Principle*, Oxford: Clarendon Press, 72.

[19] Tomkovicz, J.J. (2011) *Constitutional Exclusion: The Rules, Rights, and Remedies that Strike the Balance between Freedom and Order*, New York: Oxford University Press, 82.

[20] Burns, R.P. (1999) *A Theory of the Trial*, Princeton, NJ: Princeton University Press, 95.

[21] Non-epistemic considerations that are said to underlie particular principles of evidence and procedure have been the subject of much discussion and debate: see e.g. Pizzi, W.T. (1999) *Trials without Truth: Why Our System of Criminal Trials Has Become an Expensive Failure and What We Need to Do to Rebuild It*, New York: New York University Press; Laudan, L. (2006) *Truth, Error, and Criminal Law: An Essay in Legal Epistemology*, Cambridge: Cambridge University Press.

With these underlying considerations in mind,[22] we may proceed now to the main **4.07** focus of this chapter: the operation of the abuse of process doctrine in the context of delayed prosecutions.

D. The Abuse of Process Doctrine and Delayed Prosecutions

The decision on abuse of process and delay in *Attorney General's Reference (No* **4.08** *1 of 1990)*[23] has been followed by over two decades' worth of further case law from the Court of Appeal on the subject. In *R v F (S)*,[24] the Court, sitting with five judges, sought to clarify the principles that trial judges ought to apply when faced with abuse of process applications in the context of delay.[25] The Court expressed the view that the instant decision as well as three of its previous decisions—*R v Galbraith*,[26] *Attorney General's Reference (No 1 of 1990)*,[27] and *R v S (SP)*[28]—'contain all the necessary discussion about the applicable principles' and '[n]o further citation of authority is needed'.[29] The principles that were thought to be encapsulated in these four decisions were summarized as follows:

    (i) An application to stay for abuse of process on grounds of delay and a submission of 'no case to answer' are two distinct matters. They must receive distinct and separate consideration....

    (ii) An application to stay for abuse of process on the grounds of delay must be determined in accordance with *Attorney General's Reference (No 1 of 1990)* [1992] QB 630. It cannot succeed unless, exceptionally, a fair trial is no longer possible owing to prejudice to the defendant occasioned by the delay which cannot fairly be addressed in the normal trial process. The presence or absence of explanation or justification for the delay is relevant only in so far as it bears on that question....

    (iii) An application to stop the case on the grounds that there is no case to answer must be determined in accordance with *R v Galbraith* [1981] 1 WLR 1039. For the reasons there explained, it is dangerous to ask the question in terms

---

  [22] For a fuller discussion of epistemic and non-epistemic justifications in the law of criminal evidence and procedure, see Choo, A.L.-T. (2013) *The Privilege against Self-Incrimination and Criminal Justice*, Oxford: Hart Publishing, 3–10.

  [23] [1992] QB 630.

  [24] [2011] EWCA Crim 1844, [2012] QB 703. See generally Samuels, A., 'Abuse of Process Applications—A Tougher Stance' (2013) 177 *Criminal Law and Justice Weekly* 154.

  [25] For earlier discussion, see Choo (2008), cited at n.6, 77–80.

  [26] [1981] 1 WLR 1039.

  [27] [1992] QB 630.

  [28] [2006] EWCA Crim 756, [2006] 2 Cr App R 23.

  [29] [2011] EWCA Crim 1844, [2012] QB 703 [47]. The Court also clarified the implications of *R v B* [2003] EWCA Crim 319, [2003] 2 Cr App R 13, and *R v Smolinski* [2004] EWCA Crim 1270, [2004] 2 Cr App R 40.

of whether a conviction would be safe, or the jury can safely convict, because that invites the judge to evaluate the weight and reliability of the evidence, which is the task of the jury. The question is whether the evidence, viewed overall, is such that the jury could properly convict....

(iv) There is no different *R v Galbraith* test for offences which are alleged to have been committed some years ago, whether or not they are sexual offences....

(v) An application to stay for abuse of process ought ordinarily to be heard and determined at the outset of the case, and before the evidence is heard, unless there is a specific reason to defer it because the question of prejudice and fair trial can better be determined at a later stage....[30]

4.09   *R v F (S)* is undeniably an important decision. In particular, it provides valuable guidance on the distinction between stay applications and submissions of no case to answer that are made pursuant to *R v Galbraith*, and on the implications of this distinction. It also confirms that stays for delay are to be granted in exceptional circumstances only; the normal situation would be for the trial to proceed and for reliance to be placed on the protections available in the course of the trial. Such protections would consist primarily of the exclusion of particular evidence considered to have been 'tainted' by the delay,[31] and the delivery of 'care warnings' to the jury. Two aspects of *R v F (S)*, however, deserve comment.

4.10   First, and more broadly, the decision appears to confirm that only *epistemic* considerations would justify a stay of proceedings on the basis of delay. This may be too narrow an approach: it may be

… argued that there is also a case for not holding a trial where it is no longer fair on the participants to require them to recount events and account for actions so far in the past. One of the purposes of criminal proceedings is not simply to establish whether the accused committed the offence charged but also to engage with the accused and hold him or her to account for certain actions. This view … would suggest that proceedings should be stopped when it is no longer possible for defendants to be called to account for events because they can no longer relate to the events at that period of time in their life.[32]

4.11   The second point is that *R v F (S)* leaves the position concerning the burden and standard of proof in abuse of process applications uncertain. The Court does not address the issue itself, but it is addressed in two of the three earlier decisions specifically endorsed by the Court. In *Attorney General's Reference (No 1 of 1990)*, Lord Lane CJ, reading the opinion of the Court of Appeal, stated that 'no stay should be imposed unless the defendant shows on the balance of probabilities that owing to the delay he will suffer serious prejudice to the extent that no fair trial can be held: in other words, that the continuance of the prosecution amounts to a

---

[30] [2011] EWCA Crim 1844, [2012] QB 703 [48].

[31] *Cf. R v Boardman* [2015] EWCA Crim 175, [2015] 1 Cr App R 33.

[32] Jackson, J. and Johnstone, J., 'The Reasonable Time Requirement: An Independent and Meaningful Right?' [2005] Crim LR 3, 23.

misuse of the process of the court'.[33] In *R v S (SP)*, however, the Court of Appeal stated:

> In our judgment, the discretionary decision whether or not to grant a stay as an abuse of process, because of delay, is an exercise in judicial assessment dependent on judgment rather than on any conclusion as to fact based on evidence. It is, therefore, potentially misleading to apply to the exercise of that discretion the language of burden and standard of proof, which is more apt to an evidence-based fact-finding process. Accordingly, we doubt whether, today, in the light of intervening authorities in relation to the exercise of judicial discretion, Lord Lane would have expressed himself as he did with regard to the burden and standard of proof.[34]

The latter approach would appear consistent with contemporary judicial thinking in relation to the discretion to exclude prosecution evidence under section 78(1) of the Police and Criminal Evidence Act 1984.[35] In *R (Saifi) v Governor of Brixton Prison*,[36] for example, the Administrative Court noted pragmatically that:

> … The power [conferred by section 78(1)] is to be exercised whenever an issue appears as to whether the court could conclude that the evidence should not be admitted. The concept of a burden of proof has no part to play in such circumstances. No doubt it is for that reason that there is no express provision as to the burden of proof, and we see no basis for implying such a burden. The prosecution desiring to adduce and the defence seeking to exclude evidence will each seek to persuade the court about impact on fairness. We regard the position as neutral and see no reason why section 78 should be understood as requiring the court to consider upon whom the burden of proof rests.[37]

Acceptance of such a view would not in any way affect the principle that any *factual* determination that is to form the basis of a decision on whether a stay should be granted must be governed by the usual rules governing the burden and standard of proof. Thus, the burden would be on the prosecution to prove beyond reasonable doubt that any fact alleged to be relevant by the defence did not exist.[38]

It is to be noted, however, that, notwithstanding *R v S (SP)*, the case law on abuse **4.12** of process continues to feature statements suggesting that it is for the defence to prove, on the balance of probabilities, that particular facts justify a stay of

---

[33] [1992] QB 630, 644.

[34] [2006] EWCA Crim 756, [2006] 2 Cr App R 23 [20].

[35] This provides: 'In any proceedings the court may refuse to allow evidence on which the prosecution proposes to rely to be given if it appears to the court that, having regard to all the circumstances, including the circumstances in which the evidence was obtained, the admission of the evidence would have such an adverse effect on the fairness of the proceedings that the court ought not to admit it.'

[36] [2001] 1 WLR 1134.

[37] Ibid. [52].

[38] See further Choo (2008), cited at n.6, 167.

the proceedings. For example, the Administrative Court noted in 2014, in the context of an abuse of process application on the basis of the non-availability of evidence:

> If there is a breach of the obligation to obtain or retain the relevant material, it is ... necessary to decide whether the defence has shown, on the balance of probabilities, that owing to the absence of the relevant material the defence will suffer serious prejudice to the extent that a fair trial cannot take place.[39]

4.13 Decisions of the Court of Appeal subsequent to *R v F (S)*—notably *R v E*,[40] *R v S (P)*,[41] *R v D (R)*,[42] *R v T (A)*,[43] and *R v Taylor*[44]—have continued to take a similar line to that taken in *R v F (S)*. In *R v Taylor*, for example, the Court stated:

> It is, we accept, undoubtedly true that the very considerable interval between the events covered by the indictment and the trial created disadvantages for the appel-lant. However, the trial process was fully capable of making due allowance for those difficulties and, properly directed, the jury was able, if appropriate, to reflect their judgment upon those difficulties in their verdicts.[45]

E. Care Warnings

4.14 The *Crown Court Bench Book* provides the following guidance on the administra-tion of care warnings pertaining to delay:

---

[39] *Morris v DPP* [2014] EWHC 105 (Admin), [2014] 2 Cr App R 21 [14]. *R (Ebrahim) v Feltham Magistrates' Court* [2001] EWHC Admin 130, [2001] 1 WLR 1293 was endorsed. See also *R v E* [2012] EWCA Crim 791 [22]. Perhaps more troubling is the apparent suggestion in *R v Moore* [2013] EWCA Crim 85 [75], in the context of a discussion of allegations of entrapment, that the defence must prove relevant facts on the balance of probabilities: 'it must be recalled that the burden of proof is on the applicant defendant, albeit the standard is only that of the balance of probabilities. Unless the relevant facts are agreed, or are assumed for the purposes of argument, it may be neces-sary therefore for an applicant to give evidence in a *voir dire*, or to cross-examine the undercover officers as to their conduct or for there to be at least agreed assumptions as to the facts. If Ms Moore wished to say, as was submitted on her behalf, that it was a clear, albeit unspoken, premise of her relationship with the undercover officers that they were taking advantage of her vulnerability and innocence to lure her into offending by the temptation of cheap goods, and that the recordings of their conversations did not reflect the true circumstances as they had to be understood, then it was for her to initiate the necessary evidence and cross-examination.'
[40] [2012] EWCA Crim 791.
[41] [2013] EWCA Crim 992.
[42] [2013] EWCA Crim 1592. See generally Corker, D., 'Delays and Historic Offences' (2013) 177 *Criminal Law and Justice Weekly* 836.
[43] [2013] EWCA Crim 1850.
[44] [2013] EWCA Crim 2398.
[45] Ibid. [79]. See also *R v E* [2012] EWCA Crim 791 [28] ('In sum, no error of principle has been relied upon ... in this appeal, and no specific features of this case suggest that this was one of those exceptional cases where incurable prejudice has been caused, for which the judge's conduct of the trial and directions to the jury cannot compensate, resulting in an unfair trial. We cannot say that the judge was wrong to consider that the appellant would be able to have a fair trial'); *R v T (A)* [2013] EWCA Crim 1850 [39] ('We do not think that this was an exceptional case justifying the grant of a stay. The trial process was capable of dealing with the difficulties raised for the defence'); and *R v Downey* (Central Criminal Court, 25 February 2014) (conclusion on first ground).

- The judge should refer to the fact that the passage of time is bound to affect memory. A witness' inability to recall detail applies equally to prosecution and defence witnesses but it is the prosecution which bears the burden of proof. The jury may be troubled by the absence of circumstantial detail which, but for the delay, they would expect to be available. Conversely, the jury may be troubled by the witness' claim to recall a degree of detail which is unlikely after such a prolonged passage of time. Whether reference should be made to such possibilities is a matter for the trial judge to assess having regard to the evidence and the issues which have arisen in the case.
- If, as a result of delay, specific lines of inquiry have been closed to the defendant the disadvantage this presents should be identified and explained by reference to the burden of proof.
- A defendant of good character will be able to assert that the absence of any further and similar allegation is significant.
- Directions must make clear that the jury *should* give careful consideration to the exigencies of delay.[46]

These, of course, are merely guidelines which are not intended to be prescrip- **4.15** tive. Considerable leeway is accorded to trial judges in this field, and the Court of Appeal displays considerable reluctance to intervene.[47] While the Court of Appeal has stressed the importance of care warnings in delay cases being tailored to the facts of the case,[48] there is a danger, as previous experience in Australia suggests, that the administration of such warnings may, in time, become 'decontextualized', taking insufficient account of the rationale for administering them or the particular circumstances of individual cases. Because of fears in Australia that care warnings were suggesting that delay would *inevitably* create forensic disadvantage, the Australian uniform evidence legislation introduced a provision designed to halt this practice.[49] This provision, section 165B,[50] states that, if the court 'is satisfied that the defendant has suffered a significant forensic disadvantage because of the consequences of delay, the court must inform the jury of the nature of that

---

[46] Judicial Studies Board (2010) *Crown Court Bench Book: Directing the Jury*, 33.

[47] See e.g. *R v T (A)* [2013] EWCA Crim 1850 [88]: 'Looking at the position overall, we take the view that, while the summing-up should, to advantage, have alluded to the specific elements of prejudice said to have been occasioned to the applicant by reason of the delay, the failure to do so was not such as to render the convictions unsafe.'

[48] See e.g. *R v S (P)* [2013] EWCA Crim 992 [24]: 'On the basis of [the] authorities, it is self-evident that no two cases are the same and whether a direction on delay is to be given and the way in which it is formulated will depend on the facts of the case. We stress, therefore, that the need for a direction, its formulation and the matters to be included will depend on the circumstances of, and the issues arising in, the trial.' See also *R v T (A)* [2013] EWCA Crim 1850 [88]: 'It is, often, not desirable to provide simply a generalised formula as to possible prejudice by reason of delay—the formula should, where appropriate, be applied to the particular facts and particular prejudice identified as arising.'

[49] See generally Cossins, A., 'Time Out for *Longman*: Myths, Science and the Common Law' (2010) 34 *Melbourne University Law Review* 69; Gans, J., Henning, T., Hunter, J., and Warner, K. (2011) *Criminal Process and Human Rights*, Sydney: Federation Press, 474–81.

[50] Considerations of s 165B may be found in *KSC v R* [2012] NSWCCA 179; *Greensill v The Queen* [2012] VSCA 306; *Groundstroem v R* [2013] NSWCCA 237; *Jarrett v R* [2014] NSWCCA 140; *Pate (A Pseudonym) v The Queen* [2015] VSCA 110.

disadvantage and the need to take that disadvantage into account when consider-ing the evidence',[51] 'but the judge must not in any way suggest to the jury that it would be dangerous or unsafe to convict the defendant solely because of the delay or the forensic disadvantage suffered because of the consequences of the delay',[52] and 'significant forensic disadvantage is not to be regarded as being established by the mere existence of a delay'.[53] This ought to provide useful lessons for trial judges in England and Wales.

F. Conclusion

4.16   While *R v F (S)* is not immune to criticism, it helpfully clarifies aspects of the abuse of process doctrine as it applies in cases of delay, while emphasizing that stays are very rarely to be granted. One commentator has remarked that 'it seems that [the only] abuse submission with a good chance of gaining traction with the court is one where the specificity of the allegation allows for the mounting of either a quasi-alibi defence or one where the absence of a witness or document can demonstrably be shown to have caused prejudice'.[54] The strategy of relying where possible on care warnings,

---

[51] Evidence Act 1995 (Commonwealth of Australia), s 165B(2); Evidence Act 1995 (New South Wales), s 165B(2); Evidence Act 2001 (Tasmania), s 165B(2); Evidence Act 2011 (Australian Capital Territory), s 165B(2); Evidence (National Uniform Legislation) Act 2011 (Northern Territory), s 165B(2).

[52] Evidence Act 1995 (Commonwealth of Australia), s 165B(4); Evidence Act 1995 (New South Wales), s 165B(4); Evidence Act 2001 (Tasmania), s 165B(4); Evidence Act 2011 (Australian Capital Territory), s 165B(4); Evidence (National Uniform Legislation) Act 2011 (Northern Territory), s 165B(4).

[53] Evidence Act 1995 (Commonwealth of Australia), s 165B(6)(b); Evidence Act 1995 (New South Wales), s 165B(6)(b); Evidence Act 2001 (Tasmania), s 165B(6)(b); Evidence Act 2011 (Australian Capital Territory), s 165B(6)(b); Evidence (National Uniform Legislation) Act 2011 (Northern Territory), s 165B(6)(b). In Victoria, s 165B of the Evidence Act (2008) (Victoria) has been repealed and replaced by ss 38–40 of the Jury Directions Act 2015 (Victoria), which are to similar effect.

[54] Corker (2013), cited at n.42, 836; *R v E* [2012] EWCA Crim 791 and *R v Dent* [2014] EWCA Crim 457, both of which are decisions in which the Court of Appeal held that the relevant abuse applications had rightly failed, illustrate this point well. See also *R v Halahan* [2014] EWCA Crim 2079 [25]: 'There is, in the present case, no doubt that contemporaneous documents were missing, principally the children's home records. However, we do not accept [the] argument that those docu-ments would necessarily have cast light on the reliability of [the complainant's] present evidence. There was first, in our judgment, no likelihood that in 1976 the staff at the children's home would have taken care to record the particulars of any complaint made by [the complainant] of the conduct of the appellant towards him. That a complaint was made was likely to have been recorded but we have no way of knowing what, if any, detail might have been included. According to [the complain-ant], the fact of a complaint came to the attention of the police. That there was an investigation into the conduct of the appellant against "boys" in 1976 was demonstrated by church and other cor-respondence but there is no evidence that it concerned any complaint made by [the complainant]. It is speculative to assume that the police had a record of the particulars of the complaint made by [the complainant] to the staff at the children's home. It was equally possible that they merely had

rather than preventing the case from going to the jury altogether,[55] is consistent with the trend in the law of evidence towards 'trusting the jury' to evaluate evidence the reliability of which may be in doubt, rather than excluding that evidence from the jury's consideration altogether.[56] Caution must be exercised, however, to ensure that care warnings do not become a substitute for stays in circumstances where nothing short of a stay would suffice to provide the defendant with adequate protection from the risk of wrongful conviction stemming from delay.

Further Reading

Corker, D., 'Delays and Historic Offences' (2013) 177 *Criminal Law and Justice Weekly* 836.

Samuels, A., 'Abuse of Process Applications—A Tougher Stance' (2013) 177 *Criminal Law and Justice Weekly* 154.

Young, D., Summers, M., and Corker, D. (2014) *Abuse of Process in Criminal Proceedings*, 4th edn, Haywards Heath: Bloomsbury Professional.

Author Biography

Professor Andrew L.-T. Choo is a Professor of Law at City University London, having previously worked at the University of New South Wales, the University of Leicester, Brunel University, and the University of Warwick. He is an academic member of Matrix Chambers. He obtained degrees in Commerce and Law from the University of New South Wales and his doctorate from the University of Oxford. His publications include *Hearsay and Confrontation in Criminal Trials* (1996), *Abuse of Process and Judicial Stays of Criminal Proceedings*, 2nd edn (2008), *The Privilege against Self-Incrimination and Criminal Justice* (2013), and *Evidence*, 4th edn (2015).

---

information that a complaint had been made. No explanation existed as to why the complaint was not followed up with an interview with [the complainant]. We do not consider that it was demonstrated to the judge that irremediable prejudice was done to the appellant's case. We do not consider that this was one of the exceptional cases in which a fair trial was no longer possible.'

[55] Such a strategy has been endorsed by Dingwall, G., 'Protecting the Accused and Delay in Sexual Abuse Cases' (1996) 7 *King's College Law Journal* 132, 135: 'The reluctance to stay proceedings due to a general prejudice caused by delay, ... and the preference of leaving the matter to the jury, with suitable direction where necessary, is, it is suggested, the optimum way of ensuring that complainants who have delayed making accusations and defendants facing difficulties in obtaining exculpatory evidence receive a fair hearing.'

[56] See e.g. Stein, A. (2005) *Foundations of Evidence Law*, Oxford: Oxford University Press, 107, who writes of the idea of 'free evaluation of evidence (or free proof). This idea is ... influential amongst practitioners, law reformers, and legal scholars. The endorsement of this idea by law reformers (both legislative and judicial) is responsible for the ongoing abolition of evidentiary rules and the flowering of discretion in adjudicative fact-finding. The abolitionist trend is especially noticeable in England.'

5

TWO ASPECTS OF THE STATUTORY RESTRICTION ON INTRODUCING A COMPLAINANT'S SEXUAL HISTORY

*Nevada McEvoy-Cooke, David Wolchover, and Anthony Heaton-Armstrong**

* The authors are grateful to Richard Merz, barrister of 9–12 Bell Yard, Temple Bar, London WC2A 2JR, and others, for their comments on earlier drafts of this chapter.

A. Introduction and Background

(1) The vexed question of balance

5.01 The question of whether or to what extent, if any, evidence of a complainant's prior sexual behaviour should be admissible in criminal trials is a vexed and thorny issue which has fuelled heated debate over many years.[1] Arguably to a significantly greater extent than in other types of grave crime it poses a challenge in the quest for balance in the pursuit of due process. How do we reconcile the imperative of protecting complainants from embarrassment through irrelevant cross-examination concerning their sexual history, ensuring thereby that they remain undeterred from giving evidence and that they give a good account of themselves, with that of safeguarding the right of the defendant to a fair trial? Where should the courts mark out the limits of judicial discretion? Section 41 of the Youth Justice and Criminal Evidence Act 1999 (YJCEA) (and its kindred provisions)—the governing legislation—introduced obvious improvements but continues to provoke controversy and criticism.[2] Space constraints necessarily preclude commentary on the range of topics considered in the well-known practitioner and academic texts[3] and the present chapter will therefore be limited to focusing on two issues fundamental to achieving a satisfactory balance: (a) problems regarding the definition of 'relevance' under section 41; and (b) the interrelationship between section 41 and the provisions of the Criminal Justice Act 2003 (CJA) governing the admissibility of bad character evidence, particularly previous sexual complaints which it is established were concocted. This chapter demonstrates the need for judicial consistency when interpreting section 41; it also highlights the requirement for further guidance on the interpretation of section 41 relevance to assist advocates and judges.

(2) The special emphasis on competing credibility

5.02 It is almost a truism to state that most allegations of serious sexual assault involve an attack by one person on another in private with no one else present. Often there will be no physical evidence but where the sexual act is undisputed and the sole issue is consensuality there may be no physical evidence of an accompanying use of force. The complainant may be attributing this either to minimal physical coercion leaving no bodily trauma, or to a pre-emptive submission to the perceived threat of violence. In such cases the outcome will necessarily be contingent on an assessment of testimonial credibility,[4] a difficult enough task made all the more so when the parties

---

[1] Dennis, I. (2010) *The Law of Evidence*, London: Sweet & Maxwell, 622.

[2] Ibid, 639.

[3] Principally, Rook, P. and Ward, R. (2010) *Rook and Ward on Sexual Offences Law and Practice*, 4th edn and 1st supp., March 2014, London: Sweet & Maxwell, 813.

[4] Ibid.; Gunby, C., Carline, A., and Beynon, C., 'Regretting it After? Focus Group Perspectives on Alcohol Consumption, Nonconsensual Sex and False Allegations of Rape' (2012) 22(1) *Social & Legal Studies*, 87–106, at 94; and Ministry of Justice (2010) *Providing Anonymity to Those Accused of*

have been in a prior relationship, particularly one involving admitted intimacy.[5] In determining the limits of that assessment a careful balance has to be struck between protecting the complainant and affording the defendant a reasonable opportunity of acquittal.

(3) The permissive approach under common law

Under the former common law regime, rape complainants would routinely find   **5.03** themselves cross-examined on their previous sexual history, immoral character, or even their state of arousal at the time of the alleged incident.[6] Supposedly aimed at demonstrating promiscuity or a propensity to lie about consensual sexual relations,[7] this intrusive scrutiny may have contributed to the low reporting rates for rape and other sexual offences.[8] It was severely criticized for engaging the 'twin myths'—the tautological supposition that 'unchaste' women are more likely to consent to sexual intercourse and the idea that they are less trustworthy.[9] The Sexual Offences (Amendment) Act 1976 contained provisions intended to shield complainants from unnecessary invasion of privacy at trial.[10] These included, notably, the rule prohibiting publication of the complainant's name and restrictions on the use of sexual history evidence.[11]

(4) Initial statutory intervention

Specifically, section 2 of the 1976 Act precluded the admissibility of evidence con-   **5.04** cerning the complainant's sexual history with individuals other than the defendant except where the trial judge was satisfied that it would be unfair to exclude it. Yet this highly discretionary approach was still deemed inadequate, with judges continuing to admit 'irrelevant and prejudicial' evidence to the detriment of the complainant.[12] It was in fact the highlighting of these failings in *Speaking up for*

Rape: An Assessment of Evidence, Ministry of Justice Research Series 20/10, *https://www.justice.gov. uk/downloads/publications/ research-and-analysis/moj-research/anonymity-rape-research-report.pdf*.

   [5] Ministry of Justice, Home Office and Office for National Statistics (2013) *An Overview of Sexual Offending in England and Wales*, London: HMSO.

   [6] See generally, Dennis cited at n.1, 626.

   [7] Ibid., 625.

   [8] Temkin, J. (2002) *Rape and the Legal Process*, Oxford: Oxford University Press, 197; and see Wolchover, D. and Heaton-Armstrong, A., 'Rape Defendant Anonymity' (2012) 176 *Crim. Law & Just. Weekly*, 5–8, 24–26, at 5.

   [9] See *Seaboyer* (1991) 83 D.L.R. (4th) 193.

   [10] Implementing recommendations of the Heilbron Committee Report: Home Office (1975) *Report on the Advisory Group on the Law of Rape* (chair, Dame Rose Heilbron) Cmnd. 6352, London: HMSO.

   [11] See Temkin, J. and Krahé, B. (2008) *Sexual Assault and the Justice Gap: A Question of Attitude*, Portland: Hart, 25; and Rook and Ward (2010) cited at n.3, 813.

   [12] Kibble, N. (2005a) 'Judicial Perspectives of Rape Complainants: Ongoing Tensions Between Conflicting Priorities in the Criminal Justice System', (2005) 62 *Journal of Criminal Law*, 190–205 at 200; see also, Rook and Ward (2010), cited at n.3, 818.

Justice, the 1998 Home Office Working Group report,[13] which inspired the enactment of section 41 of the 1999 Act. The section was designed to impose further constraints on the use of sexual history evidence and curtail inconsistent applications of judicial discretion.[14]

B. Section 41 of the Youth Justice and Criminal Evidence Act 1999

(1) Principle conditions for permitting evidence

5.05 Section 41 precludes adducing any evidence of, or questioning about, a complainant's sexual history with third parties *or* the defendant unless it falls within the statutory conditions. These allow, in certain circumstances, the introduction of such evidence or questioning:

- where it relates to a relevant issue, but not of factual consent,[15] (e.g. to establish that the defendant was not the perpetrator, or to establish his *belief* in consent);[16]
- where it serves to rebut or explain evidence adduced by the prosecution;[17] or
- where it relates to a relevant issue, that issue is an issue of consent, and where the evidence in question relates to sexual behaviour alleged to have taken place at or about the same time as the incident in question,[18] or is so similar to behaviour which took place as part of the event or to behaviour which took place at or about the same time as the event that it cannot reasonably be explained as a coincidence.[19]

(2) Additional safety hurdles

5.06 Even where these conditions are met, the evidence may not be adduced unless the trial judge is satisfied that three additional safety hurdles have been crossed:

- the evidence or questioning must relate to a specific instance of sexual behaviour;[20]
- the judge must be satisfied that its purpose is not to 'impugn the credibility of the complainant as a witness';[21] and

---

[13] Home Office (1998) *Speaking Up for Justice: Report of the Interdepartmental Working Group on the Treatment of Vulnerable or Intimidated Witnesses in the Criminal Justice System*, London: HMSO, at paras 9.63 and 9.64.

[14] Temkin and Krahé (2008), cited at n.11, 25.

[15] YJCEA s 41(3)(a).

[16] Dennis (2010), cited at n.1, 630.

[17] YJCEA s 41(5).

[18] Ibid., s 41(3)(b).

[19] Ibid., s 41(3)(c).

[20] Ibid., s 41(6).

[21] Ibid., 41(4).

- the judge must be further satisfied that its exclusion may render any conclusion as to a relevant issue unsafe.[22]

(3) Measure criticized for providing insufficient discretion to maintain balance

Section 41 brought about an undoubted improvement in the protection of com- **5.07** plainants. It serves to prevent general scrutiny of a complainant's character, life-style, or background, and significantly restricts the circumstances under which any sexual history may be admitted. Nevertheless, enactment of the section initially proved largely as contentious as the previous law. Denounced by commentators as a 'hurried piece of work, enacted to fulfil election promises', it was devoid of any critical evaluation or practical judicial insight.[23] With their over-zealous discretion viewed as one of the issues which the section was intended to address, judges were largely omitted from the Working Group upon whose recommendations the Act was formulated.[24] In an eagerness to curtail their discretion, judges were stripped of their ability to inject into the trial a more nuanced approach to achieving a fair balance between the rights of complainants and those of defendants. Instead they were restricted to adjudicating on the safety or otherwise of outcomes based on pre-determined categories of evidence which Parliament deemed relevant.[25] This disproportionate 'blanket exclusionary'[26] approach arguably undermined the true objective of the Act's implementation, which was to combat the *inappropriate* use of irrelevant sexual history evidence. This was therefore seen to be favouring complainants over defendants,[27] potentially compromising the right of the latter to a fair trial[28] in preventing them from advancing an important part of their response[29] to an allegation gravely imperilling their liberty.

(4) A judicial attempt to meet the criticisms: discretion restored

The conflict between protecting complainants and affording defendants a fair and **5.08** balanced trial was addressed in *R v A*[30] in which the House of Lords established a test of admissibility compatible with fair trial provisions, re-injected judicial discretion into the law, and ultimately saved the legislation from its restrictive

---

22 Ibid., 41(2)(b); see also, *R v DB* [2012] EWCA Crim 1235.
23 Birch, D., 'A Better Deal for Vulnerable Witnesses?' [2000] Crim LR, 223–49, at 226–7.
24 See ibid.
25 Birch, D. and Underhill, G., '*R v A*: Case Comment' [2001] Crim LR, 389–94, at 392.
26 *R v A (No 2)* [2002] 1 AC 45, (Lord Steyn) [30–32].
27 Birch (2000), cited at n.23, 226.
28 Under Art 6 of the European Convention for the Protection of Human Rights and Fundamental Freedoms (Council of Europe, Treaty of Rome, 4 November 1950).
29 Kibble, N., 'Case Comment—*R v S*' [2011] Crim LR, 671–5, at 674.
30 [2002] 1 AC 45.

unworkability.[31] Alongside the statutory gateways of admissibility, the courts may now admit evidence relevant to the issue of consent where it is satisfied that its exclusion would endanger the fairness of the trial.[32] In determining the limits of relevance, judges may now place more emphasis on individual case needs than was permitted under the 1976 Act, allowing in evidence which might otherwise have been excluded.[33] This therefore provides a broader, more structured approach. Admissibility is also further regulated under Part 36 of the Criminal Procedure Rules 2013, which obliges the defence to submit, prior to trial, a written application detailing (a) the evidence or questioning they wish to introduce, and (b) the relevant issues,[34] and which therefore facilitates proper observation of the provisions.[35]

(5) Continuing unease over the section

5.09 Despite such improvements, however, the provision continues to face criticism, most fundamentally over its structure and drafting, the complexity of which has necessitated mandatory triennial training for 'sex-ticketed' judges.[36] Whilst this may have conduced to a more appropriate and controlled use of questioning and evidence,[37] issues of interpretation and procedure continue to occupy the appellate courts and inspire academic commentary, particularly over the meaning of 'relevance'. As section 41 excludes sexual history evidence unless overtly 'relevant', identifying the ambit of the concept will require deeper study, given the almost limitless range of circumstances arising in trials, than might at first blush seem necessary.

C. Understanding 'Relevance'

(1) Inadequacy of statutory definition of 'relevant issue in the case'

5.10 Relevance is given no statutory definition beyond that in section 42(1)(a), tautologically describing a 'relevant issue in the case' as 'any issue falling to be proved by the prosecution or defence in the trial of the accused'. It would appear that evidence relating to the complainant's sexual history with parties

---

[31] See Kibble, N., 'Judicial Discretion and the Admissibility of Prior Sexual History Evidence Under Section 41 of the Youth Justice and Criminal Evidence Act 1999: Sometimes Sticking to your Guns Means Shooting Yourself in the Foot: Part 2' [2005] Crim LR, 263–74, at 263–5.

[32] *R v A* [2002] 1 AC 45, (Lord Steyn) at [46].

[33] Rook and Ward (2010), cited at n.3, 814.

[34] Rules 36.2 and 36.3.

[35] Rook and Ward (2010), cited at n.3, 814.

[36] See Rumney, P. and Fenton, R., 'Judicial Training and Rape' (2011) 75(6) *Journal of Criminal Law*, 473–81, at 473–6.

[37] Dennis (2010), cited at n.1, 639.

other than the defendant will rarely be considered sufficiently relevant so as to admit the evidence.[38] However, matters are decidedly more complex when assessing the potential relevance of evidence pertaining to previous relationships between the two parties.

(2) Previous relationship of complainant and defendant

It was stressed in *R v A* that although evidence of a previous sexual relationship **5.11** between the parties would not mean that because a complainant had previously consented she must therefore have done so on the occasion in question, there would be instances where such evidence of prior intimacy might indeed be relevant in casting light on the complainant's mindset. However, this would depend on the facts and circumstances of each case.[39] This is perfectly logical since a previous sexual relationship between the complainant and defendant can hardly, of itself, support a belief in consent or even the fact of consent. To assert that the existence of such a relationship amounts to something more than coincidence (under s 41(3)(c)(ii)) would in effect engage the 'twin myth'.[40] This is precisely the line of questioning and evidence which section 41 sought to preclude. However, to disregard evidence regarding the nature and extent of a prior, intimate acquaintance, particularly a long-lasting one which may have been filled with love and affection, could also prevent the jury from fully comprehending the true facts of the case. Thus, in *R v A*, a spectrum of relevancy was developed at one end of which was evidence of an isolated instance of prior sexual activity distant in both time and circumstances from the present case, and at the other end the more relevant evidence of a continuous, happy relationship of cohabitation, intimacy, and sexual relations.[41] Where the case in hand might fall along this scale is for the trial judge alone.[42]

(3) Benefits and difficulties over discretion in prior relationship cases

This more discretionary, nuanced, approach is highly effective as it provides **5.12** broadly satisfactory guidance to ensure that the defendant's right to a fair trial is considered but does not entail the admission of *any* evidence relating to a previous relationship without limit. It avoids the need to apply rigid definitions of relevance which would be likely to prove unworkable in practice through failing to consider the needs, circumstances, and intricacies of each individual case. What will be relevant in one case may not necessarily be so in the next and any attempts to predetermine or predict relevance could instead severely disadvantage the accused. Nevertheless, even with this guidance, difficulties have arisen in determining

---

[38] See e.g. *R v A* [2002] 1 AC 45, (Lord Hope) at [64] and [77]; *R v Mokrecovas* [2002] 1 Cr App R 226 at [20]; and Kibble (2011), cited at n.29, 674.

[39] [2002] 1 AC 45, (Lord Steyn) at [31], and Lord Hutton at [151–2].

[40] See e.g. *R v MM* [2011] EWCA Crim 1291.

[41] [2002] 1 AC 45, (Lord Slynn) at [10], Lord Steyn at [32], and Lord Hutton at [152].

[42] [2002] 1 AC 45, (Lord Steyn) at [32].

where the relevance of evidence lies, particularly in more complex cases where the matters do not relate directly to previous relationships between the parties but rather reflect the more complex spectrum of human relationships and the infinitely variable circumstances which can arise in sexual offence cases.

(4) Identifying relevant issues

5.13 In *R v T*[43] the defendant sought for the first time at trial to adduce a photograph of the complainant wearing a bikini or underwear which he alleged she had sent him on Saint Valentine's Day and which his counsel described as 'quite graphic'. His purpose was to demonstrate her motive in making a false allegation in revenge for his having failed to reciprocate her sexual interest in him. To that end he also sought to introduce various messages he alleged she had sent via social media, only one of which—consisting of the phrase *'sweet talking'*—could, in the light of the photograph, conceivably have conveyed an amorous intent. It was held that the judge had erred in refusing the application on the basis that the defence had failed to comply with the Criminal Procedure Rules requirement to make it in advance of the trial. As the defence did not involve consent but a straight denial that sexual intercourse had ever occurred, the evidence was relevant to a matter under section 41(3)(a), namely a motive to fabricate the allegation, and the judge enjoyed no discretion to refuse the evidence.[44] Non-compliance with the advance notice requirements went not to admissibility but rather to the weight of the evidence, with the defendant having to provide an explanation for his late disclosures through cross-examination.

5.14 The trial judge's error in *R v T* may be contrasted with the decision in *R v Gjoni*,[45] another case illustrative of the considerable difficulties likely to be met in applying section 41. The judge had ruled that the defendant might assert, by way of explanation for having entered the complainant's bedroom, that he had been encouraged by a friend present at the time to believe that she would agree to have sexual relations with him. However, he would not be permitted to say that his belief had been encouraged by the friend's disclosure that he himself had actually experienced consensual intercourse with her a week previously. The ruling was upheld but although it appeared to represent a strict application of the letter of section 41, the decision will hardly conduce to universal equanimity. To exclude evidence from the defendant purporting to relate a third-party disclosure that she had recently evinced an amenable disposition to consensual intercourse on slight

---

[43] [2012] EWCA Crim 2358.
[44] See *R v F* [2005] 2 Cr App R 13.
[45] [2014] Crim LR 765, and see commentary on *R v Winter* (2008) 152(2) SJ29, CA, by the editors of *Archbold: Criminal Pleading, Evidence and Practice*, London: Sweet & Maxwell, 2015 edn, para 8-246, observing that while statements made prior to the event in question may encourage a belief that the complainant would consent they are logically irrelevant to the question whether the complainant did consent.

acquaintance could be a recipe for injustice. Absent evidence of such a disclosure the defendant's declared belief might appear to have been largely speculative, based on no more than an exhortation and unexplained expression of confidence by a third party perhaps plucked out of thin air. That the defendant may claim to have been the recipient of ungallant gossip does not make it true, nor indeed that it was actually ever imparted to him. The first of these two concessions could conceivably be made by the defendant without weakening his case. Indeed, such a concession might be tactically advantageous. By way of a related illustration, the defendant's case may be that the complainant initially purported to object to sexual activity with him but then consented with self-evident relish. He may be seeking to establish that he believed her initial response was wholly simulated and that he pressed on in good faith because he had been told by his friend that the complainant had a history of pretending to object to casual sexual activity but then to 'surrender' with enthusiasm. On the basis of *Gjoni* he would be barred from explaining the specific basis for his belief that he was expected to ignore her initial protestations. This is surely to shut out a potentially key factor in explaining his state of mind.

The decision in *R v T* highlights the importance of identifying correctly the issues **5.15** to which the proposed evidence relates. It has been suggested that in spite of the dedication afforded to training, some judges appear to lack an understanding of the underlying purport of the legislation and there thus remains uncertainty as to when evidence can be admitted and in identifying where its relevance lies.[46] On the other hand, it is tolerably well known among practitioners that the great majority of section 41 applications are settled in a common-sense way through negotiation and ultimately by agreement. Although the Court of Appeal has occasionally voiced disagreement with the rulings of trial judges, that can hardly be said to amount to a failure of judicial competence. Inasmuch as confusion may sometimes be encountered, this may stem from the complex drafting of the statute, suggesting that Parliament needs to rework the text, making it clearer, better defined, more conducive to the making of appropriate decisions which do justice to both the defendant and the complainant, and more usefully accessible. More importantly, however, greater emphasis should be placed upon adherence to the Criminal Procedure Rules, even where the evidence satisfies the criteria of an exclusionary gateway.[47] This is an issue which has previously been subjected to academic critique of the section 41 provisions.[48] Through strict adherence to the safeguards, obliging parties to make written application identifying the evidence they wish to adduce

---

[46] Temkin and Krahé (2008), cited at n11, 146; Kibble (2011), cited at n.29, 674.

[47] See e.g. *R v Ogbodo* [2011] EWCA 564.

[48] See e.g. Temkin and Krahé (2008), cited at n.13, 55–56; and Kelly, L., Temkin, J., and Griffiths, S. (2006) *Section 41: an evaluation of new legislation limiting sexual history in rape trials*, Home Office Online Report 20/06, 23–24, *http://webarchive.nationalarchives.gov.uk/20130128103514/http:// rds.homeoffice.gov.uk/rds/pdfs06/rdsolr2006.pdf.*

and its relevance, judges will have more time properly to assess the applicability and potential relevance of such evidence.

5.16 It may be open to debate whether the Court of Appeal in *R v T* were right to hold that the evidence ought to have been admitted. In *R v F*[49] it was held that where the admissibility criteria under one of the section 41 gateways has been satisfied, the trial judge enjoys no discretion to refuse or limit the evidence sought to be adduced. It is for this reason that the failure to make an advance application would not have induced the judge to exclude the evidence. Yet in *R v T* the Court of Appeal seem not to have considered whether the judge could properly have excluded the material by virtue of the section 41(2)(b) safety hurdle, namely that even if evidence qualifies under an exclusionary gateway, the court must still refuse to allow it in evidence unless satisfied that to exclude it would render a conclusion from the jury unsafe.[50] Although the Valentine's Day photograph and the '*sweet talking*' message might possibly have been indicative of a romantic overture, it may be conjectured how far they could have influenced the jury's deliberations. The complainant had in a voir dire denied sending them, their late introduction could well have weakened their impact, and the value of social networking media has been doubted in academic commentary.[51] The report of *R v T* mentions that in advance of the trial the defendant had applied under section 41 to adduce evidence of a previous complaint but is silent as to whether the application was allowed. In any event, without making any finite judgement on the decision in *R v T*, it may be observed in general that allowing evidence of doubtful relevance would appear to undermine the purpose of the legislation and mirror concerns expressed by the Home Office that such safeguards might be misapplied or misunderstood.[52] That such evidence could have been admitted suggests that, in failing to offer more concrete guidance surrounding 'relevant issues', the statute as currently applied remains open to the criticism that it might not be restrictive enough in protecting complainants. This is a potential drawback which further highlights the need for Parliament to consider whether the provisions could be reworked to give greater clarity to the distinction between relevance and 'credibility'.[53]

5.17 The labelling of a motive to fabricate a complaint as a sufficiently 'relevant issue' upon which to allow cross-examination is itself a basis for some greater analysis as it undoubtedly draws upon a complainant's credibility, as explicitly prohibited under section 41(4).[54] Yet a motive to fabricate is not an issue which is to be 'proved at

---

[49] Cited at n.44.

[50] Brewis, B., Jackson, A., and Stockdale, M., 'Sexual History Evidence: Late Disclosure and Relevance' (2013) 77(1) *Journal of Criminal Law*, 13–17 at 16.

[51] See O'Floinn, M. and Omerod, D., 'Social Networking Material as Criminal Evidence' [2012] Crim LR, 486–512.

[52] Kelly, Temkin, and Griffiths, cited at n.48, 17.

[53] Hoyano, L., 'Case Comment—*R v T*' [2013] Crim LR, 596–98, at 598.

[54] See further, *R v DB* [2012] EWCA Crim 1235.

court', insofar as it is not an element of the offence itself,[55] and therefore, on the face of the legislation, should not amount to a 'relevant issue' for the purposes of admitting evidence. Nevertheless, there appears to be a firm academic argument that this term should be interpreted more broadly to accommodate the fair trial necessities of the defendant.[56] To preclude evidence intended to demonstrate a motive to fabricate a complaint in *all* cases could prevent certain defendants, who may be the subject of false accusation, from advancing a crucial part of their case and potentially their only viable opportunity for securing an acquittal. Thus, an analysis of the probative weight of the evidence in question should be undertaken by judges to determine its relevance, paying due regard to the fine balance between protection of the complainant and observation of the defendant's fair trial requirements.[57] Of course, this exercise must also be undertaken with a full and competent awareness of the safety hurdles operating under section 41. The judge must not only ensure that the evidence in question relates to a specific instance of sexual behaviour but must remain alert to the risk that its exclusion, supposedly dictated by the imperative of adducing only the most relevant and probative evidence, might nonetheless result in an unsafe verdict.

5.18 However, a distinction is to be drawn between admitting evidence in relation to a complainant's motive to fabricate an allegation in the present case, and that regarding previous false allegations.

D. False Complaints and Bad Character

(1) False allegations: mendacity or mistake

5.19 There is notable difficulty in determining when to allow in evidence relating to an allegation made in the past by the complainant which is, or has been, demonstrated to be substantially false. An allegation may be false in the sense that the maker is deliberately and consciously untruthful, or it may be no more than the product of what may broadly be termed 'mistake'. Innocent errors of perception, comprehension, and remembrance may occur for many reasons, ranging from those which any sensible and stable person might make, to 'confabulation', in essence illusions, or delusions sincerely held but resulting from personality disorders or psychological or other mental health infirmities.[58] A false sense of reality has not been unknown to result from the impact on a suggestible person of various factors: sustained therapeutic treatment, rumination in the course of diary writing and reading self-help books containing self-diagnostic and dream interpretation advice. In the context

---

[55] Rook and Ward (2010), cited at n.3, 837.
[56] Ibid., 838.
[57] See ibid., 838–9.
[58] See Levitt and CPS Equality and Diversity Unit, cited at n.73, at 17, para [22].

of testimonial narrative use of the epithet 'unreliable' may be euphemistic for mendacious but is more appropriately employed when it is uncertain if the witness was being untruthful or was merely mistaken (in the sense of delusionary).

(2) Interplay between section 41 and section 100 of the Criminal Justice Act 2003

5.20 The defence may be aspiring to introduce evidence of a false allegation of sexual misconduct brought by the complainant on a previous occasion in order to support a challenge as to the truth of the instant allegation. If the past allegation can be demonstrated with sufficient cogency to have been *deliberately* false it may become admissible under section 100 (and associated sections) of the CJA 2003 as evidence of the complainant's reprehensible conduct. Conversely, while there may be unassailable evidence that the previous allegation was false in the sense that the incident complained about never happened or that the sexual act in question did not amount to a crime (for example, because it was in fact consensual) there may be no clear evidence that the falsity was deliberate. In such a case the bad character provisions of the CJA would be irrelevant and inapplicable and the only question would be whether the court ought to allow reference to be introduced to the prior allegation under section 41[59] or in some other way.

(3) Cumulative effect of section 41 and the CJA 2003 bad character provisions

5.21 Section 41 and the CJA 2003 bad character provisions may both be applicable where, for example, the previous false allegation related not to whether the act happened at all, but whether or not there had been consent, and there was tolerably clear evidence that the falsity of the allegation was deliberate. Clearly the primary purpose would be to ask about a previous deliberately false statement and not about sexual behaviour. However, section 41 applies to prevent the defence from adducing evidence or asking questions in cross-examination about any sexual behaviour of a complainant. Since the subsidiary purpose would be inextricably linked with undisputed sexual behaviour (consensual or otherwise) the section would apply to govern its admissibility. In such a case the two provisions would arguably be cumulative, with the proposed evidence having to pass both section 41 and section 100 hurdles.

5.22 The interrelationship between section 41 and the bad character provisions of the CJA 2003 is complicated, with difficult problems apt to arise when the falsity (that is, fundamental inaccuracy) of a previous allegation either cannot be definitively established or where its false character may not necessarily be attributable

---

[59] Under ss 98 and 112. See *R v M* [2009] EWCA Crim 618, (Dyson LJ) at [7]; and *R v RT* [2001] EWCA Crim 1877, (Keene LJ) at [22], [34], and [35].

to the complainant's mendacity. It is a point upon which the volume of appeals continues to rise, indicating a significant degree of judicial uncertainty, at least at first instance, surrounding the circumstances in which such evidence may be adduced.[60]

(4) Prior allegations which were not necessarily deliberately false

In seeking to introduce a demonstratively false prior allegation which cannot be **5.23** shown to have been deliberately invented (and to which therefore the CJA 2003 bad character provisions will be inapplicable) the defence will necessarily need to resort to section 41. To that end it may be trite but it is nonetheless important to distinguish between two types of case: (a) those in which the defence amounts to a denial of the allegedly non-consensual nature of a sexual act in itself undisputed where it is sought to introduce a previous false allegation of non-consensuality as regards an otherwise undisputed sexual act, and (b) those in which the instant sexual encounter is denied outright and it is sought to introduce the prior allegation of a sexual act which never in fact occurred. In a prosecution where consensuality is in issue (but not the sexual act itself) the defence might wish to introduce the fact that a previous allegation made by the complainant that she had not consented to an otherwise undisputed sexual act was demonstrably false. If it cannot be shown that she had consciously and deliberately invented the allegation, and the CJA 2003 bad character provisions would therefore be inapplicable, the evidence would only be admissible as relevant if it passes the coincidence test in section 41(3). However, that test does not require independent proof of the falsity of the prior allegation, which is irrelevant; rather it will be the marked similarity between the complainant's prior behaviour and her behaviour in the instant case which will render the past allegation admissible. It is the factor of that similarity which may point inferentially to the falsity of both allegations of non-consensuality. If there is no similarity between the circumstances of the two allegations sufficient to exclude coincidence, it follows that the shared issue of consent between the two cases must merely be coincidental and any reference to the earlier case will be inadmissible. To some commentators this might seem to go against the grain of fairness given that section 41(2)(b) would provide no relief.[61]

By contrast with cases involving consent as the central issue, the defence may be **5.24** denying the sexual act outright and may be seeking to introduce the fact that in a previous unconnected case involving some other accused the complainant had been proved to have 'confabulated' a sexual encounter, that is, made a false allegation, albeit unintentionally, that such an encounter had taken place. As already stressed in para 5.21, section 41 generally applies to prevent the defence

---

[60] See Thomas, D.A., '*R v M*: Case Comment' [2010] Crim LR, 792–6, at 793; see also, *R v Guled Yusuf* [2010] EWCA Crim 359.

[61] *R v RT* [2001] EWCA Crim 1877, (Keene LJ) at [41]; Dennis (2010), cited at n.1, 634.

from adducing evidence or asking questions in cross-examination about any sexual behaviour of a complainant. Thus, where the proposed questions are not about sexual behaviour on a particular past occasion but are about *a previous false statement* that such behaviour occurred—such questions being aimed at showing that it never in fact happened—it follows that the section will be inapplicable to preclude the questions, which are about the *non-occurrence* of the previous sexual encounter and not about sexual behaviour as such. However, would the section forbid the defence from introducing the reference to a prior undisputed sexual encounter where the complainant had made an unintentionally false allegation that she had not consented? Although the primary purpose would be to ask about a previous false statement, nonetheless the purpose would clearly be linked inextricably with sexual behaviour, that is, a sexual act which is not disputed to have occurred. In those circumstances it would seem that the effect of the section must be to prohibit the question or evidence.

(5) Difficulties in establishing falsity of prior allegation

5.25 In cases where the defence are seeking to introduce a reference to the past allegation by the complainant of a sexual act on the basis that it is said to have been false, the judge will be faced with the difficulty of determining whether there was any proper basis for concluding that it was indeed false. That difficulty is well exemplified by *R v Garaxo*[62] in which the defence involved a fundamental denial of any encounter with the complainant, sexual or otherwise, and at the trial it was unsuccessfully sought to adduce two previous complaints to the police concerning different men. Neither man, it appears, was prosecuted and the complainant was not apparently prosecuted for making a false allegation. In one case she had failed to co-operate and in the other she sought a crime reference number 'for the social'. The case was not one in which the earlier complaints were taken in isolation of each other or were provably false and from which it was sought to deduce that the instant case must likewise have been false. Rather, it was successfully argued on appeal that all three accounts were so similar that it would have been open to the jury to conclude inferentially that they were all unreliable. Since it was the similarity of the complaints which it was contended conduced to the relevance, and therefore admissibility, of the earlier ones it was immaterial whether the falsehood in each case was intentional or the product of innocent confabulation. Moreover, in such a case as *Garaxo* it would not be necessary to adduce independent evidence demonstrating that the earlier allegations were false. By contrast with cases so factually similar as to exclude the sensible possibility of coincidence, one might ask whether section 41(3)(a) will sanction the adducing of prior sexual allegations, proved to have been false, in order to demonstrate a propensity to concoct or fantasize sexual assaults? The primary purpose would not be to impugn the complainant's credibility (which under s 41(4) would disqualify the evidence

---

[62] [2005] Crim LR 883; [2005] EWCA Crim 1170. See also *R v. Butler* [2015] EWCA Crim 854.

from admissibility) but to establish a pattern of making false statements, whether deliberate invention or innocent confabulation.

There may be more direct evidence of the falsity of a previous allegation of a sexual   **5.26**
act than inference from coincidence. A successful prosecution of the complainant
for perjury or perverting the course of justice would justly be taken as decisive
evidence of deliberate malicious invention, but such cases are rare. By contrast,
where a prosecution on the strength of the complainant's evidence had resulted in
the alleged sexual assailant's acquittal, that in itself is likely to be far from enough
to establish the falsity of the allegation. The failure by the Crown to satisfy the
criminal standard of proof might well leave egg on the complainant's face but
by definition would hardly amount to proof that the allegation had either been
deliberately invented or imagined. Still less so would a decision by the police to
take no further action or by the Crown Prosecution Service (CPS) to initiate or
discontinue proceedings as a result of doubts about the veracity of the complainant against the background of medical or social reports. All would depend on the
particular facts of the case perhaps retrievable from the police crime reports and on
the content of third-party records, notably medical, and reports by social services.
The complainant might not even have made an official complaint to police but
might have voiced it to a relative, friend, or social worker. While in the absence of
knowledge of the previous cases the prosecution bear the duty of disclosure to the
defence of prior complaints (assuming police files contain reference to them) many
cases will conceivably not be known to the police and will not be discoverable even
by diligent and objective police enquiries. We further consider this issue at paras
5.33 and 5.34.

The admission of evidence under the bad character provisions, requires   **5.27**

> material such that, depending on the answers given by the complainant in cross-
> examination, the jury could have been satisfied that the previous complaint was
> untrue, or that there was material which was capable of founding an inference that
> the complaint was untrue.[63]

This is not an exercise in subsidiary investigation, seeking to explore the factual   **5.28**
veracity of a complainant's prior allegations, but rather provides a test of 'reasonable inference'[64] for the jury where judges must decide, upon the basis of the available material, whether a jury could be satisfied as to the allegation's falsity.[65] It is not
an exercise of judicial discretion,[66] yet this should still require some level of close
analysis in ensuring their decisions are based upon sufficiently probative material,
rather than mere speculation. For example—as already mentioned—the fact of
an acquittal regarding the allegation should not constitute a 'proper evidential

---

[63] *R v M* [2009] EWCA Crim 618, (Dyson LJ) at [22].
[64] Rook and Ward, (2010), cited at n.3, 863.
[65] *R v M* [2009] EWCA Crim 618, (Dyson LJ) at [23].
[66] Ibid.

basis', as this reverses the burden of proof.[67] Furthermore, in *R v Davarifar*[68] it was asserted that the opinion of the CPS was irrelevant to this exercise as it was for the court alone to determine an evidential basis.[69]

5.29 Whilst this does not always directly engage section 41, in remembering that the purpose of the YJCEA was to protect complainants from the use of detrimental, unnecessary, and painful evidence against them at trial,[70] it is arguable that the threshold of admissibility for evidence which would present to the jury details of a complainant's sexual history, is placed too low.[71] Kelly et al. have argued that only demonstrably false accusations should be admitted.[72] Yet it is almost a truism, and has long been acknowledged, that allegations of rape are at once difficult to prove and difficult to rebut,[73] a state of play which is hardly any less true now than it was in Hale's day before the advent of modern techniques of forensic medical examination.[74] Thus one must question how and in what instances will such allegations be accepted as 'demonstrably false'? This approach might risk setting the threshold too high, depriving a jury of relevant evidence upon which to base their sensible decisions of credibility and reliability, and potentially disadvantaging defendants to whom such evidence might provide their best chance of acquittal. A potential improvement could be found in refocusing training or amending the criteria in keeping with that adopted in the Canadian model where a complainant can only be cross-examined as to prior fabrication in order to demonstrate a pattern of falsity.[75] This could help ensure that, whilst following the evidential basis test, only evidence of the greatest probative value to an issue in point, would be put to the jury.

5.30 A more intractable difficulty involves the not uncommon situation where previous allegations of sexual assault made by the complainant have not been investigated to the extent necessary to enable it to be established whether they were false or, indeed, whether there in fact was any allegation made at all.[76] This may be because they were not reported to the police originally, or there was confusion as to what

---

[67] *R v BD* [2007] EWCA Crim 2668, at [22–3].
[68] [2009] EWCA Crim 2294.
[69] Stanley Burnton LJ at [10].
[70] *R v Abdelrahman* [2005] EWCA Crim 1367, (Maurice Kay LJ) at [27].
[71] Thomas (2010), cited at 60, 795.
[72] Kelly, Temkin, and Griffiths, cited at n.48.
[73] Belknap, J., (2010) 'Rape: Too Hard to Report and Too Easy to Discredit Victims' (2010) 16(12) *Violence Against Women*, 1335–44, at 1339; Levitt, A. and Crown Prosecution Service Equality and Diversity Unit (2013) *Charging Perverting the Course of Justice and Wasting Police Time in Cases Involving Allegedly False Rape and Domestic Violence Allegations*, London: CPS, 26.
[74] An 'accusation easily to be made and hard to be proved, and harder to be defended by the party accused, tho never so innocent': Hale, Sir M. (1736) *History of the Pleas of the Crown* (two vols) London: Sollom Emlyn (printed 1736 by order of Parliament, 60 years after the author's death), i, 634.
[75] *R v Riley* (1992) 11 O.R. (3rd) 151 CA.
[76] Levitt, A. and Crown Prosecution Service Equality and Diversity Unit, cited at n.73, 31.

was being alleged, or because, having been reported to the police, any consequent investigation was limited owing to, for example, the complainant's declared wish not to pursue it. It is arguable that as the law stands evidence of such complaints is not admissible owing to lack of evidence as to falsity and that this might unfairly disadvantage defendants in some circumstances.[77]

(6) Probative value

Even where the evidential basis test is satisfied, to qualify under the bad character **5.31** provision, evidence must be deemed substantially probative to a matter of substantial importance.[78] For these purposes, the complainant's credibility may constitute a significant matter in the proceedings, but the greater difficulty lies in deciphering probative value.[79] In accordance with the judgment in *R v S*, 'substantial' has been held to demand 'more than trivial ... but ... not ... conclusive probative value'.[80] This provides a higher threshold than that under the 'evidential basis' test, obliging the courts to consider the overall context and relevance of the evidence within individual cases before evidence which might significantly prejudice the complainant can be admitted.[81] In doing so, the courts will have to consider factors such as the similarities between the previous allegation and the current case, their proximity in time,[82] and, in light of the other evidence against the defendant, how valuable such evidence might be to his case.[83] This appears to strike a fair balance in considering the potential prejudicial effects of admitting such evidence on the complainant and affording the accused his right of defence and fair trial.[84] Yet given the potential prejudicial effects upon the complainant, there remains a lack of consensus as to when evidence of prior falsity will be admitted under the bad character provisions.[85] The extent of this confusion can be traced back to the need for Parliamentary guidance as to when prior false allegations will be deemed a relevant matter in issue.

This problem may be especially acute where bad character provisions and section **5.32** 41 overlap. Although bad character evidence strictly falls outside the ambit of the YJCEA, in the context of trials of sexual offences it will normally constitute material of the kind with which section 41 is primarily concerned: sexual behaviour having an adverse bearing upon the complainant's credibility. This is, of course, an ambiguous area since the circumstances will naturally vary from one case to the next. However, statutory reform to remedy this issue could fall foul of the

---

[77] See e.g. *R v Knight* [2013] EWCA Crim 2486.
[78] CJA 2003, s 100.
[79] Kibble (2011), cited at n.29, 821.
[80] [2009] EWCA 2457, (Aiken LJ) at [45].
[81] Kibble (2011), cited at n.29, 821; see also, *R v Dizaei* [2013] EWCA Crim 88.
[82] CJA 2003, s 100(3).
[83] See e.g. *R v Miller* [2012] EWCA Crim 1153, (Pitchford LJ) at [20].
[84] See *R v Stephenson* [2006] EWCA Crim 2325, (Hughes LJ) at [27].
[85] See discussion in Kibble (2011), cited at n.29, 821–2.

same criticism as met section 41: that trying to fit particular cases into predetermined, exhaustive categories of relevance is not feasible. The problems cast up by the provision are capable of being remedied, therefore, not by statutory revision but rather by additional guidelines. These might be formulated with input from seasoned judges and practitioners to provide greater clarity as to both when and why such evidence should be deemed substantially relevant and probative when falling under either the YJCEA or the CJA provisions. In either instance judges will be expected to keep in mind the complainant's vulnerable position.

(7) Difficulties with false allegations

5.33 There is one further point of analysis regarding the interrelationship between bad character and sexual history evidence. The law currently dictates that a complainant may be cross-examined as to a previous allegation of rape where it was held to be false, as this goes towards his or her credibility as a witness. Yet if the court is not satisfied that such previous assertions were false, any such questioning is excluded by section 41. Upon initial analysis, this appears logical as it only allows such questioning or evidence to lend weight to a defendant's claim that he has been falsely accused or to demonstrate that this particular complainant may be less credible, rather than allowing unjust and potentially detrimental evidence of the fact that the complainant may have previously been the victim of a serious sexual offence. In order to be admitted under the CJA 2003, the previous conduct must constitute 'reprehensible behaviour'.[86] In *R v Renda*, this was held to consist of behaviour denoting 'culpability or blameworthiness'.[87] This suggests that the complainant must have acted with some level of deliberation or motive, as demonstrated in the judgment of *R v Davarifar* where it was stated that had the complainant's previous allegations amounted to a calculated lie, the threshold under CJA 2003 would have been crossed. Yet it suggested an air of considerably less certainty where the allegations had been made as a result of alcoholism and inherent personality problems.[88]

5.34 Where a complainant's previous allegation has been shown to be unreliable, or where there has been a demonstrable pattern of repeated allegations, this might become a relevant factor which ought to be the subject of admissible evidence, albeit not of 'reprehensible behaviour' as such. This therefore serves as a reminder to the courts to pay close attention to the probative value and relevance of the evidence, carefully evaluating the relevant similarities and links between past and present allegations to establish whether it is appropriate to introduce it at court. In doing so, the courts should balance the relative weight and usefulness of the evidence against any careless and prejudicial inferences that a complainant may be

---

[86] CJA 2003, s 112.
[87] [2005] EWCA Crim 2826, at [24].
[88] [2009] EWCA Crim 2294, (Stanley Burton LJ) at [11].

apt to lie when, in fact, the prior allegation may have been made for reasons wholly collateral to the present case and thus should hold no relevance at trial.

E. Conclusion

It is clear that greater clarity is needed for both judges and practitioners in applying **5.35** the use of section 41 and, equally important, in the relationship between section 41 and bad character provisions. Whilst measures have been implemented in an attempt to achieve this, for example through mandatory training, it is imperative to ensure that greater levels of guidance are provided to assist judges in their understanding of the safeguards, key terminology, and the true objectives of the legislation, particularly surrounding the interpretation and understanding of 'relevance'.

Section 41 is an inherently complex piece of legislation, with ambiguous ter- **5.36** minology and a complicated structure of safeguards and hurdles. As already mentioned, this often results in uncertainty in the law's application, in particular because, as two of the present authors have observed from their practitioner experience, first instance rulings will escape appellate scrutiny when the defendant is acquitted. It is arguably the lack of clear guidance surrounding the intricate technicalities of the legislation which fuels such inconsistencies between judges. Some may become distracted by complicated procedural rules and thus may become blinded as to the law's true objective, potentially resulting in unnecessarily restrictive decisions compromising the defendant's fair trial. It is therefore imperative that greater levels of guidance and clarity are produced in order to unify judges' approaches to sexual cases, particularly surrounding the meaning of 'relevance' and the crossover between section 41 and bad character provisions; whether stemming from Parliamentary intervention, through a Practice Direction or through judgment of the appellate courts. This must, however, retain the fundamental judicial discretion required to address the particulars of each individual case and must further respect the balance between the rights of the complainant and defendant.

Author Biography

Nevada McEvoy-Cooke is a law graduate who has recently completed her master's degree in Criminal Law and Criminal Justice with distinction from the University of Sussex. Her main areas of research have focused on sexual violence, hate crime, and the use of restorative justice. She has previously worked as a research assistant at the International Network for Hate Studies, collating research on discrimination and bias-motivated crimes. She has also worked within a social services triage unit for the safeguarding and welfare of children and young adults.

6

BAD CHARACTER PROVISIONS
AND THEIR APPLICATION
TO SEXUAL OFFENCES

David Ormerod QC, HHJ Martin Picton, and Andrew Roberts

A. Introduction

The Criminal Justice Act 2003 (the Act) transformed the law governing the admis- **6.01** sibility of bad character evidence (BCE). From the earliest appeals, the Court of Appeal has recognized that the impact of the Act might be keenly felt in sexual offence trials. Evidence of previous misconduct is now frequently, almost routinely, admitted against defendants via the seven admissibility 'gateways' in section 101 of the Act. This chapter explores some of the difficulties that may arise in applying the provisions of the Act in sexual cases. Particular difficulty has been experienced by the courts in identifying what constitutes 'evidence of bad character' in sexual contexts; regulating the means by which BCE is to be proved; adopting a coherent approach to cross-admissibility; and directing juries as to the uses of BCE. The Act also produced a significant change to the admissibility of BCE against non-defendants, although these changes will not be considered here. This chapter examines the admissibility of BCE relating to defendants, and explores the significance of the changes in cases involving sexual offences.

(1) Sexual misconduct as evidence

6.02 Before examining the provisions of the Act, it is important to note both the potential significance of admitting BCE in a sexual offence trial, and the risks associated with its reception. Often, the only people able to provide direct evidence regarding the matters that gave rise to the charges will be the complainant and the accused. In such cases, where a jury is presented with contradictory accounts of the events in question, knowledge of the previous sexual behaviour of a party may influence its assessment of whether some disputed activity has taken place or, as the case may be, whether what took place was consensual. Evidence that on some previous occasion a defendant engaged in conduct similar to that alleged by the complainant can be used as the basis of an inference that D has a tendency or propensity to act in that way.

6.03 Where a number of similar complaints derive from independent sources, it is possible for those instances of evidence of alleged bad character to be mutually supportive, or cross admissible. The probative force of each in relation to the other lies in the perceived improbability of the complainants all being mistaken or proffering fabricated accounts. While extraneous sources of information can be helpful, reception of such evidence carries a significant risk. Empirical research suggests that when presented with evidence of convictions for certain sexual offences, there is a likelihood that juries will engage in prejudicial reasoning. In a study involving the use of simulated or 'mock' juries, jurors were presented with various forms of BCE.[1] The study suggested that when presented with evidence that the defendant had a recent conviction for a similar offence, jurors were more likely to believe the defendant to be guilty of the offence charged. Evidence of a recent conviction of dissimilar offence led to lower perceived probability of guilt than was the case where jurors were not presented with any evidence of previous convictions. However, this effect did not extend to cases in which the previous conviction was for indecent assault on a child. In such circumstances jurors were less likely to believe the testimony of the defendant, to believe that he was more deserving of punishment, and more likely

---

[1] Lloyd-Bostock, S., 'The effects on juries of hearing about the defendant's previous criminal record: a simulation study' [2000] Crim LR 734. For discussion of prejudicial effect, see Law Commission (2001) Law Commission Report No 273, *Evidence of Bad Character in Criminal Proceedings*, Cm 5257, at paras 6.33–42. See further, Honess T. and Mathews, G., 'Admitting Evidence of a Defendant's Previous Conviction (PCE) and its Impact on Juror Deliberation in Relation to Both Juror-Processing Style and Juror Concerns over the Fairness of Introducing PCE' (2012) 17 *Legal and Criminological Psychology*, 360.

to convict, even in cases in which he was charged with a dissimilar offence. There appears to be no rational basis for this phenomenon[2] and the most plausible explanation is that the juror's conclusions were a manifestation of *'moral prejudice'*—a conclusion that is the result of antipathy towards the defendant rather than an exercise of logic.[3] Perhaps mindful of the risk that the evidence might lead to juries reasoning in these prejudice-based ways, it was observed in one of the first appellate court judgments (*R v Hanson*[4]) that:

> The starting point should be for judges and practitioners to bear in mind that Parliament's purpose in the legislation, as we divine it from the terms of the Act, was to assist in the evidence based conviction of the guilty, without putting those who are not guilty at risk of conviction by prejudice. It is accordingly to be hoped that prosecution applications to adduce such evidence will not be made routinely, simply because a defendant has previous convictions, but will be based on the particular circumstances of each case.[5]

In *Hanson* and the subsequent early appeals in *R v Weir*[6] and *R v Highton*,[7] the   **6.04**
Court of Appeal provided valuable guidance and imposed important boundaries on the operation of the bad character provisions. The principles established in those cases lie at the heart of many subsequent decisions and they repay careful reading. The Court identified several matters of importance including the significance of early preparation by the Crown coupled with the provision of details of the bad character it sought to adduce,[8] as well as a co-operative engagement by the defence in that process. The Criminal Procedure Rules, then recently created, provided a foundation for the Court in that regard.[9] The cases also recognized the need for careful directions to be given to the jury in order to avoid prejudice-based convictions.[10]

In *Hanson* the Court emphasized that the Crown had to decide whether it pro-   **6.05**
posed to rely simply upon the fact of a previous conviction as evidence of bad character or also upon its circumstances. The fact of prior conviction(s) might suffice where the number and/or circumstances of them were sufficiently apparent from

---

[2] As the Law Commission (2001) observed, cited at n.1, para 6.37.
[3] On this form of prejudice as distinct from prejudicial reasoning, see Palmer, A., 'The Scope of the Similar Fact Rule', (1994) 16 *Adelaide Law Review*, 161.
[4] [2005] EWCA Crim 824.
[5] Ibid., [4].
[6] [2005] EWCA Crim 2866.
[7] [2005] EWCA Crim 1985.
[8] See more recently *R v Vickers* [2012] EWCA Crim 2689 at [38] (Treacy LJ): 'it is imperative that a judge is supplied with meticulously accurate information about a defendant's previous convictions'.
[9] In particular, requiring any defendant who challenged the conviction or caution to give notice to that under Crim PR 35.3(4)(b). In extreme instances the Crim PR have led to the exclusion of evidence for the defence because of such a failure: *R v Musone* [2007] EWCA Crim 1237. A sexual case in which late notice has led to evidence being excluded is *M* [2006] EWCA Crim 1509.
[10] Guidance is provided in the Judicial Studies Board (2010) *Crown Court Bench Book, https://www.judiciary.gov.uk/wp-content/uploads/JCO/Documents/Training/benchbook_criminal_2010.pdf.*

its description to justify a finding that it might establish propensity.[11] However, where the Crown needed and proposed to rely on the circumstances of the previous convictions, those circumstances and the manner in which they were to be proved had to be set out in the application.[12]

6.06   This need for timely preparation was reiterated in *Bovell and Dowds*[13] where the court highlighted the necessity of compliance with the timetables set in the Criminal Procedure Rules. The court in that case also emphasized the need for evidence-based convictions and observed that bad character ought not to be used to bolster a weak case. In *Hanson*, Rose LJ described 'weak' in terms of there being *'no or very little evidence'* and in *Darnley*[14] the court recognized that in determining whether a case was 'weak' the judge should apply the familiar *Galbraith* test.[15]

(2) A preliminary question: what is 'bad character'?

6.07   As we will see, the Act establishes seven grounds or 'gateways' for the reception of evidence of a defendant's bad character. However, as the Court of Appeal in *Edwards*[16] noted, the first inquiry will often be whether the evidence is 'bad character' at all. The provisions regulating admissibility of what appears to be BCE apply only to evidence that concerns 'bad character' as that term is defined in the Act. Section 98 explains that references to a person's 'bad character' are to evidence of 'misconduct', or of a disposition towards it, and 'misconduct' is defined in section 112 as meaning the commission of an offence or 'other reprehensible behaviour'. Some guidance on the interpretation of the approach to bad character was offered in the case of *Renda*. The Court was prepared to accept 'as a matter of ordinary language, the word "reprehensible" carries with it some element of culpability or blameworthiness'.[17] The absence of a clear definition of BCE has led to some difficult decisions in the context of sexual offences. One striking example is the case of *Fox*[18] where the disputed evidence was F's notebook in which he had recorded sexual fantasies involving young girls. The Court of Appeal held that it left the

---

[11] Admissibility decisions concerning s 101(1)(d) and (g) are subject to duties to ensure that reception would be just (s 103(3)) and would not have an adverse effect the fairness of proceedings (s 101(3)). Problems have arisen in sexual cases where the Crown cannot readily prove the details of the earlier alleged offending without calling the complainant in that incident (as in *R v Woodhouse* [2009] EWCA Crim 498) or applying to rely on hearsay accounts of the earlier trial—*R v Humphris* [2005] EWCA Crim 2030; *R v RML* [2013] EWCA Crim (30 April).

[12] See on the significance *R v Lamaletie* [2008] EWCA Crim 314. Problems may also arise in establishing the detail of the earlier offending which resulted in conviction overseas. See also *R v Jasionis* [2010] EWCA Crim 2981. See on this s 144 and sch 17 of the Coroners and Justice Act 2009.

[13] [2005] EWCA Crim 1091.

[14] [2012] EWCA Crim 1148.

[15] [1981] 1 WLR 1039.

[16] [2005] EWCA Crim 3244.

[17] [2005] EWCA Crim 2826. President of the Queen's Bench Decision, The Rt. Hon. Sir Igor Judge, [24].

[18] [2009] EWCA Crim 653.

impression of a '*dirty old man*', but that its content was '*evidence of thoughts rather than deeds*' and it was for that reason not to be treated as '*bad character*' and fell to be admitted, if at all, under the common law.[19] In general terms, it is clear that BCE encompasses previous convictions,[20] and formal cautions,[21] as well as evidence on charges being tried concurrently,[22] and evidence relating to offences for which a person has been charged, or for which the person was subsequently acquitted,[23] or which were stayed as an abuse of process.[24]

Two important, and to some extent problematic, exceptions are excluded from **6.08** this definition of BCE. Section 98(a) and (b) provides that BCE does not include evidence that 'has to do with the alleged facts of the offence with which the defendant is charged' or is 'evidence of misconduct in connection with the investigation or prosecution of that offence'. The terms in which this first category of evidence is defined are problematic because the scope of the exception is unclear and this lack of clarity is reflected in the case law. In *Tirnaveanu*[25] the court emphasized the need for a temporal nexus as between the offence and the evidence it was sought to adduce. In *McNeill*[26] it was suggested by Rix LJ that the words 'has to do with' were susceptible to a 'prima facie broad application' within the context of the legislative scheme. They embraced anything directly relevant to the crime charged, provided it was 'reasonably contemporaneous with and closely associated with' the alleged facts of the offence. The point at which the evidence becomes temporally remote from the events in question may be difficult to identify with any certainty. In *McKintosh*,[27] the Court of Appeal held that evidence that the defendant was alleged to have been in possession of a firearm, and had shown the complainant this weapon months before the alleged rape had taken place, fell within the exception set out in section 98(a). It was evidence that had to do with the alleged facts of the offence since it explained why V feared the accused and why she did not complain immediately.

Misconduct that formed part and parcel of the event in which the defendant com- **6.09** mitted the offence charged, but is not something that must be proved to secure a conviction for that offence, may nevertheless be evidence that has to do with the

---

[19] Having regard to s 112 this is a surprising result.

[20] Section 74 of PACE 1984 provides that the fact that the defendant has a previous conviction gives rise to a rebuttable presumption against him that he was guilty of the offence; as against a non-defendant it is generally conclusive proof.

[21] *S* [2006] EWCA Crim 756.

[22] Standing Committee B, col 546. *Cf. Stirland v DPP* [1944] AC 315; *Maxwell v DPP* [1935] AC 309.

[23] This reflects the state of the previous law following *Z* [2000] 2 AC 483.

[24] *Smith* [2005] EWCA Crim 3244 (sexual assaults not prosecuted following letter of No Further Action).

[25] [2007] EWCA Crim 1239. In cases where the evidence relates to D's motive, there may be no need for such temporal nexus: *Sule* [2012] EWCA Crim 1130.

[26] [2007] EWCA Crim 2927.

[27] [2006] EWCA Crim 193.

facts of the offence charged. In *Brand*,[28] for example, where on a retrial of charges of rape and kidnapping evidence of the defendant's conviction for theft of the victim's handbag at the first trial was treated by the Court of Appeal as being to do with the alleged facts of the offence. Similarly, in *W*,[29] evidence of an assault conviction secured at the first trial was admissible on a retrial of the rape charge.[30] In *Housen*,[31] evidence concerning the taking of cocaine by the appellant and the complainant around the time of the alleged offending was held not to be evidence to which the provisions of the Act applied because it had to do with the facts of the offence. Care will be needed in sexual cases where counts are dropped from the indictment to ensure that the evidence being exempted from BCE by section 98 has to do with the facts of the offences still charged.[32]

6.10   Section 98(b) allows for the admissibility of evidence of '*misconduct in connection with the investigation or prosecution of that offence*' outside of the BCE regime, and may arise in sexual cases as well as any other. Threats or contact with witnesses, or attempts to blackmail a complainant, could fall within section 98(b).[33]

6.11   If evidence falls outside the definition of evidence of 'bad character' in sections 98 and 112 because it falls within the exceptions in section 98(a) and (b), common-law principles of admissibility will govern whether the evidence should be admitted.[34] Counter-intuitive thinking may be necessary: adopting a broad view of what constitutes bad character may actually be beneficial to the accused since the evidence, which may be highly prejudicial, will then only be admissible if the Crown can satisfy section 98 or one of the relevant gateways under section 101. A striking example is *R v Manister*,[35] where the Court of Appeal accepted that the trial judge was wrong to conclude that an earlier sexual relationship between the appellant (aged 34) and a girl of sixteen was evidence of bad character when he stood trial for sexually assaulting a 13-year-old girl five years later. The Court decided that there was nothing reprehensible about the appellant engaging in a lawful relationship with a girl who was old enough to give valid consent. However, the Court of Appeal went on to explain that as a consequence, admissibility turned simply on relevance. The Court took the view that the appellant's sexual interest in teenage girls was relevant as to whether he would engage in a sexual relationship with the 13-year-old complainant. Likewise, the appellant's alleged sexually charged conversation with a 15-year-old was also held to be admissible on the same basis—not

---

[28] [2009] EWCA Crim 2878.

[29] [2006] EWCA Crim 2308.

[30] It was admissible at common law going to the defendant's presence at the time alleged and the question whether he had been violent to his wife.

[31] [2012] EWCA Crim 1962.

[32] *B* [2010] EWCA Crim 1251.

[33] *R v Apabhai* [2011] EWCA Crim 917.

[34] Section 99 abolished the common-law rules governing the admissibility of bad character evidence only.

[35] [2005] EWCA Crim 2866.

as bad character but as relevant to the issue of M's attraction to young girls.[36] This prejudicial evidence of similar sexual conduct with a teenage girl was admitted without satisfying the more demanding section 101 tests. If the evidence is not 'bad character' within section 98, the 2003 Act does not apply and neither do the notice provisions under Part 35 of the Criminal Procedure Rules. Prosecutors may therefore sometimes face difficult decisions. As the question of what constitutes bad character is a difficult and fact-dependent one, it is perhaps advisable to err on the side of caution by complying with the notice requirements.

Finally, it should be noted that uncertainty in the definition of BCE also impacts **6.12** on the evidence relating to non-defendants. In the sexual offences context, several cases exemplify this. For example, it might be alleged that a complainant had a mental illness,[37] that a complainant had taken an overdose,[38] or that a young complainant's behaviour on Facebook or at school was BCE. However, the Court of Appeal has doubted that 'a piece of exaggeration to fellow pupils after some everyday classroom misbehaviour attains the level of "reprehensible" behaviour envisaged in s 112(1), read with s 98'.[39]

(3) Admissibility of evidence of defendant's bad character in trials for sexual offences

If incriminating evidence is captured by the definition of BCE provided by sections **6.13** 98 and 112 of the Act, then its route into the trial is via one of seven gateways set out in section 101. The first two of these rarely create any problems. Section 101(1)(a) enables evidence to be adduced by agreement, explicitly or implicitly,[40] but it is important that the judge is informed of any such agreement.[41] A defendant who wishes to adduce evidence of his own bad character is able to do so using section 101(1)(b). However, the defendant needs to be cautious about the implications of doing this, as—once admitted—the evidence is capable of being used for any relevant purpose.[42]

The remaining gateways provide for the reception of evidence of a defendant's bad **6.14** character where: it will enable the jury to understand other evidence in the case and its value for understanding the case as a whole is substantial; it is relevant to an important matter in issue between the prosecution and the defence; it has substantial probative value in relation to a matter in issue between co-defendants; it will correct a false impression given by the defendant; or the defendant has made an

---

[36] Ibid., at [100]. See also *R v Ahmad* [2012] EWCA Crim 288 (texts to young girls).

[37] See *R v Tine* [2006] EWCA Crim 1788, in which it was held that such evidence was not BCE for the purposes of the Act.

[38] See *R v Hall-Chung* (2007) 151 SJ 1020, CA (such evidence was not BCE because it did not constitute 'reprehensible behaviour': s 112).

[39] *R v V* [2006] EWCA Crim 1901, at [41].

[40] *Marsh* [2009] EWCA Crim 2696.

[41] *J* [2010] EWCA Crim 385.

[42] *Highton* [2005] EWCA Crim 1985; *Speed* [2013] EWCA Crim 1650.

attack on the character of another person. The operation of some of the gateways is straightforward, others less so. The law relating to some has particular significance in trials involving sexual offences. With this in mind, the following sections deal with four of the gateways that allow in BCE: that is, relevant to a matter in issue between prosecution and defence; has substantial probative value in relation to an important matter in issue between co-defendants; where a defendant has made an attack on the character of another; and where it is important explanatory evidence. We begin with by far the most important gateway in terms of the volume of applications and the controversy that may be generated thereby.

B. Bad Character Evidence which is Relevant to an Important Matter in Issue between Prosecution and Defence

(1) Important matter in issue

6.15 Under section 101(1)(d), bad character is admissible against the defendant if it relates to '*an important matter in issue*' between the Crown and defence. This is a significantly lower admissibility threshold than that which had to be met under the common law '*similar fact*' rule—even in its more liberal later form in *DPP v P*.[43] As noted in *Somanathan*:[44]

> If the evidence of a defendant's bad character is relevant to an important issue between the prosecution and the defence (section 101(1)(d)), then, unless there is an application to exclude the evidence, it is admissible. Leave is not required. So the pre-existing one stage test which balanced probative value against prejudicial effect is obsolete (see also section 99(1)).[45]

6.16 From the earliest case law concerning this section it has been made clear that the prosecution can rely on BCE even where it is not 'similar fact'.[46] It can rely on such evidence where the misconduct on an earlier occasion either does not constitute an offence of the same *description*, or of the same *kind*,[47] terms that are discussed further at paras 6.18 to 6.21.

(2) Propensity

6.17 Gateway (d) should not be understood as one that is synonymous with the admissibility of propensity evidence.[48] The prosecution might seek to use evidence of

---

[43] [1991] 2 AC 447.
[44] [2005] EWCA Crim 2866.
[45] Ibid., [36].
[46] See particularly, *R v Hanson* [2005] EWAC Crim 824, *R v Edwards* [2005] EWCA Crim 1813, *R v Highton* [2005] EWCA Crim 1985, *R v Renda* [2005] EWCA Crim 2826, and *R v Weir* [2005] EWCA Crim 2866.
[47] See s 103.
[48] See for discussion, *Bullen* [2008] EWCA Crim 4.

previous misconduct for a purpose other than propensity reasoning. Such evidence might be used to rebut a defendant's denial that he had knowledge of certain matters—for example, a conviction for possession of controlled drug could be used to rebut a defendant's claim that (when he was again found in possession of that drug) he had just been given something to look after and did not know what it was.

However, evidence of bad character is frequently adduced under gateway **6.18** (d) because the evidence is relevant to a matter in issue by reference to its capacity to demonstrate a propensity. Section 103 of the Act provides that the question as to whether a defendant has a propensity that makes it more likely that the defendant committed the offence with which he is charged, can be a matter in issue between the prosecution and defence for the purposes of section 101(1)(d). In *Hanson*, the Court of Appeal suggested that where BCE is tendered as a foundation for propensity reasoning there are three questions to be considered:

1. Does the history of conviction(s) establish a propensity to commit offences of the kind charged?
2. Does that propensity make it more likely that the defendant committed the offence charged?
3. Is it unjust to rely on the conviction(s) of the same description or category; and, in any event, will the proceedings be unfair if they are admitted?[49]

(a) Does the history of conviction(s)/misconduct establish a propensity?

The first of the *Hanson* questions asks whether the evidence that the prosecution **6.19** relies on as a foundation for propensity reasoning does in fact establish that the defendant has such a propensity. A better question might be 'what is the strength of the inference that can be drawn from the evidence, if accepted, as to a propensity on the part of the defendant?'[50] Generally speaking, the greater the number of occasions on which it can be shown that a person has behaved in a particular manner, the more reliable a foundation the BCE provides for an inference that the person has a propensity to behave in that way.

Section 103(2) of the Act provides that a defendant's propensity to commit offences **6.20** of the kind charged can be established by evidence that he has been convicted either of an offence of the same *description*, or an offence in the same *category*, as the offence charged. It is explained that two offences will be of the same description as each other if the statement of the offence in a written charge or indictment would, in each case, be in the same terms.[51] Offences will be of the same category if they both belong to the same category prescribed in an order issued by the Secretary

---

[49] Ibid., [7]. See its clear application in *NE* [2008] EWCA Crim 1641.
[50] These are roughly the terms in which the corresponding question in the inquiry into the admissibility of tendency evidence under Australian uniform evidence legislation was framed by the Federal Court of Australia in *Jacara v Perpetual Trustees WA* [2000] FCA 1886.
[51] Section 103(4)(a).

of State for the purposes of the Act. So far, only one order has been made, but significantly for present purposes, one of the categories of offences prescribed in the order comprises a wide range of sexual offences against persons under the age of 16 years.[52]

6.21 Although section 103 tells us that convictions for offences of the same description and category can be used to establish a propensity, it leaves unanswered a number of important questions. It is silent on whether propensity can be inferred from: (i) relatively old convictions; (ii) a single conviction, acquittal, or allegation; (iii) conduct which occurred after the offences with which the defendant is charged; or (iv) evidence of an acquittal or an allegation of misconduct.

6.22 **(i) The age of the convictions** Section 101(3) imposes on trial judges a duty to exclude BCE that the prosecution seeks to adduce through gateway (d) where it appears that the evidence would have such an adverse effect on the fairness of the proceedings that it ought not to be admitted. Section 103(5) provides that in considering whether such evidence should be excluded, the court is to have regard to the length of time that has elapsed between the previous offences and the offences with which the defendant is charged. The fact that the previous convictions are a number of years old will not necessarily preclude admission,[53] however the older a conviction the weaker the support it lends to an inference regarding propensity. It may support an inference that the defendant had a propensity at the time of the previous conviction, but a question that might be asked is whether it can provide a foundation for an inference that the defendant has that propensity some years or decades later. In *Hanson*, it was said that the fairness of proceedings was likely to be affected by the reception of old convictions that shared no special feature with the offences charged, unless despite their age it could properly be said that they show a continuing propensity.[54] In *Murphy*,[55] it was suggested that in some cases the factual circumstances of just one conviction as long as 20 years previously might be relevant to showing propensity. However, it was thought that the previous conviction would have to demonstrate some 'very special and distinctive feature, such as a predilection on the part of the defendant for a highly unusual form of sexual activity'.

6.23 It is not clear how the distinctiveness of old convictions can have a bearing on the question as to the longevity of that propensity. The better view might be that while a propensity to commit certain types of criminal offences might dissipate when a person experiences various positive life events such as regular employment, stable relationships, and parenthood, others will not. Acquisitive crime might, for example, fall into the former category, and sexual offences into the latter. In *Sully*,[56]

---

[52] Criminal Justice Act 2003 (Categories of Offences) Order 2004, S.I. 2004/3346.
[53] *Adams* [2006] EWCA Crim 2013.
[54] *Hanson*, cited at n.4, [11].
[55] [2006] EWCA Crim 3408.
[56] [2007] 151 Sol J 1564.

at the defendant's trial in 2007 for indecent assault on a young girl, the prosecution sought to introduce the defendant's convictions for similar offences in 1968 and 1974. Relying on the decision in *Murphy*, the Court noted that there were distinctive and similar features in the conduct which led to those convictions, the defendant having placed his hand up the skirts of two young girls and touched their bottoms.

(ii) Number of previous incidents required to establish a propensity How **6.24** many previous incidents of misconduct are required to establish that a defendant has a propensity? The starting point here is the observation in *Hanson* that no minimum number of events is required to demonstrate a propensity to engage in particular conduct, albeit that the fewer the convictions relied upon (and the greater the lapse in time), the weaker the inference that the defendant had a propensity as at the time of the disputed behaviour.

However, it is not uncommon for a single conviction for a sexual offence to be taken **6.25** to demonstrate a propensity. In *Pickstone* (heard with *Hanson*),[57] a conviction for rape twelve years previously was considered sufficient. In *Miller*[58] D argued that his one conviction for gang rape ten years earlier, when he was a teenager, was not admissible under section 101(1)(d) at trial for rape of his 11-year-old niece. The trial judge and Court of Appeal (Criminal Division) disagreed. D was prepared to agree admission in any event—he alleged that V made the complaint against him because she knew he had the conviction. Similarly, in *Kang*[59] evidence of a single caution for consensual sex with a girl under 16 was rightly admitted as demonstrating a propensity to be sexually interested and to have sexual relations with young girls.

(iii) Post-incident conduct If a propensity is taken to be an enduring trait, **6.26** characteristic, or mode of behaviour, there appears to be no reason why evidence of misconduct should be restricted to proof that the defendant had that propensity at some previous point in time. Evidence of subsequent misconduct can be taken as a manifestation of a pre-existing propensity, and there should be no bar to relying on evidence of this misconduct to establish that the defendant previously had a relevant propensity.

In *A*,[60] at his trial for sexual assault on his daughter in the 1980s, BCE of the **6.27** defendant posing on the internet in 2000 purporting to be a 20-year-old woman, seeking incest-related stories from other women, was rightly admitted. It was capable of demonstrating his sexual interest in incest. Similarly, in *B*[61] BCE was admitted of D's recent acquisition of indecent images of children found when he was investigated for earlier offences of sexual assaults on children.

---

[57] Hanson, cited at n.4.
[58] [2010] EWCA Crim 1578.
[59] [2013] EWCA Crim 1609.
[60] [2009] EWCA Crim 513.
[61] [2011] EWCA Crim 1630.

6.28 (iv) **Misconduct other than a conviction**   Although the guidance provided in *Hanson* is concerned with previous convictions, it is clear from the terms in which bad character is defined in the Act that BCE is not restricted to evidence of previous convictions. Even a single caution might suffice to establish a propensity, as in *R v Woodhouse* where an eleven-year-old caution for sexual assault on a young boy by touching his penis in the course of labouring, was capable of demonstrating a propensity.[62] A single caution for indecent exposure thirteen years previously was found to be sufficient in *Toller*[63] when the defendant stood trial on a charge of engaging in sexual activity in the presence of a child. Depending on the facts, even a single previous acquittal might be admissible under section 101(1)(d). In *L*,[64] at trial for rape where D's defence was consent, BCE was admitted of a single incident in which he had been acquitted of a similar alleged rape involving a girl of similar age to the present complainant.

(b) Does the propensity make it more likely that the defendant committed the offence charged?

6.29 The answer to the second *Hanson* question will depend on the reasoning in support of which it is tendered. It was observed in *McDonald* that:

> some care is required when considering whether bad character evidence is to be used 'simply to bolster a weak case.' Where the bad character consists of convictions, the degree of similarity between those convictions and the offences being tried will be a relevant consideration … the more specific the similarities between the previous convictions and the index offence, the more relevant are those convictions and the more substantial the argument for their admission in evidence. If, for example, the *modus operandi* in the previous offences was highly unusual, and the same *modus operandi* was followed in the index offence, that may of itself be evidence that the defendant committed the index offence.[65]

6.30 The caution here is against the possible use of a conviction to support a line of reasoning that a previous conviction that is only loosely related to the offence with which the defendant is charged increases the likelihood that he committed that offence. A case that appears to come close to a line that might be drawn between permissible and impermissible use of previous convictions in this respect is *Morgan*. Evidence of the defendant's convictions some eight years earlier for rape and indecent assault on young girls in his trust was held rightly to have been admitted at his trial for oral and anal rape of a 4-year-old he was babysitting. The defendant 'had a propensity to seek sexual gratification by attacking vulnerable children at a time when he was in a position of trust'.[66]

---

[62] [2009] EWCA Crim 498.
[63] [2014] EWCA Crim 899.
[64] [2007] All ER (D) 81 (Jul).
[65] [2011] EWCA Crim 2933, at [10].
[66] [2009] EWCA Crim 2705, at [3] and [16].

Where the fact-finder is invited to find that the defendant committed the crime with **6.31** which he is charged because the previous convictions demonstrated a propensity to commit this kind of offence and he allegedly acted in accordance with that propensity on the occasion that gave rise to the offences charged, attention should be focused on the similarities.[67] In *R v C*[68] for example, a previous conviction from several years previously for sexual assault (passionately kissing a child aged 14) ought not to have been admitted where C was charged with sexual assault on two women in a hostel by rubbing the breasts of one and removing the underwear and fondling the other. His conviction was not probative of a propensity to commit sexual assaults of the kind under consideration. To the extent that it could be said to be probative of a general inability to recognize the normal boundaries of sexual propriety its probative force was, at best, weak but the prejudicial effect of admitting a conviction of this kind was likely to be very significant. Similarly, in *R v Benabbou*[69] it was held that D's prior conviction for taking part in the gang rape of a stranger, eight years earlier, ought not to have been admitted at his trial for individually raping two complainants known to him. The prejudicial effect of this dissimilar conviction outweighed what limited probative value the prior conviction could be said to possess.[70]

It is also worth emphasizing that the propensity that the BCE is alleged to demon- **6.32** strate need not be the propensity to commit the offence. It may be a propensity to engage in some particular behaviour that was demonstrated in the commission of the offence. For example, suppose the defendant has previously been shown to engage in some unusual ritualistic (but lawful) behaviour immediately before committing the offence. That propensity may make it more likely that the defendant committed the offence with which he is charged with an offence in which similar ritualistic conduct was exhibited by the offender (the previous conviction in such circumstances might also support coincidence reasoning, which will be dealt with below).

Evidence of previous convictions or misconduct does not have to bear striking simi- **6.33** larities to the offence charged to support a conclusion that the defendant committed that offence. As noted above, the relevance and probative value of the propensity evidence will depend on the reasoning in support of which it is tendered. In *R v Burdess*,[71] for example, it was held that a previous conviction for rape was properly

---

[67] See e.g. *R v Tully* [2006] EWCA Crim 2270, where the defendants were on trial for robbery of a cab driver with a knife. DD had previous convictions for robbery and joint enterprises together. These were properly admitted, but the trial judge went too far in admitting D1's previous twenty-three dishonesty convictions and D2's twenty-six previous dishonesty convictions since they did not make it more likely that DD committed the offence charged—there was no similarity whatsoever.

[68] [2009] EWCA Crim 2726.

[69] [2012] EWCA Crim 1256.

[70] The victim of the prior rape, and one of the complainants of the current offending, were both described as being lesbians. That did not rate a mention in the judgment as having any relevance and so presumably was regarded by the Court as merely coincidental rather than evidence of targeted behaviour.

[71] [2014] EWCA Crim 270.

admitted when it demonstrated D's willingness to run risks of discovery in the course of the sexual attack—by raping the victim in her bed with her partner present. That was relevant to the present case where the Crown alleged that B raped V in his bedroom while other members of his family slept in adjoining rooms. The Court of Appeal held that both the previous rape and the present rape 'have in common a distinctive and unusual feature. The appellant chooses to commit sexual offences of this nature in unusual circumstances which other rapists would avoid'. In *R v Pickering*,[72] the Court declined even to grant leave to appeal in circumstances where the trial judge had admitted evidence of the defendant engaging in online communications (albeit not explicitly sexual) with young girls as being probative of him having an unhealthy interest in them. The evidence was held to be properly supportive of the proposition that he had sexually abused his goddaughter.

6.34   It should not be overlooked that propensity evidence can only be admitted through gateway (d) where it is relevant to some matter that is in issue. It follows that where it relates to a matter that has been conceded by the defendant(s) such evidence is inadmissible. In the case of *R v G*,[73] the defendants were charged with conspiring to rape a young boy. The evidence included text messages between them describing a desire to rape the particular boy. It was admitted that the defendants had a sexual interest in young boys; the defence was that the text message exchanges represented an expression of fantasy and not a genuine intent. The Court of Appeal, *obiter*, suggested that in those circumstances there was no point in admitting as BCE pleas of guilty to making and possessing indecent images of children since the defendants' sexual interest in young boys was admitted. If the judge had analyzed the matter, he would 'have been bound to conclude that the admission of those offences would not assist' in relation to the two issues—agreement and intent—and they should not have been admitted.[74]

(c) Is it unjust to rely on the conviction(s) of the same description or category and, in any event, will the proceedings be unfair if they are admitted?

6.35   As the foregoing analysis demonstrates, the judge's role in determining admissibility under gateway (d) will not always be an easy one. The relevance and probative value of BCE will depend on the nature of the argument in support of which it is adduced. The need for close assessment of the relevant facts underlines the importance of the Crown providing meticulous details of the BCE in timely applications to adduce. As previously mentioned, section 103(3) provides a trial judge with discretion to exclude BCE that is adduced to establish that the defendant has a propensity where he or she concludes that it would be unjust to allow it. This provision enables a judge to exclude BCE where he or she is not satisfied that the evidence the prosecution seeks to introduce does have the potential to establish the relevant propensity.

---

[72] [2013] EWCA Crim 913.
[73] [2012] EWCA Crim 1756.
[74] Ibid., Aikens LJ at [45].

Section 101(3) imposes a broader duty to exclude evidence which would have an adverse effect on the fairness of proceedings. In *Hanson*, it was said that when considering what was just under section 103(3), and the fairness of the proceedings under section 101(3), a judge might take into consideration, inter alia, the degree of similarity between the previous conviction and the offence charged, and the respective gravity of the past and present offences. The judge always had to consider the strength of the prosecution case: where there was no or very little other evidence against a defendant, it was unlikely to be just to admit his previous convictions, whatever they were. A consideration that will have a bearing on the fairness of proceedings is the *cogency* of the evidence that is led in order to establish a propensity.

In *McKenzie*,[75] the Court of Appeal observed that there were particular problems **6.36** where the allegations of previous misconduct had not given rise to any investigation. In such instances the evidence is liable to be 'stale and incomplete', particularly where the incidents in question had occurred some time ago and the evidence lacked sufficient detail. In such circumstances it would be difficult for the defendant to rebut the allegations, but the jury might be left thinking that there was 'no smoke without fire'. In *Weir*, it was said that in such circumstances, the operation of the exclusionary mechanism in section 101(3) was vital for ensuring the compatibility of the statutory scheme with the requirements of Article 6 of the European Convention on Human Rights. As to the application of this provision, the court indicated that evidence of a defendant's behaviour which he is not readily able to rebut, for example, information obtained from an unidentified third party, would generally be excluded.

The concept of fairness is sufficiently broad to encompass a further considera- **6.37** tion that might be relevant to the operation of section 101(3). There is a tension between, on the one hand, the court being satisfied of the probative value of allegations of previous misconduct, and on the other, the costs exacted by the process of proof. The greater the number the alleged incidents of misconduct, the greater their probative value in this respect. But where an inquiry into the reliability of several undocumented incidents is required, there is a real risk that the trial will lose its focus and the jury will be distracted from what ought to be the main issues in the case.

C. Cross Admissibility

(1) Meaning of cross admissibility

It is commonplace in trials for sexual offences for the indictment to contain mul- **6.38** tiple counts and often to involve multiple complainants. If the indictment against

---

[75] [2008] EWCA Crim 758

the defendant contains more than one count, the issue arises as to whether the evidence relating to one count is 'cross admissible' in relation to another, and if so what uses the jury may legitimately make of it. Cross admissibility is not an appropriate term to describe the circumstances when evidence from a previous incident that does not form part of the present indictment is adduced as BCE under the Act.[76]

(2) The bad character directions issue

6.39 Where two or more counts are contained in an indictment, section 112(2) of the Act provides that the bad character provisions have effect as if each offence were charged in separate proceedings. BCE adduced in support of one count may be relevant (as it was before the Act) to other counts on the indictment because it negates coincidence or rebuts a defence and/or (since the Act) because it establishes a propensity to commit the offence charged in the other counts. However, a question which has caused difficulty is whether, in a case in which evidence supporting one count is cross-admissible to support another count, a bad character direction is required and, if so, in what terms.

6.40 The issue gave rise to a number of seemingly inconsistent decisions under the Act, with confusion exacerbated by the loose use of terminology and the ambiguity over whether the evidence was being used as 'propensity' evidence or for some other purpose under section 101(1)(d).[77] The position, as now settled by numerous decisions of the Court of Appeal, is that evidence from one count may be admissible in relation to another in one or both of the following ways.[78] First, where independent but similar complaints of sexual offences are made against the same person, the jury may be permitted to consider the improbability that those complaints are the product of mere coincidence or malice. That is to say, a complainant's evidence in support of one count is relevant to the credibility of another complainant's evidence on another count. Secondly, where a jury are sure that a defendant is guilty in relation to one count they may permissibly go on to reason that this finding establishes that the defendant has a propensity to commit that kind of offence and further whether that propensity makes it more likely that he committed an offence of a similar kind contained in another count in the indictment. On either approach, the evidence which is being adduced is evidence of bad character against the defendant under section 101 of the CJA 2003.[79] Whatever line of reasoning about which the jury may be directed, however, or even if both approaches are left open to them, the jury

---

[76] See *R v Suleman* [2012] EWCA Crim 1569.

[77] See, inter alia, *Chopra* [2006] EWCA Crim 2133; *DM* [2008] EWCA Crim 1544; *Wallace* [2007] EWCA Crim 1760; see also, Fortson, R. and Ormerod, D., 'Bad Character Evidence and Cross-admissibility' [2009] Crim LR 313–34.

[78] See *N(H)* [2012] EWCA Crim 1568, at [31].

[79] See *McAllister* [2008] EWCA Crim 1544 at [13].

must reach separate verdicts on each count, and where there is more than one defendant, in respect of each defendant.[80]

(3) Cross admissibility in cases rebutting coincidence

As the first approach described above recognizes, it is not always the case that the probative value of count 1 in relation to count 2 derives from the proof that D had a propensity to commit offences of that kind. In *Freeman and Crawford*[81] it was said that limiting cross admissibility to this kind of reasoning would be too restrictive. While the jury should be reminded that it must reach a verdict on each count separately, in doing so it may have regard to the evidence relating to any other count. **6.41**

In such cases the jury is not being invited to reason that the evidence from count 1 only derives its probative force in respect of count 2 because it demonstrates that D has a propensity. The jury is asked to recognize that the evidence in relation to a particular offence on an indictment may appear stronger and more compelling when all the evidence, including evidence relating to other offences, is looked at as a whole.[82] The probative force of the evidence flowing from one count to another derives from the fact that there are a number of sources of complaint which may make it more probable that each is accurate provided the sources are genuinely independent. If they are, then the fact that similar behaviour is being asserted by more than one person may very well make it more likely that it happened. **6.42**

(4) Collusion and contamination

The probative value of cross-admissible coincidence reasoning lies in the improbability that independent complainants should make similar allegations against the defendant and all be mistaken as to what in fact occurred, or have severally resolved to fabricate an account that falsely implicates the defendant. The more independent the sources of evidence, the greater the unlikelihood of coincidence. In *H*, it was observed that 'the reality is that independent people do not make false allegations of a like nature against the same person, in the absence of collusion or contamination of their evidence'.[83] **6.43**

However, if there has been collusion or contamination the probative value may be negligible or at least significantly undermined. The effect of contamination on the reliability of evidence being used to support coincidence-type reasoning might be such that the fairness of proceedings would be adversely effected if it were to be admitted and that it ought to be excluded under section 101(3). The problem of contamination may **6.44**

---

[80] As to the procedure for cross-admissibility, it should be noted that the Crown needs to comply with the Crim PR r 35 obligations so that the judge is in a position to assess the likely uses of the evidence between the counts. See also guidance provided by Pitchford LJ in *R v Suleman* [2012] EWCA Crim 1569.

[81] [2009] 1 Cr App R 11, [2008] EWCA Crim 1863, at [20].

[82] *McAllister*, cited at n.79, at [14].

[83] [2011] EWCA Crim 2344, at [24].

not become evident until BCE has been admitted. Such circumstances are addressed by section 107. If at any time after the close of the prosecution case, the court is satisfied that evidence is contaminated, section 107 requires a directed acquittal, or the jury to be discharged and a retrial ordered, where in light of the importance of the evidence, the contamination is such that the defendant's conviction of the offence would be unsafe.[84] Section 107(5) explains that evidence is contaminated if it is either false or misleading in any respect (or is different from what it would otherwise have been) as a result of (i) an agreement or understanding between the person giving the evidence and another (or others), or (ii) the person giving evidence being aware of anything alleged by one or more others whose evidence may be, or has been, given in the proceedings.

6.45 Otherwise, for the purposes of assessing admissibility and cross admissibility, the allegations are to be assumed to be true unless no jury could reasonably find them to be so.[85] However, the jury will need to be told that they must exclude collusion or innocent contamination as an explanation for the similarity of the complaints before they can assess the force of the argument that they are unlikely to be the product of coincidence.[86]

6.46 Several important points are worth noting. First, the fact that complainants have discussed the allegations does not necessarily mean that they will have colluded or that the evidence is contaminated as so to render it inadmissible.[87] Secondly, it is important the direction focuses on the relevant risk of collusion and/or contamination. In *Cross*[88] D was convicted of historic sexual abuse against the young daughters of a family friend. There was no doubt that both teenage sister complainants had discussed the conduct against them. The judge concluded that the mere fact that the girls had spoken together did not necessarily rob what they had separately said of independence, and he concluded that whether it did or not was properly a matter for the jury. He rightly directed the jury on cross admissibility on the basis of rebutting coincidence (i.e. not propensity) and included a warning. However, having given what the Court of Appeal described as textbook direction, the judge then oversimplified things in a subsequent passage by not emphasizing that the jury must also be sure there was no unintended influence by one witness on the other. Similarly, in *Lamb*,[89] a teacher's convictions were quashed when the judge had referred to '*collusion*' when what was in issue was inadvertent '*contamination*' between the two sixth-form girls he had allegedly kissed at leavers' balls. The Court of Appeal allowed the appeal because the judge had emphasized at length in his direction to the jury that they had to consider *collusion*, by which he made clear that he meant false fabrication, even though that issue

---

[84] Section 107(1).
[85] Section 109.
[86] *N* [2011] EWCA Crim 730.
[87] *AT* [2013] EWCA Crim 1850. See also *PR* [2010] EWCA Crim 2741.
[88] [2012] EWCA Crim 2277.
[89] [2007] EWCA Crim 1766.

had not been suggested in cross-examination and even though there was, as the judge reminded the jury, no evidence of such collusion. Crucially, the judge did not go on to direct the jury about the possibility of *innocent contamination*, even though that alternative was a standard part of the Judicial Studies Board recommended direction.

(5) Cross admissibility in cases based on propensity reasoning

In the second of the two approaches described above, evidence from one count **6.47** is admissible against another under section 101 as evidence of propensity as if the counts were being tried as separate trials.[90] In such cases it will usually be that the jury is invited to consider the count on which the evidence is strongest first. If the jury conclude that the defendant is guilty upon that count then that decision may permit the further conclusion that the defendant had a propensity to commit that kind of offence. If so, his propensity may be relevant to the jury's consideration of other counts in the indictment charging similar offences.

It is important to note that in such cases the jury is being invited to reason from **6.48** propensity. They reason: being sure D committed the offence on count 1, that established he has a propensity to do x, that propensity is demonstrated by the offender who committed count 2, therefore I am sure D committed count 2.[91]

(6) Cases of both coincidence and propensity

In some rare cases it may be appropriate to direct the jury that cross-admissible **6.49** evidence is capable of being used both to rebut coincidence *and* for propensity-type reasoning. Considerable care is needed with directions in such cases.[92] If the jury is invited to consider both coincidence and propensity uses of the evidence from one count against others, it is important to avoid 'double accounting'. The jury cannot use evidence from count 1 to rebut coincidence and therefore conclude that D committed count 2, and then having become sure of guilt on count 2, use their conclusion of his guilt on that count as evidence of his propensity so as to convict D on count 1.

In *Nicholson* N was a hospital nurse charged with various sexual offences. He **6.50** was alleged to have sexually assaulted women patients as they came round from anaesthetic.[93] Two allegations made by patients who were not coming round from

---

[90] *Wallace* [2008] 1 WLR 572; [2007] EWCA Crim 1760; *Chopra* [2007] 1 Cr App R 225; [2006] EWCA Crim 2133.

[91] In contrast to the coincidence-based reasoning where the jury do not have to reason from propensity, albeit they reason to a propensity: in both categories of case, the jury reach the *conclusion* that D has a propensity, but only in the second category does their *reasoning process* involve reference to D's propensity.

[92] Although rare and needing careful handling, there are numerous cases in which directions on both approaches have been upheld on appeal. See e.g. *R v PJW* [2013] EWCA Crim 406; *R v Nicholson* [2012] EWCA Crim 1568.

[93] [2012] EWCA Crim 1568.

anaesthetic led to acquittals. N was convicted of the offences against the others. N argued that the complainants had experienced false memories as a side effect of the anaesthetic. Experts agreed that such false memories were rare. The judge directed the jury that it was necessary to consider each count separately, rather than lumping the evidence together. The judge explained how the jury might approach the evidence on:

(i) **Coincidence.** He pointed out that when considering the evidence of any one of the complainants, the jury was entitled to ask what were the chances of the other women, who were unconnected but had made similar allegations in the same hospital, experiencing false memory. He indicated that if the jury concluded that the memory of a particular complainant might have been false it was entitled to take that into account when considering whether another complainant's allegation arose as a result of false memory.

(ii) **Propensity.** He also explained that if the jury was sure of N's guilt in respect of any one complaint, it was open to it to conclude that N had a tendency to commit sexual offences in the circumstances alleged and that was relevant to whether another complainant had described a true or a false memory. The judge also gave a conventional warning about the limitations of propensity evidence.

6.51 The Court of Appeal upheld the convictions. The judge's directions made it quite clear that whilst the evidence of one witness might be treated as supportive of another, the jury was not permitted to lump the evidence together to reach a blanket conclusion upon all of the counts. In a situation where a jury was being invited to consider the evidence of several complainants for an assessment of the unlikelihood of coincidence, care needed to be taken by the judge before also giving a propensity direction. A conclusion, partly based upon the unlikelihood of coincidence, that a defendant was guilty upon one count, and therefore had a propensity to commit such offences, might enhance the probability of guilt upon other counts, but the jury had to be aware of the risk of overvaluing the accumulation of inference.

D. Co-defendant's Use of Evidence of the Defendant's Bad Character

6.52 The Act does not grant exclusive use of evidence of a defendant's bad character to the prosecution. Gateway (e) enables a co-defendant to adduce such evidence where it has 'substantial probative value' in relation to an 'important matter in issue' between the defendants. On its face, gateway (e) appears to impose more stringent conditions—substantial probative value—on the admissibility of a co-defendant's use of evidence of a defendant's bad character than those to which prosecution use of the evidence would be subject were it to seek reception of that evidence through gateway (d)—relevance. It was noted in *Musone*,[94] however, that the Explanatory Notes which accompanied the Criminal Justice Bill suggested that the reference to 'substantial' probative value was intended to ensure only that evidence that has little probative value would be excluded.

Co-defendants proposed use of evidence of a defendant's bad character will most often arise in cases in which cut-throat defences are being run, with each claiming that the other committed the offences with which they are jointly charged. The leading case on the state of the law prior to enactment of the Act is *Randall*, in which it was said that: **6.53**

> It is difficult to support a proposition that evidence of propensity can never be relevant to the issues. Postulate a joint trial involving two accused arising from an assault committed in a pub. Assume it to be clear that one of the two men committed the assault. The one man has a long list of previous convictions involving assaults in pubs. It shows him to be prone to fighting when he had consumed alcohol. The other man has an unblemished record. Relying on experience and common sense one may rhetorically ask why the propensity to violence of one man should not be deployed by the other man as part of his defence that he did not commit the assault. Surely such evidence is capable, depending on the jury's assessment of all the evidence, of making it more probable that the man with the violent disposition when he had consumed alcohol committed the assault. To rule that the jury may use the convictions in regard to his credibility but that convictions revealing his propensity to violence must otherwise be ignored is to ask the jury to put to one side their common sense and experience. It would be curious if the law compelled such an unrealistic result.[95]

In a trial involving co-defendants accused of sexual offences, where cut-throat defences are being run, convictions that assist one defendant by establishing that the other has a propensity that makes it more likely that he committed the offence, may be admissible through gateway (e). While evidence of a defendant's propensity that is adduced by the prosecution through gateway (d) is subject to a duty to exclude where its reception would adversely affect the fairness of proceedings, there is no corresponding exclusionary provision where such evidence is adduced by a co-defendant. There is a real risk in a joint trial for sexual offences that a defendant will attempt to adduce evidence of a co-defendant's previous sexual misconduct that has little (but enough) probative value but is highly prejudicial. Where those convictions are being relied upon to support an inference that the co-defendant had a propensity that makes it more likely that he was the one who committed the offence, some control over the fairness of proceedings can be exercised by paying close attention to whether the evidence really establishes a propensity and whether that propensity makes it more likely that the co-defendant committed the offence. **6.54**

---

[94] [2007] EWCA Crim 1237, at [46].
[95] *R v Randall* [2003] UKHL 69, Lord Steyn, [22]

E. Admissibility of Evidence of a Defendant's Bad Character where an Attack has been Made on the Character of Another Person

6.55 The Act has effected a significant change in the law in respect of the consequences for a defendant of attacking the character of another person. The law that it replaced permitted a defendant to be cross-examined on aspects of his character where 'the nature or conduct of his defence was such as to involve imputations on the character of the prosecutor or the witnesses for the prosecution'.[96] However, if the defendant chose not to give evidence he was free to cast imputations without any risk of the jury hearing about any aspect of his own bad character. The Act changes this position. Section 101(1)(g) enables evidence of the defendant's bad character to be adduced if 'the defendant has made an attack on another person's character'.

6.56 The provision is of potentially broad application. In trials for sexual offences the person whose character is most likely to be attacked by the defendant is the complainant's, but as the terms of the section make clear, an attack on any person's character can lead to evidence of the defendant's bad character being admitted. In *Williams*,[97] for example, the appellant having been released from prison after serving a term of imprisonment for unlawfully taking and indecently assaulting a young boy, was subject to a Sexual Offences Prevention Order. This prohibited him from 'carrying out lengthy and sustained observations of children outside of his home address'. The police mounted a surveillance operation which resulted in the appellant being charged with breaching the Order. At trial the prosecution made an application to adduce evidence of the appellant's two previous convictions for abducting young boys and indecently assaulting them. The trial judge permitted evidence of one of these convictions to be given but the other was excluded on the grounds that it was too prejudicial. However, during cross-examination of the police who gave evidence for the prosecution case, the appellant alleged that he was the victim of a conspiracy, and that the police officers were trying to 'stitch him up'. Thereafter the prosecution successfully applied to adduce evidence of the appellant's convictions for a number of offences of dishonesty. The rationale for allowing in evidence of such offences was explained in *Lamaletie*.[98] There the Court of Appeal stated that the purpose of admitting evidence of the defendant's bad character through gateway (g) where he has attacked the character of another person, is to assist the jury in deciding who to believe. So although the gateway appears to be of broad application, allowing BCE to be adduced where an attack is made on *any* person's character, the rationale for doing so does not necessarily apply in

---

[96] Criminal Evidence Act 1898, s 1(3)(ii).
[97] [2007] EWCA Crim 1951.
[98] [2008] EWCA Crim 314.

circumstances in which the person whose character has been attacked is someone who will not give evidence in the proceedings.[99]

The opportunity that a defendant will have to attack the character of a complainant **6.57** in a trial for sexual offences will be limited by the provisions of the Youth Justice and Criminal Evidence Act 1999. In a trial in which the defendant has been charged with a sexual offence, section 41 of that Act prohibits, except with the leave of the court, adduction of evidence, either in chief or in cross-examination, concerning the sexual behaviour of the complainant. Where leave is given, gateway (g) will only allow BCE to be adduced where the defendant has 'made an attack on the character' of the complainant for the purposes of the bad character provisions. Section 106 explains that the defendant is taken to have done this where he adduces evidence that the other person has committed an offence or has behaved, or is disposed to behave, in a reprehensible way. Of course, the cross-examination of a complainant on his or her sexual behaviour will not necessarily constitute an attack on his or her character. It is only where the defendant asserts, or invites, an inference that the complainant's sexual behaviour is 'reprehensible', that is to say immoral or blameworthy.

It should also be noted that gateway (g) may also be triggered where evidence is **6.58** given of a defendant's attack on the character of a complainant during the course of questioning under caution.[100] In *Ball*,[101] for example, evidence of the defendant's bad character was adduced in the course of his trial for rape after evidence was given of his assertion during a police interview that the complainant was 'easy', 'a slag', and that most of the men in the public house that they both frequented had had sexual intercourse with her. A defendant has no right to demand, and the prosecution no obligation to remove, reference to such things as might trigger the operation of gateway (g) simply so as to avoid that consequence.[102]

F. Bad Character Evidence as Important Explanatory Evidence

Section 101(1)(c) is an important provision, allowing for the admissibility of **6.59** what had become known under the common law as 'background' evidence.

---

[99] In *R v Nelson* [2006] EWCA Crim 3412, the Court of Appeal observed that while the wording of s 101(1)(g) did not confine the gateway to situations in which a defendant had attacked the character of a prosecution witness, the trial judge still had a discretion as to whether the jury should hear about a defendant's bad character when he had made imputations about the character of a non-witness. It suggested that it would be unusual for evidence of a defendant's bad character to be admitted when the person whose character was attacked was someone who was neither a witness nor victim. The fairness of the proceedings would normally be materially damaged by so doing.
[100] For earlier consideration of imputations cast in interview see Wolchover, D. and Heaton-Armstrong, A. (2006) 'Gateway (g): casting imputations and putting in the defendant's form' [2002] 2 *Archbold News*, 6–9.
[101] One of the consolidated appeals heard with *R v Renda* [2005] EWCA Crim 2826.
[102] See *R v Dixon* [2012] EWCA Crim 2163, in which it was held that evidence of the defendant's previous convictions were properly admitted through gateway (f) where the record of the

A paradigmatic illustration of this gateway in operation in sexual cases is *R v Allanson*[103] where the defendant's previous conviction was adduced to explain the background to the rape committed on the day he was released from prison. It was important explanatory evidence as to how he came to be in the complainant's house, she having agreed at the request of a friend of his that he could reside with her, and having driven him there from a public house where he had been celebrating his release. The section clearly has a broader reach in sexual cases. For example, at the defendant's trial for the attempted rape of his partner in *R v Pronick*,[104] evidence of a previous rape allegedly committed against D's partner (of which no complaint had been made at the time) by D was held to have been properly admitted at trial for attempted rape of her (along with evidence of various acts of violence) as explanatory evidence under section 101(1)(c).

6.60 However, great care needs to be taken in the application of gateway (c). First, it is a narrow gateway as its terms make clear—the evidence must be *important* explanatory evidence. Section 102 provides that it will be *important* only if (a) without it, the court or jury would find it impossible or difficult properly to understand other evidence in the case, and (b) its value for understanding the case as a whole is substantial.

6.61 A spate of cases, many of them involving sexual offences, suggests that the Court of Appeal has concerns that BCE is being 'smuggled' into proceedings inappropriately under section 101(1)(c).[105] A recognition of the need to keep section 101(1)(c) within sensible bounds can be found in *R v Saint*[106] where evidence of D's interest in 'dogging' and 'swinging' was admitted under gateway (c) at D's trial for raping a young woman in a car park. However, the Court of Appeal held that the gateway did not provide a vehicle for such evidence, which it considered to be both irrelevant and 'gratuitously prejudicial'.[107]

6.62 Secondly, there is a danger in reliance on gateway (c) when the evidence in question is really admissible, if at all, under gateway (d). In *R v D*,[108] it was acknowledged that the admissibility of evidence through gateway (d) was subject to more stringent safeguards than that under gateway (c) namely those in section 101(3) and section 101(4) and where appropriate, section 103(3).[109] As the court noted in *Saint*:

---

defendant's police interview was adduced in its entirety. During that interview the defendant had made a false denial regarding his criminal record. If evidence of previous convictions is admissible through gateway (f) in such circumstances, there would appear to be no reason an attack on a person's character in similar circumstances would not lead to the reception of bad character evidence through gateway (g).

[103] [2009] EWCA Crim 395.
[104] [2006] EWCA Crim 2517.
[105] For example, in *Jalland* [2006] EWCA Crim 3336; *Broome* [2012] EWCA Crim 2879.
[106] [2010] EWCA Crim 1924.
[107] Ibid., at [22].
[108] [2008] EWCA Crim 1156.
[109] Ibid., at [34].

It is important not to confuse 'important explanatory evidence' under section 101(1)(c) and propensity evidence which is a subset of evidence which is 'relevant to an important matter in issue between the defendant and the prosecution'.[110]

These concerns were echoed in relation to sexual cases in *R v Lee*,[111] where preju- **6.63**
dicial evidence that L had been secretly filming his step-daughter in the shower was adduced to explain why he had left home. It was not important explanatory evidence; it was not '*impossible*' as required by section 102 to understand the other evidence—allegations of him sexually assaulting her years before—without consideration of the secret filming evidence. The evidence was instead potentially admissible as evidence of propensity under section 101(1)(d).[112]

The admissibility decision is, of course, highly fact-specific and hence there are **6.64**
numerous decisions in which the Court has approved its use in sexual cases. In *Morris*,[113] for example, the court were unpersuaded by an argument based upon *Lee* that the trial judge had been wrong to admit evidence of the appellant's conviction in 2010 of child sex offences when he stood trial in 2013 for offences committed between 1979 and 1982. The complainant said that it was learning of that conviction that finally persuaded her she should report what the appellant had done to her when she had been a child. The court determined that a jury would have found it '*impossible*' to understand the case absent that detail notwithstanding the prejudicial nature of the events underpinning the later conviction.

To guard against the misuse of section 101(1)(c), it is essential for judges to address **6.65**
with advocates, as soon as the question of admissibility is raised, the question of how it is proposed that the BCE is to be used and how the jury is to be directed. This will focus attention on the true uses of the evidence and help identify an appropriate gateway.

G. Conclusion

The trial of sexual offences is the area of the criminal law that most commonly **6.66**
engages the changes wrought by the 2003 Act in respect of BCE. Prior to the Act the courts were assiduous in seeking to protect defendants from the prejudice that prior sexual misconduct had the potential to generate. The landscape has fundamentally changed. Juries are now to be trusted as being able to assess such evidence,

---

[110] *R v Saint* [2010] EWCA Crim 1924, at [14].
[111] [2012] EWCA Crim 316.
[112] A more recent example still is *R v Sheikh* [2013] EWCA Crim 907 where the Court of Appeal deprecated the use of s 101(1)(c) to adduce evidence of a rape conviction when D was charged with breach of the Sexual Offences Prevention Order imposed as a result of that rape.
[113] [2014] EWCA Crim 419.

and to apply it properly, in the context of directions that are designed to prevent them from permitting 'prejudice' to impact on the decision-making process.

Author Biographies

Professor David Ormerod QC is a Law Commissioner for England and Wales. He is seconded from Queen Mary, University of London where he is Professor of Criminal Justice. He is the Editor-in-Chief of the *Criminal Law Review* and *Blackstone's Criminal Practice* and the author of Smith and Hogan's *Criminal Law* (14th edn 2015). He is a door tenant at 18 Red Lion Chambers. He lectures regularly for the Judicial College.

HHJ Martin Picton has been a Circuit Judge for approaching ten years. He is the Course Director of the Judicial College's Serious Sexual Offences Seminar and Joint Director of the Vulnerable Witness Course. He regularly lectures to the Judiciary and legal practitioners on topics relevant to the trial of, and sentence for, sexual crimes.

Andrew Roberts is a Senior Lecturer at Melbourne Law School, University of Melbourne, having previously held positions at the Universities of Warwick and Leeds. His research interests lie in criminal evidence and procedure, particularly identification evidence and expert testimony, on which he has published widely. He is a member of the Editorial Board of the *International Journal of Evidence & Proof*, and provides commentary on cases that are reported in *Criminal Law Review*.

7

EXPERT EVIDENCE IN TRIALS OF SEXUAL OFFENCES

Paul Roberts and Tony Ward

A. Expert Evidence and Scientific Proof of Sexual Offences

English law has enjoyed a very long and productive association with expert wit- **7.01** nesses and forensic science.[1] However, this partnership has always been unequal, and there have been strains and stresses and moments of mutual distrust and loss of confidence over the years. Fact-finding, with or without the assistance of expert testimony, must answer to the dictates of justice in criminal adjudication.[2] Common law judges have consistently emphasized, as one foundational normative requirement, that expert witnesses must never trench upon the proper, constitutional role of lay fact-finding in criminal trials. Yet in practice, pinpointing the boundary line between the legitimate province of expert testimony and the jury's sovereign realm as fact-finder is often no easy matter.

Describing the role of expert evidence in trials of sexual offences is largely an **7.02** exercise in extrapolating general evidentiary doctrines to the specific practical

---

[1] Hand, L., 'Historical and Practical Considerations Regarding Expert Testimony' (1901) 15 *Harvard Law Review*, 40. Generally, see Roberts, P. (ed.) (2014) *Expert Evidence and Scientific Proof in Criminal Trials*, Franham, Surrey: Ashgate.

[2] Roberts, P., 'Renegotiating Forensic Cultures: Between Law, Science and Criminal Justice' (2013) 44 *Studies in the History and Philosophy of Biological and Biomedical Science*, 47.

contexts of trials of rape, sexual assault, and related offences. These are all serious, or very serious, crimes with penalties on a par with homicides and aggravated physical assault; but in contrast to other grave crimes, which are often witnessed by third parties and generally leave compelling physical traces (corpses or broken limbs, etc.), sexual offending typically takes place in private and is often difficult to prove to the criminal standard, especially in relation to adults where consent is in issue. Allegations of sexual victimization may be stalemated as 'he said, she said' or 'one person's word against another's'.[3] Forensic science or other expert witness testimony may be capable of filling in perceived gaps in the evidence; where, for example, complainants do not wish to co-operate fully with the prosecutor, or may be regarded as lacking credibility.[4] In an adversarial litigation system, opportunities for the defence to call counter-expertise, on any point of genuine controversy or difficulty, in reply to the prosecution's expert evidence are implied by the accused's general fair trial right to present an effective defence.[5] Part B further elucidates the application of general evidentiary principles to trials of sexual offences in England and Wales.

7.03 It is no coincidence that many of the leading English cases on DNA evidence concern convictions of rape. In the UK, the search for an unknown 'stranger' rapist has been greatly facilitated by an extensive National DNA Database (NDNAD) enabling crime stain DNA to be searched speculatively against the profiles of previous arrestees.[6] DNA profiling evidence poses some difficult issues concerning probabilistic reasoning which are taken up in Part C.

7.04 In reality, the *identity* of the perpetrator is *not* in issue in the vast majority of indictable sexual offences committed against adults, which are perpetrated by intimates or acquaintances.[7] In cases involving allegations against known perpetrators, in addition to factual medical evidence of any physical injuries or traces, there may be scope for expert evidence to bolster the credibility of the complainant (albeit that English law has traditionally disfavoured such testimony as inadmissible 'oath-helping'). In addition, prosecutions of sexual offences against children may call upon a range of child-specific experts, including child psychologists (with varying specialisms) and paediatricians. Legal issues pertaining to the admissibility and uses of expert evidence of witness credibility are addressed in Part D.

---

[3] *Cf.* Saunders, C.L., 'The Truth, the Half-truth, and Nothing Like the Truth: Reconceptualizing False Allegations of Rape' (2012) 52 *British Journal of Criminology*, 1152.

[4] As emphasized in the *CPS Policy for Prosecuting Cases of Rape* (revised 2012), para 5.3, *http://www.cps.gov.uk/publications/prosecution/*.

[5] Jackson, J.D. and Summers, S.J. (2012) *The Internationalisation of Criminal Evidence*, Cambridge: Cambridge University Press, 361–2.

[6] Williams, R. and Johnson, P. (2008) *Genetic Policing: The Use of DNA in Criminal Investigations*, Cullompton, Devon: Willan Publishing.

[7] See Ministry of Justice et al. (2013) *An Overview of Sexual Offending in England and Wales—Statistics Bulletin*, 16.

B. Admissibility and Judicial Directions

To be received as evidence in a criminal trial, expert testimony must, on first prin- **7.05**
ciples, be both (i) relevant to a live fact in issue; and (ii) not otherwise excluded by
an applicable exclusionary rule. 'Logic and common sense' are the overriding criteria of relevance in law.[8] These are open-ended and contestable standards, requiring
contextual application to the instant facts.

The baseline position is that English law's general exclusionary rules apply to expert **7.06**
evidence, as to any other kind of evidence. For example, expert evidence obtained
through an illegal search or which conveys information about the accused's extraneous bad character could be vulnerable to exclusion on familiar grounds.[9] The
trial judge's versatile jurisdiction to exclude unfairly obtained evidence pursuant
to section 78 of the Police and Criminal Evidence Act 1984 (PACE) in principle applies, but (perceived) evidential reliability has been known to trump concerns for due process in this context.[10] Expert evidence might contain hearsay. The
strictures of the common-law exclusionary rule have traditionally been relaxed in
relation to expert testimony,[11] and the hearsay provisions of the Criminal Justice
Act 2003 introduced further liberalization. English law has not followed US
Constitutional jurisprudence in demanding face-to-face confrontation even for
lab technicians undertaking routine testing.[12] However, trial courts should remain
astute to prevent gratuitous hearsay (e.g. narratives of contested facts) from being
laundered through expert testimony.[13] Article 6(3)(d) of the European Convention
on Human Rights might theoretically be engaged, though it is hard to think of
realistic scenarios in which an expert's hearsay could be the 'sole or decisive' evidence against the accused.

Few tailor-made rules of admissibility apply to expert evidence. The conventional **7.07**
view, that expert testimony is admissible by way of exception to the 'opinion evidence rule' requiring witnesses to stick to the facts and keep their opinions to
themselves, is largely an empty formalism, because the distinction between 'facts'
and 'opinions' is so elusive where expertise is concerned. If a doctor reports observing 'a transection of the hymen', for example, or a forensic scientist states that

---

[8] Roberts, P. and Zuckerman, A. (2010) *Criminal Evidence*, 2nd edn, Oxford: Oxford University
Press, ch 3.2.

[9] See Chapter 6.

[10] *A-G's Reference (No 3 of 1999)* [2001] 2 AC 91, HL, the effect of which is deliberately preserved
by the new PACE 1984 s 63S (replacing s 64) (see James Brokenshire MP, HC Debs, Public Bill
Committee, 7th sitting, col 276, 5 April 2011).

[11] *R v Abadom* [1983] 1 WLR 126, CA; Criminal Justice Act 1988, s 30.

[12] *Melendez-Diaz v Massachusetts*, 129 S Ct 2527 (2009): *cf.* Criminal Justice Act 2003, s 127.

[13] See e.g. *R v Hirst* [1995] 1 Cr App R 82, CA, discussed by Roberts, P., 'Will You Stand Up in
Court? On the Admissibility of Psychiatric and Psychological Evidence' (1996) 7 *Journal of Forensic
Psychiatry*, 63.

two physical traces 'match', are these statements of (medical or scientific) fact, or expressions of professional opinion? Either interpretation is conceptually plausible.

7.08   There is one overriding principle in this area, more resembling an elementary precept of rationality than a mere rule of law. Expert evidence, of fact or opinion, is admissible when it is both relevant and *helpful* to the fact-finder in discharging its adjudicative responsibilities.[14] Although some commentators have fussed and cavilled over the precise language in which the 'helpfulness' standard has been expressed in particular judgments,[15] the principle itself could not be simpler, and should remain so. In practice, admittedly, trial judges are often obliged to make close judgement-calls, weighing up the anticipated probative value of the evidence in resolving disputed facts, against its potential for mischief. The Court of Appeal is unlikely to interfere, unless the trial judge's decision has strayed off into *Wednesbury* unreasonableness.[16] Whilst judicial rulings sometimes provide more concrete guidance in relation to discrete issues,[17] individual admissibility determinations (including those upheld on appeal) are not, for the most part, best characterized as new legal precedents, but rather as contextual applications of the settled legal principle. Different approaches might well be taken in subsequent cases by trial judges confronted with alternative matrices of facts, arguments, and evidence.

7.09   Expert witness testimony must also be proffered by a genuine, properly qualified expert.[18] The test of expertise is substantive, not formal. That is to say, provided that the expert actually has the relevant specialist knowledge or expertise it does not matter how, when, or where such expertise was acquired.[19] Education, training, and formal qualifications may be the standard ways of demonstrating expertise to the court's satisfaction, but none of them is strictly necessary to *constitute* expertise. The Court of Appeal sometimes appears to favour working forensic practitioners over experts perceived as scholastics or theoreticians,[20] but this may depend on the particular type of expertise in question. Impressionistically, medical doctors (including psychiatrists) may, in general, command greater judicial confidence than clinical psychologists or behavioural scientists.[21]

---

[14]   *R v Turner* [1975] QB 834, CA.

[15]   See e.g. Mackay, R.D. and Colman, A.M., 'Equivocal Rulings on Expert Psychological and Psychiatric Evidence: Turning a Muddle into a Nonsense' [1996] Crim LR 88; Mackay, R.D. and Colman, A.M., 'Excluding Expert Evidence: A Tale of Ordinary Folk and Common Experience' [1991] Crim LR 800.

[16]   *Associated Provincial Picture Houses Ltd v Wednesbury Corporation* [1948] 1 KB 223. Also now see Criminal Justice Act 2003, s 67 (pertaining to interlocutory appeals).

[17]   For one example, partly turning on a contextual question of statutory interpretation, see *R v Land* [1999] QB 65, CA (expert evidence not 'helpful' where the statutory test contained in Protection of Children Act 1978, s 2, contemplated lay assessment of a photographed child's *apparent* age).

[18]   Crim PR, r 19.3(1)(a) (replacing old r 33 from 5 October 2015).

[19]   *R v Silverlock* [1894] 2 QB 766, CCR.

[20]   *R v Reed and Reed; R v Garmson* [2010] 1 Cr App R 23, [2009] EWCA Crim 2698, [101]–[110].

[21]   *Cf. R v Gilfoyle* [2001] 2 Cr App R 57, CA.

It used to be said that experts are forbidden from expressing any opinion on the 'ulti-   **7.10**
mate issue' (or issues) which the jury has to decide. This stricture was intended to
preserve the jury's fact-finding independence, but it could backfire if it forced experts
to express themselves in unfamiliar or convoluted language, perversely diminishing
their assistance to the court. The Court of Appeal has repeatedly disavowed the rule in
recent years,[22] and the better view is that a hard-and-fast ultimate issue rule no longer
exists at common law, if it ever truly did. The fundamental precept is that expert witnesses should confine their evidence to matters of genuine expertise. For example,
experts testifying about a complainant's capacity to consent should not stray into discussing the complainant's consent in fact[23] or whether her incapacity to consent would
have been obvious to others.[24]

Many academic commentators, drawing on authoritative official reports and some   **7.11**
decided cases, argue that English criminal trial procedure currently over-exposes fact-
finders to the risk of relying on faulty science or misleading expert testimony.[25] After
a wide-ranging consultation exercise, the Law Commission proposed the introduction of a new admissibility rule for expert evidence,[26] inspired by the US Supreme
Court's *Daubert* standard.[27] The Government declined to enact the Commission's
draft Criminal Evidence (Experts) Bill, baulking at the potential cost implications of
imposing a new 'gatekeeping' responsibility on trial judges. Instead, the Consolidated
Criminal Practice Direction was amended to spell out a range of methodological and
contextual factors to which trial judges should have regard when assessing the reliability of 'expert opinion evidence', as a precondition to its admissibility.[28] The revised
Practice Direction stresses that: 'Nothing at common law precludes assessment by
the court of the reliability of an expert opinion by reference to substantially similar
factors to those the Law Commission recommended as conditions of admissibility,

---

[22] *R v Atkins* [2010] 1 Cr App R 8, [2009] EWCA Crim 1876, [14]; *R v Stockwell* (1993) 97 Cr
App R 260, 265–6, CA. See also, *R v Ugoh* [2001] EWCA Crim 1381, [19]–[21] (medical expert
should not have told jurors that it 'would have been obvious to anyone who was with her' that a rape
complainant was too drunk to consent, not because this touched on an 'ultimate issue', but simply
because it was not appropriately 'helpful' to the jury in assessing the evidence in the case).
[23] *R v A (G)* [2014] EWCA Crim 299, [2014] 1 WLR 2469, [30].
[24] *R v Ugoh* [2001] EWCA Crim 1381, [19]–[21].
[25] See e.g. Edmond, G. et al., '*Atkins v The Emperor*: The "Cautious" Use of Unreliable "Expert"
Opinion' (2010) 14 *International Journal of Evidence & Proof*, 146; Roberts, A., 'Drawing on
Expertise: Legal Decision-Making and the Reception of Expert Evidence' [2008] Crim LR 443;
Beecher-Monas, E., 'Reality Bites: The Illusion of Science in Bite-Mark Evidence' (2009) 30 *Cardozo
Law Review*, 1369; Ormerod, D., 'Sounding Out Expert Voice Identification' [2002] Crim LR 771.
[26] Law Commission (2011) *Expert Evidence in Criminal Proceedings in England and Wales*, Law
Com 325, London: The Stationery Office.
[27] *Daubert v Merrell Dow Pharmaceuticals*, 509 US 579 (1993).
[28] Consolidated Criminal Practice Direction, [2015] EWCA Crim 1567, CPD V 19A.5 mentions
such factors as 'the extent and quality of the data on which the expert's opinion is based', the validity
of the scientific method(s) employed, soundness of inferential reasoning, statistical methodology
(where salient), publication and peer review, expert disagreement, divergence from orthodox practice, etc. These criteria largely reproduce those proposed by the Law Commission, and chime with
standard epistemological accounts, e.g. Beecher-Monas, E., 'The Heuristics of Intellectual Due
Process: A Primer for Triers of Science' (2000) 75 *New York University Law Review*, 1563.

and courts are encouraged actively to enquire into such factors.'[29] In other words, trial judges *already* have the responsibility at common law, flowing from the elementary principles of relevance and helpfulness, to scrutinize the methodological credentials of scientific or other expert evidence.[30] Scientific tests that cannot, in fact, produce reliable results do not constitute evidence capable of establishing a *relevant*, logical and common-sense connection to the facts in issue. Nor is 'the bare *ipse dixit* of a scientist, however eminent'[31] *Turner*-helpful to the jury in arriving at an epistemically well-warranted verdict, if the probative significance of the expert's testimony cannot be evaluated rationally. Whether or not trial judges in England and Wales will in practice adopt a more proactive approach to scrutinizing the reliability of expert evidence remains to be seen. A shift in traditional judicial attitudes and culture will be required, and this in turn may depend on appropriate judicial training and institutional support for active gatekeeping.[32]

7.12 Well-informed critics, both lawyers and forensic experts, have long contended that adversarial criminal trials are a ludicrous way of attempting to resolve genuine scientific disagreements between bona fide experts.[33] Since their introduction in 2005, the Criminal Procedure Rules (CrimPR), with their central philosophy of promoting more thorough pre-trial preparation through proactive judicial trial management, have had especial pertinence for expert evidence. Part 19 of the CrimPR makes explicit provision for clarifying, and if possible resolving, scientific issues through pre-trial conferences between experts and the production of agreed joint reports. The latest iteration of Part 19 also requires extensive pre-trial disclosure, not only of expert reports themselves, but also of contextualizing information needed to assess reliability and facilitate judicial gatekeeping.[34] Recognizing that courtroom 'battles of experts' typically produce more heat than light, the Court of Appeal is constantly reminding trial judges to make effective use of these, still relatively novel, departures from traditional adversarial litigation practice.[35] An allied development is 'Streamlined Forensic Reporting'.[36] The quest for clarity and simplification in expert evidence is understandable and broadly welcome, though it should be said that speed and

---

[29] CPD V 19A.4.

[30] Ward, T., 'Expert Evidence and the Law Commission: Implementation without Legislation?' [2013] Crim LR 561.

[31] *Davie v Edinburgh Corporation* 1953 SLT 54, 57.

[32] Dennis, I., 'Editorial: Tightening the Law on Expert Evidence' [2015] Crim LR 1; Ward, T. '"A New and More Rigorous Approach" to Expert Evidence in England and Wales?' (2015) 19 *International Journal Evidence & Proof* 228.

[33] Regarding previous reform proposals, see Roberts, P., 'Forensic Science Evidence After Runciman' [1994] Crim LR 780; Spencer, J.R., 'Court Experts and Expert Witnesses: Have We a Lesson to Learn from the French?' (2002) 45 *Current Legal Problems*, 213; Kenny, A., 'The Expert in Court' (1983) 99 *Law Quarterly Review* 197.

[34] Crim PR Part 19.3 and 19.4 (replacing the old Part 33 from 5 October 2015).

[35] See e.g. *R v Reed and Reed* [2010] 1 Cr App R 23, [2009] EWCA Crim 2698.

[36] ACPO and CPS (2013) *National Streamlined Forensic Reporting Guidance, Version 2.0. http:// www.cps.gov.uk/legal/s_to_u/scientific_evidence.*

efficiency are not always dependable allies of factual rectitude or procedural due process in criminal adjudication.[37]

As well as ruling on admissibility, trial judges instruct juries in how to approach   **7.13** particular pieces of evidence and proffer general guidance on jurors' fact-finding responsibilities.[38] Such instructions may be given at convenient points during the course of the trial, and figure prominently in trial judges' final summings-up before the jury retires to deliberate and produce a verdict. Juries in England and Wales are directed that the prosecution bears the burden of proof, and that jurors must acquit the accused unless the evidence has made them sure that he is guilty as charged. Several more specific 'forensic reasoning rules' pertain specifically to expert evidence.[39]

The most fundamental precept is that the jury is the ultimate arbiter of disputed   **7.14** facts, and must be clearly instructed to form its own view, even in relation to uncontradicted scientific, technical, or other expert evidence.[40] Although expert witness testimony may be impressive and cogent, jurors can reasonably be expected to exercise their critical faculties in deciding whether, and to what extent, to rely on it. It is especially important that trial judges impress upon juries their responsibility to make up their own minds in relation to 'factual' issues incorporating normative evaluations,[41] or where expert evidence has traversed 'ultimate' material issues, such as the complainant's capacity to consent.[42]

Where experts called by the adversarial parties are at loggerheads, the jury must do   **7.15** its common-sense best to interpret the experts' disagreement in the light of all the evidence in the case and the contextual relevance of expert testimony to the charges and contested facts. Ultimately, in cases of enduring uncertainty or doubt, the criminal burden and standard of proof weigh in favour of an acquittal.[43] It is sometimes argued that cases involving disagreements between experts should attract a special judicial direction, but the Court of Appeal has resisted the notion that there is any ubiquitous form of words that must be used to cover this situation.[44] The judge is merely required to summarize, fairly and fully, any factual disagreement between the (expert) witnesses, indicate the potential salience of that disagreement

---

[37] McEwan, J., 'From Adversarialism to Managerialism: Criminal Justice in Transition' (2011) 31 *Legal Studies*, 519.

[38] Judicial Studies Board (2010). *Crown Court Bench Book: Directing the Jury, https://www.judiciary. gov.uk/publications/crown-court-bench-book-directing-the-jury-2/.*

[39] On forensic reasoning rules, see generally Roberts and Zuckerman, *Criminal Evidence*, above n.8, ch 15.3.

[40] *R v Allen* [2005] EWCA Crim 1344; *Davie v Edinburgh Magistrates* [1953] SC 34. But *cf R v Brennan* [2015] 1 WLR 2060, [2014] EWCA Crim 2387. [43]–[44].

[41] For example, findings of 'gross negligence' (*R v Misra and Srivastava* [2005] 1 Cr App R 21, [2004] EWCA Crim 2375) or diminished 'mental responsibility' (*R v Dietschmann* [2003] 1 AC 1209, HL, interpreting the old version of Homicide Act 1957, s 2).

[42] *R v Ugoh* [2001] EWCA Crim 1381, [23].

[43] *R v Cannings* [2004] 1 WLR 2607, CA.

[44] *R v Hookway and Noakes* [2011] EWCA Crim 1989.

for contested issues in the proceedings, and leave the rest to the jury's innate wisdom and sense of justice.

C. DNA (and Other Forensic Science) Probabilities

7.16 Although all empirical information is inherently probabilistic, evidence adduced in criminal trials has not traditionally been expressed in terms of numerical probabilities.[45] In recent decades, however, modern forensic science has introduced mathematical probabilities into criminal courtrooms with unprecedented regularity. The advent and expansion of DNA evidence,[46] with its explicit 'random match probability' (RMP), was pivotal in this regard, but quantified probabilities of random matches are not, in principle, confined to DNA profiling. On the contrary: *all* pattern recognition evidence—fingerprinting, tool marks, ballistics, hair, fibres, glass, facial-mapping, dentition, and so on—is subject to random matching, unless the questioned pattern is verifiably and demonstrably unique and could only be attributed to a single source. But this is almost never true in nature.[47] It follows that whenever physical evidence is being used to prove the identity of an alleged offender, statistically warranted random match probabilities could be provided by expert witnesses (if the necessary research has been done), and arguably *should* be[48]—albeit that English courts have not been particularly receptive to this contention.[49]

7.17 It remains an open question whether expanding recognition of the probabilistic basis of much forensic science evidence will impact on the way in which expert witnesses write their reports and testify at trial in English criminal proceedings.[50] In the meantime, RMPs are routinely being given for DNA profiling evidence, if for no other. The courts have consequently been confronted with practical questions about the way in which quantified probabilities for random matches should be presented to jurors.[51]

---

[45] There are arcane exceptions, such as cases involving gambling and lotteries: Eggleston, R. (1997) *Evidence, Proof and Probability*, reprinted 2nd edn, London: Butterworths, ch. 2.

[46] See Roberts, P., 'Forensic Science and Criminal Justice' in Hucklesby, A. and Wahidin, A. (eds) (2013) *Criminal Justice*, 2nd edn, Oxford: Oxford University Press.

[47] Even this slight qualification would be too conservative for scientists who endorse the maxim that 'nature never repeats herself'.

[48] Saks, M.J. and Koehler, J.J., 'The Coming Paradigm Shift in Forensic Identification Science' (2005) 309 *Science*, 892.

[49] *R v T* [2011] 1 Cr App R 9, [2010] EWCA Crim 2439.

[50] See further, Jackson, G., Aitken, C., and Roberts, P. (2015) *Case Assessment and Interpretation of Expert Evidence*, RSS Practitioner Guide No 4, London: Royal Statistical Society, *http://www.rss. org.uk/statsandlaw*.

[51] Generally, see Aitken, C., Roberts, P., and Jackson, G. (2010) *Fundamentals of Probability and Statistical Evidence in Criminal Proceedings*, RSS Practitioner Guide No 1, London: Royal Statistical Society, *http://www.rss.org.uk/statsandlaw*; Redmayne, M. (2001) *Expert Evidence and Criminal Justice*, Oxford: Oxford University Press.

Besides diffuse worries that jurors might overestimate (or undervalue[52]) explic- **7.18**
itly probabilistic and/or statistical information, a more focused concern is that
juries, lacking familiarity or confidence with probabilities, might perpetrate
logical reasoning errors, the most notorious of which is the so-called 'prosecutor's fallacy' (PF) (in reality, by no means confined to prosecutors). PF involves
a confusion between two very different probabilities: (i) the probability that a
person will match crime scene DNA if he is *not* its donor (this is the RMP); and
(ii) the probability that a person is *not the donor* if he matches. The RMP for a full
DNA profile for biologically unrelated individuals is conventionally reported
as 1 in 1 billion. But it is an elementary fallacy (statisticians call it 'transposing
the conditional') to interpret this as saying that the probability that anybody
other than the profile-matcher could be the donor of crime stain DNA is one in
a billion. The essential point to grasp is that 'matching' characteristics do not
uniquely identify a particular individual, but rather specify a pool of potential
suspects (delimited by an appropriate RMP). Thus, as a purely mathematical
extrapolation, if there are seven billion people in the world, the probability that
any one of them is the donor is only $1/7 = 0.14$. Elementary and seriously distorting as PF may be, anecdotal evidence suggests that it occurs in practice with
alarming regularity. English courts have attempted to insulate the jury from
PF by insisting that a forensic scientist 'should not be asked his opinion on the
likelihood that it was the defendant who left the crime stain, nor when giving
evidence should he use terminology which may lead the jury to believe that he is
expressing such an opinion'.[53]

Even when technological advances support exceedingly small RMPs, random **7.19**
matches remain live possibilities, not least because the growth of the NDNAD
increases the probability that two or more individuals on the database will adventi-
tiously share the same profile. Complex DNA mixtures, and Low Template DNA
(LTDNA) profiles generated from very small amounts of genetic material, present
additional technical challenges and interpretational difficulties, which are still in
the process of being satisfactorily assimilated into forensic practice.[54]

It might be thought, and some have argued, that jurors could be assisted in their **7.20**
interpretation and evaluation of probabilistic evidence by being introduced to the
reasoning protocols—in particular, Bayes' theorem, a formula for updating conditional probabilities in the light of new evidence—that some forensic scientists use
when interpreting their own findings and formulating their testimony. However,
English courts have strongly resisted any such development, most notably in the

---

[52] *Cf.* Saks, M.J. and Kidd, R.F., 'Human Information Processing and Adjudication: Trial By
Heuristics' (1981) 15 *Law and Society Review*, 123.
[53] *R v Doheny and Adams* [1997] 1 Cr App R 369, 374, CA.
[54] Puch-Solis, R., Roberts, P., Pope, S., and Aitken, C. (2012) *Assessing the Probative Value of
DNA Evidence*, RSS Practitioner Guide No 2, London: Royal Statistical Society, *http://www.rss.
org.uk/statsandlaw*.

rape case of *Adams*,[55] where the Court of Appeal emphatically reiterated the conventional common law position: juries are the constitutionally authentic finders of fact in criminal trials on indictment, and they should proceed by ordinary, 'common-sense' inferential reasoning.[56]

D. Expert Evidence of Witness Credibility

7.21 Assessing witness credibility is traditionally conceived as the jury's province par excellence. General common-law doctrine prohibits parties from calling evidence designed to bolster the credit of their own witnesses, which has been anathematized as illegitimate 'oath-helping'.[57]

(1) Civil and family court proceedings

7.22 The generic common law rule does not apply in civil courts, including the family courts which often deal with contested allegations of sexual abuse;[58] though strong judicial admonitions against over-reliance on expert evidence of credibility have been issued.[59] Family court judges sit without juries, and perhaps translate their scepticism about certain kinds of expert evidence into judgements of weight rather than categorical inadmissibility.[60] Moreover, questions of fact are determined 'on the balance of probabilities'. Techniques such as Statement Validity Assessment, employed extensively in German courts and elsewhere,[61] might be robust enough to inform assessments of the *probability* that a child is telling the truth about sexual abuse, but would not necessarily meet the more exacting criminal standard of proof.[62]

(2) Admissibility in criminal trials

7.23 Expert evidence 'which tends to convey to the jury the expert's opinion of the truth or otherwise of the complaint'[63] remains inadmissible in criminal proceedings as a

---

[55] *R v Adams* [1996] 2 Cr App R 467, CA; *R v Adams (No 2)* [1998] 1 Cr App R 377, CA.

[56] More recently, see *R v T* [2011] 1 Cr App R 9, [2010] EWCA Crim 2439, critically discussed by Redmayne, M., Roberts, P., Aitken, C., and Jackson, G., 'Forensic Science Evidence in Question' [2011] Crim LR 347.

[57] *R v Robinson* (1994) 98 Cr App R 370, 374–5, CA.

[58] *Re M & R* [1996] 4 All ER 239.

[59] *D v B (Flawed Sexual Abuse Inquiry)* [2007] 1 FLR 1295; *A London Borough Council v K* [2009] EWHC 850 (Fam), [162].

[60] *Re M & R* [1996] 4 All ER 239, 253.

[61] Köhnken, G., 'Statement Validity Analysis and the "Detection of Truth"' in P.A. Granhag, and L.A. Strömwall, (eds), (2004) *The Detection of Deception in Forensic Contexts*, Cambridge: Cambridge University Press.

[62] Vrij, A. (2008) *Detecting Lies and Deceit: Pitfalls and Opportunities*, 2nd edn, Chichester: John Wiley & Sons Ltd, ch. 8.

[63] *R v Chanson* [2012] EWCA Crim 1478, [12].

result of two overlapping rules. One is *Turner's* threshold 'helpfulness' requirement.[64] The other is the general prohibition on self-serving evidence of a witness's good character (embracing virtuous veracity), whether given by an expert or lay witness.[65] The common law rule of practice about a witness's good character encapsulates the general principle that courts should not be diverted by evidence of 'collateral' matters, relevant only to the credibility of a witness;[66] but the courts recognize that the objection to collateral evidence can sometimes be relaxed when dealing with sexual offences.[67] Similarly, *Turner*-helpfulness expresses the general principle that evidence should not be admitted when its tendency to distort the fact-finding process (its anticipated 'prejudicial effect') outweighs its probative value.

Allowing an expert to state or directly imply that a witness is credible does risk **7.24** distorting the fact-finding process, because jurors might too readily defer to the expert's evaluation rather than thinking for themselves. Yet in some cases this risk is relatively slight, while the probative value of the evidence is, or could be, considerable. In *R v S (VJ)*,[68] a paediatrician testified that the complainant's demeanour in a video interview was not unusual for an autistic child, and that somebody with her degree of autism 'would find it difficult to invent a story ... [or] to retain it in her memory for any significant period of time'.[69] This evidence was admitted—unfortunately for reasons not clearly explained—whereas in *R v Robinson*[70] quite similar evidence, deriving from personal acquaintance with the child rather than general scientific knowledge, was ruled inadmissible. Both decisions, however, are consistent with treating *Turner*-helpfulness as a principled general standard rather than a rigid formalism. Information about the typical characteristics of autism is plausibly more 'helpful' than a psychologist's impressionistic assessments of an individual child.[71]

Whether admissibility standards are conceptualized as rigid rules or flexible princi- **7.25** ples, certain forms of expert evidence directly addressing, or implicitly bearing on, questions of witness credibility are clearly admissible at common law. First, English courts have always distinguished between a witness's *unwillingness* to tell the truth and a medical *incapacity* to do so.[72] Thus, an expert witness was permitted to testify that

---

[64] See para 7.08.
[65] *R v Beard* [1998] Crim LR 585.
[66] *R v Francis* [2013] EWCA Crim 2312; *R v Edwards* [1991] 1 WLR 207, CA; *Hobbs v Tinling* [1929] 2 KB 1, CA.
[67] *R v Funderburk* [1990] 1 WLR 587, CA; *R v Tobin* [2002] EWCA Crim 190, [15].
[68] [2006] EWCA Crim 2389.
[69] Ibid. [9].
[70] (1994) 98 Cr App R 370, CA.
[71] See further, Ward, T., 'Usurping the Role of the Jury? Expert Evidence and Witness Credibility in English Criminal Trials' (2009) 13 *International Journal of Evidence & Proof*, 83; Roberts, P., 'Towards the Principled Reception of Expert Evidence of Witness Credibility in Criminal Trials' (2004) 8 *International Journal of Evidence & Proof*, 215.
[72] *Toohey v Metropolitan Police Commissioner* [1965] AC 595, 608, HL; *R v Pinfold and Mackenny* [2004] 2 Cr App R 5, CA.

a rape complainant suffering from Huntington's chorea tended to confabulate when her memory failed.[73] Expert evidence is also admissible to rebut evidence or cross-examination to the effect that a witness is unreliable owing to mental abnormality.[74]

7.26 Secondly, English courts have sometimes admitted expert testimony on general factors potentially affecting the credibility of certain kinds of witness. Evidence of good and bad practice in interviewing child witnesses and the dangers of excessive or suggestive questioning has been received on this basis.[75] Expert evidence explicating the distorting potential of hypnosis has also been admitted.[76] By contrast, 'social framework' behavioural science evidence of general factors affecting the reliability of eyewitness identification is *not* normally received in England and Wales. Such information as jurors are thought to require to supplement their own common-sense evaluations is provided by the judge in summing up, through *Turnbull* warnings[77] and related forensic reasoning rules.

7.27 Thirdly, evidence of post-traumatic stress disorder (PTSD) appears to be admissible on the basis that it is a 'psychological injury' consistent with the complainant's alleged victimization,[78] even though such a diagnosis typically presupposes the expert's acceptance of the complainant's account of her experiences (which, as unverified hearsay, would not be admissible at common law). Evidence of PTSD has also been admitted to explain a complainant's retraction.[79] It is debatable whether expert evidence contextualizing reactions to sexual victimization should be confined to diagnosable conditions like PTSD.[80] If evidence about the effects of 'prolonged interrogation' on 'normal' people can be adduced by the defence in an attempt to have a confession excluded,[81] it might be thought that expert evidence of 'normal' reactions to rape or sexual abuse would be equally 'helpful' to jurors. The Court of Appeal, however, has been predictably cautious, preferring that such matters be addressed in the judge's summing up rather than risking a proliferation of—possibly contested—expert opinions on collateral matters of witness credibility, which the common law jury is supposed to be competent to determine for itself.[82]

---

[73] *R v Archibald* [2002] EWCA Crim 858, [4] (Crown Court trial discussed by Hoyano, L. and Keenan, C. (2007) *Child Abuse*, Oxford: Oxford University Press, 894–5, footnote 129).

[74] *R v Robinson* (1994) 98 Cr App R 370, 374–5, CA.

[75] *R v D, The Times* 15 November 1995; *G v DPP* [1998] QB 919, 926–7, DC.

[76] *R v Clark* [2006] EWCA Crim 231.

[77] *R v Turnbull* [1977] QB 224, CA.

[78] *R v Eden* [2011] EWCA Crim 1690.

[79] *R v X* [2007] EWCA Crim 3226, [18].

[80] Ellison, L. and Munro, V.E., 'Turning Mirrors into Windows? The Impact of (Mock) Jury Education in Rape Trials' (2009) 49 *British Journal of Criminology*, 363; Cossins, A. 'Expert Witness Evidence in Sexual Assault Trials: Questions, Answers and Law Reform in Australia and England' (2013) 17 *International Journal of Evidence & Proof*, 74.

[81] *R v Blackburn* [2005] EWCA Crim 1349, [2005] 2 Cr App R 30, [30].

[82] *R v Doody* [2008] EWCA Crim 2394; *R v ER* [2010] EWCA Crim 2522, discussed by Rook, P. and Ward, R. (2010) *Sexual Offences: Law and Practice*, 4th edn, London: Sweet & Maxwell, 1.221–31, 20.16–23.

(3) Memory experts

Expert evidence of illnesses affecting memory, such as Alzheimer's disease, is plainly **7.28**
admissible.[83] However, the diagnosis of illness and its effects on memory must steer
clear of any implication that the expert is pronouncing on the credibility of the very
allegations the jury must assess.[84] The Court of Appeal is markedly less receptive
to evidence about the normal workings of memory, particularly in childhood. In
R v H[85] the Court admitted expert evidence describing the rarity of detailed memories of early childhood, but excluded parts of the expert's testimony addressing the
particular circumstances of the complainant's allegations.[86] The Court stressed,
moreover, that this was an exceptional case.[87] Subsequent case law stresses orthodox approaches to evaluating witness credibility, focusing on demeanour.[88] In *R v*
Anderson, Hallett LJ opined that, in light of emergent methodological criticisms, it
was doubtful whether *R v H* 'would be decided the same way today',[89] the expert's
research foundation being too flimsy to support testimonial conclusions about the
capacity of young children to form detailed memories.[90] These dicta leave open
the possibility that background expert evidence more securely rooted in relevant
research literature might still be admissible.[91]

The chasm separating lay understandings of cognition and memory from prevail- **7.29**
ing scientific wisdom is described elsewhere in this volume.[92] Yet judges continue
to assert that the 'difficulties of recollection of our early childhood are familiar to
us all', instructing juries to '[l]ook at all of the evidence fairly and apply your collective knowledge of life in deciding where the truth lies'.[93] Is this strategy irrational
or contrary to the interests of justice? Memory 'experts' do not speak with one
voice, and many clinicians who might be called to give evidence in criminal proceedings hold views which scientific researchers consider unsound.[94] Scientifically
questionable prosecution testimony from clinicians (often unchallenged by the
defence) appears to have expanded after New Zealand courts became more receptive to expert evidence of witness credibility.[95] Recalling the fundamental values
and traditional principles of English criminal procedure, one may wonder whether

---

83 *R v D* [2002] EWCA Crim 190, [2003] QB 90.
84 *R v H* [2014] EWCA Crim 1555.
85 [2005] EWCA Crim 1828 (also known as *R v X (Childhood Amnesia)* [2006] 1 Cr App R 10).
86 See Conway, M., 'On Being a Memory Expert Witness: Three Cases' (2013) 21 *Memory*, 566.
87 *R v H* [2005] EWCA Crim 1828 [28].
88 *R v S; R v W* [2006] EWCA Crim 1404. See also *R v H* [2014] EWCA Crim 1455.
89 *R v Anderson* [2012] EWCA Crim 1785, [9].
90 *R v E* [2009] EWCA Crim 1370, [39]. Also see *R v DPMC and DJW* [2010] NICA 22, [9]–[11].
91 But *cf. R v H* [2011] EWCA Crim 2344, [2012] 1 Cr App R 30, [41].
92 See Chapters 21, 22, and 23.
93 *R v H* [2012] Cr App R 30, [41].
94 See Chapter 23 para 23.05.
95 Zajac, R., Garry, M., London, K., Goodyear-Smith, F., and Hayne, H. 'Misconceptions
about Childhood Sexual Abuse and Child Witnesses: Implications for Psychological Experts in the
Courtroom' (2013) 21 *Memory*, 608.

juries are really helped by such testimony (even supposing that it is not gainsaid by counter-expertise) to arrive at just and true verdicts in contested criminal trials.

E. Conclusion

7.30 Increasing reliance on forensic science evidence and expert witness testimony is a hallmark of modern criminal proceedings. Such reliance extends a very long-standing common law precept that 'if matters arise in our law which concern other sciences or faculties, we commonly apply for the aid of that science or faculty which it concerns'.[96] Circumstantial features of indictable sex crimes often place a premium on scientific proof (notably including DNA profiling evidence) in bringing offenders to justice, and also, sometimes, in exonerating the innocent. The admission and use of expert evidence in trials of sexual offences are governed by the generic common-law standards reviewed in this chapter. Logical relevance and institutional 'helpfulness'[97] are the primary criteria of legal admissibility. Trial judges have now also been supplied with detailed guidance on assessing the reliability of expert evidence and the procedural framework for undertaking more active scrutiny at the admissibility stage,[98] should they choose to exploit these opportunities for proactive gatekeeping. Jurors, for their part, require careful judicial guidance on the appropriate uses of expert testimony adduced in criminal trials, always emphasizing their own ultimate responsibility for fact-finding, even in relation to uncontested scientific evidence. Certain forms of expert testimony, such as DNA match probabilities, may require more extended judicial directions to steer jurors away from notorious, but tempting, reasoning fallacies.

7.31 Judges have sometimes been too trusting of novel forms of forensic science, yet possibly too sceptical of the behavioural sciences. In either scenario, juries are left to grapple unaided with the very difficult evidential issues sometimes arising in trials of sexual offences. It should be borne in mind, however, that expert evidence on matters such as memory, witness credibility, and the 'typical' behaviour of victims has variable probative value, relative to the facts in issue in the instant proceedings, which may be difficult for juries (or judges) to assess; that it can easily trespass on the jury's constitutionally-mandated role as fact-finder; and that judges have a duty to protect the accused (and, arguably, complainants too) from unfair prejudice. Judges therefore have good reasons to be cautious in applying English law's broad, context-sensitive principles governing the admissibility of expert evidence. So long as decisions applying those principles to particular facts are not treated as creating

---

[96] *Buckley v Rice Thomas* (1554) 1 Plowden 118, 124, CB (Saunders J).
[97] *R v Turner* [1975] QB 834, CA.
[98] See paras 7.11 and 7.12.

rigid precedents, the law should remain flexible enough to admit any kind of expert evidence that is genuinely reliable, probative, and helpful to the jury.

Further Reading

Roberts, P. and Zuckerman, A. (2010) *Criminal Evidence*, 2nd edn, Oxford: Oxford University Press, ch. 11.

Rook, P. QC and Ward, R. (2014) *Rook and Ward on Sexual Offences*, 4th edn, London: Sweet & Maxwell, chs 20–4.

Royal Statistical Society Practitioner Manuals on *Communicating and Interpreting Statistical Evidence in the Administration of Criminal Justice*, *http://www.rss.org.uk/statsandlaw*.

Author Biographies

Paul Roberts is Professor of Criminal Jurisprudence at the University of Nottingham School of Law, and an Adjunct Professor in the Faculty of Law, University of New South Wales, Sydney. His extensive publications include Roberts and Zuckerman, *Criminal Evidence*, 2nd edn, (Oxford University Press, 2010), Roberts (ed.), *Expert Evidence and Scientific Proof in Criminal Trials* (Ashgate, 2014), and Roberts and Hunter (eds), *Criminal Evidence and Human Rights* (Hart, 2012). Beyond academia, he has served as a consultant to the Law Commissions of England and Scotland, the Crown Prosecution Service and the Forensic Science Regulator.

Dr Tony Ward is Reader in Law at the University of Hull and Co-Director of the Experts & Institutions research centre and the International State Crime Initiative. His publications include Green and Ward, *State Crime* (Pluto, 2004), Johnstone and Ward, *Law and Crime* (Sage, 2010) and many articles on expert evidence.

8

DEFENDING SERIOUS SEXUAL ASSAULT: ETHICAL AND EFFECTIVE ADVOCACY

Pamela Radcliffe*

* The author would like to thank Professor Gisli Gudjonsson, Professor Penny Cooper, Dr Emily Henderson, and Bridget Pettitt for their helpful comments that served to improve this chapter. Unless otherwise stated, all opinions, comments, and practical suggestions are those of the author.

A. Introduction

8.01 'Effective advocacy is at the heart of our adversarial system of justice.'[1] Unsuitable advocacy methods are unjust and do not accord with the overriding objective in criminal cases.[2] Inappropriate questioning techniques generate unreliable witness testimony; they are also potentially abusive. Irresponsible advocacy is being corrected by the legal profession. Ethical and effective advocacy is the only 'just' way to 'test' witness testimony.

8.02 The Ministry of Justice (MOJ) recently declared that by March 2015, it will 'devise a requirement' that all publicly funded advocates instructed in 'serious sexual offences' must undertake 'approved specialist training'.[3] When this training will be implemented is uncertain.[4] Advocates defending sexual cases require specialized skill sets[5] in addition to a sound understanding of substantive law and the rules of evidence and procedure. In cases of serious sexual assault, sentencing tariffs are usually in double figures. Advocates have an overriding duty to the justice system to prepare and conduct cases to the highest professional standards.

8.03 Pre-trial cross-examination of children will be introduced in all crown courts subject to positive evaluation of pilot schemes. Reform is long overdue.[6] The objective is to enhance testimonial accuracy and reduce witness distress. The mechanics and nature of the adversarial trial are undergoing radical overhaul.

8.04 This chapter describes the current 'revolution'[7] in the courtroom and identifies new initiatives and guidance for advocates. Justice is only served via ethical and effective advocacy. Trial advocacy is the culmination of the advocate's task. This chapter emphasizes that pre-trial preparation is the 'touchstone' for good quality advocacy. The chapter focuses on complainants. Knowledge of the substantive law and procedural rules is presumed.

---

[1] Jeffrey, B. (2014) *Independent criminal advocacy in England and Wales: Jeffrey Review Final Report* (Sir Bill Jeffrey), *https://www.gov.uk/government/publications/independent-criminal-advocacy-in-england-and-wales*.

[2] The Criminal Procedure Rules 2015, *https://www.justice.gov.uk/courts/procedure-rules/criminal*.

[3] MOJ, (2014) *Our Commitment to Victims*, *https://www.gov.uk/government/uploads/system/uploads/attachment_data/file/354723/commitment-to-victims.pdf*.

[4] Cooper, P., 'Ticketing Talk Gets Serious' (2014) *Counsel*, November 2014, 12 (discussing the possible content of future training).

[5] The Advocacy Training Council for the Bar (2011) *Raising the Bar: The Handling of Vulnerable Witnesses, Victims and Defendants in Court*, Final Report, para 1.3, *http://advocacytrainingcouncil.org/vulnerable-witnesses/raising-the-bar*.

[6] Gibb, F., 'Child victims will give evidence on film to avoid trauma of trial' *The Times*, 15 September 2014. See also para 8.21.

[7] See lecture by Lord Judge: Judge, I. (2013) *The Evidence of Child Victims: The Next Stage*, General Council of the Bar of England and Wales Annual Law Reform Lecture, 21 November 2013.

B. Criticisms

(1) Treatment of adult complainants

'Cross-examination' is no stranger to controversy; it continues to be a source of **8.05**
public and academic concern.[8] Historically, criticism has focused on the impact
of inappropriate questioning. Rape victims have long complained to researchers of
their brutal treatment at barristers' hands. Methods perceived as unfair are: repetitive questioning, unnecessary questioning on intimate details of the rape, attempts
to twist witness interpretation, exploiting minor inconsistencies and perpetuat-
ing rape myths by remarking on 'seductive' clothing or conduct such as excessive
drinking.[9] In 1996 Temkin identified conduct and attitudes evinced by prosecution and defence counsel, giving cause for concern.[10] Since these studies were conducted, research has concentrated on the inappropriate questioning of children
and other vulnerable witnesses.[11] Questioning on prior sexual history is now safeguarded by section 41 Youth Justice and Criminal Evidence Act (YJCEA) 1999.
(See Chapter 5.)

In a report commissioned by the MOJ following adverse media criticism of a **8.06**
series of gang grooming child-exploitation trials between 2011 and 2013, cross-
examination was identified as a source of concern causing unwarranted trauma
to victims of sexual violence.[12] The suicides of two adult rape victims in January
2013[13] and February 2014[14] reinforced the need for change.

'Inappropriately aggressive' questioning and 'bad practice' persists, but is not **8.07**
perceived to be a 'widespread issue'.[15] However, advocates are not 'off the hook'.

---

[8] Langbein, J.H. (2003) *The Origins of Adversary Criminal Trial*, Oxford: Oxford University Press.
[9] Temkin, J. (2002) *Rape and the Legal Process*, Oxford: Oxford University Press, 8–10.
[10] Temkin, J. and Krahe, B., 'Rape, Rape Trials and the Justice Gap: Some views from the
Bench and Bar' in (2008) *Sexual Assault and the Justice Gap: A Question of Attitude*, Oxford: Hart
Publishing, 125–42, citing e.g. at n.10, 129, a QC informant: 'But there are barristers still who
defend who simply want to destroy a complainant. And I mean that. ... And section 41 has gone a
long way to stopping that, but people will still try and do it, because that's the way.'
[11] Prof. John Spencer has long advocated reform: Spencer, J.R. and Lamb, M.E. (2012) *Children
and Cross-Examination: Time to change the rules*, Oxford: Hart Publishing. See also Spencer, J. and
Flin R. (1993) *The Evidence of Children: The Law and the Psychology*, London: Blackstone Press.
[12] MOJ, (2014) *Report on review of ways to reduce distress of victims in trials of sexual abuse*, para
15, *https://www.gov.uk/government/uploads/system/uploads/attachment_data/file/299341/report-on-
review-of-ways-to-reduce-distress-of-victims-in-trials-of-sexual-violence.pdf*.
[13] Gentleman, A., 'Prosecuting sexual assault: Raped all over again' *The Guardian*, 13 April
2013, *http://www.theguardian.com/society/2013/apr/13/rape-sexual-assault-frances-andrade-court*.
Frances Andrade, a historic abuse victim, committed suicide shortly after giving evidence. The
robust cross-examination provoked a media storm, but the cross-examination did not breach professional boundaries.
[14] Pidd, H. and Perraudin, F., 'Police chief calls for rape cases rethink after woman's death' *The
Guardian*, 4 February 2014.
[15] MOJ, *Report on review of ways to reduce distress of victims* cited at n.12, para 15.

'Embedding specialization', further training, and proper preparation are identified as the way forward, rather than the introduction of specialist courts.[16] The 'resonating feedback' emphasized 'the need for a cultural change in the courtroom'.[17]

8.08 Submitting evidence to the Jeffrey Review, the Council of Her Majesty's Circuit Judges reported that the diminishing level of basic competence displayed by advocates was a matter of 'serious concern to the judiciary'.[18] However, no 'hard research evidence' on advocate quality exists.

(2) Treatment of children and other vulnerable witnesses

8.09 Research on the negative impact of advocate questioning on young witnesses, the learning disabled, and those with cognitive difficulties is extensive.[19] Ellison identified the following core types of defects in cross-examination:[20]

(i) 'inappropriate language', where sophisticated language, not tailored to cognitive needs, causes confusion or is age inappropriate;

(ii) 'coercive questioning', primarily controlling questioning techniques via leading and suggestive questioning causing unreliable or inaccurate answers; and

(iii) intimidation tactics, a 'hostile' approach, utilizing certain tones of voice, eye contact, repetitive questioning, pre-emptive interruption, and rapid-fire questions.

8.10 Plotnikoff and Woolfson reported that a significant proportion of young people perceived they were not well served by the trial process.[21] Their recommendations and good practice guidance have informed recent advocacy training guidance and other witness protection measures.[22] Keane also deprecates the abusive nature of cross-examination and identifies the need for reform.[23] Henderson's recent research reveals that the profession is 'listening' and reacting to criticism,

---

[16] Ibid., para 38.

[17] Ibid., para 31.

[18] *Jeffrey Review* cited at n.1, para 2.5.

[19] See n.11.

[20] Ellison, L., 'The mosaic art?: Cross-examination and the vulnerable witness' (2001) 21(3) *Legal Studies*, 353–75, 354.

[21] Plotnikoff, J. and Woolfson, R. (2009) *Measuring up? Evaluating implementation of young witnesses in criminal proceedings*, London: NSPCC and the Nuffield Foundation, *http://www. nuffieldfoundation.org/sites/default/files/measuring_up_report_wdf66579(1).pdf*. Of 172 young people (under 16) interviewed, 49% described the defence advocate as sarcastic, rude, aggressive, or cross; 49% did not understand some questions, (a problem for all age groups); and 58% felt that the advocate was trying to put words into their mouths.

[22] See Plotnikoff, J. and Woolfson, R., 'Cross-examining children—Testing not trickery' (2010) *Archbold Review*, issue 7, 6 August.

[23] Keane, A. 'Towards a Principled Approach to the Cross-examination of Vulnerable Witnesses' [2012] Crim LR 6, 407–20; Keane, A., 'Cross-examination of vulnerable witnesses— towards a blueprint for re-professionalisation' (2012) 16(2) *E&P*, 175–98.

although 'barriers to good practice' remain. She concludes there is a 'pressing need' for further guidance and training support to teach advocates alternative questioning methods.[24]

C. Recent Reforms and New Guidance

(1) Registered intermediaries and ground rule hearings

Intermediaries were introduced in 2009 to improve communication between **8.11** counsel and vulnerable witnesses.[25] The Advocate's Gateway[26] provides guidance on the use of Intermediaries.[27] Registered Intermediaries (RIs) assess the specific needs of the witness and report to the court. They may recommend trial modifications or advise on appropriate questioning methods. The RI attends at trial and actively assists the witness during live oral evidence if required.

Police investigators should identify whether RIs are required at the outset of the **8.12** criminal investigation. RIs are able to advise on the conduct of the Achieving Best Evidence (ABE) interview by producing a preliminary report.[28] However, as observed in Chapter 1, investigators are not always efficient at identifying vulnerable witnesses.

Research suggests that the take-up of RIs at trial is generally poor[29] and that even **8.13** when they do participate, advocates do not always appear to follow their advice.[30] Henderson opines that given the unlikelihood of counsel acquiring appropriate questioning skills, a neutral third party (e.g., the RI) could interview the vulnerable

---

[24] Henderson, E., 'Jewel in the Crown' (2014) *Counsel*, November 2014, 10–12. After informally reviewing this chapter Henderson further comments that increased engagement between non-legal academics/linguists and legal professionals will enhance the quality of training.

[25] Implementing s 29 YJCEA 1999, and see MOJ, (2012) *The Intermediary Procedural Guidance Manual*.

[26] Advocacy Training Council for the Bar, *Raising the Bar*, cited at n.5. See *http://www. theadvocatesgateway.org* and *http://lexiconlimited.co.uk/intermediary-issues*.

[27] For further discussion, see Plotnikoff and Woolfson, *Measuring up?* cited at n.21.

[28] MOJ (2011) *Achieving Best Evidence in Criminal Proceedings: Guidance on Interviewing Victims and Witnesses, and Guidance on using Special Measures*, paras 2.194–200.

[29] Henderson, H., 'All the proper protections—the Court of Appeal rewrites the rules for the cross-examination of vulnerable witnesses' [2014] Crim LR 91 ('[Intermediaries are] ... only generally used in a very few difficult cases').

[30] Cooper concluded in 2010 that, 'A "Ground Rules are made to be broken" attitude may be prevalent amongst cross-examining counsel', *http://www.city.ac.uk/__data/assets/pdf_file/0006/92499/ Tell-Me-Whats-Happening-2-RI-Survey-2010-FINAL-VERSION-14062011.pdf*, 15. In the 2012 Registered Intermediary Survey, RI survey respondents reported that the majority of counsel failed to adhere to 'no leading question' recommendations. *http://www.city.ac.uk/__data/assets/pdf_ file/0008/126593/30-April-FINAL-Tell-Me-Whats-Happening-3.pdf*. She notes that 'most' intermediaries reported that grounds rules were contravened at trial and that judges did not spot the errors. For latest findings and recommendations, see Cooper, P. (2014) 'Highs and Lows 4th Intermediary Survey' updated 13 October 2014, Kingston University, London.

witness. She suggests this might increase the ultimate reliability of vulnerable witness testimony.[31]

8.14 Ground Rule Hearings (GRHs) comprise a pre-trial hearing in which the judge, counsel, and RI decide how to implement the Intermediary's recommendations. The court can now give directions to assist any witness including the defendant, to give 'complete, coherent and accurate evidence'.[32] GRHs may facilitate consideration of other pre-trial issues, including the identification of lead defence counsel in multi-defendant cases. GRHs must take place whenever an Intermediary is instructed and are good practice when any young witness is involved.

8.15 Practitioners and Intermediaries report that GRHs typically occur the day before trial. If GRHs do not take place in good time, trial delays and other setbacks ensue. Cooper's research suggests GRHs would be more effective if they occur earlier.[33] The 2014 MOJ report posits whether GRH should be widened to cover more or all sexual violence cases.[34]

(2) A series of cases from the Court of Appeal

8.16 A series of judgments from the Court of Appeal Criminal Division have shaped new advocacy guidance.[35] Very young children are now giving evidence. Testimonial competence depends on the individual characteristics of each child.

(3) Advocate's Gateway and the Advocacy Toolkits

8.17 The Advocate's Gateway, hosted by the Advocacy Training Council, launched 'Advocacy Toolkits' in April 2013.[36] These contain essential guidance for all advocates in cases involving young and vulnerable witnesses. The Toolkits provide procedural information on GRHs together with detailed guidance on a spectrum of issues including handling very young witnesses and questioning those with communication needs. The website also provides instructive videos on ground rules hearings and cross-examination.

---

[31] Henderson, 'All the proper protections' cited at n.29. After informally reviewing this chapter, Henderson further commented that training, intermediaries, ground rules, and firm judicial management, indicate 'there is a very good chance of excellent practice now' and that questioning by a neutral third party might remain an option in the most complex cases.

[32] The Criminal Procedure (Amendment) Rules 2015 (S.I. 2015/13) subject to meeting the criteria of the YJCEA 1999.

[33] Cooper, *Highs and Lows* cited at n.30. See also The Criminal Procedure (Amendment) Rules 2015 (S.I. 2015/13) adds new rules to Part 3 of the Criminal Procedure Rules 2014, in respect of 'ground rules hearings'.

[34] MOJ, *Report on review of ways to reduce distress of victims* cited at n.12, Recommendation (i) 1.1.

[35] *R v Barker* [2010] EWCA Crim 4; *R v W and M* [2010] EWCA Crim 1926; *R v Wills* [2011] EWCA Crim 1938; *R v E* [2012] EWCA Crim 563.

[36] *http://www.theadvocatesgateway.org*. See also *http://lexiconlimited.co.uk/intermediary-issues*.

(4) Criminal Practice Directions 2013

These directions issued by the Lord Chief Justice,[37] emphasize that 'procedural **8.18** manoeuvres' have no part in a fair trial and that parties should identify matters in issue as early as possible. They provide detailed procedural guidance on case management, pre-trial applications, and vulnerable witnesses. Active judicial intervention to redress unfairness is also encouraged.[38]

(5) Judicial College Bench Checklist: Young witness cases

This is a short, practical pre-trial checklist[39] to guide judges and advocates when **8.19** discussing trial timetable, special trial measures, and 'ground rules' for appropriate questioning. Additional guidance is found in the Equal Treatment Bench Book.[40]

(6) Mind guidance on achieving justice for victims and witnesses with mental distress

Guidance issued by Mind, the mental health charitable foundation, on achieving **8.20** justice for victims and witnesses with mental distress compliments the advocacy 'Toolkits'.[41] The guidance contains further checklists and case studies to assist advocate handling of a person suffering mental distress. It also has a helpful section on 'Asking the right questions' of medical experts when considering whether the quality of oral testimony may be affected by witness perception, memory recall, concentration etc. Other charities also provide guidance.[42]

(7) Pre-trial cross-examination of young and vulnerable witnesses

As at July 2015 the report on pilot studies has not yet been published.[43] However, **8.21** initial results indicate the new procedure is working well.[44] Procedural guidance on this anticipated reform will also follow. The twin objectives of section 28 are to enhance testimonial accuracy by facilitating questioning whilst memory recall is fresh, and reduce witness distress by interviewing outside the courtroom. The success of this reform is heavily dependent on the prosecution complying with disclosure duties as early as possible.

---

[37] [2013] EWCA Crim 1631 Court of Appeal (Criminal Division).

[38] Criminal Practice Directions: Amendment No 4 issued July 2015, now replaces CPD 1 General Matters 3A Case management, *https://www.judiciary.gov.uk/publications/criminal-practice-directions-amendment-no-4/*.

[39] January 2012, *https://www.judiciary.gov.uk/publications-and-reports/guidance/2012/jc-bench-checklist-young-wit-cases*,

[40] November 2013, *https://www.judiciary.gov.uk/publications/equal-treatment-bench-book/*.

[41] Mind (2010) *Achieving justice for victims and witnesses with mental distress: A mental health toolkit for prosecutors and advocates.*

[42] National Autistic Society (2011) *Autism: A guide for criminal justice professionals*, *http://www.cps.gov.uk/publications/docs/mind_toolkit_for_prosecutors_and_advocates.pdf.*

[43] YJCEA 1999, s 28.

[44] See Gibb, 'Child victims will give evidence on film to avoid trauma of trial' cited at n.6.

(8) The treatment of adult complainants

8.22 There is no new guidance for trial treatment of non-vulnerable adult complainants. Prosecuting advocates are now advised to intervene if they consider cross-examination 'inappropriate or too aggressive'.[45] Other judicial measures to reduce witness distress include imposing time limits on cross-examination, and intervention during questioning to stop or caution the advocate, as justice requires.

(9) The introduction of professional standards monitoring: QASA

8.23 This future quality assurance measure will enable judges to monitor advocate performance. Advocates will be graded according to the level of expertise exhibited.[46]

D. Advocate Training and the Adversarial Trial

8.24 This section considers the implications of traditional advocate training for the adversarial trial. Advocates in sexual cases may be either solicitors or barristers. There is currently no common advocate training. Barristers remain the predominant professional advocate in serious sexual offences.

(1) Traditional legal education

8.25 Research reveals two consistent threads of concern:

(i) advocates display inadequate knowledge of child linguistic development, mental health disorders, learning disabilities, and cognitive processes; and

(ii) cross-examination involves abusive 'unjust' methods.

A brief look at legal and professional education provides some insight.

8.26 The Bachelor of Laws degree traditionally involves learning 'black-letter' substantive law. Inter-disciplinary modules teaching basic cognitive psychology, linguistics, or child development are uncommon. Barristers learn the rudiments of advocacy during practical training on their postgraduate course. After qualifying, they undertake twelve months of pupillage. Thereafter, the advocate is permitted to practice without supervision or external regulation. No professional monitoring or external assessment of advocacy performance has existed previously. This is now being addressed.[47]

---

[45] Crown Prosecution Service (2013) *The Code of Practice for Victims of Crime*, October 2013, *https://www.gov.uk/government/uploads/system/uploads/attachment_data/file/254459/code-of-practice-victims-of-crime.pdf* 37, para 3.2.

[46] The Quality Assurance Scheme for Advocates. This is not yet in force but is being developed by the Bar Standards Board, the Solicitors Regulation Authority, and the Institute of Legal Executives Professional Standards.

[47] Advocacy training for solicitors is summarized in the *Jeffrey Review*, cited at n.1, 26–7.

Voluntary training for advanced advocacy in sexual cases has been in place for **8.27** some years providing updates in substantive law, and forensic and medical issues. More recently, modules on questioning children and vulnerable witnesses have been provided.

(2) The adversarial model and trial safeguards

The adversarial trial 'pitches' the prosecution and defence advocates against each **8.28** other in an oral contest before the jury. 'The purpose of the trial process is to identify the evidence which is reliable and that which is not, whether it comes from an adult or child.'[48]

'An advocate's duty is to present his case as forcefully as he can without becom **8.29** ing personally identified with it or forming or expressing any opinion about it. Nevertheless, he is entitled to conduct a case in a way which *suggests* that he believes in it. This is part of his persuasive role.'[49] The advocate's objective is not a quest for the truth, but rather to persuade the jury to reach their decision from his case perspective, and not his opponent's.

Both the defendant and the complainant enjoy legal protection via European **8.30** law. The defendant enjoys the right to a fair trial, including the right to examine witnesses 'against him'.[50] European legislation extends various protections to victims,[51] including that Member States 'shall ensure … [protection of] the dignity of victims during questioning and when testifying'.[52]

The Code of Conduct of the Bar of England and Wales also safeguards the com **8.31** plainant's position,[53] as does the trial judge. Advocates 'must not abuse their role as an advocate'. They must act with 'honesty and integrity'.[54] They must not 'make statements or ask questions merely to insult, humiliate or annoy a witness or any other person'.[55] Advocates are also instructed 'not [to] make a serious allegation against a witness whom you have had an opportunity to cross-examine unless you have given that witness a chance to answer the allegation in cross-examination'.[56]

---

[48] *R v Barker* [2010] EWCA Crim 4 per The Lord Chief Justice of England.

[49] Stone, M. (2009) *Cross-Examination in Criminal Trials* (3rd edn) West Sussex: Tottel Publishing, 2.

[50] ECHR Article 6.

[51] Directive 2012/29/EU of the European Parliament and of the Council of 25 October 2012, establishing minimum standards on the rights, support and protection of victims of crime, and replacing Council Framework Decision 2001/220/JHA, *http://eur-lex.europa.eu/legal-content/EN/TXT/?uri=CELEX:32012L0029.*

[52] ECHR Article 6, cited at n.50, ch. 4, Article 18, right to protection.

[53] Bar Standards Board Handbook, in force from 6 January 2014, *https://www.barstandardsboard.org.uk/media/1553795/bsh_handbook_jan_2014.pdf.*

[54] Ibid., The Core Duties, CD1 and 3.

[55] Ibid., rC7.1.

[56] Ibid., rC7.2.

The Criminal Procedure Rules 2014[57] also provide for the 'appropriate treatment and questioning of a witness or the defendant'.

8.32 An adversarial 'battle' atmosphere sometimes permeates the courtroom. Such an environment is hostile and unhelpful for all involved. Against this backdrop, a less experienced advocate may be overly timorous; fearful of causing the witness distress he or she may not explore relevant matters. Alternatively, the advocate may 'over-compensate' and become too aggressive, or appear to be bullying. Either approach risks causing injustice.

E. Paving the Way for Ethical and Effective Advocacy

(1) The aim of defence advocacy in a sexual case

8.33 This section presumes unequivocal, 'not guilty' instructions. The core aim of advocacy is to 'test' the evidence and expose unreliability whilst complying with the Code of Conduct.[58] Techniques used to achieve this aim are: (i) 'destroying' the witness's evidence by confronting them with irrefutable evidence of dishonest testimony; (ii) weakening the evidence, by 'teasing out' material inconsistencies; or (iii) undermining it, by attacking the witness's credit, to show they cannot be trusted as a truthful witness.[59] In practice, it is uncommon to discover evidence that completely refutes a sexual allegation. For this reason, advocacy tends to rely on the second and third of these techniques.

8.34 In sexual crime the focus of the advocate's questioning is to test the reliability and credibility of the complainant's ABE testimony. Evidential 'reliability' and 'credibility' should not be conflated. They require separate consideration by the advocate. Witness testimony may be inconsistent and unreliable in parts, but overall witness credibility may be unimpeachable. Identifying the nature, cause, and impact of apparently unreliable evidence will assist the advocate to decide if it is 'fair' to cross-examine upon it at trial.

(2) 'Inadequate preparation is the enemy of good advocacy'

8.35 All elements of advocacy, including the formulation of legal arguments, questioning, and speeches, depend upon timely and effective preparation;[60] this in turn is

---

[57] *https://www.justice.gov.uk/.../procedure-rules/criminal/.../2014* para 3.9(6) Amended by the Criminal Procedure (Amendment) Rules 2015 (S.I. 2015/13).

[58] Bar Standards Board Handbook, cited at n.53 and *http://www.sra.org.uk/solicitors/handbook/code/content.page.*

[59] Munkman, J. (1951) *The Technique of Advocacy*, London: Stevens & Sons, (reprinted 1986 by Sweet & Maxwell, London and Fred B Rothman & Co, Littleton, Colorado) 52.

[60] *Jeffrey Review* cited at n.1, 9.

contingent upon the defence team working together. If the solicitor is not the trial advocate, counsel should be instructed as early as possible after charge.

How and when a strand of evidence was obtained may be critical. Examining the **8.36** integrity of the investigative process is vital. This involves investigating each strand of prosecution evidence to consider if it may have been rendered unsafe or unreliable by methodological factors, for instance, interview bias, exposure to contamination, inaccurate reporting, or unsound forensic procedures. One unsafe strand may impact upon the safety of another.

In summary, ethical and effective advocacy in sexual cases extends well beyond **8.37** mere questioning about the alleged abusive incident. It also involves 'testing' the reliability of expert scientific testimony, medical evidence, interview techniques and the evidence-gathering processes.

(3) Investigating the prosecution case

Lord Justice Auld, in his review of the criminal courts of England and Wales, **8.38** observed: '[T]he criminal process is not a game. It is a search for the truth according to the law, albeit by an adversarial process in which the prosecution must prove guilt to a heavy standard.'[61]

Sexual crime may be grouped into three main categories: **8.39**

  (i) assault by a stranger;
 (ii) assault upon an adult by a person known to the complainant:
        (a) in a social context, for instance a casual meeting or during a relationship, or
        (b) in a professional context, for instance by a doctor or dentist; and
(iii) assault upon a child, or young person by:
        (a) a friend or family member,
        (b) a professional, or
        (c) via exploitation, (e.g. gang grooming cases).

Each category of case may use different investigative methods and generate varying **8.40** evidence and unused material. The key questions in each category are:

• Is the evidence reliable?
• Is the process by which it has been obtained sound?
• Is the instructed expert suitably qualified?
• Have all expert procedures been carried out according to accepted professional standards?
• Is the expert opinion founded on up-to-date knowledge?

---

[61] Auld, R. (2001) *Review of the Criminal Courts of England and Wales, http://www.criminal-courts-review.org.uk*, ch. 1, Introduction, para 12.

(4) Adult/child complaints of assault/abduction by a stranger

8.41 This genre of offence typically generates a large quantity of technical evidence, for instance, mobile phone cell-site evidence, advance number plate recognition, forensic crime scene evidence, for example, DNA, fibre, footprint, fingerprint, and CCTV. These investigations are usually investigated as major incidents and use HOLMES.[62] The most likely defence is 'mistaken identity'. The advocate must always maintain objectivity.

8.42 The very first issue in these cases is:

- Has the prosecution proved beyond reasonable doubt that a crime occurred?

8.43 Other issues to consider are:

- Is the crime scene investigation scientifically sound?
- Were sampling techniques or the exhibit audit trail appropriately conducted?
- Is the eye-witness evidence reliable? Reliability of eye-witness testimony, is fraught with risk and will need careful scrutiny to check whether procedures were carried out correctly.
- If there is no CCTV or other evidence corroborating that an assault occurred, then the advocate should check whether investigators scrutinized the reliability of the actual complaint.
- If the complainant suffered injuries, did the medical examiner consider if they could have been self-inflicted?
- Does the complainant have any mental health, neurological, or other medical disability that may have impaired his or her memory recall?[63]

Cases inform us that witnesses do sometimes concoct 'extreme' false complaints and even inflict injuries upon themselves.[64] It is not intended to imply here, that false reports are necessarily prevalent. Recent academic analysis highlights the research challenges in this field.[65] The interests of justice require investigators and justice professionals to be open-minded and neutral when carrying out their respective duties.

---

[62] Home Office Large Major Enquiry System.

[63] Is the impairment one that may be addressed by use of special measures, or is there a risk it may undermine the reliability of the complaint itself? If the latter, then a s 78 Police and Criminal Evidence Act 1984 application to exclude part or all of the evidence should be considered.

[64] *R v Brooker, trainee barrister*, 26 June 2014, BBC News Bristol (false rape complaint with self-inflicted injuries). See also *R v Warburton* (false claims of rape and self-inflicted injuries), *http://www.yourlocalguardian.co.uk/news/10265752*.

[65] Lisak, D., Gardinier, L., Nicksa, S.C., and Cote, A.M., 'False Allegations of Sexual Assault: An Analysis of Ten Years of Reported Cases' *Violence Against Women* (2010) 16(12) 1318–34; Saunders, C., (2012) 'The Truth, The Half-Truth, and Nothing Like the Truth. Reconceptualising False Allegations of Rape' (2012) 52(6) *Br J Criminol*, 1152–71.

(5) Adult complaints of assault by a known adult

Assaults committed in a public context may also generate technical evidence as **8.44** above and the same considerations as in para 8.43 apply. Blood alcohol evidence may also feature.

Other issues are as follows: **8.45**

(a) *Unused material and unexplored avenues of enquiry* Advocates should examine the unused material schedule for discarded forensic evidence or potential witnesses who may have seen the defendant with the complainant at or near the relevant time. Were potential witnesses spoken to? Was a statement taken? The defence team should investigate any unexplored avenue of enquiry.

(b) *Recent complaint evidence* Assaults committed in private may present no other evidence apart from the complainant's word and recent complaint evidence. If the complainant reports in interview that he or she did tell 'X' about it, but there is no evidence to support this, further disclosure requests should be considered. The reality may be that he or she did not 'complain', or that what he or she reported was materially inconsistent with the complaint to the police. Either scenario may adversely affect credibility. Alternatively, the omission may be an investigative oversight. Proceeding with caution is advised.

(c) *The integrity of the ABE[66] video and statement taking process* Video transcripts and copy statements should always be checked against both the original and pre-interview notes. Material inconsistencies between documents, (e.g. the original crime report) including internal inconsistencies within the ABE interview, will need to be identified and evaluated. Compliance with the guidelines should be checked. If the witness is vulnerable or suggestible, breaches of the guidance may affect the reliability of the overall account. Consideration should also be given to the impact of any confirmation bias.[67] Records of any conversations that took place prior to the assault should always be sought.

(d) *Identifying the 'trigger' for the complaint and events leading to the official complaint* This is a critical part of preparation. Tracking what was said, and when and to whom it was said, may reveal evidence of possible memory contamination, collusion, or memory 'distrust',[68] particularly in cases of delayed complaints. Did any other person make a complaint at or around the same time? Did the witnesses speak to each other? Are the allegations similar?

---

[66] MOJ, *Achieving Best Evidence* cited at n.28.
[67] Kassin, S.M., Dror, I.E., and Kukucka, J. (2013) 'The forensic confirmation bias: Problems, perspectives, and proposed solutions' *Journal of Applied Research in Memory and Cognition*, 2/2013, 42–52, *http://cognitiveconsultantsinternational.com/Dror_JARMAC_forensic_bias.pdf*.
[68] See Chapter 1.

(e) *Identifying any prior history of false complaints* See Chapters 3 and 5.

(f) *Investigating any relevant prior sexual history evidence* See Chapters 3 and 5.

(g) *Investigating any prior and post friendship/contact, (dependent on instructions) between the parties or references by the complainant about the defendant, to third parties* This covers electronic media, Facebook, Twitter etc. to investigate any comments suggestive of consensual contact, that nothing at all happened, or any other different account.

(h) *Identifying any relevant mental health or disability issues* Investigate whether the complainant suffers from any cognitive or mental health issues. These may affect testimonial reliability and/or questioning technique. Was/ is the adult taking any medication, alcohol, or illicit drugs that may impair memory, perception, or the reliability of the account given to the police? Full disclosure of any pre-existing medical conditions that may impact on witness testimony should be sought. A statement from the treating medical professional/therapist, detailing professional qualifications, treatment methodology, and any records of treatment sessions, should be requested.

(i) *Complaints of assault by professionals* Advocates must identify precise professional records, recording equipment or other oral testimony that may assist the defence when making disclosure requests.[69] Knowing what information is or may be relevant within professional records is crucial.

(6) Complaints by children against non-professionals

8.46 The alleged perpetrator may be father, brother, mother, friend or other relative. Paragraphs 8.42 to 8.45 apply.

8.47 An understanding of family law is helpful if there has been an investigation into the same complaint by the family court.[70] The family court usually gathers considerable contextual data and often receives expert opinion(s) to assist evaluate the complaint.[71] Spencer refers to the criminal court having a 'snapshot' approach by comparison; he comments that the criminal courts might assist fact-finders better if some of the methods in the civil courts were adopted.[72]

8.48 Even if the child has not been the subject of care or custody proceedings, ongoing divorce proceedings, proximate to the complaint, may yield relevant information within pleadings or reports. Full instructions should be taken on family history

---

[69] See Chapters 3 and 9.

[70] See Chapters 10 and 16. Also consider the new disclosure protocol: Crown Prosecution Service, President of the Family Division and Senior Presiding Judge for England and Wales (2013) *2013 Protocol and Good Practice Model—Disclosure of information in cases of alleged child abuse and linked criminal and care directions hearings*, October 2013, http://www.cps.gov.uk/publications/docs/third_party_protocol_2013.pdf.

[71] A good example is *A London Borough Council v K* [2009] EWHC 850 (Fam).

[72] Spencer and Lamb cited at n.11, 198.

and relationships between individuals including the complainant and the defendant, both prior to and post the complaint.

The ABE interview[73] A good working knowledge and understanding of the ABE **8.49**
guidance is fundamental. Transcript accuracy and ABE compliance should be
verified. The significance of this preparation is not always fully understood by
advocates. If material breaches have occurred, then a potential legal argument on
admissibility may lie.[74] The course of future action will depend upon the nature
and extent of the breaches as well as the individual characteristics of the child. If
material breaches are discovered, then an expert report should be considered. If in
doubt whether an expert is required, approach an expert for a preliminary view.
Legal argument on the admissibility may be required.

The importance of context The reader is referred to Chapter 1 para 1.26. **8.50**
Consideration of contextual issues will inform advocates on appropriate disclosure
requests and focus on specific areas for client instructions.

(7) Complaints by children against professionals

Preparation will involve synthesizing documentary disclosure for the profession **8.51**
concerned, for instance teacher, dentist, doctor, carer, scout leader etc. with the
points made in paras 8.42 to 8.45. The reader is also referred to Chapter 9, where
complaints involve medical professionals.

(8) Gang grooming, child exploitation, and trafficking cases

The criminal justice system has been slow to recognize and prosecute these cases. **8.52**
Professional training is now underway. The prevalence of such cases, including
international child trafficking, is growing. The Rotherham Report revealed serious
failings in the criminal justice treatment towards victims of sexual exploitation
and gang grooming. Obtaining and evaluating witness testimony from these complainants is challenging for investigators and fact-finders.[75]

Case experience and research informs us that: **8.53**

(i) honest witnesses are not necessarily unimpeachable;
(ii) children and young people may refuse to acknowledge abuse, out of guilt or
shame; and
(iii) lies may be told in order to shield others, from fear of intimidation or
retaliation.

---

[73] MOJ (2011) *Achieving Best Evidence*, cited at n.28.
[74] See (2015) *Archbold Criminal Pleading, Evidence and Practice*, London: Sweet & Maxwell,
para 8-91.
[75] Jay, A. (2014) *Independent Inquiry into Child Sexual Exploitation in Rotherham 1997–2013*
(Alexis Jay OBE) 21 August 2014.

Defence advocates should take care when considering material that reveals inconsistencies. These may be more apparent than real. The CPS are aware of the difficulties in these cases and have instructed investigators to obtain as much corroborative evidence as possible.

(9) Historic or non-recent sexual complaints

8.54 The prevalence of historic or delayed complaints of sexual abuse has increased in recent years. There is no legal definition of what constitutes a 'historic' complaint. The hallmark of 'historic' or delayed complaints is that there is little or no surviving evidence to either support or counter the complainant's word. The complainant is often an adult drawing on long-term memory recall. Many years and sometimes decades may have elapsed between the alleged incident and the official complaint. The difficulties posed by long-term memory recall are addressed in Chapters 1, 21, 22, and 23. Alternatively, the delayed complaint of childhood abuse may come from a young person. (See Chapter 16.)

8.55 These cases require a proactive defence. The difficulty of mounting an abuse of process argument founded on delay is addressed in Chapter 4. The defence is commonly a simple 'nothing happened'. The 'trigger' for the complaint, is an important starting point for preparation. Instructions will be more far-reaching than those for 'contemporary' cases. Creating a chronology of significant events, and a table showing the relative ages of all significant family members/witnesses/parties, at the time of the alleged abuse are of great assistance to advocates and the court.

F. Cross-examining the Adult Complainant

(1) Cross-examination—traditional approaches

8.56 Cross-examination is the apex of the advocate's task and the focus of current concerns. Cross-examination of the complainant is usually unavoidable.

8.57 Cross-examination is an extemporary exercise. The 'perfect' cross-examination does not exist. However, the quality and effectiveness of the questioning improves with advance preparation. Identifying the specific questions to be asked in especially sensitive areas of the evidence will ensure greater fairness and effectiveness. If the advocate is in doubt about the fairness of a question, he or she would be well advised to discuss it with the judge at the plea and case management hearing (PCMH) or GRH.

8.58 The golden rule of cross-examination is to control the witness by the use of leading questions.[76] However, this is not necessarily fair or consistent with an ethical model

---

[76] Morely, I. (2005) *The Devil's Advocate: A short polemic on how to be seriously good in court* London: Sweet & Maxwell (reprinted 2007) 154: 'Always ask leading questions. Always. Never ask an open question.'

of advocacy in sexual cases. Leading questions, suggesting the desired answer are the main source of criticism identified earlier in the chapter. They have scant probative value and do not 'test' the evidence; the objective of cross-examination. They generate inaccurate answers and can cause confusion. The advocate needs to be discriminating with this advocacy tool.

(2) 'Putting the defence case'

'Putting the defence case' is the practice of relaying the defence account to the complainant for their response. The practice of saying to the witness, 'I suggest to you that' or mounting a series of assertions is now deprecated.[77] Again, it is advisable to canvass the issue with the judge well before trial as to whether this is necessary. Relevant considerations will be the complainant's mental health and cognitive understanding. If the defence possess independent evidence capable of undermining a material part of the complainant's account, then fairness suggests, this should be 'tested' with the witness.

8.59

(3) A few practical pointers

The object of cross-examination is to elicit facts, not invite argument or bully etc. There may well be questions of fact essential to the defence case that need to be explored. Important areas for genuine examination may relate to events prior to or following the alleged incident. For instance, there may have been a disagreement that occurred after 'consensual intercourse', or other relevant behaviour.

8.60

(4) Cross-examining on the details of the alleged crime

Whether or not this has to be done will depend on the nature of the defence and whether the incident is accepted as having occurred at all. If the defence is 'consent', it will be necessary to explore the defence instructions with the complainant. Cases do occur where unreliable/false allegations are made because of extreme embarrassment after the event, possibly because of the nature of conduct agreed to.[78] These cases are difficult for all concerned, given the public setting. Again, a sensitive approach is advised, taking into account the personal characteristics of the witness.[79]

8.61

---

[77] *R v Farooqi* [2013] EWCA Crim 1649.

[78] See the case of *R v Dodd*, described in Spears, N. (2012) 'Woman who falsely claimed she was raped by three men because she regretted having sex with them jailed for two years.' *Daily Mail*, 17 September 2012, *http://www.dailymail.co.uk/news/article-2204712*.

[79] Vulnerable witnesses may falsely present as having legal 'capacity' to make correct choices on special measures, where this is not the case. See Brown, H. (2014) *The death of Mrs A.: A Serious Case Review*, Report by Professor Hilary Brown for Surrey County Council: Safeguarding Adults Board, April 2014 (Mrs Andrade chose to conceal her mental health history from the court and to give evidence in open court, with tragic consequences.)

8.62 Where intimate details do need to be explored, advocates should consider, with the judge and witness, whether the public be excluded for that part of the questioning.[80] The judge should be forewarned of this issue at the PCMH or GRH.

(5) Professional duties and advocate manner

8.63 Advocates must be conscious of their professional code of conduct at all times and conduct their case in a way that minimizes witness distress.

8.64 The advocate should remain calm, not argue with the complainant, and be reasonable with the court. If the advocate adheres to these simple rules, the jury will be more willing to listen and engage with the defence case.

G. Cross-examining Children and Vulnerable Witnesses

8.65 There is now extensive guidance on how children should be questioned. Readers are advised to proceed with care and sensitivity at all times. Advocates need to consider the relevance of background 'contextual' issues. (See also Chapters 1 and 16.) Questioning the child on the detail of the alleged sexual assault will rarely be required.[81]

H. Conclusion

8.66 Increased understanding about the impact of inappropriate advocacy methods has underlined the necessity for ethical advocacy.

8.67 Early defence preparation, and consideration of the individual characteristics of complainants, coupled with sensitive judicial case management, will facilitate effective advocacy.

8.68 The traditional practice of asserting to witnesses that they are 'lying' or 'fantasizing' should be avoided completely with child and vulnerable witnesses, and should generally be curbed. It is an ineffective forensic device for evaluating unreliability.

---

[80] YJCEA 1999, s 25.
[81] As to correct approach for children, see *R v Barker* [2010] EWCA Crim 4; *R v W and M* [2010] EWCA Crim 1926; *R v Wills* [2011] EWCA Crim 1938; *R v E* [2012] EWCA Crim 563; and 'Toolkits', cited at para 8.17 and n.36. For the most recent Court of Appeal approach to questioning children and vulnerable witnesses see *R v Cokesix Lubemba, R v JP* [2014] EWCA Crim 2064, *R v Sandor Jonas* [2015] EWCA Crim 562 and *R v FA* [2015] EWCA Crim 209.

Commonality of advocate training will ensure consistency of good quality **8.69**
advocacy.

There is scope for empirical research on advocacy standards in sexual cases. **8.70**

Further Reading

Kapardis, A. (2014) *Psychology and Law: A Critical Introduction* (4th edn) New York: Cambridge University Press.

9

SEXUAL ALLEGATIONS AGAINST MEDICAL PROFESSIONALS

*Brendan Finucane QC, Fiona Horlick, and James Leonard**

A. Introduction and Overview

Sexual allegations against medical professionals fall into three broad **9.01** categories—allegations made by patients, allegations made by professional colleagues or others in the working environment, and lastly those made by persons unconnected to the professional's working life. The investigative methodology and trial process will vary depending on the category of complaint. The relationship between medical professionals and their patients is unique. Medical professionals are in a position of trust with regard to their patients. Those patients might be vulnerable and frightened as well as being physically or mentally ill. They may be unsure whether a procedure or examination is medically justified or not.

---

* Any unsubstantiated opinions contained within this chapter represent the authors' own views based upon their extensive professional experience.

Occasionally, patients develop relationships, real or imagined, with those who treat them. The range of factual matrices can be challenging for those investigating allegations and for the trial process. In respect of the second category, namely professional complaints, investigators should acquire a sound knowledge of the working environment in question. This knowledge will inform the investigation, including lines of enquiry, disclosure requests, and their deployment within the trial process. The third broad category requires no particular specialist knowledge as the medical professional will be investigated as a private person.

9.02 No practicing medical professional is immune from prosecution of sexual offences and the context of each professional environment gives rise to differing problems relating to an understanding of the case and to disclosure. Within the medical profession there will sometimes be wide variations. The working practice of doctors or nurses practising in hospitals will differ significantly from doctors and nurses who are in private practice, and will be different again from those working in general practitioner's (GP's) practices. Although each profession may have some commonality of documents, each specialty, for instance, paediatrics or gerontology, will have its own unique record system. In addition, despite overarching guidance issued by professional regulators, for instance the General Medical Council (GMC), working and record-keeping practices may vary widely between different health authorities.

9.03 Allegations against medical professionals involving both patients and workplace colleagues are also frequently 'hydra-headed', spawning multiple concurrent litigation, for instance, criminal, regulatory, civil, employment, and internal disciplinary proceedings, and more recently, the Disclosure and Barring Service. Each of these proceedings will generate official records of potential relevance to the criminal investigation. Disclosure protocols will vary between each proceeding, as will the lawyers for each side. Additionally, there may be a prior history of sexual allegations against the professional (that may assist the police or the accused professional), requiring further investigation. Accordingly, when it comes to criminal cases there may well be a raft of other material that needs to be considered.

B. Investigations

(1) Allegations about conduct while at work

9.04 Allegations involving medical professionals in their working environment— patients and colleagues—come both directly and indirectly to the attention of the police. The workplace for medical professionals will have mandatory complaints procedures. A sexual complaint against a medical professional to someone within the working environment will be investigated. The quality and extent of that investigation will vary enormously. For example, a complaint made to the practice manager of a small GP surgery may be communicated immediately to the very person against whom the allegation has been made allowing that medial professional ample time to prepare himself before the police become involved. On the other hand, a hospital NHS Trust may have a sophisticated system in which a complaint is rapidly escalated to the police. Indeed, the guidance for all Trust investigations, 'Maintaining High Professional Standards in the Modern NHS', instructs Trusts to report all potential criminal cases to the police provided they have the agreement of the complainant.[1]

(2) Internal investigations

There may well be situations where an internal investigation takes place. There are **9.05** obvious implications both for evidence-gathering and for the potential contamination of witness testimony. Internal investigators are rarely trained to the level typical for specialist police investigators. Internal investigators are unlikely to have any familiarity with the criminal rules of evidence; they are likely to ask leading questions, put other accounts to the witness or keep no or inadequate records or notes. Police investigators and those involved later in the criminal process should be alert to these deficiencies.

(3) Investigation by regulators

It is difficult to conceive of individuals who hold themselves out as medical pro- **9.06** fessionals not now being regulated by one of the statutory bodies. All relevant professions have a regime of accreditation, registration, and regulation by their professional regulator.[2] This enables each profession to control who enters the profession and once they are part of that profession, the manner in which they practice. The ultimate sanction is the removal of an individual professional's 'licence' to practice, either temporarily or permanently. The police must report any arrest, charge, or caution of a professional to their appropriate regulator. Many professionals are also obliged to self-report and failure to do so may well constitute misconduct. A complaint of sexual misconduct may also be, and indeed often is, made direct to the regulator. Once the regulator is informed, by whatever route, of a sexual allegation, the regulator's mechanism of control will come into action. For the mature regulatory regimes, such as the GMC, the likely first response will be an immediate referral to an 'interim orders' hearing before a panel or committee. The purpose of an interim orders hearing is to decide whether it is necessary to restrict or even suspend the professional's ability to practice whilst a fuller investigation of the sexual allegation is conducted by the regulator. Thereafter, the regulator will

---

[1] *http://www.dhsspsni.gov.uk/hrd_suspensions_framework.pdf.*
[2] *http://www.gmc-uk.org/doctors/index.asp; http://www.gmc-uk.org/concerns/index.asp; http://www. gdc-uk.org/Dentalprofessionals/Pages/default.aspx; http://www.gdc-uk.org/Aboutus/Whoweregulate/ Pages/default.aspx; http://www.nmc-uk.org/Nurses-and-midwives/; http://www.pharmacyregulation. org/; http://www.optical.org/en/Registration/index.cfm; http://www.osteopathy.org.uk/; http://www. hcpc-uk.org.uk/aboutregistration/regulators/healthandcare/.*

investigate the allegation, which can take a considerable amount of time. If the police are conducting an investigation, this will 'stop the clock' with regard to the regulator's own investigation (aside from an interim order) and the regulator will usually await the outcome of any police investigation or subsequent trial. However, the regulator may still be in possession of potentially disclosable material.

(4) Police investigations

9.07 Records, working environment, medical knowledge, guidance issued by the professional regulators and the professions themselves are just some of the factors which will be of essential importance at all stages of the trial process and this applies equally to the police investigation. Information can be both lost and misunderstood at this critical stage and the authors suggest that police investigators seek specialist assistance at an early stage from a prosecutor with the requisite knowledge, and if necessary, from an expert. For example, a patient may believe she has been sexually assaulted during an examination but an expert would say that the examination was a legitimate and clinically indicated examination properly performed. Conversely, some aspect of the complaint might appear to the unknowledgeable to be normal but would ring alarm bells to anyone with knowledge of medical practice. The factors referred to above will be explored in more detail in this chapter.

C. Working Environments

9.08 The opportunity to perpetrate a sexual offence on a patient or work colleague or the likelihood of an allegation of such being correct is dictated by the working environment. Although it may be a matter of common sense that sexual impropriety is, for example, more likely if a male doctor sees a female patient alone in her home than in a curtained-off cubicle in a busy A&E department, knowledge of how each working environment functions is essential to a proper understanding of a potential case. Factors such as the physical layout, procedures and policies, record keeping, and the presence or absence of other people such as other staff and patients all vary according to the type of environment. There are then further variations within each category. Typical environments are: hospitals; GP surgeries; dentists' surgeries; clinics run by other health professionals; out-of-hours services; and home visits. Private practice is another area and one in which rules and regulations may be very much less rigorous.

D. Records

(1) The requirement for accurate record keeping

9.09 In cases involving medical professionals and patients there are almost invariably going to be patient records which may well be of huge significance to the criminal investigation and any subsequent trial. Medical professionals are obliged to keep contemporaneous and accurate patient records. For example, the GMC issues guidance on record keeping; this is available on the GMC website.[3] Although records made by medical professionals vary enormously in quality, all would and should know of the obligation to keep records. Aside from clinical records made by medical professionals, there will many other types of records. Records are explored in more detail below and in the case studies.

(2) GP records

For those unfamiliar with GP patient records, it is worth explaining something of their history and application. Prior to computerization, patient records were hand-written. For GPs the change came circa 2000. The old handwritten records were on cards and referred to as 'Lloyd George' cards. For any patient who saw a GP prior to the changeover, the cards should still exist albeit with scant entries and unreadable writing. GP computer systems have evolved and there are rival systems. Sometimes GP practices migrate from one system to another and information is lost in the process. Modern systems are often very sophisticated with each patient record having multiple 'layers' that further sift and sort the information. Various health professionals, not only the GP, will make entries on these records. These records may also contain scans of hospital records or downloads of clinical tests such as blood tests. The purpose of the 'layers' is to limit the information immediately confronting a GP, so that when the file is initially inspected, critical information such as allergic reactions, or long-term serious medical problems, together with the most recent consultations, present first. The entire clinical history is, of course, available to the clinician upon further inspection. However, it must be realized that paper printout of the records will usually not show all the information on the system nor will it give any real idea of what a health professional will actually see on the screen when the patient records are opened on the computer. An optical copy of the records will be necessary. **9.10**

Computer records can also be reviewed to show audit trails. The audit trail can show when information was entered, whether it has been subsequently altered or deleted either innocently or not, and the 'login' details of the individual who made every entry, deleted information, and/or altered what is recorded. This can be important where, for example, a GP tries to justify an examination that a patient says was a sexual assault by later adding to the clinical record. Furthermore, GP surgery computers will show when a patient was booking in for an appointment, when the patient arrived, and how long the consultation lasted. This might be important to show that where a patient is alleging that the doctor kept her in his surgery for forty-five minutes and sexually assaulted her, she was actually only in there for seven minutes. **9.11**

---

[3] *http://www.gmc-uk.org/guidance/ethical_guidance/13427.asp.*

(3) Hospital records

9.12 Hospital records can be extensive and with contributions from a wide variety of personnel. For example, if a patient arrives at the Accident & Emergency Department (A&E), they will first be seen by reception and then by a triage nurse, both of whom will make separate records. After this, an A&E doctor will conduct an examination and input more notes onto the records. The patient may then be admitted and once on the ward will be seen by a variety of personnel—doctors, nurses, healthcare assistants, physiotherapists and so on. All will or should make notes. Then there will be operation notes, theatre notes, and anaesthesia records. All, some, or none of these records might be of importance depending on the allegation.

(4) Clinical content

9.13 Assuming a record is contemporaneous, its content may be highly significant both for what it does contain and for the absence of some material element. Again, this will be fact-specific. For example, a patient may allege that she consulted a doctor for a vaginal discharge and that he sexually assaulted her during the examination. If the record shows no complaint of vaginal discharge and that in fact, the complaint was of a swollen elbow, then the police, the prosecution, and the defence will all go on to assess the complainant's credibility in the light of the content of the record.

E. Disclosure of Records

(1) Disclosure prior to police interview

9.14 Police officers frequently conduct interviews with medical professionals without either obtaining or disclosing the patient notes. It is often not taken into account that medical professionals will examine thousands of patients over the course of their career; a GP will see hundreds of thousands. No medical professional can be expected to remember each patient or each patient encounter and will need sight of the patient records to either answer questions or make a prepared statement, or make an informed decision whether to remain silent in interview. It is often thought imperative that a medical professional be given the chance to consider the records that exist in relation to a particular patient before making any comment in a police interview. It may be easier for a potential defendant to prepare a written statement whilst making 'no comment' to all other questions if he or she has had sight of the notes. Some solicitors experienced in advising the medical professions in interview whilst at the police station will insist on access to the records before any interview is conducted. However, if on examination, the records are inadequate or in some way do not support the potential defendant's instructions, there is a chance that insisting on advance disclosure may exacerbate rather than advance the defendant's predicament. Much will depend on what the individual interviewee knows or recalls (without having seen the records) about the complainant. If he or she has no recollection of the individual concerned at all, it is difficult to proceed without first seeing the records that are available.

(2) Disclosure prior to trial

It is absolutely essential to both the prosecution and the defence that full records **9.15** are obtained well before trial. The prosecution will need to do this in order to make a proper assessment of whether the criteria are satisfied for charging and then later to discharge their disclosure obligations. The defence will need disclosure in order to mount a proper defence and potentially to instruct an expert. It is a matter of immense frustration that the Crown (both the CPS and police) often appear to be ignorant or obstructive in obtaining such important information. There are concerns from both sides that such failures lead to trials being adjourned despite numerous disclosure requests with the obvious knock-on effects of delay, expense, and the emotional toll on witnesses and the defendant and there is always the spectre of miscarriages of justice.

F. Experts

(1) Prior to charge

In some cases of alleged sexual impropriety, the medical professional may be **9.16** suggesting that his or her conduct has arisen out of a clinically indicated and properly executed (but misunderstood) medical examination. If that is the case, it is good practice to seek an expert opinion on the potential defendant's instructions as soon as possible, ideally (although rarely in practice) before he is actually interviewed or at least before he chooses whether to answer any questions. The clinical credibility of the client's account may not be obvious to the legal advisor at the police station. If the records are not provided by way of disclosure in advance, that may justify an interviewee making 'no comment'. The course of the police interview will then tend to reveal the nature of the allegation being made. At the end of the first interview, police will almost invariably bail the accused professional until a second interview. If the first interview has revealed the nature of the complaint and also (whether privately in instructions or as a result of questions being answered) the interviewee's account of what has occurred, it is highly advisable to obtain an expert's report on the issues thus far revealed before returning for a second interview. This applies equally to the police as it does to defence solicitors. From the prosecution point of view such a report combined with the advice of specialist counsel may lead to the complainant being asked further questions either by way of another Achieving Best Evidence or a further statement.

(2) At trial

9.17   Experts are a common feature of professional conduct hearings for professionals and should normally be retained and instructed long before the trial process
is embarked upon. It is surprising that the prosecution instructs experts in cases
infrequently even where a need for them may seem obvious. There is perhaps a tendency in cases involving GPs to think that because every member of the jury will
have been to the GP it is not necessary to seek expert opinion. Such a path can and
does lead to the prosecution falling apart at the seams at trial. Prosecutors should
always approach a prosecution on the basis that they need to give a jury confidence
that the assault complained of is outside the ambit of any clinically indicated or
executed examination. Because a doctor or dentist necessarily comes into contact
with a patient physically when performing a perfectly proper examination, it may
well be important to establish that the physical contact complained of is anything
but proper. Likewise, as already detailed in para 9.16, it is essential that a medical
professional's instructions are tested and evaluated by reference to an experienced
expert before being offered up for cross-examination.

G. Disclosure

9.18   Aside from the subject of records as set out in Section D, there may be other areas
of disclosure in cases involving medical professionals. As discussed in para 9.05,
there may be internal investigations before a complaint reaches the police and
the obtaining and potential disclosure of that material will need to be sought.
Furthermore, the order in which the criminal and disciplinary (that is action taken
by a professional regulator) aspects of the same case occur is not clear-cut and so
reliance cannot be placed upon complete disclosure having taken place in one or
the other. Disciplinary cases may lead to criminal cases and vice versa. Criminal
prosecutions are governed by the Criminal Procedure and Investigations Act 1996
(CPIA), the Attorney General's *Guidelines on Disclosure*[4] and in addition, from
3 December 2013, the *Judicial Protocol on the Disclosure of Unused Material in
Criminal Cases* under CPD Disclosure 22A[5] according to which all applications
for disclosure must be dealt with by virtue of section 8 of the CPIA. The protocol
reminds courts and the parties that complainants do not waive their right to confidentiality, nor their right to respect for private and family life under Article 8 of
the European Convention on Human Rights,[6] by making a complaint against the
accused. However, problems arise in regulatory proceedings because of the varying

---

[4] *https://www.gov.uk/government/publications/attorney-generals-guidelines-on-disclosure-2013.*
[5] *http://www.judiciary.gov.uk/wp-content/uploads/JCO/Documents/Protocols/Disclosure+
Protocol.pdf.*
[6] European Convention for the Protection of Human Rights and Fundamental Freedoms,
Council of Europe, Rome, 4 November 1950, Cm 8969.

attitudes of the different regulatory bodies. All of them would claim to have in place appropriate disclosure regimes, but when dealing with a professional charged in disciplinary proceedings, with what is in effect a criminal offence (and the prospect of it actually becoming so), they often dispute the relevance of the Attorney General's *Guidelines*, claiming that the matter that is being dealt with by them is a civil matter. Not surprisingly, some of their staff are wholly unfamiliar with the provisions of the Attorney General's *Guidelines*, or the general principles behind them, and appear to have little or no training in relation to disclosure generally, even in civil proceedings. There is, for instance, no published document setting out the disclosure regime of the GMC and in *R (Johnson) v Professional Conduct Committee of the Nursing and Midwifery Council*[7] the Court held that there was no free-standing duty on those bringing disciplinary proceedings to gather evidence in favour of registrants as well as evidence against them (distinguishing *Jespers v Belgium*[8]). Fortunately, the prosecution of disciplinary and regulatory cases is often undertaken by counsel or higher court advocates who do have knowledge of disclosure and are able to assess material appropriately for disclosure. However, this is not always the case and they may not be provided with all the relevant material to review—the only real safeguard is constant vigilance.

H. Professional Guidance

Those involved in investigating, prosecuting, and defending medical profession-als should be aware of the plethora of guidance issued by the professional regula-tors and by the individual bodies of expertise of each aspect of the professions. For example, the GMC issues its own guidance as will each Royal College cover-ing each speciality within the medical profession. The GMC guidance is readily available on the GMC website.[9] The overarching guidance for doctors is called *Good Medical Practice*.[10] This and all other guidance is periodically updated and where the complaint is historic it will be necessary to judge the complaint and the alleged conduct by the guidance which existed at the time. Further, whereas it would be almost inconceivable for a doctor to conduct an 'intimate examina-tion' of a patient's breasts or genital area without a chaperone in this day and age, it would have been commonplace a few years ago. Medical professionals are expected to be aware of guidance applicable to their field and have an obligation to keep their knowledge up to date. Adherence or lack of adherence to guidance and to the norms of behaviour within the profession may be an important evi-dential factor. **9.19**

---

[7] (2008) EWHC 885 (Admin).
[8] (1981) 27 DR 61.
[9] *http://www.gmc-uk.org/guidance/ethical_guidance.asp.*
[10] *http://www.gmc-uk.org/Good_medical_practice___English_0914.pdf_51527435.pdf.*

I. Case Studies Regarding GPs

(1) Dr C

9.20 In 2003 complaints were made regarding inappropriate examinations by Dr C of the genitalia of pre-pubescent girls during consultations at his surgery. The police investigated in 2003/4 but took no further action. However, the GMC brought disciplinary proceedings against him in respect of the allegations which were found proved and he was erased from the Register. The GMC proceedings received very considerable publicity including on television in that part of England. Following the conclusion of the GMC proceedings other girls came forward making similar claims and eventually Dr C was arrested for the second time. Upon his arrest his computer was seized and was found to contain indecent material and records of thousands of visits to pre-teen pornography sites. There was further publicity upon the second arrest. Some of the complainants, both at the time of the GMC hearing and subsequently, had commenced civil proceedings against Dr C. Some were members of families where there had been social services intervention, as a consequence of sexual abuse by other members of the family, and had received therapy and counselling, where there had been either no mention of any allegation against Dr C, or such allegations against Dr C had emerged as a result of the discovery of the other abuse. Others had received therapy in relation to what they alleged had occurred with Dr C. Yet further girls had made allegations against Dr C to various agencies, including the GMC, but refused, or their parents would not permit them, to make statements in the criminal proceedings. The prosecution instructed a leading expert in respect of the medical aspects of the allegations. It will be apparent that there were a considerable number of aspects of disclosure to be considered: the medical records for all the complainants; school records; social service files; psychotherapy and counselling files; all the papers in the GMC proceedings; the various civil proceeding documents, including the expert psychiatric and other reports prepared both for the complainants and on behalf of Dr C in relation to their claims for damages; and finally, the case file in the original police investigation in 2003/4 when no action had been taken. The disclosure also had a bearing on the medical justification and appropriateness of the examinations.

(2) Dr L

9.21 Apart from his work as a GP, Dr L also examined applicants for positions in the ambulance, fire, and police services, in relation to both driving and other duties involving heavy lifting. Between 1999 and 2014 he carried out some 10,000 such examinations. The DVLA requirements necessitated intimate physical examinations for both men and women. In 2002/3 a number of women in one cohort of applicants for the ambulance service who were in dispute with the ambulance service had complained about the necessity for such examinations and the appropriateness of how they were carried out by Dr L. The GMC investigated and concluded that the examinations were necessary and appropriately carried out, although there should have been better communication of the purpose and nature of the examination. As a result of the Jimmy Savile investigation in 2013, a number of other women, some from the same cohort of applicants for the ambulance service as the original complainants, and a couple of others who had been applicants for the fire service came forward and complained about the appropriateness of the manner in which the examinations had been carried out. Dr L was duly arrested, with accompanying publicity, and later charged and committed for trial. During the process the police wrote to all 5,000 or so of the patients in Dr L's practice asking them to come forward if he had behaved inappropriately towards them. None did, but the defence were aware of the fact that some patients had responded to the letter sent by the police in terms that were very supportive as to the manner in which Dr L had carried intimate examinations of them. The police were reluctant to disclose these. There were further ongoing difficulties about disclosure of all the relevant clinical records. Further, the Crown refused to call or tender the chaperones who were present at every single examination of the patients and who were thus primary witnesses of the allegedly abusive examinations.

(3) Dr M

Dr M was accused of sexually assaulting a young female patient on a number of **9.22** occasions over an eighteen-month period which encompassed her pregnancy and subsequent appointments with her baby. She disclosed the allegations to the police. During the police investigations, the officer in the case asked the GMC if they had any relevant informationon the doctor. The GMC disclosed to the police that there had been a number of complaints made over the years which they had investigated. In all but one case they had either taken no action or written a letter of advice to Dr M. However, one complaint dating ten years previously was that made by a receptionist in an out-of-hours GP clinic where Dr M did some extra work in the evenings. The receptionist first complained to her employer that Dr M had sexually assaulted her on a number of occasions. The employer investigated by first taking a brief statement from the receptionist and interviewing Dr M and later reported him to the GMC. No report was ever made to the police. The GMC investigated, took statements, and then had a full hearing at which the allegations were found not proved. The officer in the case in the index trial tracked down the receptionist who was willing to support a criminal allegation. Dr M was charged with these allegations as well and they were joined to that of the patient. Disclosure relating to the original case relating to the receptionist became of significance and the loss of material led to the abuse of process argument at trial. In particular, the recording of the evidence that the receptionist gave at the original GMC hearing along with that of other material witnesses including Dr M (whose recollection of events had been eroded since then by the passage of time) had been destroyed and there was no transcript in existence.

(4) Dr B

9.23 A patient made an allegation both to the GMC and to the police that Dr B had sexually abused her on frequent occasions over a fourteen-year period. The terms in which she made the complaint to the GMC were materially different to that made to the police. The prosecution obtained very limited patient records relating to the patient. Dr B's recollection was that the patient had a significant psychiatric history and therefore the defence made vigorous attempts to get the patient's full medical notes from birth (she was in her late 50s at the time of the complaint). Further disclosure did reveal references to psychiatric difficulties and shortly before trial her psychiatric notes were obtained. These revealed multiple difficulties and allegations of rape dating from when she was a young girl. The defence instructed a consultant psychiatrist who examined the notes and eventually conducted an interview with the complainant. The psychiatrist's opinion was that the complainant suffered from a borderline personality disorder materially affecting the reliability of her evidence. Analysis of the full GP notes demonstrated that consultations for specific complaints at which the complainant said that various sexual assaults took place had not taken place at all.

J. Conclusion

9.24 Investigating, prosecuting, and defending sexual allegations against medical professionals requires specialist knowledge and expertise. The interests of potential and future victims, medical professionals, and the public demand that such cases are rigorously investigated and only pursued to trial on the basis of an informed expert decision. It is essential that specialist lawyers and experts be involved from an early stage.

Author Biographies

Brendan Finucane QC has extensive advocacy experience in serious crime and professional and disciplinary regulatory work. He has appeared in high-profile, sensitive, and complex cases before the General Medical Council and General Dental Council, the Crown Court and Coroner's Courts representing health-care professionals. He has advised the Medical Protection Society in relation to the redrafting of the GMC rules, and the British Osteopathic Association. He has appeared frequently appeared in the Court of Appeal. He regularly lectures to solicitors and in-house lawyers.

Fiona Horlick is praised by the directories for her unrivalled advocacy skills and her 'unbending will to succeed' as well as for her charisma and her ability to handle clients with sensitivity. Her practice encompasses international business crime, professional discipline and regulation, medical crime and health and safety regulatory crime. She has extensive experience as an advocate before juries, tribunals, and in appellate courts including the Court of Appeal and the Privy Council, and at inquests. Fiona is co-editor and contributing author to the prestigious LexisNexis publication *Lissack and Horlick on Bribery* the second edition of which was published in October 2014.

James Leonard is a Professional Discipline specialist. In the General Medical Council he represents clients up to consultant level in relation to performance, health, and conduct issues with a particular emphasis on conduct which includes misconduct relating to dishonesty, fraud, and suspected sexual impropriety. He has represented senior members of the dental profession in the General Dental Council. He has a background in serious crime (and is a veteran of innumerable cases of murder, manslaughter, sexual offences, and investment/tax fraud). When dealing with conduct allegations against professionals which involve criminal behaviour, he appears in the Crown Court.

In 2014, he was awarded the accolade of Chambers and Partners Professional Discipline Junior of the Year.

10

SEXUAL ALLEGATIONS AND EVIDENCE GATHERING IN THE FAMILY COURT

Alex Verdan QC, Sam King, Cleo Perry, and Rebecca Foulkes

A. Introduction

This chapter will provide a summary of how allegations of child sexual abuse are **10.01**
handled within the family courts. It will look at the procedure adopted in litigating
such allegations and the types of evidence upon which judges must routinely rely.
This chapter will also highlight the tensions and differences that exist between the
litigation of these allegations within the family and criminal courts.

Allegations of child sexual abuse are litigated within two types of family pro- **10.02**
ceedings: *private law proceedings*, where (most usually) separated parents or
(occasionally) family members are in dispute about the arrangements for the
care of a child, or *public law proceedings*, where a local authority has initiated
proceedings against a parent or other family member who is caring for reasons
of child protection.

When an allegation of child sexual abuse is made within family proceedings, the **10.03**
court will determine at an early stage whether that allegation needs to be proved.

This decision is within the court's discretion but only rarely would a court decline to hold a fact-finding hearing in respect of an allegation of child sexual abuse. The obvious exception is where the allegation has already been the subject of a conviction following a criminal trial. In contrast, an acquittal does not preclude the allegation being litigated again within the family court because the family court operates on a lower standard of proof.

10.04 Fact finding is a discrete hearing held to enable the court to determine the allegation that has been made. The focus of the hearing is on the factual aspects surrounding the allegation and not what orders will best serve the long-term interests of the child, which will come later. The purpose of such a hearing is to provide a factual matrix upon which any expert instructed in the proceedings can make recommendations and the court can make a decision as to what arrangements will be in the child's best interests.

10.05 An allegation of child sexual abuse could be made against a parent, who is automatically a party to the proceedings, or against another family member or the new partner of a parent. Generally, such a person will not automatically be a party to the proceedings but, at the point that the court decides whether to undertake fact-finding, it will also decide whether the alleged perpetrator should be permitted to intervene in the proceedings, so that he or she can participate within the fact-finding hearing and be legally represented if he or she so chooses. Because of the strict rules in respect of legal aid funding provision and the costs of litigation, many litigants have to represent themselves.

10.06 In private law proceedings the burden of proving the allegation of child sexual abuse lies on the party who is making or relying upon the allegation. In public law proceedings the burden will usually lie on the applicant local authority, which has to satisfy the court that the threshold to justify public law orders has been passed by establishing that the child is suffering, or is likely to suffer, significant harm.[1] To assist the court, the party on whom the burden lies is directed to produce a schedule[2] setting out succinctly the allegations which the court is being invited to determine. When the court ultimately gives judgment on the allegations, it will usually do so by reference to this schedule.

10.07 The standard of proof to be applied is the ordinary civil standard, namely the balance of probabilities. This issue was comprehensively considered by the House of Lords in *Re B (Care Proceedings: Standard of Proof)*[3] which laid to rest any suggestion that there is a heightened standard to be applied the more serious the allegation being litigated.

---

[1] Children Act 1989, s 31.
[2] Commonly called a *Scott* schedule.
[3] [2008] UKHL 35, [2009] AC 11.

B. The Written Evidence

(1) The record of the complaint

At the outset, the practitioner must seek to understand what allegations have been made, when, by whom, and to whom. All too often, allegations are reported in general terms within witness statements prepared specifically for the family proceedings and without the source material being made available. If a note has been taken of an allegation, it is vital that a copy of that note is obtained. If a child has made an allegation to a professional, there should be a written record. Where an allegation of child sexual abuse is made to a professional that person should have made a referral to the local authority in whose area the child lives detailing the allegation. The local authority's record of the referral must be sought as well as the referring professional's own note.

10.08

Confidentiality issues may arise where the allegations come from someone other than the subject child. An example of the difficulties which may occur as a consequence are well illustrated in *Re A (A Child) (Family Proceedings: Disclosure of Information)*.[4] Following a contact order, the subject child was having unsupervised overnight contact with her father. When the subject child was 8 years old the local authority contacted the mother informing her that serious allegations of sexual abuse had been made against the father. The complainant (X) wished to remain anonymous. The mother was advised that she should no longer permit unsupervised contact. The local authority sought to establish public interest immunity so that it would not be required to disclose the identity of X and the details of the allegations. X had an unusually complex presentation. She suffered from a range of physical symptoms for which there was no apparent cause and a range of psychological difficulties. The physical symptoms were therefore considered to be either due to, or at least substantially exacerbated by, her psychological difficulties. In the opinion of X's treating consultant psychiatrist, disclosure and a requirement for her to give live evidence would be detrimental to her physical and mental health.

10.09

The Supreme Court upheld the order for disclosure, finding that X's privacy rights were not a sufficient justification for the grave compromise of the fair trial and family life rights of the parties which non-disclosure would entail. The allegations had to be properly investigated and tested so that the subject child could either be protected from any risk of harm which her father may present to her or could resume her normal relationship with him; that could not be done without disclosing to the parents and to the children's guardian[5] the identity of X and the detail and history

10.10

---

[4] [2012] UKSC 60, [2013] 2 AC 66.
[5] A practitioner with social work experience appointed by the court to represent the subject child's interests within the proceedings independent of the other parties.

of the allegations which she had made. In the context of the instant case, whereby the State was acting in support of important public interests and X was currently under the supervision and specialist care of a consultant physician and psychiatrist who would do the utmost to mitigate any further suffering, it would not violate her rights under Article 3 of the European Convention on Human Rights to order disclosure to the parents and the children's guardian of X's identity and of the records of the substance of her sexual abuse allegations.

(2) The importance of 'contextual' evidence

10.11   It is important to understand the specifics of the allegation. What exactly does the child say has occurred? What amount of detail has he or she provided? The context of the allegation is equally important because it is by reference to that context that the court is able to evaluate the quality of the allegation. In considering the context, the practitioner needs to consider the following:

- The person to whom the child first made an allegation.
- How and in what context that allegation came to be made.
- How the allegations have evolved since then and the consistency of those allegations.
- Is there any evidence of coaching or rehearsal or any suggestion from the circumstances that there might have been?
- What is the degree of the child's own sexual knowledge?
- What was the child's emotional state at the time that each allegation was made?
- How did the person to whom the child made each allegation respond?
- Is there any other evidence that would corroborate the child's account?

10.12   Due to the absence of research into the issue, the prevalence of false allegations within family proceedings is unknown. However, practitioner reports and case law show that they do occur. Two striking examples are *Doncaster MBC v Haigh, Tune and X*[6] in which the mother invented allegations of sexual abuse and coached the subject child to make allegations against her father, and *A London Borough Council v K*[7] in which the mother came, through a process of distorted thinking, to believe wrongly that the children had been sexually abused by their father and set about proving it.

10.13   The retraction of an allegation normally requires careful and specific consideration.[8] The fact that an allegation is subsequently retracted does not prevent a judge from accepting that the allegation is in fact true. However, it does give rise to questions which must be addressed sufficiently fully and directly in the judge's reasons to demonstrate that the fact of the retraction has been given proper weight in the judge's

---

[6] [2012] 1 FLR 577.
[7] [2009] EWHC 850 (Fam).
[8] *Re W (Fact Finding: Hearsay Evidence)* [2013] EWCA Civ 1374.

conclusions. That advice is particularly pertinent where the only evidence before the court about the complaint is hearsay.

If the allegation has been referred to a local authority, then the local authority **10.14** may undertake an investigation to enable it to decide whether to take any further action to safeguard or promote the child's welfare, including issuing public law proceedings.[9] If the allegation has also been made to the police then this may be a joint or single agency investigation.

(3) Achieving Best Evidence interviews

If there is a police investigation of the allegation, then there may be an Achieving **10.15** Best Evidence (ABE) interview of the child. This is not always the case; if, for example, the age and understanding of the child concerned precludes it, it will not be undertaken. Where an ABE interview has taken place, it is common for the recording and transcript of that interview to be disclosed by the investigating police force into the family proceedings subject to the applicant providing a written undertaking to protect against its unauthorized use. This evidence is important because it may be the only opportunity for the judge to actually see the child discussing the allegations. To evaluate the weight of any allegation made within the ABE interview, the practitioner is advised to familiarize him or herself with the ABE guidelines.[10]

In family proceedings, breaches of the ABE guidelines will not automatically lead **10.16** to the ABE interview being excluded but a judge is likely to attach less weight to what has been alleged within it if there have been clear, demonstrable breaches.

(4) Allegations arising within therapeutic contexts

On occasion a child may make an allegation of sexual abuse within a therapeutic **10.17** context. Therapeutic treatment is commonly undertaken by children who have suffered trauma or abuse or have behavioural issues, whether or not caused by sexual abuse. In such a situation, the context and therapeutic methodology should be scrutinized with care. In *D v B and others (Flawed Sexual Abuse Enquiry)*[11] the High Court endorsed the need to treat sexual allegations arising in therapy with care. In that case, the mother and the child received counselling and support on the basis that the child had been sexually abused by the father. The trainee play therapist, who had participated in the counselling sessions of the mother, carried out

---

[9] Children Act 1989, s 47.
[10] Ministry of Justice (March 2011) *Achieving Best Evidence in Criminal Proceedings. Guidance on interviewing victims and witnesses, and guidance on using special measures*. Or the ABE guidance that was in place at the time the ABE was conducted. The guidance was originally drafted and published in January 2002, revised in 2007, and updated in 2011.
[11] [2006] EWHC 2987, [2007] 1 FLR 1295.

the therapy sessions with the child. The child was told prior to the therapy that the purpose was to tell the therapist how the father had hurt her. The judge found that the recordings of the therapy sessions required extremely careful handling since they were solely therapeutic and were never intended to bear any forensic function. There had been no attempt at open-ended questions to support and encourage the child, the sessions came after a lengthy period in which the assumption had been made and established with the child that the alleged abuse had taken place, the sessions had been heavily influenced by the mother and during them the child had her allegations of abuse confirmed and reinforced. However, the judge made it plain that he did not proceed upon the basis that therapeutic sessions can never provide a source of forensic evidence. The issue is one of weight. Disclosure of any written or audio records of the therapeutic sessions should be requested.

(5) Disclosure of information between the CPS and the family court

10.18 Where the allegations have been the subject of a police investigation, disclosure of police material into the family proceedings will routinely be sought. Since 1 January 2014 the management of this process has been governed by a new protocol and good practice model.[12] The 2013 protocol applies to cases involving criminal investigations into alleged child abuse (both sexual and non-sexual) and/or family proceedings concerning a child. It seeks to facilitate timely and consistent disclosure of information and documents from the police and the CPS into the family justice system[13] and the reverse, subject to the Family Procedure Rules 2010 (and relevant practice directions),[14] the Criminal Procedure Rules 2013 and the common law duty of confidentiality.[15]

10.19 The 2013 protocol is comprehensive in scope. It provides that as soon as reasonably practicable and, in any event, on issue of proceedings, the local authority will provide formal notice to the police single point of contact (SPOC) of the contemplation or existence of family proceedings.[16] Where criminal proceedings have been commenced (or are contemplated), the police will immediately forward a copy of the notice form to the CPS and the CPS will give due priority to making charging decisions in cases involving family proceedings.[17] Within five working days of the commencement of a relevant investigation, the police will provide to the local authority SPOC, details of the criminal investigation.[18] The protocol places an

---

[12] Crown Prosecution Service, President of the Family Division and Senior Presiding Judge for England and Wales (October 2013) *2013 Protocol and Good Practice Model: Disclosure of information in cases of alleged child abuse and linked criminal and care directions hearings.*

[13] Ibid., para 3.3.

[14] In particular, Family Procedure Rules 2010, Practice Direction 12G.

[15] *2013 Protocol and Good Practice Model*, cited at n.12, para 3.5.

[16] Ibid., para 4.1.

[17] Ibid., para 4.2.

[18] Ibid., para 5.1.

ongoing duty to keep the local authority informed in respect of charging decisions and relevant court directions and timetables.[19] It provides a system for voluntary disclosure by the police/CPS to the local authority and into the family justice system.[20] It is hoped that the 2013 protocol will remedy past difficulties with police disclosure.[21]

The 2013 protocol is expected to apply to both public and private law proceedings **10.20** and it is anticipated that there will be an expectation of consistency in any family proceedings dealing with alleged child abuse (both sexual and non-sexual).

It should be noted that, via the family proceedings, there may be disclosure of **10.21** evidence gathered for the criminal investigation not only to a defendant but also to a witness. This raises an inevitable tension between the need to determine family proceedings in a timely manner and the requirement to preserve the integrity of an upcoming criminal trial.

C. The Oral Evidence

The family court's assessment of the truth of the allegation will be significantly **10.22** influenced by the oral evidence heard, which will invariably include evidence from the alleged perpetrator and often from the child making the allegation.

(1) The parties and section 98 of the Children Act 1989

A party to public law proceedings is not excused from giving evidence on the **10.23** ground that doing so might incriminate him or herself or his or her spouse.[22] However, a statement or admission made in such proceedings shall not be admissible in evidence against the person making it or his or her spouse in proceedings for an offence other than perjury.[23] The meaning and effect of section 98 have been considered on two occasions by Munby J (as he then was).[24] He made clear that section 98(2) gives protection only against the use of such statement or admission 'in evidence'; it does not, for example, protect against use in a police investigation. Further, he suggested that putting inconsistent statements to a witness in order to challenge his or her evidence or attack his or her credibility does not amount to using those statements 'against' him or her within the meaning of the section. Finally, he confirmed that it is ultimately for the judge in the Crown court, who is conducting the criminal proceedings, and not for the judge in the family court to

---

[19] Ibid., paras 5.2, 5.3, and 5.4.
[20] Ibid., para 6.
[21] See e.g. *A London Borough Council v K and others* [2009] EWHC 850.
[22] Children Act 1989, s 98(1).
[23] Children Act 1989, s 98(2).
[24] *Re X (Children)* [2007] EWHC 1719 (Fam), [2008] 1 FLR 589 and *Re X (Disclosure for Purposes of Criminal Proceedings)* [2008] EWHC 242 (Fam), [2008] 2 FLR 944.

decide whether or not, and to what extent, section 98(2) applies in any particular situation.

10.24 This approach has recently been endorsed by Keehan J in a decision that post-dates the introduction of the 2013 Protocol. Keehan J provides guidance to family and criminal practitioners in respect of the need for an alleged perpetrator to file a response to threshold or a narrative statement.[25]

(2) Children

10.25 Children giving oral evidence remain a less common feature of family proceedings than of criminal proceedings although the frequency is rising. In *Re W (Family Proceedings: Evidence)*[26] Lady Hale said that in public law proceedings a balance must be struck between the Article 6 requirements of fairness, which normally allows for the challenging of evidence, and the Article 8 right to respect for family life, with neither right having precedence. In striking the balance, experience shows that the court will not require the child to give evidence in the majority of cases but this is not a presumption or even a starting point.

10.26 In light of *Re W*, when deciding whether a child should give evidence, the court's principal objective should be achieving a fair trial. With that objective in mind, the court should carry out a balancing exercise between the following primary considerations:

- the advantages that it will bring to the determination of the truth; and
- the damage it may do to the welfare of this or any other relevant child.

(3) Family Justice Council guidelines on child witness testimony

10.27 The Family Justice Council has produced guidelines in relation to children giving evidence[27] which provide an extremely helpful framework for family courts and practitioners considering this difficult issue. There are no specific age limits on a child giving evidence but the child's age, maturity, vulnerability, understanding, capacity, and competence are relevant factors to be considered by the court. If the decision is made that a child should give oral evidence, it is generally appropriate for special measures, such as videolink, to be used.

10.28 If the child does not give live evidence, the court is obliged to warn itself that the hearsay evidence of a child's allegations has to be handled with the greatest care and looked at closely,[28] reminding itself that:

---

[25] *A Local Authority v DG and IK and HL* [2014] EWHC 63 (Fam) [42].

[26] [2010] UKSC 12, [2010] 1 WLR 701.

[27] Family Justice Council (December 2011) *Guidelines in relation to children giving evidence in family proceedings.*

[28] *R v B County Council ex p P* [1991] 1 WLR 221.

- however good the procedures are for interviewing children, they are never more than simply interviews; and
- the ABE interviews do not constitute evidence which has been tested in court.[29]

(4) The weight to be given to hearsay evidence

In the case of *Re W (Children) (Abuse: Oral Evidence)*, Wilson and Wall LJJ (as they then were) stated that, where evidence of a child stands only as hearsay, the lack of a facility to test it would make it intrinsically less credible.[30] Rimer LJ went further, stating that a judge deprived of the testing of evidence by cross-examination was deprived of a crucial element of the trial process essential to the making of a fair decision and that a failure to call a child to give oral evidence may mean the case will not be proved.[31] On appeal to the Supreme Court, Lady Hale added that the family court has to give less weight to the evidence of a child because he or she has not been called.[32]   **10.29**

Hearsay evidence is admissible within family proceedings.[33] However, the degree to which a judge can place weight on any single piece of hearsay evidence must be carefully considered. Where an adult's evidence is central to a finding sought, then that adult would normally be expected to give direct evidence (perhaps with assistance or special measures). If direct evidence is not given, the judge must have regard to the reasons for its absence in weighing the hearsay evidence on which reliance is placed instead.[34]   **10.30**

(5) Vulnerable adults and special issues

Particular care is also needed where the person making the allegations is a vulnerable adult. In the matter of *Re A (A Child) (Family Proceedings: Disclosure of Information)*,[35] having endorsed the decision to permit disclosure of the identity of the young adult (X) making the allegations against the father and the detail of those allegations, the Supreme Court went on to consider the question of X giving oral evidence. The Supreme Court found that it did not follow from disclosure being permitted that she would have to give live evidence in person in the proceedings. If disclosure alone were not sufficient to deal with matters there were a number of options available. If she were required to give live evidence then up-to-date medical evidence could be provided to ensure her fitness to do so and there were other methods available for her evidence to be received aside from the normal   **10.31**

---

[29] *B v Torbay Council* [2007] 1 FLR 203 [16–17].
[30] [2010] EWCA Civ 57, [2010] 2 FLR 256 [15].
[31] Ibid., [46–48].
[32] [2010] UKSC 12, [2010] 1 WLR 701 [26].
[33] See e.g. the Children (Admissibility of Hearsay Evidence) Order 1993 and the Civil Evidence Act 1995.
[34] *Re W (Fact Finding: Hearsay Evidence)* [2013] EWCA Civ 1374.
[35] [2012] UKSC 60, [2013] 2 AC 66.

courtroom confrontation.[36] The object of the procedure was to enable witnesses to give their evidence in the way which best enabled the court to assess its reliability; it was certainly not to compound any abuse which may have been suffered. A form of closed material procedure in which full disclosure was made to a special advocate appointed to protect X's interests but not to the father himself was not an option available in civil proceedings.[37] Even if it had been theoretically possible to do so, it would not have met the minimum requirements of a fair hearing in this case.

10.32 Following the Supreme Court decision, the case was remitted to the Family Division of the High Court.[38] It was determined that X should give evidence in person at the fact-finding hearing at which she was assisted by an intermediary. She gave evidence for two days to her considerable distress leading the judge to the conclusion that she should not be called for a third day which had the effect of significantly curtailing the cross-examination put on behalf of the father. The allegations were found against the father.

10.33 This decision has been the subject of a successful, appeal to the Court of Appeal.[39] In summary, the factors which led the Court of Appeal to its decision were the inadequacy of X's evidence about the allegations (both the lack of any ABE interview and/or narrative statement and the complete failure of the cross-examination of her on behalf of the father), the absence of any other evidence which directly supported or corroborated X's allegation of sexual abuse coupled with the fact that in at least one central respect her accounts were not reliable and the lack of balance in the judge's appraisal of the many factors which needed to be taken into account in the weighing of X's evidence. Gloster LJ cautioned that the need for the trial process to be carefully and considerately managed in such a way as to enable vulnerable witnesses to give their evidence in the best way possible and without being subjected to unnecessary distress should not come at the price of depriving alleged perpetrators of their right to a fair trial in which they participate and a proper opportunity to present their case in accordance with natural justice and Article 6 of the European Convention on Human Rights.[40]

D. Expert Evidence

10.34 The starting point for the instruction of an expert within family proceedings is rule 25.1 of the Family Procedure Rules 2010. That rule permits the instruction of

---

[36] Such as by the use of videotaped conversations with ABE-trained police officers or social workers, by the use of supplemental written questions put to her in circumstances approved by her treating psychiatrist, or by the use of screens or videolink so as to avoid a face-to-face confrontation between the complainant and the alleged perpetrator.

[37] *Al Rawi v Security Service* [2011] UKSC 34, [2012] 1 AC 531.

[38] *Re A (Vulnerable Witness: Fact Finding)* [2013] EWHC 2124 (Fam), [2014] 1 FLR 146.

[39] *Re J (A Child)* [2014] EWCA Civ 875.

[40] Ibid., [109].

experts only 'if necessary'. Within a fact-finding context, most such applications relate to veracity (i.e. whether the child is likely to be telling the truth), propensity (i.e. whether the alleged perpetrator is likely to have committed the abuse) and paediatrics.

Within the family court, judges' attitudes to the use of veracity experts vary con-   **10.35** siderably. Some consider that such experts add little to the case and that they are in effect carrying out a quasi-judicial function. Other judges disagree with that view and consider that, in such a complex area, the court is assisted by expert evidence.

In the authors' experience, expert evidence as to propensity is rarely seen in family   **10.36** proceedings. The reasons for that are summarized in *Re B*,[41] in which the court held that expert psychological or psychiatric evidence is admissible only to assist the court in drawing inferences and conclusions where the tribunal of fact lacks the necessary expertise to do so, and that evidence as to propensity will rarely be relevant or admissible as probative of the factual issue whether an alleged perpetrator committed a particular act of abuse where it is essentially an issue of credibility.

Paediatric evidence is not often present in cases in which child sexual abuse has   **10.37** occurred and evidence from paediatricians where sexual abuse is alleged remains of limited value in the majority of cases; it neither proves nor disproves sexual abuse and normally is simply consistent or not consistent with it. Furthermore, in the vast majority of cases such evidence does not assist with the identification of the perpetrator.

In *Leeds City Council v YX & ZX (Assessment of Sexual Abuse)*[42] Holman J (relying   **10.38** on the then new guidelines produced by the Royal College of Paediatrics and Child Health[43]) expressed concern about relying on purely physical evidence saying 'the medical assessment of physical signs of sexual abuse has a considerable subjective element, and unless there is clearly diagnostic evidence of abuse (e.g. the presence of semen or a foreign body internally) purely medical assessments and opinions should not be allowed to predominate'.[44]

E. Conclusion

The impact of a family court finding either that sexual abuse has taken place or that   **10.39** it has not will have life-long implications for the family life of everyone involved. Recent changes to the family justice system are designed to make the process of

---

[41] [1999] 1 WLR 238.
[42] [2008] EWHC 802 (Fam).
[43] The Royal College of Paediatrics and Child Health (March 2008) *The Physical Signs of Child Sex Abuse: An evidence-based review and guidance for best practice*. A second edition was published in 2015. See Chapters 18 and 19.
[44] Cited at n.42, 143.

resolving these issues easier. However, child sexual abuse allegations will continue to present challenges to family courts and practitioners who are seeking to determine, in a fair and just manner, the likelihood of abuse having taken place whilst ensuring that children are protected from the harm that arises both from sexual abuse and from unjustified allegations.

Further Reading

The Family Court Practice (2014) Bristol: Jordan Publishing.
Hershman and McFarlane: Children Law and Practice Bristol: Jordan Publishing.

Author Biographies

Alex Verdan QC specializes in complex and serious children cases; both private law and public law. In particular, those involving intractable residence and contact disputes; internal relocations and leave to remove from the jurisdiction; serious emotional abuse; child fatalities and significant injuries and serious abuse with disputed medical evidence and often with linked criminal proceedings; allegations of sexual abuse including false allegations; and factitious illness. He has been in practice for over twenty-five years, took silk in 2006, and sits as a deputy high court judge. He is also a qualified family mediator.

Sam King was called to the bar in 1990. She specializes in children's work and represents all parties in complex private and public law proceedings. The scope of her work includes child fatalities, non-accidental injuries, sexual abuse, and cases involving fabricated illness and false allegations of abuse. In the private law arena she is regularly instructed in cases involving intractable disputes about the arrangements for the children. She has a particular interest in proceedings related to non-traditional family structures and in fertility law, including surrogacy.

Cleo Perry specializes in children work, including public law proceedings in which she regularly acts for children, parents, and local authorities, and public and private international law, in all levels of court. In practice she deals with cases involving complex legal issues, child fatalities and significant abuse, including historical sexual abuse or multiple injuries. She also deals with complex private law proceedings.

Rebecca Foulkes is a specialist family law practitioner. She was called to the Bar in 2001 and specializes in children work. She has particular expertise in complex public and private law children work, in which she represents local authorities, parents, and children's guardians.

11

INTERNATIONAL CASE STUDIES

Part I: Canada

Justice Bruce Durno and Amy J. Ohler

A. Witness Testimony in the Multicultural and Constitutional Context

Over the past twenty-five years Canadian criminal law has undergone significant **11.01** changes to encourage and facilitate the participation of sexual assault complainants in the adjudication of offences. Following the constitutional entrenchment of the Canadian Charter of Rights and Freedoms (the *Charter*)[1] in 1982, these changes were examined in terms of constitutional values, balancing the rights of the complainant against the fair trial rights of the accused. The facility of these reformed practice and procedures to respond to the evolving needs of complainants was most recently tested in a constitutional challenge on behalf of a sexual

---

[1] Part I of the Constitution Act, 1982, being Schedule B to the Canada Act 1982 (UK), 1982, c 11.

assault complainant who wished to testify while wearing a niqab.[2] The case also questioned the value of demeanour in assessing credibility.

(1) The legislative context

11.02 Parliament has enacted legislation to facilitate the presentation of evidence and to encourage the participation of complainants by taking steps to reduce potential harm as result of testifying.[3] *The Criminal Code*[4] permits young complainants, or those with a mental or physical disability, to testify from outside the courtroom using closed circuit television and to be accompanied by a support person while testifying.[5] There are mandatory publication bans on the names of the complainant or anything that might tend to identify her or him.[6] Where the accused is not represented by counsel, the Crown can apply to have a lawyer appointed to cross-examine the complainant. Where the witness is under 18 years of age there is a presumption the accused shall not cross-examine the witness.[7] For older witnesses the Crown must show the appointment of counsel is required in order to obtain a full and candid account from the witness of the facts complained of.[8] Any *Charter* challenges to the legislation referred to have been unsuccessful.

(2) Hearsay evidence reforms

11.03 Alongside the legislative changes, the last twenty years have seen a hearsay revolution in Canada. With Supreme Court of Canada judgments in 1990 and 1993,[9] the principled exception to the hearsay rule was applied to permit the admission of child witness' complaints to adults on a substantive basis. Videotaped witness statements are often taken under oath and warning from sexual and domestic assault complainants as well as other witnesses. Where the witness recants or cannot be located, prosecutors can now apply to have the statement admitted on a substantive basis.[10]

(3) The requirement of an oath

11.04 To give evidence in a court proceeding in Canada, it is necessary to swear an oath or affirm to tell the truth.[11] To accommodate the members of our multicultural

---

[2] *R v N.S.*, [2012] 2 S.C.R. 531 (SCC); 2012 SCC 72.
[3] These procedural changes must be understood alongside changes to the admissibility of evidence of a complainant's prior sexual activity with the accused or any other person contained in s 276 of the *Criminal Code*, R.S.C. 1985, c. C-46, and upheld in *R v Darrach*, [2000] 2 S.C.R. 443 (SCC), 2000 SCC 46. See also Rook, P. and Ward, R. (2010) *Rook and Ward on Sexual Offences*, 4th edn, London: Sweet & Maxwell, paras 19.140–19.148.
[4] RSC 1985, c. C-46.
[5] Ibid., s 486.2 and 486.1.
[6] Ibid., s 486.4.
[7] Ibid., s 486.3(1).
[8] Ibid, s 486.3(2).
[9] *R v Khan*, [1990] 2 S.C.R. 531 (.CC), and *R v K.G.B.* [1993] 1 SCR 740 (SCC).
[10] Young complainants may also adopt a videotaped statement under s 715.1 of the *Criminal Code*.
[11] Canada Evidence Act, RSC, 1985, c. C-5, s 13; s 14.

society, court registrars have numerous oaths and affirmations for various religions or cultures. Courtrooms in the Province of Ontario now have copies of the Bible, the Koran, Sikh holy books and the Bhagavad Gita. For some of Canada's First Nation persons there are eagle feathers upon which to swear an oath. Witnesses may affirm or swear on a holy book.

Young witnesses and witnesses whose capacity is in question may testify on prom- **11.05** ising to tell the truth.[12] The Supreme Court of Canada considered these legislative requirements in the context of a sexual assault prosecution involving a mentally disabled adult complainant.[13] A majority of the Court found that it was unnecessary and undesirable to conduct an inquiry into a mentally disabled witness' capacity to understand the duty to tell the truth and that such inquiries would immunize categories of offenders from prosecution based on their choice of victim.[14]

(4) *R v N.S.*—The niqab in the courtroom

Against this background, the most recent Supreme Court of Canada judgment **11.06** dealing with the testimony of a sexual assault complainant reflects the challenges of balancing the witness' rights against those of the accused person. The case also illustrates the tensions and changes caused by Canadian society's rapid evolution and by the growing presence of new cultures, religions, traditions, and social practices.

In *R v N.S.*, a young Muslim woman alleged that her uncle and cousin had sexually **11.07** assaulted her. She attended court to testify at their preliminary inquiry wearing a niqab that only revealed her eyes. The complainant told the judge she wished to testify wearing the niqab for religious reasons.

After conducting an inquiry, the presiding judge concluded her religious belief **11.08** was 'not that strong' and ordered her to remove her niqab. The complainant then applied to the Superior Court for extraordinary relief, *certiorari* to quash the order and *mandamus* to require the preliminary inquiry judge to permit her to testify wearing her niqab. She argued that the order to remove her niqab violated her right to religious freedom under the section 2 of the *Charter*. As such, she applied for relief under section 24(1) of the *Charter* which provides broad discretion to a judge to craft any such remedy as the court considers appropriate and just in the circumstances.

The Superior Court Justice quashed the order that she be made to testify without **11.09** her niqab, and the Court of Appeal for Ontario agreed, returning the case to the preliminary inquiry judge for reconsideration. The complainant then appealed

---

[12] Ibid., s 16; s 16.1.
[13] *R v D.A.I.*, [2012] 3 S.C.R. 726 (SCC); 2012 SCC 5.
[14] Ibid., at para 67.

to the Supreme Court of Canada. The seven judges hearing the appeal produced three judgments: four and two judge rulings dismissed the appeal, while one judge dissented, holding that unless the witness' face was directly relevant to the case such as where her identity was in issue, no witness should be required to remove her niqab.

11.10 The four judge majority judgment rejected as untenable the extreme approaches of always requiring the removal of the niqab or that the niqab was never removed. Instead, the Court found the answer lay in a just and appropriate balance between the freedom of religion and trial fairness, based on the particular facts of the case. A witness who for sincere religious beliefs wants to testify wearing a niqab in a criminal proceeding will be required to remove it if (i) it is necessary to prevent a serious risk to trial fairness because reasonably available options will not prevent the risk; and (ii) the salutary effect of requiring her to remove the niqab outweighs the deleterious effects of so doing.[15]

11.11 Four questions guide the inquiry: first, would requiring the witness to remove the niqab interfere with her religious freedom? For the witness to rely on her *Charter*-guaranteed fundamental freedom of conscience and religion, the witness must show her desire to wear her niqab is based on a sincere religious belief, not whether the belief is strong.[16]

11.12 Secondly, would permitting the witness to wear her niqab create a serious risk to trial fairness? The Canadian legal system includes a deeply rooted presumption that seeing a witness' face is important to a fair trial because it enables effective cross-examination and contributes to credibility assessments. The court was not prepared to accept that demeanour evidence does not have a role to play in assessing a witness' credibility. However, a majority of the court was not prepared to find it paramount either. Instead, the majority adopted a case-specific approach, depending on the nature of the witness' evidence. It might be necessary for a witness to testify without her niqab where her evidence is contested. If wearing the niqab does not pose a serious risk to trial fairness, a witness who wears one for religious reasons may do so.[17]

11.13 Thirdly, if both religion and trial fairness are engaged on the facts, the judge should consider whether there is a way to accommodate both rights and avoid a conflict between them, and whether there are reasonably available options that would conform to the witness' religious convictions yet still prevent a serious risk to trial fairness. In this regard, it is incumbent on the parties to lead evidence as to possible accommodations.[18]

---

[15] Cited at n.2, at para 46.
[16] Ibid., at para 11.
[17] Ibid., at paras 18–29.
[18] Ibid., at paras 31–3.

Fourthly, and only if there are no reasonably available options, a judge is to con-   **11.14**
sider whether the salutary effects of requiring the witness to remove the niqab
outweigh the deleterious effects of doing so. The deleterious effects include the
harm done by limiting the witness' sincerely held religious beliefs and practices.
The judge is directed to consider the importance of the religious practice to the
witness, the degree of state interference with that practice, and the courtroom
situation including the number of people present and measures that would limit
facial exposure. A judge is also directed to consider broader societal concerns
such as discouraging niqab wearing women from reporting offences and partici-
pating in the justice system. The salutary effects of requiring the removal of the
niqab include the accused's fair trial rights and safeguarding the reputation in the
administration of justice.[19] The result of this weighing in any particular case will
depend on a variety of factors.

The two concurring judges adopted one of the extremes rejected by the four major-   **11.15**
ity judges, finding there should be a clear rule that niqabs may not be worn at any
stage of a criminal trial. The minority found that a general rule excluding niqabs
would be consistent with the principle of public openness of the trial process and
safeguard the integrity of that process. For the minority, wearing a niqab does not
facilitate acts of communication. Rather, it shields the witness from interacting
fully with the parties, counsel, the judge and jurors; wearing a niqab is incompatible with the accused's rights, the nature of the Canadian public adversarial trials
as well as with the constitutional values of openness and religious neutrality in contemporary, yet diverse, Canada. To require a case-specific determination dependent on the nature of the evidence would add yet another layer of complexity to an
already complex trial process.

Noting the variety of accommodations currently in place to accommodate the   **11.16**
needs of witnesses, a single judge would have made a clear rule that niqabs may be
worn at any stage of a criminal trial, including where a niqab-wearing woman is
the accused, except where identity is in issue. Furthermore, under the principled
exceptions to the hearsay rule, it is not uncommon for the courts to admit into
evidence statements given out of court by persons who are not available to testify,
absent any ability to assess demeanour at all.[20]

(5) The practical result

In spring 2013, when the preliminary inquiry resumed, the presiding judge con-   **11.17**
ducted a voir dire and determined the complainant should remove her niqab. She
appealed again. However, the appeal was abandoned when a compromise was
reached: the witness would remove her niqab, provided the courtroom was not

---

[19] Ibid., at paras 34–45.
[20] Ibid., at paras 92–110.

open to the public, and only the accused, their counsel, the prosecutor, judge, and court staff would be present.

(6) Conclusion

11.18 The Canadian approach to witness testimony in sexual assault offences is continually evolving. The impact of the *Charter* on the development of the law has been significant, both in safeguarding the rights of the accused, and accommodating the testimony of complainants in recognition of the larger societal interest in prosecuting these offences to sound conclusions.

Part II: New Zealand

Judge Gerard Winter

A. Introduction

11.19 We lawyers were taught that only a proper confrontation of a crown witness in front of a jury could secure a fair trial. The jury system has been described throughout the common law world as a 'palladium'[21] and a 'bulwark of civil liberty',[22] it is said to be 'an integral and indispensable part of the criminal justice system'.[23] It is, however, failing to achieve justice for the child victims of sexual crime. Children have something to say about their lives.[24] When a child is given the opportunity to be heard without traditional confrontation, 'the court will then see the child as a real person, rather than as the object of other people's disputes or concerns'.[25]

11.20 New Zealand has modified the processes for the receipt and delivery of child evidence in criminal jury trials. More recently, the New Zealand Law Commission has questioned the relevance of jury trials and confrontation of witnesses for the fair prosecution of sexual crime. We will follow the story of two real Pacifica children, Tom and Tama, and ask whether these young and vulnerable children were given the freedom to tell their story. We will ask what more could be done to deliver justice for these children and the accused.

---

[21] Blackstone, W. (1765–1769) *The Commentaries on the Laws of England* (4 vols) facsimile edn (introduction by Katz, S.N.), Chicago: University of Chicago, bk iv, 349.

[22] Starkie, T. (1880) *The Trial by Jury*, Boston: Little, Brown & Company, 3.

[23] *R v Mirza* [2004] AC 1118, 1131–1132 (HL).

[24] Parkinson, P. and Cashmore, J. (2008) *The Voice of a Child in Family Law Disputes*, Oxford: Oxford University Press.

[25] Hale, B., 'Children's Participation in Family Law Decisions Making: Lessons from Abroad' (2006) 20(119) *Australian Journal of Family Law*, 124.

B. Tom and Tama

Tom and Tama were Pacific Island brothers.[26] Their parents left their Island home **11.21**
and lived with the boys in Australia until they separated and the mother fled to
New Zealand with her five children. The father remained in Australia. The mother
worked two jobs to support the family, pay her church tithe, and remit money back
to their island village. Her long hours at work meant these younger boys had to live
with their grandparents. The grandparents spoke little English. Their home ran
under a disciplined rule of unquestioning obedience and respect for your elders. It
was in this context that the sexual offending against the boys occurred. Tom was
ten and Tama eight years old. Their similar sexual abuse continued on a regular
basis for one year.

When he had the children alone their 40-year-old Uncle would kiss him them on **11.22**
the mouth inserting his tongue as he did so. He would have the boys kiss him all
over his body as he grabbed and squeezed their genitals. He forced his penis into
the 8-year-old child's mouth telling him to 'suck it'. Uncle would frequently sodo-
mize both boys. The children's grandmother discovered some of this abuse. The
police were called.

The boys gave a recorded evidential interview within a matter of days in a child- **11.23**
friendly investigation unit. The unit was furnished in a relaxed style with low slung
couches, chairs, and bean bags. The design minimized any size difference between
adults and children. Toys, books, paper, and pens were on and about a low coffee
table. A specialist interviewer was used.

The children first established their knowledge of truth and lies. A promise to only **11.24**
tell the truth was explored and made. The children were asked not to guess at any
answer but to tell the interviewer if they did not know or were unsure about anything. Rather than a script driving discussion the interviewer used focused story-
telling about events using simple language and answer centric prompts. The child's
story was at times clarified by the use of visual aids.

This process when coupled with New Zealand's codified approach to evidence[27] **11.25**
allowed the recorded interviews to be replayed as the children's evidence-in-chief
at the jury trial later that year. Thereafter, supplementary questions or cross-
examination was by way of a closed circuit television system operated between a
remote site and the courtroom. No adverse comment about the use of this process
was allowed.

---

[26] To protect the children's identity names have been anonymized and case detail altered.
[27] Evidence Act 2006, which allows the admission of any out of court statement at trial that is
relevant, probative, and relatively non-prejudicial.

11.26   The separate interviews showed bright boys willing to use simple language and slang to describe their sexual abuse. Tom explained what happened when he was 'bum jacked' by use of drawings and a doll. Congruently and unprompted he talked about how sore his bottom was during and after the abuse.

11.27   Tama talked not only of his abuse but also of seeing the abuse of his brother. In his words his brother and he were 'humped' by their Uncle. Tama was also able to talk about otherwise inexplicable bruising to his neck and chest describing these as 'hickies'. These marks left on his skin after abuse were noticed by relatives. When cross-examined about these marks and asked why he didn't tell anyone about his uncle's abuse the child talked about being ashamed. He said he could not tell because 'I knew they will be, like, "Oh, shame, you're ugly, you've gotta boyfriend."' The boys said their uncle had offered them money for sexual favours.

11.28   A support person remained with the boys in the video suite while they were then cross-examined. The cross-examination, while confrontational, was judicially moderated and quickly demonstrated that both Tama and Tom had a good command of their story. When counsel concentrated on attacking the truthfulness of the boy's evidence about dates, times, frequency, and duration of the abuse little ground was gained. The uncle gave no evidence. The jury swiftly returned verdicts of guilty on all counts. The uncle was sentenced to fifteen years imprisonment.

C. Could We Do Better?

11.29   A psychological report prepared after the trial but before sentence addressed the potential impact on the children from the criminal offending and trial.

11.30   Tom described the offending as 'being gay'. However, he reported that he did not worry about 'being gay' and that he understood that the offending against him and his brother was 'bad and wrong'. Tom denied any current psychological distress or anxiety. He reported no bad dreams or any re-experiencing phenomena that might be associated with a history of sexual trauma. Tom reported no fear in relation to the accused or any other person. He reported being very happy in his life.

11.31   Tama was at pains to present as well and without any problems. He regarded the offending as 'rude stuff'. Tama found the physical aspects of the abuse very painful saying he had 'cried' because it 'hurt a lot'. He wanted his uncle punished for the offending.

11.32   The boys had no symptoms that reached a threshold for any diagnosis of post-traumatic stress disorder (PTSD), or any depressive or anxiety disorder. It is known that sexually abused children and adolescents who do not exhibit symptoms may develop psychological problems later on in life. These 'sleeper effects', do not fully manifest until adulthood. That said, these children showed little additional distress as a result of the trial process.

D. Reforms

Until 1990 the New Zealand justice system made it very difficult for children to testify and displayed deep suspicion of their testimony. Much has changed in the last two decades. This case study demonstrates the broad discretions now available to lessen a child's trauma in giving evidence before a jury. At a very basic level it may be concluded that this jury trial process was less traumatic for Tom and Tama than the face-to-face confrontation of a traditional trial.[28]   **11.33**

Although children now regularly testify by way of pre-recorded evidence and appear in court by the use of CCTV there continues to be controversy about the efficacy of an adversarial jury trial to confront a child's testimony. Judges still frequently intervene or complain about defence counsels developmentally inappropriate or badgering questions of these vulnerable witnesses.[29]   **11.34**

In an effort to address these concerns a second wave of reforms has been proposed.[30] The New Zealand Minister of Justice, referring to an Auckland University of Technology research paper,[31] observed: **11.35**

> We simply must do better to ensure that the estimated 750 children who give evidence in criminal courts each year—the majority of them complainants in sexual offending cases—are not re-brutalised by their participation in the process. They are in the criminal justice system through no fault of their own and they deserve special protection.

The Minister expects that the new processes will resemble an inquisitorial system by requiring the judiciary to play a more active role in determining whether questions to be put to child witnesses are appropriate. Along with the proposed reforms relating to improving the questioning of child witnesses, reforms designed to reduce the impact of time delays, and other enhancements relating to child witnesses and their evidence were also announced.   **11.36**

The New Zealand Law Commission has recently expressed its concern over the profound limitations of the adversarial jury trial system. It was these concerns   **11.37**

---

[28] Commencing with the Evidence Amendment Act 1989 and the Summary Proceedings Act 1989 a new pathway was created for the receipt, admissibility, and comment upon child testimony.

[29] Recent research on practice in the New Zealand criminal courts has demonstrated a high level of inappropriate and unsafe questioning of child witnesses, particularly during cross-examination: Institute of Public Policy (2010) *Child Witnesses in the New Zealand Criminal Courts: A Review of Practice and Implications for Policy*, Auckland: University of Auckland.

[30] The Guidelines and the Cabinet Paper are posted at *http://www.justice.govt.nz/policy/ justice-system-improvements/child-witnesses-in-the-criminal-courts*.

[31] Cited at n.29.

that led to the Commission's current reference and issues paper, *Alternative Pre-trial and Trial Processes: Possible Reforms.*[32] The Law Commission canvassed a range of proposals aimed at simplifying the trial procedure and improving the experience for both accused persons and victims. Particularly in light of research on sexual offending trials the Commission considered 'that options beyond the traditional trial/verdict/sentence model are required to deal with the large number of sexual offending cases that are not, and never will be, amenable to satisfactory resolution through that model, no matter what reforms may be made to it'.

11.38 The Commission reached the view that reforms to the current jury trial process were necessary to improve the confidence of certain categories of victims in the process, encourage participation, and curb adverse outcomes. The Commission considered that two reforms for sexual offending cases offer a justifiable move away from an adversarial jury trial process. The commission suggested a sexual violence court that operates after a guilty plea but before sentence (see section 5); and an alternative process for sexual offence cases outside the criminal justice system (see section 6).

E. Conclusion

11.39 Tom and Tama had the freedom to tell their story relatively unscathed by the modified jury trial process. Their example may offer some comfort to other children brought into the New Zealand criminal justice system through no fault of their own. However, the present system barely protects child victims of sexual crime and so the Ministers proposed reforms are welcomed.

11.40 The right to trial by jury is a well-established tradition that provides important safeguards to citizens in the criminal justice system. However, the current system is not the only way of safeguarding those interests. Furthermore, the current jury system is not achieving its purposes, particularly in the area of sexual crime against children. A specialist sexual violation sentencing court has the potential to not only provide equal protection of the interests safeguarded by the right to trial by jury, but also the interests of the many child victims of sexual abuse. Long-term judicially monitored and rehabilitative sentences may provide a better outcome for children and the public interest. However, further research is required before any alternate process for sexual offence cases might become generally acceptable.

---

[32] Law Commission (2011) *Alternative Pre-Trial and Trial Processes: Possible Reforms.* Issues paper No. 30, Wellington: New Zealand Law Commission (NZLC IP30), *http://www.lawcom.govt.nz/sites/default/files/projectAvailableFormats/NZLC%20IP30.pdf.*

Part III: South Australia *R v Maiolo*:
Collusion, Concoction, and the Elephant(s) in the Room

*Robert Kane**

A. Introduction

The common law afforded some protection from the undoubted prejudice to **11.41** an accused facing multiple complainants alleging sexual misconduct. In South Australia, recent legislative amendments have eroded those protections to the point where, in practical terms, an accused in such a situation is required to prove their innocence.

It is reasonable to suspect that in a trial involving allegations of sexual misconduct **11.42** by a number of complainants the rhetorical question 'why would the complainant(s) lie?' will be very much at the forefront of a jury's deliberations. In *Palmer v R*,[33] the High Court of Australia considered the question of the propriety of cross-examination of an accused as to whether a complainant had a motive to lie, and whether it was proper to invite a jury to speculate upon that basis.

In a joint judgement, the majority stated: **11.43**

> .... a complainant's account gains no legitimate credibility from the evidence of motive. If credibility which the jury would otherwise attribute to the complainant's account is strengthened by an accused's inability to furnish evidence of a motive for a complainant to lie, the standard of proof is to that extent diminished.[34]

It is contended that these considerations are particularly apposite where an accused is faced with multiple complainants alleging sexual impropriety.

Whilst courts have long grappled with questions relating to the admissibility of **11.44** similar fact evidence in sexual cases, it is plain that the common law has long recognized that criminal propensity is prejudicial to an accused as it may be used as sufficient of itself to prove the commission of the alleged offence. Accordingly, the law has recognized that the criterion of admissibility of similar fact evidence is that its probative force clearly transcends its merely prejudicial effect.[35] Furthermore, as the majority of High Court of Australia held in *Hoch v R*:

> In cases where there is a possibility of joint concoction there is another rational view of the evidence. The rational view—*viz.* joint concoction—is inconsistent

---

* My thanks to Judge Michael Boylan, Gilbert Aitken and Ben Sale for their comments.

[33] (1998) 193 CLR 1.
[34] Ibid., at 9.
[35] *Perry v R* (1982) 150 CLR 580; *Sutton v R* (1984) 152 CLR528; *Hoch v R* (1988) 165 CLR 292.

both with the guilt of the accused person and with the improbability of the complainants having concocted similar lies. It thus destroys the probative value of the evidence which is a condition precedent to its admissibility.[36]

The majority held that the admissibility of similar fact evidence in a case involving multiple complainants alleging sexual abuse depends on the evidence having the quality that it is not reasonably explicable on the basis of concoction. The court held that whilst an examination on the voir dire may sometimes be necessary:

> ... if the depositions or statements indicate that the complainants have a sufficient relationship to each other and had opportunity and motive for concoction, then as a matter of common sense and experience, the evidence will lack the degree of probative value necessary to render it admissible.[37]

11.45 That notwithstanding, the Parliament of South Australia has recently enacted legislation which has abolished the test enunciated by the High Court in *Hoch v R*. Section 34S(b) of the Evidence Act,[38] provides that evidence *may not* be excluded under the Division if the only ground for exclusion is that the evidence may be the result of collusion or concoction. Under the *Hoch* test a trial judge was required to subject the proposed evidence to a threshold test where there was a suggestion of collusion or concoction. Under the new legislation such questions are now a matter for the jury.

B. *R v Maiolo*

11.46 The proceedings against Mr Maiolo have, to date, been the subject of three appeals and five trials.

11.47 In *R v Maiolo*, the accused was charged with sexual offending against four female complainants. The first complainant, 'SZ' was the daughter of the accused and 'TZ'. The other three complainants ('RX,' 'MX', and 'DX') were the sisters of TZ and the aunts of SZ.

11.48 The accused met TZ in 1986 and commenced a relationship which continued until 1993. Their daughter, SZ was born in 1987. From 1986 to 1993, the accused would visit the home of TZ's mother where RX, MX, and DX also resided. On the Crown case, RX, MX, and DX would also visit the accused and TX, and stay overnight from time to time.

11.49 In 1993, the appellant ended the relationship with TX and commenced living in a relationship with TX's sister, RX, who was approximately 20 years old at the time. The relationship between the accused and RX continued until 1998. The daughter

---

[36] Ibid., at 296.
[37] Ibid., at 297.
[38] 1929 South Australia.

of the accused, SZ, would spend every second weekend with him and her aunt RX from 1993 to 1996. The evidence at trial was that as a result of commencing a relationship with the accused, RX became estranged from her family.

In 1996, SZ made allegations of sexual misconduct against her father. At the time of her initial complaint, SZ was nine years old. The complaint was made to her mother TZ, on an occasion when the accused had come to take her on an access visit. **11.50**

Mr Maiolo was charged with sexual offending against his daughter in 1996. However, in 1997, the Director of Public Prosecutions entered a *nolle prosequi* with respect to all counts alleging sexual offending against his daughter. **11.51**

In 2008, SZ contacted the police with respect to reopening the proceedings against her father. It was after this time that SZ's aunts, namely RX, MX, and DX all spoke with the police alleging sexual misconduct by the accused between 1987 and 1993. It was common ground that this was the first time that their allegations had been reported to the police. **11.52**

The first trial against the accused was heard in 2011. That trial concerned the allegations of all four complainants. There was no application for severance but the trial judge, of his own volition, and before the summing up, ruled that the evidence in relation to the various complainants *was not* cross-admissible and summed up on that basis. On appeal, the Court held that if an application for severance had been made, it would in all probability have been granted. Accordingly, the Court of Criminal Appeal held that in all the circumstances no directions by the trial judge as to the evidence not being cross-admissible could safeguard against the prejudice to the appellant in the various counts being heard together.[39] Nonetheless, the Court did recognize that there might be a 'strong argument' that the evidence was cross-admissible.[40] **11.53**

Upon the resulting re-trial an application for severance as between the evidence of the various complainants was made, but refused, the trial judge being of the view that the evidence *was* cross-admissible. As a consequence, the issue of collusion and concoction between the various complainants was the primary thrust of the defence case. **11.54**

On the evidence, the complainants RX, MX, and DX had been aware of the allegations made by their niece SZ in the period 1996 to 1997. Indeed, RX had been present during the accused's record of interview with the police in 1997. Furthermore, on their evidence RX, MX, and DX had been upset or angry with respect to the decision by the Director of Public Prosecutions to discontinue the prosecution of the accused in 1997. **11.55**

---

[39] *R v Maiolo* [2011] SASFC 86.
[40] Ibid.

11.56   Unsurprisingly, one of the principal points made on the defence case was that RX, MX, and DX, having not only been aware of the allegations made by their niece in 1996, but also being upset with respect to the Director of Public Prosecution's decision not to proceed with the prosecution, said nothing to the authorities as to their own allegations until 2008 to 2009. Furthermore, the evidence was clear that there had been contact between SZ, MX, and DX on the one hand and RX and MX on the other, prior to any of SZ's aunts reporting their own allegations to police. In the event, the accused was convicted on all counts.

11.57   The convictions were the subject of a successful appeal in 2013.[41] Inter alia, the Court of Criminal Appeal held that the evidence of SZ was not cross-admissible with the evidence of the other three complainants and ordered retrials.[42]

C. Conclusion

11.58   It is contended that the evidence in *R v Maiolo* at a bare minimum, would have involved a serious consideration of the threshold test posited in *Hoch v R*. The legislative abolition of the *Hoch* test is a serious erosion of an accused's right to a fair trial.

11.59   In South Australia it is now the position that questions of collusion and concoction are a matter for the jury. As a result, an accused in practical terms is now required to 'prove' collusion and concoction in a trial involving multiple complainants. Juries are now directed that if they find collusion and concoction as a reasonable possibility they should consider the evidence with respect to the evidence of each complainant individually. In other words, the potentially exculpatory evidence is not cross-admissible. The case of *R v Maiolo* demonstrates that the question of cross-admissibility is a topic upon which reasonable minds can differ. The common law has long recognized that prejudicial evidence should be kept from a jury because it is just that—*prejudicial*. It is contended that the abolition of the safeguards enunciated by the High Court of Australia in *Hoch v R*, significantly diminish the rigour with which the common law approached the often difficult questions posed by multi-complainant sexual cases.

11.60   Returning therefore to the (impermissible) rhetorical question 'why would the complainant(s) lie?' abolition of the *Hoch* test may well have erected almost insurmountable hurdles for an accused facing sexual allegations from multiple complainants. The absence of a motive for lying is not proof that there was no such motive and the question is not only deeply prejudicial but effectively reverses the onus of proof.[43] Abolition of the *Hoch* test will surely result in juries speculating on that very question.

---

[41]   See *Maiolo (No 2)* [2013] SASFC 36.
[42]   The accused was convicted on all counts on both retrials.
[43]   *R v E* (1996) 39 NSWLR 450 at 464, cited with approval in *Palmer v R*, cited at n.34.

Further Reading

Elizabeth A. Sheehy (ed.) (2012) *Sexual Assault Law in Canada: Law, Legal Practice and Women's Activism*, Ottawa: Ottawa University Press.

Author Biographies

Justice Bruce Durno has been a justice of the Superior Court of Justice (Ontario) since 1998. Justice Durno graduated from Harvard University, Cambridge, Massachusetts in 1971 and the University of Toronto Law School in 1974. Prior to his appointment he was a criminal law defence counsel for twenty-three years and was the President of the Ontario Criminal Lawyers' Association from 1994 to 1998. From 2000 to 2008 he was the Regional Senior Judge for the Central West Region of the Province of Ontario, where he currently presides.

Amy J. Ohler, B.A., M.A., LL.B, Judicial Law Clerk, Ontario Court of Appeal (2008–2009), Judicial Law Clerk Superior Court of Justice (Ontario) (2009–2010), LL.M (Cantab), Pegasus Scholar (2011). Ms Ohler practices primarily in criminal appeals at Fenton, Smith Barristers in Toronto, Ontario, Canada. She is also a Special Lecturer in the Faculty of Law at the University of Windsor, in Windsor, Ontario, Canada where she teaches Criminal Law and Feminist Legal Theory.

Judge Gerard Winter C.R.H is a lawyer, academic and jurist and has presided over significant constitutional, criminal, land, and human rights cases. His work on law reform, Pacific regional legal systems, codified law for post conflict states, constitutional revision and the Universal Periodic Review of human rights has provided him with a sound understanding of the policy, design, management, and operation of parliaments, courts, and justice systems. He returned home in 2010 and now lives in Karaka, South Auckland, with his wife, Katherine, and two of their five sons.

Robert Kane was called to the Bar in 1995 and is a member of Mitchell Chambers, Adelaide. He practices at all levels of the criminal justice system from summary matters to appeals. He has an extensive practice in trials, criminal appeals, and coronial inquests both in South Australia and other jurisdictions. He has appeared in a wide range of cases ranging from murder to people smuggling to white collar fraud. He has a particular interest in matters involving historic allegations of sexual abuse.

12

INSTITUTIONAL ABUSE INQUIRIES

Robert R. Spano, Jon F. Sigurdsson, and Gisli H. Gudjonsson CBE

A. Introduction   12.01

The abuse of children in residential care has been a major social (and criminological) issue which emerged in the late 1980s, continued throughout the 1990s and shows no sign of abating in the twenty-first century. Despite the subsequent media and official furore, there is a paucity of knowledge and literature on the subject.[1]

The above paragraph refers to a review of a book about public inquiries into the **12.02** abuse of children in residential care. The book, written by Brian Corby, Alan Doig, and Vicki Roberts,[2] demonstrates that until the 1990s public inquiries were almost exclusively focused on the death of children who had been physically abused whilst residing with their parents or carers in the community. However, since 1990 the focus of public inquiries has shifted onto the abuse of children in residential care. These residential establishments have included approved schools, local authority homes, and residential schools for children with intellectual disabilities and/or behavioural problems.

---

[1] Gallagher, B. (2002) 'Public Inquiries into Abuse of Children in Residential Care' (book review) 20 *Research, Policy and Planning*, 35–6.

[2] Corby, B., Doig, A., and Roberts, V. (2001) *Public Inquiries into Abuse of Children in Residential Care*, London: Jessica Kingsley Publishers.

12.03 Claire McLoone provides a historical perspective on the origins of institutional-ized care for children in Ireland during 1914 to 2000 and offers a sociocultural analysis of how and why the Irish Roman Catholic Church perpetuated the abuse of children in the care of its institutions.[3] Peter Sidebotham and Jane Appleton have drawn parallels between the extensive institutional abuse perpetrated by the high profile celebrity Jimmy Savile and those of the Catholic Church.[4] The authors emphasize the importance of not ignoring or covering up abuse, learning from past mistakes, and accepting the fact that: 'No institution, whether religious or secular, public or private, is immune from the dangers of child abuse.'

12.04 The purpose of the present chapter is to briefly review institutional abuse inquiries and discuss a public inquiry, appointed by the Prime Minister of Iceland in 2007 on the basis of an Act of Parliament, having the task of investigating sexual, physi-cal, and emotional maltreatment allegations in a number of children's homes in Iceland from the 1950s onward. The chapter will describe the investigation con-ducted, the methodology adopted and implemented by the Committee set up for these purposes, the recommendations made, and the outcome of the settlements reached. The recommendations will serve to assist those who work in this field, whatever their role, and will cross international boundaries.

B. Institutional Abuse Inquiries and Investigations

(1) A review of public inquiries

12.05 Corby et al. provide a comprehensive review of public inquiries into abuse of chil-dren in residential care in the UK with a particular focus on the North Wales Tribunal of Inquiry. The authors set out five key principles for achieving trust in inquiries.[5] These are:

1. They need to be carried out by an independent body in order to avoid issues of interest and bias.
2. The findings of inquiries need to be made open to the public, whilst protect-ing the identities of the individuals involved.
3. The inquiry's findings need to be written up and made available to both local and national bodies so that lessons can be learned from them.
4. Inquiries should be held without delays.

---

[3] McLoone, C. 'Say nothing! How pathology within Catholicism created and sustained the institutional abuse of children in 20th Century Ireland' (2012) 21 *Child Abuse Review* 394–404, published online in Wiley Online Library (*wileyonlinelibrary.com*) doi: 10.1002/car.2209.

[4] Sidebotham, P. and Appleton, J.V. 'Editorial: Understanding complex systems of abuse. Institutional and ritual abuse' (2012) 21 *Child Abuse Review*, 389–93, published online in Wiley Online Library (*wileyonlinelibrary.com*) doi: 10.1002/car.2253.

[5] Corby, Doig, and Roberts, *Public Inquiries*, cited at n.2.

5. Inquiries should have the power to make recommendations for compensation of victims of abuse.

(2) Home Affairs Committee Report

In a detailed Report published in October 2002,[6] a House of Commons Home **12.06** Affairs Committee provides a detailed review and recommendations regarding the investigation and trial of people accused of sexual abuse in children's homes. These included audio or video recording of police interviews with alleged victims, anonymity for the accused, tighter rules of evidence, and wider powers for the Criminal Cases Review Commission (CCRC) to review alleged miscarriages of justice cases. The Report also addresses risks associated with 'trawling'[7] the 'compensation factor',[8] and allegations dating back many years ('historical cases').[9]

(3) The 'Longcare Inquiry'

This inquiry relates to an investigation by the Thames Valley Police into offences of **12.07** ill-treatment and willful neglect of residents in a care home for people with intellectual disabilities.[10] The importance of this inquiry is that residents who were suspected of having been abused 'were assessed by clinical psychologists to ascertain their understanding of the oath and their suitability as competent witnesses in criminal proceedings', and 'Medical opinion was obtained on the suitability of the residents as witnesses with advice on how to question them, if at all'.[11] A video-recorded police interview was conducted for those residents found to be suitable for interview. The psychological evaluation of forty-nine residents found that thirty-seven (76%) were able to complete the assessment and of those, seventeen (46%) were considered competent to be interviewed by police and act as witnesses in court.[12] The psychological evaluation also found a strong relationship between IQ and the understanding of the oath. In fact, most of those residents with an IQ score of 60 or above had a basic understanding of the oath, compared with one third of those with an IQ score between 50 and 59. None

---

[6] House of Commons Home Affairs Committee (2002) *The conduct of investigations into past cases of abuse in children's homes* (HC 836-I and HC 836-II) London: The Stationery Office.

[7] This is defined in the Report as follows: 'Trawling, as we understand it, refers to the process when the police go one step further and contact potential witnesses who have not been named or even mentioned. In a trawl, the police will contact all, or a proportion of, those who were resident at the institution under investigation during the period when the abuse was alleged to have occurred.' Ibid., 8.

[8] The principal risk addressed in the Report relates to the prospect that compensation induces some individuals to fabricate or exaggerate allegations of abuse and how this risk can be minimized by a better 'working relationship between personal injury solicitors and the police'. Ibid., s 41, para 141.

[9] The Committee rejected a statutory time limit, but recommended that after a period of ten years, prosecutions should only proceed with the court's permission. Ibid., s 41, para 139.

[10] *Independent Longcare Inquiry*, (June 1998), Published by Buckinghamshire County Council.

[11] Ibid., Annex 5, para A5.9.

[12] Gudjonsson, G.H., Murphy, G.H., and Clare, I.C.H., 'Assessing the capacity of people with intellectual disabilities to be witnesses in court' (2000) 30 *Psychological Medicine*, 307–14.

of those with an IQ score below 50 had a basic understanding of the oath and would therefore not have been competent to act as witnesses.[13]

C. Breidavik

12.08 Breidavik, previously a farm and fishing base in the extreme west part of Iceland, was purchased by the Icelandic Government in 1952 and became a residential establishment for behaviourally disordered boys and later (in 1972) also for girls. The home was closed in 1979 and it is estimated that it housed a total of 158 children.[14]

12.09 In the first half of 2007, a number of reports in the Icelandic media described accounts of individuals that had been placed as children in Breidavik. They alleged that they had suffered ill-treatment during their stay. On 13 February 2007 the Government of Iceland decided to submit a Bill to Parliament providing for a comprehensive inquiry into the running of the children's home from 1950 to 1980 and, if need be, into other similar children's homes and special schools. The terms of reference of the inquiry will be further described in Section D.

12.10 In 1974, Gisli Gudjonsson conducted a follow-up study of seventy-one boys sent to Breidavik by the Reykjavik Children's Welfare Committee between 1953 and 1970, which comprised 64 per cent of all boys sent to Breidavik during that period.[15] There were three main reasons for the boys' admission to Breidavik: delinquent behaviour (79% of the boys had been reported to the police), home circumstances (i.e. the parent(s) had difficulty managing the child's behaviour), and truancy from school. Truancy from school was never the only reason for admission to Breidavik. Gudjonsson's follow-up study, which included a detailed analysis of the boys' background and their criminal records after leaving Breidavik, revealed that 75 per cent of the boys were subsequently convicted of a criminal offence, which indicated that Breidavik was a failure as a residential establishment for these boys.

---

[13] Gudjonsson, G.H. and Gunn, J., 'The Competence and Reliability of a Witness in a Criminal Court' (1982) 141 *British Journal of Psychiatry*, 624–7.

[14] Skýrsla nefndar samkvæmt lögum nr. 26/2007. Könnun á starfsemi Breiðavíkurheimilisins 1952–1979 Reykjavik, 31 January 2008 (The report of the committee in accordance with law no 26/2007. Inquiry into the operation of the Breidavik care home 1952–1979 Reykjavik, 31 January 2008).

[15] Gudjonsson, G.H. (1975) *Delinquent boys in Reykjavik: A follow-up study of boys sent to an approved school*, BSc Dissertation, Department of Psychology, Brunel University. See also, Gudjonsson, G.H. 'Delinquent Boys in Reykjavik: A Follow-up Study of Boys Sent to an Institution' in Gunn, J. and Farrington, D.P. (eds) (1982) *Abnormal Offenders, Delinquency, and the Criminal Justice System*, Chichester: John Wiley & Sons Ltd, 203–12.

D. The Breidavik Committee

(1) The role and function of the Committee

The Breidavik Inquiry was conducted by a Committee of experts appointed by the   **12.11**
Prime Minister of Iceland on 2 April 2007 on the basis of Act No 26/2007, promulgated by the Icelandic Parliament. The Committee was composed of a professor
of law, as chairman, a professor and senior lecturer of psychology, and a professor
of social work. The role of the Committee was fourfold:[16]

1. to investigate the circumstances of the placement of children at Breidavik;
2. to verify, as far as possible, whether the children at Breidavik were subjected
   to ill-treatment during their stay;
3. to assess whether public monitoring and supervision of the children's
   home at Breidavik was satisfactory and in conformity with applicable legal
   standards; and
4. to put forth proposals on possible government responses in light of the
   Committee's conclusions.

The Committee's procedures were composed of six essential elements: **12.12**

1. compilation of documentary evidence from government and municipal institutions and memorandums from experts;
2. on-site investigation of Breidavik;
3. interviews with individuals who were placed as children at Breidavik;
4. interviews with former staff members at Breidavik and other government
   officials;
5. analysis of information compiled in the form of documentary evidence, testi-
   monials, and expert reports; and
6. assessment and proposals on the basis of the Committee's substantive
   conclusions.

(2) Methodology

In adopting its methodology for the assessment of evidence and its probative   **12.13**
value, the Committee first took account of the fact that this was the first time an
inquiry of this nature had been conducted in Iceland. Secondly, looking to examples from other countries, the Committee found that similar inquiries had not

---

[16] Skýrsla nefndar samkvæmt lögum nr. 26/2007. Könnun á starfsemi Breiðavíkurheimilisins
1952–1979 Reykjavik, 31 January 2008 (The report of the committee in accordance with
law no 26/2007. Inquiry into the operation of the Breidavik care home 1952–1979 Reykjavik,
31 January 2008).

been conducted in a consistent manner but had been adapted to take account of the special nature of each inquiry and the domestic situation in each case. Thus, the Committee concluded that an inquiry of this nature should be based on the facts and special circumstances in the country in question as well as adapting procedures and methodologies to take due account of the special features of the legal system in which the inquiry took place.

12.14 When further assessing its preferred methodology, the Committee considered that its role was to establish, as far as possible, the veracity of allegations of facts taking place several decades previously in an Icelandic society very different from that of the present. Its role was thus to verify, *as a general matter*, whether children were ill-treated in the homes and special schools. Hence, its role was not to analyze and establish the truth of each and every account, as such an approach would not yield safe and reliable outcomes. Therefore, the Committee concluded that its preferred methodology would involve assessing, *holistically*, whether documentary evidence and testimony could provide a basis for holding that it was *more likely than not* that children were ill-treated at Breidavik during their stay. The approach was therefore one of ascertaining the *existence of patterns of abuse* during certain periods and not to opine on whether a particular (named) individual had been the subject of ill-treatment.

12.15 When defining the scope of its role, and especially the *concept of ill-treatment*, the Committee concluded that account should be taken of the internationally recognized norms of human rights that Iceland was obliged to follow during the period in question. As Iceland had already ratified the European Convention on Human Rights (ECHR) in 1953, the Committee decided that in the interpretation of the concept of ill-treatment, as provided for by Act No 26/2007, account should be taken of Article 3 of the ECHR, which bans torture and other forms of inhuman or degrading treatment or punishment. Further, in assessing the substance of the provision, the Committee looked to the jurisprudence of the European Court of Human Rights. With this in mind, the Committee considered that the concept of ill-treatment should include any act or omission which could be considered, objectively, to be inhuman or degrading. Thus, any form of direct physical force against a child as punishment, where unnecessary pain or suffering was inflicted, would be considered ill-treatment, unless the act was held to be a legitimate measure aimed at preventing violence or the imminent threat of violence or destruction of property. Also, the concept of ill-treatment would include other acts of intimidation or degradation of a child or any act or omission that was capable of constituting an abuse of a child and a violation of its dignity.

(3) Issues of credibility

12.16 According to Act No 26/2007, the Committee was allowed to interview the former residents and employees of Breidavik and anyone else the Committee believed had information that could be useful in its work, provided they consented.[17] As stated above, the purpose of the investigation was not to assess the truthfulness/credibility of the individual accounts of the former residents and employees of Breidavik about specific incidents. The individual accounts about the same specific incidents were sometimes quite different and were not supported in any written documents. In fact, none of the documents that the Committee obtained from the government or local councils shed light on whether ill-treatment and/or violence had occurred at some point at Breidavik.

(i) *The appointment of an expert to the Committee*

The Committee decided to request an independent external evaluation of the indi- **12.17** vidual accounts by witnesses before reaching its final conclusions. This evaluation was carried out by Professor Gisli Gudjonsson, one of the authors of this chapter. Gudjonsson was asked to evaluate in general terms the credibility of the accounts given by the former residents and employees in order to assist the Committee in deciding whether or not ill-treatment and physical and sexual violence had occurred at some point in the history of Breidavik. Gudjonsson also included a review of the most recent scientific literature on the credibility of witness accounts, which guided the Committee's work and conclusions. By this approach the Committee believed that the overall assessment of the accounts and its final conclusions were as far possible founded on solid grounds.

(ii) *The interviews of former residents*

It was decided to invite all the former residents of Breidavik about whom the **12.18** Committee had information, for an interview, instead of selecting a limited sample. This was done to ensure that all those who so wished, would have a viable opportunity to give information about their stay and experience at Breidavik. The main objective of the interviews was to gather information in order to be able to assess, as far as possible, whether, and to what extent, children who were admitted to Breidavik, were mistreated or victimized during the stay. The objective was also to further the Committee's understanding of the operation of the home in general, and of the antecedents and consequences of the residents' stay. The organization of the interviews aimed at meeting these objectives. Efforts were made to define as much as possible the conduct of the interviews in line with the aims of the Committee.

According to available information, 158 children were admitted to Breidavik **12.19** during the years between 1952 and 1979. Of these, the Committee interviewed

---

[17] Skýrsla nefndar samkvæmt lögum nr. 26/2007. Könnun á starfsemi Breiðavíkurheimilisins 1952–1979 Reykjavík, 31 January 2008 (The report of the committee in accordance with law no 26/2007. Inquiry into the operation of the Breidavik care home 1952–1979 Reykjavik, 31 January 2008).

eighty (51%), thirty-three (21%) were deceased, eleven (7%) could not be found, nineteen (12%) were not interested in being interviewed, ten (6%) could not be interviewed because they lived abroad and four (3%) did not turn up for the pre-arranged interview. One former resident requested to submit a written statement of his stay at the home.

12.20   As preparation for the interviews, all the former residents were telephoned and given general information about the Committee, its role and the planned interview. Those who agreed to be interviewed received a letter containing the same information and the timing of the interview. Those who could not be contacted by telephone were sent a letter containing information about the Committee and its role and an invitation to be interviewed about their experience at Breidavik. The Committee prepared a checklist of items considered necessary to obtain critical background information about possible ill-treatment and violence at Breidavik. The interviews were generally conducted by one of the Committee's members and a legally qualified secretary of the Committee. In the interviews, the former residents were asked about their stay in general, the antecedents of their admittance, daily life at Breidavik, mental and physical care provided, education, punishment, communication with other residents, staff, and family during their stay, and in detail about alleged ill-treatment and physical and sexual violence. At the beginning of each interview the legally qualified secretary explained the resident's legal status according to Act No 26/2007. In particular, it was emphasized that those who were interviewed would be entitled to refuse to answer questions if their responses included admissions or indications that they had committed criminal offences, or that there might be damage to their reputation. A written consent and permission to record the interviews was obtained. Such permission was granted in all cases except two. Usually the interview lasted about one hour, but the length was guided by the needs of each interviewee.

(iii) The interviews of staff

12.21   According to Act No 26/2007, all public employees, for example, medical doctors and other health-care employees, who would otherwise be entitled to confidentiality, were obliged to provide the Committee with information upon request, and the same went for those who had retired. Therefore the Committee decided to interview a selected sample of former employees of Breidavik (i.e. managers, teachers, and staff performing general duties at the home), who were considered likely to have information that could shed light on incidents and circumstances in the operation of Breidavik. In deciding which employees should be interviewed, consideration was given if the former resident's accounts warranted indications that ill-treatment and physical and sexual violence had occurred in certain periods of Breidavik's operation. Efforts were made to interview former employees and other public employees through all the years the home was operational so that an overall picture of the home could be obtained. The interviewing of the former employees at Breidavik was conducted in a similar manner as the interviews with the former residents.

(4) Outcome and recommendations

The Committee published its comprehensive and detailed Report on Breidavik **12.22**
on 31 January 2008. The members held a press conference on that day in order to
highlight the importance of immediately disseminating to the public the conclusions reached by the Committee in accordance with its philosophy of transparency,
the importance of which should not be underestimated for the proper conduct of
inquiries of this nature. The main conclusions of the Report were the following:

1. *Ill-treatment by residents and staff* The Committee concluded that during certain periods of activity, some children placed at Breidavik were ill-treated by
   other residents and/or by the staff members, particularly in the period from
   1964 to 1972.
2. *Governmental supervision and monitoring* As regards governmental supervision
   and monitoring of the home, the Committee held that when looking to the legal
   provisions on governmental supervision of the home, in force at the material
   time, account had to be taken of the fact that the substance and scope of supervision of childcare institutions was relative in nature. It had to be assessed in light
   of the nature and structure of the particular institution, the particular group of
   children it was meant to serve, the requirements of specialized knowledge of the
   staff members, the internal and external conditions of confinement provided by
   the institution, and the aims that its activity was meant to pursue. Furthermore,
   a distinction was made between external supervision by governmental organs
   and municipal childcare committees and internal monitoring by the director
   of the institution and staff members. As regards Breidavik, the Committee concluded that the monitoring and supervision of the activities of Breidavik, both
   from an external and an internal viewpoint, was lacking in general.

On the basis of its conclusions, the Committee set out an array of *proposals and* **12.23**
recommendations directed to the Icelandic Government.

1. *Damages* The Committee invited the Government to assess whether and to
   what extent damages should be awarded to the former residents of Breidavik
   on a non-pecuniary basis. On the basis of the Committee's proposal,
   Parliament subsequently enacted a law providing for damages to all former
   residents of Breidavik and other childcare institutions and special homes that
   the Committee subsequently investigated.[18]
2. *Provision of treatment* The Committee highlighted the importance of assessing
   whether and to what extent it was necessary to provide the former residents
   with mental health treatment. Both during and after the publication of the
   Committee's report, such treatment was provided to the former residents.

---

[18] Lög nr. 47/2010 um sanngirnisbætur fyrir misgjörðir á stofnunum eða heimilum sem falla
undir lög nr. 26/2007 (Law no 47/2010 about compensation for wrongdoing whilst in institutions
or in homes falling under law no 26/2007).

3. *Reform* The Committee emphasized the need for reform of the current system of external and internal monitoring of childcare facilities and homes. The Committee put forth several proposals in that regard, most of which have subsequently been followed with legislative amendments in the area of childcare law.

(5) The continued work of the Committee with regard to other care homes

12.24 Having concluded its first inquiry under Act No 26/2007, as regards the children home at Breidavik, the Committee subsequently opened inquiries into eight other children's homes as well as the special school for deaf children in Iceland. The Committee published three further reports on 31 August 2009,[19] 31 August 2010,[20] and 21 November 2011,[21] concluding its work under the original composition with the last-mentioned report in 2011. The Committee's four reports, prepared over a period of five years, cover approximately 1,700 pages.

12.25 The Committee consistently applied the same methodology as originally conceived during the Breidavik inquiry, as the members believed that it was the correct approach in light of the aims of its statutorily mandated work. In its last Report from 21 November 2011, the Committee gave a comprehensive review of all of its activities, conclusions, proposals, and recommendations.

E. Conclusion

12.26 The Grand Chamber of the European Court of Human Rights has recently held that States Parties to the ECHR, which comprise forty-seven European States, are required to take measures designed to ensure that individuals within their

---

[19] Skýrsla nefndar samkvæmt lögum nr. 26/2007. Áfangaskýrsla nr. 1. Könnun á starfsemi Heyrnleysingjaskólans 1947–1992, vistheimilisins Kumbaravogi 1965–1984 og skólaheimilisins Bjargs 1965–1967 Reykjavík 31 August 2009. (The report of the committee in accordance with law no 26/2007. Progress Report no. 1. Inquiry into the operation of the School for Deaf Children from 1947 to 1992, the Kumbaravogur care home from 1965 to 1984, and the Bjarg boarding school from 1965 to 1967. Reykjavik 31 August 2009).

[20] Skýrsla nefndar samkvæmt lögum no 26/2007. Áfangaskýrsla nr. 2. Könnun á starfsemi vistheimilisins Silungapolls 195-1969, vistheimilisins Reykjahlíðar 1956–1972 og heimavistarskólans að Jaðri 1946–1973. Reykjavik 31 August 2010. (The report of the committee in accordance with law nr. 26/2007. Progress Report no 2, Inquiry into the operation the Silungapollur care home from 1950 to 1969, the Reykjahlid care home from 1956 to 1972, and the Jadar boarding school from 1946 to 1973, Reykjavik 31 August 2010).

[21] Skýrsla nefndar samkvæmt lögum nr. 26/2007. Áfangaskýrsla nr. 3. Könnun á starfsemi Upptökuheimilis ríkisins 1945-1971, Unglingaheimilis ríkisins 1971-1994 og meðferðarheimilisins í Smáratúni og á Torfastöðum 1979–1994 Reykjavík 21 November 2011. (The report of the committee in accordance with law no 26/2007. Progress Report no 2. Inquiry into the Government's Children's Home from 1945 to 1971 and 1971 to 1994, and the Smaratun and Torfastadir treatment homes from 1979 to 1994. Reykjavik 21 November 2011).

jurisdiction are not subjected to torture or inhuman or degrading treatment, including such ill-treatment administered by private individuals. The required measures should, at least, provide effective protection in particular of children and other vulnerable persons and should include reasonable steps to prevent ill-treatment of which the authorities had or ought to have had knowledge. This positive obligation of protection assumes particular importance in the context of the provision of an important public service such as primary education, school authorities being obliged to protect the health and well-being of pupils and, in particular, of young children who are especially vulnerable and are under the exclusive control of those authorities. It is thus an inherent obligation of government to ensure their protection from ill-treatment, especially in a primary education context, through the adoption, as necessary, of special measures and safeguards.[22]

European States respect this positive obligation by instituting public inquiries into **12.27** allegations of child abuse in public institutions. It is important in this respect to appreciate that public inquiries into events in the distant past are difficult enterprises fraught with conceptual as well as logistical limitations. The experience gained in Iceland demonstrates the importance of setting realistic goals at the outset so as not to create unwarranted expectations. Furthermore, care must be taken in constructing a clear and foreseeable mandate for inquiries of this nature, drafting efficient procedural rules that respect fundamental safeguards under the rule of law, as well as securing necessary resources in the form of human knowledge and expertise. Although there are inherent limitations in seeking to establish events arising in different societies from the present, the importance of social acceptance and awareness of child abuse in public institutions can never be underestimated.

Further Reading

Corby, B., Doig, A., and Roberts, V. (2001) *Public Inquiries into abuse of Children in Residential Care*, London: Jessica Kingsley Publishers.

Gudjonsson, G.H. 'Delinquent Boys in Reykjavik: A Follow-up Study of Boys Sent to an Institution' in Gunn, J. and Farrington, D.P. (eds) (1982) *Abnormal Offenders, Delinquency, and the Criminal Justice System*, Chichester: John Wiley & Sons Ltd, 203–12.

Vrij, A. 'Criteria-based content analysis. A qualitative review of the first 37 studies'. (2005) 11 *Psychology, Public Policy, and Law*, 3–41.

Wolfe, D.A., Jaffe, P.G., Jetté, J.L., and Poisson, S.E. 'The impact of child abuse in community institutions and organizations: Advancing professional and scientific understanding' (2003) 10 *Clinical Psychology: Science and Practice*, 179–91.

---

[22] *O'Keefe v Ireland* [GC] No 35810/09, ss 144–7, 28 January 2014.

Author Biographies

Robert R. Spano is a Judge of the European Court of Human Rights. He holds a Candidate of Law degree from the University of Iceland and a Master of Jurisprudence from the University of Oxford (University College). Prior to becoming an international judge, Spano served provisionally as Parliamentary Ombudsman of Iceland from 2009 to 2013. He is a professor of law at the University of Iceland and was Dean of the faculty from 2010 to 2013. From 1997 to 2012, he chaired the inquiry, set up by Parliament, tasked with investigating allegations of ill-treatment in children's homes run by the State from 1947 to 1992. He has also been an independent expert to the Lanzarote Committee on child sexual abuse of the Council of Europe.

Jon F. Sigurdsson, PhD, is Professor of Psychology and Clinical Director at Reykjavik University and Professor at the University of Iceland and Landspitali–The National University Hospital of Iceland. Between 2001 and 2013 he was the Head of Clinical Psychology Services at Landspitali and between 1988 and 2001 he was a Prison Psychologist at the National Prison and Probation Administration in Iceland. He has been adviser to the Ministry of Welfare, the Althingi Ombudsman, and the Police and the Government Agency for Child Protection. He has been a member of two committees investigating ill-treatment of children in Iceland, the committee set up in 2007 by the Icelandic Parliament, referred to in this book chapter, and the Investigative Committee of the Catholic Church in Iceland set up in 2011 to investigate the reactions and practice of the Catholic Church in Iceland regarding allegations of sexual abuse and other violent acts of ordained servants and other employees of the Church.

Gisli H. Gudjonsson CBE, PhD, is an Emeritus Professor of Forensic Psychology at the Institute of Psychiatry, Psychology and Neuroscience King's College London and an Honorary Consultant Clinical and Forensic Psychologist at Broadmoor Hospital. Prior to his retirement from King's College on 1 January 2012 he was the Head of Forensic Psychology Services for the Lambeth Forensic Services and Medium Secure Unit at the South London and Maudsley NHS Trust (SLaM). He has been awarded two lifetime achievement awards and was appointed a Commander of the Order of the British Empire (CBE) in the Queen's Birthday 2011 Honours List for services to clinical psychology.

PART II

INVESTIGATIVE AND SCIENTIFIC PERSPECTIVES

13

ANALYZING AND IMPROVING THE TESTIMONY OF VULNERABLE WITNESSES INTERVIEWED UNDER THE 'ACHIEVING BEST EVIDENCE' PROTOCOL

Graham Davies, Ray Bull, and Rebecca Milne

A. Introduction

Between 2011 and 2012, some 33,000 children and young people were cited as witnesses in the criminal courts of England and Wales.[1] Many of these witnesses were appearing in cases of alleged sexual or physical abuse and would have been interviewed by police officers or social workers trained in the official guidance given **13.01**

---

[1] Association of Chief Police Officers (2010) *Advice on the Structure of Visually Recorded Witness Interviews*, London: National Strategic Steering Group on Investigative Interviewing, ACPO.

in *Achieving Best Evidence in Criminal Proceedings* or *ABE*. Adherence to interviewing protocols is essential to elicit best evidence, given the demonstrable impact of suggestive or otherwise inappropriate questioning on the reliability of testimony of children and young people.[2] We begin by considering the evolution of the protocol and the reasons for the changes introduced in successive revisions and their impact on performance. We consider the new legal provisions which give juvenile complainants of sexual or physical violence the option of giving their evidence live in court and its implications for evidence and procedure. We identify the most common failings in interviews and how these can best be addressed before turning to how interviewers can be trained to adhere to the requirements of the protocol and to monitor and maintain the quality of their interviews.

B. The Evolution of *Achieving Best Evidence*

(1) The origins of the guidance

13.02 The incoming Labour Government in 1997 had signalled the priority it attached to greater support for victims and witnesses within the criminal justice system. An interdepartmental document[3] recommended a number of reforms and these were included in the Youth Justice and Criminal Evidence Act, 1999.[4] This Act introduced a range of procedural innovations, termed Special Measures, most available at the discretion of the judge, to assist vulnerable witnesses of all ages in giving their evidence at court. One measure, the admission of pre-recorded videotaped interviews as a substitute for evidence-in-chief had been introduced for juvenile witnesses in the 1991 Criminal Justice Act, but now became available to vulnerable witnesses of all ages. The conduct of such interviews with children had been the subject of an earlier guidance document, the *Memorandum of Good Practice* (1992)[5] and a decision was reached that revised guidance was required to accommodate the new legislation.

(2) Departures from the *Memorandum of Good Practice*

13.03 In addition to detailing the Special Measures, *Achieving Best Evidence in Criminal Proceedings*,[6] launched in 2002, also embodied a number of other changes, reflecting the perceived need for 'rebalancing the criminal justice system in favour of the

---

[2] Ceci, S.J. and Bruck, M. (1995) *Jeopardy in the Courtroom: A Scientific Analysis of Children's Testimony*, Washington: American Psychological Association.

[3] Home Office (1998) *Speaking Up for Justice: Report of the Interdepartmental Working Group on the Treatment of Vulnerable and Intimidated Witnesses in the Criminal Justice System*, London: the Home Office.

[4] Available at *http://www.legislation.gov.uk/ukpga/1999/23/contents*.

[5] Home Office (1992) *Memorandum of Good Practice for Video Recorded Interviews with Child Witnesses for Criminal Proceedings*. London: HMSO.

[6] Home Office (2002) *Achieving Best Evidence in Criminal Proceedings: Guidance for Vulnerable or Intimidated Witnesses, including Children*, London: The Home Office.

law-abiding majority.'[7] The new guidance was not confined to the conduct of investigative interviews, but also sought to place the investigative interview within the wider context of witness care. There was a greater emphasis upon the planning required before the interview took place and in particular, any special needs of the complainant which ought to be taken into account. There was also formal recognition that some limited pre-interview contact between the interviewer and the witness was necessary to ensure the interviewee was able to provide information relevant to the enquiry and prepared to speak about it within a recorded interview, though it was emphasized that this contact should be properly recorded. There was also recognition that the criminal justice system's obligation to the witness did not end with the interview: witnesses would need support and preparation, particularly if the matter was to go to the criminal court. This might include a familiarization visit to the courtroom and an explanation from the Crown Court liaison Officer or the Young Witness Service to establish any special needs and answer any questions about the trial process.

(3) The wider ambitions of *ABE*

Another new theme concerned to whom the guidance was directed. The recommendations in the *Memorandum of Good Practice* were directed exclusively toward those conducting interviews with children. *ABE* sought to engage the wider legal community as an audience for its recommendations, particularly judges and advocates who, it was hoped, would follow its recommendations on such matters as style and pacing of questions and the need to take account of special needs at court. In the main, prosecutors, judges, and magistrates have shown themselves ready to invoke Special Measures to assist witnesses, including the use of intermediaries to assist very young witnesses or those with communication disorders.[8] However, the style of questioning by advocates at court continued to be a source of concern, despite the *ABE* recommendations.[9] There are refreshing signs of a greater awareness among the Bar of the special difficulties vulnerable witnesses face in giving their best evidence, particularly under cross-examination[10] and the development of relevant training materials.[11] The conflict for advocates between adequately representing their client's case and taking account of prosecution witness vulnerabilities creates an inevitable tension not easily resolved. In 2013, new guidance on prosecuting cases of child sexual abuse was issued, including a recommendation

13.04

---

[7] Office for Criminal Justice Reform (2006) *No Witness No Justice: The National Victim and Witness Care Programme*, London: Office for Criminal Justice Reform.

[8] Plotnikoff, J. and Woolfson, R. (2007) *The Go-Between: Evaluation of Intermediary Pathfinder Projects*, http://lexiconlimited.co.uk/wp-content/uploads/2013/01/Intermediaries_study_report.pdf.

[9] Spencer, J.R. and Lamb, M.E. (2012) *Children and Cross-examination: Time to Change the Rules?* Oxford: Hart Publishing.

[10] *Raising the Bar: The Handling of Vulnerable Witnesses, Victims and Dependents in Court* (2013), http://www.advocacytrainingcouncil.org/images/word/raising%20the%20bar.pdf.

[11] *A Question of Practice 2013* provides a film and 'toolkits' covering case management and questioning of young and/or vulnerable witnesses, http://www.theadvocatesgateway. org/a-question-of-practice.

that only trained specialists be employed as prosecutors, and preliminary hearings be established to agree ground rules covering the length and content of cross-examination prior to trial.[12]

(4) The phased approach to interviewing

13.05   The new guidance gave an opportunity to address some issues which had arisen from extensive practical experience of using the *Memorandum* to interview children. The *Memorandum* had advocated a four-phased model of interviewing. The first phase involves *rapport building* in which the *ground rules* for the interview are also introduced. These rules include the importance of telling the truth and the interviewee informing the interviewer if they do not understand a question or do not know the answer. Following completion of this phase, the interviewer moves on to the *free narrative* phase, where the focus of the interview is raised through an indirect prompt, such as: 'Do you know why you are here today?' Explicitly raising the particular allegation with the interviewee is specifically discouraged. Free narrative is developed and extended through *active listening strategies* ('I see. So what happened next?'). When the interviewee has exhausted their spontaneous account, the third, *questioning* phase begins with an emphasis on the use of open questions. *ABE* recommends that other types of question, such as specific or closed ('either/or') questions should only be used to expand upon issues already raised from free narrative and leading questions should be avoided. In the final or *closure* phase, the interviewer summarizes what the interviewee has said, as far as possible in their own words, before offering reassurance and thanks.[13]

(5) Did interviewers adhere to the *Memorandum* guidance?

13.06   Research using transcripts of actual investigative interviews with children revealed that interviewers experienced difficulties in adhering to the precepts of the *Memorandum*. Davies and colleagues examined a sample of 40 interviews conducted during the first two years under the *Memorandum*.[14] Rapport was generally satisfactorily established, but many of the ground rules were omitted. All four phases of the interview were clearly present in just 30 per cent of interviews, with the free narrative and closure phases being most frequently omitted. Where a clear questioning phase existed, only 30 per cent began with an open question and closed or specific questions predominated. Later surveys showed a general overall improvement in compliance with the *Memorandum*, which reflected improved training and

---

[12] Crown Prosecution Service, (2013) *Guidelines on Prosecuting Cases of Child Sexual Abuse Issued by the Director of Public Prosecutions, http://www.cps.gov.uk/consultations/csa_guidelines_v2.pdf.*

[13] Bull, R. (1996) 'Good practice for video recorded interviews with child witnesses for use in criminal proceedings' in Davies, G., Lloyd-Bostock, S., McMurran, M., and Wilson, C. (eds) *Psychology, Law and Criminal Justice*, Berlin: de Gruyter, 100–17.

[14] Davies, G., Wilson, C., Mitchell, R., and Milsom, J. (1995) *Videotaping Children's Evidence: An Evaluation*, London: Home Office.

practical experience.[15] However, some weaknesses persisted: a marked absence of open questions beyond the initial prompt to tell what had happened and a continuing over-reliance on specific and closed questions.[16] There was also a continuing failure to cover ground rules beyond the admonition to tell the truth.[17]

(6) Changes in *ABE* designed to increase compliance

The *ABE* guidance retained the same four-phase approach to questioning recom-   **13.07**
mended by the original *Memorandum*, but sought to increase compliance through the introduction of checklists for ground rules and closure points and semi-scripted elements were offered to assess interviewee's understanding of truth and lies and for initially raising the issue of concern. There was increased emphasis on the importance of asking open questions throughout the interview and of the dangers of over-using closed and specific questions. There was also recognition that a 'one size fits all' approach provided by the original *Memorandum* gave insufficient recognition to developmental differences, and thus *ABE* included additional guidance on interviewing pre-school and children with learning disabilities and endorsed alternative interviewing procedures, such as the *Cognitive Interview*[18] and the *National Institute of Child Health and Development (NICHD) Protocol*,[19] which shares an emphasis on the importance of open-ended questions and semi-scripted interview prompts.

(7) Has *ABE* made interviewers more guidance-compliant?

No systematic evaluation has been commissioned on the effectiveness of *ABE* subse-   **13.08**
quent to its introduction in 2002. The new guidance was supplemented by a training pack emphasizing its distinctive features and uses with different groups of vulnerable witnesses.[20] However, training of police officers in the demands of the new interviewing techniques remains a cause for concern with little systematic training or regular monitoring of standards, a position aggravated by recent reductions in police funding.[21] A recent study directly compared the quality of interviews under

---

[15] Davies, G.M. and Westcott, H. (1999) *Interviewing Child Witnesses under the 'Memorandum of Good Practice': A Research Review*, Police Research Series, no 115, London: Home Office.

[16] Sternberg, K.J., Lamb, M.E., Davies, G.M., and Westcott, H.L. '"The Memorandum of Good Practice": Theory versus application' (2001) 25 *Child Abuse and Neglect*, 669–81.

[17] Westcott, H.L. and Kynan, S., 'Interviewer practice in investigative interviews for suspected child sexual abuse' (2006) 12 *Psychology, Crime and Law*, 367–82.

[18] Fisher, R.P. and Geiselman, R.E. (1992) *Memory Enhancing Techniques for Investigative Interviewing: The Cognitive Interview*, Springfield, IL: Charles C. Thomas.

[19] Lamb, M.E., Hershkowitz, I., Orbach, Y., and Esplin, P.W. (2008) *Tell Me What Happened: Structured Investigative Interviews with Child Victims and Witnesses*, Chichester: John Wiley & Sons Ltd.

[20] Welsh Assembly Government (2004) *Training Pack: Achieving Best Evidence in Criminal Proceedings for Vulnerable and Intimidated Witnesses including Children*, Cardiff: Welsh Assembly.

[21] Criminal Justice Joint Inspection (2012) *Joint Inspection Report on the Experience of Young Victims and Witnesses in the Criminal Justice System*, https://www.justiceinspectorates.gov.uk/cjji/inspections/joint-inspection-report-on-the-experience-of-young-victims-and-witnesses-in-the-criminal-justice-system/#.VdxCg-BOFbw.

ABE and the *Memorandum*,[22] but found no general improvement in compliance. The *ABE* interviews included more of the ground rules than did those conducted under the *Memorandum*, but there was no observable difference in the proportion of open questions employed. Lamb and colleagues also noted the continuing low levels of open questions used by *ABE* trained interviewers, which they contrasted with the numbers achieved under the *NICHD Protocol*, with its more explicit emphasis upon rigorous practice in the use of scripted open-ended questions.[23]

C. The 2007 Revision of *ABE*

13.09 One of the more unexpected findings of a Home Office survey of vulnerable and intimidated witnesses[24] concerned the incidence of intimidation. No separate figures were reported for child sex complainants, but overall, two thirds of all vulnerable witnesses reported that they had actually experienced or feared intimidation, mainly from defendants (36%) or their families (21%). These findings were reflected in the first revision of *Achieving Best Evidence* in 2007,[25] where an entirely new chapter was devoted to the topic. However, the focus was exclusively upon intimidated adults, particularly key or 'significant' witnesses whose interviews were from now on to be routinely videotaped. However, all the recommendations concerning the planning and conduct of interviews with children remained in place, but with a renewed plea for a greater emphasis upon appropriate training for specialist interviewers.

D. The 2011 Revision of *ABE*

13.10 A further revision of the guidance in 2011[26] took account of changes resulting from the Coroners and Justices Act (2009)[27] and the advice of the Association of Chief

---

[22] Hill, E.S. and Davies, G.M., 'Has the quality of investigative interviews with children improved with changes in Guidance? An exploratory study' (2013) 7 *Policing*, 63–71.

[23] Lamb, M.E., Orbach, Y., Sternberg, K.J., Aldridge, J., Pearson, J., Stewart, H.L., Esplin, P.W., and Bowler, L., 'Use of a Structured Investigative Protocol Enhances the Quality of Investigative Interviews With Alleged Victims of Child Sexual Abuse in Britain' (2009) 23(4) *Applied Cognitive Psychology*, 449–67.

[24] Hamlyn, B., Phelps, A., Turtle, J., and Sattar, G. (2004) *Are special measures working? Evidence from Surveys of Vulnerable and Intimidated Witnesses* (Home Office Research Study 283) London: Home Office.

[25] Office for Criminal Justice Reform (2007a) *Achieving Best Evidence in Criminal Proceedings: Guidance on Interviewing Victims and Witnesses, and Using Special Measures*, London: Office for Criminal Justice Reform.

[26] Ministry of Justice (2011) *Achieving Best Evidence in Criminal Proceedings: Guidance on interviewing victims and witnesses, and guidance on using special measures*, London: Ministry of Justice, *http://www.cps.gov.uk/publications/docs/best_evidence_in_criminal_proceedings.pdf.*

[27] Coroners and Justice Act, 2009, *http://www.legislation.gov.uk/ukpga/2009/25/section/125.*

Police Officers.[28] The traditional role of the investigative interview—to elicit the witness's account—is maintained, but an additional component has been added on case-specific questions arising from other witness statements or information received, answers to which would assist police investigations. This second component can form part of the main interview or constitute a separate, second interview with the witness, but would not be shown in court. The need for this latter feature is unlikely to arise in most cases of familial sexual abuse, but might be required in major investigations of child sexual exploitation involving organized groups of offenders. The new guidance takes account of judges' recommendations that the main rapport phase be conducted off-camera, although it recommends that any ground rules discussed should be referred to in the visual record. There is also more advice and increased caution in the use of props such as models, dolls, and photographs, and extended coverage of the Enhanced Cognitive Interview.

E. Impact of the Relaxation of the 'Primary Rule'

(1) The new legal position

The Coroners and Justices Act, 2009[29] raised the age limit for recording investigative interviews with witnesses concerning sexual and violent offences from 17 to 18 years. However, the most far-reaching change for children was the relaxation of the 'primary rule': the presumption set out in the Youth Justice and Criminal Evidence Act 1999[30] that children giving evidence in such cases would give their evidence-in-chief through a recorded investigative interview. In future, there would be some discretion over the way that children testified in such cases: they would not necessarily be required to use this Special Measure: children would be permitted to request that their evidence be given in the traditional manner in open court or from behind a screen in open court. The 1999 Act proposed three tests as to a need for Special Measures: whether the witness was vulnerable (children automatically qualify); whether access to Special Measures would improve the quality of their evidence; and what Special Measure(s) would be likely to maximize this quality. The Coroners and Justices Act, 2009 required judges dealing with requests to give evidence in open court to consider: **13.11**

- the age and maturity of the witness;
- their understanding of the consequences of giving evidence on the day at court;
- the relationship of the child to the defendant(s);
- the social, cultural, and ethnic background of the child; and

---

[28] Association of Chief Police Officers (2010) *Advice on the Structure of Visually Recorded Witness Interviews,* London: National Strategic Steering Group on Investigative Interviewing, ACPO.
[29] Cited at n.27
[30] Cited at n.4.

- the nature and circumstances of the offence, together with any other relevant factors.[31]

(2) The impact of choice on court procedure

13.12 A minority of children wish to confront an accused and give their evidence in open court[32] and the 2009 legislation facilitates this outcome. However, the initiative for requesting open court testimony lies with the child complainant, although the final decision is made by the court.[33] It should be noted that rule changes now allow the recorded interview to be supplemented at court by additional questions put to the witness covering new matters or relevant issues not raised by the child or interviewer in the original recording. It is not explicit in the legislative guidance what standing any existing recording might have if the child is permitted to give their evidence in another way: presumably they could view their recording prior to trial (although some children are still denied this facility, irrespective of the method they chose to testify[34]).

(3) The impact on the quality of evidence

13.13 The court will need to have regard to the differences in the way in which evidence is taken at court compared to how it is elicited in an investigative interview. Prosecutors will have a clear notion as to what evidence they want the child to provide to the court, which may not correspond with what the witness, or indeed the police, regard as relevant and worthwhile. It is noteworthy that in the Home Office survey on vulnerable witnesses, 98 per cent of witnesses who gave their evidence via a pre-recorded interview felt they had been given the opportunity to say everything that they wished, which was true for only 53 per cent who gave evidence-in-chief at court, a reflection of the very different approaches adopted in the two settings.[35]

13.14 One question frequently raised by prosecutors is their belief in the greater impact and immediacy of testimony given in open court compared to that mediated by an electronic recording and the relative impact on the sentiment of juries.[36] While some research studies support the view that live testimony has greater impact, the overall outcome is equivocal, with the suggestion that any immediate impact is neutralized

---

[31] Cited at n.27.

[32] Plotnikoff, J. and Woolfson, R. (2009) *Measuring Up? Evaluating Implementation of Government Commitments to Young Witnesses in Criminal Proceedings*, http://www.nuffieldfoundation.org/sites/default/files/measuring_up_report_wdf66579(1).pdf.

[33] Hoyano, L.C.H., 'Coroners and Justices Act, 2009: Special measures take two: Entrenching unequal access to justice?' [2010] 210 Crim LR, 1–19.

[34] Plotnikoff and Woolfson (2009)cited at n.32, 68.

[35] Hamlyn et al. (2005) cited at n.24.

[36] Davis, G., Hoyano, L., Keenan, C., Maitland, L., and Morgan, R. (1999) *An Assessment of the Admissibility and Sufficiency of Evidence in Child Abuse Prosecutions*, London: Home Office.

by the process of jury discussion and decision-making.[37] There is also the question of the likely quality of evidence given on the day of trial compared to an earlier recording. Despite best efforts, delay is still a frequent feature of sexual assault trials[38] and there is research evidence that the passage of time has a disproportionately adverse effect upon the testimony of younger children.[39] The requirement to give evidence in open court may also lead to reluctance by the CPS to permit children to undergo therapy in the interim.[40] Indeed, any factors which are likely to increase witness anxiety levels are likely to have an adverse effect upon the quality of evidence given in open court. In short, those who urge the primacy of oral evidence by children may not be comparing like with like. In our view, it is in the children's best interests for the courts generally to continue to rely upon a pre-recorded interview, not least because it obviates the need for judges to explain why child A is giving her testimony via a pre-recorded interview, whereas child B is testifying in open court.

F. Common Interviewer Failings

(1) Compliance with guidelines

The difficulties interviewers experience in complying with the *ABE* are not unique; **13.15** trained interviewers from other countries which employ similar guidelines also exhibit difficulties in complying with the requirements of good interview practice.[41] Common difficulties encountered from the analysis of investigative interviews include: omitting important information from the opening and closure phases;[42] using too few open questions and too many closed questions;[43] resorting to suggestive and multiple questions;[44] and employing concepts and vocabulary inappropriate to the age and development of the child.[45] This may

---

[37] Davies, G.M., 'The impact of television on the presentation and reception of children's evidence' (1999) 22 *International Journal of Law and Psychiatry*, 241–56.

[38] Criminal Justice Joint Inspection (2012) cited at n.21.

[39] Flin, R., Boon, J., Bull, R., and Knox, A., 'The effects of a five month delay on children's and adults' eyewitness memory' (1992) 83 *British Journal of Psychology*, 323–36.

[40] Criminal Justice Joint Inspection (2012), cited at n.21.

[41] Craig, R., Scheibe, R., Raskin, D., Kircher C., and Dodd, D., 'Interviewer questions and content analysis of children's statements of sexual abuse' (1999) 3 *Applied Developmental Science*, 77–85; Warren, A., Woodall, C., Hunt, J., and Perry, N., '"It sounds good in theory, but …": Do investigative interviewers follow guidelines based on memory research?' (1996) 3 *Child Maltreatment*, 231–45.

[42] Westcott, H.L. and Kynan, S., 'Interviewer Practice in Investigative Interviews for Suspected Child Sexual Abuse' (2006) 12 *Psychology, Crime and Law*, 367–82.

[43] Powell, M. and Guadagno, B., 'An examination of the limitations in investigative interviewer's use of open-ended questions' (2008) 15 *Psychiatry, Psychology, and Law*, 382–95.

[44] Thoresen, C., Lonnum, K., Melinder, A., Stridbeck, U., and Magnussen, S., 'Theory and practice in interviewing young children: A study of Norwegian police interviews 1985–2002' (2006) 12 *Psychology, Crime and Law*, 629–40.

[45] Korkman, J., Santtila, P., Drzewiecki, T., and Sandnabba, N.K., 'Failing to keep it simple: Language use in child sexual abuse interviews with 3–8-year-old children' (2008) 14 *Psychology, Crime and Law*, 41–60.

seem surprising, given the substantial resources often devoted to training and mentoring. One explanation may lie in the failure of interviewers to acknowledge how different are the requirements of formal investigative interviewing with witnesses and victims, compared to normal conversation with a child or peer. In order to develop these new and specialized skills, it is necessary for the interviewer to inhibit overlearned habits and replace them with interrogative techniques consistent with best practice in interviewing victims and witnesses.

13.16 While many countries follow the phased approach to interviewing exemplified by *ABE*, the quality of relevant training and guidance varies considerably. In England and Wales, national guidance on interviewing procedures has been available to the police and social services for over twenty years, first in the *Memorandum of Good Practice*[46] and from 2002, the *ABE*. Is there any indication that refining and developing interview protocols have improved performance by professionals? As has been noted earlier, one study which directly compared *Memorandum* and *ABE* interviews found some positive changes,[47] but many of the old problems persisted. While, in our experience as expert witnesses at court, really egregious interviewing practices are infrequently encountered, more skilled and appropriate interviewing techniques need to be consistently applied to obtain evidentially richer accounts from witnesses.

(2) The views of lawyers

13.17 Burrows and Powell have examined the views of Australian prosecutors on the interviews used at court.[48] The lawyers reported that they thought interviews with child witnesses were too long and needed to be more focused on the legal points necessary to secure a conviction. The prosecutors felt that interviewers tried to gather far too many event details using specific or closed questions. Similar concerns have been expressed in the UK[49] and in New Zealand.[50] Of course, questioning about the information required to enable each separate act of abuse is desirable. However, the prosecutors believed that too many unnecessary questions were asked about

---

[46] Bull, R., 'Interviewing children in legal contexts' in Bull, R. and Carson, D. (eds) (1995) *Handbook of Psychology in Legal Contexts*, Chichester: John Wiley & Sons Ltd.

[47] Hill and Davies (2013) cited at n.22.

[48] Burrows, K. and Powell, M. (2014a) 'Prosecutors' recommendations for improving child witness statements about sexual abuse' (2014) 24 *Policing and Society*, 189–207; Burrows, K. and Powell, M. (2014b) 'Prosecutors' perceptions on improving child witness interviews about abuse' in Bull, R. (ed.) *Investigative Interviewing*, New York: Springer, 229–41.

[49] Criminal Justice Joint Inspection (2012) cited at n.21; Stern, V. (2010) *The Stern Review: A report by Baroness Vivien Stern CBE of an independent Review into how Rape Complaints are handled by Public Authorities in England and Wales*, http://webarchive.nationalarchives.gov.uk/20110608160754/http://www.equalities.gov.uk/PDF/Stern_Review_acc_FINAL.pdf.

[50] Hanna, H., Davies, E., Henderson, E., Crothers, C., and Rotherham, C. (2010) *Child witnesses in the New Zealand Criminal Courts: A Review of Practice and Implications for Policy*, The Law Foundation: New Zealand, http://www.ipp.aut.ac.nz/__data/assets/pdf_file/0020/119702/Child-Witnesses-in-the-NZ-Criminal-Courts-full-report.pdf.

such matters as the colour of clothing, bedding, and furniture at the scene of the offence which often generated minor inconsistencies, both within and across interviews or with later testimony at court, to the detriment of the prosecution's case.

Burrows and Powell noted that the prosecutors attributed these shortcomings to poor interview planning and case preparation, inadequate interviewer engagement and listening skills, and a limited understanding of precisely what information was required for judicial proceedings. They also noted that for prosecutors, the persuasiveness of open-ended questioning was important, because too many closed questions could result in accounts that were more difficult for a jury and/or judge to follow. For the complainant's account to be maximally persuasive, they argued that it should be largely in a narrative form from the child. There is some support for the prosecutors' view from psychological research on children's recall. Kulfkosky and colleagues reported that greater narrative cohesion in young children's accounts of a staged event was associated with increased accuracy,[51] while Castelli and colleagues found that interviewer questioning style affected mock jurors' ratings of the credibility and reliability of an alleged child victim of sexual abuse.[52] Children's speech style as well as content may also influence perceptions of credibility.[53]

13.18

(3) Promoting adherence to good practice

For several years now, police officers in England and Wales have only been permitted to interview children and other vulnerable witnesses after several years of policing experience, during which time they will have undergone extensive training. The amount and quality of training hold the key to effective practice. The *NICHD Protocol*[54] aims to provide more concrete and detailed guidance than previous guidelines such as the *ABE*. There is a stronger emphasis on learning and applying semi-scripted questions and on peer review and feedback as ways of promoting adherence to good practice. Commendably, considerable resources were made available by American agencies, first in the initial development of the protocol, and later, in assessing its effectiveness and the compliance of interviewers with its requirements. Police officers trained rigorously in the use of the *NICHD Protocol*, but with only limited experience of interviewing children in sexual abuse investigations, used more open questions and fewer option posing and suggestive questions than those undergoing traditional training.[55]

13.19

---

[51] Kulkofsky, S., Wang, Q., and Ceci, S., 'Do better stories make better memories? Narrative quality and memory accuracy in preschool children' (2008) 22 *Applied Cognitive Psychology*, 21–38.

[52] Castelli, P., Goodman, G.S., and Ghetti, S., 'Effects of interview style and witness age on perceptions of children's credibility in sexual abuse cases' (2005) 35 *Journal of Applied Social Psychology*, 297–319.

[53] Ruva, C.L. and Bryant, J.B., 'The impact of age, speech style, and question form on perceptions of witness credibility and trial outcome' (2004) 34 *Journal of Applied Social Psychology*, 1919–44.

[54] Lamb, et al. (2008) cited at n.19.

[55] Lamb, et al. (2009) cited at n.23.

G. Conclusion

13.20 Police and criminal justice agencies once thought of interviewing as an inherent skill that all officers possessed. Any training simply involved learning through observation or workplace mentoring, but experience confirmed that it was insufficient to nurture effective interviewing skills.[56] As a consequence formal interview training was introduced in the UK and elsewhere.[57] Research has repeatedly demonstrated that interviewers find difficulty in adhering to the protocols taught on such courses; the more practical the training course, the more likely skills will be transferred into the workplace.[58] Such training is intensive and time-consuming and each participant must first develop their skills on the basis of constructive feedback and then overlearn them to ensure ready availability and compliance.[59]

13.21 Traditionally, officers are introduced to interviewing at recruit school by learning to write hand-written statements, a process which encourages a closed-questioning style where the conduct of the interview is controlled by the interviewer.[60] This technique then becomes a default option for officers whenever they encounter difficulty in interviews in unfamiliar and unpractised settings. Police officers need to learn to inhibit these ineffective questioning habits in order to develop and deploy new techniques. Research has shown that the demands of developing an open-questioning style and the complex distinctions between open-ended and closed questions both contribute to lack of adherence.[61] In order for these new skills to be maintained, it is also essential to institute refresher training and continuous assessment.[62] Only by addressing these underlying issues for non-compliance is it likely that a lasting improvement in the quality of investigative interviewing will be achieved.

---

[56] Baldwin, J., 'Police interview techniques' (1993) 33 *British Journal of Criminology*, 325–52.

[57] Milne, R., Shaw, G., and Bull, R. 'Investigative interviewing: The role of research,' in Carson, D., Milne, R., Pakes, F., and Shalev, K. (eds) (2007) *Applying Psychology to Criminal Justice*, Chichester: John Wiley & Sons, 65–80.

[58] Guadagno, B.L., Hughes-Scholes, C.H. and Powell, M.B., 'What themes trigger investigative interviewers to ask specific questions when interviewing children?' (2013) 15 *International Journal of Police Science and Management*, 51–60.

[59] Powell, M.B., Wright, R., and Clark, S., 'Improving the competency of police officers in conducting investigative interviews with children' (2010) 11 *Police Practice and Research: An International Journal*, 211–26.

[60] Westera, N., Kebbell, M., and Milne, R., 'Interviewing witnesses: Will investigative and evidential requirements ever concord?' (2011) 13 *British Journal of Forensic Practice*, 103–13.

[61] Wright, R. and Powell, M.B., 'Investigative interviewers' perceptions of their difficulty in adhering to open-ended questions with child witnesses' (2006) 8 *International Journal of Police Science and Management*, 316–25.

[62] Griffiths, A., Milne, R., and Cherryman, J., 'A question of control? The formulation of suspect and witness interview question strategies by advanced interviewers' (2011) 13 *International Journal of Police Science and Management*, 1–13.

Further Reading

Bull, R. (ed.) (2014) *Investigative Interviewing*, New York: Springer.

Lamb, M.E., Hershkowitz, I., Orbach, Y. and Esplin, P.W. (2008) *Tell Me What Happened: Structured Investigative Interviews with Child Victims and Witnesses*, Chichester: John Wiley & Sons Ltd.

Lamb, M.E., La Rooy, D.J., Malloy, L.C., and Katz, C. (2011) *Children's Testimony: A Handbook of Psychological Research and Forensic Practice*, Chichester: John Wiley & Sons Ltd.

Author Biographies

Graham Davies is Professor Emeritus of Psychology at the University of Leicester. His research interests focus on the testimony of children and adults and the support of vulnerable witnesses at court, on which topics he has published some ten books and over 150 articles in scientific journals. He led the writing team responsible for the original version of *Achieving Best Evidence in Criminal Proceedings* (2002). He is a Fellow of the British Psychological Society, a former president of the European Association of Psychology and Law, and the founding editor of the journal *Applied Cognitive Psychology*.

Ray Bull is Professor of Criminal Investigation at the University of Derby. In 2005 he received a Commendation from the London Metropolitan Police for 'Innovation and professionalism whilst assisting a complex rape investigation'. In 2008 he was the recipient of the Award from the European Association of Psychology and Law for his lifetime contribution to the study of psychology and law and is its current president. In 2012, he became the first Honorary Life Member of the International Investigative Interviewing Research Group. In 2010, he was made an Honorary Fellow of the British Psychological Society in recognition of his contribution to the discipline of psychology.

Rebecca Milne is a Professor of Forensic Psychology at the Institute of Criminal Justice Studies at the University of Portsmouth. She is Director of the Centre of Forensic Interviewing and works closely with the police and other criminal justice organizations, both in the UK and abroad. Rebecca is a member of the Association of Chief Police Officers, Investigative Interviewing Strategic Steering Group and was part of the writing team which developed the 2007 revision of *Achieving Best Evidence in Criminal Proceedings*. In 2009, Rebecca received the Tom Williamson Award from ACPO for her outstanding achievements in the field of investigative interviewing.

14

INVESTIGATIVE PRACTICE

Gavin E. Oxburgh and Ian Hynes

A. Introduction

Rarely has witness testimony been so pivotal to the investigative process as it is in **14.01** cases of sexual assault.[1] Often there is little or no independent evidence save for the word of the complainant victim and suspect.[2] This evidence then becomes the investigative touchstone and sexual assault trials depend upon the receipt of good quality witness testimony. It is, therefore, necessary that all evidence is obtained fairly and ethically,[3] with the overall aim of achieving best evidence,[4] whilst also securing information (and perhaps intelligence) relevant to the overall investigation.

---

[1] Walsh, D. and Oxburgh, G.E., 'Investigative interviewing of suspects: Historical and contemporary developments in research' (2008) 92 *Forensic Update*, 41–5.

[2] Benneworth, K., 'Repertoires of paedophilia: Conflicting descriptions of adult child sexual relationships in the investigative interview' (2007) 13 *International Journal of Speech, Language and the Law*, 189–211; Kebbell, M., Hurren, E.J., and Mazerolle, P., 'Sex offenders' perceptions of how they were interviewed' (2006) 4 *Canadian Journal of Police & Security Services*, 67–75.

[3] Gudjonsson, G.H., 'Psychological vulnerabilities during police interviews. Why are they important?' (2010) 15 *Legal and Criminological Psychology*, 161–75.

[4] Ministry of Justice (2011) *Achieving best evidence in criminal proceedings: Guidance on interviewing victims and witnesses, and guidance on using special measures*, http://www.cps.gov.uk/publications/docs/best_evidence_in_criminal_proceedings.pdf. See also Chapter 13.

14.02 Recent investigations in England and Wales involving online child sexual exploitation (CSE) and allegations of historical child sexual abuse (HCSA; e.g. Operation Yew Tree—enquiry into Jimmy Savile et al.), have become increasingly reliant on witness testimony alone. Thus, the effective investigation of sexual offences demands an increasingly strategic, rationalized, and transparent process, using a scientifically informed approach based upon current research. The objective is securing the 'best evidence' from forensically appropriate interviews, whilst minimizing the risk of miscarriages of justice either for complainant victims or the suspects. This is vital for all victims and witnesses, especially vulnerable witnesses and those with special needs.[5] Requirements and modifications for vulnerable and 'special measures' witnesses must be identified prior to the investigative interview.

B. The Investigative Process

14.03 An investigation demands commitment to enquire in detail, to observe carefully, and to examine all evidence systematically and objectively. Investigations are a 'journey' and there is a skill attached to the conversion of information into evidence, and occasionally, there is an inevitable erosion (or reduction) of that evidence, particularly if it is witness testimony that is to be relied upon. This can be subject to attrition due to various reasons including external influence, organizational and managerial constraint, and resource availability. Whilst there has been a growing reliance on the traditional sciences to underpin and direct investigations (e.g. DNA etc.), it follows that officers should test the validity of the information they are being given to check its accuracy, reliability, and trustworthiness—a task that is often difficult in the early stages of an enquiry. The validity can be checked internally or externally, and can also be physically checked (e.g. CCTV, bodily injuries, etc.). On passing this test, the evidence becomes *hard fact*,[6] with *soft facts* including any of the elements unearthed during interviews, including any utterances and assertions within accounts of witnesses, which are often difficult to underpin with *hard facts*.

14.04 Of increasing impact on the investigation process is social media as a means of communication, and the use of mobile devices, including smartphones, SMS text messaging and instant communication tools/applications. Thus, it follows that there is inevitably a strand of the investigation that focuses on communications data, with the role of the Digital Media Investigator (DMI) assuming significant investigative value.[7]

---

[5] Ministry of Justice (2013) *Code of practice for victims of crime* (Presented to Parliament pursuant to section 33 of the Domestic Violence, Crime and Victims Act 2004) London: The Stationery Office.

[6] Shepherd, E. and Griffiths, A.G. (2013) *Investigative Interviewing: The conversation management approach*, 2nd edn, Oxford: Oxford University Press.

[7] Cook, T. and Tattersall, A. (2014) *Senior Investigating Officers' Handbook*, 3rd edn, Oxford: Oxford University Press.

To effectively investigate all forms of sexual assault requires investigation teams to **14.05** have a a a clear understanding of what information may be potentially relevant in such cases.[8] Thus, the starting point is to examine the complaint in full detail to gather all appropriate evidence that may help in ascertaining whether any crime has actually been committed. Such enquiries should be conducted by officers who have been appropriately trained and in accordance with the Professionalising Investigation Programme (PIP), which was introduced in England and Wales in 2007.[9] The PIP aims to improve the professional competence of all those who are tasked with conducting investigations. There are four levels of training identified based on investigation activities, with PIP Level 2 being dedicated for the investigation of serious and complex crime/incidents (such as sexual offences).

There is now a range of special measures intended to enable adult witnesses, in **14.06** certain cases, to supply and present their evidence in the most appropriate and effective manner; highly relevant given relatively recent legislation for victims of serious sexual offences to provide pre-recorded video evidence-in-chief.[10] However, although all such victims will be eligible to apply for their visually recorded interview to be admitted as their evidence-in-chief, the police will not make an automatic decision to do so—decisions will be taken on a case-by-case basis following receipt of the witness' views.[11] Investigators should also be aware of the available advice on visually recorded interviews.[12]

Police investigations have evolved to being somewhat 'silo' in nature and process, **14.07** not particularly helpful when considered in the context of memory contamination. A brief exploration of this process exemplifies the opportunity for memory contamination. An alleged victim is likely to report the offence initially to a friend, then perhaps to a counsellor or medical practitioner, and eventually to the police. The case will then be referred to a police officer who will attend to commence a primary investigation and might secure a 'first account' to inform the initial actions. The witness is likely to be medically examined and the enquiry will then be transferred to specialist investigators. Only at this stage of the process is consideration likely to be made as to how the interviewee's best evidence (for any future court proceedings) should be secured, yet the witness has been interviewed at every stage of the process thus far with all the attendant memory erosion already referred to.

---

[8] Westera, N. and Kebbell, M., 'Investigative interviewing in suspected sex offences' in Bull, R. (ed.) (2014) *Investigative interviewing*, New York: Springer, ch 1.

[9] McGrory, D. and Treacy, P., 'The Professionalising Investigation Programme' in, Haberfield, M.R., Clarke, C.A., and Sheehan, D.L. (eds) (2012) *Police organization and training: Innovations in research and practice*. New York: Springer, ch. 8.

[10] The Coroners and Justice Act (2009).

[11] Crown Prosecution Service (January 2015) *A Protocol between the Police and Crown Prosecution Service in the investigation and prosecution of allegations of rape, http://www.cps.gov.uk/publications/ agencies/cps_acpo_rape_protocol_v2-1.pdf.*

[12] ACPO National Investigative Interviewing Strategic Steering Group (2010) *Advice on the structure of visually recorded interviews*, Wyboston, UK: ACPO.

Once the interview/s have been completed, it is entirely possible that the Crown Prosecution Service (CPS) will direct a clarification interview before the witness is exposed to providing evidence-in-chief and subjected to cross-examination. When considering the (proper) imperative to keep a witness updated on the *general* progress of an investigation great care needs to be taken to prevent witness memory contamination whilst fulfilling that obligation. There are various reasons why sharing information with interviewees is ill-advised. In the current context, the necessity for the investigator to prevent witness memory corruption, must override the interviewee's understandable wish to be updated on detail of investigative findings. Preventing memory contamination is essential for good memory retrieval and optimizes future good quality, reliable witness testimony.

C. Interviewing Strategies and the PEACE Model of Interviewing

(1) Interviewing strategies

14.08 The primary purpose of an investigative interview is to secure the most reliable accounts and to assist those making the charging decision to decide if there is sufficient and reliable evidence to charge the suspect/s. The investigative interview is, thus, a central and significant aspect of the criminal justice process[13] and forms an integral part of the overall investigation.[14] The obtaining of such accounts is enhanced by the application of good investigative interviewing techniques, underpinned by seven key principles.[15] Principle two is perhaps of particular note in the context of sexual offence investigations when there is an increasing imperative to put the victim at the centre of the investigation and consideration.[16]

14.09 Investigators in England and Wales are encouraged to rely on an investigative mindset—open-minded and non-judgmental—and to resist confirmation bias,[17] the potentially damaging impact of which is exemplified later in this chapter. They should look for other explanations and not become too focused on restricted hypotheses. In tandem with the National Decision-making Model,[18] investigators

---

[13] Oxburgh, G.E. and Dando, C.J., 'Psychology and interviewing: What direction now in our quest for reliable information?' (2011) 13 *British Journal of Forensic Practice*, 135–44; Milne, R. and Bull, R. (1999) *Investigative interviewing: Psychology and practice*, Chichester: John Wiley & Sons Ltd.

[14] Walsh and Oxburgh (2008) cited at n.1.

[15] College of Policing (2014) *Investigative interviewing*, *http://www.app.college.police.uk/app-content/investigations/investigative-interviewing*.

[16] 'Those with clear or perceived vulnerabilities should be treated with particular care, and extra safeguards be put in place.'

[17] Hill, C., Memon, A., and McGeorge, P., 'The role of confirmation bias in suspect interviews: A systematic evaluation' (2008) 13 *Legal and Criminological Psychology*, 357–71.

[18] Cook and Tattersall (2014), cited at n.7, 31.

are essentially encouraged to adopt the 'ABC' principle throughout the journey of any investigation:[19]

- Assume nothing;
- Believe nothing;
- Challenge everything.

In the context of sexual offence investigations, 'believe nothing' might at first appear harsh and is certainly controversial in the current climate. Clearly there is a competing requirement of listening to the victim with empathy, whilst remaining impartial at all times, but investigative decision-making encourages healthy scepticism, to take nothing for granted or at face value. All the evidence should be reviewed and corroboration sought wherever possible.[20]

As investigators develop their professional skills, those charged with responsibility to investigate serious sexual offences will adopt a process aligned to the ACCESS model of investigation, which is a mnemonic acronym of the six stages of problem solving involved in any investigation.[21] It is cyclical in nature and is key to the investigation of serious and complex crime. Officers should: Assess the information they have to formulate an action plan; Collect all evidence available; Collate the available evidence; Evaluate and review the information; Survey and conduct a methodical and comprehensive overview of the investigative outcomes; and Summarize everything in a written record and/or verbal briefing that spells out the case succinctly as it currently stands. The prevailing expectation is that all the above processes are conducted ethically, with integrity, and are proportionate. **14.10**

(2) The PEACE model of interviewing

The PEACE model of interviewing was introduced in the early 1990s (Planning and preparation, Engage and explain, Account, clarify and challenge, Closure, Evaluation)[22] and came about as a consequence of well publicized miscarriages of justice arising (primarily) from interviews with suspects[23] (e.g. the Guildford Four, 1989—known as 'one of the worst miscarriages of justice in recent history'[24]—and the Birmingham Six, 1975). Throughout the majority of all miscarriages of justice, there is a common thread of vulnerability. The PEACE model is now widely used in many countries worldwide and is used to interview witnesses and suspects. **14.11**

---

[19] CENTREX (2005) *Practice Advice on Core Investigative Doctrine*, Cambridge: National Centre for Policing Excellence.
[20] Cook and Tattersall (2014), cited at n.7, 31.
[21] Shepherd and Griffiths (2013), cited at n.6, 9.
[22] Milne and Bull (1999), cited at n.13.
[23] Gudjonsson, G.H. (2003) *The psychology of interrogations and confessions: A handbook*, Chichester: John Wiley & Sons Ltd.
[24] Ewing, C. and McCann, J. (2006) *Minds on trial. Great cases in law and psychology*, Oxford: Oxford University Press, 54.

Witness interviews should always be structured using the PEACE model[25] and Table 14.1 below outlines how the PEACE model is comparable with the phases of the Achieving Best Evidence framework.[26]

Table 14.1 Table outlining the comparability of the PEACE model and ABE framework

PEACE Model of Interviewing	Achieving Best Evidence Framework
Planning and preparation	Planning and preparation
Engage and explain	Establishing rapport
Account, clarify, and challenge	Initiating and supporting a free narrative account through appropriate questioning
Closure	Closing the interview
Evaluation	Evaluation

14.12 There are essentially three distinct methods of witness interviewing within the PEACE model: (i) the Cognitive Interview (CI);[27] (ii) the Enhanced Cognitive Interview (ECI);[28] and (iii) Conversation Management (CM).[29] The CI is a way of interviewing co-operative victims/witnesses to assist them in reporting what they remember from a particular event,[30] and helps to minimize mis-interpretation and uncertainty that is sometimes seen in the questioning process during interviews. It consists of a set of four instructions:[31]

1. report everything;
2. mentally reinstate the context of the 'to-be-remembered' event;
3. recall events in a variety of different temporal orders; and
4. change perspective.

14.13 Not all instructions need to be used in every interview—one instruction should be used well rather than all the instructions used poorly, and one aspect may 'work' better on some witnesses than others. The CI consistently enhances memory retrieval and elicits genuine memories without generating inaccurate accounts of information or confabulations.[32] However, no known research has been conducted

---

[25] College of Policing (2014), cited at n.15.
[26] Association of Chief Police Officers (2009) *National Investigative Interviewing Strategy*, London: The Stationery Office; College of Policing (2014), cited at n.15.
[27] Fisher, R. and Geiselman, R. (1992) *Memory-enhancing techniques for investigative Interviewing: The cognitive interview.* Springfield: Charles Thomas.
[28] Hill, Memon, and McGeorge (2008), cited at n.17.
[29] Shepherd and Griffiths (2013), cited at n.6, 13.
[30] Tulving, E., 'Cue-dependent forgetting.' (1974) 62 *American Scientist*, 74–78; Tulving, E. and Thomson, D.M., 'Encoding specificity and retrieval processes in episodic memory' (1973) 80 *Psychological Review*, 352–73.
[31] Ministry of Justice (2011), cited at n.4, App I, 186.
[32] Kohnken, G., Milne, R., Memon, A., and Bull, R., 'The cognitive interview: A meta-analysis' (1999) 6 *Psychology, Crime and Law*, 3–27; Dando, C.J., Wilcock, R., Behnkle, C., and Milne, R.,

using the CI specifically relating to sexual offences, although there is no reason to doubt its efficacy with this group of witnesses. The ECI adds to the CI and includes an additional framework for building rapport and effective communication.[33] In simple terms, the ECI discourages the interviewer from interrupting the witness, instead, allowing them to control the flow of information, whilst the interviewer actively listens.[34]

CM is an approach to interviewing that maximizes spontaneous disclosure. It is an **14.14** ethical and effective approach and is a tool that is applicable to any interviewing context. It combines empirical research findings in cognitive and social psychology, with research into reflective practice and skilled practitioner performance. CM combines an awareness of the dynamics of conversation and a commitment to ethical conversation—respecting and treating the interviewee as a conversational participant.[35]

(3) Questioning strategies

The questioning style expected of a competent investigative interviewer (i.e. trained **14.15** to at least PIP level 2 and regularly conducts sexual offence investigations) should ensure they secure an untainted and forensically robust account from a witness. An effective questioning style encourages (when appropriate) going straight to the main topic of the interview and dealing with the 'to-be-remembered events' that are often at the forefront of the interviewee's mind and which may be evidentially vital. Thus, the first interviews are more often impactive and evidential in nature, and deal with the crucial elements of the offence. Interviewers are then encouraged to take a short break before conducting an additional interview in which to address the more detailed elements of the enquiry. As such, building a rapport with the interviewee is vitally important and should never be neglected—rapport very often starts well before any interview (e.g. in telephone calls to arrange the interview etc.) and continues throughout the course of the interview/s.[36] However, anecdotal evidence suggests that such an approach is not suitable for all interviewees, with the more vulnerable perhaps requiring much more in terms of rapport and questioning strategies. That said, police officers appear to find it more difficult to build rapport with those suffering from mental disorders due to such interviews being more cognitively challenging.[37]

'Modifying the cognitive interview: Countenancing forensic application by enhancing practicability' (2011) 17 *Psychology, Crime and Law*, 491–511.

[33] Ministry of Justice (2011), cited at n.4, App I, 186.

[34] Memon, A., Meissner, C.A., and Fraser, J., 'The cognitive interview: A meta-analytic review and study space analysis of the past 25 years' (2010) 16(4) *Psychology, Public Policy and Law*, 340–72.

[35] Shepherd and Griffiths (2013), cited at n.6, 14.

[36] Ministry of Justice (2011), cited at n.4, App I, 188; Bull, R., 'Obtaining information expertly' (1992) 1 *Expert Evidence*, 5–12.

[37] Oxburgh, L.D., Milne, R., and Cherryman, J. (in prep) 'Investigative interviewing, communication, and mental disorder: Current perspectives from practitioners'.

14.16 During the planning stage for an interview, interviewers should always develop a questioning strategy, which can be defined as the structured use of *appropriate* types of questions,[38] which are relevant to the subject matter under investigation. However, a questioning strategy should always take account of the interviewee, interviewer/s, and overall interview situation—no interview is the same.[39] Interviewers are encouraged to use a questioning 'funnel' or 'spiral' throughout each topic, commencing with an *open* question (e.g. 'tell', 'explain', 'describe'), supplemented, if and where needed, by *probing* questions (e.g., 5WH—'who', 'what', 'when', 'where', 'why', and 'how'). However, these latter questions are sometimes also known as *specific-closed* questions.[40] Interviewers should not use *inappropriate* forms of questioning such as: (i) leading; (ii) multiple; (iii) forced-choice; or (iv) opinion/statements.[41] Investigators are trained that if *open* questions do not succeed in eliciting recall of the event, they should default to *probing* questions (*specific–closed*), reverting back to *open* questions as and when appropriate.

(4) Planning and preparation

14.17 The planning and preparation stage is argued as being the single most important part of any interview and is fundamental to the efficacy of *any* investigative interview.[42] From selection of appropriate and competent interviewers, to location of interview, questioning strategy, special measures for the most vulnerable (e.g., use of appropriate adults, intermediaries), knowledge of the available evidence and so on, are all vital aspects that must be considered. Appropriate investment at this stage will pay dividends thereafter, alleviating the need for re-interviews and clarification. The interviewer/s should have a clear understanding of the purpose of the interview (e.g. to establish if any offence has occurred) and should consider when and where it will take place (e.g. in the police station, specially adapted suite, or indeed at a witness' home using portable recording equipment). If there are two interviewers, they should be clear as to each other's roles, which should be explained to the interviewee.

14.18 Skilled interviewers will be aware of the possible need for specialist support throughout the whole process, recognizing that in many cases, especially in

---

[38] Ministry of Justice (2011), cited at n.4, 78, para 3.44.

[39] Griffiths, A.G., Milne, R., and Cherryman, J., 'A question of control? The formulation of suspect and witness interview question strategies by advanced interviewers' (2011) 13 *International Journal of Police Science and Management*, 255–67.

[40] Ministry of Justice (2011), cited at n.4, 78, para 3.47.

[41] Oxburgh, G.E., Myklebust, T., and Grant, T.D., 'The question of question types in police interviews: A review from a psychological and linguistic perspective' (2010) 7 *Speech, Language and the Law*, 45–66.

[42] Ministry of Justice (2011), cited at n.4, para 2.1, 10; Shepherd and Griffiths (2013), cited at n.6, 10, para 1.2.2; Clarke, C. and Milne, R. (2001) *National evaluation of the PEACE investigative interviewing course*, Police Research Award Scheme PRAS/149; Clarke, C., Milne, R., and Bull, R., 'Interviewing suspects of crime: The impact of PEACE training, supervision and the presence of a legal advisor' (2011) 8 *Journal of Investigative Psychology and Offender Profiling*, 149–62.

HCSA, the interview process might last many days or weeks. Specialist interviewers are advised that if there is any doubt whatsoever about capacity, mental health, well-being, or learning difficulties, then specialist support should be sought from specialist interview advisors.[43] An emerging area of challenge is the recording of intermediaries' assessment interviews, during which evidence and information can be collected, and disclosures made. Recording of the process can potentially rebut challenges of witness coaching for example.

D. Special Investigative Challenges

There are many investigative challenges when dealing with sexual offences, not least the impact on investigating officers, who report such interviews as being more emotive and problematic than other interviews they conduct.[44] This is primarily due to the abhorrent nature of such offences and the painful emotions that arise from the information that is often provided.[45] Officers have to try and make sense of this information, psychologically, which may make subsequent interviews of a similar nature more emotionally difficult to conduct.   **14.19**

(1) Investigating allegations of historical child sexual abuse

In recent years, there has been extensive debate and media attention surrounding child abuse per se, but more specifically HCSA, some of which relate to extremely serious crimes committed over many years, sometimes decades, and by well-known individuals (e.g. Jimmy Savile, Rolf Harris et al.). The police have a duty to investigate thoroughly all complaints that are made to them, and justice for the victims is absolutely vital. Some of the victims in such crimes have experienced terrible ordeals that were committed against them when they were at their most vulnerable. Those involved in the Criminal Justice System have a duty of care to ensure that justice reflects the severity of these offences, taking account of the psychological difficulty faced by many victims who come forward and make a complaint. Victims must feel that the CJS will not only take their complaints seriously, but also that they will receive a fair hearing.[46]   **14.20**

---

[43] College of Policing (2014), cited at n.15.

[44] Oxburgh, G.E., Ost, J., Morris, P., and Cherryman, J., 'Police officers' perceptions of interviews in cases of sexual offences and murder involving children and adult victims' (2013) 16(1) *Police Practice and Research: An International Journal, http://dx.doi.org/10.1080/15614263.2013.84 9595.* (First published on-line on 13 October 2013.)

[45] Oxburgh, G.E., Ost, J., Morris, P., and Cherryman, J., 'The impact of question type and empathy on police interviews with suspects of homicide, filicide and child sexual abuse' (2014) 21(6) *Psychiatry, Psychology and Law, http://dx.doi.org/10.1080/13218719.2014.918078.* (First published on-line 10 July 14.)

[46] Secretary of State for the Home Department (2003) *The Conduct of Investigations into Past Cases of Abuse in Children's Homes.* The Government reply to the fourth report from the Home Affairs Committee, Session 2001–2002 HC 836, Cm 5799.

14.21 At the time of writing, there is no national guidance available to investigators involved in cases of HCSA. However, such investigations have become increasingly reliant on witness testimony alone. Unfortunately, there is no common definition of 'historical', and boundaries can become blurred. Definitions can extend from, 'a long time after the abuse has occurred'[47] to, 'an allegation of abuse which is made by a person who at the time of making the allegation is an adult, i.e., 18 years or over, and, at the time of the abuse, the complainant was under 18 years of age; and, where the abuse was either intra-familial, committed by another carer, or by another professional.'[48]

14.22 One also has to be cognisant of memory decay, together with the loss of potential corroborative evidence in such witnesses, and investigators must address any material inconsistencies[49] to clarify if the allegation may be false, to establish if there is a cognitive or memory encoding problem, a misunderstanding, or perhaps mistaken identity of the alleged offender. If the investigation ensues a 'long time' after the crime was committed, there is a greater risk of and opportunity for memory distortions, which may reduce the accuracy of the information obtained. Such errors can be detrimental to both the victim/witness and the suspect/s. Research has also shown that any discussions between the complainant and other people (regardless of intent) may cause memory 'source errors' where the complainant unwittingly integrates the information provided by these 'sources' into their own 'account' that they later supply to the police.[50] Although unintentional, friends and family, medical examiners, therapists/counsellors, legal advisors and the media are all potential sources of memory contamination that might lead to genuinely held, but false, memory beliefs about their autobiographical memory. Thus, it is essential to establish what factors, if any, may have influenced a person's memory. Similarly, the investigator should always establish if there is any corroborating evidence that can help verify the victim's account.

E. Dealing with Inconsistencies and Re-interviews of Witnesses

14.23 The starting point has to be an understanding that memory is fallible, that it is not like a video-recording, that it is reconstructive in nature, and that different

---

[47] National Centre for Policing Excellence (2005) *Code of practice on the National Intelligence Model*, London: NCPE.

[48] Greater Manchester Police (2012) *Public Protection Division*, Public Protection Investigation Unit Handbook.

[49] Ministry of Justice (2011), cited at n.4, 94, para 3.130.

[50] Loftus, E.F. and Palmer, J.C., 'Reconstruction of automobile destruction: An example of the interaction between language and memory' (1974) 13 *Journal of Verbal Learning and Verbal Behaviour*, 585–9; Gabbert, F., Memon, A., and Allen, K., 'Memory conformity: Can eyewitnesses influence each other's memories for an event?' (2003) 17(5) *Applied Cognitive Psychology*, 533–43; Loftus, E. and Banaji, M.R., 'Memory modification and the role of the media' in Gheorghiu, V., Netter, P., Eysenck, H.J., and Rosenthal, R. (eds), (1989) *Suggestibility: Theory and research* New York: Springer-Verlag, 279–93.

witnesses will interpret events very differently.[51] This is the case even if all witnesses are present at the same event (see Chapters 21 and 23). There are also four factors that have to be considered in all interviews: (i) the social effects (the impact/effect of the interview on a particular witness); (ii) the cognitive effects (the effects of the interview on the memory of the witness); (iii) the emotional effects (the anxiety that might be caused during the interview and testifying at court); and (iv) the motivational effects (is the witness willing to co-operate with the interviewer and the police in general?).

The issue of clarifying and/or challenging discrepancies and the re-interviewing of witnesses, is one of the three 'golden rules' considered to be vital for the success of an open-minded, thorough, and ethically fair investigation. The other two are the lawful and effective recording and application of significant statements made by a suspect during the course of the enquiry, and the (still) undervalued impact of a thoroughly researched and prepared pre-interview briefing (disclosure) to a suspect, or their legal representative, prior to conducting the interview. **14.24**

If a person's account is at odds with other facts known to the investigation team, it should not be automatically supportive of a stance that they are being deliberately misleading (or indeed lying); they may well be, but it is equally important to drive out any lies and/or false allegations, or recall of false or implanted memory, as it is to verify the account detail. What is important is to identify any inconsistencies or areas for clarification as early as possible and address/challenge them during the investigative interview. Failure to do so exposes the opportunity for possible miscarriages of justice, and leaves the witness open to further challenge should they reach the point of cross-examination, potentially setting them up to fail and adding no value to the investigation process. **14.25**

It is generally held that responsibility for any re-interviewing rests with the police investigation team until the case clearly sits with the CPS to progress to trial, and any intended re-interview should be subject to discussion with the CPS and a written record of rationale made.[52] However, it should be noted that thereafter, responsibility primarily rests with the CPS, although safeguards should always be in place to ensure that the CPS representative is appropriately trained to conduct a forensically robust re-interview, taking into consideration the importance of the differing interview methods, and questioning strategies and the fallibility of memory. What is clear is that there should be consistency in such interviews, their methodology, and manner of recording and presentation, whilst also recognizing the potential of special measures[53] and video-recorded cross-examination in advance of trial. **14.26**

---

[51] Bartlett, F.C. (1932) *Remembering: A study in experimental and social psychology,* Cambridge: Cambridge University Press.
[52] Ministry of Justice (2011), cited n.4, 94, para 3.130.
[53] Youth Justice and Criminal Evidence Act 1999.

(1) Disclosure challenges

14.27 In the context of investigation of HCSA or protracted sexual offences, the challenges around 'disclosure' of third-party material has never been greater, with all regions and authorities adopting different strategies and policies. The imperative is for all material to be available to investigators as soon as possible in the investigation process, meeting obligations to 'Record, Retain, and Reveal.'[54] From a practical perspective, such information is crucial to inform the planning stage when preparing for an interview if only to minimize inconsistencies and reduce the number of (re)interviews.

F. Conclusion

14.28 Conducting sexual offence investigations is not as straightforward a task as some may think. The importance of understanding the fallibility of memory, the debate surrounding false and recovered memories, especially when investigating allegations of HCSA, cannot be underestimated. The PEACE model of interviewing and ABE framework highlight how much the police service in England and Wales have developed both professionally and morally, no longer using cohersive and psychologically unsafe tactics to obtain information from victims, witnesses, and suspects of crime. Carefully planning and preparing effectively for an interview is fundamental to its overall efficacy with the potential to impact on numerous elements of the interview process itself. This is especially so for the most vulnerable.

14.29 Rarely has the CJS seen such volatility and cultural change in investigative practice as those driven out by the learned experiences of well publicized recent allegations of HCSA (e.g. Yew Tree et al.), and those into child sexual exploitation (Rochdale et al.). Crucially, at the time of writing, the College of Policing has withdrawn much of the existing ex-National Policing Improvement Agency core doctrine to be replaced with Authorised Professional Practice (APP). Aside from change driven out by those enquiries and reviews, the biggest change must be to the prevailing third-party disclosure protocols, so as to ensure that investigators have as many material facts as possible at their disposal as early as possible in the investigation process to reliably and accurately inform investigative decision-making from the outset, in turn enabling proper threshold decision-making by prosecutors. Perhaps a third significant challenge is the streamlining of process that determines a serious sexual offence investigation, and the removal of as many layers as possible to ensure consistency and seemlessness throughout that process—many police forces have

---

[54] Office of the Attorney General (2013) *Attorney General's guidelines on disclosure: For investigators, prosecutors and defence practitioners, https://www.gov.uk/government/publications/attorney-generals-guidelines-on-disclosure-2013*, 7, para 15e.

made significant strides towards this in recent years with the creation of specialist serious sexual offence investigation units.

Further Reading

Oxburgh, G.E., Myklebust, T., Grant, T.D., and Milne, R. (2015) *Communication in investigative and legal contexts: Integrated approaches from psychology, linguistics and law enforcement*, Chichester: John Wiley & Sons Ltd.

St-Yves, M. (2014, edn) *Investigative interviewing: The essentials*, Canada: Carswell.

Ridley, A.M., Gabbert, F., and La Rooy, D.J. (2013) *Suggestibility in legal contexts: Psychological research and forensic implications*, Chichester: Wiley-Blackwell.

Shepherd, E. and Griffiths, A.G. (2013) *Investigative interviewing: The conversation management approach*, Oxford: Oxford University Press.

Author Biographies

Dr Gavin E. Oxburgh is a Consultant Forensic Psychologist, a Chartered Psychologist, and Chartered Scientist. He is a Senior Lecturer in Psychology at Newcastle University and the Chair and Founding Director of the International Investigative Interviewing Research Group (*http://www.iiirg.org*). He previously served with the Royal Air Force Police, where he was a senior detective specializing in the investigation of sexual offences. A registered expert witness, he works closely with various agencies worldwide, including police forces and government departments. He has recently developed training for investigators from the International Criminal Court, the United Nations High Commissioner for Refugees, and the United Nations Development Programme.

Ian Hynes was a Specialist Investigative Interview Advisor for eight years following a thirty-year career in Greater Manchester Police as a detective within various Criminal Investigation Departments, being deployed throughout the UK and abroad in various capacities. He has an outstanding record of developing, implementing, and managing ground-breaking training and operational initiatives to ethically secure investigations, thereby reducing opportunities for miscarriages of justice. His success has been based on applying his experience to address contemporary compliance, governance, and operational competency issues with effective training packages and operational strategies. He is now Chief Executive Officer of IntersolGlobal (*http://www.intersolglobal.com*).

15

PROVIDING FOR THE NEEDS OF WITNESSES

Bridget Pettitt, Lina Wallace, Amanda Naylor, and Mark Castle OBE

A. Introduction

15.01 The ability of victims[1] and witnesses to provide testimony is crucial to the criminal justice system. However, it has only been recognized over the past twenty years that appropriate support and preparation of victims and witnesses helps them to give better evidence, when in court, but also in the often long build-up to the trial.[2] 'The additional stress of coping with an unfamiliar situation is likely to reduce the ability of witnesses to participate and respond to questioning, or to effectively recall events in order to assist the fact-finding process of the criminal justice system.'[3] Sexual violence has a profound effect on victims' mental and physical health, and for some, the experience of going through the criminal justice system can be as traumatic as the original crime.[4] Many commentators question the appropriateness of the adversarial approach in such sensitive cases, and believe that an inquisitorial approach, or in certain cases the use of restorative justice, would be more suitable.[5] Indeed, the former Director of Public Prosecutions, Sir Keir Starmer QC, described the current criminal justice system as being unable to protect vulnerable victims and called for a total change in approach.[6] Other commentators feel that with modification the criminal justice system is well equipped to deal with sensitive cases.[7]

15.02 This chapter explains how the needs of witnesses should be addressed throughout to mitigate any impact of the actual trial process, and to help give their best evidence. This chapter provides an overview of the needs of, and the support available for, victims and witnesses. It goes on to describe good practice in supporting witnesses, and outlines some of the barriers to providing good support.

(1) Context

15.03 Over the past twenty years there have been a range of policies and initiatives designed to improve the provision for witnesses and victims. Key to these are the Victims Code, the Witness Charter, and the Prosecutor's Pledge. There are

---

[1] Throughout this chapter we use the term 'victim' rather than 'complainant'. As Victim Support our work is predicated on the assumption that the complainant is a victim of a crime, but this does not imply a pre-verdict assumption that all complainants are necessarily victims of the accused.

[2] Home Office (1998) *Speaking up for Justice: Report of the Interdepartmental Working Group on the treatment of Vulnerable or Intimidated Witnesses in the Criminal Justice System*, London: Home Office.

[3] Ministry of Justice (2011) *Achieving Best Evidence in Criminal Proceedings. Guidance on interviewing victims and witnesses, and guidance on using special measures*, London: Ministry of Justice, 99, para 4.1.

[4] Parsons, J. and Bergin, T., 'The impact of criminal justice involvement on victim's mental health' (2010) 23(2) *Journal of Traumatic Stress*, 182–8; Rumney, P., 'Male rape in the courtroom: issues and concerns' (2001) Crim LR, 205–13.

[5] Smith, O. and Skinner, T., 'Observing Court Responses to Victims of Rape and Sexual Assault' (2012) 7(4) *Feminist Criminology*, 298–326.

[6] BBC News 8 January 2014, *http://www.bbc.co.uk/news/uk-25647046*.

[7] Personal communication from Mr John Riley, Barrister, at 23 Essex Street, London.

also commitments to improved rights of victims to challenge decisions to drop charges, improved communications to victims, and enhanced approaches for victims with mental health problems and disabilities.[8] Complainants of sexual assault are defined as 'intimidated' witnesses in the Youth Justice and Criminal Evidence Act 1999 and are thus entitled to special measures with the agreement of the court. Many witnesses in sexual violence cases will also be 'vulnerable'— children, and adults with a mental disorder, learning disability, or physical disability. Special measures include the use of screens, live TV link, giving evidence in private, removal of wigs and gowns, the use of video-recorded interviews, and the use of intermediaries. Section 28 of the Act—video-recorded cross-examination, has not yet come into force, but is currently being piloted.[9] Section 41 of the same Act restricts the circumstances in which evidence or questioning about a victim's previous sexual history may take place.

(2) Achieving Best Evidence

The Achieving Best Evidence Guidance refers to specific support needs for victims   **15.04** of sexual violence and outlines the responsibilities of legal representatives towards vulnerable and intimidated witnesses:

- to ensure they are put at ease as much as possible;
- to assist the court to make informed decisions about any special measures directions or necessary steps to assist a witness, and to inform the judge of any special requirements;
- to avoid delays for example by making applications for disclosure of relevant records early;
- to follow guidelines on appropriateness, manner, and tone when cross-examining witnesses and on appropriate language use;
- to avoid and challenge adjournments where this will have an adverse effect on the witness, the need for regular breaks, and to protect the witness from inappropriate questioning by drawing the judge's or magistrate's attention to it; and

---

[8] Ministry of Justice (2013) Code of Practice for Victims of Crime, London: The Stationery Office, *https://www.cps.gov.uk/publications/docs/victims_code_2013.pdf*; Ministry of Justice (2013) The Witness Charter: Standards of care for witnesses in the criminal justice system, London: The Stationery Office, *https://www.gov.ukgovernment/publications/the-witness-charter-standards-of-care-for-witnesses-in- the-criminal-justice-system*; Crown Prosecution Service (2005) The Prosecutors' Pledge, *https://www.cps.gov.uk/publications/prosecution/prosecutor_pledge.html*, Published online: CPS; Crown Prosecution Service (2013). Victims' Right to Review Scheme, http://www.cps.gov.uk/victims_witnesses/victims_right_to_review/index.html; Crown Prosecution Service (2009) Supporting victims and witnesses with a learning disability published online: CPS; Crown Prosecution Service (2009) Supporting victims and witnesses who have mental health issues, London, *https://www.cps.gov.uk/publications/docs/supporting_victims_and_witnesses_with_mental_health_issues.pdf*.

[9] See details of the pilot at: *http://webarchive.nationalarchives.gov.uk/20130128112038/http://www.justice.gov.uk/legal-aid/newslatest-updates/crime-news/moj-pilot-on-pre-recorded-cross-examination-of-vulnerable-witnesses*.

- to perform duties in relation to proper handling of video-recordings of evidence, to ensure they don't fall into the wrong hands.[10]

B. Needs of Victims and Witnesses

15.05 Pursuing a crime through the criminal justice system can be emotionally beneficial for the victim or witness: having their experience believed and validated, to have a voice, and to have justice in terms of retribution of the offender, as well as safety and protection from the perpetrator. Although the outcome of the trial is very important, procedural justice—the sense that they have been treated fairly and equitably and with respect—is an important factor for improvements in emotional well-being.[11]

15.06 There is evidence, however, that aspects of the criminal justice system itself may exacerbate the trauma of the original crime. Sexual violence has a substantial effect on victim's mental and physical health; and can leave victims with persistent emotional and mental health problems.[12] People with pre-existing mental health problems are also at far greater risk of violent or sexual assault than those without.[13] Facing the perpetrator in court and remembering details of the crime can trigger secondary responses to the initial trauma.[14] This 'secondary victimization' where the victim feels blamed by the justice system and other society around them, may be particularly acute for victims and witnesses of sexual crimes.[15]

15.07 Victims and witnesses of sexual assault will have individual support needs which vary considerably according to their own response to the crime, the seriousness of the incident, the relationship they have with the defendant and their own resilience and support network.[16] Their needs may also change over time. This section

---

[10] Ministry of Justice (2011) Achieving Best Evidence in Criminal Proceedings. Guidance on interviewing victims and witnesses, and guidance on using special measures, *http://www.cps.gov.uk/publications/docs/best_evidence_in_criminal_proceedings.pdf*, 103, para 4.15.

[11] Clark, H., 'What is the justice system willing to offer? Understanding sexual assault victim/survivors' criminal justice needs' (2010) 85 *Family Matters*, 28–37; Tyler, T., 'Procedural Justice and the Courts' (2008) 44 *Court Review*, 25–31.

[12] Parsons, J.M. and Bergin, T., 'The impact of criminal justice involvement on victim's mental health' (2010) 23(2) *Journal of Traumatic Stress*, 182–8.

[13] Pettitt, B., Greenhead, S., Khalifeh, H., Drennan, V., Hart, T., Hogg, J., Borschmann, R., Mamo, E., and Moran, P. (2013) *At risk, yet dismissed: the criminal victimization of people with mental health problems*, London: Victim Support and Mind.

[14] Parsons and Bergin (2010), cited at n.12; Campbell, R., Wasco, S.M., Ahrens, C.E., Self, T., and Barnes, H.E., 'Preventing the "Second Rape": Rape Survivors' Experiences With Community Service Providers' (2001) 16(12) *Journal of Interpersonal Violence*, 1239–59.

[15] Campbell, R., 'What really happened? A validation study of rape survivors' help-seeking experiences with the legal and medical systems' (2005) 20 *Violence and victims*, 55–68.

[16] Ministry of Justice (2013) *Support for victims: Findings from the Crime Survey for England and Wales*, London: Ministry of Justice.

is based on research with victims and witnesses who have been through the court process[17] and experiences and case studies from professionals at Victim Support working with witnesses on a daily basis.

(1) Becky—a case study in child sexual abuse

Becky[18] (aged 15) was a victim of childhood sexual abuse inflicted by her family members. She had learning difficulties, and therefore required specialist care throughout her case. All four defendants pleaded not guilty and were tried together. Becky's carer was told by police and social services that pre-trial counselling was not allowed.   **15.08**

During the trial, Becky was subjected to three days of cross-examination via video link by four different barristers. Due to her learning difficulties, the barristers were provided with instructions from the judge to only ask one question at a time, and to wait for Becky to respond before asking the next question. She was not provided with an intermediary and the court was adjourned many times due to one barrister not heeding instructions from the judge and firing multiple questions at Becky, leaving her confused and upset in what was already a stressful ordeal. The judge in the case warned the barrister and threatened to hold him in contempt of court should he continue. However, the harm of aggressive questioning had already taken its toll on Becky. This also resulted in a prolonged cross-examination period for Becky, and having to repeat her ninety-mile round trip over several days.   **15.09**

A frustrating element of the trial for Becky's carer was the limited information provided to the court on Becky's circumstances. While Becky spent some time at a special needs residential home, the court referred to this incorrectly as boarding school thus giving the jury no explanation of Becky's learning difficulties. The court held that Becky's difficulties could only be disclosed during summing up. As a result, there was a risk that jury members would not take into consideration Becky's additional difficulties during cross-examination which may have harmed her credibility. In contrast, one of the defendant's health was brought up as a mitigating factor in court.   **15.10**

Lack of continuity of professionals within the police service, witness care, and court services left Becky with no consistent support throughout the trial and Becky had to repeat her experiences to many different people within the same profession. Becky's carer is still struggling with social services and her GP to ensure Becky has continued counselling for her trauma from one individual on a constant basis. Currently, Becky's carer is receiving emotional support from a Victim Support   **15.11**

---

[17] Hunter, G., Jacobson, J., and Kirby, A. (2013) *Out of the shadows: victims' and witnesses' experiences of attending the Crown Court*, London: Victim Support and Institute for Criminal Policy Research, Birkbeck University of London; see also Jacobson, J., Hunter, G., and Kirby A. (2015) *Inside Crown Court: Personal experiences and questions of legitimacy*, Bristol: Policy Press.

[18] Names have been changed.

volunteer, which helps her to support Becky while they wait to be allocated a counsellor from the Child and Adolescent Mental Health Services (CAMHS).

(2) Pre-trial needs

15.12 There is often a long delay between reporting a crime to the police and coming to court, and the witness may have ongoing fears for their safety or may be worried about repercussions and reprisals from the defendant or their family.[19] The incident may have also disrupted their lives in other ways, especially if the defendant is a family member, involving additional housing and emotional difficulties.

15.13 Victims and witnesses are often extremely anxious about going to court. Many are still coming to terms with the personal impact of the crime, in addition to the fact that the defendant has pleaded not guilty. They are going to have to confront what happened, and to revisit the incident, and are concerned about the way they, or their family members, may be treated. Victims of sexual assault have to face describing intimate, personal actions, in a public arena, and may be dealing with a range of conflicted emotions: anger, embarrassment, self-blame, and fear of being judged. For example, in one case the Witness Service supported a man who met another male in a club, returned to the defendant's home and was sexually assaulted with a weapon. This was devastating for the victim and he was worried about the major part his sexuality was likely to play in the trial.

(3) The need for pre-trial therapy

15.14 Many victims of sexual violence require therapy or may be in a therapeutic relationship already. Often victims do not enter into therapy as they believe, or are advised, that it may prejudice their case by the defence claiming that they have been coached or that their recollections are not their own but a result of false memories from the session. In the example of Becky in section (1) above, pre-trial counselling was denied her by the police and social services in spite of clear guidance by the Crown Prosecution Service (CPS) relating to access to therapy for children. The guidance from the CPS states that the mental health need of the victim should be regarded as paramount.[20]

(4) Information about the case and procedures

15.15 Being kept informed about the case and its progress is crucial for victims and witnesses. In sexual assault cases it is particularly important for witnesses to know

---

[19] Hunter, et al. (2013), cited at n.17.
[20] CProsecution Service, Department of Health and Home Office (2001) *Provision of therapy for vulnerable or intimidated adult witnesses prior to a criminal trial—Practice guidance: Implementing the Speaking up for Justice Report, http://www.cps.gov.uk/publications/prosecution/pretrialadult.html*; Crown Prosecution Service, Department of Health, and Home Office (2001) *Provision of Therapy for Child Witnesses Prior to a Criminal Trial: Practice Guidance, http://www.cps.gov.uk/publications/prosecution/therapychild.html*.

about issues that affect their safety, for example, about the defendant's bail conditions. Although there are a range of commitments from different agencies to keep victims and witnesses informed, research findings show that they often feel kept in the dark.[21] Information about the criminal justice process, for example, concepts such as the burden of proof and the role of the prosecuting counsel, is often missing, and this can lead to anxiety, but also to unrealistic expectations, and therefore disappointment in the outcome.[22] Good information allows witnesses and victims to make informed decisions, improves their engagement with the criminal justice system and prepares them for the process.[23]

(5) During trial

Witnesses have often never been in a court before and this means they can feel nervous about giving evidence and coming face to face with the defendant. Although in most courts there are separate waiting areas, many prosecution witnesses, including victims, describe encountering the defendant or the defendants' supporters in the public areas of the court, or just outside the court. These encounters can be extremely distressing. The mother of one sexual violence victim described the court experience in the following account: **15.16**

> We left at the same time as the perpetrator and he came out of the same entrance as us. My daughter came face-to-face with him, and he and his family wanted to set about her and were hurling abuse at her. And she went to the pub and she broke a glass and she started self-harming in the toilets and we had to call an ambulance. I think it was the trauma of just coming out of the court at the same time.[24]

(6) Waiting to give evidence

The delay leading up to the trial is often compounded by having to wait at court to give evidence. Often witnesses are required to attend court at the start of the business day and then may not be called to give evidence until later in the afternoon, the next day, or in some cases days or weeks later. This can be extremely stressful, and inconvenient in people's busy lives. Having separate waiting spaces for the witness offers a 'safe haven' away from the defendant. **15.17**

(7) The role of the prosecutor

Research conducted with prosecution witnesses in the UK found that many, especially victim-witnesses misunderstand the role of the prosecution barrister, **15.18**

---

[21] Victim Support. (2011) *Left in the dark; Why victims of crime need to be kept informed*, London: Victim Support; Skinner, T. and Taylor, H., '"Being Shut Out in the Dark": Young Survivors' Experiences of Reporting a Sexual Offence' (2008) 4(2) *Feminist Criminology*, 130–50.

[22] Hunter, et al. (2013), cited at n.17.

[23] Clark, (2010), cited at n.11.

[24] Pettitt et al. (2013), cited in n.13, 42.

and incorrectly thought of them as representing them as individuals rather than acting on behalf of the Crown, and this raised their expectations in terms of how much contact they would have with them and their involvement in the case.[25]

(8) Giving evidence and being cross-examined

15.19 Going into court and giving evidence is extremely daunting, as the following account attests:

> It's just very frightening, very daunting when you walk in and you see all the chairs and the benches and everything set out, and then you see all these people with their wigs on and the gowns. It's just very, very frightening.[26]

Victims and witnesses describe being cross-examined as being put on trial themselves, being blamed for the incident, and believing that the defence barrister is trying to discredit them.[27] They often feel constrained by the way they gave evidence that they are unable to give a complete picture of the incident, and its impact on themselves. The following account is illustrative:

> He kept saying to me: 'It didn't really happen. You really wanted it to happen, didn't you?' Trying to discredit your character; they're trying to prove that his person is innocent and I'm the guilty person. And I kept going back, 'I did not ask him to do that. I did not invite him to my room. He assaulted me. He sexually assaulted me.'[28]

(9) Post-trial

15.20 The needs of witnesses after the trial relate to being kept informed of the outcome of the trial, and where appropriate, the sentence hearing. Although this is a clear duty for the Witness Care Units, witnesses and victims talk about being poorly informed and finding out about the outcome through other means—occasionally even from the defendant's friends and family or on social media. A clear concern is their safety after the court hearing itself, and fears of reprisals and repercussions from the defendant or their supporters.

15.21 For many, as described in para 15.19, the impact of going through cross-examination and being in court can have a detrimental impact on their emotional and physical health. They need ongoing support to cope with this, especially where there is an unsatisfactory outcome.

---

[25] Hunter, et al. (2013), cited at n.17; Clark, (2010), cited at n.11; Stern, V. (2011) *The Stern Review, A report by Baroness Vivian Stern CBE of an independent review into how rape complaints are handled by public authorities in England and Wales*. London: Government Equalities Office and Home Office.
[26] Hunter, et al. (2013), cited at n.17, 18.
[27] Ibid., 12; Stern, V. (2011), cited at n.25.
[28] Hunter, et al. (2013), cited at n.17, 22.

(10) Specific needs of child witnesses

Children and young witnesses have specific needs in the criminal justice process. **15.22**
Many in abuse cases are likely to be giving evidence against close family relations;
they are likely to have problems understanding the questions, and the power dynamics make it hard for them to say that they do not understand or to disagree with an
adult. Over three-quarters of children in one study felt anxious about giving evidence,
just over half had stress symptoms, and many felt their education was affected.[29]
For some, the stress of being cross-examined can prevent them being able to think
and articulate their point. Children are automatically entitled to special measures,
and there are specific good practice guidelines in managing young witness cases and
questioning children.[30] However, as in the case of Becky shown in section (1), these
special measures are sometimes not provided—for example, the lack of an intermediary in spite of her learning difficulties—or offer insufficient protection.

C. Support Available for Victims and Witnesses

There is a wide range of support available for all witnesses and specialist support for **15.23**
sexual violence witnesses.

(1) Witness Care Units

Witness Care Units provide information to victims and witnesses whose case is **15.24**
proceeding to court. They are staffed jointly by the police and the CPS, conduct
assessments, and provide tailored support to all victims and witnesses.

(2) The Witness Service

The Witness Service was developed by Victim Support in 1989 to operate inde- **15.25**
pendently of the police and courts. It provides support to prosecution and defence
witnesses, primarily through trained volunteers, in magistrates and crown courts
across England and Wales. In 2013, Victim Support provided help and support
to around 200,000 prosecution and defence witnesses, including 39,825 vulnerable and intimidated witnesses. Citizen's Advice have provided the service,
commissioned by the Ministry of Justice, since April 2015. It provides pre-trial
visits which enables witnesses to become familiar with the court room, and
the roles of people in court and court procedures; a quiet place for witnesses to
wait before giving evidence, separate from the defendant; an escort to the court
room or live TV link room; and an opportunity to receive further information and support post-trial. The Service provides emotional support before and
during the trial, at verdict, and at sentence where appropriate. Where special

---

[29] Plotnikoff, J. and Woolfson, R. (2009) *Measuring up? Evaluating implementation of
Government commitments to young witnesses in criminal proceedings. Good practice guidance in managing young witness cases and questioning children*, London: NSPCC and The Nuffield Foundation.
[30] Ibid.

measures are being provided for vulnerable and intimidated witnesses, the Witness Service may explain how these work and demonstrate them in pre-trial visits, and often identify vulnerable and intimidated witnesses at pre-trial stage who may not have been identified previously. In seven areas of the country, Victim Support provides a specialist service for young witnesses. It provides intensive pre-trial and post-trial support, often in outreach settings, to help young witnesses understand the court system, develop coping strategies, prepare for cross-examination, come to terms with the verdict and move on positively in their lives post trial.

(3) Specialist independent sexual violence advisers

15.26 In some areas there are specialist 'independent sexual violence advisers' (ISVAs) to co-ordinate support and risk management for victims of these crimes. They are generally based in voluntary sector organizations such as Rape Crisis, and Sexual Assault Referral, Centres which provide mental health care, counselling, and a forensic examination for victims of sexual violence.

(4) Sexual Offence Investigative Technique officers

15.27 Sexual Offence Investigative Tenique (SOIT) officers are specially trained police officers who provide technical and pastoral support to rape victims and also function as a bridge between the criminal case and procedure.

(5) Registered Intermediaries

15.28 Registered Intermediaries may be involved where a vulnerable witness needs support to communicate their evidence in court. They complete communication assessments, advise both defence and prosecution of the witness's communication needs, and assist in the live TV link room or court, intervening where necessary to ensure the witness is able to give their best evidence.

(6) Other support

15.29 Other support may be provided by family liaison officers or the officer in charge of the case.

D. Good Practice in Supporting Witnesses

(1) Co-ordination and communication

15.30 With vulnerable and intimidated witnesses in sexual violence cases, there is often a range of different agencies involved, and good inter-agency communication and joint working is key to ensure the best outcomes for witnesses.

15.31 The milestone 'Oxford Grooming case', (*R v ZA and others*) which was brought to light by Operation Bullfinch and was tried at the Central Criminal Court in 2013, provides an apt illustration of how strong multi-agency co-ordination and communication can ensure that vulnerable young witnesses are robustly supported. Six young witnesses were supported over the two years it took to bring the trial to court and during the four-month trial period and post-trial. The Kingfisher Sexual Exploitation Team, social workers, police, and health professionals worked alongside Victim Support to ensure that all aspects of support were addressed. This included practical accommodation and transport issues, special measures, trial preparation, and emotional support for young witnesses who had serious emotional and behavioural challenges.

(2) Information for witnesses

It is essential for the witnesses to be kept informed about the case, the potential **15.32** timing of the trial and the criminal justice procedures. Early engagement with the Witness Service through enhanced outreach can facilitate this, as the following account illustrates:

> A very vulnerable victim of sexual violence couldn't face coming to court. It was only on her second pre-trial visit to court that she felt strong enough to look in the court room. She was convinced that defence would 'annihilate' her. We explained the roles of key personnel within the courtroom so she had an overall unbiased view of, in particular the role of both prosecution and defence counsel and what her role was in the process. She went away to think about the information given to her and called up several times to ask questions. She then came up with her own support plan factoring in practical needs (breaks, crying in toilet to let off steam) and emotional support, (volunteer always being present and checking how she was feeling).

(3) Early identification and needs assessment of vulnerable witnesses and applications for special measures

Early assessment of the needs of a witness is essential if they are to be afforded **15.33** the level of support that they require. Victims and witnesses should be allowed to identify what kind of special measures they think would work best for them, and to have a realistic idea of what they will entail. Counsel, as well as other court staff, need to be informed early of a witness's vulnerability in advance, which is often not possible when they are given instruction late.[31] Witness requests should be granted by the court as soon as possible so that witnesses know in advance what will occur. It is particularly important to obtain intermediaries early for child witnesses, so that they can be allocated and build a rapport with the child well before trial.

(4) Case study of ongoing support: a young witness's story

Jessica (a pseudonym) is a very young girl who was sexually assaulted and had to **15.34** go to court. She was allocated a trained volunteer, Rachael, through the Witness

---

[31] Personal communication from Mr John Riley.

Outreach Service, previously part of Victim Support who provided court preparation support for two to three months. Jessica was visited three times at her family
home before the trial; Rachael used a number of resources and activities to help
Jessica express her feelings and advise how she could deal with them, for example, the 'Let's go to court' booklet, 'Feelings face' activity, along with 'Hannah's
bag of worries' game and flashcards. Jessica was asked to pack a small bag of her
favourite toys, books, and food to be taken to court. Rachel also assisted in finding
additional emotional support for the family, obtaining police assistance to deal
with harassment by the defendant's associates, and sourcing help for housing problems. Rachael arranged a pre-trial visit attended by Jessica, the Witness Service at
court, the intermediary (who had been assigned to the case by the CPS), and the
chief usher who showed how the TV link worked. Jessica gave her evidence really
well. At the last home visit, Rachael talked about the trial and the verdict; a not
guilty verdict was returned, and Jessica and her family were very disappointed. The
last activity that Jessica was given was a jigsaw puzzle, with a few pieces missing.
She tried to complete it but of course couldn't because of the missing pieces. This
helped Rachael explain why the defendant was found not guilty; it was not the fact
that she had not been believed nor was in any way to blame, but there may had been
some evidence missing in the case and the full clear picture could not be seen. The
service provided a follow-up call to see how things were for Jessica and her family.

(5) Training for defence advocates and judges on cross-examination for sexual violence cases and the impact on vulnerable witnesses and victims

15.35 Judges and prosecution barristers participate in specific training on managing rape
trials which needs to be refreshed every three years. Recently, a proposal has been
made for judges and defence barristers to be trained on how to deal with vulnerable
and intimidated witnesses.[32] Further guidance on cross-examination of vulnerable
and intimidated witnesses can be found in the Equal Treatment Bench Book and
the Advocates Gateway.[33]

(6) Waiting times and procedures in court

15.36 Often it is not possible to shorten the waiting times for witnesses. One solution
used in several courts has been not to call vulnerable and intimidated witnesses to
give evidence until the afternoon of the trial, and to finish evidence on the day even
if they have to sit late. In another court, the witness care manager in court allowed

---

[32] See Bar Council announcement for barristers *http://www.barcouncil.org.uk/media-centre/news-and-press-releases/2013/july/bar-council-encourages-creation-of-a-'required-training-programme* and *http://www.bbc.co.uk/news/uk-23595398* for specialist training for the Judiciary.
[33] Judicial College (2013) *Equal Treatment Bench Book*, London: Judicial College, *http://www.judiciary.gov.uk/Resources/JCO/Documents/judicial-college/equal-treatment-bb-2013.pdf*; see also *http://www.theadvocatesgateway.org/*.

some witnesses, mainly children, to wait in other areas in close proximity of the court building such as coffee shops and libraries, alleviating the stress of waiting around at the court.[34]

In some courts, there are discreet ways in which the court may be alerted to any **15.37** problems within the live link room, for instance, if the witness is becoming distressed, the witness may show an orange card. Witnesses can use a traffic light system, green, orange, and red to give non-verbal clues of the need to stop giving evidence. In some pilot areas, child witness can give evidence using a remote live link from another location—for example where they gave their ABE interview. This avoids the risk of meeting the perpetrator and allows more flexibility whilst waiting to give evidence.

(7) Creative and responsive use of special measures

In some instances, one type of special measure is not sufficient. For example, some **15.38** child witnesses may become very distressed that the defendant can see their evidence on screen from the live TV link room. In some cases screens have been used as well as the live link so that the defendant cannot see the witness' evidence on the TV screen. In another example, a child with learning difficulties found it easier to be cross-examined when the prosecution barrister was present in the live TV link room which enabled the child to pick up on visual clues and understand the questions better.

(8) Ground rules hearings and judges/court staff protecting the witnesses

When being cross-examined or questioned in a way that is aggressive or confusing, **15.39** the intervention of the judge is likely to be appreciated, as the following account illustrates:

> The judge was like the referee.... When he didn't understand anything, or he didn't understand a question that the barrister had asked me or didn't see the point in it he was quick to the mark and said, 'I don't actually think that is a relevant question.' To me he was very patient; when things did get a bit emotional he stopped everything. He was very understanding.[35]

Ground rules hearings are a meeting in advance of the trial which agrees the approach to the trial, for example, how questions can be put to a vulnerable witness. The trial judge can also eliminate repetitive questioning by multiple counsel (via agreement) by appointing a lead counsel to cross-examine or otherwise limit questioning. These hearings are compulsory when intermediaries are involved, and it is good practice for them to be used with any vulnerable or intimidated witness.[36]

---

[34] Victim Support Case Study.
[35] Hunter, et al. (2013), cited at n.17, 23.
[36] See resources at the Advocates gateway, *http://www.theadvocatesgateway.org/*.

(9) Additional support

15.40 Many of the things that may enable witnesses to give good testimony may seem relatively minor to the court process but are significant for the individuals. For example, in a (domestic violence) case, a pregnant victim-witness found that sipping milk sustained her through giving evidence; in another case a child was comforted by the presence of a dog in the live link room and even simple breathing techniques can play a part. In each of these cases it was thought that these small adaptations were significant in helping the witness to relax sufficiently to concentrate on their testimony. Sufficient time with a trusted supporter needs to be allowed to establish these calming influences, and a degree of flexibility of the court to permit these requests. It is often at the pre-trial visit that these needs and solutions are identified. Some courts also allow the prosecution victim-witness to come in through a different entrance (the judge's entrance) to prevent the inadvertent meeting with the defendant outside the court.

E. Barriers to Effective Support

15.41 There are a range of policies, initiatives, and support mechanisms to improve the experience of witnesses and victims. However, in many of the descriptions in section E it is clear that there are often barriers to effective support and protection for witnesses. Late identification of the witness and their needs means it is not possible to provide sufficient pre-trial support and to address needs that might be significant in achieving best evidence on trial day. This can also mean they may not be able to have a pretrial visit which makes it difficult for witnesses to make informed decisions about their own needs, and council are not aware of the needs of the witnesses.

15.42 Many victims of sexual violence have mental health problems, learning difficulties, or other disabilities that have not been flagged by the police or witness care units. In this scenario supporters are often not equipped with the specialist knowledge and opportunities for appropriate special measures, for example intermediaries are missed or delayed. Special measures have been greatly appreciated by victims, especially the use of screens, and live links. However, often these are not being requested, or are requested, and granted at the last minute, adding stress and uncertainty for victims and witnesses. Technical problems have at times caused failure of special measures, for example, live TV links not working, screens being wrongly positioned, or audio failure with the DVD of witness testimony. Continuity of intermediaries, and counsel, is important to offer support to vulnerable witnesses, however, the listing system and the fees structure is not designed to assist counsel retain cases.[37]

---

[37] Personal communication from Mr John Riley.

Separate waiting facilities for witnesses are greatly valued. However, in some courts **15.43** these facilities are not available due to the constraints of the building. Waiting times and cancellations continue to be a significant stress for witnesses. People need to be able to plan and manage their anxieties and expectations. People describe having to put their 'lives on hold' and not being able to move on from the crime. This stress of waiting can be exacerbated by frequent changes and cancellation at the last moment, as this account clearly shows:

> It was due to start on the Wednesday. It was cancelled, so we thought we were going on the Thursday, and on the Wednesday evening they cancelled the Thursday, so we were scheduled for the Friday. And those two days were hell, absolute hell not only for [the daughter]: you are so upset and so worried and you'd get keyed up for this day, and it's awful enough anyway and then you're cancelled and cancelled again.[38]

The impact of the long waits and cancellations can be greatly mitigated by good communication, and being kept informed about what is happening with the case. It is particularly important for witnesses to be aware of availability of special measures and whether these would be granted.

F. Conclusion

The evidence of harrowing victim and witness experiences calls for an overhaul **15.44** in the approach taken to the criminal justice system; a system where witnesses are not exposed to having their personal credibility questioned, and where they have their experience validated, to have a voice, and gain safety from the perpetrator and justice. Improvements in the existing system are moving in the right direction and this paper shows the crucial role that all criminal justice agencies work together and communicate effectively in the best interest and protection of vulnerable and intimidated witnesses. The examples here show the key role supporters can play, including the Witness Service working in partnership with other criminal justice professionals. The Witness Service provide invaluable support to witnesses and victims in sexual violence cases and should be part of the process at an early stage; as such, lawyers should be active in involving the Witness Service early on in any prosecution and ensure that they are provided with key details and updates concerning the victim and the case regularly.

Further Reading

Crown Prosecution Service (2009) *Supporting victims and witnesses with a learning disability*; and (2009) *Supporting victims and witnesses who have mental health issues*; Prosecution Guidance, published online.

---

[38] Hunter, et al. (2013), cited at n.17, 14.

Hunter, G., Jacobson, J., Kirby, A. (2013) *Out of the shadows: victims' and witnesses' experiences of attending the Crown Court*, Birkbeck University of London: Victim Support and Institute for Criminal Policy Research.

Ministry of Justice (2011) *Achieving Best Evidence in Criminal Proceedings. Guidance on interviewing victims and witnesses, and guidance on using special measures.* Published online: London: Ministry of Justice.

Ministry of Justice (2013) *Code of Practice for Victims of Crime*, London: The Stationery Office.

Plotnikoff, J. and Woolfson, R. (2009) *Measuring up? Evaluating implementation of Government commitments to young witnesses in criminal proceedings. Good practice guidance in managing young witness cases and questioning children*, London: NSPCC and The Nuffield Foundation.

Author Biographies

Bridget Pettitt is a former researcher at Victim Support and has recently co-authored a report on people with mental health problems as victims of crime. She is a visiting Researcher at the Institute of Psychiatry and an Honorary Research Associate at Kingston University and St George's London.

Lina Wallace is Senior Manager for Witness Service Development at Victim Support and has had nineteen years' experience of managing and developing Witness Services in London Courts.

Amanda Naylor is the Manager of Victim Support's Children and Young People's Service and supports the development of Victim Support's Young Witness Service.

Mark Castle OBE is the CEO of Victim Support, having previously been the Chief Executive of the Association of Police and Crime Commissioners (APCC) and CEO of the Association of Police Authorities (APA). He previously served in the Army for thirty-one years leaving as a Brigadier.

16

UNDERSTANDING WHAT CHILDREN SAY: AVOIDING THE PITFALLS OF CHILD TESTIMONY

Harry Zeitlin

A. Introduction

The significance given to child statements within legal proceedings has varied **16.01** immensely over time. There have been tendencies either to ignore child statements, or conversely to overvalue them; sometimes adult qualities have been inappropriately attributed to child functioning. This brief review of the historical development of the treatment of child statements by professionals within the justice process highlights the requirement for objective interpretation and treatment of children's communications.

16.02   In the late 1960s and early 1970s increasing weight was given to statements by children as evidence of sexual abuse and hence also criminal activity by an adult. Eventually any statement by a child that could even remotely relate to abuse was taken almost as proof. This immense over-identification of abuse led to a number of inquiries of which the Cleveland Inquiry[1] was the most renowned. 'Cleveland' was a landmark that heralded the introduction of guidance for professionals conducting interviews with children and interpreting the significance of child statements. It also assisted understanding in circumstances where distressed adult interpretation could misrepresent the significance of child statements.[2]

16.03   Unfortunately, at the same time, the realization of over-identification led to a phase of extreme caution over considering abuse—until the next dramatic case with the pendulum swinging back and forth. There is now, a quarter century later, in the 'mid twenty tens' once again great agitation to identify child abusers and castigation of the previous 'laissez-faire.' Current investigations include the Independent Inquiry, Home Office Review, Rochdale inquiry, Savile BBC review, Savile NHS Inquiry, Jersey inquiry, Police Operation Yewtree, Police operations Fairbank, Fernbridge and Cayacos, Department of Education inquiry, and sundry others.[3]

16.04   Part of the difficulty is linked to the impact of the thought of child abuse on adult objectivity, though there is limited objective research.[4] This chapter will consider from a clinical standpoint, those aspects in which the significance of children's statements differs from adults, evaluation of the validity of child statements and the reasons for the need for caution in interpretation. Many of the issues are covered to some extent in other chapters. However, the overall focus of this chapter will be on appropriate good practice both in facilitating children to describe their memory of events and also on avoiding misinterpretation. Case examples are used, as far as possible to relate the data to practice.

B. Understanding the Complex Nature of Child Witness Testimony

16.05   'Children have a right to be heard.'[5] This phrase, referring to the voice of the child is one often used and sometimes taken to imply that court decisions should accord

---

[1] Butler-Sloss, E. (1988) *Report of the Inquiry into Child Abuse in Cleveland 1987*, Cm. 412, London: HMSO. See also: Royal College of Psychiatrists 'Child psychiatric perspectives on the assessment and management of sexually mistreated children: Report of the Royal College of Psychiatrists Working Party on Child Sexual Abuse' (1988) 12(12) *Bulletin of the British Journal of Psychiatry*.

[2] Jones, D.P.H. (1992) *Interviewing the sexually abused child. Investigation of Sexual Abuse*, 4th edn, London: Gaskell.

[3] BBC News review, November 2014.

[4] See e.g. Pillai, M., 'An evaluation of "confirmatory" medical opinion given to English courts in 14 cases of alleged child sexual abuse' (2007) 14(8) *Journal of Forensic & Legal Medicine*, (Nov), 503–14.

[5] Parkinson, P. and Cashmore, J. (2008) *The Voice of a Child in Family Law Disputes*, Oxford: Oxford University Press.

with what the child actually says. This sounds correct but unfortunately is a long-standing problem that mixes several issues together. It risks conveying a presumption that what a child says under all circumstances will reflect 'outside' reality, that it indicates what the child really wants, and that the child can determine what is best. It also assumes that interrogation of the child will do no harm 'provided they tell the truth'.

Children's statements can be relevant to many aspects of legal proceedings, both **16.06** civil and criminal, but much of the literature relates to evidence in cases of allegations of child abuse. A smaller but significant amount links to civil proceedings in cases of parental dispute, most often with contact issues. In the 1970s 'disclosure' became a key word in the investigation of allegations of sexual abuse of children. It sounded right until it was appreciated that 'disclosure' was inappropriate in cases where the child in question had not been subject to abuse. Identifying evidence that abuse has occurred is not the same as enabling children to reveal *their perception* of abusive behaviour to which they had been subjected.

Failing to listen objectively to the child's word, allied with professional over- **16.07** interpretation, risks compromising child health, as was revealed in 'Cleveland'.

'Cleveland' was the first major inquiry to prompt examination of two core issues **16.08** of concern, namely, how to interpret and understand child statements and how to interpret and understand physical characteristics observed in child genital examinations. Criteria were used that were related, 'sensitive' to abuse but not 'specific'.[6] Reflex anal dilatation was perhaps the classic example.[7] This physical feature had been misunderstood as an indication of abuse, whereas contemporary medical understanding was aware that these anal signs were also associated with other physical conditions, unrelated to sexual interference.[8] It was, however, during the time of intense concern considered to be an indicator of sexual abuse of any form. 'Cleveland's' recommendations still have resonance today.

'Cleveland' criticized professionals for 'the certainty and over-confidence with **16.09** which they pursued the detection of sexual abuse in children referred to them'.[9] Butler-Sloss also highlighted the difficulties for professionals in this area. 'It is difficult for professionals to balance the conflicting interests and needs in the enormously important and delicate field of child sexual abuse.'[10] Importantly, the

---

[6] Dziak, J.J., Coffman, D.L., Lanza, S.T., and Runze, L. (2012) *Sensitivity and specificity of information criteria* Methodology Centre and Department of Statistics, Penn State Technical Report Series, Pennsylvania: Pennsylvania State University, 12–119. The terms, 'sensitive' and 'specific' are long-established concepts in epidemiology.

[7] Claydon, G.S., 'Reflex anal dilatation associated with severe chronic constipation in children' (1988) 63(7) *Archives of Diseases in Childhood*, 832–6.

[8] Ibid.

[9] Report, cited at n.1, Pt 3, Final Conclusions, 243, para 7.

[10] Ibid., 244, para 15.

report further cautioned, 'If there is a suspicion of child sexual abuse in the mind of the professional, the danger of false identification ought not to be forgotten.'[11]

16.10 Techniques in questioning children were developed that 'enabled' children to reveal what had happened—at least in the mind of the questioner. Unfortunately, there are a number of factors that affect a child's perception of events and recall. These include the child's developmental status, aspects of the development of memory, a child's understanding of events, external influences on a child's perception of events both socially and in the manner of questioning, and a child's use of fantasy in dealing with stressful and painful experiences.

16.11 In summary, there's no reason to contradict a statement that children should be heard. It remains important to know the feelings and perceptions of the child. However, it is also essential to consider what might affect the reliability of the child's perception and recall.

C. Child Memory

16.12 The psychology of memory is dealt with elsewhere in Chapters 21, 22, and 23. There is a growing body of information about memory and the nature of memory with increasing awareness of its complexity. In general terms, however, children's memory tends to be partial and fragmented before the age of three with considerable variation according to age and developmental status.

16.13 From the age of 6 to 8 into teenage years there is better co-ordination both of memory and of the circumstances surrounding memories, particularly autobiographical ones.[12] It is important, therefore, to remember that a child's memory of events may appear to be precise but may be incomplete and relate an incident to incorrect surrounding circumstances.

16.14 Children's memories are influenced not only by the actual event but by subsequent experience particularly the statements of important others. The latter may include parents, peers, and enthusiastic interrogators.

Case example 1

16.15 *A 7-year-old girl said that she hated her father who had shouted at her and hit her. Her parents had separated four years before, contact had been stopped by the mother 2½ years before and the father was now seeking re-establishment of contact through the court. The mother said the father was an impulsive violent man but that she was*

---

[11] Ibid., Recommendations 8 (c)(vi), 251.
[12] Goldstein, G., Alan, D., Thaler, N., Luther, J.F., Panchalingam, K., and Jay, W., 'Developmental aspects and neurobiological correlates of working and associative memory' (2014) 28(4) *Neuropsychology*, 496–505.

stopping contact because of what her daughter said. When interviewed for an expert report, the child repeated the statement but when asked to describe her father she said she couldn't remember him or anything about him. She commented that it would be best to ask her mother.

In this case the child remembered what she had been told or perhaps just overheard **16.16** and incorporated it as true memory. Variations on this pattern are very common in acrimonious parental contact cases. It is difficult to distinguish between genuine fearfulness of the father, suppression of memories of abuse, and memory derived from discussion.

This particular example indicates that the child should be permitted to speak in **16.17** an unpressurized environment. Statements by a child need to be interpreted from the perspective of the child and that will also depend on the developmental status of the child.

D. Developmental Status

There is an immense difference in all skills but particularly including memory and **16.18** receptive and executive language across the age range from birth to 18. There's also considerable variation in these parameters in any one age group. In order to understand the significance of a child's communication it is important to evaluate the child's developmental status.

It is remarkably easy to make assumptions about a child's developmental status and **16.19** to assume either that it can be determined by age or that the child's understanding would be the same as that of the interviewer. It is not uncommon for those involved in the legal processes within the courts as well as police officers and social workers to have little training in interviewing children, with the risk of misjudging developmental status.[13]

Case example 2

Following an allegation of possible child abuse a police officer formally interviewed **16.20** *a child. The police report concluded that the 5-year-old child confirmed that she had been digitally abused by the accused. The report included a statement that the child's understanding had been confirmed. The police interview had been recorded on tape. Reviewing the tape: the child was told, 'You must not tell a lie. Is that a skirt?' The child was wearing a skirt and nodded. 'If you said you were wearing trousers that would be a lie. OK?' The officer smiled and nodded to which the child responded by smiling and nodding. 'Did he touch you?' The officer smiled and nodded as an indication of*

---

[13] Handley, G. and Doyle, C., 'Ascertaining the wishes and feelings of young children: social workers' perspectives on skills and training' (2014) 19(4) *Child & Family Social Work*, 443–54.

requiring a reply (perhaps unaware of doing so), to which the child smiled and nodded. Taken as assent. 'Did he touch you on your …' etc., through a range of questions each with a reciprocated smile and nod. The child actually had a very limited comprehension or vocabulary and as it eventually turned out had not experienced the alleged abuse nor did she understand what a lie was.

E. Mental Health Status

16.21 The range of mental health disorders in children differs to some extent from those of adults and in many respects is more difficult to identify. It would not be appropriate here to evaluate the possible impact of each form of disorder.[14]

16.22 The mental state of the child is still likely to have a significant impact on the child's perception and on reporting of events. Examples of common conditions would include attention deficit hyperactivity disorder (ADHD), oppositional defiant disorder (ODD), conduct disorder, mood disorders, anxiety disorders, drug and substance misuse, post-traumatic stress disorder (PTSD) et cetera. These may affect a range of functions within the child such as impulsivity, attentiveness to events, perception, and so on. The child's mental health status may also have a significant effect on the child's response and vulnerability to adverse events. It is therefore important for an appraisal of the child's mental state to take place, even if only to record the fact and conclusion of the assessment.

Case example 3

16.23 *A boy of 14 was brought to the clinic by his mother who said that he had told her he was very worried that he might abuse his sister or mother. Clinically he was pubertal and he explained that he now thought about girls a lot. He particularly thought about his mother and his sister. However, the lad had been attending for some time for a different reason. He had difficulty in coping with change, showed repetitive behaviour, and was rigid in his relationships with difficulty in understanding others' feelings. He showed a fairly typical picture of Asperger's Syndrome. When asked to speak more about his feelings he repeated openly that he thought about all females but then in an agitated manner stressed that it was absolutely out of the question that he would ever do anything to his female family members. He showed very considerable relief when told of the process of coming to terms with sexual feelings and there being 'an incest taboo'. The main problem was of his conscious and public expression of the feelings rather than a risk of abusing his female relatives.*

---

[14] For further reading, see Rutter, M., Bishop, D., Pine, D., Scott, S., Stevenson, J.S., Taylor, E. A., and Thapar, A. (2010) *Rutter's Child and Adolescent Psychiatry*, 5th edn, Singapore: Wiley-Blackwell.

F. Child Awareness or Otherwise of Significance of Adult Behaviour

A very young child's perception of the significance of adult behaviour is likely to be **16.24** very different to that of an adult. The child's perception will change with increasing independence and contact with the outer world and, of course, with the advent of puberty. There is a very real risk of assuming that the child's perception of abusive behaviour may be the same as that of an adult.

Case example 4

Misunderstanding a child's perception of an event: A mother alleged that the elderly **16.25** *man in the ground floor flat put his hand up the skirt of her 5-year-old child as she went upstairs to their flat. The event probably occurred on two occasions but the child was unaware of its significance and thought the man was playing. The child was in due course questioned and asked, inter alia, whether the man had touched her sexually. She said she did not know. It was explained to her what that meant and she was told what a horrible thing he had done.*

The man had committed an offence but it was not an appropriate setting for either **16.26** self-protection training or sex education and the investigating interview had a far more sexualizing effect on the child than the event itself.

G. Parent Misinterpretations (Motivated)

Adults may misinterpret both what the child means and what the child actu- **16.27** ally says. The commonest examples of this are probably in cases of acrimonious parental separation within contact disputes. The parents, particularly the mothers, under these conditions experience very powerful emotions. There is likely to be interpretation of children's statements to fit the adult feeling. The child is also likely to perceive and copy the nature of the parental feeling.

Case example 5

A 6-year-old girl and 4-year-old boy, children of separated parents, returned from a **16.28** *contact visit to their father. The mother reported to social services that her daughter had told her that the father had defecated on her during a contact visit. The social worker asked the girl in the presence of the mother if father had pooed on her. The girl said yes. The social worker asked 'Did he touch you', to which the girl replied 'yes, he did'. 'Where did he touch you?' 'On my bottom,' and contact was stopped. The same questions were asked by a psychologist and the girl gave the same reply. The case went to court with the issue of abuse during contact. When seen late in the day for an assessment for* *the court she was tired and played very actively with the dolls house. When asked what she was doing she said, 'It was in the bathroom.' Encouraged to go on she said that she had been in the bath with her brother and 'there it was on the floor. The poo.' (So what happened?) 'Dad asked who did it. I said it wasn't me. My brother said it wasn't him and Dad said "that only leaves me." So dad had pooed on us.' (And then?) 'Dad got a flannel, put soap on it and rubbed it over my bottom.'*

16.29   It is best if children are interviewed alone.[15] There is evidence that children are influenced by adults who are important to them, such as the parent.[16] Children may say what pleases that adult and subsequently also come to consider that what they have said is true. In this case the true memory appeared to be still present even though the statement that dad had pooed on her had been repeated by her many times.

H. Psychological Stress on Vulnerable Children

16.30   Reference is made in para 16.27 to the circumstances of children in acrimonious contact disputes. In these circumstances children may also have distortion of their perceptions and statements because of powerful psychological stress. There is a relatively constant pattern of events in contact conflict cases. The parents separate with powerful disagreement that has become acrimonious. The mothers experience psychological distress at not being able to totally remove involvement of an ex-partner whom they feel has been in some way abusive to them; this is then projected onto the child.

16.31   After some contact there is an allegation that the father is dangerous to the child, that he will remove the child, and that he had never really had much involvement with the child. Fathers most often express extreme frustration and powerlessness.

16.32   Children are placed in an impossible situation; they cannot be loyal to both parents if brought into their parents' conflict. The children begin to rationalize an attachment to one parent and rejection of the other. It is particularly noticeable when children in these circumstances are interviewed in the presence of the parent to whom they show allegiance.

Case example 6

16.33   *(Irrational) fearfulness in children involved in acrimonious contact dispute. Parents had separated two years previously and both children (girl aged 12 and boy aged*

---

[15]   It is preferable that the interviewer has met with the child prior to the interview, to reduce potential anxiety.

[16]   In order to optimize the quality of the witness testimony, the parent or carer may be located near but not in the interview room.

10) had continued contact. The boy gradually objected to going to the father and then adamantly refused. He would become frantic when the time for contact was due. When interviewed he said that the father was terrible and would never let him do what he wanted. He said the father would lurk outside the school—he had seen the bushes shake and he knew he was there.

The indications were that the father was a somewhat rigid and controlling man but there was no indication of frightening or dangerous behaviour. The boy had first been interviewed in the presence of the mother. The main focus of the interview was what his father had done that would be the cause of the boys apparent terror. *There was no opportunity for him to explain what it was like to be expected to be loyal to both sides in a battle.*   **16.34**

I. Interviewer Misinterpretation

That children are abused both physically and sexually is horrifying to most people working in the field. As noted above, investigators experience considerable psychological pressure not to overlook possible cases of child sexual abuse. The pressure may result in listening to the child but not actually hearing what the child says.   **16.35**

Case example 7

Over-identification: a child admitted to hospital was found to have excoriation of the vulva. The child was 'heard' to say that it was scratched. This was taken as sufficient evidence to start an enquiry into abuse of the child. The child had, in fact, said that she scratches herself. It was only later the correlation was made with the medical history of the little girl who suffered from cystic fibrosis. After a course of long-term antibiotics the child acquired an infection of vulval Candida Albicans, that is, 'Thrush' which in turn caused irritation and triggered the scratching.   **16.36**

The investigator's horror at the thought of a little girl having her vulva scratched led to direct action that could have been averted, if recent medical history been considered. The very simple link was only made after referral to social services and commencement of legal proceedings.   **16.37**

Reference has been made above to oscillations between over-reaction and under-reaction. The following case was relatively recent. It illustrates a response to a minor's behaviour that denies the significance of child behaviour.   **16.38**

Case example 8

Under-identification of abusive events: a girl of 13 attended a Child and Adolescent Mental Health Service (CAMHS) clinic for falling school performance. The busy parent described how her daughter would go out at night 'to friends' and return with more   **16.39**

259

money than her parents had given her. When asked, the child said that she could not remember how she received it. She was also noted to have messages from unknown 'males' on her mobile phone.

16.40   The local social service office declined to investigate saying that it was not uncommon behaviour amongst teenagers. The child was actually being induced into prostitution.

J. Time Sequence and Constructing a Timeline

16.41   Time sequencing of recalled data presents two problems. First, there appears to be a degree of flexibility in children for very early memories but also probably for many into early teenage years, in the way that memory of events is linked to surrounding environment.[17]

16.42   Secondly, in evaluating the significance of child memories there is a very powerful 'pressure' to make as good a link as possible. If a link is close in time then causation is likely to be assumed.

16.43   In considering the validity of children's statements, very careful examination of time sequencing can help. Children's recall of past events may be linked to a range of influences and have a distorted time sequence. It is important to construct a precise timeline that includes all available data. Case example 9 illustrates the difficulties.

Case example 9

16.44   *The value of a precise timeline: In a compensation case an older teenager, who had been taken into care as a child for neglect, claimed to have been abused in a children's home soon after he went there. He repeatedly used the phrase that 'it had happened in the attic'. It had been noted from the social service records that as a child he had referred to the phrase 'it happened in the attic' during the month that he was first in care but it was not until the court hearing had commenced it was seen that the entry in the social service record was two weeks before he went to the children's home.*

16.45   What had happened in the attic related to the child's experience prior to being placed in the home. It was probable that rather than deliberately lying, the child's account was impaired by the impact of severe neglect on his development and mental state. It was most likely in his parental home that something, maybe abuse, actually happened in the attic, but the associations changed in his mind to the location in the children's home. When this was pointed out to the judge there was

---

[17]   Wang, Q. and Peterson, C., 'Your earliest memory may be earlier than you think: Prospective studies in children stating of the earliest childhood memories' (2014) 50(6) *Developmental Psychology*, 1680–6.

chaos in court but after discussion the case was closed. In the analysis of any data it is essential to construct a very careful timeline looking at the detailed sequencing of events and carefully place child statements as far as possible according to otherwise validated data.

K. Media Impact on Children

Parents and interviewers have the most direct effect on the nature and content of **16.46** childrens' statements, however, the internet, social media, and television, play an increasingly important role in shaping child behaviour and understanding. A high proportion of children now spend increasing amounts of time each day either watching television or playing media-based games. There is a long-standing literature on the impact of media violence[18] and recognition of some of the parameters that have an increased effect on children's behaviour[19] and the child's perception of the appropriateness of the behaviour of others. The parameters include the developmental status of the child, degree of parental supervision, and extent to which the child feels involved in the portrayed activities.

Belson identified a causal link between watching aggressive conduct and viewer **16.47** behaviour in 1978[20] and these concerns remain. Cardwell refers to 'this societal ill' in 2013.[21] Extreme aggressive behaviour, nudity, and sexual scenes are increasingly commonplace on mainstream television.

In the late 1980s, at the time of 'Cleveland', the fact of a child displaying knowl- **16.48** edge of the mechanics of sexual intercourse added great probative weight to any suspicion or complaint of sexual abuse. However, over the last twenty years it has become increasingly unlikely that a child of six will not witness simulated sex on television.

Consequently, explicit sexual detail referenced within a child's statement needs to **16.49** be carefully evaluated. Young children are more likely to experience difficulty distinguishing between reality and fantasy. A further cause for concern is the increasing interactive experience inherent in popular social media games. There is a real risk that the child perceives violence against others as an acceptable and even reasonable norm. Research on controlling the adverse effects of video games and other social media is essential.

---

[18] Belsen, W.A. (1978) *Television violence and the adolescent boy*, Farnborough, Hants: Saxon House.

[19] Breuer, J., Scharkow, M., and Quandt, T., 'Tunnel Vision or Desensitization?: The Effect of Interactivity and Frequency of Use on the Perception and Evaluation of Violence in Digital Games' (2014) 26(4) *Journal of Media Psychology: Theories, Methods, & Applications*, 176–88,.

[20] Belsen, (1978), cited at n.19.

[21] Cardwell, M.S., 'Video Media-Induced Aggressiveness in Children' (2013) 106(9) *Southern Medical Journal*, 513–17.

Case example 10

16.50 *A boy of 17 had stabbed another boy. The quiet boy of low normal ability described in detail that he carried a knife and when the older boy rushed at him 'of course' he took out the knife and stabbed him. (Why carry a large knife?) 'It's what you do; everyone does.'*

L. A Protocol for Using Child Evidence

16.51 The following looks at possible ways of minimizing the difficulties in assessing child statements. The prime purpose of interviewing a child is two-fold, to listen to what the child says, and to examine and assess the child's internal perceptions and feelings. A thorough and objective evaluation of a child's statement is required before it may be accepted as evidence of fact; this requires consideration of a variety of internal and external factors about and surrounding the child.

16.52 (1) **Evaluation of the child's status**

    (a) Consider the child's developmental status, particularly expressive and receptive language.

    (b) Conduct a basic appraisal of the child's mental state.

    (c) Appraise the child's environment. Is the child exposed to the opinion of important adults?

    (d) Does the child show evidence of particular influences, for example, peer group, media?

16.53 (2) **Spontaneity**

    (a) Has the child made any spontaneous statement, and if so how was it recorded?

    (b) Has the child made a spontaneous action, for example, drawing?

    (c) Consider all possible explanations for the child's spontaneous statement/action.

    (d) How was the child questioned/interviewed?

16.54 (3) **The child's expectation of the interview**

    (a) Is the child aware of the purpose of the interview?

    (b) Who informed the child of the reason for the interview?

    (c) Does the child know the interviewer?

    (d) Has the child being told that there will be a consequence?

    (e) Who else was present at the interview?

16.55 (4) **Questioning children**

    (a) Was the interviewer trained?

    (b) Was there a careful record of the interviewing?

    (c) Did the interview technique use open or closed questioning?

(5) Consider all possible explanations   **16.56**

(a) Give reasons for each possible explanation.
(b) Indicate relative probabilities or reason for exclusion of other explanations.
(c) Indicate particular reasons for explanation given.

M. Conclusion

It remains of value and importance to hear what children involved in legal proceed-   **16.57**
ings have to say. There is a range of factors that affect a child's perception of past
and present events and the memory that they retain. The statements of children
can help clarify events that they have seen and experienced personally but interpreting what they actually mean may not always be a straightforward process.

Training is needed to enable interviewers to listen to the child without creating   **16.58**
pressure or distress and causing psychological harm. Consideration should be
given to the child's mental state and external influences that may have operated
on the child's mind, when evaluating what the child has said. The range of influences on a child's memory and thinking are complex and suggest that only in rare
cases should the court's decision rest solely on the child's word. The child or young
person's perception of events may reflect an internal reality that includes confusion
and distress rather than an accurate account of events.

Evaluating childrens' statements with care will enhance understanding of the   **16.59**
import of childrens' statements in civil law cases and the identification of those
child testimonies that can assist the court in the conviction of child abusers and
other offenders in criminal cases. Nonetheless, courts should exercise considerable
caution not to place the responsibility for their decisions onto the shoulders of
the child.

Further Reading

Simcock, G., Hayne, H., 'Age-related changes in verbal and non-verbal memory during
early childhood' (2003) *Developmental Psychology*, Volume 39(5), 805–14.
Cowan, N. (2009) *The development of memory in infancy and childhood*,
New York,: Psychology Press, US 2nd edn 43–68, xii, 410.

Author Biography

Professor Harry Zeitlin, BSc., MBBS, M.Phil, MD, FRCP, FRCPsych, was
educated at the (Royal) London Hospital and Maudsley Hospital. He held his first
academic post in child psychiatry in London University at Westminster Children's

Hospital from 1973 to 1990. He was a professor at University College London from 1990 to 2001. He has been an expert witness since 1976 at the invitation of the Official Solicitor. He was the originator and coordinator of Royal Society of Medicine course on expert witness for child mental health professionals and was a member of the independent panel of psychiatrists for the Cleveland Inquiry. He has conducted research and written on various topics including long-term outcome for childhood disorders, drug and substance misuse in young people, sexual abuse, and acrimonious parental contact disputes.

17

FORENSIC SCIENCE, FORENSIC MEDICINE, AND SEXUAL CRIME

Jason Payne-James, Mary A. Newton, and Christine Bassindale

A. Introduction

The investigation into sexual crimes involves the need for documentation and inter- **17.01**
pretation of both scientific and medical evidence. There is significant variation in
the documents available for recording information and the training to undertake
interpretation is conducted by a range of organizations making consistency difficult to maintain. In addition, standards of scientific and medical assessment may
be adversely affected by inappropriate, inexperienced, or incompetent practitioners. The chapter provides information on appropriate standards that should be
sought when prosecuting or defending such cases, and identifies further relevant
reference sources. The chapter provides an overview of the nature of sexual crime
on an international basis. It provides an overview of the principles for collection,
sampling, and documentation of such forensic scientific and medical evidence.
Examples of classification of injury, interpretation of injury, and findings after
sexual crimes will be provided predominantly in relation to adults.

B. Types and Incidence of Sexual Crime

17.02   Pertaining to intimate partner sexual violence, many studies from a variety of backgrounds including forensic medicine, criminology, sexual assault referral centres, public health, and criminology have explored this and the data obtained are variable.[1]

17.03   Adult male sexual assault has been studied widely (and particularly in prison and the military) and although a minority of overall sexual assault complaints is well-recognized.[2]

17.04   False allegations of sexual assault, although rare, do occur.

C. Principles of Forensic Science and Forensic Medicine

17.05   For the sexual assault complainant and suspect and those tasked with prosecuting or defending such cases, it is important to understand the scope and limitations that forensic science and forensic medicine may contribute. In the UK there is great variability in the skills and competences of doctors and nurses conducting forensic medical examinations of complainants and suspects of alleged sexual assault. Some doctors and nurses are competent to undertake sexual assault examination, recording of injuries and sample taking, but do not have the extended skills to interpret the range and variety of findings in the context of a criminal case. They can provide evidence entirely appropriately as professional witnesses of fact, but cannot provide opinion (expert) evidence. This is a distinction often missed by the examiner, police investigators, the Crown Prosecution Service (CPS), and defence legal teams.

17.06   Forensic medical and forensic scientific examination potentially assists the investigation of sexual crime in a variety of ways including identifying perpetrators, corroborating accounts, excluding accounts, and confirming detail. The forensic medical assessment comprises a comprehensive examination, identifying injury, obtaining appropriate samples for forensic scientific assessment, and contemporaneous documentation (which may include photo-documentation). The forensic scientific input is directed at analyzing scenes, recovering relevant evidence, and using a wide variety of analytic and technical methods (including fibre analysis, DNA analysis, and toxicology) to assist the investigation.

17.07   Much of the work of the medical and scientific professionals utilizes Locard's Exchange Principle (also known as Locard's theory) which states in simple form,

---

[1] Hamby, S., 'Intimate Partner and Sexual Violence Research: Scientific Progress, Scientific Challenges, and Gender' (2014) 15(3) *Trauma Violence Abuse*, 149–58; Newton, M., 'The forensic aspects of sexual violence' (2013) 27 *Best Practice and Research Clinical Obstetrics and Gynaecology*, 77–90.

[2] Peterson Z.D., Voller E.K., Polusny M.A., and Murdoch M., 'Prevalence and consequences of adult sexual assault of men: review of empirical findings and state of the literature', (2001) 31(1) *Clin Psychol Rev*, 1–24. doi: 10.1016/j.cpr.2010.08.006. Epub 2010 Aug 27.

that 'every contact leaves a trace'.[3] This forms a basis for the recovery and inter-pretation of forensic scientific and medical evidence. In a sexual crime setting, if the crime perpetrator comes into contact with the scene (or someone within that scene), then something will be brought into the scene and something will be taken away. It is for the forensic practitioners to consider the given accounts, identify what contact may have occurred, harvest relevant samples in an evidentially sound way, submit the samples for forensic scientific analysis and interpret the findings. The principle can be applied in all settings, for example, by linking a suspect's DNA profile to that obtained from forensic seminal fluid obtained from a complainant's vagina, by identifying hair from a balaclava used in a stranger sexual assault.

D. Examination of Complainants and Suspect

From a forensic medical perspective, complainants (victims) and suspects (assail-ants) must have an appropriate primary clinical forensic medical assessment, in an appropriate clinical forensic medical facility conducted by a healthcare profes-sional with specific training, knowledge, experience, mentorship, supervision and who has been competence tested in sexual offences medicine. They ought to be offered a choice of examiner (in particular choice of gender of their examiner).   **17.08**

At present in the UK a complainant of sexual assault will generally be assessed and examined in a purpose-built Sexual Assault Referral Centre (SARC). In general, UK SARCs provide the examiners, whether doctors or nurses, with some mentorship and supervision (the quality and quantity of which is dependent on the local model of care and resources of the service). In 2015 the Royal College of Paediatrics and Child Health (RCPCH) along with the Faculty of Forensic & Legal Medicine (FFLM) published a document titled 'Service specification for the evaluation of children and young people who may have been sexually abused'. The client group which fall under this document are children and young people up to their eighteenth birthday. As part of the quality standards within the document it is stated that a 'medical practitioner with appropriate competencies' must only see this client group in keeping with the United Nations Convention on the Rights of the Child (UNCRC).[4] Purpose-built SARCs have fixtures and fittings that are durable with washable surfaces, and can be cleaned between forensic examinations. Practically, it is important to monitor equip-ment and examination areas to identify if any significant levels of DNA are present, and subsequently whether cross-contamination between cases could be considered a possibility. Comparison of DNA results obtained from the environmental samples with all relevant staff profiles could also identify any gross contamination.   **17.09**

---

[3] Petherick, W.A., Turvey, B.E., and Ferguson, C.E. (2010) *Forensic Criminology*, London: Elsevier Academic Press.

[4] <http://www.rcpch.ac.uk/system/files/protected/page/Service%20Specification%20for%20 the%20clinical%20evaluation%20of%20CYP%20who%20may%20have%20been%20sexu-ally%20abused_September_2015_FINAL.pdf>

17.10   The examination of potential suspects in sexual assault investigations is much more ad hoc than that of complainants and little information has been recorded on this. The arrested suspect is generally examined in a custody suite medical examination room. Examiners are from a range of widely variable healthcare practitioners, dependent on how the particular police service has commissioned their forensic medical services. The nature of this provision will change as these healthcare services are eventually transferred to the NHS, and their are serious concerns that this transfer will not be appropriately funded.[5]

17.11   No studies appear to exist for the recommended standards for forensic facilities available for the examination of suspects in sexual assault investigations.[6] On this issue there is no equality of arms. This is also the case when reviewing the experience and competence of those undertaking forensic medical examinations which can vary widely. The examiners must be aware of their primary duties of consent and confidentiality and place those duties in the context of providing medical care, documenting injury, and retrieving, preserving and interpreting evidence in appropriate formats for court. Practitioners must abide by their relevant professional guidelines (e.g. as determined by the General Medical Council or the Nursing & Midwifery Council). The Faculty of Forensic and Legal Medicine (the body which is tasked with setting standards in these areas of work) has recently produced 'Quality Standards for Nurses: Sexual Offence Medicine' which identifies expected standards of nurse examiners[7] and 'Quality Standards in Forensic Medicine' for registered medical practitioners.[8]

17.12   Any doctor or nurse who is undertaking a forensic medical examination related to any form of sexual assault and who is interpreting findings and providing expert opinions should have an awareness of the range and frequency of sexual practices in the general population; a detailed knowledge of normal anatomy, development and physiology; an awareness of social, cultural, religious, ethnic, and sexual orientation activities or practices that may affect interpretation or the nature of physical findings. An example where this may be relevant may be in those females who have been subject to female genital mutilation which may take a number of forms.[9] There are data which look at the incidence of sexual acts undertaken in consensual relationships such as fellatio, cunnilingus and anilingus and it is important that examiners are aware of the range and nature of sexual behaviours.[10]

---

[5] Payne-James, J.J., Green, P.G., Green N., McLachlan, G.M., Munro, M.H., and Moore, T.C., 'Healthcare issues of detainees in police custody in London, UK' (2010) 17 (1) 11–17.

[6] Newton, (2013), cited at n.1.

[7] *http://fflm.ac.uk/upload/documents/1395839844.pdf.*

[8] *http://fflm.ac.uk/librarydetail/4000113.*

[9] RCN, RCN, RCOG, Equality Now, Unite (2013) *Tackling FGM in the UK: Intercollegiate recommendations for identifying, recording and reporting,* London: Royal College of Midwives.

[10] Evans, B.A., Bond, R.A., and Macrae, K.D., 'Sexual behaviour in women attending a GU medicine clinic' (1998) 64 *Genitourin Med,* 43–8; Bolling, D.R., 'Prevalence, goals and complications of heterosexual anal intercourse in a gynecologic population' (1977) 19 *J Reprod Med,* 121–4.

The Faculty of Forensic and Legal Medicine have produced for adult female **17.13** and male forensic sexual assault examination pro forma (which include body diagrams) which may be adapted or provide models for individual practitioner's use.[11]

E. The Examination

Medical examinations follow a basic format of history taking, examination, **17.14** sample taking and further medical management. This basic format will change according the individual circumstances of each examinee. It is essential that all information is recorded including details of the initial call-out (who made the referral, the date and time, contact details), the nature and timing of the alleged assault, and when an examination can be commenced. In the UK there is no agreed single national standard for the paperwork utilized to record details of the forensic medical assessment. Proper record keeping is useful for advocates reviewing a case as it provides information to assess the quality/reliability of the examination. It is also important for forensic clinical governance and peer review of a case and or the examiner. If the assault is recent and there is an expected delay in full examination it may be appropriate for non-medical personnel who have been trained to use 'Early Evidence Kits'. The first appropriately trained person to encounter the complainant may need to enable the collection of certain samples of potentially early evidence. Samples may include sanitary wear, urine for toxicology, samples from the oral cavity if oral penetration has been alleged (usually oral rinse), hand and fingernail samples and non-intimate skin samples and clothing. The taking of early evidence samples prior to a medical examination will be dictated by the general demeanour and the needs of the complainant. There are also evidence persistence time frames to take into consideration. Urine and oral rinse samples need to be collected within the first six hours of an alleged assault. In general, if the complainant reports very soon after the offence it is better to leave the entire evidence gathering to the medical examiner where possible as this provides a holistic consistent approach and ensures continuity of evidence.

If there are injuries that require treatment beyond the skills or capabilities of those **17.15** in the SARC or police station, these should be prioritized by referral to hospital (and if general anaesthesia is required appropriate consents should be sought prior to any operative intervention, for sampling). Wherever possible, the examinee should be given the option of choosing the gender of the examiner, although this is often not possible.

---

[11] *http://fflm.ac.uk/upload/documents/1276183431.pdf; http://fflm.ac.uk/librarydetail/4000095.*

F. Consent

17.16 The importance of obtaining informed consent is a complex but vital preliminary issue.[12] Appendix A shows a suggested form of consent taken from the FFLM pro forma.

17.17 It is essential that the examinee is fully aware of the nature of and the reasons for any examination and sampling, and the potential for use and disclosure of that information in court. It is essential that an appropriate chaperone be present when undertaking an examination of someone of the opposite gender. Many forensic physicians would advise that the presence of a chaperone is required in all medical examinations of complainants and suspects of sexual assault. This is less of a challenge in SARCs where a variety of individuals (e.g. crisis workers, sexual offence trained police officers) are usually available, however, this may not be the case in the police station setting. The use of interpreters is often crucial in understanding the events that are alleged to have occurred.

G. History Taking

17.18 The medical history should include questions about general health, pre-existing skin conditions, previous illness, and operations. In females, a full obstetric history should be taken documenting information such as dates and nature of menstrual periods, previous pregnancies, and mode of delivery. Medication and allergy history is important to identify features that may mimic or modify the possible effects of injury (e.g. anticoagulants and aspirin associated with bruising) and contraceptive history (since the risk of pregnancy needs to be assessed and managed as soon as practicable).

17.19 Accounts of the alleged sexual assault are obtained from the complainant, accompanying police officers, or attending support workers. A complainant's initial account and their responses to direct questions should be recorded verbatim. An examiner should carefully explain that further questions and detail are necessary to inform and determine the most appropriate forensic sampling and to determine whether there is any potential risk of sexually transmitted infection or pregnancy. Specific questions should be asked about any additional recent sexual or physical contacts or activities undertaken that were not covered by previous questions. These will affect a forensic strategy for both sample collection during the medical examination and subsequent examination by forensic scientists. These questions are often documented as direct prompts on the medical examination paperwork. If the examinee makes reference to items that were discarded at the scene (e.g. tissues, tampons, underwear) this should be documented and the police advised.

---

[12] Dhai, A. and Payne-James, J.J. 'Problems of capacity, consents and confidentiality' (2013) 27 *Best Practice & Research Clinical Obstetrics and Gynaecology*, 59–75.

Direct questions should be directed at establishing whether there are any as yet **17.20** unrecognized or undisclosed injuries. There are some differences of opinion about the necessity for taking a sexual history but in general this is considered important in enabling the interpretation of forensic evidence and some clinical findings, and informing some aspects of the medical aftercare.

A detailed drug and alcohol history, in general and surrounding the assault is **17.21** essential in assisting determining some issues such as ability to consent to sexual contact, or to identify or exclude substances in possible drug-facilitated sexual assault (DFSA) cases. Numerous studies have shown that ethanol is the most prevalent toxicological finding in urine/blood from victims of sexual assault, and high ethanol concentrations are often detected. The authors concluded that among the patients suspecting proactive DFSA, very few had sedative drug findings not explained by voluntary intake. Such studies are useful in showing that, as the authors concluded, DFSA was opportunistic in many cases, rather than proactive.

H. Physical Examination

(1) External examination

All complainants and suspects of sexual assault should, with consent, undergo a full **17.22** external examination. All findings (e.g. marks, scars, abnormalities) should be documented. Examination includes measuring height and weight and noting the general appearance including the nature of the skin and hair (e.g., any matting which may represent lubricant or ejaculate). The examinee's demeanour and behaviour should be documented, although it is not anticipated that the nature of that demeanour and behaviour will be used to identify the accuracy or credibility of any account. Speech nature and content should be documented as should any physical abnormality which may limit or modify an individual's capabilities. Handedness should be recorded.

A detailed examination should review the following and the presence or absence of **17.23** injuries noted: scalp/hair, face, eyes (reflecting the eyelids), ears (external and ear canal), nostrils, mouth, lips, the mouth cavity, teeth, neck, back of torso, buttocks, upper and lower limbs, hands/wrists (fingernails), feet/ankles, front of torso, breasts, and abdomen. This part of the examination is essential as extra-genital injuries are far more common that injuries to the anus or genitalia in sexual assault cases.

Table 17.1 lists the main features which should be considered for any injury identified.[13] **17.24**

The injuries should be classified with consistent terminology. An example of such **17.25** a classification is shown in Table 17.2.[14]

---

[13] Payne-James, J.J., Crane, J., and Hinchliffe J., (2011) 'Injury assessment, documentation and interpretation' in Stark, M.M. (ed.) *Clinical Forensic Medicine: A Physician's Guide* New Jersey: Humana Press, 129.
[14] Ibid., 131.

Table 17.1 Main features to be documented for each injury

How the injury was sustained

Part of the body used or implement used (if implement, whether it is still available)

When the injury was sustained

Whether the injury been treated (and if so details of any treatment)

Clothing worn

Location (site, position)

Type (e.g. bruise, abrasion, laceration)

Orientation

Shape, colour, surface, any signs of healing

Size (use metric values)

Symptoms: pain, tenderness, stiffness

Table 17.2 Classification of injuries

wheals and erythema (reddening)

bruises (contusion, ecchymosis)

haematoma

petechiae

abrasions (grazes)

linear abrasions

scuff/brush abrasions

point abrasion

lacerations

tears

fissures

incisions

slash

chop

stab wounds

mixed and patterned injuries

miscellaneous

burns

17.26 This examination also identifies further areas for potential evidential sampling (e.g. for saliva at the sites of patterned injuries allegedly caused by biting, and for semen at the site of ejaculation).

(2) Systemic examination

17.27 A more general medical examination reviewing the cardiovascular, respiratory, abdominal, and nervous system should then be undertaken and the findings documented. These findings may identify features that may suggest intoxication with drugs and alcohol.

I. Anogenital Examination

The two main purposes of the anogenital examination are (a) to identify and document injuries which may have been sustained during any alleged assault and (b) to obtain relevant samples for submission for forensic scientific analysis to assist in confirming contact with another person. Anogenital examination includes visual assessment (sometimes aided by a colposcope which provides an illuminated, magnified view) of the female genitalia (including, with consent, the use of a disposable, plastic speculum), the perianal region, anus, anal canal, and rectum (which necessitates the use of a disposable, plastic proctoscope), and the male genitalia (including scrotum, testes, penis). During the examination, samples may be taken from all these areas as indicated by both the history and the clinical assessment.   **17.28**

It is a common assumption that sexual assault of any nature will result in injury to the victim whether adult or child.[15] This is not correct and sexual assault (including rape) often occurs without any visible physical injury either genital or extra-genital. Conversely, consensual sexual activity (sexual activity between consenting adults) may result in injury. The presence or absence of injuries in association with allegations of sexual assault do not necessarily indicate by themselves one way or another whether the particular activity was consensual or non-consensual. There is now a substantial body of research in adults and those of younger ages which document the type of injury seen and the frequency with which the injuries have been noted following clinical examination of complainants of sexual assault and examples are given below.   **17.29**

A number of studies of injuries after consensual sex have been undertaken. The research showed genital injuries occur in women following consensual penile–vaginal intercourse, although injuries have, in one study been observed three times more frequently in the group reporting non-consensual penile–vaginal intercourse; however, most complainants of penile–vaginal rape will not sustain any genital injury. Most women do not have visible genitoanal injuries. The risk of sustaining genitoanal injury during a sexual assault is higher among women without prior sexual intercourse experience and among women exposed to anal penetration. The amount of violence or force associated with the assault in terms including whether it involves penetrative sex by a penis or another object is a poor predictor of genitoanal injury.[16]   **17.30**

Documentation of all injury should be in written form, defining the injury site, position, type, features and size, supplemented by body diagrams and photographs.   **17.31**

---

[15] Payne-James J.J. (2016) 'Sexual Offenses, Adult: Injuries and Findings after Sexual Contact.' In: Payne-James J. and Byard R.W. (eds.) *Encyclopedia of Forensic and Legal Medicine*, 2nd edition, Vol. 4, pp. 280–5. Oxford: Elsevier.

[16] Evans, S., Carabott, R., Marsh, N., Kemp, A., Payne-James, J.J., and Vanezis, P., 'Guidelines for photography of cutaneous marks and injuries: a multi-professional perspective' (2014) 37 *J. Vis Commun Med.*, 3–12; Payne-James, J.J., Hawkins, C., Bayliss, S., and Marsh, N., 'Quality of photographic images for injury interpretation: room for improvement?' (2012) *Forensic Sci Med Pathol*, DOI 10.1007/s12024-012-9325-2.

Photography is useful in capturing positioning, size, and colouration of injuries. It is equally important to document the absence of any injury as it is not easy to recall individual patient examinations when it is likely that court proceedings may take place a significant time after a medical examination has been conducted. Photography of injuries must be undertaken by those with the training, skills, and expertise to produce images that will assist a court in determining the weight of evidence. Photographs should be correctly labelled, in focus, properly lit, have close-up and distance views and always have ruled and colour scales included.[17] Copies used in court proceedings and for interpretation should be of the best quality so that injuries, marks, or abnormalities are nor missed, or possibly worse, misinterpreted.[18]

17.32 Photo-documentation of genital injuries (usually using a colposcope with a camera attachment) is recommended. The images should also be of adequate quality to demonstrate the clinical findings and if for some reason they do not, this should be recorded in the clinical notes. All images must be stored and managed securely to ensure respect for the privacy of the subjects of the images. Recommendations have been jointly devised jointly by the Faculty of Forensic and Legal Medicine, the Royal College of Paediatrics and Child Health and the Association of Chief Police Officers for this purpose.[19]

17.33 Medical care must be arranged appropriately to address (a) treatment of injuries, (b) risk of pregnancy, and (c) sexually transmitted infection (including hepatitis and HIV). Most SARCs will have clear protocols and guidance on these matters and in their absence the examiner must ensure (and document how) they have sought and provided appropriate advice and instructions to the examinee.

J. Forensic Sampling

17.34 Forensic science can help determine the nature of sexual acts, the gender and possible identity of the assailant and potential links with other offences. From the medical examination the majority of samples taken are biological (e.g. samples from the mouth, vulva, vagina, anus, penis as swabs), and/or blood and urine for toxicology.

17.35 In recent years, DNA methodologies based on polymerase chain reaction have allowed the production of DNA profiles in sexual assault cases that were not previously examined. In April 2009 a recommendation was put forward by the European Network of Forensic Science Institutes (ENFSI) and the associated European DNA Profiling working group to the EU Police Co-operation working party for a new generation of DNA profiling chemistries to be designed. The reasoning behind this recommendation was to aid the sharing of DNA profiles between countries, increase the discrimination power between profiles and to increase the robustness of the DNA profiling

---

[17] Evans, et al. (2014), cited at n.15.
[18] Payne-James, et al. (2012), cited at n.15.
[19] *http://fflm.ac.uk/librarydetail/4000099.*

chemistries. The new DNA chemistries are adopted by England and Wales Forensic Science Providers from summer 2014. Northern Ireland introduced one of the new technology systems, known as DNA-17 in December 2013. Due to the increased sensitivity of the systems it is anticipated that more background DNA will be detected. As such, extra care should be taken within the working environment of where forensic samples are collected. The use of dedicated forensic sampling kits or modules is imperative together with up-to-date guidance on how samples are retrieved including the consideration for appropriate background controls where appropriate.[20]

When dealing with trace samples from complainants or suspects of sexual assault, **17.36** it is important to identify which areas to target for sampling. From the medical examination perspective it is appropriate to target any part of the body where contact may have occurred (e.g. licking, kissing, sucking, biting, squeezing, scratching, ejaculation, attempted penetration, penetration). The uses of non-invasive detection systems such as Polilight[21] and others are used in some jurisdictions to initially examine the subject in a further attempt to identify areas for sampling.

Sexual assault evidence collection kits vary in content but must be regularly reviewed. **17.37** The Faculty of Forensic and Legal Medicine has a multi-professional Forensic Scientific Committee which meets to discuss the content of forensic kits used to sample complainants and suspects of sexual assault. The methodology of sampling is important and the Science Committee regularly updates its recommendations for the collection of forensic specimens from complainants and suspects.[22]

Financial constraints are clearly and worryingly influencing police services and the **17.38** CPS in deciding whether to pay for sexual assault evidence collection and subsequent forensic analysis.

For forensic sampling from a complainant or suspect of sexual assault, most trace **17.39** samples are collected using swabs. Swabbing of a non-genital skin area that is dry has always required moistening of the swab to traverse the sampling area a number of times. Further research into optimal collection methods and swab types would be beneficial given the tiny amounts of trace evidence often recovered in sexual assault investigations. What is clear is that the scientific data for persistence of trace evidence whether on skin, hair, nails, or genitalia are relatively limited and that the best option is, if in doubt, take a sample.

The nature and the extent of licking, kissing, or biting may result in saliva (which **17.40** contains salivary amylase) being transferred. Identifying salivary amylase is the only

---

[20] Hopwood, A.J., Puch-Solis, R., Tucker, V.C., Curran, J.M., Skerrett, J., Pope, S., and Tully, G. 'Consideration of the probative value of single donor 15-plex STR profiles in UK populations and its presentation in UK courts' (2012) 52(3) *Science & Justice*, 185–90.
[21] Vandenberg, N., Roland, A.H., and Van Oorschot, R.A.H. 'The Use of Polilights in the Detection of Seminal Fluid, Saliva, and Bloodstains and Comparison with Conventional Chemical-Based Screening Tests' (2006) 51 *J Forensic Sci*, 2.
[22] *http://fflm.ac.uk/upload/documents/1393618480.pdf.*

means currently for the forensic scientist to identify the presence of a substance as potentially being saliva. It is now common practice to carry out a double-swabbing technique of potential saliva stain which result in a sample from which a DNA profile may be obtained.[23]

17.41 Currently, if the sexual assault involves an unknown assailant, and injuries including bites on the skin are present that are attributed to direct contact by the assailant, then if the complainant has not showered or bathed, some recommendations suggest sampling the area up to seven days after the incident. Minitapes (sterile, clear adhesive tape) can lift potential cellular material from the skin by being pressed repeatedly onto the surface of skin to collect any loosely adhering cellular material.[24] These techniques may appear simple but poor training and lack of competence or update training of examiners can limit the success rates of the samples collected.[25] Similarly, with the storage and transfer of samples, that is, standard operating procedures pertaining to safe and appropriate sample storage and proper chains of custody are essential to ensure the integrity of evidence.

K. Presentation of Evidence

17.42 The findings and evidence from the medical and scientific examinations is initially presented by the examiner in written form, either as a report or as a statement. Doctors and nurses undertaking forensic medical examination will generally have training, knowledge, skills, and expertise to be professional witnesses of fact, regarding their findings. Thus they can undertake a general and ano-genital examination and appropriately document and record findings. Many do *not* have the skills, experience or training to provide expert opinion about the evidence, particularly with regard to interpretation of injury, or absence of injury and the effects and significance on the presence or absence of semen or DNA on samples, or the effects and significance of drug and alcohol present in samples. Expert opinion in this setting may require a substantial clinical experience, associated with research and publication experience. Many healthcare professionals are very happy to provide professional—witness of fact—evidence about their findings, but do not feel that they should provide expert opinion. So, increasingly, it is common for doctors and nurses who do not feel they are appropriately experienced to give opinion evidence (quite correctly) to include in their statement a phrase such as: 'This statement is based on my professional opinion. I am not able to offer an expert opinion with regard to interpretation of these findings.' Some practitioners

---

[23] Sweet, D. et al., 'An improved method to recover saliva from human skin: the double swab technique' (1997) 42 *J. Forensic Sci. Soc.*, 320–2.

[24] Kenna, J., Smyth, M., McKenna, L., et al., 'The recovery and persistence of salivary DNA on human skin' (2011) 56 *J. Forensic Sci.*, 170–5.

[25] Raymond, J.J., Van Oorschot, R.A.H., Walsh, S.J., et al., 'How far have we come with trace DNA since 2004? The Australian and New Zealand experience.' (2011) 4 *Aust. J. Forensic Sci.*, 231–44.

may be coerced by police, CPS or lawyers to give opinion outwith their expertise. This can have unfortunate consequences in court. Expert opinion now appears to be sought at an earlier stage, so that the expert can have early access to all evidence and the medical assessment findings. Such early expert opinion enables prosecutors to make earlier decisions on possible outcomes and decide whether to proceed with a case, and enables defence teams to assist in advising clients, for example, to put in an early guilty plea.

L. Conclusion

Forensic science and forensic medicine provide important components in the **17.43** investigation of sexual crime. As this chapter shows within the footnotes there are many sources of standards and evidence bases. The limitations of chapter size preclude inclusion of all the standards and evidence-base available. However, the nature of any scientific or medical examination should be compared by appropriate experts against such contemporaneous standards and evidence bases. Financial constraints impact significantly on the quality of forensic medical and forensic scientific processes in sexual assault examination. Close scrutiny should be made of these processes when prosecuting or defending in cases of alleged sexual assault.

Appendix A

Table 1 Consent to history, examination and report

I, [name] consent to a forensic examination, as explained to me by [ ].

I understand that the forensic examination will include (delete if not applicable)

(a) A full medical history and complete examination;

(b) Collection of forensic and/or medical specimens;

(c) Taking of notes, photographs/videos/digital images for recording and evidential purposes (including second opinions from medical experts and peer review). I have been told that any sensitive photographs, videos and/or digital images will be stored securely and only be made available to other non-medical persons on the order of a judge;

(d) I understand and agree that the doctor/nurse may provide a statement/report for the police;

(e) I understand and agree that a copy of the medical notes may be given to professionals involved in the case (e.g. police or lawyers) and may be used in a court;

(f) I agree to the use of my anonymised photographs/videos/digital images/medical notes for teaching;

(g) I agree to the use of my anonymised photographs/videos/digital images/medical notes for audit and research;

(h) I have been advised that I may halt the examination at any time.

Signed

Date

If verbal consent Signature & Name of Witness

Further Reading

Fraser, J. and Williams, R. (2009) *Handbook of Forensic Science* Cullompton, Devon: Willan Publishing.

Author Biographies

Dr Jason Payne-James is a specialist in Forensic and Legal Medicine. He has honorary posts at Cameron Forensic Medical Sciences, Barts & the London School of Medicine and Dentistry, and in Adult and Paediatric Emergency Medicine at St George's Hospital, London. He is external Consultant to the National Crime Agency; Forensic Medical Examiner—Metropolitan Police Service; Editor—*Journal of Forensic & Legal Medicine*; and President of the Faculty of Forensic & Legal Medicine. Previously, he was Examiner for the Diploma in the Forensic and Clinical Aspects of Sexual Assault. He has co-edited or co-authored publications including the *Encyclopedia of Forensic & Legal Medicine* (1st and 2nd editions) and the 13th edition of *Simpson's Forensic Medicine*.

Mary A. Newton is an independent forensic consultant with thirty-five years of specialist knowledge in rape and serious sexual assault. She is an Honorary Fellow of the Faculty of Forensic and Legal Medicine for significant contribution to research and continuous development of the forensic medical examination kits, and is a member of their scientific committee. She became an Honourable Steering Group Advisor to the UK Association of Forensic Nurses in 2012. In July 2012 she was invited to work for the Home Office on behalf of the Forensic Regulator on issues related to contamination in the forensic medical examination arena.

Dr Christine Bassindale is a consultant forensic physician with twenty-five years specialist experience in sexual assault in the UK and Australia. She is a Fellow of the Faculty of Forensic and Legal Medicine. She was previously the Principal Forensic Physician to Lancashire Constabulary, Founder Clinical Director of the Lancashire Sexual Assault Forensic Examination (SAFE) Centre, Consultant Forensic Physician to Cumbria Constabulary, and Clinical Lead of the Medical and Forensic Service, Perth, Western Australia.

18

THE INTERPRETATION OF CLINICAL SIGNS OF SEXUAL ABUSE IN CHILDREN

*Jacqueline Yek-Quen Mok**

A. Introduction

'Sexual abuse' is defined as the involvement of dependent, developmentally immature **18.01** children and adolescents in sexual activity that they do not fully comprehend and to which they are unable to give informed consent; or that violate the social taboos of family roles. There is an imbalance of power between abuser and abused, and an element of control by the trusted adult. The UN Convention on the Rights of the Child (1989) defines a child as 'every human being below the age of eighteen years unless, under the law applicable to the child, majority is attained earlier'.[1] No single law defines the age of a child across the UK but specific age limits are set out in relevant

---

* The author wishes to thank Professor Joyce Adams of the University of California San Diego School of Medicine, for critically reviewing the chapter and providing helpful comments.

[1] *http://www.unicef.org.uk/Documents/Publication-pdfs/UNCRC_PRESS200910web.pdf.*

laws or government guidance. In England, safeguarding guidance refers to children up to their eighteenth birthday.[2]

18.02 Sexual abuse ranges from violent assault to gentle seduction. There may be physical contact, including penetration or non-penetrative acts such as masturbation, kissing, rubbing and touching over clothing. It may involve non-contact activities, such as in the production of sexual images, watching sexual activities, encouraging children to behave in sexually inappropriate ways, or grooming a child in preparation for abuse (including via the internet). Perpetrators can be adult males, females or other children.

18.03 In the UK, data collected for the year between 2012 and 2013 show that there were 23,663 sexual offences against children recorded by the police.[3] Radford and colleagues (2011) conducted interviews of 1,761 young adults (18–24 years); 2,275 children (11–17 years) and 2,160 parents of children aged less than 11 years between March and December 2009 in the UK.[4] They found that:

- a quarter of young adults experienced sexual abuse (contact and non-contact) by an adult or by a peer during childhood;
- one in six children aged 11–17 have experienced sexual abuse;
- one in ten children aged 11–17 have experienced sexual abuse in the past year;
- one in three children aged 11–17 who experienced contact sexual abuse by an adult did not tell anyone else about it; and
- four out of five children aged 11–17 who experienced contact sexual abuse from a peer did not tell anyone else about it.

B. Diagnosis of Child Sexual Abuse

18.04 The Butler-Sloss inquiry (1988)[5] raised the profile of Child Sexual Abuse (CSA) within the UK, highlighting the need for professional agreement on the significance and accurate interpretation of physical signs. CSA should rarely, if ever, be diagnosed on the basis of physical signs alone. The medical evaluation of children who allege sexual abuse should be part of a multi-agency process, which spans the investigative, diagnostic, and therapeutic needs of the child and family.

---

[2] Department for Education (2015) *Working Together to Safeguard Children: A guide to inter-agency working to safeguard and promote the welfare of children*, London: HMG. Ref DFE-00130-2015, *https://www.gov.uk/government/uploads/system/uploads/attachment_data/file/419595/ Working_Together_to_Safeguard_Children.pdf.*
[3] Jütte S., Bentley H., Miller P., and Jetha N. (2014) *How safe are our children?* NSPCC report.
[4] Radford, L., Corral, S., Bradley, C., Fisher, H., Bassett, C., Howat, N., and Collishaw, S. (2011) *Child abuse and neglect in the UK today*, London: NSPCC.
[5] Butler-Sloss, E. (1988) *Report of the Inquiry into Child Abuse in Cleveland 1987*, London: HMSO.

Although there is a large literature reporting on the physical signs in sexual assault, **18.05** they are difficult to compare because of differences in methodology and inconsistencies in terminology. It is important for the courts to understand the strength of the evidence and the likelihood that a physical sign has been caused by the alleged abuse. Legal and other professionals, who rely upon expert evidence of this kind, should be aware of the issues that continue to give rise to debate, such as the terms used to describe clinical findings, understanding what is normal, techniques in examination, and interpretation of physical signs.

(1) Inconsistent use of terminology to describe physical signs

Doctors are often asked to determine whether penetration has occurred; and how **18.06** often a child has been abused. More often than not, the physical appearances will be normal or non-specific. The medical report must avoid terms which can be misinterpreted and lead to confusion. Subjective descriptions such as a 'lax' sphincter or a 'gaping' hymenal opening are unhelpful.

Clinicians must use recommended terminology to describe the genitalia and to inter- **18.07** pret ano-genital findings, so that those who examine children for alleged sexual abuse can understand what is meant by each other's descriptions. Heger, et al., in a review of findings in girls selected for non-abuse, called for a thorough understanding of normal studies and a consistent application of established terminology, which can prevent the misinterpretation of non-specific or congenital findings as post-traumatic changes.[6]

(2) Interpretation of clinical signs

Since CSA was recognized in the 1970s, many changes have occurred in the way **18.08** clinical signs are interpreted. This has led to a better understanding of what is normal and what constitutes non-specific findings. A comprehensive list of clinical and laboratory findings seen in abused and non-abused children was first drawn up in 1992 (the Adams Classification System) and developed over the years. The latest revision is the result of examining published data and consensus amongst experienced physicians.[7] The classification system can be summarized as:

- **Findings documented in newborns, or commonly seen in non-abused children:**
  - (a) normal variants;
  - (b) findings commonly caused by medical conditions other than trauma or sexual contact; and
  - (c) conditions mistaken for abuse.

---

[6] Heger, A.H., Ticson, L., Guerra, L., Lister, J., Zaragoza T., McConnell, G., and Morahan, M., 'Appearance of the genitalia in girls selected for non-abuse: Review of hymenal morphology and non-specific findings' (2002) 15 *Journal of Paediatric and Adolescent Gynaecology*, 27–35.

[7] Adams, J.A., Kellogg N.D., Farst K.J., et al. 'Updated Guidelines for the Medical Assessment and Care of Children Who May Have Been Sexually Abused' (2015) *Journal of Pediatric and Adolescent Gynecology*, doi: 10.1016/j.jpag.2015.01.007.

- **Findings with no expert consensus on interpretation with respect to sexual contact or trauma:**
  (a) complete anal dilatation with relaxation of both the internal and external anal sphincters, in the absence of other predisposing factors such as constipation, encopresis, sedation, anaesthesia, and neuromuscular conditions;
  (b) notch or cleft in the hymen rim, at or below the three or nine o'clock location, which is deeper than a superficial notch and may extend nearly to the base of the hymen, but is not a complete transection; and
  (c) genital or anal condyloma acuminata, Herpes Type 1 or 2 lesions in the absence of other indicators of abuse.
- **Findings caused by trauma and/or sexual contact:**
  (a) acute trauma to external genital/anal tissues, which could be accidental or inflicted, for example, fresh laceration or extensive bruising;
  (b) residual (healing) injuries, for example, perianal scar;
  (c) injuries indicative of acute or healed trauma to anogenital tissues, for example, acute laceration; bruising; healed hymenal transection;
  (d) presence of infection transmitted by sexual contact, for example, gonorrhoea; and
  (e) diagnostic of sexual contact, for example, pregnancy; sperm identified in specimens taken directly from the child's body.

This system provides a useful tool in interpreting clinical findings, and helps physicians to achieve some consistency in terminology.

C. Normal Anatomy

(1) Normal female anatomy

18.09 To recognize signs of trauma, the clinician must have a sound knowledge of normal ano-genital anatomy and its variants. Contemporary textbooks provide little insight into the female genital anatomy, which vary considerably from newborn to adolescence. In the newborn, effects of maternal oestrogens result in prominence of the labia and clitoris, with a redundant and fleshy hymen. In early infancy, the labia majora (outer lips) gradually cover the introitus (entrance to the vagina) to form a protective pad. As maternal oestrogen effects wear off in childhood, the labia majora appear flattened and the labia minora (inner lips) are seen as thin folds. With the onset of puberty, oestrogens cause the labia and hymen to become fleshy again.

18.10 There is no internationally accepted definition of the term 'vagina'. The general public often refers to the female external genitalia as the 'vagina'. The medical definition is 'a muscular canal which lies between the hymen and the cervix (neck of the womb) at its upper end'. The legal definition of the vagina includes the vulva (external female genitalia) as well as the 'medical' vagina. For legal purposes, therefore, 'penetration of the vagina' means penetration between the labia (outer lips) and does not have to involve penetration of the hymen.[8]

The hymen is a rim of tissue at the lower end of the vagina. Unless 'imperforate' **18.11** (a very rare congenital anomaly), every hymen has an opening (hymenal orifice) which varies in size depending on the shape of the hymen. The hymen changes with age and pubertal status. In a prepubertal child, it is thin and delicate. As puberty approaches, oestrogens cause the hymen to become fleshy and elasticated (stretchy) with a tendency to fold outwards.[9] Abundant oestrogenized hymenal tissue also tends to wrinkle and fold over itself. Careful examination techniques are required to define the hymenal anatomy in the pubertal girl.

During the medical examination, any sign considered to be significant should be **18.12** described and documented, using the clock face to denote its location. With the child lying on her back, the centre of 'the clock' is represented by the hymenal orifice. Twelve o'clock is uppermost towards the abdomen while six o'clock denotes the posterior position towards the anus; three o'clock is towards the child's left and nine o'clock to her right. This 'anatomical position' does not change as the child changes position, that is, twelve o'clock always represents the area closest to the abdomen.

(2) Normal male anatomy

The external male genitalia include the penis and scrotum. The penis consists of **18.13** the shaft and glans (head) which is sheathed by the prepuce (foreskin). The urethra runs throughout the penile shaft and opens at the meatus. The scrotum is a wrinkled pouch within which lie the testes.

(3) Anal anatomy

The anal canal is the terminal part of the large intestine, extending from the rectum **18.14** to the anal orifice. The anus is normally closed but opens for the passage of gas or faeces. Two muscles control the opening and closure of the anus—the involuntary internal sphincter and the external sphincter which is under voluntary control. It is the contraction of the external anal sphincter that causes the appearance of anal folds.

D. How do Doctors Diagnose Sexual Abuse?

(1) Absence of signs

The police and legal profession have traditionally placed great emphasis upon find- **18.15** ings from the medical examination. However, paediatricians have long recognized

---

[8] Sexual Offences Act 2003, s 79(9).
[9] Myhre, A.K., Myklestad, K., and Adams, J.A., 'Changes in Genital Anatomy and Microbiology in Girls between age 6 and age 12 Years: A Longitudinal Study' (2010) 23 *Journal of Paediatric and Adolescent Gynaecology*, 77–85.

that many abused children will have no findings diagnostic of sexual abuse and that a normal or negative physical examination does not exclude the possibility of sexual abuse. There are three different reasons for normal ano-genital findings in a child who describes sexual abuse: (1) no abuse occurred; (2) abuse occurred, but it did not cause any injury; (3) abuse occurred, and there were injuries, but the injuries healed by the time the child was examined, leaving no residual indicators of injury. The medical examination is only a part of the jigsaw. Physical evidence is neither essential for, nor predictive of conviction. The child's history is the single most important factor in the accurate diagnosis of most cases of sexual abuse.

18.16 With the introduction of standard terminology and photo-documentation, practice and research have become more reliable. The rates of 'abnormal findings' have decreased as previously reported abnormal findings have been recognized as non-specific findings, present also in control subjects carefully selected for non-abuse.[10] Abnormalities of the genital tract associated with abuse may be minor and non-specific, occurring also as a result of inflammation, infection, or poor hygiene. 'Normal' or 'non-specific' examinations have been reported in up to 99 per cent of children referred for evaluation of CSA. Some forms of CSA will leave no physical signs.

18.17 On the other hand, normal examination does not exclude previous injury as many injuries heal without physical signs. Ano-genital signs are more likely to be found in children reporting penetrative abuse and in those examined within 72 hours of the last episode of abuse. Other factors that might influence physical findings include the position of the child in relation to the abuser, size of the object inserted relative to the size of the orifice, degree of force used, use of lubricant, and frequency and duration of abuse. The pubertal hymen is much more elasticated compared to the prepubertal hymen, and therefore more likely to accommodate any object inserted without damage. Also, residual injuries caused by sexual abuse during the prepubertal years may be hidden in the abundant folds of the pubertal hymen. A medical examination must always be considered even if the abuse happened many years ago, with careful attention to defining the hymenal anatomy.

(2) Signs of sexual abuse—what does the research evidence tell us?

18.18 The Royal College of Paediatrics and Child Health published an evidence-based review of the physical signs of CSA in 2008, with an updated edition published in 2015.[11] The literature on physical findings in CSA was systematically identified, critically appraised, and synthesized up to March 2014.

18.19 In general, acute signs such as abrasions, bleeding, redness, and swelling are more likely to be detected in children examined soon after the alleged abuse, but

---

[10] Royal College of Paediatrics and Child Health (2015) *The Physical Signs of Child Sexual Abuse: An updated evidence-based review and guidance for best practice*, 2nd edn London: RCPCH, ch. 7.
[11] Ibid.

children rarely disclose immediately. When acute signs were reported, few studies distinguished between accidental and inflicted injury. The significance of some of the more commonly reported and debated signs have been summarized from the evidence-based review.[12]

Each sign must be considered with the overall clinical picture, the child's statement, **18.20** social and family history, and a detailed multi-agency assessment. The presence of more than one clinical sign in a child, especially if documented over time, should lead to a suspicion that the child may have been the victim of CSA. For example, in a child who describes sexual abuse, has signs of genital or anal injury *and* has a sexually transmitted infection (genital warts or herpes simplex), the combination of factors greatly increases the likelihood that the child has been the victim of sexual abuse.

(i) Abrasion

An abrasion is a superficial injury involving the outer layers of the skin or mucous **18.21** membrane, caused commonly by friction between a rough surface and the skin. Abrasions on the genital area have not been reported in prepubertal girls selected for non-abuse.[13] Although the evidence in the abused population is limited, when genital abrasions are found, sexual abuse should be considered in the differential diagnosis.

(ii) Bruising

Bruising must be differentiated from pigmented lesions and some dermatological **18.22** conditions. A bruise is the result of leakage of blood into the surrounding tissues when blood vessels are damaged. Different terms used to describe bruises include haematoma, contusion, ecchymosis, and petechiae. Because bruises fade, they are more likely to be found when the child is examined soon after the assault. Bruises cannot be 'aged' by their colour. Genital bruising has not been reported in a study of non-abused prepubertal girls.[14] When found on the genitalia, other causes including CSA must be excluded.

(iii) Cleft/notch on the hymen

These superficial indentations on the rim of the hymen do not extend to its base. **18.23** During examination, the finding of a notch or cleft must be confirmed by using a different technique (e.g. labial separation and labial traction) or with the child in a different position (e.g. prone knee-chest and supine frog-legged position). The term notch/cleft should be used only to describe a defect where there are no signs of acute injury.[15]

---

[12] Ibid., chs 3 and 5.

[13] Myhre, A.K., Berntzen, K., and Bratlid, D., 'Genital anatomy in non-abused preschool girls' (2003) 92 *Acta Pediatrica*, 1453–62.

[14] Ibid.

[15] *The Physical Signs of Child Sexual Abuse*, cited at n.10, ch. 3.

18.24 Absence of hymenal tissue in the anterior portion is a normal finding in a crescent-shaped hymen and should not be interpreted as an anterior cleft, notch, or transection. Superficial notches in the posterior hymen have been reported in both prepubertal girls with a history of vaginal penetration and prepubertal girls selected for non-abuse.[16] This would suggest that superficial notches are normal variants. However, two studies[17] have found that lacerations and tears to the hymen can heal to leave slight notching/narrowing on the hymen. Shallow notches may represent healing of partial tears to the hymen; but when seen for the first time, it is difficult to be certain whether the superficial notch represents a normal variant or a healed injury, unless an acute injury was seen in a previous examination and followed to healing.

(iv) Erythema/redness/inflammation

18.25 This sign is caused by dilatation of the capillaries and subsides with time. It is 'non-specific', as it has been reported in both sexually-abused and non-abused girls. There are many causes and if caused by trauma, erythema resolves quickly and early examination is crucial.

(v) Size of the hymenal orifice

18.26 Larger hymenal openings are wrongly believed to imply repeated penetrative intercourse. The hymen consists of elastic tissue which in pubertal girls can stretch without tearing. Studies have shown a substantial overlap in diameter size between girls who allege sexual abuse and those selected for non-abuse. The hymenal orifice also changes shape and size depending on its morphology, the examination position and technique, state of relaxation of the child, age of the child, and skill of the examiner. Therefore measurement of the hymenal orifice diameter is of no value in diagnosing CSA.

(vi) Hymenal width

18.27 This is the visible amount of hymenal membrane from its free margin to its base attachment to the vagina. Vaginal penetration is thought to damage the hymen partially or completely, locally or in a generalized manner. Most studies have focused on the width of the posterior hymen. Measurement of the width of the hymen is not recommended due to the difficulties in obtaining accurate measurements, especially if the hymenal tissue is narrow. There is insufficient evidence to determine the significance of a 'narrow' posterior hymenal width.[18]

---

[16] Berenson, A.B., Chacko, M.R., Wiemann, C.M., Mishaw, C.O, Friedrich, W.N., and Grady, J.J., 'A case-control study of anatomic changes resulting from sexual abuse' (2000) 182 *American Journal of Obstetrics and Gynecology*, 820–34.

[17] Heppenstall-Heger, A., McConnell, G., Ticson, L., Guerra, L., Lister, J., and Zaragoza, T., 'Healing patterns in anogenital injuries: A longitudinal study of injuries associated with sexual abuse, accidental injuries, or genital surgery in the preadolescent child' (2003) 112 *Pediatrics*, 829–37; McCann, J., Miyamoto, S., Boyle, C., and Rogers, K. 'Healing of Hymenal Genital Injuries in Prepubertal and Adolescent Girls: A Descriptive Study' (2007) 119 *Pediatrics*, e1094–106.

[18] *The Physical Signs of Child Sexual Abuse*, cited at n.10, ch. 3.

An 'attenuated hymen' was believed to be a sign of repeated penetration. The terms **18.28** 'attenuation' or 'worn away' are not helpful terms to use when describing the width of the hymen and are therefore not recommended. The term 'narrow' is preferred and should only be used in comparison to either a previous examination of the same child or in comparison to other areas of the hymen. When seen, an apparently absent or 'narrow' posterior hymenal rim should be confirmed using other examination techniques or positions.[19]

(vii) Laceration/tear

This term refers to a wound made by tearing through the full thickness of skin, **18.29** mucous membranes or deeper structures of the body, caused by blunt force trauma. When acute, it may be associated with bleeding and/or bruising of the edges of the wound. Genital lacerations have not been reported in prepubertal girls selected for non-abuse. In girls who allege penetration, lacerations are seen more commonly to the posterior fourchette/fossa navicularis than to the hymen or other genital tissues. When genital lacerations are seen, penetrative abuse should be strongly suspected unless there is a convincing history of an accidental penetrating injury. Hymenal lacerations/tears can heal completely without scarring or may heal to leave a notch, cleft, or transection.[20]

(viii) Oedema/swelling

This refers to excess fluid in the tissues caused by trauma, inflammation, or infec- **18.30** tion. It resolves with time and will be missed if there is delay in the examination. There is insufficient evidence to determine the significance of this non-specific sign.

(ix) Scar/fibrous tissue

Scar tissue is the result of a previous injury which has healed. The timing of an **18.31** injury cannot be inferred from the presence of scar tissue. Older case reports have documented hymenal scars at the site of acute injuries in girls who have been followed up, suggesting that scars are associated with sexual abuse. However, a recent study showed that healing of hymenal injuries did not result in scarring of the hymen.[21]

(x) Transection

A hymenal transection is a healed defect in the membrane that extends through the **18.32** width of the hymen to its base. It is not the same as a cleft which does not extend to the base of the hymen. There is good evidence that hymenal transections are associated with CSA in prepubertal girls. A case-control study of prepubertal girls found a hymenal transection in one girl who alleged vaginal penetration but not in

---

[19] Ibid., ch.11.
[20] McCann et al., cited at n. 17.
[21] Ibid.

any selected for non-abuse.[22] When hymenal transections are found, penetrative injury should be strongly suspected.

(3) Sexual abuse of boys

18.33 Injury to the male genitalia as a result of sexual abuse is not well reported. Inflicted genital injury in boys may be the result of physical or sexual abuse and include burns, bruises, incised wounds, lacerations, or scars. Penile injuries are the most common inflicted injuries while scrotal and testicular injuries predominate in accidental injuries. Without a clear account of an accident, the possibility of CSA must be considered.[23]

(4) Anal signs

18.34 There are no good quality studies comparing signs in anally-abused children with those selected for non-abuse. Many studies fail to report data on anal signs according to the type of abuse. Acute signs of trauma (erythema, bruising, oedema) disappear quickly and will be missed unless the child is examined within seventy-two hours of an episode of trauma. Perianal bruising, lacerations and scars have been seen only in sexually-abused children and not in those selected for non-abuse.

18.35 Where anal signs are present, other possible causes must be excluded. Findings must be interpreted in the broad context of the clinical history, the child's allegation, and a multi-agency assessment. As with genital signs, absence of anal signs does not exclude the possibility of digital or penile penetration.

(i) Fissure or laceration?

18.36 A fissure has been defined as a superficial defect (split) in the perianal skin, located on the anal verge and does not extend into the subcutaneous tissue. A laceration refers to a deep defect in the perianal skin, located on the anal verge and extends into the subcutaneous tissue. Although fissures and lacerations are assumed to be distinct, the difference between the two is not well defined and the terms are used interchangeably. The evidence base is limited for both signs. Fissures resulting from constipation cannot be distinguished from those caused by anal abuse. It is impossible to distinguish trauma caused by a descending constipated stool from trauma ascending from the outside as in penetrative anal abuse. In the context of an alleged anal assault, a fissure may provide corroboration only if other causes (constipation, diarrhoea, skin conditions) are ruled out. Anal lacerations are associated with acute sexual assault and have not been reported in children selected

---

[22] Berenson et al., cited at n.16.
[23] Hobbs, C.J. and Osman, J., 'Genital injuries in boys and abuse' (2007) 92 *Archives of Disease in Childhood*, 328–31.

for non-abuse. A recent study of 1,115 children referred for possible sexual abuse compared the frequency of anal features between children with and without anal penetration. A positive association was confirmed between anal penetration and soiling, anal lacerations, and anal fissures.[24] It should be noted that in subjects who reported anal symptoms such as constipation or soiling, neither anal fissures nor total anal dilation were significantly associated with probable anal penetration.

(ii) Perianal venous congestion

This refers to the collection of venous blood in the perianal tissues in a relaxed **18.37** child examined for less than 30 seconds. It may be localized or diffuse and is not influenced by the examination position. It has been described in a relatively high proportion of children who have been sexually abused but its prevalence in non-abused children is less well defined. It is non-discriminatory for sexual abuse. In a study by Myhre et al.,[25] the percentage of children with venous pooling was almost identical in the group without and with probable anal penetration.

(iii) Reflex anal dilatation

This incompletely understood phenomenon must be interpreted with caution and **18.38** in context. It is best demonstrated by parting the buttocks gently and observing for <30 seconds. A positive result is obtained when the external anal sphincter contracts briefly, followed by dramatic relaxation of both external and internal sphincters to reveal a cylindrical opening into the rectum. It is a dynamic sign.

Reflex anal dilation (RAD) is reported more often in those who allege anal abuse **18.39** compared to unspecified CSA. Information on the prevalence of RAD in non-abused children is scant. The variation in frequency of RAD reported may be due to the use of different examination techniques and different thresholds of dilatation used by researchers. Lack of study detail makes it difficult to determine whether studies are describing dynamic reflex anal dilatation or the more static appearance of a dilated anus.

In one study of non-abused prepubertal children, dilatation was classified as total, **18.40** external, or intermittent. Total dilatation (presumed to represent RAD) was observed in less than 1 per cent of children examined in the left lateral position and in 5 per cent examined in the prone knee-chest position. No data were available in the supine position.[26] If RAD is seen, anal abuse should always be considered in the context of the history, medical assessment, and other anogenital signs.[27]

---

[24] Myhre, A.K., Adams, J.A., Kaufhold, M., Davis, J.L., Suresh, P., and Kuelbs, C.L., 'Anal findings in children with and without probable anal penetration: A retrospective study of 1,115 children referred for suspected sexual abuse' (2013) 37 *Child Abuse & Neglect*, 465–74.

[25] Ibid.

[26] Myhre, A.K., Berntzen, K., and Bratlid, D., 'Perianal anatomy in non-abused preschool-children' (2001) 90 *Acta Paediatrica*, (1321–8).

[27] Ibid.

(iv) Reduced anal tone

18.41 Many terms have been used to describe the state of the anus which looks open to a variable degree, implying reduced tone. These include 'visibly relaxed anus', anal laxity, and anal gaping. The terms imply a static finding but are seldom defined and have been described in anally-abused children and also in chronic constipation, neurological disorders, and with some anaesthetic agents. To be exact, anal tone can only be measured accurately using manometry, which is seldom advised during routine examinations.

(v) Other anal signs

18.42 Other anal signs which have been described in textbooks and in clinical practice include 'anal twitching', 'anal winking', 'deficits in the anal margin', 'smoothing', 'thickening', 'irregularity of fold pattern', 'funnelling', 'anal verge deficit', 'distorted' or 'disrupted' anus. The lack of consistency in terminology and absence of definitions make it difficult to know what authors are describing and therefore impossible to compare studies. These terms are best abandoned.

E. Abuse or Accident?

18.43 Most accidental injuries are relatively easy to distinguish from those caused by sexual assault because there is usually a clear description of the accident and the majority of unintentional injuries involve external structures (labia, perineum, posterior fourchette, anal margin). Questions arise when injuries are found in the hymen or vestibule. This is particularly relevant when the child is young and unable to give an account of events. There have been reports of unusual accidents where children were run over by slow-moving vehicles and sustained acute perianal and hymenal injuries identical to those seen in sexual assault. After healing, it is impossible to distinguish between trauma caused by assault or an accident. This underlines the importance of a thorough history from the child and carers, and an understanding of mechanisms of injury.

F. Case Studies

Case example 1 Inadequate examination

18.44 *A 13-year-old girl disclosed sexual abuse by her mother's partner, from the age of 10. Alleged acts included oral sex, fondling, digital-vaginal penetration, penile-vaginal and penile-anal penetration. The ano-genital examination was conducted using a colposcope with contemporaneous DVD recording. The labia minora, posterior fourchette and vestibule were described as 'generally red and inflamed with a particularly friable, red,* *ragged area on the posterior fourchette. This stretched into a linear scar extending into the perineum. The hymen had superficial notches at the 5 and 7 o'clock positions. There was an apparent anterior transection at the 12 o'clock position.' The doctors concluded that the 'ano-genital examination revealed an abnormal pre-pubertal hymen which would be consistent with the allegations made by the child'.*

(i) Comment

The doctors make no mention of the appearance of the hymen, nor have they com- **18.45** mented on negative findings. An 'apparent transection in the 12 o'clock position' requires explanation. Absence of hymenal tissue in the anterior portion is a normal finding in a crescent-shaped hymen and should not be interpreted as an anterior transection.

The presence of a scar in the posterior fourchette is a sign of previous acute genital **18.46** trauma. However, from the description above, the finding could also have been a labial adhesion that was being pulled apart by the examiner's 'stretching' of the tissues.

The 'superficial notches' on the hymen could be normal variants. In the context **18.47** of the allegations, the notches could also represent healed partial tears caused by digital or penile penetration of the hymen.

The report is incomplete without an examination of the perianal area, which may **18.48** or may not have been carried out. However, photo-documentation was available and this allowed a review which did show that the anus was examined and found to be normal. The distensibility of the anal canal means that penile-anal penetration can occur and leave no abnormality.

Case example 2 Misinterpretation of clinical signs

A 6-year-old girl whose mother sought medical attention because of vaginal bleeding **18.49** *over three days, associated with tummy ache, itching and burning on passing urine. Three years previously, she had been examined by a doctor because of maternal con-cerns regarding CSA. No signs of injury were documented and the hymenal orifice was reported to measure about 0.4 cm in diameter, 'circumference intact'.*

In relation to the present concerns, a forensic paediatric examination was con- **18.50** *ducted and labial traction showed a thin rim of hymenal tissue, described as 'irregular and smooth edged'. The section of hymenal tissue between 7 o'clock and 9 o'clock was 'very thin and fibrous with the appearance of scar tissue'. At 4 o'clock there was 'an area of active bleeding with apparent laceration to the hymenal tissue'. Internal vaginal structures were clearly visible. The doctors concluded that 'these findings are indicative of both very recent and previous injury and/or penetration of her vagina'.*

(i) Comment

18.51 The 'thin rim' implies that the width of hymenal tissue is narrower than that expected because the hymen has been 'worn away'. It is difficult to say with certainty if the hymenal rim was narrow ('thin') for the following reasons—the child was not examined in the prone knee-chest position; and no images were captured before any manipulation was performed to allow comparison between the hymenal rim with different techniques (i.e. labial separation and labial traction).

18.52 The clear visibility of internal vaginal structures implies that the hymenal diameter was large. The doctors also compared their examination to an examination of three years ago when the hymenal diameter was recorded as 0.4 cm. The doctors' conclusion was that a large hymenal opening implied that penetration had occurred.

18.53 There is evidence that the hymenal orifice increases with age, but there is substantial overlap in the range of hymenal diameters between sexually abused and non-abused prepubertal girls. The hymen is an elastic tissue which stretches, making it impossible to measure accurately. The hymenal opening also varies with the examination position, technique, state of relaxation of the child, and the skill of the examiner. The diameter of the hymenal orifice is non-discriminatory for sexual abuse and therefore cannot be used to diagnose sexual abuse.

18.54 The expert recommended that the child was examined again to verify the presence of scar tissue and to establish by a different position if the hymenal rim was indeed narrow. No scar tissue was found at follow-up. It is likely that in the original examination, the light reflex from the colposcope was interpreted as 'scar tissue'. Examination in the prone position revealed the hymen to have a good posterior rim.

G. Conclusion

18.55 Expert medical testimony may help to interpret the presence or absence of physical signs, but the overall effect on the legal outcome is unknown. Increased communication and joint training between the legal and medical professions may improve understanding and usage of consistent terminology. A medical expert should be able to demonstrate relevant training or experience in sexual abuse cases that are similar to ones in which he or she has been called on to provide expert testimony. Irresponsible medical testimony must be avoided, such as use of unique theories of causation, unusual interpretations of medical findings, alleging non-existent physical signs, deliberate omission of pertinent facts, lack of awareness of current research, or misquoting of medical literature.

Author Biography

Dr Jacqueline Yek-Quen Mok retired from clinical practice in 2011. She was Lead Paediatrician for Child Protection in Edinburgh, and Part-time Senior Lecturer, Department of Child Life and Health, University of Edinburgh. She has published widely on various aspects of child maltreatment and appeared as an expert witness for both the prosecution and defence in cases involving child physical and sexual abuse. In May 2010 she was made the David Jenkins Professor in Forensic and Legal Medicine. She received the Crown Office and Procurator Fiscal Service Excellence Award for services to the people of Scotland in April 2011. She is current Chair of the Royal College of Paediatrics and Child Health Scottish Child Protection Committee.

19

CHILD AND ADOLESCENT SEXUAL ASSAULT EXAMINATIONS: GOOD PRACTICE AND KEY ISSUES

Mary Pillai and Jean Price

A. Introduction

The chapter reviews the role of paediatricians and forensic medical examiners in **19.01** cases of alleged or suspected child sexual abuse. It references the current professional guidance of which decision-makers in the investigative process and legal professionals should be aware when considering the reliability of expert opinions. It clarifies the tension between the medical and the forensic role and the risk that opinion may reflect emotional involvement in the case. The duties of a doctor include advocacy for the child, which may conflict with his or her independence and impartiality.

19.02 The evidence base on normality, trauma, and healing is very limited. Available studies, in the main, consist of small numbers of children and are of variable quality with no consistent methodology or terminology. Most child sexual assault examinations reveal only normal anatomical findings. Possible explanations for this may be disclosure delay and consequent pre-examination healing, or that the sexual abuse of children predominantly involves activities that avoid injury or forming part of a grooming process. This chapter will seek to expose myths and misunderstandings and so assist professionals to achieve the best possible expert evidence. Case examples are given to help clarify the potential for interpretation of findings and presentation of evidence to introduce bias into the Court process.

B. What is Normal?

19.03 The special examination techniques needed to visualize the hymen are only ever performed in the context of examining a child for suspected sexual abuse. A medical examination for other reasons would rarely or never include visualization of the hymen. This has considerable potential to bias interpretation of findings by leading examiners to assume that any minor variations found reflect the suspicion or allegation, because of lack of knowledge of the range of normal variation. Rates of anatomic variations reported as abnormal ranged from 98 per cent in one centre,[1] to 15 to 20 per cent reported in other centres in the 1990s,[2] to less than 5 per cent in much larger studies published since 2000.[3] The validity of interpretation of any finding as indicative of abuse can only be established by testing against the non-abused population. The best available controlled studies comparing non-abused girls with those referred for suspected abuse have confirmed that many of the

---

[1] Hobbs, C.J., Wynne, J.M., and Thomas, A.J., 'Colposcopic genital findings in prepubertal girls assessed for sexual abuse' (1995) 73 *Archives of Disease in Childhood*, 465–9.

[2] Adams, J.A., Harper, K., Knudson, S., and Revilla, J., 'Examination findings in legally confirmed child sexual abuse: It's normal to be normal' (1994) 94 *Pediatrics*, 310–17; Kellogg, N.D., Parra, J.M., and Menard, S., 'Children with anogenital symptoms and signs referred for sexual abuse evaluations' (1994) 94 *Archives of Pediatric and Adolescent Medicine*, 310–17; Bowen, K. and Aldous, M., 'Medical evaluation of sexual abuse in children without disclosed or witnessed abuse' (1999) 153 *Archives of Pediatric and Adolescent Medicine*, 1160–4.

[3] Berenson, A., Chacko, M., Wiemann, C.M., Mishaw, C.O., Friedrich, W.N., and Grady, J.J., 'A case control study of anatomic changes resulting from sexual abuse' (2000). 182 *American Journal of Obstetrics and Gynecology*, 821–34; Heger, A., Ticson, L., Velasquez, O., and Bernier, R., 'Children referred for possible sexual abuse: medical findings in 2384 children' (2002) 26 *Child Abuse and Neglect*, 645–59.

findings reported as 'abnormal' or 'supportive' in the past are normal non-specific variations.[4]

C. Professional Guidance

Paediatric specialist training in the UK now includes a considerable element of **19.04** child protection, but does not always include forensic sexual abuse examination. Cases requiring this type of examination will generally be referred to a paediatrician with special responsibility for child protection. In many circumstances they will jointly examine the child with a forensic medical examiner or another paediatrician with specialist safeguarding knowledge. Within the UK, the need for guidance on interpretation of anatomical findings was highlighted in the 1980s by serious flaws in practice detailed by the Cleveland Enquiry.[5] The Royal College of Physicians (RCP) publication 'Physical Signs of Sexual Abuse' followed in 1991 and was updated in 1997.[6] More detailed guidance on the conduct of the examination was first issued in 2002 in a joint document by the Association of Forensic Physicians (from 2005 the Faculty of Forensic and Legal Medicine—FFLM) and the Royal College of Paediatrics and Child Health (RCPCH). This was updated in 2004, 2009, and 2012[7] and incorporated into the evidence-based review published in 2008.[8]

In the USA there has been a different approach to professional guidance. A con- **19.05** sensus document called 'the Adams Classification' was first published in 1992 and has been regularly updated. It is intended as a tool to assist medical providers in making clinical determinations of the possible significance of findings in children examined for suspected sexual abuse.[9] Although it is also based on information currently available in the medical literature, it is a consensus view of leading American practitioners in the field, rather than an evidence-based review of the published literature. The American Academy of Pediatrics (AAP) has also published and periodically updated guidance since 1991.[10]

---

[4] Berenson et al. (2000), cited at n.3; Heger et al. (2002), cited at n.3.

[5] Butler-Sloss, E. (1988) *Report of the inquiry into child abuse in Cleveland 1987.* Cm 412 London: HMSO. For a summary see *B.M.J., 297:6642* (July 16, 1988), 190–91.

[6] Royal College of Physicians of London (1997) *Physical signs of sexual abuse in children: a report of a working party,* 2nd edn, Suffolk: Lavenham Press.

[7] RCPCH and FFLM (2012, October) *Guidelines on Paediatric Forensic Examinations in Relation to Possible Child Sexual Abuse, http://fflm.ac.uk/upload/documents/1352802061.pdf.*

[8] Royal College of Paediatrics and Child Health (May 2015) *The Physical Signs of Child Sexual Abuse: An evidence-based review and guidance for best practice,* 2nd edn. London: RCPCH. (1st edn 2008).

[9] Adams, J.A. 'Medical evaluation of suspected child sexual abuse' Updated. (2011) 20 *Journal of Child Sexual Abuse,* 588–605.

[10] Jenny, C. and Crawford-Jakubiak, J.E. (2013) *The Evaluation of Children in the Primary Care Setting when Sexual Abuse is Suspected.* Committee on Child Abuse and Neglect, e558–e567.

19.06 The RCPCH guidance was produced in collaboration with the Royal College of Physicians of London and the FFLM.[11] It aims to review the international evidence-base critically, and it is recommended to be used in conjunction with relevant up-to-date literature, particularly that produced by the RCPCH and FFLM.[12] A key component in current RCPCH guidance is a recommendation that 'any doctor who undertakes a forensic assessment of a child who may have been subject to abuse must have particular skills.'[13] Skills include competence and detailed understanding of the following:

- consent (for forensic examination) and confidentiality as they relate to children and young people;
- normal ano-genital anatomy and changes with puberty;
- the diagnosis and differential diagnosis of physical signs, based on current research;
- relevant forensic sampling and how these should be packaged;
- photo-documentation and the requirements for storage of sensitive images;
- accurate and precise documentation, statement writing and presentation of evidence in court; and
- prescribing post-exposure prophylaxis.

The guidance clarifies that 'a single doctor examination may take place provided the doctor has the necessary knowledge, skills and experience for the particular case.' This includes keeping up to date with newly published work. Doctors lacking any particular skill should enlist the assistance of another doctor with complementary skills. The doctor should include information about their experience and practice with any statement.

19.07 Although there is now a much larger literature on child sexual abuse (CSA) than a decade ago, there is still comparatively little data detailing the anatomical and microbiological data in normal non-abused children and cases of sexual abuse. A major limitation has been that there are no high quality studies. This is understandable since children cannot be randomized to receive abuse. The categorization of children as abused or non-abused between papers is very variable with no consistent methodology or terminology. The difficulty of assigning a child to a control, (non-abuse) group in order to conduct research makes it unlikely any research ethics committee would approve this type of study in the UK. Consequently the evidence base addressing what is and is not normal is likely to remain limited.

---

[11] Cited at n.8.
[12] *http://www.rcpch.ac.uk/child-health/standards-care/child-protection/publications/child-protection-publications*; FFLM (February 2014) Quality standards for doctors undertaking paediatric sexual offence medicine (PSOM), *http://fflm.ac.uk/upload/documents/1393326841.pdf*.
[13] Cited at n.8, 224.

D. Training Issues

(1) Paediatricians and general practitioners

Case assessments may involve doctors from varying specialities. After qualification **19.08** as a medical practitioner paediatric training takes a further eight years in addition to two foundation years and may, although will not necessarily, include disciplines helpful in CSA assessment such as paediatric gynaecology, dermatology, and psychiatry. So far very few practitioners involved in CSA work have completed the Diploma in the Forensic and Clinical Aspects of Sexual Assault (DFCASA), launched in 2011.[14]

(2) Forensic medical examiners

Since 2006 most police forces in England and Wales have outsourced the work **19.09** of forensic examination and forensic sample collection to private companies.[15] This work was formerly conducted by General Practitioners appointed as standing Forensic Medical Examiners. There being no set career structure or training for paediatricians and forensic doctors engaged in CSA examinations this has resulted in a lack of uniformity of experience, knowledge, and training. Clinical Forensic Medicine is still not recognized by the GMC as a medical speciality.

With the increasing recognition since the 1970s that CSA is a hidden paediat- **19.10** ric problem[16] more paediatricians and other medical practitioners have become involved in CSA investigations. However, particularly for those working in the NHS, the inconvenience of attending court often at short notice, coupled with the pressure from lawyers to provide a firm opinion on a subject beset with uncertainty, has tended to deter many from undertaking such work.

E. Aims of the Forensic Medical Examination

Any allegation of CSA requires investigation, and in most cases a medical exami- **19.11** nation, as to which there are broadly four aims.

(1) Documentation of injury (including negative findings)

Documentation of the injury involves a visual anatomical inspection and a **19.12** clear written description of any injury. Photodocumentation, preferably with a

---

[14] See *http://fflm.ac.uk/education/licentiatesom/*.

[15] Pillai, M. and Paul, S., 'Facilities for Complainants of Sexual Assault throughout the United Kingdom' (2006) 13 *J. Clin. Forensic Med.*, 164–71.

[16] Kemp, C.H. 'Sexual Abuse, another hidden paediatric problem' (The 1977 Anderson Aldrich lecture) (1978) 62 *Pediatrics*, 382–9.

colposcope, is considered best practice.[17] This requires parental consent and, where the child has achieved sufficient understanding, it is also good practice to obtain the child's consent. Children, especially adolescents, will be anxious lest intimate photographs are available in court. Currently there is no guarantee against dissemination of sensitive images. Images should normally only be available to expert witnesses and not used in court. Where, exceptionally, the court decides that photographic images would be helpful, the examining doctor should be consulted and present to assist with interpretation. Forensic images should be stored securely and in accordance with guidance.[18] It is good practice that a line diagram of any abnormal anatomical finding is included in a medical report.

(2) Collection of evidence

19.13 Forensic samples may include clothing, linens, body swabs (for DNA, semen, microbiology), saliva, hair, and blood if the examination occurs within 72 hours of the (last) alleged event.[19] These must be appropriately labelled.[20]

(3) Therapeutic purposes

19.14 An Examination should be holistic and include a full medical, social and emotional assessment and onward referral as appropriate. This may involve giving reassurance to both the child and a parent about harm, and advice and, where appropriate, provision of post-exposure prophylaxis against pregnancy and sexually transmitted infection, including blood born viruses.

(4) Safeguarding

19.15 Lastly a key purpose is to address child protection issues.

F. Context and Timing of the Examination

19.16 Most examinations follow a request by police and often form part of a child protection enquiry. Among prepubertal children, most examinations are historic (more than seven days since the last alleged event). When the alleged sexual abuse occurred within seventy-two hours or there is an acute injury, the examination should be performed as soon as possible to allow forensic evidence

---

[17] FFLM and RCPCH (2012, October); *Guidelines*, cited at n.7.
[18] FFLM. (2014, May) 'Guidance for best practice for the management of intimate images that may become evidence in court' *http://fflm.ac.uk/upload/documents/1400752731.pdf.*
[19] FFLM (2015, January) 'Recommendations for the collection of forensic specimens from complainants and suspects', *http://fflm.ac.uk/upload/documents/1422637185.pdf.*
[20] FFLM (2013, October) 'Labelling Forensic Samples', *http://fflm.ac.uk/upload/documents/1380634869.pdf.*

collection.[21] With patchy provision of forensic sexual assault services, particularly for children, it is not always possible to arrange a prompt examination.

Body swabs collected in prepubertal children more than twenty-four hours after a   **19.17**
sexual assault are unlikely to yield forensic evidence, and nearly two thirds of the
forensic evidence may be recovered from clothing, linens, or the environment where
the offence occurred.[22] When more than seventy-two hours have passed and no acute
injuries are present, forensic sampling is not indicated in prepubertal children, so the
examination can be arranged at the first convenient time. However, any unwashed
clothing or linen should be collected, as it may yield forensic evidence until washed.

Where possible a video interview should precede the examination, to avoid con-   **19.18**
taminating the child's evidence. Knowledge of the alleged acts allows the examiner to plan their intervention and assess which forensic samples may be required.
However, in acute cases any delay may risk loss of forensic evidence, so the examination takes priority. However, it is then important that the medical examiners
avoid leading questions or anticipating the investigative interview. They should
make a contemporaneous note of any spontaneous comments by the child. In historical abuse there is no urgency and the video evidence should be completed first.

G. The Examination Position

(1) Prepubertal girls

Traditionally the genitalia of prepubertal girls are examined with the child in   **19.19**
supine frog-legged position (the child lying on the back with knees bent and legs
apart). Where necessary, the examiner uses labial separation and traction to expose
the hymen. In the circumstance that a defect is found or suspected the supine
position may not give adequate information about the posterior rim of the hymen.
So, if the child is willing, the knee-chest position should be used. Real defects
can most reliably be differentiated from pseudo defects in the knee-chest position.
Photographic illustrations of the effect of position are available in the literature.[23]
Where the prepubertal hymen appears to have a defect, failure to visualize with the

---

[21] FFLM and RCPCH (2013, May) Sexual Offences: Pre-pubertal Complainants, *http:// fflm.ac.uk/upload/documents/1369999406.pdf*; FFLM and RCPCH (2013, May) 'Sexual Offences: Post-pubertal Complainants', *http://fflm.ac.uk/upload/documents/1369999423.pdf*.

[22] Christian, C.W., Lavelle, J.M., De Jong, A.R., Loiselle, J.L., Brenner, L., and Joffe, M. 'Forensic evidence findings in prepubertal victims of sexual assault' (2000) 106 *Pediatrics*, 100–104. Giardet R, Bolton K, Lahoti S, et al. 'The collection of forensic evidence from pediatric victims of sexual assault.' (2011) 128(2) *Pediatrics*, 233–8; Thackeray J, Horner G, Benzinger E., and Scribano P. 'Forensic evidence collection and DNA identification in acute child sexual assault.' (2011) 128(2) *Pediatrics*, 227–32.

[23] Heger, A., Emans, S.J., and Muram D. (2000) *Evaluation of the sexually abused child.* 2nd edn, New York: Oxford University Press, 130.

child in knee-chest position may result in a diagnosis of hymen abnormality where the hymen is normal (Case 5). In either position the hymen may not open and examination techniques such as separation or traction of the labia may be required to help open and visualize the hymen.[24]

(2) Post-pubescent girls

19.20 In adolescent girls the knee-chest position is generally not appropriate or help-ful. Pubertal changes mean that defects in the hymen can more appropriately be examined for using either a moistened cotton tip swab or the balloon of a catheter.

(3) Rectal

19.21 Within the UK the anus is examined using buttock separation (usually for 30 seconds) with the child in left lateral position, or supine knee chest for very small children, However, in USA supine or prone knee-chest position has more often been used and this may account for some differences in findings.

H. Photo-documentation

(1) Purpose: to provide a permanent record

19.22 Photo-documentation of the clinical examination allows examiners to review their findings, seek second opinions, and engage in peer review.[25] It may avoid re-examination necessitated by interpretational disagreement and an erroneous finding of sexual abuse. However, the need for a cautious approach to photographs was highlighted in *Re Y*, where it was established that photographs misled several doctors to a diagnosis of sexual abuse.[26] Images may not display the true depth of field and are not the same as examining the child directly. Live examination must remain the gold standard. It is essential that the images are of adequate quality to demonstrate the clinical findings, and if the images do not demonstrate the clinical findings the reason for this should be recorded in the clinical notes. Video recording is likely to be more dynamic than still photography, but as yet there is no published data evaluating which of these two methods of photodocumentation is better.

---

[24] RCPCH (2008, March and 2015, May) *The Physical Signs of Child Sexual Abuse: an evidence-based review and guidance for best practice*, London: RCPCH, 130.

[25] FFLM (2014, March) 'Peer Review in Sexual Offences including Child Sexual Abuse cases and the implications for the disclosure of Unused Material in criminal investigations and pros-ecutions', *http://fflm.ac.uk/upload/documents/1396515960.pdf*. RCPCH roles and competencies of health care staff March 2014.

[26] [2003] EWHC 3090 (Fam), (Holman J.) (evidence of abuse; use of photographs).

(2) Colposcopy

Similarly, colposcopy—illuminated magnification to produce high quality **19.23** photographs—requires a cautious approach. Although the courts and legal profession may in general have relied on it to permit a definitive diagnosis it does not lessen the primacy of skilled examination and interpretation. The key to capturing the relevant image is using the correct examination technique and position, and assistance in photographing the demonstrated findings.

I. The Significance of Normal Findings

Historically, there was a tendency to conceptualize sexual abuse of girls in adult **19.24** terms of penile vaginal penetration. This raised an expectation as to findings but current evidence has negated such an expectation. Most sexually abused children present with normal findings since CSA may embrace a range of non-penetrative and therefore potentially non-injurious exploitative sexually gratifying activities. This is perhaps understandable given that abusers may be only too well aware that injuring the child carries the high risk of discovery and loss of access. Historically, these concepts were not understood. Those investigating need to understand the child's perception of genital anatomy to avoid confounding an expectation of findings (see para 19.25). Investigators also need to understand that healing may occur in a relatively short time, for example, a few days.

J. Interpreting What Children Say

There is need to consider what the vagina is to a prepubertal child. Before men- **19.25** struation commences most girls will have little understanding of the complexities of external and internal genital anatomy or exactly what and where the vagina is. Most will be unaware of it as a separate orifice internal to the structures comprising the vulva. Young girls will not therefore understand the difference between vaginal penetration and that within the vulva or between the labia. Forensically however there are very important differences in that contact with a blunt object passing between the labia will not be likely to result in significant tissue trauma (e.g. hymenal laceration). An examination soon after the event may reveal inflammation or even vestibular abrasion, but often there will be no visibly abnormal findings.

K. Evaluating the Reliability of Medical Evidence

In both criminal and civil proceedings considerable weight is typically given to the **19.26** medical evidence in resolving disputes over events. It is essential that the scientific basis of any opinion be explored to safeguard the integrity of the fact-finding process and increase the prospects of the court achieving a just verdict. Clinical findings must be accurately recorded and described using correct and consistent terminology. For their interpretation it is important that due consideration be given to the limited size of the evidence-base. Small numbers always demand cautious interpretation and an understanding that outliers in the normal population will be in grave danger of being labeled 'abnormal'.

19.27   GMC guidance is clear that doctors must always act in the patient's best interests.[27] The forensic duty of gathering evidence and providing opinions may conflict with various aspects of the medical role. For example, the duty of disclosure may conflict with that of confidentiality. The role of advocacy may well conflict with the duty of impartiality to the court, especially the duty to disclose evidence that may not support the doctor's opinion. Opinion may reflect emotional involvement, which may compromise the doctor's objectivity, induce bias and promote over-interpretation of clinical observations. The GMC has not really addressed how the independence expected by the courts can encompass the advocacy detailed in *Good Medical Practice*.[28] To address all of this a support system is key to good practice, particularly participation in peer review, yet this remains an area still to be clarified judicially.[29]

L. Cases

Case example 1 Illustrating the changes in medical understanding and interpretation

19.28   *A 5-year-old who had supposedly slipped and struck her vulva on a bidet had a genital abrasion and an irregular hymen edge. A paediatrician deemed the latter including the hymen orifice size as reflecting actual or attempted penetration. They also deemed that there was abnormal reflex anal dilatation (RAD).*

(i) Comment

19.29   This case occurred in the early 1990s when there was no published data on the range of hymen measurements in children. Evaluation of the current evidence base would clarify that the findings described at three examinations of this child fall into the range found in non-abused children and should be regarded as non-specific. Until publication of the evidence-based review in 2008,[30] it

---

[27] GMC (March 2013). *Good Medical Practice, http://www.gmc-uk.org/Good_medical_practice___English_0914.pdf_51527435.pdf.*

[28] Ibid.

[29] White, C. 'Medical Evidence: Children' in (2014) Rook, P. and Ward, R. *Sexual Offences, Law and Practice*, 4th edn, London: Sweet & Maxwell, 521–33.

[30] Cited at n.8.

was commonplace for doctors to report hymen measurements and opine their status in respect of normality. However, almost always no description was given of how the measurements were made. The hymen opening size is difficult to measure and varies with type of hymen, the position of the child, the method of examination and degree of relaxation and co-operation of the child. The evidence-based review clarified there is considerable overlap in hymen measurements in abused and non-abused children.[31] For this reason measurement is generally considered unhelpful. The RCPCH has recommend RAD of >1cm 1991, >1,5cm 2008 and in 2015 refers to dynamic dilatation involving both sphincters (no stool present) as being associated with anal abuse. The AAP suggests that RAD >2 cm indicates penetrating trauma but are more cautious in their updated guidelines 2015. Of note this child did not fulfil any of these criteria.

Case example 2 The potential for a misleading history to influence interpretation of findings

In 2004 a 7-year-old stated that she had been 'touched on her privates'. An experienced   **19.30**
paediatrician described her hymen as 'gaping' with an orifice diameter of 7 mm and suggestive of previous penetration, while a hymenal bump and tag were said to be consistent with healing or previous trauma.

(i) Comment

In many cases prior to publication of the RCPCH guidance (2008) the hymen   **19.31**
was described as 'gaping'. This is a subjective impression rather than an objective measure. It may be interpreted as the hymen orifice appeared open, such that a view could be obtained into the vagina. The ease with which the hymen orifice and vagina can be seen with a child lying supine in the frog-legged position is very variable, and its significance is unknown. Hegar et al. describe this as a normal finding.[32] This terminology should therefore no longer be used. A number of published studies have sought to establish the range of findings in normal non-abused girls.[33] A transverse diameter of 7 mm is well within the normal range. Research evaluating examination of the hymen in the diagnosis of previous penetration

---

[31] Ingram, D.M., Everett, V.D., and Ingram, D.L. 'The relationship between transverse hymenal orifice diameter by the separation technique and other possible markers of sexual abuse' (2001) 25 *Child Abuse and Neglect*, 1109–20. See also Heger et al. (2000), cited at n.23.

[32] Hegar, A.H., Ticson, L., Guerra, L., et al., 'Appearance of the genitalia in girls selected for non-abuse: a review of hymenal morphology and non-specific findings' (2002) 15 *J. Pediatric Adolesc Gynecol*, 27–35.

[33] McCann, J., Wells, R., Simon, M., and Voris, J. 'Genital findings in prepubertal girls selected for non-abuse: a descriptive study' (1990) 86 *Pediatrics*, 428–39; Berensen, A., Heger, A., Hayes, J., Bailey, R., and Emans, S. 'Appearance of the hymen in prepubertal girls' (1992) 89 *Pediatrics*, 387–95; Gardner, J.J. 'Descriptive study of genital variations in healthy, non-abused premenarchal girls' (1992) 120 *J. Pediatrics*, 251–7; Berenson, A.B. and Grady J.J. 'A longitudinal study of hymenal development from 3 to 9 years of age' (2002) 140 *J Pediatr*, 600–7.

has not included or commented on 'gaping'.[34] This is probably because subjective impressions cannot be reliably measured and do not show high levels of inter-observer agreement. The suggestion that the mound of tissue and a hymen tag at 6 o'clock may represent healing of previous trauma is completely unsupported in the published data on healing of hymen trauma.[35] Possibly there may have been confusion with the interpretation of anal skin tags, which have been reported at the site of healed injury. A review of available data on non-abused children published in 2002 showed that the findings of a hymen tag and a mound of tissue are common non-specific findings.[36]

**Case example 3 Inconsistent medical opinion—
the range of medical opinion**

19.32 *A 10-year-old and her siblings from a family with no risk factors or evidence of abuse were placed in care after the girl had mentioned genital soreness to her GP and a paediatrician and a second doctor had diagnosed an absent hymen, conclusive of chronic sexual abuse. A court-appointed examiner identified a narrow rim hymen and found that the two doctors had over-estimated the hymen orifice by 300 per cent.*

(i) Comment

19.33 Subsequently consent was given for use of the images in this case for educational review. Of seventy-two forensic physicians and thirty-five gynaecologists or paediatricians, thirty-seven stated the anatomy was normal, twenty-four that it was abnormal and forty-seven were uncertain.

Case example 4 Selective admission of opinion

19.34 *Six months after the last of several alleged rapes, a 12-year old complainant was jointly examined by a paediatrician and a forensic doctor. She was in early to mid puberty. They described the right hymen margin 'blunt' with a small hymen notch posteriorly, which the paediatrician called 'a small healed tear'. The paediatrician opined there had been penetration. The forensic doctor stated the hymen was intact and opined the findings inconclusive. Only the paediatrician's evidence was admitted during court proceedings.*

---

[34] Ingram, et al. (2001), cited at n.32; Berenson, A.B., Chacko, M.R., Wiemann, C.M., et al. 'Use of Hymenal Measurements in the Diagnosis of Previous Penetration' (2002) 109 *Pediatrics*, 228–35.
[35] McCann, J., Mlyamoto, S., Boyle, C., and Rogers, K., 'Healing of hymenal injuries in prepubertal and adolescent girls: A descriptive study' (2007) *Pediatrics, 119e*, e1094-e1106; Heppenstall-Hegar, A., McConnell, G., Ticson, L., et al. 'Healing patterns in anogenital injuries: a longitudinal study of injuries associated with sexual abuse, accidental injuries or genital surgery in the preadolescent child' (2003) *Pediatrics, 112*, 829–37.
[36] Cited at n.33.

(i) Comment

Use of the term 'tear' was not appropriate since this implies causation. The doctor **19.35** should describe what they see impartially avoiding terms that assume causation. The forensic doctor described the hymen as 'intact'. In the past both the lay and medical understanding of this term was that vaginal penetration had not occurred. Current medical knowledge has clarified that one cannot determine virginal status from examination of the hymen.[37] However, in the past it was thought that penetration of the hymen would leave defects (notches/clefts or loss of hymen tissue) that could be confirmed by examination. Thus the description by one doctor of the hymen as 'intact' was inconsistent with the description of the other who described and interpreted a posterior hymen notch as evidence of a past penetrating injury. It is difficult to reconcile the differences in the anatomical description given by the two doctors. Admitting only one of these two opinions had potential to undermine the safety of any conviction. Moreover, the descriptive terminology of the hymen edge as 'blunt' is meaningless. It may imply the edge was less clear to see on one side compared with the other but this is subjective and has no known clinical significance.

Case example 5 The importance of examination position

Employing only a supine, frog-leg examination of a 4-year old, paediatricians found **19.36** *no visible hymen towards the back and concluded there had been hymen penetration. Another practitioner's examination employed both supine and knee-chest positions and revealed hymen tissue in the area in question and indicated no conclusive evidence of abuse.*

(i) Comment

Whenever there are concerns regarding possible abnormalities in the hymen these **19.37** should be corroborated by examining the child using another technique. In prepubertal children the recommended way would be the prone knee-chest position. This allows gravity to pull on the tissues and smooth out any apparent abnormalities. In this case the CPS did not proceed with the possible sexual abuse, but did continue with allegations of neglect.

M. Conclusion

Medical evaluation requires consideration of the child's medical and social history, **19.38** on-going medical and psychological needs, as well as collecting forensic evidence

---

[37] Adams, J.A., Botash, A.S., and Kellogg N. 'Differences in hymenal morphology between adolescent girls with and without a history of consensual sexual intercourse' (2004) 158 *Arch Pediatr Adolesc Med*, 280–5.

and addressing therapeutic need and child protection concerns. There are significant gaps in training and peer support for doctors undertaking this work, particularly the forensic role. Controversies and disagreements certainly still exist, but a body of knowledge has gradually been developed on the epidemiology, manifestations, and sequelae of the sexual misuse of children. Although the total evidence base is still relatively small, variations of normal in anal and genital anatomy have been better clarified. Twenty years ago, the assumption appears to have been that CSA in prepubertal girls mirrored adult sexual activity. Given the very different dimensions of prepubertal genital anatomy it was expected that there should be signs. This appears wrong. We have learned that the physical examination, while a key component of the evaluation, is most often normal even in the face of a history that would suggest genital injuries should be present and where the perpetrator admits to some form of sexual act.[38] The key to this may lie in interpreting the child's understanding of genital anatomy and sexual acts. A child's story of what happened remains one of the most important aspects of the evidence.

Author Biographies

Dr Mary Pillai has been a Consultant in Obstetrics and Gynaecology since 1993. From 1996 to 2014 this included a specialist service for paediatric gynaecology and for ten years this also included forensic sexual assault examinations. Her practice is based in Gloucestershire and currently encompasses sexual reproductive health and fetal medicine. She represented the Faculty of Forensic and Legal Medicine on the Royal College of Paediatrics and Child Health Project Board producing the second edition of 'The Physical Signs Of Child Sexual Abuse', published in May 2015.

Dr Jean Price, now retired, was formerly a Consultant Paediatrician for Southampton City Primary Care Trust. She has worked in the field of child sexual abuse since 1983, and played a leading role in the development of CSA services within Hampshire and Devon. Dr Price co-chaired the Female working group that produced the RCPCH 2008 and 2015 guidance. "The physical Signs of Child Sexual Abuse – An evidence-based review" published May 2015. She is a leading authority in the field of child protection and lectures on child abuse issues within the UK and internationally. She is frequently asked to act as an expert witness in both Family and criminal proceedings.

---

[38] Muram, D. 'Child sexual abuse; relationship between sexual acts and genital findings' (1989) 13(2) *Child Abuse and Neglect*, 211–16; Bruni, M. 'Anal findings in sexual abuse of children (a descriptive study)' (2003) 48(6) *J. Forensic Sci*, 1343–6.

20

COMMON PSYCHIATRIC, PSYCHOLOGICAL, AND LEARNING DISORDERS AND TREATMENT

Harry N.W. Wood and Keith Rix

A. Introduction

Mental disorder affects about 25 per cent of the population in any one year.[1] At **20.01** least one in four complainants, witnesses and defendants, will have a mental disorder. So criminal justice personnel need to understand how mental disorder affects the victims and perpetrators of, and witnesses to, sexual offences. Furthermore, the risk of involvement in sexual offending, as complainant or alleged perpetrator, is increased in individuals with mental disorder.[2] In addition, sexual trauma can cause or contribute to mental disorder and the processes of investigation and prosecution can cause or exacerbate disorder.[3]

This chapter describes the main groups of mental disorders and learning difficulties **20.02** encountered in witnesses, complainants, and defendants which have implications

---

[1] McManus, S., Meltzer, H., Brugha, H., Bebbington, P., and Jenkins, S. (2009) *Adult Psychiatric Morbidity in England, 2007*, Leeds: NHS Information Centre.

[2] Ward, T.D., Polaschek, L., and Beech, A.R. (2006) *Theories of Sexual Offending*, Chichester: Wiley-Blackwell.

[3] Bornstein, B., Hullman, G., and Miller, M. 'Stress, Trauma, and Wellbeing in Court: Where do we go from here?' in (2013) Miller, M and Bornstein, B (eds), *Stress, Trauma, and Wellbeing in the legal system*, Oxford: Oxford University Press.

for different stages of the criminal process. It also introduces the drugs used to treat mental disorders.

20.03 The World Health Organization will soon issue a revised classification of mental disorders (The International Classification of Diseases, ICD). The widely used American Diagnostic and Statistical Manual (DSM) classification was recently revised.[4] A simpler framework should be more helpful, at least as far as sexual offending is concerned. The simpler framework employed in this chapter should be more helpful, at least as far as sexual offending is concerned. It categorizes diagnoses in a straightforward way that should be helpful for lawyers and recognizable by their experts. Table 20.1 indicates the prevalence of the disorders.

Table 20.1 Lifetime prevalence rates of mental and behavioural disorders

Condition	Lifetime Prevalence Rates
Learning (intellectual) disability	1%
Pervasive developmental disorders: Autism Spectrum Disorder	1.8% in men and 0.2% in women
Personality disorders	6% overall; 3.6% Cluster A, 1.5% Cluster B, 2.7% Cluster C
Organic disorders: Acute (e.g. delirium tremens)	Delirium: 10% in adults over 65 who are admitted into hospital for a general medical condition
Organic disorders: Chronic (e.g. dementia)	Dementia: 2%–4% in over 65s, 20% in over 85s
Psychotic disorders: mood incongruent (e.g. schizophrenia, delusional disorder)	Schizophrenia: 0.5%–1% Delusional disorder: 0.03%
Psychotic disorders: mood congruent (e.g. mania, depressive psychosis, bipolar disorder)	Mania: Depressive psychosis: Bipolar Disorder: 0.4%–1.6%
Psychotic disorders: other (e.g. schizoaffective disorder)	Schizoaffective disorder: less common than schizophrenia
Depressive disorder	10%–25% in women and 5%–12% in men
Generalized anxiety disorder	5%
Panic disorder	1.5%–3.5%
Phobic disorders	5%
Posttraumatic Stress Disorder	1%–14%
Attention Deficit Hyperactivity Disorder (ADHD)	3%–5% in school-age children 4% of adults have some symptoms, these are severe in 1.7% of cases
Eating Disorder	Anorexia nervosa: 0.5%–1% in young adult females, rates for males are not known Bulimia nervosa: 1%–3% in young adult females, the rate for males is approximately one tenth of this

---

[4] American Psychiatric Association (2013) *Diagnostic and Statistical Manual of Mental Disorders* (5th edn), Washington DC: American Psychiatric Association.

B. The Limitations of Psychiatric Diagnosis

The diagnosis of psychiatric and psychological problems is more difficult than in **20.04** other branches of medicine. Diagnoses cannot be confirmed with a physical test. Diagnosis often depends mainly, sometimes entirely, upon self-reported *symptoms* and little on objectively observable *signs*. Whereas in clinical practice it is often reasonable to assume that most patients give a reliable history, it should not be assumed that in the forensic setting defendants, witnesses and complainants will give a reliable history. Their account may be self-serving. One of the important skills of the forensic psychologist/psychiatrist is to make allowances for unreliability.

Mental disorders are usually the manifestation of the combination of biological fac- **20.05** tors, particularly genes, and a variety of influences on development from conception to adulthood. They are influenced by gender, gender orientation, race, culture, social and economic circumstances, personal identity and the reactions of others, and by other factors creating tension between lawyers and their experts. The resulting biographic, holistic, and deterministic 'medical' model may be at odds with the 'legal model' with its emphasis on free will, rationality and decontextualization as in 'the reasonable man' (not woman).[5]

Psychiatric diagnoses sometimes appear variable. The lawyer may find a range of **20.06** diagnoses in someone's medical records. This can result from the use of different classificatory systems. Persistent/recurring conditions may be consistently and repeatedly diagnosed over time, for example, recurrent depressive illness, schizophrenia, and dementia. These can be termed, 'life-time diagnoses'. Other conditions, such as adjustment disorders, alcohol misuse or dependence, brief psychotic illnesses and phobic disorders, come and go or occur against the background of life-long disorders. They can be termed, 'episode diagnoses'. Sometimes a lifetime diagnosis can only be made by looking back and comparing a number of episode diagnoses.

The categorical approach to psychiatric classification gives the mistaken impression **20.07** that diagnosis is all about the presence or absence of mental disorder. It obscures the fact that many disorders occur on a continuum between normality, whatever that is, and illness, so, annoyingly for lawyers who want to know whether the defendant is, or is not, mentally ill, there are grey areas. DSM 5 reconfigures some

---

[5] Rix, K.J.B. 'Psychiatry and the law: Uneasy bedfellows' (abridged version of the Presidential Address given to the Leeds and West Riding Medico-Legal Society on 1 October 2003). (2006) 74 *Medico-Legal Journal*, 148–59.

divisions along dimensional rather than categorical lines with uncertain implications for the courts.

C. The Main Areas of Mental Disorder

(1) Learning disabilities[6]

20.08 Individuals with learning disabilities present with a significantly reduced ability to understand new or complex information and to learn new skills, and have a reduced ability to cope with independent living. In the UK a diagnosis of learning disability is made on the basis of the presence of the following criteria:[7]

- an IQ (Intelligence Quotient), as measured on a recognized psychometric test of intelligence, of less than 70;
- a significant impairment in adaptive functioning; and
- the problems began before the age of 18 years.

20.09 A range of levels of disability is described in the diagnostic manuals, although, given issues associated with the measurement of IQ in individuals with more severe disability, it has been suggested that we should limit this to 'mild', (IQ score 50 – 69) and 'severe', (IQ score less than 50).[8] People with severe learning disability tend to be completely dependent upon the support of professional carers and are less likely to give evidence in court but, if they are, would be significantly limited in their ability to do so.

20.10 The difficulties that individuals with learning disabilities have are of significance when it comes to taking part in criminal proceedings. These include difficulties in expressive and receptive communication, a lack of understanding of social norms and expectations, limitations in memory, difficulties in areas of academic functioning, for example, in reading and writing, and a tendency towards passivity often manifesting as a tendency to accept what others say.[9] Personality characteristics that are associated with learning disability that hinder the individual's ability to act as a witness include acquiescence (answering, 'yes', when uncertain), confabulation (filling in the gaps of one's memory with distortions and fabrications that one believes to be true), compliance, and suggestibility.[10] It is important,

---

[6] Also now more commonly known as intellectual disabilities.

[7] British Psychological Society (2000) *Learning Disability: Definitions and Context*, Leicester: BPS.

[8] See ibid.

[9] Murphy, G.H. and Clare, I.C.H. 'The effect of learning disabilities on witness testimony' in (2006) Heaton-Armstrong A., Shepherd E., Gudjonsson G., Wolchover D. (eds), *Witness testimony: psychological, investigative and evidential perspectives*, Oxford: Oxford University Press.

[10] Clare, I.C.H. and Gudjonsson, G., 'Interrogative suggestibility, confabulation and acquiescence in people with mild learning disabilities (mental handicap): Implications for vulnerability during police interrogation' (1993) 32 *British Journal of Clinical Psychology*, 295–301.

however that people with learning disabilities are afforded the same opportunities in life, including full access to justice.

As with other mental disorders it is often not evident that an individual has learn- **20.11** ing disability on the basis of their physical appearance and initial presentation. People with learning disabilities may not be aware that they have this condition. In other cases, individuals become skilled at concealing their difficulties. It is important, therefore, that comprehensive psychological assessment is conducted in cases in which there are doubts about an individual's ability to take part in the investigative process.

(2) Developmental disorders

(a) Pervasive developmental disorder

Pervasive developmental disorders involve severe and persistent impairment in **20.12** areas of development. Deficits commonly relate to social and communication skills. There may sometimes be obsessional behaviours, interests, and activities, and an additional learning disability. Difficulties begin within the first few years of life.

The autism spectrum disorders (ASD) are a group of pervasive developmental dis- **20.13** orders including autism and Asperger's syndrome. ASD is associated with significant impairments in non-verbal and verbal communication, social difficulties, and obsessional interests/routines. Although individuals with ASD are not thought to present any greater risk of offending behaviour[11] their social deficits make them especially vulnerable to exploitation. Furthermore, the traits that are associated with ASD complicate any task that is dependent upon verbal communication. ASD and their specific difficulties can make it particularly difficult to act as a witness.

Individuals with ASD share many of the difficulties that were identified in associa- **20.14** tion with learning disability. In addition to this, the associated social impairment can cause the individual to appear disingenuous. Individuals with ASD find it difficult to empathize. Their social presentation can be egocentric and suggest a lack of concern. Their non-verbal behaviour and facial expressions might indicate an emotional response that is not congruent with the subject matter and which is not always consistent with how they actually feel. This can include smiling or, even, laughing when discussing issues that are embarrassing or distressing. When this is the case it is important that the court is made aware of the impact that this can have on the individual's presentation.

---

[11] Gunasekaran, S. and Chaplin, E., 'Autism spectrum disorders and offending' (2012) 6(6) *Advances in Mental Health and Intellectual Disabilities*, 308–13.

(b) Attention Deficit Hyperactivity Disorder

20.15 Attention Deficit Hyperactivity Disorder (ADHD) is a behavioural disorder in which the individual presents with inattention, impulsivity, and hyperactivity. DSM 5 has updated its definition of ADHD to reflect the experience of adults with this condition.[12] ADHD has been associated with increased risk of involvement in the criminal justice system generally[13] and specifically in relation to sex offences in adolescence[14] and adulthood.[15]

20.16 The effects of ADHD are such that the individual would be significantly impaired in their ability to take part in the legal process. Concentration is limited and the individual is easily distracted. Full assessment in relation to this is essential and, if appropriate, the prescription of pharmacological treatment might facilitate the individual's participation. In cases where this condition is apparent the court would need to consider special measures in the form of shorter sessions and regular breaks.

(3) Personality disorder

20.17 Personality disorder can be defined as, 'the failure to achieve adaptive solutions to life tasks'.[16] Individuals who have personality disorder experience difficulties in:

* their sense of self and representations of others;
* their ability to form, manage, and maintain close or intimate interpersonal relationships; and
* their ability to function adaptively within the social world.

20.18 A number of supposedly discrete personality disorder diagnoses have been identi-fied in ICD and DSM, including antisocial personality disorder and borderline personality disorder which are associated with high co-morbidity (i.e. co-existing disorders). The ten discrete personality disorder diagnoses described in DSM 5 have been divided into three clusters:

(A) Odd and eccentric (paranoid, schizoid, schizotypal);
(B) Dramatic and emotional (antisocial, borderline, histrionic, narcissistic); and
(C) Anxious and fearful (avoidant, dependent, obsessive-compulsive)

---

[12] American Psychiatric Association cited at n.4.
[13] Young, S. and Ward, J., 'ADHD and offenders' (2011) 12(1) *World Journal of Biological Psychiatry*, 124–8.
[14] Hilarski, C. and Wodarski, J. (2006) *Comprehensive Mental Health Practice with Sex Offenders and their Families*, New York: Routledge.
[15] Langevin, R. and Curvoe, S. 'Psychopathy, ADHD, and brain dysfunction as predictors of lifetime recidivism among sex offenders' (2011) 55(1) *International Journal of Offender Therapy and Comparative Criminology*, 1–26.
[16] Livesely, J.W. (2003) *Practical Management of Personality Disorder*, New York: The Guilford Press, 19.

Many of the features associated with personality disorder make it difficult for the **20.19** individual to take part in criminal proceedings. For example, a man charged with serious sexual offences was advised by his solicitor not to answer questions put to him by the police. At trial psychiatric evidence was admitted to the effect that he had a paranoid personality disorder and on the basis of the ruling in *R v Argent*[17] the trial judge ruled that the jury could not draw an adverse inference from his silence under the provisions of section 35(1) of the Criminal Justice and Public Order Act 1994.[18] The grounds for affording a defendant this protection include mental capacity, state of health, tiredness, and personality.

In extreme cases individuals can present in a manner which looks like psycho- **20.20** sis. Individuals may experience the hallucinations and altered experience that are associated with serious psychiatric illness. The specific features of other types of personality disorder, not least of paranoid personality and of the Cluster B personality disorders, can make it difficult for the individual to provide an accurate account of events. Individuals with narcissistic personality disorder, for example, seek to present themselves in an impressive manner, driven by their need for admiration. Histrionic personality disorder is associated with a desire to be the centre of attention and a willingness to use one's presentation to pursue this. This can include using physical appearance to impress, and presenting in a flirtatious and/ or dramatic manner. Both presentations can include making statements that are either exaggerated or untrue. False confessions or testimony that seems hollow and insincere can be associated with these presentations. Again, the court would need to be made aware when these issues were apparent.

As with most mental disorder, individuals with personality disorder may not be **20.21** aware that they have a diagnosable condition. Again, appearance and initial presentation may not immediately alert legal professionals to their difficulties.

(4) Organic disorders

The brain is the organ of the mind. Organic disorders are conditions in which the **20.22** function of the organ is disrupted by disease, such as Alzheimer's dementia, head injury, or a systemic disease, such as septicemia which affects the brain as well as other organs.

(a) Acute organic disorders

Acute organic disorders, with a relatively short and abrupt onset and duration, usu- **20.23** ally involve such severe brain disruption that conscious level is altered or clouded, manifesting in subtle and fluctuating impairments of attention, concentration, and memory with almost dream-like experiences. At the other extreme, it may take

---

[17] [1997] 2 Cr App R 27.
[18] Rix, K.J.B., 'Silence in interview: Psychiatry and the *Argent* conditions' (1998) 5 *Journal of Clinical Forensic Medicine*, 199–204.

the form of frank confusion and disorientation as occurs, for example, in delirium tremens, which is the most extreme alcohol withdrawal state.

(b) Chronic organic disorders

20.24 Chronic organic disorders usually have a more gradual onset, do not resolve completely or at all, and do not usually manifest with clouding of consciousness. Their characteristic symptoms are persistent, sometimes progressive defects of cognition—impairments of attention and concentration, memory, reasoning, judgement, abstract thinking, and orientation. Other features depend on the nature of the disorder. Many organic disorders also manifest in changes of personality and behaviour. They may be of particular significance if it appears that a vulnerable person in a care home or a brain injury rehabilitation unit has been sexually abused by another resident or a member of staff. There may be issues as to fitness to be interviewed and/or fitness to plead and stand trial in an elderly person charged with sexual offences. This may be an issue in cases involving allegations of historical sexual abuse that predate the onset of cognitive deterioration.

(5) Substance misuse disorders

20.25 Table 20.2 shows how drugs of misuse can be categorized and Table 20.3 shows the range of disorders that can be associated with these. Combining the two lists produces a grid of bewildering complexity. A few combinations illustrate their relative frequency and importance in the investigation of sexual offending.

20.26 Alcohol intoxication is probably the most common and most important disorder to require attention. Voluntarily self-induced intoxication is not a defence. However, where the complainant or the defendant or both were intoxicated it will be more difficult to establish whether or not the complainant consented or what the defendant perceived as to consent.

20.27 So common are alcohol and opioid dependence that frequently the processes of arrest and detention in police stations interrupt alcohol or substance use and, without, or sometimes in spite of, medical management, precipitate withdrawal states in those who have a physical dependence on the drug. Whereas a mild opioid withdrawal state, no worse than a bad cold, may not affect the reliability of answers to questions, more severe withdrawal states can have serious implications for the reliability of police interviews. In such cases, challenges to the admissibility or reliability of interviews often call for assistance from experts as familiar with Code C of the Police and Criminal Evidence Act 1984 as with their profession's diagnostic manuals and who can detect, from the analysis of interview transcripts and audio or visual records, the subtle influences of abnormal mental states on thinking and speech.

20.28 A common scenario will soon be one in which the complainant or suspect has been under the influence of an unknown, little known, or barely understood, substance, known as a, 'legal high', which may have had a significant effect on their think-ing, mood, reactions, or behaviour. There is a confusing and daily changing list of substances believed to be, 'legal', although some are not, the effects of which are not limited to elevation of mood and which could be allocated to many of the cat-egories in Table 20.2. To make matters worse, although the problem is not limited to this scenario, the substance taken may not be the same as was advertised. If you find an expert who claims to be up to date on legal highs, they are fooling you. It is not possible.

Table 20.2 Drugs involved in psychoactive substance misuse

Group	Examples
Alcohol	
Sedatives and hypnotics	Benzodiazepines such as diazepam, temazepam
Opioids	Heroin, morphine, dihydrocodeine
Cannabinoids	Cannabis, 'skunk'
Stimulants	Cocaine, 'Crack', and amphetamines
Hallucinogens	LSD, hallucinogenic 'magic' mushrooms
Volatile solvents	Gas, glue
Anabolic steroids and other body-building drugs	
Tobacco	

Table 20.3 Levels of substance misuse disorders

Acute intoxication	Inebriation; being 'drunk,' or, 'stoned'
Harmful use	e.g. binge drinking
Dependence	• Psychological dependency • Physical dependency
Withdrawal states	• With/without delirium • With/without convulsions
Longer-term effects of substance misuse	• Psychotic disorder • Amnesic disorder • Personality change • Cognitive impairment • Flashbacks

(6) Psychotic disorders

Delusions and hallucinations are the hallmarks of the psychoses. A delusion is **20.29** a false belief held with total conviction and inappropriate to the patient's intel-ligence, social background, and sub-cultural beliefs. A hallucination is a false perception lacking an adequate basis in external stimuli. Hallucinations occur in various modalities such as the auditory modality (e.g. voices) and the visual modality (e.g. seeing animals or insects).

20.30 A broad distinction is made between psychoses in which the hallucinations or delusions or both reflect, or are congruent with, a pathologically altered mood state, for example, mania in which delusions of grandeur reflect the elated mood and depressive psychosis where the person hears voices calling them, 'wicked', 'evil', or 'Devil's disciple'. Where there is no major mood disorder and psychotic symptoms do not reflect prevailing mood, the psychoses are termed mood incongruent psychoses.

(a) Mood incongruent psychotic disorders

20.31 (i) **Delusional disorder** In delusional disorder, there are persistent and relatively fixed delusions that occur with mainly normal functioning. Commonly the delusions are of persecution, for example, a belief that agencies are conspiring against the person. There may be grandiose delusions, for example, the belief that the person is responsible for an invention that is going to change the course of mankind. In the context of domestic violence, and sometimes sexual violence, there may be delusions about the fidelity of a partner (sometimes misnamed, 'delusional jealousy'; the jealousy *is* real and far from delusional but the reason for it is delusional). Hallucinations are rare and, according to some, inconsistent with the diagnosis. Personality tends to be preserved.

20.32 Although such conditions may warrant investigation when they arise in the context of sexual offending, they are not incompatible with the ability of a complainant or witness to give reliable evidence and a defendant with a delusional disorder may be fit to plead and stand trial. Just because a man is deluded about being a great inventor does not mean that he is less reliable in his evidence about a sexual assault he has witnessed or suffered. If, however, he is heterosexual and labours under the delusional belief that he has to submit to various homosexual acts to be recruited to MI5, there may well be an issue as to his reliability as a complainant in a case of alleged homosexual assault.

20.33 Being deluded does not necessarily mean that someone is not fit to be interviewed, as the issue is whether or not the disorder might render a confession or evidence unreliable (*R v O'Brien*,[19]) or that someone is unfit to plead and stand trial, *R v Robertson*[20]). Although someone with delusional disorder may appear to the lay person, indeed to the educated professional, as 'insane', it does not follow that they are legally insane according to the M'Naghten Rules.[21] Even a man who rapes his 15-year-old daughter in the delusional belief that the mixing of their bodily fluids will enhance her resistance to sexually transmitted infections and protect her from

---

[19] [2000] All ER (D) 62.
[20] [1968] 3 All ER 557, CA.
[21] *M'Naghten's Case* (1843) 10 Cl & F 200.

extra-marital pregnancy, albeit that he is suffering from a defect of reasoning due to disease of the mind, may be aware of the nature and quality of the act and know that it is against the law.

(ii) Schizophrenia   In the most common form of schizophrenia, hallucinations   **20.34** and delusions have particular characteristics which enable schizophrenia to be distinguished from other non-organic psychoses, such as third-person auditory hallucinations, voices in the form of a running commentary, or the delusional belief that thoughts are being broadcast or transmitted. There are often other distinctive symptoms such as disorganization of the thought processes manifesting in incoherence of speech, idiosyncratic use of words, neologisms, that is, new words constructed by the patient, often forming part of a private language, and incongruous or inappropriate affect or mood. Schizophrenia is so common that it will occur coincidentally in both the victims of sexual crimes and the perpetrators. With emerging evidence that child sexual abuse can play a part in its aetiology, it may be particularly likely to affect, for example, complainants in historical child abuse cases. Although it raises issues as to the reliability of complainants and victims, it will seldom be the case that a person with schizophrenia is incapable of giving reliable evidence as to a sexual assault, although it may be necessary to seek an expert psychiatric opinion. Marked thought disorder could cause difficulties in understanding the evidence of alleged victims and alleged perpetrators who suffer from this condition.

R v Shulman,[22] is the case of a young man with schizophrenia and no criminal   **20.35** record, at least in the UK. He was convicted of the rape, false imprisonment, and section 47 assault of a prostitute, and was made the subject of an indeterminate sentence in prison, where without further treatment his schizophrenia became worse. His forename was Jacob. Study of the transcripts of his evidence, and his interruptions of the court proceedings, along with notes of conferences with counsel, revealed evidence of schizophrenic thought disorder. There was evidence to suggest that, having, heard, 'Rachel', whispered to him at a cash point, he believed, when he met his victim, that she was the Biblical Rachel whom Jacob had married, and that when he locked her in his flat, she was Penelope who was going to wait faithfully for her Odysseus to return. The Court of Appeal quashed his convictions, made a finding of unfitness to plead and unfitness to stand trial, and ordered his detention in hospital with restrictions on discharge.

(b) Mood congruent psychoses

(i) Mania and hypomania   Mania is characterized not only by particular delu-   **20.36** sions, such as religious and grandiose delusions, and sometimes by particularly pleasant hallucinations, such as heavenly music, but also by other symptoms which

---

[22] [2010] EWCA Crim 1034.

in many ways are the polar opposites of symptoms of depressive illness: elated instead of depressed mood; hyperactivity instead of slowness of movement; pressure of speech instead of delayed or slow speech; a subjective awareness of accelerated or crowded thinking instead of slowness or poverty of thought; subjectively enhanced clarity of thought instead of impaired concentration; disinhibition instead of lack of motivation; excesses of appetite, for drink as well as food, instead of impaired appetite; hypersexuality instead of reduced libido; inappropriate optimism instead of hopelessness, and so on.

20.37   In its milder form known as hypomania, frank psychotic symptoms are usually, or by convention, absent and the other symptoms milder. Usually there are episodes of depressive illness; when these occur along with manic and hypomanic episodes the diagnosis is known as bipolar I disorder. Where only depressive and hypomanic episodes occur, the diagnosis is known as bipolar II disorder.

20.38   Manic and hypomanic illnesses are important in sexual offending. The combination of hyperactivity, disinhibition, hyper-sexuality, and grandiose ideas/delusions can result in sexual behaviour which is out of character and may give rise to an allegation of sexual offending. Such manic illnesses may be obvious, although a defence of insanity may be difficult or impossible to prove. Hypomanic illnesses can be missed and although conviction may still be the outcome, it means that important mitigation is missed and more importantly so are opportunities for treatment and the prevention of further episodes.

20.39   **(ii) Depressive psychosis**   The cardinal symptoms of a depressive illness are the triad: depressed mood; loss of the capacity for enjoyment and loss of interest in usually pleasurable activities; and tiredness and lack of motivation. There is usually a combination of related symptoms: insomnia, pessimism and hopelessness, loss of appetite, loss of weight, impaired attention and concentration, reduced self-esteem and self-confidence, reduced libido, and suicidal ideas. In depressive psychosis what distinguishes psychotic from non-psychotic depressive disorders are hallucinations or delusions or both. The person may believe that they are responsible for world disasters. They may hear voices accusing them of being wicked. The severely depressed defendant needs careful assessment to ensure that as a result of their psychosis they do not admit to offences they have not committed.

20.40   **(iii) Other psychotic disorders**   The other commonly encountered psychotic disorder is schizoaffective disorder in which episodes have sufficient schizophrenic symptoms and manic or depressive symptoms to satisfy diagnoses of both schizophrenia and affective disorder, hence diagnoses of schizo-mania and schizo-depressive illness or, if manic and depressive symptoms are present in sufficient number, schizoaffective illness, mixed type.

(7) Non-psychotic disorders

(a) Depressive disorders

The symptoms of depressive disorders have been described in para 20.39. As well **20.41**
as making a distinction between psychotic and non-psychotic depressive illness,
an important distinction, at least in terms of treatment, is between those who
have 'biological' or 'somatic' symptoms of depression and those who do not. These
are: loss of interest or pleasure in activities which are normally enjoyable; lack
of emotional reactivity to normally pleasurable surroundings and events; early
morning waking; depression worse in the morning; psychomotor retardation or
agitation; loss of appetite; weight loss; and loss of libido. These symptoms are predictive of a response to physical treatments such as electroconvulsive therapy and
antidepressant drugs.

(b) Anxiety and phobic disorders

Anxiety disorders, which feature psychological symptoms, including worry, fear **20.42**
and foreboding, and physical symptoms, for example, blushing, choking, difficulty
breathing, and palpitations, are usually separated into generalized anxiety disorder, panic disorder and phobic disorders, such as agoraphobia and social phobia.

On paper and in the eyes of many psychiatrists, anxiety and depressive disorders **20.43**
seem clearly distinguishable. In practice, especially in people seen at the primary-
care level, anxiety and depressive symptoms often co-exist and to an extent that it
can be argued that the distinction is meaningless.

(c) Trauma and stressor-related disorders

Trauma such as sexual abuse or violence can have significant effects upon an indi- **20.44**
vidual's mental health and psychological functioning.[23] Therefore the effects of
traumatization are important. Experiencing or witnessing a serious sexual assault
will constitute a traumatic event and may give rise to a variety of symptoms. Also,
many perpetrators of this type of offence are victims of sexual abuse themselves,
that is they may have been suffering from the effects of traumatization at the time
of the offence.[24]

Individual responses to traumatic events vary from no reaction through to disa- **20.45**
bling distress that does not improve with the passage of time.[25] The nature of the
specific trauma is one factor that influences how people react; being the victim of

---

[23] Mason, F. in (2010) *Rook and Ward on Sexual Offences* (1st Suppl: Law and Practice, 4th Edn)
London: Sweet & Maxwell.

[24] Jespersen, A.F., Lalumiere, M.L., and Seto, M.C., 'Sexual abuse history among adult sex
offenders and non-sex offenders: A meta-analysis' (2009) 33 *Child Abuse and Neglect*, 179–92.

[25] See Hilarski and Wodarski, cited at n.13.

a serious sexual assault is particularly likely to result in a clinically significant reaction. Women are more likely than men to experience significant symptoms.

20.46   Symptoms commonly associated with a significant post-traumatic response include anxiety, hyperarousal, hypervigilance, depression, insomnia, decreased appetite, attempts to avoid potential reminders of the traumatic event, poor concentration, re-experiencing intrusive images (nightmares, flashbacks) of the traumatic event, feelings of guilt, and self-blame. Some of these symptoms are obviously more significant when it comes to considering the individual's ability to take part in the investigative process. Symptoms that are commonly associated with a diagnosis of post-traumatic stress disorder (PTSD) can affect the individual's ability to provide a coherent and consistent account, their ability to recall the details of what happened, and feelings of shame and inappropriate self-blame.

20.47   Confronting a traumatic event in the process of giving evidence can have a re-traumatizing effect on someone with PTSD. This could result in intrusive ideation, that is, distressing memories of the event, and in an increased level of arousal. The individual may seek to avoid going to court or retract aspects of their account. They may decide not to disclose the full extent of their experience in an attempt to manage the resulting arousal making them seem insincere and unreliable. However, the increase in arousal can help the individual recall details in full so this can facilitate justice.

20.48   The courts do, however, need to identify the presence of symptoms resulting from trauma in order to fully understand potentially misleading aspects of the witness' presentation and to allow the court to support the witness in an appropriately empathic manner.

D. Prescribed Drugs

20.49   The term, 'psychotropic drugs' refers to drugs intended to affect the functioning of the mind. However, other prescribed drugs can also affect the mind, sometimes in their prescribed doses, sometimes if taken in excess and sometimes if the prescribed dose is omitted.

20.50   Psychotropic drugs, classified very simply according to their primary action, fall into three categories: (a) antipsychotic drugs, of which some are sometimes also prescribed for mood-stabilization, sedation or impulse control, for example, chlorpromazine, risperidone, olanzapine; (b) antidepressants and mood stabilizers, so called because respectively they elevate depressed mood and prevent or reduce the risk of relapse or recurrence in affective disorders, such as citalopram and fluoxetine which are antidepressants, and lithium and sodium valproate which are mood stabilizers; and (c) sedative-hypnotics, drugs of, or related to, the benzodiazepine family, which are used, or are meant to be used, for the short-term treatment of acute anxiety and sleep disturbance, such as the sedatives diazepam, lorazepam and chlordiazepoxide and the hypnotics temazepam, zopiclone, and zaleplon (the 'z' drugs).

If witnesses or defendants are being prescribed psychotropic drugs, it is important **20.51** to establish that they are or were taking them as prescribed. It may matter that a witness, perhaps a complainant, or a defendant, was so anxious that they have not taken their medication before giving evidence.

The effects of missing one dose or more will depend on the drug. Missing one or **20.52** even a few doses of an antipsychotic or antidepressant drug may not make a significant difference. Missing one or a few doses of a benzodiazepine tranquilizer or hypnotic may result in a withdrawal state that has implications for the reliability of admissions, instructions to solicitors, or evidence at trial.

Many participants in criminal proceedings will be on prescribed medication. **20.53** Assiduous research may identify a rare side effect that could possibly have implications for their capacity to give evidence. Before instructing a clinical pharmacologist, toxicologist, or other medical expert, spending public money in search of a red herring, it is prudent to find out whether or not the side effect has been, or is being, suffered and indeed whether or not the drug has been, or is being, taken.

E. Conclusion

Justice for victims, perpetrators and alleged perpetrators of sexual offences depends **20.54** on the recognition of the psychiatric and psychological disorders and learning disorders that can influence the effective participation of complainants, witnesses, and defendants in criminal proceedings. Forensic psychologists and psychiatrists can provide invaluable assistance.

Further Reading

Gudjonsson, G.H. (2003) *The Psychology of Interrogations and Confessions. A Handbook*, Chichester: John Wiley & Sons Ltd.
Rix, K.J.B. (2011)*Expert Psychiatric Evidence*, London: RCPsych Publications.

Author Biographies

Dr Harry N.W. Wood, MSc, DClinPsy, is a Consultant Clinical Psychologist and Forensic Psychologist working in a low secure hospital and from The Grange consulting rooms in West Yorkshire. He completed his doctorate at University College London in 2002 and has subsequently worked in low, medium, and high secure hospitals, working in services for offenders with learning disabilities and in personality disorder services. He reports to the courts on a regular basis and receives instructions from both prosecution and defence. He is an affiliate lecturer at the University of Huddersfield and a Clinical Consultant to the editorial board of the *Journal of Criminal Psychology.*

Professor Keith J.B. Rix, BMedBiol (Hons), MPhil, LLM, MD, FRCPsych, Hon FFFLM, is a retired consultant forensic psychiatrist and a former consultant psychiatrist at HM Prison, Leeds. His forensic interests began in the 1960s when he lived in hostels with ex-offenders and assessed prisoners for admission. He established the Leeds Magistrates' Court Mental Health Assessment Scheme and the city's forensic psychiatry service. He provided expert evidence for thirty years, including evidence in capital cases in the Caribbean and Africa, and he is the author of *Expert Psychiatric Evidence.* He was a lecturer at De Montfort Law School, Leicester, and Visiting Professor of Medical Jurisprudence, Institute of Medicine, University of Chester.

21

NEUROLOGICAL MEMORY DISORDERS

Nigel North and Simon B.N. Thompson

A. Introduction

Human memory is a complex entity that has until recently been poorly understood **21.01** in many areas of academic and professional study. Recent advances in the field of neurosciences, cognitive psychology and neuro-imaging have resulted in a more comprehensive understanding of disorders of memory. The role of human memory in the human psyche and human behaviour is vital. Almost all aspects of cognitive function rely to a greater or lesser extent on some contribution of memory.

B. The Neuroanatomical Basis of Memory

21.02 The study of lesions or damage in the brain has been used to understand the neuroanatomical basis of memory. Individuals who have sustained damage to their brain have been studied and information has been gathered regarding the effects on memory function.

21.03 Advances in brain scanning and imaging have resulted in a greater understanding of the neural basis for many areas of cognitive functioning including memory. Techniques such as Positron Emission Tomography (PET) and Functional Magnetic Resonance Imaging (fMRI) have enabled us to measure the activity of specific neural units in specific areas of the brain.

21.04 The brain consists of a huge network of communicating nerve cells (neurons) which transmit impulses using neurotansmitters. The transmission is both chemical and electrical. Memory probably starts as an activation of neurons which encode information using different brain structures.

21.05 Current models of memory stress the importance of modular systems within the brain which works in an integrated manner. There is no single locus in the brain where all memories reside and many parts of the brain are involved in acquiring, processing, encoding, storing, and retrieving information.

21.06 However, the hippocampus is crucial because it forms part of a structure known as the medial temporal lobe and is important for remembering new episodes or event. Some models regard the brain as a series of functional zones arranged in a hierarchy.[1] Moving up from a very basic level of sensory motor processing are 'convergence zones' that receive input from sensory motor regions and code for 'coherent entities' such as entire objects.

21.07 At the top of the hierarchy are zones that code for the co-occurrence of entities that constitute an entire event.

21.08 Areas related to memory include: cerebellum, amygdala, basal ganglia, frontal lobes, temporal lobes, parietal lobes, and the occipital lobe.[2] Damage, through disease or injury, may occur in any or all of these areas leading to effects on memory.

---

[1] Baddeley, A.D. 'Working memory' (1992) 255 *Science*, 556–9; Baddeley, A.D. and Hitch, G.J. 'Working Memory' in Bower, G.A. (ed.) (1974) *Recent advances in Learning and Motivation*, New York: Academic Press, viii, 47–89.

[2] Baddeley, A.D (1992), cited at n.1.

C. The Psychology of Memory

(1) Memory types

(i) Short-term and long-term memory

Short-term memory, now elaborated into the concept of working memory,[3] is the **21.09** system which allows a person to remember a new telephone number whilst dialling it as long as there are no distractions. Long-term memory, on the other hand, allows a familiar telephone number to be remembered from day to day and year to year.

(ii) Semantic and episodic memory

Different types of knowledge appear to be stored differently. A distinction drawn ini- **21.10** tially between episodic and semantic memories, and more latterly, a contrast between procedural and declarative memories, has gained acceptance. Episodic memories are for particular events, while semantic memories are for 'context-free' facts. For example, knowing the components of one's breakfast is an episodic memory: knowing that the word 'breakfast' means a morning meal is a semantic memory.[4]

(iii) Declarative and procedural memory

Both semantic and episodic memories may be subsumed under this heading which **21.11** represents the memory for facts. Procedural memory is a memory for skills and routines and may include some types of sensory stimuli. For example, knowing how to drive a car is a procedural memory, knowing how the engine works is declarative memory.

(iv) Autobiographical memory

Recollections from the life of an individual are stored in autobiographical mem- **21.12** ory, based on a combination of episodic and semantic memory. Autobiographical memory helps an individual to use past personal experiences as a way of solving current problems, developing and maintaining social bonds through shared experiences, and creating and maintaining a coherent self-identity over time.

(v) Sustained and selective attention

A specific component of the memory process is the ability to attend to stimuli. **21.13** Attention needs to be sustained at times, and at other times needs to be able to

---

3 Ibid.
4 Nyberg, L., Backman, L., Erngrund, K., Olofsson, U., and Nilsson, L.G., 'Age differences in episodic memory, semantic memory, and priming: relationships to demographic, intellectual, and biological factors' (1996) 51(4) *Journal of Gerontology*, 234–40.

move or shift, re-engage and disengage. If there are problems with attention then there will be problems with memory.

(2) Structure of memory

21.14   There have been many models of memory and the way in which it is structured. These models have attempted to integrate the different types of memory and have tried to explain how the various components are related, in order to explain both 'normal' and 'abnormal' memory functioning.

21.15   A particular problem in explaining memory is the relationship between short-term and long-term memory systems. Baddeley and colleagues proposed a model to help us understand the relationship between long-term and short-term memory.[5] It was proposed that the concept of short-term memory should be replaced by the term '*working memory*'.

21.16   Working memory was assumed to have an 'attentional controller' called the 'central executive' which functions to co-ordinate and schedule mental operations. This incorporates the notion of a 'scratch pad' system which is able to hold and manipulate information simultaneously.

21.17   A cluster of peripheral systems support the 'central executive system' including the 'Articulatory Loop System' and the 'Visuospatial Sketchpad', responsible for recycling verbally decodable information, and temporary storage and manipulation of visual and spatial information, respectively.

21.18   The central executive system devotes varying degrees of processing resources such that we can talk about one topic whilst remembering statements about another.

21.19   The 'working memory' model not only explains how this aspect of memory works but also explains how information can be consolidated and transferred to a long-term store to be retrieved when necessary. 'Working Memory', therefore, holds a limited amount of information for a very short period of time in an accessible state. Through a process of rehearsal and manipulation, information undergoes a process of consolidation and this is then stored in long-term memory.[6]

21.20   Cellular and molecular changes take place rapidly in the sets of neurons that constitute the brain network and are reorganized over a much longer period.

21.21   The functioning of memory may be altered by a wide range of illnesses, injuries, and psychological conditions which may interrupt the process at various levels.

---

[5] Baddeley and Hitch (1974), cited at n.1.
[6] Krishnan, K.R., 'Organic basis of depression in the elderly' (1991) 42 *Annual Review in Medicine*, 261–6.

D. Common Memory Disorders and How
They May Manifest Themselves in an Individual

(1) Memory and 'normal' ageing

Ageing brings with it changes, not just in an individual's appearance but also to **21.22** the higher mental functions or cognitive functions. Memory can also be affected, sometimes because the individual has failed to receive information correctly or sometimes because it can no longer be effectively encoded or stored.[7] The effect of ageing on memory, particularly episodic memory, is very often one of the first cognitive functions to be noticed by others and can cause considerable distress to the individual and to relatives, close friends, and carers.

Deterioration in memory functioning is characteristic of dementia but it can also **21.23** represent the decline in memory seen in the ageing process. Generally, older people can learn as much as younger people but more time is needed for them to achieve the same level of learning as they cannot process and 'absorb' information as quickly as younger people.[8] Sometimes this speed reduction becomes noticeable and marked and may accompany the onset of depression.[9] If memory has changed noticeably and continues to do so it can be an indication of a dementing process, particularly if it is accompanied by other failures in cognitive function.

Intellectual decline associated with ageing is noticeable in four areas of cognitive **21.24** ability:

1. The primary or working memory capacity of older people differs little from younger adults,[10] except when the amount of material to be remembered exceeds the normal primary storage capacity of six or seven items.
2. Diminished ability for abstract and complex conceptualization is a common problem.[11]
3. Mental inflexibility and the ability to change mental set may become an issue with age.[12]
4. General behavioral slowing affects a range of cognitive functions as well as memory.[13]

---

[7] Nyberg, et al., cited at n.4.
[8] Salthouse, T.A. and Meinz, E.J., 'Ageing, inhibition, working memory, and speed' (1995) 50(6) *Journal of Gerontology*, 297–306.
[9] Krishnan (1991), cited at n.6.
[10] Larner, A.J., 'Neurological signs of ageing' in Sinclair, A., Morley, J.E., and Vellas, B. (eds) (2012) *Pathy's principles and practice of geriatric medicine*, 5th edn, Chichester: John Wiley & Sons Ltd.
[11] Ibid.
[12] Caine, D. and Watson, D.G., 'Neuropsychological and neuropathological sequelae of cerebral anoxia: a critical review' (2000) 6 *Journal of the International Neuropsychological Society*, 86–99.
[13] Larner (2012), cited at n.10.

21.25 Longitudinal studies of cognitive function indicate that there is considerable variability in 'normal' older adults across different skills. The concept of 'normal' in ageing, therefore, may be difficult to define and may be subject to interpretation across different cultures, different environments, and between genders.[14] Clearly, there needs to be considerable thought given to the definition of 'normal' when we are trying to make diagnose pathology or impairment.

(2) Amnesic syndrome and sub-types

21.26 'Global Amnesia' refers to a marked and defined deficit in memory in the context of well-preserved intelligence.

21.27 People with amnesias demonstrate normal performance on tasks of immediate memory and working memory.[15]

21.28 Global amnesia occurs when the medial temporal lobes as well as a number of other subsidiary structures such as the diencephalon and basal forebrain are injured or damaged. This damage may be caused by traumatic vascular and disease processes such as anoxia, encephalitis, cerebrovascular accidents, Korsakoff's syndrome, and rupture and/or repair of aneurysms in of one particular artery in the brain (anterior communicating artery).

(3) Korsakoff syndrome

21.29 This condition results for a depletion in a particular vitamin (thiamine) usually resulting from the overuse of alcohol. The condition is characterized by an acute phase in which the patient is disorientated, confused, lacking in any motivation and unable to maintain coherent conversation. Following this acute stage the individual is left with a dense amnesia; frequently, he or she provides a history which is a confabulation. The sufferer will have profound and global learning difficulties. They may be able to repeat information without any delay but the presence of interference or delay of only a few seconds will result in impaired performance on recall. There is usually a retrograde memory loss often extending back many years.[16]

21.30 It is unlikely that people with this condition will recover completely although there can be substantial recovery over a period of years, as long as the individual refrains from alcohol. However, most authors agree that a percentage of people, even with abstinence, will not improve from this condition.[17]

---

[14] Ibid.
[15] Kopelman, M.D., 'Remote and autobiographical memory, temporal context memory and frontal atrophy in Korsakoff and Alzheimer patients' (1989) 27 *Neuropsychologia*, 437–60.
[16] Ibid.
[17] Victor, M., Adams, R. D., and Collins, G.H. (1971) *The Wernicke-Korsakoffe Syndrome*, Philadelphia: F.A. Davis.

(4) Herpes Simplex Encephalitis

This condition occurs as a result of a virus which causes haemorrhagic lesions **21.31**
in the brain. The person initially experiences a 'flu-like' illness which then
leads on to profound confusion and disorientation. The area of damage centres
around the hippocampus and the sufferer is often left with a dense amnesia.
They may find it difficult to acquire any new knowledge either verbally or
visually although they may have completely preserved IQ. A patient known
as S.S., for example, experienced dense memory loss as a result of infection
from the Herpes Simplex Encephalitis (HSE) virus. He was not able to form
any new declarative memories and was unable to retain any episodic information regarding significant family members. He also failed to acquire any new
semantic knowledge. Despite his dense amnesia he retained a full scale IQ
of 130 (superior intelligence range) some thirty years after the onset of his
amnesia.[18]

(5) Anoxia

Anoxia occurs as a result of reduced oxygen to the brain. This may be the result of **21.32**
factors such as cardiac or respiratory arrest, strangulation or hanging, drowning,
or carbon monoxide poisoning.

People who have been anoxic may demonstrate problems with memory as the hip- **21.33**
pocampus is particularly vulnerable to insult. The greater the degree of oxygen
deprivation, the greater is the degree of cognitive impairment. A wide range of
memory impairment may be seen after anoxic injury.

However, this type of injury is often widespread and non-selective. Lesions may **21.34**
be found in many areas of the brain and therefore people may present with more
generalized cognitive deficits and changes in behaviour and personality.[19]

(6) Retrograde amnesia

Retrograde amnesia is a loss of memory for events that occurred before the onset of **21.35**
brain injury or illness. The pattern of memory loss may be very variable, for example, the period of memory loss may be relatively short such as a few hours or days,
or may be very extensive. In the latter scenario an individual may have an inability
to recall events for several decades before an event. It can be very difficult to make
an accurate assessment of retrograde amnesia and formal tests have been devised to
aid in the assessment of this condition.

---

[18] O'Connor, M. and Verfaellie, M., 'The amnesic syndrome: Overview and subtypes' in
Baddeley, A.D., Kopelman, M.D., and Wilson, B.A. (2005) *Memory disorders for clinicians.*
Chichester: John Wiley & Sons Ltd.
[19] Caine and Watson (2000), cited at n.12.

(7) Post-traumatic amnesia

21.36 Post-traumatic amnesia refers to the early period of time following an injury to the head. It often refers to the emergence from coma in which there is difficulty in recording and retrieving information relating to daily events. Post-traumatic amnesia is often used as a measure of the severity of head injury. It has also been found to predict the presence and chronicity of memory impairment, for example durations of post-traumatic amnesia of longer than two weeks are associated with long-term memory deficits.[20]

21.37 Post-traumatic amnesia is often evaluated by asking a person to describe their first memory after an accident and to identify when their memory resumed continuously. This retrospective approach may be inaccurate due to problems with confabulation and/or difficulty with monitoring reality. This latter issue may be a problem when individuals have spent some time in a hospital intensive care ward or been given large amounts of analgesic medication following an accident. Often talking to family and friends or using formal assessment tools such as the 'Galveston Orientation and Amnesia Test (GOAT) may be useful to assess this condition.[21]

(8) Transient memory loss

21.38 Transient memory loss manifests as a sudden attack of impaired anterograde memory accompanied by repetitive questioning and comments. The person is incapable of retaining information regarding the environment around them and they may be disorientated for time and place. Confusingly, however, they are able to use contextual cues in their environment and general world knowledge in order to make inferences regarding their situation. When facing a failure in their memory the individual may guess what they should remember.

21.39 The episodes of transient global amnesia are brief in duration lasting less than twenty-four hours, with no recollection of the amnesic period following its resolution.

21.40 In about one third of people the condition is triggered by a precipitating event such as stress, extreme physical exertion, or exposure to extreme heat or cold. Other conditions have also usually been ruled out as causing the condition, such as head injury, epilepsy, drug or alcohol intoxication or stroke.[22] This is a rather confusing condition and sufferers may be viewed, incorrectly, as malingering or faking the condition due to its transitory nature.

---

[20] Brooks, N., McKinlay, W., Symington, C., Beattie, A., and Campsie, L., 'Return to work within the first seven years of severe head injury' (1987) 1 *Brain Injury*, 5–19.

[21] Levin, H.S., O'Donnell, V.M., and Grossman, R.G., 'The Galveston Orientation and Amnesia Test' (1979) 167 *Journal of Nervous and Mental Disease*, 675–84.

[22] Hodges, J.R. and Warlow, C.P., 'Syndromes of transient amnesia: towards a classification. A study of 153 cases' (1990) 53 *Journal of Neurology, Neurosurgery and Psychiatry*, 834–43.

E. Unusual Memory Disorders

(1) Psychogenic amnesia and functional memory loss

Psychogenic amnesia refers to memory impairments due to psychologically based **21.41** factors such as extreme depression or 'pseudodementia'. It may encompass individuals with prolonged memory impairment or transient and discrete episodes of memory loss. These transient amnesias may be specific to certain situations and events such as amnesia for an offence[23] or amnesia for rape or childhood sexual abuse.[24]

The term 'dissociative amnesia' is often applied to situations in which there is a **21.42** brief, discrete episode of memory loss following a traumatic event in the personal history of an individual.[25] In contrast, psychogenic amnesia or psychogenic fugue state is a condition in which the individual has a sudden onset of a loss of all autobiographical memories which may include their own identity. The individual may be found wandering around with no recollection of who they are or what they are doing. This condition may occur in the context of extreme stress, or depression.[26]

This is a very controversial area, particularly in relation to offenders. It is a highly **21.43** specialist field and requires appropriate, in-depth assessment of the individual in order to ascertain the relative contributions of psychological factors, organic factors, and social factors in relation to the condition. The area of controversy, not surprisingly, involves the detection of malingering for which there are now sophisticated assessment approaches available.[27]

F. Cognitive Assessment

In assessing memory problems it is important to try to build up as comprehensive **21.44** picture as possible of the nature and extent of these difficulties. This may include a combination of face-to-face interviews with the individual involved, interviews

---

[23] Pyszora, N., Barker, A., and Kopelman, M.D., 'Amnesia for criminal offences: a study of life sentence prisoners' (2003) 14 *Journal of Forensic Psychiatry and Psychology*, 475–90.

[24] Goodman, G.S., Ghetti, S., Quas, J.A., Edelstein, R.S. et al., 'A prospective study of memory for child sexual abuse' (2003) 14(2) *Psychological Science*, 113–18.

[25] American Psychiatric Association (2013) *Diagnostic and statistical manual of mental disorders*, 5th edn, Washington, DC: APA.

[26] McKay, C.M. and Kopelman, M.D., 'Psychogenic amnesia: when memory complaints are medically unexplained' (2009) 15 *Advances in Psychiatric Treatment*, 152–8.

[27] Gudjonsson, G. and Young, S. 'Suboptimal effort and malingering' in Young, S., Kopelman, M., and Gudjonsson G. (eds) (2009) *Forensic Neuropsychology in Practice. A Guide to Assessment and Legal Processes*, Oxford: Oxford University Press, 267–99; Thompson, S.B.N., 'Malingering and deception: Treated patients seeking compensation for injuries and trauma in cognitive rehabilitation settings' (2003) 21(2) *Journal of Cognitive Rehabilitation*, 6–10; Thompson, S.B.N., 'Effortless effort: current views on assessing malingering litigants in neuropsychological assessments' (2011) 2(7) *Rehabilitation*, 1–5. Doi: WMC002014.

with family and friends, the completion of memory questionnaires looking at the type of memory problems reported but also their behavioural effects, and finally a battery of cognitive assessments.

(1) Interviewing the subject and associates

21.45 The initial assessment of memory problems in an individual is usually undertaken by asking the person concerned about their memory. Questions regarding the type of memory difficulties an individual may have, their history, and the impact they may have on the life of a person.

21.46 This can be further explored by asking a close friend, relative, or carer of that person about any memory difficulties they have noticed. This approach can be helpful, particularly in situations where there is a lack of insight into the presence of memory problems.

21.47 It may become apparent on interview that memory difficulties do exist. There may be repetition of information, obvious confabulation or clear evidence that material is being forgotten during the conversation. There may be awareness of the difficulties by the individual or a lack of awareness or insight.

(2) Questionnaires and rating scales

21.48 Following on from the interview there are a number of questionnaires and rating scales that may be helpful in gaining greater understanding of the individual's memory function. A number of such scales exist, such as the Neurobehavioural Functioning Inventory,[28] The Cognitive Symptoms Checklists,[29] The Cognitive Behaviour Rating Scales,[30] and the Everyday Memory Questionnaire.[31]

21.49 These scales have been specifically designed to provide an insight into the type of memory problems arising. They are designed to be completed by the individual with memory problems and in some of them the scale can also be completed by family or friends giving a more comprehensive picture of perceived memory functioning.

(3) Psychometric testing

21.50 In many situations a more formal assessment of memory functioning is required and a wide range of standardized tests are available for this purpose. Access to

---

[28] Kreutzer, J.S., Seel, R.T., and Marwitz, J.H. (1999) *Neurobehavioural Functioning Inventory*, San Antonio, Texas: The Psychological Corporation.

[29] O'Hara, C., Harrell, M., Bellingrath, E., and Lisicia, K. (1993) *Cognitive Symptoms Checklists*. Odessa, Florida: Psychological Assessment Resources Inc.

[30] Williams, J.M. (1987) *Cognitive Behaviour Rating Scales Manual, Research Edition*. Florida, Odessa: Psychological Assessment Resources Inc.

[31] Sundeland, A., Harris, J.F., and Gleave, J., 'Memory failures in everyday life following severe head injury' (1984) 6 *Journal of Clinical Neuropsychology*, 127–42.

psychometric testing is closely controlled and, therefore, an appropriately qualified individual will need to administer, score, and interpret these tests.

The range of tests available may examine different aspects of memory function- **21.51** ing. The Rivermead Behavioural Memory Test,[32] for example, is designed to establish the level of an individual's procedural memory functioning but does not provide much information about specific memory deficits.

More specific tests, such as the Wechsler Memory Scale,[33] allows for the identifi- **21.52** cation of visual or auditory memory deficits, the individual's ability to learn new items and visuospatial deficits. There are also tests available for specific groups of people. For example, the Middlesex Elderly Assessment of Mental State[34] is a useful screening tool for dementia. An in-depth discussion of the range of tests available is beyond the scope of this chapter and can be found elsewhere.[35]

(4) Assessing other areas of cognitive function

In addition to memory, there are a number of other areas of cognitive function- **21.53** ing they may need to be examined using a variety of assessment techniques. These other areas of cognitive functioning may include attention, perception, language, executive functioning, speed of thinking, mood, and insight. When assessing individuals with memory problems the issues of malingering or 'lying' must also be considered.

G. Impact of Mood on Memory

(1) Anxiety and depression

Many people who are experiencing problems with memory may also have diffi- **21.54** culties with anxiety, or depression, or both. Sometimes memory problems can be explained by the presence of mood disorder which can have an adverse effect on cognition. But even in situations where there is a clear and demonstrable problem with memory perhaps due to some organic factor this situation can be further exacerbated by the presence of anxiety or depression.

In fact, depression can lead to enormous difficulties in assessing whether a person **21.55** has a dementia-type disorder or a depressive disorder. Individuals can wrongly be

---

[32] Wilson, B.A., Cockburn, J., and Baddeley, A. (1991) *Rivermead Behavioural Memory Test Manual*, 2nd edn, Bury St Edmunds: Thames Valley Test Co.

[33] Wechsler, D. (2009) *Wechsler memory Scale-Fourth edition. Administration and scoring manual*, San Antonio, Texas: The Psychological Corporation, Pearson Inc.

[34] Golding, E. (1989) *The Middlesex Assessment of Mental State*, Bury St Edmunds: Thames Valley Test Company.

[35] Lezak, M.D. (2012) *Neuropsychological Assessment*, 5th edn, Oxford: Oxford University Press.

diagnosed with dementia, when in fact they have a depressive disorder and the term 'pseudodementia' is often used in this situation.[36]

21.56 Whilst there is much debate concerning the exact nature of cognitive difficulties arising from both anxiety and depression it is clear that people with mood disorders do show a range of difficulties with their memory.

(2) Post-traumatic stress disorder

21.57 Post-traumatic stress disorder can occur following trauma;[37] this may include being the victim of violent crime, a disaster, road traffic collision, and even some medical procedures.[38] It is characterized by re-experiencing the traumatic event through nightmares, flashbacks, and intrusive thoughts, a marked avoidance of thinking, talking, or reminders of the event, and symptoms of persistent arousal such as an exaggerated startle response, feelings of nervousness, and anxiety and irritability.

21.58 In addition, however, there are a range of cognitive difficulties that may occur such as difficulties recalling aspects of the traumatic event itself, problems with anterograde memory, problems with attention and concentration, and problems with autobiographical memory.[39]

21.59 A thorough assessment of the individual is required in order to assess the relative contribution of organic factors to memory problems and the contribution of post-traumatic stress disorder, if it is present.

(3) Recognition of anxiety, depression, and post-traumatic stress disorder

21.60 Anxiety and depression represent an enduring problem rather than a transitory one. Individuals who develop an anxiety disorder will be constantly tense, worried, and on edge. They feel that something 'awful' is about to happen to them, they find it extremely hard to sit at ease and feel relaxed, and feel restless for much of the time. They will frequently experience feelings of panic in which their heart will race, they may find they are hyperventilating and they feel that the world is pervasively dangerous. They are often plagued by fears and worries and the range of feelings they experience interfere with their daily life. If these symptoms have been present for a month or longer then this is regarded as being a significant anxiety disorder.

---

[36] Fischer, P. 'The spectrum of depressive pseudodementia' (1996) 47 *Journal of Neural Transmission*, supplement, 193–203.

[37] American Psychiatric Association (2013), cited at n.25.

[38] Taylor, S. (2006) *Clinician's guide to PTSD: A cognitive-Behavioural approach*, New York: The Guilford Press, 3–23.

[39] Ibid., at 24–40.

Similarly, a depressive disorder is characterized by continuous low mood or sad- **21.61**
ness, feelings of hopelessness and helplessness, low self-esteem, frequent tearful-
ness, feelings of guilt, irritability, loss of drive or motivation, difficulty making
decisions and loss of pleasure in life. Symptoms such as these which have been
present for a month or longer constitute a significant depressive disorder.

It is the continuous nature of the symptoms that distinguish anxiety and depres- **21.62**
sion from feeling sad or worried; these last two states are transient and do not
interfere with daily life.[40]

Screening tools have been developed in order to help in the detection of anxiety **21.63**
and depression. Scales such as the Hospital Anxiety and Depression Scale have
been developed in order to detect states of anxiety and depression.[41]

The symptoms of post-traumatic stress disorder have been described in para 21.57. **21.64**
Screening tools also exist for the detection of this condition such as the Revised
Impact of Events Scale.[42] This is a short scale which assesses three main components
of post-traumatic stress disorder: avoidance, intrusion, and hyperarousal.

H. Neurological Conditions Affecting Memory

(1) Intellectual disability

Intellectual disability is a term used internationally and corresponds with the **21.65**
term 'learning disability',[43] frequently used in health and social care contexts
in the UK. People with learning disability may have a wide range of cognitive
difficulties. For an individual to be considered as having a learning disability, a
number of criteria have to be met. These include a significant impairment of intellectual functioning, a significant impairment of adaptive or social functioning
and an age of onset within the developmental period before adulthood. It also
includes an IQ score of less than 70 (two standard deviations below the population mean).[44]

There is evidence to suggest that many people with intellectual disability, when com- **21.66**
pared to the general population, are at greater risk of experiencing significant impairments in visual and verbal memory and executive functioning and have a more limited

---

[40] American Psychiatric Association (2013), cited at n.25.
[41] Zigmond, A.S. and Snaith, R.P., 'The Hospital Anxiety and Depression Scale' (1983) 67 *Acta Psychiatrica Scandinavica*, 361–70.
[42] Horowitz, M.J., Wilner, M., and Alverez, W., 'Impact of events scale: A measure of subjective stress.' (1979) 41 *Psychosomatic Medicine*, 209–18.
[43] Thompson, S.B.N. (1993) *Eating disorders: a guide for health professionals.* London: Chapman and Hall, 195.
[44] World Health Organization (1992) *ICD-10: Classification of Mental and Behavioural Disorders: Clinical Descriptions and Diagnostic Guidelines*, Geneva: World Health Organization.

understanding of, and ability to use, language.[45] They may also be at increased risk of additional difficulties, such as epilepsy, autistic spectrum problems, and other mental health difficulties. They are also more likely to be socially disadvantaged.[46]

21.67 It is important in working with individuals who have an intellectual disability to obtain a comprehensive assessment of their cognitive abilities. Due to the heterogeneity of people with intellectual disability it is not possible to make generalizations and assessment of each individual person is important in understanding any cognitive difficulties they may have.

(2) Dementias

21.68 The diagnosis of dementia that is generally accepted by clinical psychologists and psychiatrists includes demonstrable evidence of impairment in short-term and long-term memory. Impairment in short-term memory (i.e. the inability to learn new information) may be indicated by an inability to remember three objects after five minutes. Long-term memory impairment (i.e. the inability to remember information that was known in the past) may be indicated by an inability to remember past, personal information, for example, what happened yesterday or one's birthplace.[47]

21.69 An individual with dementia may demonstrate other changes or difficulties:

1. impairment of short-term and long-term memory;
2. impairment of abstract thinking;
3. impaired judgement;
4. disturbances of higher cortical function (e.g. aphasia, apraxia, agnosia, constructional difficulty); or
5. personality change.[48]

21.70 Dementia is commonly regarded as a single disease, when in fact it is a syndrome with a number of different sub-types. People often think of dementia as being due to Alzheimer's-type dementia, which requires a specific diagnosis to be made. Individuals with this type of dementia appear to pass through several stages which include an initial stage of 'forgetfulness' often accompanied by anxiety,[49] followed by increasing memory loss for recent events[50] and finally a severe disorientation

---

[45] Thompson, S.B.N. (2006) *Dementia and memory: a handbook for students and professionals*, Aldershot: Ashgate, 57.

[46] Murphy, G.H. and Clare, I.C.H., 'Adults' capacity to make legal decisions' in D. Carson and R. Bull (eds) (2003) *Handbook of Psychology in Legal Contexts*, 2nd edn, Chichester: John Wiley & Sons Ltd, 31–66.

[47] American Psychiatric Association (2000), cited at n.25.

[48] Ibid.

[49] Greene, J.D.W., Hodges, J.R., and Baddeley, A.D., 'Autobiographical memory and executive function in early dementia of the Alzheimer type' (1995) 33 *Neuropsychologia*, 1647–70.

[50] Goldblum, M.C., Gomez, C.M., and Dalla Barba, G., 'The influence of semantic and perceptual encoding on recognition memory in Alzheimer's disease' (1998) 36(8) *Neuropsychologia*, 717–29.

and a loss of motivation, purpose, and willpower.[51] Sufferers of dementia may also demonstrate disorders of mood such as anxiety and depression.[52]

Clearly, an individual with dementia, whatever the type, may have significant **21.71** problems with memory which may have particular implications in terms of giving evidence.

(3) Stroke

Strokes may affect any aspect of cognitive functioning, depending on which part of **21.72** the brain is affected. Memory difficulties, however, are a frequently reported problem following a stroke. A stroke may directly affect memory by damaging brain areas associated with memory processes such as the limbic system or indirectly affecting other brain areas upon which memory is dependent such as the attentional system.

Episodic memory (the period of time before and after a stroke) may be severely **21.73** affected. This may lead an individual to have significant problems in remembering specific time periods in their life. They may also have problems resulting in problems with visuospatial memory resulting in great difficulty in the recognition or the recalling faces. Individuals following stroke, may be left with verbal and non-verbal memory difficulties, attentional difficulties, or problems with executive function.[53]

(4) Head injury

Head injury is a complex phenomenon. The consequences of mild traumatic brain **21.74** injury can impede physical, emotional, social, marital, and vocational functioning. Because of the nature of their deficits this group of people may become 'lost' to health and social care and remain in the community trying to cope with their difficulties which can have severe adverse effects on their families.[54]

The most common cognitive problems following mild and moderate head injury **21.75** include speed of information processing and divided attention as well as difficulties with slowed reaction time, short-term and long-term verbal memory and visuospatial short-term and long-term memory. After severe head injury the cognitive impairments tend to be widespread, have a significant adverse effect on the daily life of individuals and are usually permanent.[55] The cognitive problems cannot be

---

[51] Baddeley, A.D., Bressi, S., Della Sala, S., and Logie, R., 'The decline of working memory in Alzheimer's disease' (1991) 114 *Brain*, 2521–42.

[52] Thompson, S.B.N. (1997) *Dementia: a guide for health care professionals*, Aldershot: Arena.

[53] Lincoln, N.B., Kneebone, I.I., Macniven, J.A.B., and Morris, R.C. (2012) *The Psychological Management of Stroke*, Chichester, John Wiley & Sons Ltd, 87–108.

[54] British Society of Rehabilitation Medicine (2003) *Rehabilitation following acquired brain injury: National clinical guidelines*, London: Royal College of Physicians.

[55] King, N.S. and Tyerman, A., 'Neuropsychological presentation and treatment of head injury and traumatic brain damage' in Halligan, P.W., Kischka, U., and Marshall, J.C., (eds) (2003) *Handbook of Clinical Neuropsychology*, Oxford: Oxford University Press, 487–505.

seen in isolation from the array of social, occupational, and behavioural difficulties that may arise.

(5) Neurological disease

21.76 There are a wide range of neurological diseases which may have a significant impact on memory functioning and excellent reviews can be found in a number of recent works.[56] Some of the common neurological problems that have an adverse effect on memory include Parkinson's disease, which has been shown to have an adverse effect on autobiographical memory,[57] epilepsy and its treatment which may affect a wide range of memory functions depending on the type of seizures being experienced,[58] and multiple sclerosis which has been found to have specific impairments in long-term verbal and non-verbal memory.[59]

21.77 In addition, there are a wide range of medical conditions and their treatment which may result in impairment of memory functioning. There are some excellent texts available regarding this area.[60] Certainly, new research has highlighted some interesting results in terms of medical/psychiatric conditions and memory deficits. Analgesia or having undergone surgery, have for example, been shown to lead to a specific type of amnesia[61] and eating disorders have been shown to lead to wide-ranging cognitive dysfunction.[62]

I. Insight and Awareness of Deficit

(1) Recognition of loss of insight

21.78 Many people who have problems with their memory resulting from injury or illness are acutely aware of their problems and difficulties. Some, however, have little or no insight into their memory difficulties. It may be tempting to conclude that they have failed to remember they have a deficit; however, it is clear from a number of studies

[56] Larner, A.J. (2013) *Neuropsychological Neurology: The neurocognitive impairments of neurological disorders*, 2nd edn, Cambridge: Cambridge University Press.
[57] Souchay, C. and Smith, S.J., 'Autobiographical memory in Parkinson's disease: A retrieval deficit' (2013) 7 *Journal of Neuropsychology*, 164–78.
[58] Ibid.
[59] Rao, S.M., Bernadin, L., and Unversagt, F., 'Cognitive dysfunction in multiple sclerosis: frequency, patterns and predictions' (1991) 41 *Neurology*, 685–91.
[60] Anthony, D., Flemminger, S., Kopelman, M., Lovestone, S., and Mellors, J. (2012) *Lishman's organic psychiatry: A textbook of neuropsychiatry*, Chichester: Wiley-Blackwell.
[61] Kemp, S., Agostinis, A., House, A., and Coughlan, A.K., 'Analgesia and other causes of amnesia that mimic post-traumatic amnesia (PTA): A cohort study' (2010) 4 *Journal of Neuropsychology*, 231–36.
[62] Zakzanis, K.K., Campbell, Z., and Polsinelli, A., 'Quantitative evidence for distinct cognitive impairment in anorexia nervosa and bulimia nervosa' (2010) 4 *Journal of Neuropsychology*, 89–106.

that some people have a loss of insight that cannot be accounted for by a failure to remember.[63]

If individuals lack insight into their memory difficulties then this creates a number **21.79** of difficulties in their ability to act as a witness and recall information. Insight is most easily assessed by the use of self-report measures (which have been described in paras 21.45 to 21.49). If these scales are completed by the individual with suspected memory problems and also completed by a close family member then the scores can be compared. This comparison may demonstrate agreement or disagreement between the raters or it may reveal that an individual underestimates the severity of a memory disorder whilst recognizing that there are some difficulties. It must also be remembered that insight may change over time and that an individual who lacks insight may regain this over time.

Lack of insight can be a very difficult condition to manage as the individual lacks **21.80** awareness of it. It is important to rule out other factors that may be exacerbating the problem such as the presence of anxiety, depression, or post-traumatic stress disorder. It may be important to gain some information about medications the person may be taking as these may affect insight.[64] Reducing the stress of a situation, providing cues to a situation, and ensuring the person is not fatigued may also help in improving insight.

J. Helping a Witness with Memory Problems

(1) Special considerations

Some individuals who have severe memory impairments may need special considera- **21.81** tions if they are to provide evidence. These are well documented in relation to facilitating vulnerable witnesses in criminal proceedings and individuals with memory problems may need to be considered in this way.[65] For some people their memory impairments may be so severe that they need to be assessed in order to ascertain whether they have the ability to act as a witness.

It is important in assessing individuals with memory problems to look for an **21.82** underlying disorder relating to physical and mental health. There may also be other factors involved such as drugs and/or alcohol which may adversely affect memory. There is also the possibility of malingering and for all memory difficulties a cognitive assessment using a battery of psychometric tests can be invaluable not only in

---

[63] O'Keefe, F.M., Murray, B., Coen, R.F., Dockree, P.M., Bellgrove, M.A., Garavan, H., Lynch, G.T., and Robertson, I. H., 'Loss of insight in frontotemporal dementia, cortico basal degeneration and progressive supranuclear palsy' (2007) 130 *Brain*, 753–64.

[64] Lincoln et al. (2012), cited at n.53.

[65] Ministry of Justice (2011) *Achieving best practice in criminal proceedings: Guidance on interviewing victims and witnesses and guidance on using special measures*, London: Home Office.

understanding the problem and its possible causes but also in gaining a perspective on those who are malingering or 'faking'.

K. Conclusion

21.83 Human memory is a pivotal concept within the context of providing testimony. It is a complex cognitive function which is often poorly understood. Recent advances in a number of fields have increased our understanding of memory both in terms of how it is organized in the brain and also how it can be assessed. It is subject to a wide range of influences of both a psychological and pathological nature and it is important to have an understanding of the nature of memory, its vagaries and apparent contradictions if we are to facilitate evidence giving by people who may have memory problems and/or impairments in the field of sex cases.

Further Reading

Brown, J.M. and Campbell, E.A. (2010) *The Cambridge Handbook of Forensic Psychology*, Cambridge: Cambridge University Press.

Gunn, J. and Taylor, P.J (eds) (2014) *Forensic Psychiatry: Clinical, Legal and Ethical Issues*, 2nd edn, Florida: Taylor & Francis.

Larner, A.J. (2013) *Neurological Neurology: The Neurocognitive Impairments of Neurological Disorders*, 2nd edn, Cambridge: Cambridge University Press.

Author Biographies

Professor Nigel North is a Consultant Clinical Psychologist and Neuropsychologist at Salisbury District Hospital, Salisbury and Visiting Professor at Bournemouth University, United Kingdom. His interests focus on the impact of illness and injury on the cognitive function of adults as well as the cognitive effects of posttraumatic stress disorder. He has published on a wide range of topics including unilateral spatial neglect, spinal cord injury, brain injury, and psychosocial oncology.

Professor Simon BN Thompson is Associate Professor of Clinical Psychology & Neuropsychology at the Faculty of Science & Technology, Bournemouth University, United Kingdom. Visiting Professor at Université Paris X Ouest Nanterre La Défense, Paris, France. His research interests span Alzheimer's disease, stroke, and the neurology of yawning. He has written fourteen books and over 150 publications in international peer-reviewed journals and magazines. He is an expert witness in medical negligence and neuropsychology and University External Examiner for faculties of medicine and psychology. He has talked at international conferences, BBC Radio, and on film.

22

MEMORY AND RELIABILITY: DEVELOPMENTS AND CONTROVERSIAL ISSUES

R. Christopher Barden

A. Introduction

22.01 Reliance on science is essential to proper legal process. The science of memory is particularly important. Criminal investigations must often focus on individual memory reports in the absence of corroborative evidence. Controversial theories involving the notion of 'repressed-recovered memories' (RRM) include multiple personality disorder (MPD), dissociative identity disorder, traumatic amnesia, dissociative amnesia, betrayal trauma theory, and related concepts. Such theories have generated some of the most contentious, complex, and forensically challenging issues in the recent history of the mental health and legal systems.

22.02 Co-ordinated, multidisciplinary efforts in legislation, litigation, licensing regulation, education (public and professional), and science (memory research) abruptly ended the widespread abuses of the RRM-MPD therapy movement while generating important legal and mental health reforms. The experienced application of recent legal reforms is often essential in such complex cases. These reforms include *Daubert/Kumho* reliability–validity hearings applying the doctrines of several historic US Supreme Court cases.[1] These hearings assess the reliability, validity, and admissibility of expert witness testimony and protect the legal system from unreliable information. The innovative, multidisciplinary, science-litigation team methods and practices that ended the RRM-MPD treatment industry (i.e. the 'memory wars' malpractice suits) also provide a highly effective model for litigating controversial memory cases in civil, criminal, administrative, and family law systems.[2]

22.03 This chapter will clarify terminology, analyze current methodological issues, and discuss how to forensically assess and effectively litigate controversial theories of memory. Criteria for selecting effective expert witnesses who can properly articulate the opinions of the relevant scientific community are included. Scientific information is provided to preclude the use of unreliable, untested interviewing protocols for children (e.g. the RATAC or 'CornerHouse' protocol) while increasing reliance upon validated methodologies (e.g. the US National Institute of Child Health and Human Development (NICHD) interviewing protocol).[3] Finally, this chapter offers advice on avoiding unreliable clinical judgement methodologies including impressionistic assessments of witness credibility.

---

[1] *Daubert v Merrell Dow Pharmaceuticals, Inc.*, 509 U.S., 113 S. Ct. 2786 (1993); *Kumho Tire Co., Ltd v Carmichael*, 119 S. Ct 1167 (1999).

[2] Barden, R.C., 'Informed consent in psychotherapy: A multidisciplinary perspective' (2001) 29(2) *The Journal of the American Academy of Psychiatry and the Law*, 160–6; Barden, R.C., 'Reforming Mental Health Care: Ending "Recovered Memory" Treatments Brought Informed Consent to Psychotherapy' (2014) 31 *Psychiatric Times*, 6.

[3] Lamb, M.E., Orbach, Y., Hershkowitz, I., Esplin, P., and Horowitz, D., 'A structured forensic interview protocol improves the quality and informativeness of investigative interviews with children: A review of research using the NICHD Investigative Interview Protocol' (2007) 31 *Child Abuse & Neglect*, 1201–31.

B. Science and Law are Essential Elements of Modern Civilization

The greatest achievements of civilization include science and law. These essential **22.04** systems are enhanced when applied as integrated, multidisciplinary processes. History shows that legal professionals acting upon pseudoscientific notions, and scientists operating beyond legal restraints, pose significant risks to society. In contrast, science-informed professionals, including judges, attorneys and expert witnesses, assist the legal process with reliable, ethical, and relevant scientific methods and knowledge.[4]

C. Controversial Theories of Memory: Terminology and Methodological Limitations

Some of the most controversial theories in psychotherapy, criminal investiga- **22.05** tions, and civil litigation posit that memories of horrific trauma can be accurately encoded but later (a) repressed, blocked, dissociated, or 'split off' from the victim's awareness thus becoming involuntarily inaccessible to memory; (b) stored for years in a highly stable, reliable format; and (c) later (even after decades) somehow 'recovered' and accurately reported to therapists, investigators, and courts of law. Despite dozens of studies over decades, the notion that people can reliably encode traumatic experiences without being able to recall them still lacks credible empirical support. Although repressed-recovered memories (RRM), traumatic amnesia, dissociative amnesia, betrayal trauma theory,[5] multiple personality disorder (MPD) or other versions of this theory remain testable hypotheses, the key foundation of these theories—the notion of 'repressed-recovered memories'—has never been credibly supported by methodologically rigorous, peer-reviewed, published studies.[6]

RRM-MPD and related controversial notions fail *Daubert-Kumho* analysis **22.06** because they lack an acceptable, reliable, documented error rate. This a key issue in *Daubert-Kumho* legal analysis.[7] RRM-MPD notions also fail *Daubert-Kumho*

---

[4] Grove, W.M. and Barden, R.C., 'Protecting the Integrity of the Legal System: The Admissibility of Testimony from Mental Health Experts Under Daubert/Kumho Analyses' (1999) 5(1) *Psychology, Public Policy and Law*, 234–42. Excerpts reprinted in Fisher, G. (Prof. Stanford Law School) (2002) *Evidence*: University Casebook Series New York: Foundation Press–West Group, 688.

[5] McNally, R.J., 'Betrayal trauma theory: A critical appraisal' (2007) 15 *Memory*, 280–94.

[6] McNally, R.J. (2003) *Remembering Trauma*, Cambridge, MA: Belknap Press/Harvard University Press; Pope H., Oliva P., and Hudson J., 'Repressed memories: The scientific status of research on repressed memories' in Faigman, D.L., Kaye, D.H., Saks, M.J., and Sanders, J. (eds) (2012) *Science in the law: social and behavioral science issues*, St. Paul, MN: West Group, 807–913; Piper A., Lillevik L., and Kritzner R., 'What's wrong with believing in repression? A review for legal professionals' (2008) 14 *Psychology Public Policy and Law*, 223–42.

[7] Grove and Barden (1999), cited at n.4.

analysis because they have never been 'generally accepted' by the relevant scientific community.[8] In sharp contrast to general acceptance, RRM-MPD notions have been so controversial they generated the 'memory wars' of the 1990s, spreading contentious issues from psychotherapy into science, law, legislation, journalism, and public policy.[9]

22.07 When litigating RRM-MPD and related notions, informed attorneys and experts ensure that courts are aware of the complex and exceptionally troubled history of RRM-MPD research. Methodological errors, state licensing prosecutions-revocations, admissions of gross misconduct, destruction of data, federally pros-ecuted research fraud, irrational ideas, malpractice litigation, and other indicia of unreliability in the RRM-MPD movement have been publicly documented via peer-reviewed publications, exhaustive trial cross-examinations, and expert affidavits.[10]

22.08 When conducting investigations of complex memory reports, it is important to dis-tinguish RRM-MPD and other controversial theories from memory impairments that are generally accepted among scientists including: (1) ordinary forgetfulness; (2) behaviour that is falsely viewed as amnesia such as lying to escape punishment; (3) incomplete encoding due to hyper-focus on salient details (e.g. a robbery victim might remember the gun but not the criminal's visage); (4) global amnesia (total memory loss from a limited time period); and (5) biological amnesia (drug and alcohol intoxication, head injuries, early-childhood neurological developmental processes).

D. *Daubert-Kumho* Hearings Assess the Relevance, Validity, and Admissibility of Controversial Memory Theories

22.09 As noted in para 22.02, the historic *Daubert-Kumho* rulings of the US Supreme Court were designed to require judges to make a reasoned assessment of the reli-ability, validity, and admissibility of expert witness methods, conclusions, and theories.[11] These cases are based upon the essential principle that 'scientific' testi-mony, methods, and evidence should be excluded if the underlying methodology

---

[8] Grove and Barden (1999), cited at n.4; Piper, et al. (2008), cited at n.6.

[9] McNally (2003), cited at n.6.; Grove and Barden (1999), cited at n.4.

[10] Belluck, P., 'Memory Therapy Leads to a Lawsuit and Big Settlement.' *The New York Times*, 6 November 1997 (award of $10.6 million), 1, col. 1. See also citations to the work of McNally, Loftus, Pope, Hudson, and Piper in this chapter. See also cross-examination of Daniel Brown, PhD by R.C. Barden, PhD, J.D. in *Rhode Island v Quattrocchi*, C.A. No P92-3759 (R.I. 1999) (on remand from R.I. Supreme Court 681 A.2d 879 (R.I. 1999)); Cross-examination by R.C. Barden, PhD, J.D. of Bessel van der Kolk, MD in *Rivers v Father Flanagan's Boys* Town, Doc 1024, Case No 743, Nebraska State Court Judge Sandra L. Dougherty, 25 November 2005; Cross-examinations by R.C. Barden, PhD, J.D. of James Chu, MD and Constance Dalenberg, PhD, in *John Doe v Archdiocese of St. Paul*, Case No 62-C9-06-003962, 8 December 2009, and similar cases. See also Affidavits of Harrison G. Pope, Jr, MD, Richard J. McNally, PhD, and R. Chris Barden, PhD, J.D. reviewing the testimony of Daniel Brown, PhD, in *Anonymous v Vella*, 2007, US District Court of Nebraska, Case No 8:04CV-269 and see Grove and Barden (1999), cited at n.4.

[11] *Daubert* (1993), cited at n.1; *Kumho* (1999), cited at n. 1.

and conclusions are irrelevant, unreliable (no reasonable error rates), illogical, improperly applied to the facts of the case, or not generally accepted by the relevant *scientific* (not clinical) community. In these landmark cases, the legal system began the long overdue process of creating powerful incentives for legal professionals to learn and properly apply scientific methodological analysis. Even in jurisdictions where *Daubert-Kumho* principles have no precedential value, similar methods can be used to effectively exclude, expose, or limit contaminative, unreliable evidence thus protecting the integrity of any legal system.

E. Multidisciplinary, Science-litigation Teams

Until the legal education system trains a generation of science-informed attorneys, multidisciplinary science-litigation teams will remain the most effective method for litigating controversial theories of memory. History shows that few traditionally trained lawyers, judges, therapists, or clinician expert witnesses have proven capable of effectively dealing with the methodological complexities posed by controversial memory issues such as RRM-MPD.[12] In contrast, multidisciplinary, science-litigation teams have proven remarkably successful in excluding controversial RRM-MPD evidence from courtrooms following detailed, science-informed *Frye-Daubert-Kumho* hearings.[13] In contrast, cases where RRM-MPD expert opinions have been admitted document a range of serious litigation errors.   **22.10**

More specifically, cases where RRM-MPD testimony and evidence are admitted into evidence often demonstrate most or all of the 'top fifteen', often-fatal, science litigation errors including: **22.11**

(1) Juris Doctor-only attorneys seem quite unable to cross-examine PhD's and MD's properly with regard to complex scientific issues;
(2) failing to explain to the court, aggressively and persuasively, the documented history of criminal prosecutions, licensing prosecutions, admissions of research fraud, and admissions of data destruction in the RRM-MPD movement;[14]

---

[12] Hagen, M. (1997) *Whores of the Court: The Fraud of Psychiatric Testimony and the Rape of American Justice*, New York: Harper Collins Press.

[13] Barden (2001a), cited at n.2; Barden (2014), cited at n.2. See, e.g., *Hamanne, et al. v Humenansky*, Ramsey County Mn, No C4-94-203, Judge Betrand Poritsky, 30 June 1995; *Carlson v Humenansky* (Minnesota Trial Ct), Judge Betrand Poritsky (January, 1996); *Engstrom v Engstrom*, California App., 2nd App. Dist., Div 2, (CA 1997); *State of New Hampshire v Hungerford and State of New Hampshire v Morahan*, 698 A.2d 1244 (N.H. 1997); *State of New Hampshire v Walters*, 697 A.2d 916 (N.H. 1997); *Franklin v Stevenson*, 987 P.2d 22 (1999); *Rhode Island v Quattrocchi*, C.A. No P92-3759 (R.I. 1999); *New Hampshire v Bourgelais*, Docket No 02-S-2834, 4 April 2005; *Rivers v Father Flanagan's Boys Town*, Doc 1024, Case No 743, Nebraska State Court, 25 November 2005; *John Doe (Keenan) v Archdiocese of St. Paul*, 817 N.W.2d 150 (Minn. 2012).

[14] Affidavit of R. Chris Barden, PhD, J.D. reviewing the documented history of errors, including criminal and licensing troubles, in RRM-MPD research in *Anonymous v Vella*, 2007, US District Court of Nebraska, Case No 8:04CV-269.

(3) failing to create a truly multidisciplinary team with expert witnesses—both scientists and also clinicians—from both psychology and psychiatry including special expertise in ethics, psychological testing, diagnostics, human memory, clinical judgement errors, and licensing issues;

(4) failing properly to clarify the severe methodological limitations of psychiatric diagnostic systems (e.g. DSM and ICD);

(5) failing to document—including preparing persuasive, summary graphic depictions in real time in front of the court—the many methodological errors of 'pro-repression' research studies;

(6) failing to distinguish highly cited scientists from controversial clinicians;

(7) failing to document that in the most completely and competently litigated cases courts have uniformly excluded RRM-MPD notions as unreliable, controversial, and lacking a known error rate;

(8) failing to explicate fully the serious errors of logic, analysis, and methodology demonstrated by those few courts permitting RRM-MPD testimony;[15]

(9) failing to distinguish members of the relevant scientific community from clinician-nonscientists;

(10) failing to share with the court the opinion of the relevant scientific community as documented in the Amicus Briefs of the National Committee of Scientists for Academic Liberty and the International Committee of Social, Psychiatric, Psychological, Cognitive Science, Neuroscience, and Neurological Scientists;[16]

(11) failing to obtain a numerical advantage in expert witnesses (easily done as few science experts will testify for 'repressed memory' while many will testify against it);

(12) failing to have a local, poplar clinician expert explain to the court that scientific principles and methods apply across state borders thus national science experts can be trusted;

(13) failing to explicate fully the history of fads and frauds in mental health care (e.g. from dream analysis to lobotomies to primal screaming to 'multiple personality' treatments) over the past hundred years;[17]

(14) failing to properly explain the full history of the 'memory wars' reform efforts including the co-ordinated multidisciplinary wave of internationally reported malpractice lawsuits;[18] and

---

[15] See Hagen (1997), cited at n.12, and see e.g. *Isely v Capuchin Province*, 877 F. Supp. 1055 (E.D. Mich. 1995); *Shazade v Gregory* (930 F. Supp. 673, D. Mass. 1996).

[16] Barden, R.C. (2006) Amicus Curiae Brief of the National Committee of Scientists for Academic Liberty, for Defendants and Appellants, Elizabeth Loftus, et al., Supreme Court of the State of California, February 2006. See also, Barden, R.C. (2009) 'Brief of the International Committee of Social, Psychiatric, Psychological, Cognitive Science, Neuroscience, and Neurological Scientists as Amicus Curiae in Commonwealth v Shanley', at *http://tillers.net/ev-course/materials/shanley.amicus. pdf.* Copies also available at *rcbarden@mac.com.*

[17] Singer, M.T. and Lalich, J. (1996) *Crazy Therapies*, San Francisco: Jossey-Bass.

[18] Barden, R.C. (2001a), cited at n.2; Barden, R.C. (2014), cited at n.2.

(15) failing competently to investigate and expose licensing and ethics viola-
tions of each of the therapists and experts involved in the case (this requires
significant ethics and licensing expertise in psychology, psychiatry, and
social work).

These are only the most obvious and general errors, many more errors lurk for the
unprepared, uni-disciplinary litigator. In sum, even the most experienced JD-only
litigators would be most unwise to attempt such hearings without detailed, multidisciplinary consultation.

As Grove and Barden (1999) noted over a decade ago, 'In the world of *Daubert/*   **22.12**
Kumho analyses, science-intensive litigation teams should be the minimal standard
of legal practice, to help ensure that these complexities are properly addressed.'[19]

F. Selecting Expert Witnesses from
the Relevant Scientific Community

Effective science-litigation teams include: (1) a local attorney to handle local   **22.13**
legal issues and filings; (2) an expert scientist-attorney to handle complex science
(*Daubert-Kumho*) issues and the examinations and cross examinations of expert
witnesses with advanced degrees (i.e. Master of Social Work, MD, PhD); and
(3) science and also clinical expert witnesses from the relevant fields of knowledge including psychology and psychiatry. Choosing appropriate experts is an
essential task in this process. The most effective expert witnesses for scientific litigation are members of the relevant scientific community. Such witnesses should
optimally have :

(1) obtained several substantial state, federal, or private scientific research grants
    as a 'principal investigator';
(2) authored original scientific research in credible scientific journals published
    by national science-professional associations (i.e. American Psychological
    Association, American Psychiatric Association, American Medical Association
    and Association for Psychological Science) not specialty clinical journals;
(3) been frequently cited in credible peer-reviewed science journals by colleagues;
(4) participated actively in the editorial process of credible scientific (not clinical)
    journals;
(5) received national science awards from credible scientific (not clinical) national
    associations;
(6) given invited addresses at credible national science (not clinical) conventions;
(7) participated in previous *Daubert-Kumho* hearings;

---

[19] Grove and Barden, cited at n.4, 239.

(8) served on research grant review panels; and

(9) practised as licensed clinicians who can offer standard of care opinions regarding treatment issues.

Some experts have also served on relevant state licensing boards. Although few experts will meet all of these standards, the best will meet many of them.

22.14 Tragically, too many of the 'experts' testifying in courtrooms today meet few, if any, of these important standards. Most are clinicians who lack sufficient knowledge of scientific methodology, have no history of credible research grant funding, have never published in a credible scientific (not clinical) journal, and, if they have published, are not often cited by members of the relevant scientific community. Decades of research projects on the limitations of 'clinical judgement' have documented why clinician-therapist 'experts' often offer little reliable evidence to courts of law.[20]

G. Science–Litigation–Policy Teams Reformed the US Emergency Medical and Mental Health Systems

22.15 The power of multidisciplinary science-litigation teams has been well documented. A series of internationally reported, multidisciplinary reform projects began in the early 1990s. The first project brought important improvements to US health care. Multidisciplinary analysis led to model legislation that generated legislative and regulatory reforms to the US Emergency Medical System for Children. This process was assisted by peer-reviewed medical-legal publications, media exposes (e.g. national news magazines and television programmes), malpractice litigation, and involved citizen groups. In just a few years, these co-ordinated efforts reformed a complex multi-billion dollar industry. Several US Surgeon Generals have noted these reforms saved the lives of thousands of children.[21]

22.16 Energized by the unexpectedly rapid success of emergency medical system reforms, similar reform processes were applied to the US mental health system. Responding to an unprecedented epidemic of injuries from RRM-MPD 'treatments', a national wave of co-ordinated malpractice lawsuits, media reports, integrated licensing actions, and scientific publications quickly collapsed this once rapidly growing and highly profitable therapy industry. In addition to the wave of

---

[20] Garb, Howard N. (1998) *Studying the clinician: Judgment research and psychological assessment*, Washington, DC: American Psychological Association Press, 333 doi: 10.1037/10299-002, 39–83; Dawes, R.M. (1997) *House of Cards: Psychology and Psychotherapy Built on Myth*, New York: Free Press; Grove, W.M. and Meehl, P.E. 'Comparative efficiency of informal (subjective, impressionistic) and formal (mechanical, algorithmic) prediction procedures: The clinical-statistical controversy' (1996) 2(2) *Psychology, Public Policy, and Law*, 293–323.

[21] Barden, R.C., Kinscherff, R., George, W., Flyer, R., Seidel, J., and Henderson, D., 'Emergency medical care and injury prevention systems for children: An economic-medical-legal-psychological analysis and legislative proposals' (1993) 30(2) *Harvard Journal on Legislation*, 461–97.

lawsuits, science-legal litigation team members participated in a range of reform activities including: assisting state officials in licensing prosecutions,[22] working to block insurance payments for controversial 'treatments,'[23] organizing *Daubert/ Kumho* legal hearings to exclude evidence related to RRM-MPD theories, enforcing informed consent protections for psychotherapy patients,[24] working on citizen education efforts with groups like the False Memory Syndrome Foundation,[25] and energizing a rapidly growing body of scientific research on trauma, memory, false memory, and eyewitness testimony.[26]

Following months of multidisciplinary team litigation, in August 1995 a Minnesota **22.17** jury in *Hamanne v Humenansky* returned a verdict of $2.67 million compensation for emotional damages from RRM-MPD therapy.[27] Dozens of cases were quickly placed with attorneys across the US as the *Hamanne* case had (finally) demonstrated the financial viability of psychotherapy malpractice litigation. In January of 1996, the same Minnesota multidisciplinary litigation team obtained a $2.54 million compensation jury verdict for emotional damages from RRM-MPD therapy.[28] These 'Minnesota Twins' multi-million dollar jury verdicts, reported throughout the world via newspapers, television, and radio, quickly generated a wave of similar, co-ordinated legal actions and media exposes. Multidisciplinary, science-litigation team methods, practices, and procedures were disseminated via detailed consultations with local lawyers in co-ordinated cases across the US.

In 1996, two former RRM-MPD patients received widely reported settlements **22.18** including a $1.57 million settlement in Oregon and a $1 million settlement in Missouri.[29] On 4 March 1997, a Wisconsin RRM-MPD patient followed the 'Minnesota Twins' template and settled for $2.4 million.[30] In August 1997,

---

[22] AP News Wire Chicago, 'Psychiatrist [Braun] loses license over satanic allegations' 8 October 1999; *Georgia Board of Psychology v George Greaves, PhD* (1994) Docket Number 93-598 (consent to Licence Revocation signed 4 April 1994); Lerner, M., 'Psychologist barred from treating cases involving false memories' *Minneapolis/St. Paul Tribune*, 3 June 1999.

[23] DiStefano, J.N. 'Pennsylvania liquidates the American Psychiatric Association Insurance Trust' (2003) *Philadelphia Inquirer*.30 June, D-1.

[24] Barden, R.C. (2001a), cited at n.2; Barden, R.C. (2014), cited at n.2.

[25] See e.g. *http://www.fmsfonline.org*, Pamela Freyd, PhD, Director, Memory and Reality: Reconciliation Conference, Co-Sponsored by The False Memory Syndrome Foundation and The Johns Hopkins Medical Institutions, Baltimore, MD 9–11 December 1994.

[26] Loftus, E.F. and Davis, D., 'Recovered memories' in (2006) 2 *Annual Review of Clinical Psychology*, 469–98; McNally, R.J. (2003), cited at n.6; Pope et al. (2012), cited at n.6.

[27] Gustafson, P., 'Jury awards patient $2.6 million: Verdict finds therapist Humenansky liable in repressed memory trial' *Minneapolis St. Paul Tribune*, August 1 1995.

[28] Gustafson, P. 'Jury awards $2.5 million in lawsuit against psychiatrist: "Memories" were induced' *Minneapolis/St. Paul Tribune*, 25 January 1996, 1B.

[29] *Fultz v Carr and Walker* (1996), Circuit Court, Multnomah County Oregon, Case 9506-04080; *Rutherford v Strand* et al., Circuit Court of Green County, Missouri, Case 1960C2745; AP Newswire. 'Family [Springfield, Missouri] torn by false repressed memories settles for $1 million' *Lubbock, Avalanche-Journal*, 3 March 1996.

[30] AP newswire, '$2.4 Million Settlement Reached Over Multi-personality Diagnosis' *Chicago Times*, Tribune News Services, 4 March 1997.

a Texas jury raised the stakes by awarding $5.8 million for RRM-MPD therapy injuries.[31] In October 1997, a federal grand jury in Houston returned multiple criminal indictments against several RRM-MPD therapists included allegations of health care fraud that included 'bizarre and outlandish (RRM-MPD) treatment sessions'. The most influential battle of 'Memory Wars I' (1994–1997) concluded in November of 1997 when the Burgus family accepted a $10.6 million settlement for damages suffered during years of RRM-MPD treatment. This record settlement was reported on page one, column one, of *The New York Times* and highlighted in major magazines, television programmes, and on radio throughout the world.[32] Following the *Burgus* settlement, many other RRM-MPD cases were quickly, quietly, and confidentially settled across the US. By the end of 1997, co-ordinated, multidisciplinary reform processes had largely collapsed the once-burgeoning RRM-MPD therapy industry.

22.19 The 1997 collapse of the RRM-MPD industry included the closing of clinics, the surrender of licences, and a well-documented, precipitous decline in RRM-MPD research publications.[33] In just a few years, co-ordinated science-litigation teams saved tens of thousands of families from horrific emotional abuses by RRM-MPD 'therapists', shut down the once rapidly growing RRM-MPD treatment industry, and protected the integrity of the US legal and health care systems.[34] It is essential for historians to note that in contrast to the tragic damages of the RRM-MPD epidemic, the cleansing wave of successful reform lawsuits and licensing actions resulted in historic, lasting reforms in the US mental health system. Such reforms included a new focus on empirically supported therapies, new research on the nature of human memory, model applications of *Daubert-Kumho* legal proceedings to exclude unreliable social science theories, and the long overdue enforcement of informed consent protections for psychotherapy patients. By making 'failure to obtain proper informed consent' one of the key allegations in a national wave of lawsuits and licensing prosecutions, reformers forced the mental health system to (finally) protect the fundamental human right of informed consent for all health care patients—including those in psychotherapy.[35]

---

[31] Smith, M., '5.8 million awarded in Carl lawsuit, claims therapists implanted false memories of satanic ritual abuse' *Houston Chronicle*, 15 August 1997.

[32] Belluck, P. (1997), cited at n.10.

[33] Pope, H.G., Bodkin, S.B., and Hudson, J.I., 'Tracking Scientific Interest in the Dissociative Disorders: A Study of Scientific Publication Output 1984–2003' (2006) 75 *Psychother Psychosom*, 19–24 doi: 10.1159/000089223.

[34] Barden, R.C. (2001a), cited at n.1; Barden, R.C. (2014), cited at n.1.

[35] Barden, R.C., 'Reforming the Mental Health System: Coordinated, Multidisciplinary Actions Ended "Recovered Memory" Treatments and Brought Informed Consent to Psychotherapy' *Psychiatric Times*. 31(6): 6 June 2014.

H. Science–Litigation Teams ended Criminal Prosecutions Based upon Uncorroborated 'Recovered Memories', 'RRM-MPD', and Related Controversial Notions

At the peak of the RRM-MPD therapy epidemic many US citizens were prosecuted **22.20** based solely upon RRM allegations lacking any reliable corroborative evidence. Widespread prosecutions based solely on RRM-MPD testimony ended in the US following the 1995–1997 wave of malpractice lawsuits, subsequent licensing prosecutions, and international media reports as well as the landmark hearing in *Rhode Island v Quattrocchi*.[36]

The *Quattrocchi* hearings reportedly remain the most complex, lengthy, and exhaus- **22.21** tively litigated *Daubert-Kumho* hearings on memory issues in history. Following several weeks of technical, detailed, methodological analyses of many dozens of research studies plus extensive examinations and cross-examinations of multiple (seven) expert witnesses including a number of internationally acclaimed scientists, the court ruled that RRM-MPD and related theories and practices were unreliable, controversial, and not generally accepted by the relevant scientific community—thus ending the case. US criminal prosecutions based solely on RRM-MPD testimony became rare in the US following the *Quattrocchi* decision.[37]

I. Science–Litigation Teams ended the Rebirthing–Coercive Holding–Attachment Therapy Industries

Energized by national reform successes in the emergency medical and mental health **22.22** fields, from 2001 to 2005, multidisciplinary litigation teams next worked to collapse the controversial Rebirthing-Coercive Holding-Attachment Therapy industry in the US. Such 'therapies' were based on yet another controversial theory of memory—that coercive, painful, physical pressure could 'release trauma memories locked within muscles'. Litigation, prosecution, education, and legislation efforts to halt such practices resulted in lengthy prison sentences (sixteen years each) for several leading 'rebirthing' therapists,[38] licensing restrictions for other therapists,[39]

---

[36] C.A. No P92—3759 (R.I. 1999).

[37] Mooney, T., 'Recovered Memory Rejected: Judge rules out key element in landmark [*Quattrocchi*] case' *The Providence Journal (Rhode Island)*, 28 April 1999.

[38] Janofsky, M., 'Girl's Death Brings Ban on Kind of "Therapy"' *The New York Times*, 18 April 2001; Lowe, P., 'Rebirthing team convicted: Two therapists face mandatory terms of 16 to 48 years in jail' *Rocky Mountain News*, 21 April 2001.

[39] Hyde, J., 'Utah jettisons holding therapy' *Deseret Morning News*, 11 February 2005.

a legislative ban on such practices,[40] and the state's expert witness warning millions of citizens about such dangerous 'treatments' via a national television interview.[41] Once again, decisive, co-ordinated, actions by multidisciplinary science-litigation teams produced rapid, enforced, lasting reforms to protect the public as well as the integrity of the legal and mental health systems.

J. The Current Opinion of the Relevant Scientific Community Regarding RRM-MPD and Related Controversial Theories of Memory

22.23 The opinion of the relevant scientific community on RRM-MPD issues was first documented in the amicus brief of the National Committee of Scientists for Academic Liberty submitted to the Supreme Court of the State of California in February of 2006. An updated opinion was documented in the amicus brief of the International Committee of Social, Psychiatric, Psychological, Cognitive Science, Neuroscience, and Neurological Scientists submitted to the Supreme Court of the State of Massachusetts in 2009. A broad collection of internationally acclaimed scientists—many in the top 1 per cent of the most cited scientists in the world in psychology, psychiatry and neuroscience—joined both briefs. Their joint statement in 2006 concluded:

> [T]his unsupported theory [RRM-MPD] has caused incalculable harm to the fields of psychology and psychiatry, damaged tens if not hundreds of thousands of families, severely harmed the credibility of mental health professionals, and also misled the legislative, civil, criminal and family legal systems into many miscarriages of justice. The debate over 'repressed and recovered memories of trauma' is one of the most contentious, important and newsworthy debates in the history of psychology, psychiatry and the mental health system . . . Despite the clinical beliefs of some therapists, there is simply no credible, methodologically sound, replicable scientific evidence for the claim that victims repress and recover memories of traumatic events . . . Decades of research and scientific debate have clarified over and over again, that the notion of traumatic events being somehow 'repressed' and later accurately recovered is one of the most pernicious bits of folklore ever to infect psychology and psychiatry. This folklore provided the theoretical basis for 'recovered memory therapy'—arguably the worst catastrophe to befall the mental health field since the lobotomy era.[42]

22.24 Similarly, experts in the UK reviewed the field of RRM-MPD and 'trauma memory' research and concluded: 'Despite clinical support and popular belief that memories can be "blocked out" by the mind, no empirical evidence exists to

---

[40] Josefson, D., 'Rebirthing therapy banned after girl died in 70 minute struggle' (2001) 322 (7293) *British Medical Journal*, 1014, 28 April.

[41] Barden, R.C. (2001b) 'Little Girl Lost: 10 Yr Old Dies From Controversial Rebirthing Therapy' *ABC NEWS* 20/20 (Interview by Barbara Walters and Deborah Roberts), 15 June.

[42] Quoted in Barden (2006), cited at n.16, 18–19.

support either repression or dissociation [of complete trauma memories].'[43] The best and most recently updated summaries of relevant research document these ongoing controversies as well as the ongoing general skepticism regarding RRM-MPD and related notions.[44]

K. Disease Classification Systems do not Provide Evidence of Validity or Error Rates for RRM-MPD or Other Controversial Theories of Memory

When litigating issues related to controversial theories of memories, informed pro- **22.25**
fessionals help courts understand that disease classification systems (DSM, ICD) are not scientifically valid, methodologically sound, scientific journal publications of research. The DSM and ICD classification systems were designed to serve essentially as 'dictionaries' compiled to improve the reliability of diagnostic terms. Reliability, validity, and error rates data for such notions as RRM-MPD, 'traumatic amnesia', 'dissociative amnesia', 'dissociative identity disorder', or related concepts are simply not provided in the DSM or the ICD.[45]

L. Public Statements from Professional Associations Document Controversy but no General Acceptance for RRM-MPD Theories

Public statements of professional associations including the American Medical **22.26**
Association, the Canadian Psychological Association, the Australian Psychological Association, and others document a controversial, contentious debate over the existence and reliability of RRM-MPD and related concepts. None document general acceptance or a published, reliable error rate.[46]

M. Misinformation on the Nature of Memory Remains Widespread

Misinformation about the essential nature of human memory remains wide- **22.27**
spread in the public as well as in the mental health and legal professions. For example, a recent (2012) survey of licensed psychologist clinicians in Norway

---

[43] Brandon S., Boakes J., Glaser D., and Green R., 'Recovered Memories of Childhood Sexual Abuse: Implications for Clinical Practice' (1998) 172 *British Journal of Psychiatry*, 296–307, 302.

[44] Pope H.G. Jr, et al. (2012), cited at n.6; Piper A., et al. (2008), cited at n.6; Loftus, E.F. and Davis, D. (2006), cited at n.26; McNally, R.J. (2003), cited at n.6.

[45] Grove and Barden (1999), cited at n.4.

[46] Piper A., Lillevik L., and Kritzner R. (2008), cited at n. 6; Barden, R.C., cited at n.16.

found that a substantial number still cling to the unreliable, controversial notion that 'recovered repressed memory' reports involve actual, accurate, memories. Similarly, research finds that a majority of US citizens mistakenly believe 'memory works like a video camera', with nearly half thinking 'memory is permanent', and a majority even believing the controversial notion that 'memory can be enhanced through hypnosis'.[47] Such unreliable, unscientific ideas pose serious hazards to the integrity of the legal process and should be countered by informed expert witness testimony.

N. Professionals are Often Unreliable 'Lie Detectors'

22.28 Too many investigators, police officers, psychotherapists, physicians, judges, and lawyers continue to believe they are highly reliable 'experts' at discerning truthful memory reports.[48] In contrast, informed litigators and expert witnesses help courts understand the relevant research findings noting that 'professionals are [often] more confident in their veracity judgements but *are no more accurate* [than laypersons]'.[49]

O. Tested, Valid, and Reliable Interview Protocols (NICHD) are Available to Avoid Improperly Contaminating Children's Memories

22.29 Another important memory-related controversy involves investigative interviews of children. For centuries, children were poorly served and infrequently protected by the legal system. From the 1960s to the 1990s criminal prosecutions based upon the testimony of children grew rapidly using methods designed by crime investigators rather than developmental psychologists. Until near the end of the twentieth century, the scientific community showed little interest in the centuries-old debate over the accuracy of children's testimony. A wave of infamous criminal cases involving abusive interview practices, including the *McMartin, Kelly Michaels, Wenatchee, Little Rascals* cases and many others, generated considerable controversy and interest in science-based investigative

---

[47] Patihis, L., Ho, L., Tingen, I., Lilienfeld, S., and Loftus, E., 'Are the "Memory Wars" Over? A Scientist-Practitioner Gap in Beliefs About Repressed Memory' (2013) *Psychological Science*, doi: 10.1177/0956797613510718.

[48] Rosen, G.M. and Phillips, W.R., 'A Cautionary Lesson from Simulated Patients' (2004) 32 *Journal of the American Academy of Psychiatry and Law*, 132–3.

[49] Vrij, A., Granhag, P., and Porter, S., 'Pitfalls and opportunities in nonverbal and verbal lie detection' (2010) 11(3) *Psychological Science in the Public Interest*, 89–121, ISSN 1529-1006 10.1177/1529100610390861, 13.

interviewing methods.[50] In 1995, a group of international science and public policy experts wrote to the US Congress requesting science-based, legislative reforms to correct errors in the mental health (RRM-MPD) and investigative systems. They wrote:

> Child abuse is a serious social problem that should be dealt with in an effective and responsible manner. We strongly support the implementation of effective programs to reduce the incidence of child abuse, assist victims of abuse, and punish those who harm children. Efforts to attain these important goals must, however, be based in fact rather than prejudice, science rather than hysteria, and reason rather than political ideology.[51]

Research has long demonstrated that when properly interviewed, even young chil- **22.30** dren are often quite capable of reliable, accurate testimony. Proper interviewing procedures protect victims of abuse as well as the integrity of the legal process. Controversial, memory contaminative interviewing errors can be largely eliminated with proper training and expert witness review. A science-informed expert witness should assess methodological issues including:

(1) 'were the facts of the alleged crime first described by the witness or suggested during questioning?';
(2) 'is there a clear history of all investigative interviews documented in the videotaped interview?';
(3) 'were contaminative drawings or dolls used prior to statements of allegations?';
(4) 'did the investigator improperly repeat questions, fail to explore alternative theories, or ignore answers in an attempt to confirm preconceived theories?'; and
(5) 'did the investigator deceive the witness?'

These and other assessment issues are essential in efforts to protect children as well as the integrity of the investigative process.

With no known error rate, no general acceptance in the relevant scientific com- **22.31** munity, and no credible research support, the 'CornerHouse' (also known as the 'RATAC' method) and other outdated protocols should not survive a proper

---

[50] Bruck, M. and Ceci, S., 'Amicus brief for the case of State of New Jersey v Michaels presented by the committee of concerned social scientists' (1995) 1 *Psychology, Public Policy, and Law*, 272–322; Rabinowitz, D., 'No Crueler Tyrannies: Accusation, False Witness, and Other Terrors of Our Times' *Free Press*, 24 February 2004.

[51] Barden, R.C. (1995) Letter to the Congress of the United States of America regarding reform of the mental health system. With co-signers Paul E. Meehl, Terence W. Campbell, Richard Ofshe, Richard A. Gardner, MD, Margaret Singer, William Grove, Michael D. Yapko, Robyn Dawes, Richard Flyer, Robert Kinscherff, Mel Guyer, Francis Fincham, Thom Moore, Henry E. Adams, E. Mark Cummings, Lewis P. Lipsitt, Donald M. Kaplan, Robert R. Holt, Richard M. McFall, Hans H. Strupp, Stephen J. Lepore, Lee Sechrest, Paul Ekman, Hans J. Eysenck; with Version. II signed by Jerome Kagan, George Stricker, Debra Ann Poole, Mark L. Howe, J. Don Read, and Howard Shevrin, quoted in Dineen, T. (1996) *Manufacturing Victims*, Montreal: Robert Davies Publishing.

Daubert/Kumho litigation challenge.[52] In contrast, validated, peer-reviewed, published protocols that are generally accepted by the relevant scientific community, such as the US National Institute of Child Health and Human Development (NICHD) protocols, have become the standard of care.[53]

P. False Memories may be Errors, not Lies

22.32 A final controversial memory issue involves the distinction between false memory reports and lies. Research has shown that memory reports may well be false-but-fervently-believed-in 'memories'. As Loftus, McNally, and others have demonstrated, inaccurate memories may be just as compelling and every bit as 'real' to a witness as inaccurate, false memories.[54] The *Hamanne, Carlson Burgus, Kelly Michaels, McMartin, Wenatchee*, and many other cases vividly and tragically document how improper interviewing and negligent psychotherapy practices and procedures can produce horrific, detailed, convincing, yet utterly false 'memories' of trauma in children and adults.

Q. Conclusion

22.33 Multidisciplinary science-litigation teams have produced historic reforms in the emergency medical, mental health, and legal systems. Competent investigations, proper prosecutions, and science-informed attorneys, experts, and courts are essential to ongoing efforts to preserve and protect the integrity of the legal system.

Further Reading

Grove, W.M. and Barden, R.C., 'Protecting the integrity of the legal system: The Admissibility of Testimony from mental health experts under daubert/kumho analyses' (2000) 5(1) *Psychology, Public Policy and Law*, 234–42. Excerpts reprinted in Fisher, G. (2002) *Evidence*: University Casebook Series, Foundation Press–West Group, New York, 688.

---

[52] 'R.A.T.A.C.' signifies the components of the 'CornerHouse' interview protocol including Rapport, Anatomy Identification, Touch Inquiry, Abuse Scenario, and Closure; Todd, J. and Tomison, A., 'Comparing the NICHD and RATAC Child Forensic Interview Approaches—Do the Differences Matter?' (2011) 20(1) *THE LINK*: Official Newsletter of the International Society for Prevention of Child Abuse and Neglect (ISPCAN), Autumn; Grove and Barden (1999), cited at n.4.

[53] Lamb, et al. (2007), cited at n.3.

[54] Loftus, E., 'Our changeable memories: legal and practical implications' Science and Society (2003) 4 *Nature Reviews: Neuroscience*, 231–5; McNally, R.J., Lasko, N.B., Clancy, S.A., Macklin, M.L., Pitman, R.K., and Orr, S.P., 'Psychophysiological responding during script-driven imagery in people reporting abduction by space aliens' (2004) 15 *Psychological Science*, 493–7.

Pope H.G. Jr, Oliva P.S., and Hudson J.I., 'Repressed memories: The scientific status of research on repressed memories' in Faigman, D.L., Kaye, D.H., Saks M.J. and Sanders, J. (eds) (2012) *Science in the law: social and behavioral science issues*. St. Paul, MN: West Group, 807–913.

Barden, R.C. (2009) Brief of the International Committee of Social, Psychiatric, Psychological, Cognitive Science, Neuroscience, and Neurological Scientists as Amicus Curiae in Commonwealth of Massachusetts v Shanley. SJC No 10282, *http://tillers.net/ev-course/materials/shanley.amicus.pdf* or at *rcbarden@mac.com*.

Author Biography

Dr R. Christopher Barden, PhD, JD, is a scientist-clinician-attorney-policy expert specializing in multi-disciplinary analysis and reform. He served as the President of the National Association for Consumer Protection in Mental Health Practices (1995–2005). As a practicing trial lawyer, Dr Barden has litigated cases in dozens of states and several countries resulting in record verdicts and settlements. As an expert witness in psychology, he has participated in civil, criminal, and licensing cases in dozens of jurisdictions. As a scientist, Dr Barden is the recipient of two national science awards in child clinical psychology with research funding from the National Science Foundation, the National Institute of Mental Health, the Foundation for Child Development, the W.T. Grant Foundation, and other sources. Dr Barden has published in leading journals and texts in law, clinical psychology, developmental psychology, social psychology, psychiatry, pediatrics, surgery, public policy, and legislation.

23

HOW MISCONCEPTIONS ABOUT MEMORY MAY UNDERMINE WITNESS TESTIMONY

James Ost and Christopher C. French*

A. Introduction

Memory is at the heart of any criminal justice system, from the initial statements **23.01** provided by complainants or other witnesses, to the evidence given in court. As Professor Charles Brainerd notes, 'the science of memory is as central to the law as biology is to medicine.'[1] Police officers, barristers, judges and—ultimately—the jury are often asked to make critical decisions primarily on the basis of memory evidence.

---

* The authors thank Janet Boakes, Gisli Gudjonsson, and Pamela Radcliffe for comments that greatly improved the quality of this chapter.

[1] Brainerd, C.J., 'Murder must memorise' (2013) 21 *Memory*, 547–55, at 547.

23.02 Research consistently shows that the general public, as well as criminal justice professionals, often hold beliefs about the nature of memory that are not in accordance with scientific evidence.[2] The first section of this chapter briefly reviews misconceptions about memory and remembering and shows that they are common even amongst psychological professionals who might be expected to be familiar with the scientific literature. The second section focuses on one very common and powerful misconception—the belief that memory is an accurate record of events. The chapter concludes by outlining three areas where memory science has produced counter-intuitive findings that are relevant to understanding the credibility of witness accounts, specifically relating to detailed accounts, inconsistencies in recall over time, and so-called 'discontinuous' memories. These three issues are particularly relevant because an account that is detailed, consistent, and continuously remembered may be assumed to be accurate, and the production of an account with such features may—unconsciously—be the goal of those charged with obtaining evidence from witnesses. However, psychological science suggests that such features are not necessarily diagnostic of accuracy.

B. Common Misconceptions about Memory and Remembering

(1) Guidance on memory science

23.03 In 2010 the British Psychological Society (BPS) published a document entitled *Guidelines on memory and the law: Recommendations from the scientific study of human memory.* The purpose of that document was to 'provide a far more rigorously informed understanding of human memory than that available from commonly held beliefs' in order to 'give courts a much firmer basis for accurate decision-making'.[3] However, some argue that little attention has been paid to the report in the legal community, partly because the scientific findings are perceived to be 'the same as, or very similar to, commonly held beliefs, common experience and common sense'.[4] But do commonly held beliefs about memory really accord with the scientific literature? The results of several large-scale surveys examining beliefs about memory would suggest that such optimism might be premature.

---

[2] Patihis, L., Ho, L.Y., Tingen, I.W., Lilienfeld, S.O., and Loftus, E.F., 'Are the "memory wars" over? A scientist-practitioner gap in beliefs about repressed memory' (2014) 25 *Psychological Science*, 519–30; Simons, D.J. and Chabris, C.F., 'What people believe about how memory works: A representative survey of the US population' (2011) 6(8) *PLoS ONE*, e22757.

[3] British Psychological Society (2010) *Guidelines on memory and the law: Recommendations from the scientific study of human memory*, Leicester: British Psychological Society, 1.

[4] Keane, A., 'The use at trial of scientific findings relating to human memory' [2010] Crim LR, 1, 19–30, at 24.

(2) Lay understanding of memory science

One survey of 2,000 adult Norwegians regarding their beliefs and opinions about **23.04**
human memory produced mixed findings. On some issues (e.g. the date of earliest memories), the views of the general public were reasonably consistent with the
scientific literature. On other issues (e.g. the plausibility of repression of adult traumatic memories), their sample expressed beliefs that were largely unsupported by
the scientific literature.[5] A representative sample of 1,500 US citizens found that 63
per cent of respondents agreed with the statement 'Human memory works like a
video camera, accurately recording the events we see and hear so that we can review
and inspect them later' and 47.6 per cent agreed with the statement that 'Once
you have experienced an event and formed a memory of it, that memory does not
change'.[6] Neither of these statements was endorsed by a separate sample of seventy-
three experts that included sixteen professors, each of whom had over ten years of
memory research experience. A meta-analysis of twenty-three surveys assessing
lay knowledge of eyewitness issues concluded that estimator variables (those not
under the control of the criminal justice system such as the influence of alcohol on
eyewitness memory) were more frequently beyond the knowledge of a jury.[7] Even
when surveys indicate that potential jurors do demonstrate reasonable agreement
with expert opinion, the question remains about whether that information would
be integrated appropriately into their decision-making in a real case.[8] The problem
does not end with jurors. Surveys of other professional groups find that they too,
hold beliefs about memory that are not in accordance with the scientific literature.

(3) Professionals' understanding of memory science

A survey of US and Norwegian judges' knowledge and beliefs about a range of eye- **23.05**
witness issues found that both groups had limited knowledge of the scientific literature.[9] Likewise, a survey of ninety-nine judges in Scotland found a large degree
of variability in their consistency with expert opinion about memory.[10] A survey
of 220 professionals, including social workers, psychiatrists, and clinical psychologists found that 68 per cent of them agreed with the statement that 'everything one
experiences is permanently recorded in one's brain' (with 84% of the social workers

---

[5] Magnussen, S., Andersson, J., Cornoldi, C., De Beni, R., Endestad, T., Goodman, G.S.,
Helstrup, T., et al., 'What people believe about memory' (2006) 14 *Memory*, 595–613.
[6] Simons and Chabris, cited at n.2.
[7] Desmarais, S.L. and Read, J.D., 'After 30 years, what do we know about what jurors know?
A meta-analytic review of lay knowledge regarding eyewitness factors' (2011) 35 *Law and Human
Behavior*, 200–10.
[8] Cutler, B.L., Penrod, S.D., and Dexter, H.R., 'The eyewitness, the expert psychologist, and
the jury' (1989) 13 *Law and Human Behavior*, 311–32.
[9] Magnussen, S., Wise, R.A., Raja, A.Q., Safer, M.A., Pawlenko, N., and Stridbeck, U., 'What
judges know about eyewitness testimony: A comparison of Norwegian and US judges' (2008) 14
Psychology, Crime & Law, 177–88.
[10] Houston, K., Hope, L., Memon, A., and Read, J.D., 'Expert testimony on eyewitness evidence: In search of common sense' (2013) 31 *Behavioral Sciences and the Law*, 637–51.

agreeing with this statement).[11] Likewise, a survey of 858 licensed psychologists in Norway revealed that the average number of correct responses given by this sample (63%) was no different from a parallel survey of judges (63%) and not much higher than a survey of the general public (56%).[12] Interestingly, the beliefs of psychology professors also differed as a function of their training and professional orientation.[13] Professors responsible for teaching an experimental curriculum gave responses that were more in line with the scientific literature than did professors with a clinical (psychodynamic) specialism.[14] Similarly, a survey of psychiatrists found that the vast majority of them reported beliefs that were wildly inconsistent with the memory literature (e.g. that 'blocked memories' can result in physical symptoms like non-epileptic seizures).[15]

23.06 Despite the fact that—among memory scientists—there is a clear consensus on many (but not all) memory-related phenomena, results of surveys with samples of the general public and professionals (including psychologists, psychiatrists, and lay therapists) repeatedly indicate that many of them hold erroneous beliefs about memory. How to deal with such evidence in court therefore presents a challenge for the legal system.

C. The Reconstructive Nature of Autobiographical Memory

(1) Remembering is naturally error-prone

23.07 Over a hundred years of scientific research attest to the fact that memory does not operate like a video camera, accurately recording events as they occur, allowing us to mentally 'rewind' experience and inspect the contents. Remembering is a reconstructive process.[16] While we may remember the general outline (or 'gist') of an event, the specific details fade rapidly.[17] This means that when we attempt to recall an event from our past, what we report might be accurate at the level of 'gist' (i.e.

---

[11] Legault, E. and Laurence, J.-R., 'Recovered memories of childhood sexual abuse: Social worker, psychologist, and psychiatrist reports of beliefs, practices, and cases' (2007) 35 *Australian Journal of Clinical and Experimental Hypnosis*, 111–33.

[12] Magnussen, S. and Melinder, A., 'What psychologists know and believe about memory: A survey of practitioners' (2012) 26 *Applied Cognitive Psychology*, 54–60.

[13] Mirandola, C., Ferruzza, E., Cornoldi, C., and Magnussen, S., 'Beliefs about memory among psychology students and their professors in psychodynamic clinical and experimental study programs' (2013) 63 *European Review of Applied Psychology*, 251–6.

[14] Faust, D. and Ziskin, J., 'The expert witness in psychology and psychiatry' (1988) 241 *Science*, 31–5.

[15] Kemp, S., Spilling, C., Hughes, C., and de Pauw, K., 'Medically unexplained symptoms (MUS): What do current trainee psychologists, neurologists and psychiatrists believe?' (2013) 2 *Open Journal of Medical Psychology*, 12–20.

[16] Bartlett, F.C. (1932) *Remembering: A study in experimental and social psychology*, Cambridge: Cambridge University Press.

[17] Brainerd, C.J. and Reyna, V.F., 'Fuzzy-trace theory and false memory' (2002) 11 *Current Directions in Psychological Science*, 164–9.

someone might remember having their appendix removed during early adulthood) although the specific details (which hospital, which month, the time they were admitted, who was present) might well be incorrect. In a classic study, participants' detailed recall of the moment they heard about the explosion of the Challenger Space Shuttle changed—in some cases markedly—over the course of two and a half years, to the extent that some of them refused to believe that they had written their earlier account that had been produced the morning after the explosion.[18] It is important to note that this kind of memory error is a natural by-product of the cognitive and social processes involved in remembering and occurs in the absence of any specific external suggestion.[19] Psychological science has demonstrated that repeatedly *imagining* a strongly believed in but false event is sufficient to lead to illusory recollections.[20] This highlights the dangers inherent in sustained interviewing by therapists, police, and social services, when tenuously held memories or beliefs are subject to uncritical exploration and development.

(2) Suggestive questioning can alter memory

Psychologists have repeatedly demonstrated that suggestive questioning can alter **23.08** memory reports.[21] For example, after being exposed to a suggestive question, people misremember *details* of terrorist attacks[22] and events surrounding the death of high profile public figures.[23] These particular findings are important because they concern precisely the kinds of events that 'common sense' might suggest would be more memorable and, thus, more resistant to errors.[24] Indeed, there is evidence that even after having been told that the details they remembered were incorrect, a proportion of participants continued to insist that they can still clearly picture the event(s) in their mind[25]—a phenomenon referred to as a non-believed

---

[18] Neisser, U. and Harsch, N., 'Phantom flashbulbs: False recollections of hearing the news about Challenger' in Winograd, E. and Neisser, U. (eds) (1992) *Affect and accuracy in recall*, New York: Cambridge University Press, 9–31.

[19] Mazzoni, G. 'Naturally-occurring and suggestion-dependent memory distortions' (2002) 7 *European Psychologist*, 17–30.

[20] Goff, L.M. and Roediger, H.L., 'Imagination inflation for action events: Repeated imaginings lead to illusory recollections' (1998) 26 *Memory & Cognition*, 20–33.

[21] Frenda, S.J., Nichols, R.M., and Loftus, E.F., 'Current issues and advances in misinformation research' (2011) 20 *Current Directions in Psychological Science*, 20–3.

[22] Ost, J., Granhag, P-A., Udell, J., and Roos af Hjelmsäter, E., 'Familiarity breeds distortion: The effects of media exposure on false reports concerning the media coverage of the terrorist attacks in London on 7th July 2005' (2008) 16 *Memory*, 76–85.

[23] Sjödén, B., Granhag, P-A., Ost, J., and Roos af Hjelmsäter, E., 'Is the truth in the detail? Extended narratives help distinguishing false "memories" from false "reports"' (2009) 50 *Scandinavian Journal of Psychology*, 203–10.

[24] Porter, S. and Peace, K., 'The scars of memory: A prospective, longitudinal investigation of the consistency of traumatic and positive emotional memories in adulthood' (2007) 18 *Psychological Science*, 435–41.

[25] Smeets, T., Telgen, S., Ost, J., Jelicic, M., and Merckelbach, H., 'What's behind crashing memories? Plausibility, belief, and memory of reports of having seen non-existent images' (2009) 23 *Applied Cognitive Psychology*, 1333–41.

memory.[26] Research has shown that, in some cases, people can also report compelling false memories for the 'gist' of events[27]—that is, they remember *entire events* that did not occur. In these studies, participants' parents were asked to provide details of a number of events that did (and more importantly did not) occur in their offspring's childhood. Early research demonstrated that when questioned suggestively over a number of sessions, approximately one quarter of participants reported rich and detailed false memories of being lost in a shopping centre as a child.[28] Researchers then extended this method to show that the types of false events that participants reported included those containing very idiosyncratic suggestions (e.g. that you knocked a punch bowl over at a wedding, ruining the bride's dress)[29] and those concerning unpleasant and frightening events, such as being attacked by an animal[30] or an overnight hospitalization.[31]

(3) 'Memory recovery techniques' are problematic

23.09   So-called 'memory recovery techniques'[32] that are sometimes used to assist recall have also been shown to be problematic and have been included in a list of potentially harmful treatments.[33] Hypnosis, for example, is not a reliable means of helping clients recall traumatic or non-traumatic memories[34] and has been linked directly to the creation of false memories.[35] Guided imagery techniques, where individuals are asked to imagine an event that did not occur, have been shown to increase their subjective belief that an event occurred when it did not—a phenomenon known as 'imagination inflation'.[36] Looking at photographs of one's

---

[26] Mazzoni, G., Scoboria, A., and Harvey, L., 'Non-believed memories' (2010) 21 *Psychological Science*, 1334–40.

[27] Brainerd, C.J. and Reyna, V.F. (2005) *The Science of False Memory*. New York: Oxford University Press.

[28] Loftus, E.F. and Pickrell, J.E., 'The formation of false memories' (1995) 25 *Psychiatric Annals*, 720–25.

[29] Hyman, I.E. Jr, Husband, T.H., and Billings, F.J., 'False memories of childhood experiences' (1995) 9 *Applied Cognitive Psychology*, 181–97.

[30] Porter, S., Yuille, J.C., and Lehman, D.R., 'The nature of real, implanted, and fabricated memories for emotional childhood events: Implications for the recovered memory debate' (1999) 23 *Law and Human Behavior*, 517–37.

[31] Ost, J., Foster, S., Costall, A., and Bull, R., 'False reports of childhood events in appropriate interviews' (2005) 13 *Memory*, 700–10.

[32] Lindsay, D.S. and Read, J.D., 'Psychotherapy and memories of childhood sexual abuse: A cognitive perspective' (1994) 8 *Applied Cognitive Psychology*, 281–338.

[33] Lilienfeld, S.O., 'Psychological treatments that cause harm' (2007) 2 *Perspectives on Psychological Science*, 53–70.

[34] Lynn, S.J., Myers, B., and Malinoski, P., 'Hypnosis, pseudomemories, and clinical guidelines: A sociocognitive perspective' in Read, J.D and Lindsay, D.S. (eds) (1997) *Recollections of trauma: Scientific evidence and clinical practice*, New York: Plenum Press, 305–36.

[35] Green, J.P., Lynn, S.J., and Malinoski, P., 'Hypnotic pseudomemories, prehypnotic warnings, and the malleability of suggested memories' (1998) 12 *Applied Cognitive Psychology*, 431–44.

[36] Garry, M., Manning, C.G., Loftus, E.F., and Sherman, S.J., 'Imagination inflation: Imagining a childhood event inflates confidence that it occurred' (1996) 3 *Psychonomic Bulletin and Review*, 208–14.

childhood, when combined with a misleading suggestion, leads to much higher rates of 'false memory' than a misleading suggestion alone.[37] Forcing someone to describe a blatantly false detail or event can lead to false memories.[38] In addition, simply instructing participants to reflect on the meaning and implications of suggested events (referred to as 'conceptual elaboration') can, under certain circumstances, lead to increased rates of wholly false memory.[39]

At a general level, what all of these techniques do is lead us to generate a perceptually rich and detailed image of a past real or false event. When we are later asked about that event, we misattribute the 'source' of the memory (e.g. that it was imagined, or came to mind while we were hypnotized) and may report it as being a genuine memory.[40] In other words, we incorporate incorrect information into our mental representation of the event such that it is indistinguishable from what was originally experienced.[41] This difficulty in correctly monitoring the source of information may partially explain why scores on a constellation of personality variables (fantasy proneness, dissociation) are often positively correlated with memory errors in laboratory studies. For example, individuals who are fantasy-prone appear to be more susceptible to certain memory errors, possibly because they experience more vivid mental imagery and—as a result—may be more likely to confuse imagination and memory.[42] Likewise, there are correlations between measures of dissociation (symptoms of which include perceptual distortions about the self or environment and an inability to control mental functions such as memory) and measures of suggestibility, susceptibility to false memories, and symptom exaggeration.[43]

23.10

(4) False memories beyond the laboratory

Within the confines of the psychological laboratory, ethical standards rightly preclude attempts to suggest to participants that they had experienced potentially traumatic events like being the victim of sexual abuse in childhood. However,

23.11

---

[37] Lindsay, D.S., Hagen, L., Read, J.D., Wade, K.A., and Garry, M., 'True photographs and false memories' (2004) 15 *Psychological Science*, 149–54.

[38] Ackil, J.K. and Zaragoza, M.S., 'Memorial consequences of forced confabulation: Age differences in susceptibility to false memories' (1998) 34 *Developmental Psychology*, 1358–72.

[39] Zaragoza, M.S., Mitchell, K.J., Payment, K., and Drivdahl, S., 'False memories for suggestions: The impact of conceptual elaboration' (2011) 64(1) *Journal of Memory and Language*, 18–31.

[40] Lindsay, D.S. and Johnson, M.K., 'Source monitoring and recognition memory' (1991) 29 *Bulletin of the Psychonomic Society*, 203–5.

[41] Hyman, I.E. and Pentland, J., 'Guided imagery and the creation of false childhood memories' (1996) 35 *Journal of Memory and Language*, 101–17.

[42] Merckelbach, H., Horselenberg, R., and Muris, P., 'The Creative Experience Questionnaire (CEQ): a brief self-report measure of fantasy proneness' (2001) 31 *Personality and Individual Differences*, 987–95.

[43] Lynn, S.J., Lilienfeld, S.O., Merckelbach, H., Giesbrecht, T., McNally, R., Loftus, E.F., Bruck, M., Garry, M., and Malaktaris, A., (2014) 'The Trauma Model of Dissociation: Inconvenient Truths and Stubborn Fictions: Comment on Dalenberg et al.' (2012) 140 *Psychological Bulletin*, 896–910.

convergent evidence from a variety of sources outside the laboratory indicates that people can and do come to misremember events of a sexually abusive nature.[44] Research has shown that individuals report memories of being abducted and sexually interfered with by space aliens[45] or having been raised as a member of a satanic cult and being forced to participate in horrific acts.[46] The common element in the development of those memories of—at best—highly improbable events appears to have been a therapist who strongly endorsed or uncritically accepted such experiences as being the 'cause' of a client's presenting problems.[47] Research has shown that the beliefs of therapists can be a strong determinant of what is 'remembered' by a client in therapy.[48] Likewise, research with retractors—individuals who have repudiated their earlier claims of being sexually abused as children—suggests that the therapeutic process played a large role in the development of memories that they now realize are false.[49]

23.12 The scientific literature is thus replete with examples of the fallible and reconstructive nature of remembering (including wholly false memories of significant and negatively charged childhood events). However, in everyday life this is generally unproblematic, as there are few instances where we need to recall details from our past with such precision—usually the 'gist' will suffice.[50] Where it does pose a challenge, of course, is in investigative and legal contexts where a memory (or memories) often constitutes the only available evidence. Understanding the nature of memory is critical in such cases and failure to do so can result in potential[51] and actual[52] miscarriages of justice. Recognition of this problem has led psychologists over the last forty years to devote considerable effort to understanding the reliability of memory. The remainder of this chapter is focused on three specific

---

[44] Ost, J., 'Recovered memories and suggestibility for entire events' in Ridley, A., Gabbert, F., and La Rooy, D. (eds) (2013) *Suggestibility in Legal Contexts: Psychological research and Forensic Implications*, Chichester: Wiley-Blackwell, 107–28.

[45] Clancy, S.A. (2005) *Abducted: How people come to believe they were kidnapped by aliens*, Harvard, MA: Harvard University Press.

[46] La Fontaine, J.S. (1998) *Speak of the devil: Tales of satanic abuse in contemporary England*, Cambridge: Cambridge University Press.

[47] Bottoms, B.L., Shaver, P.R., and Goodman, G.S., 'An analysis of ritualistic and religion-related child abuse allegations' (1996) 20 *Law and Human Behavior*, 1–34.

[48] Spanos, N.P., Menary, E., Gabora, N.J., Du Breuil, S.C., and Dewhirst, B., 'Secondary identity enactments during hypnotic past-life regression: A socio-cognitive perspective' (1991) 61 *Journal of Personality and Social Psychology*, 308–20; Bottoms, B.L. and Davis, S.L., 'The creation of satanic ritual abuse' (1997) 16 *Journal of Social and Clinical Psychology*, 112–32.

[49] Ost, J. and Nunkoosing, K., 'Reconstructing Bartlett and revisiting the "false memory" controversy' in Haaken J. and Reavey, P. (eds) (2009) *Memory matters: understanding contexts for recollecting child sexual abuse*, London: Routledge, 41–62.

[50] Newman, E. and Lindsay, D.S., 'False memories: What the hell are they for?' (2009) 23 *Applied Cognitive Psychology*, 1105–21.

[51] Loftus, E.F., 'Eyewitness testimony in the Lockerbie bombing case' (2013) 21 *Memory*, 584–90. See also Wolchover, D. (2014) *Culprits of Lockerbie*, *http://www.davidwolchover.co.uk/docs/Culprits%20of%20Lockerbie.doc*.

[52] *http://www.innocenceproject.org/Content/DNA_Exonerations_Nationwide.php*.

areas where psychological science has provided evidence that is counter-intuitive and—more importantly—challenges common-sense understanding of the way memory works. These findings have clear implications for the way in which memory evidence is currently presented and evaluated in the courts.

D. Counter-intuitive Findings about Memory Relevant to Legal Proceedings

(1) Detailed accounts

A highly detailed memory report, although desirable from an investigative and legal point of view, does not guarantee that the memory is accurate. The scientific research has shown repeatedly that, although we may remember the *'gist'* of an event, the specific *details* of an event fade over time. If asked to think about, or report, the details of this event, one might try and 'fill in the gaps' in order to provide a coherent narrative. The point is that memory for the very specific details from an event that occurred many years ago would be considered unusual.[53] It is possible that these more detailed aspects of a witness's memory are either guesses about what might have happened, have been added later following discussions with other people, or are based on general knowledge not related specifically to the alleged event (e.g. general details about one's childhood home). Thus, just because a memory (or an aspect of a memory) of an event is very detailed, it does not mean that the event occurred. Nor does a lack of detail necessarily suggest that an event did not happen—research shows that we frequently do not report significant events that would presumably have been fairly memorable at the time.[54] Put simply, the level of detail in any given account of a childhood event is unlikely to be diagnostic of its accuracy. The recall of one or more highly specific details may make a memory seem credible to an observer (or a jury) but, in fact, does not guarantee that a memory is accurate, or even that the event occurred.[55] Furthermore, recent research suggests that it is extremely rare for young children (aged five to six) to freely recall certain attributes of an event (e.g. the date and time, duration of an event, and the narrative sequence of individual components of an event) and that these details do not reliably appear until children are approximately ten years of age. Thus adult accounts of childhood events that contain such details 'exceed the limits of what a child would be capable of at the time the event was encoded'.[56]

23.13

---

[53] Conway, M.A., 'On being a memory expert witness: Three cases' (2013) 21 *Memory*, 566–75.

[54] Lindsay, D.S. and Read, J.D., 'Adults' memories of long-past events' in Nilsson, L.G. and N. Ohta, N. (eds) (2006) *Memory and society: Psychological perspectives*. New York: Psychology Press, 43–64.

[55] Bell, B.E. and Loftus, E.F., 'Trivial persuasion in the courtroom: The power of (a few) minor details' (1989) 56 *Journal of Personality and Social Psychology*, 669–79.

[56] Strange, D. and Hayne, H., 'The devil is in the detail: Children's recollection of details about their prior experiences' (2013) 21 *Memory*, 431–43, at 441.

(2) Inconsistencies in recall

23.14 In the legal context, inconsistencies in an account are often used to undermine a witness' credibility,[57] are perceived by jurors and legal professionals to be indicative of inaccurate testimony,[58] and often harm mock jurors' perceptions of witness credibility, leading to increased not guilty verdicts.[59] However, research shows that these beliefs about inconsistencies are not in accordance with the findings of psychological science. To begin with there is more than one kind of inconsistent statement that a witness can make. Consider a witness who is interviewed by the police (time 1) and then called to give evidence in court (time 2). They may report details at time 2 that directly *contradict* details they reported at time 1. Alternatively, they may report additional details at time 2 that they did not report at time 1 (referred to in the psychological literature as *reminiscence*[60]). Both of these scenarios would lead to a perception that the witness is providing inconsistent testimony leading to the accuracy of their entire testimony being questioned. Furthermore, research that has systematically examined the quality of memories of events that are reported on two different occasions (e.g. time 1 and time 2) shows that *contradictory* and *reminiscent* statements are associated with different levels of accuracy.

23.15 *Contradictory* statements are typically fairly rare in laboratory studies of eyewitness memory and they are, of course, more likely to be inaccurate (only one statement can be correct). However, research shows that the overall accuracy of witnesses who make several contradictory statements is no worse than witnesses who make few such statements. *Reminiscent* statements, although also relatively infrequent in laboratory studies of memory, are more accurate than contradictory ones and—in some studies—almost as accurate as consistent details.[61] The prevalence of reminiscent statements in a report is also unrelated to the overall accuracy of the report. Even when both types of inconsistent statements (*contradictory* and *reminiscent*) are combined there is no evidence that inconsistency is predictive of inaccurate testimony.

23.16 What this research suggests is that various components of a complex event (e.g. offender's description, offender's actions) are processed independently. Thus it is entirely possible that a witness could provide inaccurate reports of one aspect of an

---

[57] Fisher, R.P., Brewer, N., and Mitchell, G., 'The relation between consistency and accuracy of eyewitness testimony: Legal versus cognitive explanations' in Bull, R., Valentine, T., and Williamson, T. (eds) (2009) *Handbook of psychology of investigative interviewing: Current developments and future directions*. Chichester: John Wiley & Sons Ltd, 121–36.

[58] Potter, R. and Brewer, N., 'Perceptions of witness behaviour-accuracy relationship held by police, lawyers and jurors' (1999) 6 *Psychiatry, Psychology and Law*, 97–103.

[59] Brewer, N. and Hupfeld, R.M., 'Effects of testimonial inconsistencies and witness group identity on mock juror judgments' (2004) 34 *Journal of Applied Social Psychology*, 493–513.

[60] Turtle, J.W. and Yuille, J.C., 'Lost but not forgotten details: Repeated eyewitness recall leads to reminiscence but not hypermnesia' (1994) 79 *Journal of Applied Psychology*, 260–71.

[61] Oeberst, A., 'If anything else comes to mind … better keep it to yourself? Delayed recall is discrediting—unjustifiably' (2012) 36 *Law and Human Behavior*, 266–74.

event (e.g. what the offender was wearing) whilst also providing accurate reports of other aspects (e.g. what the offender did). Therefore the practice of using inconsistencies to diagnose (or suggest) that a particular witness's overall testimony is unreliable is at odds with the findings of contemporary memory science.

(3) Memories 'recovered' following a period of non-awareness

Some survivors of reported childhood sexual abuse claim to have remembered epi- **23.17** sodes of childhood abuse of which they were previously unaware ('discontinuous memories'). These are sometimes described as the 'recovery' of traumatic memories that have been 'repressed' or 'dissociated'.[62] Memory science has found no evidence to support a mechanism for 'repression' or 'blocking out' of memory.[63] Despite this lack of evidence, the idea that the mind can selectively 'block out' memories of trauma continues to have considerable influence in legal contexts.[64] However, if there is no evidence that the mind 'blocks out' memory of such events what else might account for these 'recovered memory' experiences? As it turns out memory science provides a number of alternative and relatively mundane mechanisms that could account for an apparently 'discontinuous' memory of abuse.[65]

The first is that the abuse was not traumatic (or experienced as traumatic) at the time **23.18** it occurred. It may have only been in adulthood that the person comes to realize or understand what it was that they experienced.[66] In this case, events that have always been remembered are interpreted in a very different light (or 're-perceived'[67]). There is evidence that this can be very distressing[68] but it is clearly not the same as claiming the person had blocked out the traumatic memory.

A second possibility is that reminders of the abuse were absent. As the scientific **23.19** evidence strongly suggests that traumatic memories do not have any particularly special properties in terms of their memorability[69] then memories of abuse, as with any memory, will fade over time if not cued. If, for example, the person subsequently moved away from the area where the abuse occurred, or the perpetrator died, then there would be few reminders. Due to the secretive nature of childhood

---

[62] McNally, R.J. (2003) *Remembering trauma*, Cambridge, MA: Harvard University Press.
[63] Kihlstrom, J.F., 'No need for repression' (2002) 6 *Trends in Cognitive Sciences*, 502.
[64] Piper, A., Lillevik, L., and Kritzer, R., 'What's wrong with believing in repression? A review for legal professionals' (2008) 14 *Psychology, Public Policy, and Law*, 223–42.
[65] McNally, R.J. and Geraerts, E., 'A new solution to the Recovered Memory Debate' (2009) 4 *Perspectives on Psychological Science*, 126–34.
[66] Clancy, S.A. (2009) *The trauma myth: The truth about the sexual abuse of children—and its aftermath*, New York: Basic Books.
[67] Payne, D.G. and Blackwell, J.M., 'Truth in memory: Caveat emptor' in Lynn S.J. and McConkey, K.M. (eds) (1998) *Truth in memory*, New York: The Guilford Press, 32–61.
[68] Clancy, S.A. and McNally, R.J., 'Who needs repression? Normal memory processes can explain "forgetting" of childhood sexual abuse' (2005/2006) 4 *Scientific Review of Mental Health Practice*, 66–73.
[69] Shobe, K.K. and Kihlstrom, J.F., 'Is traumatic memory special?' (1997) 8 *Current Directions in Psychological Science*, 70–4.

sexual abuse, it is very unlikely that other people would provide memory cues, unless the child had disclosed the abuse to someone else at the time it had occurred.

23.20 A third possibility is that people may deliberately try to avoid thinking about the abuse. However, because intentionally trying not to think about a particular memory or event is not a particularly effective technique—because you are essentially providing yourself with a strong memory cue for the very thing you are trying to forget ('don't think about a white bear'[70])—people may avoid thinking about the abuse by distracting themselves, or focusing on other thoughts instead.

23.21 A fourth possibility is that some individuals may have forgotten that they had previously remembered the abusive episodes. This is termed the 'forgot-it-all-along' (FIA) effect and originates from a series of case studies published by Schooler and colleagues.[71] They found that some people who claimed to have suddenly 'remembered' forgotten episodes of childhood abuse had, in fact, previously disclosed that abuse to other people (e.g. spouses). The issue then is not that they had forgotten, repressed, or dissociated their memories of abuse—rather they had forgotten that they had previously remembered it. Put another way, they had underestimated their previous successful recall of those events. Experimental analogues have provided support for the FIA effect and argued that it is caused by changes in the recall context.[72]

23.22 A final possibility is that recovered memory experiences may be based on false beliefs or memories that have developed over time. For example, medical or therapeutic notes sometimes indicate that there was no mention of any abuse prior to, or during the early stages of, treatment and that beliefs and memories of abuse appear to have emerged over the course of that treatment. Whilst this does not mean those events did not happen, it does raise important questions about the reliability of that testimony (as outlined in Section C), even though it may be honestly and genuinely believed in, and compellingly presented.

23.23 In summary, the evidence is that some discontinuous abuse memories (i.e. those reported to have been recalled after a period of non-awareness) appear to be genuine. What is less clear is what it is that is responsible for the 'period of non-awareness'. There is no evidence for any kind of mechanism that 'banishes' swathes of traumatic memories from conscious awareness, although this still remains a powerful theory in some contexts. The weight of the evidence suggests that reasonably ordinary and mundane processes of remembering and forgetting can account for 'periods of non-awareness'.

---

[70] Wegner, D.M., Schneider, D.J., Carter, S., and White, T., 'Paradoxical effects of thought suppression' (1987) 53 *Journal of Personality and Social Psychology*, 5–13.

[71] Schooler, J.W., Bendiksen, M., and Ambadar, Z., 'Taking the middle line: Can we accommodate both fabricated and recovered memories of sexual abuse?' in Conway M.A. (ed.) (1997) *Recovered memories and false memories*, Oxford: Oxford University Press, 251–92.

[72] Arnold, M.M. and Lindsay, D.S., 'Remembering remembering' (2002) 28 *Journal of Experimental Psychology: Learning, Memory, & Cognition*, 521–9.

E. Conclusion

The aim of this chapter was to highlight that memory science is at the heart of the **23.24** investigative and legal process. The scientific research shows that memory science is not always well understood by key stakeholders in the criminal justice system or by those who may be called upon to assist. The reconstructive and malleable nature of memory—usually unproblematic in everyday life—presents enormous challenges when issues of justice and liberty are at stake. Memory science has shown that many common-sense assumptions about memory are not supported (or are more nuanced) when subject to rigorous and controlled investigation. If these assumptions are allowed to go unchallenged or uncorrected then there is the risk of a miscarriage of justice. This clearly highlights the need for ongoing dialogue and collaboration between memory scientists and those involved in the legal system.

Further Reading

Special issue of the Taylor and Francis journal Memory entitled 'Memory and the Law: Case studies' Volume 5, 545–617.
Howe, M.L. (2011) *The nature of early memory*, Oxford: Oxford University Press.
McNally, R.J. and Geraerts, E., A new solution to the Recovered Memory Debate (2009) 4 *Perspectives on Psychological Science*, 126–34.

Author Biographies

Dr James Ost is Reader in Applied Cognitive Psychology at the Department of Psychology, University of Portsmouth. He is a Chartered Psychologist and Associate Fellow of the British Psychological Society and a member of the Scientific and Professional Advisory Board of the British False Memory Society. He has published over thirty peer-reviewed articles and book chapters, focusing mainly on memory errors, has advised police forces on interview strategy and appeared as an expert witness in court.

Professor Chris French is the Head of the Anomalistic Psychology Research Unit at Goldsmiths, University of London. He is a Fellow of the British Psychological Society and a member of the Scientific and Professional Advisory Board of the British False Memory Society. He has published over one hundred articles and chapters covering a wide range of topics. He frequently appears on radio and television casting a sceptical eye over paranormal claims, as well as writing for *The Guardian* and *The Skeptic* magazine. His most recent book, co-authored with Anna Stone, is *Anomalistic Psychology: Exploring Paranormal Belief and Experience*.

24

PATHOLOGICAL LYING

Charles C. Dike and Reena Kapoor

A. Introduction

The Miriam-Webster Dictionary defines a lie as 'to make an untrue statement **24.01** with intent to deceive; to create a false or misleading impression; an untrue or inaccurate statement that may or may not be believed true by the speaker; and so on'. Lying is a normal human behaviour and ubiquitous in every culture, from the so-called white lies told to grease social intercourse to the defensive lies told to avoid consequences of truth-telling. In fact, deception, the ultimate goal of ordinary lies, is considered a biological need,[1] adaptive as a protective device among both humans and animals; animals, of course, do not lie, but they can engage in other forms of deception. For example, chameleons change colour to avoid predators, and some birds feign injury to divert attention from their young offspring.

---

[1] Wile, I.S., 'Lying as a Social Phenomenon' (1928) 20 *Arch. NeurPsych*, 1284–311.

24.02 Despite these adaptive uses of deception, lying is often considered rude behaviour. Yet, according to Selling, everyone lies.[2] There is general agreement that ordinary lies serve an apparent purpose to the liar, either to obtain an external reward or to avoid a negative consequence. However, a German physician, Anton Delbruck,[3] is credited with coining the term pseudologia phantastica to describe a special type of lying behaviour he observed in a group of his patients; their lies were so out of proportion and abnormal that they seemed incomprehensible to him. They were not ordinary lies. With time, pseudologia phantastica became known as pathological lying, and now it is also used interchangeably with mythomania, morbid lying, compulsive lying, and pseudologia fantastica, but it remains uncertain if all these terms describe the same exact phenomenon. Of these, pathological lying is the term most recognizable by the lay public. However, the popular understanding of what constitutes pathological lying is somewhat simplistic. For example, many people think of pathological liars as individuals who repeatedly lie to gain prestige or money, such as the infamous case of 'Clark Rockefeller'.[4] Others believe that individuals who are callous and lie on a grand scale, such as those involved in perpetrating Ponzi schemes for many years, are pathological liars. While these definitions help to create an ease of discourse about lying in everyday conversation, pathological lying as understood by clinicians is more complicated and more difficult to package into a neat definition.

24.03 Mental health professionals have been trying to understand and define this special group of liars ever since pseudologia phantastica was introduced in the literature over a century ago. In recent years, the definition of pathological lying has coalesced around certain core elements observed and agreed upon by different researchers, although the concept of pathological lying continues to undergo refinement. However, no uniform International Classification of Diseases (ICD) or Diagnostic and Statistical Manual (DSM) definition or criteria for the disorder have been created as yet.

B. Definition and Characteristics

24.04 Pathological lying can be defined as a lifestyle of repeated, extensive, and frequent lying, often fantastic in nature, for which there is no apparent external motive or

[2] Selling, L.S., 'The psychiatric aspects of the pathological liar' (1942) 1 *Nervous Child*, 335–50.

[3] Delbruck, A. (1891) *Die pathologische Luge und die psychisch abnormen Schwindler. Eine Untersuchung uber den allmahlichen Uebergang eines normalen psychologischen Vorgangs in ein pathologisches Symptom, fur Aerzte und Juristen*, 131, Stuttgart,Healy W. (trans) Healy M.T.: Pathological lying, accusation and swindling, in (1969) Patterson Smith Reprints Series in Criminology, Law Enforcement, and Social Problems, Gault R.H., Crossly F.B., Garner J.W., Montclair, N.J. Patterson Smith, (eds) 14.

[4] Belluck, P. and Rimer, S. (2008) *Ready-made Rockefeller, http://www.nytimes.com/2008/08/24/fashion/24rockefeller.html?_r=0*.

benefit. Pathological lies often appear purposeless. They can often be easily veri-fied to be untrue, and in some cases, might even be self-incriminating or damag-ing, which makes them more incomprehensible to the audience. Even when there appears to be an external reason for the lies in pathological lying, the lies are so grossly out of proportion to the apparent gain that they appear illogical. Such characteristics of pathological lying have led some researchers to conclude that the lying behaviour appears to be a gratification in itself;[5] the reward is internal to the liar.

Researchers who have grappled with this phenomenon in the past have wondered **24.05** if the pathological liar recognized his or her lies as false or believed them to be real. Some have observed that the lie is impulsive and unplanned[6] and seizes the liar suddenly, while others have proposed that in the final analysis, pathological liars lose mastery of their lies such that the lies have the worth of a real experience and cannot be differentiated from a delusion.[7] It has also been proposed that the lie in pathological lying is an expression of the desired self rather than the actual self, and with time, the desired self becomes preponderant and decisive.[8] An extension of this proposition is the hypothesis that pathological lying is a 'wish psychosis',[9] similar to a psychotic experience with impaired reality testing. All of these charac-terizations of pathological lying reflect the conundrum that confronts a clinician when faced with a pathological liar and suggests, at least in part, that the pathologi-cal liar may not have control over his lies and may believe them to be true. The ease and confidence with which the pathological liar tells lies and the apparent lack of distress associated with it despite knowledge that the lies could be easily exposed, adds credence to the notion that the pathological liar believes his lies to be true. As such, some have suggested that the pathological liar sometimes appears to lose contact with reality.[10]

---

  [5] Deutsch, H., 'On the pathological lie (Pseudologia phantastica)' (1982) 10(3) *J. Am. Acad. Psychoanal*, 369–86.

  [6] Stemmermann, A. (1906) *Beitrage und Kasuistik der pseudologia phantastica*, Geo. Reimer, Berlin, 102. Translated by Healy W, Healy M.T. 'Pathological lying, accusation and swindling' in Patterson Smith Reprints Series in Criminology, Law Enforcement, and Social Problems edited by Gault R.H., Crossly F.B., Garner J.W., and Montclair, N.J.: Patterson Smith, 26–7, 1969.

  [7] Koppen M (1898): *Ueber die pathologische Lugner*, Charite-Annalen, 8, 674–719. Translated by Healy W, Healy M.T. 'Pathological lying, accusation and swindling' in Patterson Smith Reprints Series in Criminology, Law Enforcement, and Social Problems edited by Gault R.H., Crossly F.B., Garner J.W., and Montclair, N.J.: Patterson Smith, 19, 1969.

  [8] Wendt E (LXVIII): *Ein Beitrag zur Kasuistik der pseudologia phantastica*, Allgemeine Zeitschrift fur Psychiatrie 4:482–500. Translated by Healy W., Healy M.T.: 'Pathological lying, accusation and swindling' in Patterson Smith Reprints Series in Criminology, Law Enforcement, and Social Problems edited by Gault R.H., Crossly F.B., Garner J.W., Montclair, N.J.: Patterson Smith, 33, 1969.

  [9] Vogt H (1910) *Jugendliche Lugnerinnen. Zeitschrift fur Erforschung d. jugend*, Schwachsinns Bd.3. H.5:394-438. Translated by Healy W., Healy M.T. 'Pathological lying, accusation and swin-dling' in Patterson Smith Reprints Series in Criminology, Law Enforcement, and Social Problems edited by Gault R.H., Crossly F.B., Garner J.W., Montclair, N.J., Patterson Smith, 25, 1969.

  [10] See the references cited at nn.6, 7, and 9.

24.06   Not all researchers or clinicians share this belief, however. An alternative view suggests that pathological lying is fantasy on the part of the liar, a fantasy lie communicated as reality.[11] As fantasy, the lie is a gratification in and of itself. Others have likened the impulses that drive the lying behaviour in pathological lying as similar to those that drive literary creation.[12] The pathological liar, like the author of fiction, develops and weaves plots involving different themes and often thrusts himself into the centre of these plots. Finally, the observation that the pathological liar may admit some of his lies when vigorously challenged[13] may be an indication that the liar has not lost contact with reality. However, the degree of contact with reality can be difficult to assess in some individuals, particularly those who doggedly hold firmly to their lies in the face of contrary evidence. With persistent challenge, however, the pathological liar is more likely to slightly alter his or her lies or to change topics as he or she subsequently proceeds with more elaboration of lies.

24.07   Other characteristics of pathological lying that have generated attention and speculation include the observation that the lie is impulsive and 'seizes the liar suddenly'.[14] According to Otto Fenichel, some authors have highlighted the obsessional nature of the lies and subsequently proposed that pathological liars are compelled to lie repeatedly or have obsessional falsifications.[15] A more recent question that bears further consideration is whether or not a pathological liar is addicted to lying; is pathological lying an addictive behaviour?

C. Etiological Considerations

24.08   The etiology of pathological lying is unclear. However, in reviewing theories proposed regarding the etiology, two divergent views emerge: that pathological lying is an independent phenomenon not caused by another mental disease or organic brain syndrome,[16] referred to as primary pathological lying,[17] or that pathological lying is always secondary to another disorder of the brain,[18] Secondary Pathological Lying.[19]

---

[11] See Deutsch (1982), cited at n.5.

[12] Risch B (1908): *Uber die phantastische form des degenerativen irreseins (Pseudologia phantastica)*, Allgemeine Zeitschrift fur Psychiatrie 65(4):576–639. Translated by Healy W., Healy M.T. 'Pathological lying, accusation and swindling' in Patterson Smith Reprints Series in Criminology, Law Enforcement, and Social Problems, edited by Gault R.H., Crossly F.B., Garner J.W., Montclair, N.J., Patterson Smith, 21–2, 1969.

[13] Wiersma, D. 'On pathological lying' (1933) 2(1) *Character and Personality*, 48–61.

[14] See Stemmermann (1906), cited at n.6.

[15] Fenichel, O. 'The economics of pseudologia fantastica' in Fenichel O, (ed.) (1939) *The Collected Papers of Otto Fenichel*, second series, New York: Norton.

[16] Healy, W. and Healy, M.T. (1926) *Pathological Lying, Accusation and Swindling*. Boston: Little, Brown and Company.

[17] Dike, C.C., Baranoski, M., and Griffith, E.E.H., 'Pathological Lying Revisited' (2005) 33 *J. Am. Acad. Psychiatry. Law*, 342–9.

[18] See Selling (1942), cited at n.2.

[19] See Dike et al. (2005), cited at n.17.

Neither of these theories regarding etiology is definitive, as there are reported cases of pathological lying both with and without other psychiatric or neurological impairment.[20] Central nervous system (CNS) abnormalities such as epilepsy, brain infection, electroencephalographic (EEG) changes, brain trauma,[21] and right hemithalamic dysfunction[22] have been associated with some pathological liars, but it is not clear how they are associated.

Psychodynamic theorists have suggested that pathological lying is an attempt to displace or disguise intrapsychic conflict.[23] Pathological lying facilitates the repression of emotional distress and functions as an unconscious psychological defence against traumatic memories or intolerable affect.[24] Some have observed that the lying is often worsened by stress[25] which supports the idea that the lying behaviour serves an important psychological purpose for the individual. **24.09**

D. Epidemiology

There is paucity of information on the epidemiological characteristics of pathological lying. In a study of 1,000 repeat juvenile offenders, the prevalence of pathological lying was reported as close to 1 per cent.[26] The literature has shown variability in reports of the sex ratio in pathological lying, ranging from a preponderance of females[27] to an equal ratio of males and females.[28] A review of 72 cases of pathological lying[29] showed the average age of onset of the lying behaviour as 16 and the average age at discovery as 22. The Intelligence Quotient (IQ) of pathological liars has been reported as average or below average.[30] There is no evidence that socioeconomic factors play a role in the development of the phenomenon. **24.10**

E. Treatment

The current recommended treatment for pathological lying is long-term insight oriented psychotherapy with the aim of the pathological liar developing insight **24.11**

---

[20] Ibid.

[21] King, B.H. and Ford, C.V. 'Pseudologia fantastica' (1988) 77 *Acta psychiatr. Scand.*, 1–6.

[22] Modell, J.G., Mountz, J.M., Ford, C.V., 'Pathological lying associated with thalamic dysfunction demonstrated by [99mTc] HMPAO SPECT' (1992) 4(4) *J. Neuropsychiatry*, 442–6.

[23] Ford, C.V., King, B.H., and Hollander, M.H. 'Lies and Liars: Psychiatric Aspects of Prevarication' (1988) 145(5) *The American Journal of Psychiatry* 554–62.

[24] Snyder, S., 'Pseudologia fantastica in the borderline patient' (1986) 1431(10) *The American Journal of Psychiatry*, 1287–9.

[25] See Healy and Healy (1926), cited at n.16.

[26] King, B.H. and Ford, C.V., 'Pseudologia fantastica' (1988) 77 *Acta Psychiatrica Scandinavica*, 1–6.

[27] Healy and Healy (1926), cited at n.16.

[28] King and Ford (1988), cited at n.26.

[29] Ibid.

[30] Ibid.

into his lying behaviour and its causes and consequences. Cognitive behaviour therapy (CBT) may also be used to teach the pathological liar how to identify the thinking patterns that precede the lying behaviour. However, the effectiveness of psychotherapy in treating pathological lying has not been systematically studied.

24.12 Given the proposed hypotheses regarding the characteristics of pathological lying, psychiatrists working with these individuals should carefully evaluate the presence of behaviours that would encourage a trial of psychotropic medications (as adjuncts to psychotherapy). For example, medications used by psychiatrists to decrease impulsivity or manage compulsive behaviours may be considered. Likewise, medications used to decrease cravings in substance addiction could also be tried in select cases if there are indications the pathological liar is addicted to the lies. None of these treatments are formally indicated for the treatment of pathological lying, however, so treatment is guided by clinical judgement rather than established guidelines.

F. Pathological Lying and Sexual Abuse Allegations

24.13 False accusations are not uncommon in pathological lying. As Hoyer postulated, pathological liars most often tell stories in which they are either the hero or the victim, as these types of tales create a sense of 'specialness' about the individual.[31] In some instances, the individual is portrayed as a victim of fate—for example, contracting a serious illness—but in others, a perpetrator is alleged. Published case reports document pathological liars who have falsely accused others of a wide variety of improprieties: stalking, threatening, kidnapping, physical abuse, and rape.[32] In some cases, these accusations have resulted in criminal prosecution of the alleged offender, only to have the charges dismissed after the 'victim's' lies are discovered.

24.14 Forensic mental health professionals asked to evaluate alleged victims of sexual abuse are unlikely to encounter pathological lying, even in cases where the victim's credibility is in question. As discussed in other chapters of this text, many common psychiatric and neurologic conditions are more likely to affect an individual's recollection of sexual abuse than pathological lying. For example, psychotic symptoms, cognitive deficits, or traumatic dissociation may interfere with an individual's ability to give a clear and consistent account of the abuse, creating the impression of lies. Pathological lying should be considered, but it is much further down the list of differential diagnoses.

---

[31] Hoyer, T. 'Pseudologia fantastica: A consideration of "the lie" and a case presentation' (1959) 33 *Psychiatric Quarterly*, 203–20.

[32] Birch, C.D., Kelln, B.R., and Aquino, E.C., 'A review and case report of pseudologia fantastica' (2006) 17(2) *Journal of Forensic Psychiatry and Psychology*, 299–320; see also Ford, et al. (1988), cited at n.23.

Pathological lying is also less common a reason for making false allegations of **24.15** sexual abuse than 'regular' lying. False allegations occur fairly frequently; studies estimate that 8 to 41 per cent of all rape allegations are false.[33] Motivations for making these accusations are varied, and pathological lying is only one possible explanation. Turvey and McGrath identified several others: profit, anger/revenge, crime concealment, and mitigation of responsibility.[34] Bernet has also articulated many reasons that individuals, particularly children, make false reports of sexual abuse: suggestion, indoctrination, fantasy, delusion, misinterpretation, deliberate lying, perpetrator substitution, and group contagion.[35] All of these reasons are just as likely—if not more so—to explain false accusations of sexual abuse than the relatively rare condition of pathological lying.

(1) Illustrative cases

Few case reports involving sexual abuse allegations and pathological lying have **24.16** been published in the English-language literature, but those that have may provide some guidance in understanding the intersection between the two phenomena. Some illustrative examples are shown in the following paragraphs.

(a) Ms A

A 28-year-old woman sought treatment for seizures after allegedly being beaten **24.17** and raped. Over the course of the hospital admission, it was determined by video EEG monitoring that the seizures were non-epileptic, and medical records from the time of the alleged rape were wholly inconsistent with her report. Her parents visited the hospital and reported that she had been hospitalized repeatedly under similar circumstances. In addition, she had made several calls to police as a teenager saying that she had been assaulted. Though she had been 'tied up' and was found 'unconscious', she was ultimately found to have fabricated the incidents entirely by smashing items around the house and tying herself to a chair. When confronted with this history by hospital staff and her parents, she fled.[36]

(b) Ms B

The four children of Ms B, a middle-aged French woman, were suspected by **24.18** school officials of being abused after the eldest displayed provocative and sexualized behaviour. Ms B confessed to the abuse and implicated her husband. Over the next few months, Ms B co-operated with authorities and implicated over a

---

[33] Turvey, B.E. and McGrath, M., 'False allegations of sexual assault' in Savino, J. and Turvey, B. (eds) (2011) *Rape Investigation Handbook*, 2nd edn, Waltham, MA: Academic Press, 269–92.
[34] Ibid.
[35] Bernet, W., 'False statements and the differential diagnosis of abuse allegations' (1993) 32(5) *Journal of the American Academy of Child and Adolescent Psychiatry*, 903–10.
[36] Feldman, M.D., Ford, C.V., and Stone, T., 'Deceiving others/deceiving oneself: Four cases of factitious rape' (1994) 87(7) *Southern Medical Journal*, 736–8.

dozen neighbours in the alleged sexual abuse of twenty-five children. The children were removed from their homes, the adults were detained, and eventually a trial ensued. At the trial, Ms B admitted that she had fabricated the allegations against her neighbours, saying, 'Nothing is true! I am a sick person and a liar!' Only four people (Ms B, her husband, and two neighbours) were ever convicted of the crime; the remaining charges were dismissed. The case sparked a public outcry and a parliamentary inquiry into the perceived dysfunction of France's judicial system.[37]

(c) Mr C

24.19 An 18-year-old man was admitted to a psychiatric hospital for treatment of depression and substance abuse. A week after admission, he became more depressed, stating that his brother had told him that his (Mr C's) girlfriend had been raped. He promised to murder the rapist, whom he said he knew. Within twenty-four hours, Mr C recanted the story, saying that his brother had lied to him. Hospital staff interviewed his parents and siblings separately, and all reported that Mr C had lied frequently since age 13, seemingly in an effort to enhance his self-esteem. For example, he had exaggerated his drug use and told stories about being a successful drug dealer. Later in the hospitalization, he admitted that he felt inferior to his successful siblings and only felt 'whole' when contemplating criminal activity associated with drug use.[38]

(d) Ms D

24.20 A 22-year-old woman told authorities that she had been kidnapped and held at knifepoint by a childhood friend who had become romantically and sexually obsessed with her. She insisted that the story was true even when the friend (with whom she really had been close since childhood) was arrested for the crime and spent over a year in prison. The truth was only revealed years later, after Ms D had received counselling in a secure psychiatric hospital and admitted that she had instructed the friend to abduct her as part of an elaborate ruse. Her only motivation for engaging in the hoax was that she 'loved drama'. Subsequent psychiatric evaluation revealed that Ms D had engaged in numerous other acts of lying for the sake of amusement or creating 'drama', from attending the funerals of strangers to mailing herself threatening letters supposedly written by her lovers' wives.[39]

24.21 Each of these vignettes, though very brief, illustrates the complexity of cases in which pathological lying and sexual abuse accusations intermingle. Several challenges are readily apparent.

---

[37] Bensussan, P., 'Forensic psychiatry in France: The Outreau case and false allegations of child sexual abuse' (2011) 20(3) *Psychiatric clinics of North America*, 519–32.

[38] Ford et al. (1988), cited at n.23.

[39] Hoyer (1959), cited at n.31.

(2) Pathological lying can be difficult to distinguish from other types of lying

For example, in the case of Ms B, she may have been motivated not by an internal **24.22** need for narcissistic gratification, but rather by a desire to mitigate her own responsibility in the (true) sexual abuse of her children. Although her in-court expression of being a 'sick person' and a liar could be interpreted as a self-serving attempt to be viewed as pitiful by the fact-finder, her proposal that her lying behaviour was a 'sickness' invites further exploration. Similarly, her allegations against the neighbours, which were made after her own arrest, could have been made to disperse responsibility for the crime but that would not completely explain her psychological motives for persistently accusing a dozen innocent neighbours, an observation that appears disproportionate to any perceived benefit to her.

(3) Pathological lying can coexist with other psychopathology

As these cases illustrate, personality disorders and factitious disorders frequently **24.23** occur in conjunction with pathological lying. Many have theorized that factitious disorders are inextricably linked with pathological lying, as the former is simply one category of pathological lying. The case of Ms A illustrates this pairing of disorders, as the false report of a rape serves as the pretext for physical symptoms (seizures) that garner attention and care from health-care providers. In the cases of Mr C and Ms D, borderline personality disorder is a serious diagnostic consideration.

(4) Sexual abuse allegations are often accompanied by other falsehoods

In the case of Ms D, her story was predicated on the idea of a sexual obsession, **24.24** but the alleged crime itself included kidnapping, threats, and physical assault, in addition to sexual assault. Furthermore, she had engaged in many different types of (seemingly unnecessary) deceptions over the years, from attending strangers' funerals to sending herself threatening letters. Although many of the incidents shared a similar theme of violence being threatened or perpetrated because of Ms D's sexuality, the number and variety of incidents in her lifetime makes it difficult to sort out truth from fiction. Healy and Healy's observation that pathological lying is very rarely seen as a symptom by itself as there is a tendency for the lying to be embedded in other forms of misrepresentation highlights the connection between pathological lying and other falsehoods.[40]

(5) False accusations of sexual abuse sometimes involve third parties

As in the cases of Ms B and Mr C, sometimes individuals make false reports of **24.25** sexual abuse being perpetrated against a third party (most commonly the individual's child, but not necessarily so). This phenomenon, similar to the syndrome of

---

[40] Healy and Healy (1926), cited at n.16.

Munchausen's by Proxy, may also occur in pathological lying. In fact, the DSM IV notes that pathological lying is a common symptom of factitious disorder, under which is Munchausen's syndrome. The individual in Munchausen's syndrome by proxy apparently seeks sympathy indirectly by assuming a caretaker role for an abused child. These cases are often even more complex than when a pathological liar reports self-abuse, as the child will often corroborate the statements out of a sense of loyalty to the parent. This leads to a greater risk of a false claim being believed by authorities.

24.26 Of course, believing the false tales of a pathological liar is not the only danger when investigating such cases; the opposite problem is equally dangerous. Erroneously labelling accusations of sexual assault as false can be extremely harmful to an individual. In addition, some scholars have noted that early sexual abuse may contribute to the development of pathological lying later in life,[41] so it is entirely possible that an individual making a false accusation has also suffered real abuse. As such, it is imperative to proceed cautiously and treat all potential victims with compassion and respect.

G. Evaluation of Pathological Lying in Sexual Abuse Cases

24.27 The procedure for psychiatric evaluation of an individual suspected of making false allegations of sexual abuse follows the same format as most forensic psychiatric evaluations. An interview of the subject, gathering of collateral data, psychological and/or neurological testing, and case formulation are all necessary components of the evaluation. However, concentrating on certain areas of the individual's history and presentation in cases where pathological lying is suspected can greatly aid in making the diagnosis. These considerations are outlined below.

(1) Interview of the relevant individual(s)

24.28 After discussing the limits of confidentiality in the psychiatric evaluation, the interviewer begins by taking a thorough psychiatric history. Particular attention should be paid to early relationships with caretakers, co-morbid psychiatric diagnoses, and any history of hospitalizations. In addition, a detailed history of abuse should be elicited, including the circumstances of the abuse, the perpetrator(s), reactions of loved ones (if known), and how the issue was resolved. When asking about the current abuse incident, although it is important to gather details, the

---

[41] Snyder (1986), cited at n.24.

interviewer should make sure to remain neutral and ask open-ended questions that do not suggest a particular response.

During the mental status examination, signs of feigned illness, such as implausible **24.29** cognitive deficits or psychiatric symptoms, should also be assessed. If any 'red flags' are present, these issues should be evaluated further using standardized psychological testing and/or malingering assessments (see para 24.31).

(2) Gathering of collateral data

Data from collateral sources, such as police reports, medical records, and **24.30** interviews with family members are important in any forensic psychiatric evaluation. In assessments where pathological lying is a consideration, they are absolutely essential. Every effort should be made to speak with friends and family members who have known the evaluee for a long time, as these individuals are most likely to notice patterns of repeated lying. In addition, it may be necessary to seek medical and legal records (police reports and arrest records) from other jurisdictions, as the evaluee may have moved several times in order to avoid detection of lies or to escape ridicule from others when the evaluee's lies finally box him in a corner. School records often contain invaluable information about the individual's early childhood behaviour and pattern of disciplinary problems.

(3) Psychological and other testing

Personality testing such as the Minnesota Multiphasic Personality Inventory **24.31** (MMPI-II) or the Millon Clinical Multiaxial Inventory (MCMI-III) can be helpful, both in assessing co-morbid psychiatric disorders and evaluating defensiveness or feigning of symptoms. Structured malingering tests, such as the Test of Malingered Memory (TOMM), Validity Indicator Profile (VIP), and Structured Inventory of Reported Symptoms (SIRS) can similarly assist in the evaluation. Neuroimaging or EEG testing may be relevant in some cases, particularly those where a question of acquired brain injury has arisen. Law enforcement agents may employ polygraph testing, but its use in mental health evaluations is not typical. Of course, no test can conclusively determine whether an individual has falsified a particular allegation or historical detail, but the psychological testing can help the evaluator to form a more detailed and evidence-based understanding of the evaluee.

(4) Case formulation and differential diagnosis

After all of the data has been gathered, the evaluator must formulate the case and **24.32** reach a conclusion. Table 24.1 can assist the evaluator in thinking through the differential diagnosis of lying and determining whether the current case truly involves pathological lying.

Table 24.1 Important Considerations Related to Pathological Lying in Sexual Abuse Cases

Does the accusation of sexual abuse involve obvious secondary gain? For example, is it motivated by revenge, profit, or a desire to conceal criminal activity?

Does the individual have a long-standing pattern of habitual lying about different things?

Are the reasons for lying obvious and understandable to the audience? Are the lies grossly out of proportion to any perceived benefit?

Is the individual's pattern of lying self-serving or self-destructive?

Is the lying reality-based? Have psychoses or delusional disorders been ruled out?

Does the individual have a history of mental illness?

Is there any history of varied legal entanglements?

24.33 Pathological lying should be differentiated from other psychiatric conditions that have been associated with deception. Lying behaviours that appear similar to pathological lying have been described in certain personality disorders and in factitious disorder. In those personality disorders—antisocial, borderline, histrionic and narcissistic—the core symptoms of these disorders are often the leading presentation that will call attention to the individual; the lies are not central. For example, in borderline personality disorder, the lifelong pattern of emotional instability, intense and unstable relationships, or suicidal or self-harm behaviours will aid in establishing the diagnosis. In antisocial personality disorder, the lies are often told for external gain, and only rarely are there lies that may suggest pathological lying. In addition, symptoms such as callous disregard for the feelings of others, gross and persistent disregard for social norms, rules, and obligations, and low threshold for violence and aggression, will be prominent. In histrionic personality disorder, self-dramatization, exaggerated expressions of emotion, and shallow and labile affect will accompany (and often overshadow) the lies. With regard to factitious disorder, the individual describes psychological or physical symptoms for the sole purpose of assuming a sick role. The narrowness of the lying behaviour in factitious disorder is in sharp contrast to the elaborate and sometimes fantastic lies of the pathological liar.

24.34 Other conditions that could be confused with pathological lying include malingering, Ganser syndrome, and confabulation. In Ganser syndrome, the lies are limited to approximate answers (for example, in response to 'How many legs does a dog have', the individual might say, 'three' or 'five'). In confabulation, falsifications are used to cover memory gaps derived from organic damage to the brain. With regard to malingering, the external incentives driving the lying behaviour are often apparent and understandable, unlike in pathological lying, where the motivation to lie is less clear.

Delusions are also included in the differential diagnosis of pathological lying. The **24.35** core distinction between these two conditions is whether the individual believes the stories to be true. In some cases of pathological lying, the lies may appear to rise to delusional proportions, but other psychotic symptoms (hallucinations, paranoia, and thought disorder) are unlikely. Also, in delusional disorder, the beliefs are more likely to be fixed and held with absolute conviction despite incontrovertible evidence to the contrary; unlike in pathological lying, the beliefs are unshakeable.

H. Conclusion

Exploration of lies is an essential element of any forensic evaluation, including **24.36** those involving sexual abuse. Lies can take many forms, and typically the individual's reasons for lying are understandable—avoiding consequences of illegal behaviour, revenge, protecting loved ones, or obtaining profit. Compared to these common reasons for lying, pathological lying is much rarer. Pathological lying should be suspected only in cases where the individual's lies appear excessive, frequent, purposeless, incomprehensible, or self-incriminating/self-destructive.

A thorough assessment of pathological lying is a labour-intensive process of explor- **24.37** ing the individual's life history. Gathering collateral information from close family members, friends, work colleagues, school records, hospital/mental health records, and legal records is particularly important. The presence of co-morbid psychiatric or neurological impairments, especially those that have been associated with pathological lying, should be assessed. Delusions and psychotic disorders should be ruled out. Only after this thorough, multi-source evaluation can pathological lying be diagnosed.

Even when the diagnosis of pathological lying is made, its implications in cases **24.38** of sexual abuse are not easily predicted. The diagnosis of pathological lying may alter the course of the legal case, resulting in allegations being dismissed and the complaining individual being referred for psychiatric treatment. However, this outcome is far from certain, both because pathological lying is difficult to diagnose and because individuals with pathological lying may be telling the truth about a particular allegation. Prudent forensic evaluators will proceed cautiously, stating an opinion about pathological lying in sexual abuse cases only when supported by clear evidence and a thorough evaluation.

Further Reading

Dike, C.C., Baranoski, M., and Griffith, E.E.H., 'Pathological Lying Revisited' (2005) 33 *J Am Acad Psychiatry Law*, 342–9.

Healy, W. and Healy, M.T. (1926) *Pathological Lying, Accusation and Swindling*, Boston: Little, Brown and Company.

Ford, C.V. (1996) *Lies! Lies!! Lies!!! The Psychology of Deceit*, Washington, DC: American Psychiatric Press.

Author Biographies

Dr Charles Dike, MD, MPH, FRCPsych, is Director of Whiting Forensic Division, a 232-bed forensic hospital facility of the Connecticut Department of Mental Health and Addiction Services. He is also Assistant Professor of Psychiatry in the Law and Psychiatry Division of Yale University School of Medicine, and Co-Deputy Training Director for the Yale forensic psychiatry fellowship programme. A Fellow of the Royal College of Psychiatrists of England and Distinguished Fellow of the American Psychiatric Association, Dr Dike also holds a postgraduate diploma in clinical psychiatry from the Republic of Ireland, and a Masters in Public Health from the United States.

Dr Reena Kapoor, MD, is Associate Professor of Psychiatry in the Law & Psychiatry Division, where her clinical work and scholarship focus on the intersection between serious mental illness and the criminal justice system. She has expertise in correctional psychiatry, community treatment of persons with criminal justice involvement, and management of problematic sexual behaviours. In addition, she serves as Co-Deputy Training Director for the Yale forensic psychiatry fellowship. Before joining the faculty, Dr Kapoor completed her residency training in psychiatry at Harvard Medical School and a forensic psychiatry fellowship at Yale. She is a 2003 graduate of Northwestern University's Feinberg School of Medicine.

25

CONCLUSION

The Editors

A. Witness Testimony in Sexual Cases: Aims and Objectives

'Law which can't respond to new situations ... has come adrift from justice.'[1] So **25.01** saying in a lecture ten years ago, Lord Justice Sedley nicely portrayed law as an evolving process constantly re-sculpted by the tides of contemporary societal needs and understanding, a process particularly evident in sexual crime. Statutory reforms, coupled with increased knowledge and scientific advances have contributed to make sexual crime a dynamic and specialist field.

Recent events have exposed entrenched fault-lines in professional mindset and **25.02** training. The Rotherham report[2] caused international shock[3] and national shame; social workers and investigators had failed to protect hundreds of young people

---

[1] Sedley, S. (2004) *How to push the boat out without sinking*, South Eastern Circuit lecture, 6 January 2004, available on South Eastern Circuit DVD, *The Art of Advocacy*.

[2] Jay, A. (2014) *Independent Inquiry into Child Sexual Exploitation in Rotherham (1997–2013)* (Alexis Jay, OBE). Rotherham: Rotherham Metropolitan Borough Council, *http://www.rotherham. gov.uk/downloads/file/1407/independent_inquiry_cse_in_rotherham*.

[3] Bennhold, K., 'A reign of terror and rape' *International New York Times*, 2 September 2014.

from sexual exploitation for more than a decade. Equally, the demise of publicly venerated figures such as Jimmy Savile revealed that justice professionals were beguiled and failed to investigate complaints impartially. Erroneous professional mindsets towards the victim/witness contributed to these failings. At the time of writing, an overarching public enquiry into the investigation of historic child sexual abuse is taking place in England and Wales.

25.03 Chapter 12 recounts the Icelandic experience when conducting a public inquiry into the historical institutional abuse of children in residential care. There is an absence of international guidance in this field. Understanding the approach and methodology of the Breidavik Committee provides welcome assistance for other similar inquiries.

25.04 In 2013 and 2014, public and academic criticism over mistreatment by the criminal justice system of child and vulnerable witnesses and all victims of sexual crime reached the 'tipping point'. It seemed that law had indeed 'come adrift from justice'. Children and the vulnerable were being failed by the system. There has been a groundswell of concern that the criminal justice system has not reacted to the needs of victims, that the attrition rate remains too high and the conviction rate is too low.

25.05 However, the law must react reflectively, not instinctively to these criticisms. It has not been within the scope of this book to address the questions whether rape complainants should receive independent legal representation, whether there should be separate specialist courts for sexual crime, or whether conviction rates should be improved. Its scope is strictly confined to considering the current law and practice pertaining to witness testimony.

25.06 The starting point of *Witness Testimony in Sexual Cases* has been the recognition that achieving good quality witness testimony underpins the entire criminal justice process, that is, from complaint to verdict. It is axiomatic that good quality witness testimony is central to proving sexual crime. Investigators and lawyers have different roles with varying duties; however, they are all participants within the same adversarial justice system. This system is founded on the touchstone of the presumption of innocence.

25.07 The *core approach* of this book has been to incorporate the essential spectrum of forensic issues of relevance to facilitate the professional evaluation of a sexual complaint from all professional standpoints. The book is thus *inclusive*, not selectively exclusive. Ensuring evidence is both of the best quality and is reliable is at the heart of the investigator's and prosecutor's tasks.

25.08 The *prime objective* of this book has been to assist investigators and justice professionals to understand factors that enhance the quality and probative value of witness testimony by identifying factors that assist or undermine witness accuracy and witness communication.

25.09 The *second linked objective* of this book has been to assist decision-makers to evaluate the reliability of witness testimony, that is, to distinguish unreliable evidence from reliable truthful evidence. There is no scientific test currently available to distinguish with certainty between the truthful and the untruthful witness; however, understanding the factors that underpin probative testimony provides a useful starting point.

B. The Inherent Flaws of Witness Testimony

'The probative force of testimony rests on four analytically distinct factors: (1) the **25.10** reliability of the witness's initial perceptions; (ii) the accuracy of the witness's memory; (iii) his truthfulness when testifying; and (iv) effective communication to the fact-finder.'[4] Whilst the third factor above remains an enigma, and is typically difficult to ascertain with certainty, the other three factors emerge as a strong theme throughout the chapters.

Adversarial trial under common law is traditionally and still mainly (though not **25.11** exclusively) operative through oral witness testimony. The particular challenge posed by witness testimony in sexual crime is that proof of the crime is critically dependent on it. Concerns about the flaws inherent in witness testimony hark back to antiquity, Socrates having instanced it as the illustration par excellence of his contention that true belief is distinguishable from knowledge, being subjective, inconstant and liable to flux.[5] It has been characterized as 'unreliable, subjective, misleading and impossible to evaluate by objective standards'.[6]

Testimony may be unreliable because it is mendacious; this is a not a modern **25.12** notion. Titus Oates, primarily remembered for his conviction for perjury in 1685 causing the execution of innocent men, also made unfounded sexual allegations against a schoolmaster; apparently, because he desired the job.[7] Alternatively, witness testimony may be unreliable because a witness holds honest but false beliefs arising from genuine memory flaws, or neurological or cognitive impairment. (See Chapters 1, 21, 22, 23, and 24.)

Chapters 13, 14, 15, 16, and 20 inform us that more child and vulnerable wit- **25.13** nesses (of all ages) are entering the criminal justice system. They alert us to the factors that need to be taken into account to achieve good quality testimony. These are: identifying vulnerabilities and communication difficulties from the outset and implementing relevant special measures, employing appropriate interviewing/

---

[4] Roberts, P. and Zuckerman, A. (2010) *Criminal Evidence*, 2nd edn, Oxford: Oxford University Press, 346.

[5] Plato, *Theaeteteus*, cited in Walton, D. (2008) *Witness Testimony Evidence: Argumentation, Artificial Intelligence and Law*, Cambridge: Cambridge University Press, Ch 1, 'Witness Testimony as Argumentation', 13.

[6] Ibid., 12.

[7] Ibid., 24, citing Lane, J. (1971) *Titus Oates*, Westport, CT: Greenwood Press.

questioning techniques, providing appropriate support from complaint through to post-trial and listening to the witness but not suspending critical judgement.

25.14 Lastly, the overriding objective of the Criminal Procedure Rules is that cases be dealt with 'justly'.[8] 'Justly' includes acquitting the innocent and convicting the guilty. In pursuing a 'balanced' approach, the consequences of wrongful conviction of the innocent cannot be ignored. It is integral to a fair and balanced evaluation of witness testimony that a neutral and open mindset is maintained; this extends to investigators, Crown Prosecution Service lawyers, prosecuting and defence advocates, expert witnesses, the judiciary, and the jury.

25.15 It is assumed that readers will draw their own conclusions from the chapters. The main themes that emerge will now be briefly revisited.

C. Identifying Vulnerable Witness Needs

25.16 Chapters 1, 15, 20, and 21 highlight the importance of detecting vulnerable witnesses and identifying necessary support early on. The Bradley report found that investigators performed poorly at this.[9] The absence of an intermediary or other witness support may lead to witness confusion or misunderstanding in the conduct of the Achieving Best Evidence (ABE) interview. It will undermine witness performance and testimonial quality. When vulnerabilities are identified it is essential that they are appropriately acted upon (Chapter 1). Recent research has shown that even with the Bradley reforms implemented at police stations ineffective use of risk assessment tools and health-care professionals still persists.[10]

25.17 Some vulnerable persons may mask their cognitive and mental health difficulties and these difficulties may not be readily apparent to the observer. Criminal justice professionals require training to enable them to communicate effectively with persons who may have complex psychological needs. There currently appears to be a 'knowledge gap' in this area that requires urgent attention.[11]

D. The ABE Interview and Early Considerations

25.18 Chapters 1, 13, 14, 16, 17, and 21 assist here. The visually recorded 'cognitive' interview is now regarded as an essential handmaiden of investigation into alleged

---

[8] Criminal Procedure Rules 2015, Pt 1 1.1. (1) and (2).

[9] Bradley, K. (2007) *The Bradley Report: Lord Bradley's Review of People with Mental Health Problems or Learning Disabilities in the Criminal Justice System*, London: Department of Health; 2009; see also, Burton, M., Evans, R., and Saunders, A., 'Vulnerable and intimidated witnesses and the adversarial process in England and Wales' (2007) 11 *Int. Journ. Ev. & Proof*, 1–23.

[10] Young, S., Goodwin, E.J., Sedwick, O., and Gudjonsson, G.H., 'The effectiveness of police custody assessments in identifying suspects with intellectual disabilities and attention deficit hyperactivity disorder' (2013) 11(248) *BMC Medicine*, doi:10.1186/1741-7015-11-248.

[11] See Chapter 8 on the need for advocate training.

sexual assaults.[12] It is essential that this is carefully planned and carried out in a sensitive manner. Investigators are expected to follow up assertions made in interview by open-mindedly checking them against independent sources of information. In the event of discrepancy witnesses may need to be re-interviewed. However, care is needed in respect of repeated interviewing due to suggestibility and possible contamination.[13]

Interviewing witnesses in cases of historic abuse, often dating back years or dec- **25.19** ades, is particularly problematic. Chapter 12 outlines the inherent problems in relation to institutional abuse inquires and Chapters 22 and 23 provide a review of developments, pitfalls, and controversies in memory science. This is currently a highly topical subject, given the escalation of historic complaints and their dependence on long-term memory recall. Disagreements still remain among some 'memory experts' about the credence that should be given to such memories in court, particularly in cases of 'recovered memories'. Chapter 22 provides strong conclusions about the inherent problems with such memories and how they should be treated by the courts. Others have raised concern that 'the rather one-sided focus on false memories in the research literature has led to media articles implying that memory is fundamentally unreliable'.[14]

Chapter 13 underscores the need for specialist training in the interviewing of **25.20** young children. Adherence to the ABE guidance remains patchy and inconsistent. Complying with the guidance is not merely a 'tick box' exercise. The guidance cautions that training and awareness of the rules is insufficient to improve and maintain investigator performance; regular monitoring and responsible feedback is required.

Handling sexual complaints from children requires great skill from all criminal **25.21** justice professionals. Evidence from children under five years old, is now commonly received by the courts. Credible evidence can be obtained from such young children when interviewed sensitively and expertly.[15]

Chapter 16 focuses on child testimony from a psychiatric perspective. Understan- **25.22** ding the social and family context in which the complaint arose will be fundamental. Chapter 10 shows how the family court approaches complaints from children and identifies the documentation produced.

---

[12] For a review of the strengths and limitations of the 'cognitive interview' see Geiselman, R.E. and Fisher, R.P., 'Interviewing witnesses and victims' in M. St-Yves (ed.) (2014) *Investigative interviewing:The essentials*. Toronto: Carswell.

[13] Ceci, S.J., Kulkofsky, S., Klemfuss, J.Z., Sweeney, C.D., and Bruck, M., 'Unwarranted Assumptions about Children's Testimonial Accuracy' (2007) 2 *Annu. Rev. Clin. Psych.*, 311–28.

[14] See recent comments by Professor Chris Brewin in Brewin, C., 'Child protection and the Rotherham abuse scandal' (2014) 27 *The Psychologist*, 737 (October issue).

[15] Gudjonsson, G.H., Sveinsdottir, T., Sigurdsson, J.F., and Jonsdottir, J.K., 'The ability of victims of childhood sexual abuse (CSA) to give credible evidence. Findings from a National Child Advocacy Centre' (2010) 21 *J. Forensic Psychiatry and Psychology*, 569–86.

E. The Charging Decision

25.23 Chapter 2 provides a comprehensive review of recently revised CPS guidance and duties of prosecutors. It examines the newly espoused 'merits based' approach to the charging decision.[16] The authors explain that this approach, focusing on the credibility of the account rather than the complainant,[17] is not novel. The editors note that prosecutors must, nonetheless, apply the code for prosecutors; the requirement to assess evidential reliability, accuracy, and credibility remains.[18]

25.24 The authors caution against concluding that inconsistencies are necessarily indicators of inherent unreliability. They draw attention to the CPS guidance that seemingly contradictory disclosure is, 'so commonplace that it can potentially be regarded as symptomatic of abuse rather than an indication of untruthfulness'.[19]

25.25 Chapter 21 informs us how trauma may cause genuine memory impairment and/or loss of memory recall. Any neurological memory disorders should be 'flagged up' as part of pre-interview preparation. Investigators should be alert to ensure this issue has either been eliminated or identified and assessed in all cases, not merely historic complaints.

25.26 Care must be taken not to suspend critical judgement. Further empirical research is required before conclusions may be drawn that certain features are or are not 'symptomatic' of abuse. Over-interpretation[20] and confirmation bias[21] risk compromising testimonial quality, accuracy, and subsequent evaluation. An open line of communication between prosecutors, investigators, and the trial advocate is essential at all times. Sharing information and discussing investigative progress is of paramount importance. Practitioner experience suggests that late instruction of the trial prosecution (and defence) advocate is still a cause for concern.

---

[16] For further consideration see Wolchover, D. and Heaton-Armstrong, A. 'Rape and the Prosecution Threshold.' (2014) 178 *Criminal Law and Justice Weekly, 28*, 424–5; *29*, 439–40; *30*, 459–61. In an online postscript the authors contend on the basis of anecdotal evidence that prosecuting counsel's advice to discontinue a rape prosecution is now very rarely followed: 'Rape: Farewell to the 50 Per Cent Rule', 13 September 2014, *http://criminallawandjustice.co.uk/features/Rape-Farewell-50-Cent-Rule.*

[17] See Chapter 2, para 2.11.

[18] *http://www.cps.gov.uk/publications/code_for_crown_prosecutors/codetest.html.*

[19] Chapter 2, para 2.14, citing CPS (2013) *Guidelines on Prosecuting Cases of Child Sexual Abuse.*

[20] La Fontaine, J.S. (1998) *Speak of the Devil: Tales of satanic abuse in contemporary England,* Cambridge: Cambridge University Press, 125. An older girl retracted her first account, explaining: 'You lot are into those things and the police and social workers wanted to hear them so I thought I had to say something and I went from there.'

[21] See Ceci et al., cited at n.13.

F. The Importance of Timely Disclosure

Chapter 3 identifies the various strands of disclosure that feature in sexual crime. **25.27**
The 'golden rule' of disclosure is well known: 'fairness requires full disclosure
should be made of all material held by the prosecution that weakens its case or
strengthens that of the defence'.[22] Heaton-Armstrong et al., highlight that '11th
hour' disclosure still occurs, sometimes even at the 'court door'. The complaint is
not new.[23] The importance of the defence statement and defence disclosure obligations also need to be recognized.[24]

Timely disclosure informs fair charging decisions. It also enables defence counsel **25.28**
to give advice that may lead to a change of plea, or alternatively to prepare for trial
and cross-examination. An updated Protocol between the Police and the CPS,
advises officers investigating rape complaints to be 'proactive', 'identifying and
seeking access to relevant third-party material as early as possible at the pre-charge
stage'.[25] Chapter 3, however, suggests that pre-charge disclosure of such relevant
background material is not a regular occurrence.

Chapter 9 considers sexual allegations against medical professionals. It draws **25.29**
attention to the need for correct identification and interpretation of health records
for investigation and disclosure. Where a complaint relates to a specialist field, for
instance, medicine or education, investigators may need to seek guidance from an
appropriate source to assist identify relevant documentation.

Understanding the potential evidential relevance of disclosure material is critical; **25.30**
this applies to all legal professionals, not just investigators. It requires training and

---

[22] *http://www.cps.gov.uk/legal/a_to_c/attorney_generals_guidelines_on_disclosure/.*
[23] In a review of cases conducted in 2007 jointly by the inspectorates of constabulary and the
CPS 50% were disclosure compliant: Her Majesty's Inspectorate of Constabulary and Her Majesty's
Crown Prosecution Service Inspectorate (2007) *Without Consent: A report on the joint review of the
investigation and prosecution of rape offences.* Half a decade later disclosure was still being identified as a 'contentious issue': Her Majesty's Inspectorate of Constabulary and Her Majesty's Crown
Prosecution Service Inspectorate (2012). *Forging the links: Rape investigation and prosecution. A joint
HMIC and HMCPSI review.* CJJI, *http://www.justiceinspectorates.gov.uk/hmic/media/forging-the-
links-rape-investigation-and-prosecution-20120228.pdf.*
[24] *R v Omar Bryan* [2009] EWCA 2291 illustrates the dangers of investigative bias and defence
case statement failure. The defence was consensual intercourse. The officer in the case chose not to
seize the complainant's phone because, 'it would be bad form and might jeopardize her case'. The
complainant alleged rape by a stranger in the street. Fresh evidence (available at trial), was obtained
by the Criminal Cases Review Commission. It fatally undermined the complainant's account. The
young defendant served over three years in custody.
[25] Protocol between the Police Service and the Crown Prosecution Service in the Investigation
and Prosecution of Rape, Section 13, Third Party Material, updated June 2015. The Protocol applies
to rape and all penetrative offences regardless of the victim's age and is considered good practice in
non-penetrative sexual offences, including child sexual abuse, *http://www.cps.gov.uk/legal/p_to_r/
rape_and_sexual_offences/appendix_f/.*

an open mind. In *R (on the application of JRP) v The CPS*,[26] social service records were reviewed by counsel acting for the local authority. Only two and a quarter pages were disclosed. Later, the CCRC reviewed 284 pages of relevant material, a 'large number' of which should have been disclosed. The Court of Appeal concluded that the undisclosed material 'would have had considerable bearing' on the defence case and on the jury's assessment of the complainant's credibility. Counsel 'failed to see the significance of the entries'.

G. Pre-trial Legal Issues

(1) Section 78 applications

25.31 Early disclosure enables both prosecution and defence to assess the relevance and reliability of the prosecution evidence. It equips the defence ahead of trial to assess the potential for any section 78 application to exclude witness testimony.[27] Whilst this is unlikely to be a common course of action, it should be borne in mind, particularly with historic complaints.

(2) Section 28 pre-trial cross-examination

25.32 The anticipated reform introducing pre-trial cross-examination[28] of young and vulnerable witnesses adds further impetus for compliance with prompt disclosure. At the time of writing, procedural guidance for prosecutors is awaited.

(3) Abuse of process applications

25.33 Chapter 4 provides extensive coverage of the development of the abuse of process doctrine. It is now settled that any application that the trial be stayed as an abuse of process should occur prior to trial. Decision-making in this area has evolved since the case of *R v Bell*.[29] Any 'stay' on the basis of delay remains exceptional. Chapter 2 notes that even if a 'stay' is obtained, it will not prevent the evidence within that case being used in any subsequent complaint. *R v RD*[30] indicates success only where delay has led to the loss of evidence which might support a defence, typically of alibi.[31]

---

[26] [2010] EWCA Crim 2438.
[27] Section 78 of the Police and Criminal Evidence Act 1978 provides that a court may refuse to allow evidence if, 'having regard to all the circumstances, *including the circumstances in which the evidence was obtained*, the admission of the evidence would have such an adverse effect on the fairness of the proceedings that the court ought not to admit it', (emphasis added).
[28] Pursuant to YJCEA 1999.
[29] [2003] EWCA Crim 319.
[30] [2013] EWCA Crim 1592; 2013 WL 4788714.
[31] For a discussion of the implications of the judgment see Corker, D., 'Delays and Historic Offences' (2013) 177(51/52) *Criminal Law and Justice Weekly*, (21 December) 836.

(4) Section 41 applications

Chapter 5 discusses the statutory restriction on cross-examination of the complain- **25.34**
ant's prior sexual history.[32] It explores the case law and reveals the complications
caused by statutory ambiguity. It discusses the difficulties caused to the defence
when an unproven, prior false complaint is suspected. As the authors point out, it
is well nigh impossible, in the absence of a confession or perjury conviction, for a
defendant to show a previous complaint to be 'demonstrably false' to the criminal
standard and thereby 'unlock' the restriction on admission of the previous 'false
complaint' evidence. The authors posit whether the current threshold is too high.

(5) Expert evidence

Chapters 17, 18, and 19 provide technical accounts of symptom methodology, **25.35**
recording, and assessment, an understanding of which is essential in the field of
child sexual abuse involving recent complaint. However, such examinations are usually unlikely to provide assistance in the generality of historic allegations although
anatomical evidence of past abuse may exceptionally be present. Medical professionals should demonstrate sensitivity when examining the complainant.[33] These three
chapters emphasize the need for proper training and rigorous adherence to professional guidance. Numerous case studies illustrate their points. Science is a slowly
evolving process. Catastrophic mistakes do occasionally occur.[34] It is advisable that
criminal justice professionals ensure the integrity of the scientific process being used.

Chapter 7 provides a comprehensive overview of the current approach to the admis- **25.36**
sion of expert evidence by the courts,[35] including a 'fool's mini-guide' to DNA
evidence. Understanding DNA evidence is a common lawyer 'blind-spot'. As to
the admission of expert memory evidence, the authors opine that in common with
other expert evidence, such as the 'typical' behaviour of victims, it has 'variable probative value' and is fact-specific. The chapter concludes that 'the law should remain
flexible enough' to admit 'genuinely reliable, probative and helpful' expert evidence.

H. Facilitating Good Quality Witness Testimony at Trial

Chapter 15 emphasizes the need to support witnesses in order to maximize good **25.37**
quality witness testimony. Chapter 8 highlights the requirement for advocates to

---

[32] Section 41,YJCEA.
[33] Norfolk, A., 'Doctor "sorted out golf trip as girl waited for rape exam"' *The Times*,
14 February 2013.
[34] Sims, P. and Camber, R., 'Police fear 90 cases may be tainted after crime scene officer is
arrested' *Daily Mail*, 29 August 2012. See also *http://www.mirror.co.uk/news/uk-news/dna-bungle-
sees-teen-spend-759387*('Teen spends three months in prison over rape in city he'd never visited
because of DNA bungle').
[35] See now also Crown Prosecution Service (2014) *Guidance On Expert Evidence*, 1st edn.

conduct ethical and appropriate questioning, for children and adults alike, to facilitate effective and fair communication.

I. Trial Safeguards in Respect of Unreliable Evidence

25.38 Proven false complaints of rape are few in number as against the totality of rape allegations. It follows that the risk to rape defendants of facing such a complaint is a relatively low one. Nonetheless, there is appellate authority the effect of which is to require juries under certain conditions to be warned of the risk of convicting solely on the complainant's testimony.

25.39 Prior to the Criminal Justice and Public Order Act 1994 the jury in all sexual offence cases had to be warned of the danger of convicting on the uncorroborated evidence of a complainant, irrespective of the age or sex of the complainant and even if the only issue was that of the identity of the accused. Compulsory warnings of this nature were abolished by section 32(1) of the 1994 Act, but section 32(2) preserves a discretion to give a warning. Importantly, the Court of Appeal in *R v Makanjoula (Oluwanfunso); R v Easton*,[36] responded to an invitation to give guidance as to the circumstances in which a judge may urge caution in regard to a particular witness and the terms in which that should be done.

25.40 Giving judgment, Lord Taylor of Gosforth CJ pointed out that often no special warning was required at all, but that any warning that was given was discretionary, that no single formula was to be applied and that where applicable the strength and terms of the warning depended on the content and manner of the witness's evidence, the particular circumstances of, and the issues in, the case. The nub of the guidance statement advises:

> Where … the witness has been shown to be unreliable, [the judge] may consider it necessary to urge caution. In a more extreme case, if the witness is shown to have lied, to have made previous false complaints or to bear a grudge, a stronger warning may be thought appropriate and the judge may suggest it would be wise to look for some supporting material before acting on the impugned witness's evidence. We stress that these observations are merely illustrative of some, not all, of the factors which judges may take into account in measuring where a witness stands in the scale of reliability and what response they should make at that level in their directions to the jury.[37]

25.41 It has been noted[38] that Lord Taylor had necessarily to formulate his guidance on the preserved discretion in diffident terms. He could not be heard to be retaining

---

[36] [1995] 2 Cr. App. R. 469.

[37] Ibid., 472. In *R v A* [2014] NICA 2, clear evidence of the falsity of the complainant's initial account cast doubt on her general credibility and, referring to *Makanjoula*, Girvan LJ stressed the importance of tailoring an appropriate warning to exercise more than normal caution by reference to the evidence, rather than following a set piece, or 'mantra'.

[38] Wolchover, D. and Heaton-Armstrong, A. 'Rape Trials' (2010) 177(17) *Criminal Law and Justice Weekly*, (April 24), 244–9, at 248–9.

a mandatory corroboration warning by the back door. The language he uses necessarily therefore typifies authoritative suggestion rather than prescription: trial judges will consider what *might* be appropriate. The guidance contemplates two tiers of instruction: a caution where the complainant is shown to be unreliable; or advice to look for supporting evidence where the complainant has been shown to have lied. It is stressed that appellate courts will be slow to interfere, but typically for discretion cases the absence of a suitably worded caution where the unsatisfactory nature of the complainant's evidence is clear will be potentially subject to appeal. Where there are obvious markers of untruth, for example, inconsistency or self-contradiction on key aspects of the account or conflict with other incontrovertible or even credible evidence, there may be little difficulty for the judge. However, it has been argued that even without internal or circumstantial indicators of mendacity such is the nature of discretion that the evidence of the defendant could of itself provide a foundation for a suitable warning where the judge has found it to be clearly more credible than that of the complainant.

In contrast to mendacity, it should be of equal importance for the courts to develop **25.42** careful and comprehensive directions concerning the possibility that witnesses might honestly believe in the accuracy of their complaint but in consequence of one or more of the various mental and physical conditions highlighted in other chapters of this book, may simply be mistaken. The Judicial Studies Board *Bench Book* currently makes scant reference to those factors which might induce an honestly held, but false belief.

J. Conclusion

The nature of the adversarial trial and oral tradition militates against witnesses for **25.43** the prosecution and defendants. Advocates are professional orators and witnesses are pitted against them in a theatrical forum that has changed little in the past two hundred years. It is inherently unfair in many respects. Testimony from either the complainant or defendant may be rendered unreliable by forensic scrutiny whose quest is to undermine, rather than search out the truth.

Forthcoming training measures, embedded specialization, trial modifications, **25.44** and ongoing witness support will, it is to be hoped, serve to ameliorate most if not all concerns and encourage good quality witness testimony.

Whatever efforts are made to increase the likelihood of just results in sexual assault **25.45** cases—the conviction of the guilty and the acquittal of the innocent—some errors will slip through the net. Genuine complaints to the police may result in no further action being taken or the case being discontinued owing to misplaced and ill-informed conclusions that there is no realistic prospect of conviction. Honest and accurate complainants may see their assailants acquitted on the back of a false but plausible story advanced by the defendant, as the result of an incomplete police investigation or muddled thinking by juries induced by notions of stereotypical victim behaviour. Some innocent suspects will be arrested and defendants convicted because the falsity of a complaint remains uncovered through inefficient and incomplete compliance with the requirements of the disclosure regime. As the contents of this book endeavour to establish, however, the risk of unjust outcomes can be reduced yet further by a greater degree of attendance to the complexities of witness testimony.

INDEX